W9-DGC-181

Crown and Nobility
1450–1509

To Antonio Santosuosso

Crown and Nobility 1450–1509

J. R. Lander

Edward Arnold

First published 1976
by Edward Arnold (Publishers) Ltd
25 Hill Street, London W1X 8LL

ISBN: 0 7131 5833 6

Text set in 11/12 pt Photon Baskerville, printed by photolithography, and bound in Great Britain at The Pitman Press, Bath

Contents

Preface

When preparing these essays for publication it has seemed better to reprint them in their original form, without alteration except for obvious factual errors and misprints, than to undertake extensive revisions, and to indicate in a new Introduction the various points on which my views and theories of the period have changed as a result of further research, reflection and criticism and as a result of the more recent publications of other scholars. Though this method has obvious disadvantages it avoids the inconvenience (which most scholars find both awkward and irritating) of having two different versions of the same article in print and has the advantage of demonstrating the state of knowledge and opinion at the time of the original publication.

Acknowledgements

My grateful acknowledgement and thanks are due to the following for permission to reprint the various chapters of this book:

To Martin Secker and Warburg Ltd for chapter 2, which originally appeared as the introduction to *The Wars of the Roses* (1965); to the John Rylands Library and the Manchester University Press for chapter 3, originally printed in *Bulletin of the John Rylands Library* XLIII (1960–61) 46–69; to the Editor and the Institute of Historical Research, University of London for chapters 4 and 8, *Bulletin of the Institute of Historical Research* XXXVI (1963) 119–52, XXXII (1959) 138–80; to the Editor and the Cambridge University Press for chapter 5, *Historical Journal* IV (1961) 120–51; to the Editor and George Philip and Son Ltd for chapter 6, *History* XLI (1956) 38–52; to the Editor and Longman Group Ltd for chapter 7, *English Historical Review* LXXIII (1958) 27–46; to the Editor and the University of Louisiana State University Press for chapter 9, from *Tudor Men and Institutions: Studies in English Law and Government* ed. A. J. Slavin (1972) 70–100; to the Editors and the Journal of History Co. Ltd, University of Saskatchewan for chapter 10, *Canadian Journal of History* II (1967) 1–28; to the Editors and the University of Toronto Press for chapter 11, from *Florilegium Historiale: Essays Presented to Wallace K. Ferguson* ed J. G. Rowe and W. H. Stockdale (1971) 327–67.

Abbreviations

BM	British Museum
C.	Chancery
Cal. Charter Rolls	*Calendar of Charter Rolls*
Cal. Close Rolls	*Calendar of Close Rolls*
Cal. Pat. Rolls	*Calendar of Patent Rolls*
Council and PS	Council and Privy Seal
CP	George Edward Cockayne, *The Complete Peerage* ed. V. Gibbs and others (12 vols 1910–59)
DNB	*Dictionary of National Biography*
E.	Exchequer
EETS	Early English Text Society
Foedera	*Foedera, Conventiones, Literae, etc.* ed. T. Rymer (17 vols 1703–17)
Fulman	'Historiae Croylandensis Continuatio', in *Rerum Anglicarum Scriptorum Veterum* I ed. W. Fulman (1684)
Hist. MSS Comm.	Historical Manuscripts Commission
KB	King's Bench
KR Mem. Roll	King's Remembrancer's Memoranda Roll
LTR Mem. Roll	Lord Treasurer's Remembrancer's Memoranda Roll
Paston Letters	*The Paston Letters* ed. J. Gairdner (4 vols 1910)
PRO	Public Record Office
Proceedings and Ordinances	*Proceedings and Ordinances of the Privy Council of England* ed. Sir H. Nicolas (7 vols 1834–7)
Rot. Parl.	*Rotuli Parliamentorum: ut et Petitiones, et Placita in Parliamento* ed. J. Strachey (6 vols 1767–77)
Rot. Scot.	*Rotuli Scotiae* (2 vols 1814–19)

Stevenson

Letters and Papers Illustrative of the Wars of the English in France during the Reign of Henry VI ed. J. Stevenson (2 vols in 3, Rolls Series 1861–4)

Wedgwood, *Register*

Wedgwood, *Biographies*

J. C. Wedgwood, *History of Parliament, 1439–1509* (2 vols 1936–8)

1

Introduction: aspects of fifteenth-century studies

1 Tradition and general developments

A quarter of a century ago or more, in the period immediately following the second world war, a general opinion prevailed that the fifteenth century was one of the neglected waste lands of English history and that, because of the nature of its surviving sources, it was unlikely ever to be anything else. At the same time a small number of supposedly pioneer students in the universities congratulated themselves and each other, that they had at least begun to turn the ponderously heavy clods of its virgin soil. They were almost unconsciously the victims of self-deception, or of an unwillingness to count, for since the beginning of the century and the end of the war at least 20 books and 36 major articles dealing, in whole or in part, with the fifteenth century had already been published, besides numerous others of less importance.

Yet, in another sense, the 'pioneers' of the late forties were justified in their opinions. The bulk of these earlier works had been mostly concerned with the Hundred Years War,[1] with economic history, especially overseas trade[2] (agrarian history had so far received much less attention),[3] with constitutional ideas,[4] with the development of parliament and of parliamentary procedures,[5] and to a much more limited extent with the development

[1] e.g. R. A. Newhall, 'The War Finances of Henry V and the Duke of Bedford', *English Historical Review* XXXVI (1921) 172–98; *The English Conquest of Normandy* (1924); *Muster and Review: A Problem of English Military Administration, 1420–1440*, Harvard Historical Monographs XIII (1940). B. J. H. Rowe, 'Discipline in the Norman Garrisons Under Bedford, 1422–1435', and 'John, Duke of Bedford and the Norman "Brigands"', *English Historical Review* XLVI (1931) 194–208, and XLVII (1932) 583–600. R. Doucet, 'Les Finances anglaises en France à la fin de la guerre de Cent Ans', *Le Moyen Age* XXXVI (1926).

[2] e.g. E. Power, 'The English Wool Trade in the Reign of Edward IV', *Cambridge Historical Journal* II (1926–8) 17–35; *The Wool Trade in Medieval English History* (1941); *Studies in English Trade in the Fifteenth Century*, ed. E. Power and M. M. Postan (1933).

[3] See below pp. 6 and 7 and p. 7, n. 30.

[4] e.g. S. B. Chrimes, *English Constitutional Ideas in the Fifteenth Century* (1936).

[5] e.g. H. L. Gray, *The Influence of the Commons on Early Legislation: A Study of the Fourteenth and Fifteenth Centuries* (1932). M. McKisack, *The Parliamentary Representation of English Boroughs During the Middle Ages* (1932). W. H. Dunham Jr, *The Fane Fragment of the Lord's Journal* (1935). J. C. Wedgwood, *History of Parliament, 1439–1509* (2 vols 1936–8). A. R. Myers,

of the royal council, the justices of the peace,[6] and the law courts.[7] Because of their specialized scope these studies had only marginally affected general interpretations of the period. No new synthesis had so far appeared. With the exception of K. B. McFarlane, in his chapter on the Lancastrian kings in volume VIII of the Cambridge Medieval History,[8] published in 1936, no historian had broken fresh ground with a new interpretation of politics. General histories of the period still followed an established nineteenth-century tradition.

The Yorkist age was particularly sterile ground. In 1923 Cora L. Scofield had written a monumental two volume *Life and Reign of Edward IV*[9] based on many years of laborious archival research. Her book traced in the most minute and accurate detail a political narrative of the period, but at the last, in so far as it expressed any general conclusions at all, it echoed those of the third volume of Stubbs's *Constitutional History* published 45 years earlier. C. H. Williams who wrote the corresponding chapter to McFarlane's in the *Cambridge Medieval History* merely expressed the view that the Yorkists seemed to have held many of the same ideas of reform as Henry VII but 'they hardly knew whither they were going' and 'so had little abiding influence on the country for good or ill.'[10] Henry VII's reign had been rather better served, particularly in matters of financial history,[11] but paradoxically enough, as later research was to demonstrate, those up-to-date works were themselves misleading in that they attributed entirely to Henry VII vital financial reforms which have since been traced back to 1461 and the years immediately following.[12]

Although many of its conclusions had been modified in detail, Stubbs's *Constitutional History* still set the prevailing tone upon the century, and in sonorous cadences Stubbs had asserted that 'the most enthusiastic admirer of medieval life must grant that all that was good and great in it was

'Parliamentary Petitions in the Fifteenth Century', *English Historical Review* LII (1937) 384–404, 590–613, and 'Some Observations on the Procedure of the Commons in dealing with Bills in the Lancastrian Period', *University of Toronto Law Journal* III (1939) 51–73. K. B. McFarlane, 'Parliament and Bastard Feudalism', *Transactions of The Royal Historical Society* 4th series XXVI (1944) 53–79.

[6] J. F. Baldwin, *The King's Council in England During The Middle Ages* (1913). T. F. T. Plucknett, 'The Place of the Council in the Fifteenth Century', *Transactions of the Royal Historical Society* 4th series I (1918) 157–89. B. H. Putnam, *Proceedings Before the Justices of the Peace in the Fourteenth and Fifteenth Centuries, Edward III to Richard III* (1938).

[7] M. Hastings, *The Court of Common Pleas in Fifteenth Century England* (1947).

[8] *Cambridge Medieval History* VIII (1936) ch. 11 'England: The Lancastrian Kings, 1399–1461'.

[9] C. L. Scofield, *The Life and Reign of Edward IV* (2 vols 1923).

[10] *Cambridge Medieval History* VIII (1936) ch 12, 'England: The Yorkist Kings, 1461–1485', 449.

[11] A. P. Newton, 'The King's Chamber Under the Early Tudors', *English Historical Review* XXXII (1917) 348–72. F. C. Dietz, *English Government Finance, 1485–1559*, University of Illinois, Studies in the Social Sciences IX (3) (1920).

[12] See below p. 38 and n. 207.

languishing even to death', and that it was 'a worn out helpless age that calls for pity without sympathy, and yet balances weariness with something like regrets.'[13]

In 1888 a decade after Stubbs, an Oxford cleric, W. Denton, published a book crammed with pessimistic opinions so extreme that they were very nearly caricature. The country was impoverished because its soil was exhausted. The very people were morally inferior to their ancestors, and the nobility as physically degenerate as they were ill-educated. Power had become concentrated into the hands of too few, a minority so powerful as to be almost the peers of the king himself. The rest of the nobility, encumbered with debt due to the cost of war and personal extravagance, had lost their former and legitimate influence. Although, in spite of all this England was more peaceful than other parts of Europe, disorder and violence reigned so supreme that they 'destroyed all feeling of security, and hindered any progress in the arts of peace'.[14] Even those who derided the wild extravagances of Denton's theories continued to regard the wretched century with immense distaste. As the tale went, the premature Lancastrian constitutional experiment had collapsed into near anarchy, followed by the constitutional backsliding of the Yorkists and Henry VII,[15] which created an unfortunate hiatus in English development, a despotism wholly alien to our political traditions, but mercifully of short duration.

Social deterioration went hand in hand with political weakness. A troglodyte aristocracy—ill-educated[16] and militarily-minded, its revenues badly depleted by the depopulation and agrarian depression resulting from the Black Death and subsequent outbreaks of bubonic and other forms of plague, having by the mid-1450s lost its possessions in France—turned to political gangsterism at home to recoup its fortunes in the Wars of the Roses.[17] These nobles headed the malign forces of bastard feudalism, noted as an evil particularly prevalent in this century, and condemned as immoral and faithless, 'far removed indeed from the atmosphere of responsibility, loyalty and faith which had characterised the relationship of lord and vassal in the earlier middle ages'.[18] While opinions

---

[13] W. Stubbs, *The Constitutional History of England* III (1878) 613, 618. Other works tended to modify its conclusions but made no fundamental break particularly about the later part of the century.

[14] W. Denton, *England in the Fifteenth Century* (1888) especially 153–5, 257 ff., 287.

[15] See below ch. 6, p. 162.

[16] e.g. 'In the Middle Ages the members of the ruling class were in general men of arrested intellectual development who looked to those below them in the social scale for the intelligence necessary to order and govern society'. V. H. Galbraith, 'A New Life of Richard II', *History* XXXI (1941–2) 227.

[17] M. M. Postan, 'The Fifteenth Century', *Economic History Review* IX (1938–9) 166–7.

[18] H. M. Cam, 'The Decline and Fall of English Feudalism', *History* XXV (1940) 216–33 especially 225, reprinted in *Liberties and Communities in Medieval England* (1944) 205–22. See also Sir John Fortescue, *The Governance of England* ed. C. Plummer (1885) introduction 11 ff.

differed as to the destructiveness of the civil wars,[19] it was generally held that the Yorkists though well-intentioned failed to deal with the problems of rampant disorder, aristocratic oppression and livery and maintenance.[20] Improvement came about only after 1485—that almost mesmeric, climacteric year—when recovery began with the quiet constructive work of Henry VII. His careful parsimony established the financial recovery of the monarchy and by pressure on the overmighty subject through the court of Star Chamber, he suppressed bastard feudalism with all its attendant evils of livery and maintenance and restored public order. Henry VII was in fact the only fifteenth-century king whom historians universally praised and whose reputation stood universally high, though oddly enough when contemplating his methods they could at the same time debate whether he was the last of our medieval or the first of our modern kings.

On most other aspects of life the consensus was alike distinctly pejorative. With the suppression of lollardy, religion had become excessively commercialized, mechanical and unintellectual. Monasticism, except in the prejudiced pages of Cardinal Gasquet and his disciples, had never recovered from the blows inflicted upon it by the Black Death. The parish clergy, even if not decadent and immoral, were at best unlearned and therefore more and more despised by an increasingly educated and more critical laity. Some historians, still under the influence of the nineteenth-century ecclesiologists, trenchantly asserted that gothic architecture had reached a peak of perfection between about 1180 and 1280, that the decorated style exhibited a florid decadence and that perpendicular was no more than inferior shop work, bought by the yard.[21] Although the mystery and miracle plays and lyric poetry reached a high level of perfection, post-Chaucerian courtly verse was intolerably dull and insipid. Prose writing, with the exception of that of Sir Thomas Malory, and a few others working in a traditional devotional idiom, was halting and clumsy, until Sir Thomas More evolved a rich, incomparable vernacular equally felicitous for the expression of devotion, theology and history.[22] Only one bright spot appeared in these darkened skies—Thorold Rogers's demonstration that owing to rising wages following upon the Black Death, the fifteenth century was a golden age for the labourer.[23]

Changing judgments can derive from two things—changes in taste and increasing knowledge. A generation with more catholic tastes is now capable of admiring the perpendicular as well as the early English style of

[19] See below ch. 2 pp. 61–2.
[20] See above p. 2.
[21] G. G. Coulton, *Art and the Reformation* (1928, 2nd edn. 1953) introduction, especially 9 ff.
[22] R. W. Chambers, *On the Continuity of English Prose From Alfred to More and his School*, EETS (1932).
[23] J. E. Thorold Rogers, *Six Centuries of Work and Wages: The History of English Labour* (1884, reprinted 1949) ch. 12.

gothic architecture. In this field it was architects rather than historians who led the way, for as early as 1876 George Frederick Bodley had begun to build his masterpiece, the church of Holy Angels, Hoar Cross, in a modified perpendicular style.

Fifteenth-century literature was perhaps too savagely excoriated by those blind to anything but the classical revivalism of the Renaissance, and who judged England only by the more advanced standards of Italy. There were, however, distinctive English developments in the works of the first antiquarians William Worcester and John Rous, who were the forerunners of Leland, Camden, Stow and the great seventeenth-century county historians.[24]

Although some fifteenth-century authors remained surprisingly popular for a very long time, the customary verdict can be only gently modified. Readers well into the eighteenth century still admired John Lydgate, the fifteenth century's most prolix versifier. But it is more than doubtful whether anybody but an enthusiastic literary historian will ever find much pleasure in his verbose, didactic exercises.

Intensive application to hitherto unexplored record sources has, to an even greater degree than the development of a more tolerant, catholic taste, called forth new attitudes to fifteenth-century problems. As I have written elsewhere,[25] between the death of Thomas Walsingham, the last of the St Albans school of historians, and the appearance after 1483 of the humanist authors Dominic Mancini, Sir Thomas More and Polydore Vergil, only the Second Anonymous Croyland Continuator dealing with the years 1459–86 wrote in a mode comparable to that of the traditional Latin chroniclers. Other Latin annals are short and none too well-informed and the new London chronicles in English which now replaced the monastic histories, although they mark the beginnings of a new type of vernacular literature, exhibit all the crudities generally associated with first attempts of any kind. Their meagre, ill-informed and clumsy narratives provide a far from adequate basis for the reconstruction of political events. In their pages rumour and slander are often difficult to distinguish from facts.[26] Very little remains from the period in the way of private political letters, state papers or conciliar memoranda to inform us of the workings

---

[24] K. B. McFarlane, 'William Worcester, A Preliminary Survey', in *Studies Presented to Sir Hilary Jenkinson*, ed. J. Conway Davies (1958) 196–221; T. D. Kendrick, *British Antiquity* (London 1950) ch. 2; William Worcestre, *Itineraries*, ed. J. H. Harvey (1969) introduction.

[25] J. R. Lander, *Conflict and Stability in Fifteenth Century England* (1969) ch. 1. See also below ch. 4 p. 94, for a criticism of modern political narratives of the period put together from these sources.

[26] A partial exception may perhaps be made for *The Great Chronicle of London* ed A. H. Thomas and I. D. Thornley (1938), but even so its author (most probably Robert Fabyan) had no 'inside information' on government activities of the type known to some of the earlier monastic chroniclers.

of the minds of kings and statesmen, and for most of the time we are reduced to guessing their motives from the results of their actions, at best a fallible and hazardous process. Thirty years ago the exploitation of these sources *in isolation* had apparently brought historians to a dead end. It seemed that they had very little new to yield.

Neglected archives, however, survive in enormous quantities waiting for students prepared to live laborious days. Fifteenth-century government records exist in their thousands and by the hundredweight, even by the ton. Their bulk is terrifying, and consisting as they do principally of accounts, judicial proceedings, administrative and executive orders penned in the inelegant jargon of the lawyer and the bureaucrat, they provide far from stimulating or alluring reading. Together with much less numerous private estate accounts and records, they have formed and continue to form the essential basis of fifteenth-century studies. The studies earlier mentioned on the Hundred Years' War, trade and commerce, and the development of parliament largely depend upon the use of such materials. The studies of parliament made by J. C. Wedgwood[27] and J. S. Roskell[28] were applications to the fifteenth century of the prosopological techniques so successfully used by Sir Lewis Naimer for the eighteenth-century political scene. Progress in fifteenth-century studies has in fact largely advanced through techniques similar to those developed by sociologists, though except in the work of Sylvia Thrupp there seems to have been little conscious imitation or exchange of ideas.[29] These techniques, exploiting hitherto unused and seemingly more or less intractable sources, have made possible radical reinterpretations of the governmental structure, the bases of political and social power, the state of public order and the royal finances, producing all in all a deeper and more valid background against which even the meagre chronicles of the day can be more surely interpreted.

Numerous investigations of estate accounts have destroyed earlier impressions of almost universal agricultural depression and declining agrarian incomes, putting in their place an account of highly divergent regional economies, ranging from acute depression in parts of the north and some of the midland counties, through modestly buoyant conditions on the lands of the archbishops of Canterbury, to conditions more prosperous than in earlier centuries on some of the southwestern estates of

[27] Wedgwood, *History of Parliament, op. cit.*

[28] J. S. Roskell, 'The Social Composition of the Commons in a Fifteenth Century Parliament', *Bulletin of the Institute of Historical Research* XXIV (1951) 152–72, and *The Commons in the Parliament of 1422* (1954).

[29] S. L. Thrupp, 'The Problem of Conservatism in Fifteenth Century England', *Speculum* XVIII (1943) 363–8; *The Merchant Class of Medieval London* (1948), and 'The Problem of Replacement Rates in Late Medieval English Population', *Economic History Review* 2nd series XVIII (1965) 101–19.

the duchy of Cornwall and those of Tavistock abbey.[30]

The church has also found its need of rehabilitation. The monastic vocation remained popular, so much so that after the ravages of the Black Death the rate of increase in the numbers of the religious was far greater than that of the country's population as a whole. If the monastic life was no longer as enthusiastic and austere as it had been in earlier centuries, major scandals were rare. Even in 1536 Henry VIII originally thought in terms of a reduction in the excessive number of monasteries rather than complete abolition. In fact in the preamble to the act of 1536 which dissolved religious houses worth less than £200 a year, the king went out of his way to praise the virtuous standards of life in the greater monasteries. Total abolition was in the end the result of a squalid financial scramble rather than of religious disapproval.[31] If the disbursement of money is any true guide the church was far from unpopular, for the creation of colleges and chantries and the rebuilding, either partial or entire, of numerous parish churches right up to the end of the 1520s, made the fifteenth century one of the great ages of religious benefaction.[32]

[30] Among numerous studies, see M. Postan, 'The Chronology of Labour Services', *Transactions of the Royal Historical Society* 4th series XX (1937) 169–94, reprinted in *Essays in Agrarian History* ed. W. E. Minchinton (2 vols 1968) I 73–91. J. Saltmarsh, 'Plague and Economic Decline in England in the Later Middle Ages', *Cambridge Historical Journal* VII (1941–3) 23–42. *The Cambridge Economic History of Europe* I ed. J. H. Clapham (1941). R. A. L. Smith, *Canterbury Cathedral Priory* (1943). R. H. Hilton, *The Economic History of Some Leicestershire Estates in the Fourteenth and Fifteenth Centuries* (1947). Most of these earlier works presented a picture of acute agrarian depression. Later works have produced much more varied regional results, e.g. J. M. W. Bean, *The Estates of the Percy Family 1416–1537* (1958). A. R. Bridbury, *Economic Growth: England in the Later Middle Ages* (1963). R. D. Dobson, *Durham Priory, 1400–1456* (1973) ch. 8. I. R. Raftis, *The Estates of Ramsey Abbey* (1957). F. R. H. Du Boulay, *The Lordship of Canterbury: An Essay on Medieval Society* (1966) chs 5 and 6, and 'A Rentier Economy in the Later Middle Ages: The Archbishopric of Canterbury', and 'Who were farming the English Demesnes at the end of the Middle Ages', *Economic History Review* 2nd series XVI (1963–4) 443–55, and XVII (1964–5) 427–38. H. P. R. Finberg, *Tavistock Abbey* (1951) 240–64. J. Hatcher, *Rural Economy and Society in the Duchy of Cornwall, 1300–1500* (1970) ch. 7.

[31] J. Youings, *The Dissolution of the Monasteries* (1971), introduction and document 10 '. . . considering also that divers great and solemn monasteries of this realm wherein (thanks be to God) religion is right well kept and observed . . .'. See also D. Knowles, 'The English Monasteries in the later Middle Ages', *History* XXXIX (1954) 26–38, and *The Religious Orders in England* II and III (1948, 1959). G. W. O. Woodward, 'The Exemption from Suppression of Certain Yorkshire Priories', *English Historical Review* LXXVI (1961) 385–401. T. H. Swales, 'The Opposition to the Suppression of the Norfolk Monasteries', *Norfolk Archeology* XXXIII (1962–5). C. Haigh, *The Last Days of the Lancashire Monasteries and the Pilgrimage of Grace*, Chetham Society (17) (1969). R. B. Dobson, *Durham Priory, 1400–1450* (1973) especially chs 2 and 10.

[32] E. J. Jacob, 'Founders and Foundations in the Later Middle Ages', *Bulletin of the Institute of Historical Research* XXXV (1962) 29–64. K. L. Woodlegh, *Perpetual Chantries in Britain* (1965). J. R. F. Thomson, 'Piety and Charity in Late Medieval London', *Journal of Ecclesiastical History* XVI (1965) 163–77. W. O. Ault, 'Manor Court and Parish Church in Fifteenth Century England: A Study of Village By-Laws', *Speculum* XXXXII (1967) 53–67. J. T. Rosenthal, *The Purchase of Paradise: The Social Function of Aristocratic Benevolence, 1307–1485* (1972).

Finally, if the ecclesiastical hierarchy was excessively legalistic rather than truly pastoral in its attitudes towards its flock,[33] the bishops at least within limits managed to improve the standards of the parish clergy. In the diocese of Lincoln the proportion of graduate clergy rose from fourteen to over thirty per cent between 1400 and 1500, and in a modest kind of way the standards of the rest of the clergy also improved with the spread of grammar school education.[34] They became sufficiently literate to conduct the services without error, which was a modest enough development but at least a considerable improvement on the low standards of earlier centuries.[35]

More intensive record studies are by no means confined to the fifteenth century. Indeed, similar and parallel record studies of other periods have contributed to the reassessment of fifteenth-century conditions by providing more realistic standards of comparison that those which existed two or three generations ago. The classic, unduly glowing accounts of the high middle ages and the sixteenth century were based upon the study of legislation, that is upon the intentions, even upon the pious hopes, of governments and parliaments. On the other hand, since the days of Henry Hallam (1779–1859) historians have repeatedly commented that the fifteenth was very far from being a century of legislative or institutional development, and therefore they tended to condemn its lack of significant innovation. At the same time, the early and isolated publication of part of The Paston Letters,[36] with their endless wails about violence, corruption and 'lack of governance', provided a blood-curdling scenario of fifteenth-century actualities which nineteenth-century writers in all unconscious good faith contrasted with the legislative intentions of other periods. These contrasts led them to formulate trenchant but quite illegitimate conclusions about the horrors of the dying middle ages.

If the Lives of the Berkeleys, published by subscription in a very limited edition in the 1880s, had achieved anything like the enormous circulation of The Paston Letters, historians could hardly have drawn their notorious comparison between the violence of the fifteenth century and the good order of the sixteenth. Although the worst outrages during the squalid history of the family quarrels and lawsuits occurred during the fifteenth century, the

[33] A. Hamilton Thompson, The English Clergy and their Organisation in the Later Middle Ages (1947) ch. 2. R. L. Storey, Diocesan Administration in the Fifteenth Century, St Anthony's Hall Publications (16) (1959).

[34] For the extension of education, see N. Orme, English Schools in the Middle Ages (1973) ch. 7.

[35] M. Bowker, 'Non-residence in the Lincoln Diocese in the Early Sixteenth Century', Journal of Ecclesiastical History XX (1964) 40–50 and The Secular Clergy in the Diocese of Lincoln, 1495–1520 (1968) chs 2 and 3. P. Heath, The English Parish Clergy on the Eve of the Reformation (1969) chs 5 and 6.

[36] They were partly published by James Fenn in two volumes in 1787, two further volumes were published in 1789 and a fifth by Fenn's nephew Serjeant Frere in 1823.

innumerable acts of chicanery, outrage and violence which the book relates year after year during the sixteenth,[37] hardly convey the impression of a society in which public order had markedly improved.

Conditions varied in different parts of the country from decade to decade. If Margaret Paston in East Anglia had to defend the family properties against armed attack,[38] Elizabeth Stonor in Oxfordshire led a peaceful enough life, having nothing worse to complain about than a rumour that her husband intended to bring lodgers home to Stonor. The good lady complained very bitterly indeed, on the ground familiar to housewives over the centuries, that servants were not as diligent as they used to be, and roundly said that if the rumour were true she would give up the burden of housekeeping altogether rather than submit to such an intolerable incubus.[39]

Conditions in medieval and in sixteenth-century England were at all times more or less violent. At least one foreign observer, the Venetian envoy of 1497, thought crime exceptionally widespread in England. He remarked, 'there is no country in the world where there are so many thieves and robbers' and added, 'people are taken up every day like birds in a covey, and especially in London, yet for all this they never cease to rob and murder in the streets.'[40] His opinion is hardly surprising for the execution of the criminal law had always been weak.[41] The mid fifteenth-century records of the court of king's bench show few convictions except of notorious highway robbers. During the period of his personal rule Henry VI issued hundreds of pardons to both suspected and condemned criminals in what was probably a tacit confession of weakness, for men under sentence of outlawry even for crimes as heinous as murder found it possible to live openly and unmolested for years together.[42] Except for the

<hr>

[37] J. Smyth, *The Lives of the Berkeleys* ed. Sir J. MacLean (3 vols 1883–5). The original subscribers numbered less than one hundred and fifty and, although more copies were probably printed, the volumes have never been republished.

[38] In January 1450, in the middle of a quarrel with Lord Moleyns over the ownership of Gresham, an armed gang of about a thousand men (or so the Pastons afterwards alleged) attacked Margaret Paston and twelve other people in the manor house, thoroughly pillaged it and left the place little better than a ruin. *Pastons Letters* introduction pp. xlix–li, I 105–8, 143–4. The incident is no doubt somewhat exaggerated in John Paston's account of it, as such matters generally were in petitions for redress and indictments.

[39] *The Stonor Letters and Papers* ed. C. L. Kingsford, Camden Society (2 vols 1919) I 106. The letter is undated but the editor attributes it to 1470 or slightly earlier.

[40] *A Relation or Rather a True Account of the Island of England* . . . ed. C. A. Sneyd, Camden Society (1847) 34, 36. Also, Sir John Fortescue boasted that more men were hanged in England in one year for robbery and manslaughter than were hanged in France in seven. B. Wilkinson, *Constitutional History of England in the Fifteenth Century* (1964) 328.

[41] T. F. T. Plucknett, *Edward I and Criminal Law* (1960). J. G. Bellamy, *Crime and Public Order in England in the Later Middles Ages* (1973) ch. 1.

[42] R. L. Storey, *The End of the House of Lancaster* (1960) 37, 210–16.

recently developed practice of issuing such numerous pardons, there appears to have been nothing new in all this. Judicial incompetence and judicial violence were centuries old. Any reader of the law codes of Anglo-Saxon England receives from them the impression of an outrageously violent society relying in judicial matters upon ferocious resorts to self-help.[43] Even the saintly Edward the Confessor could order Earl Godwin to take a gang of strong-arm boys into Dover to beat up the population as a punishment for an alleged insult to Count Eustace of Boulogne.[44] The Lincolnshire assize roll of 1202 reveals (most probably for one single year) 114 cases of homicide, 89 of robbery (generally with violence), 65 of wounding, 49 of rape and a number of lesser crimes. An analysis of the sessions of the peace for the same county towards the end of the fourteenth century shows that in fifteen years (1381–96) juries indicted 485 felons. Brutal crime was much more frequent in proportion to the size of the population than it is today, yet the harvest of judicial reprisal was distinctly meagre. In 1202 16 men who had fled and escaped capture were outlawed, 11 others who had taken sanctuary in churches were also outlawed, 9 criminal churchmen were handed over to the ecclesiastical courts, 8 men were sent for trial by ordeal, and of these 2 were executed. Of the 485 felons of late fourteenth-century Lincolnshire, only 81 ever came to trial and all but 5 of these were acquitted or pardoned.[45] There was obviously very little margin for much deterioration in the fifteenth century.

Yet in spite of the sad age-long record, opinion demanded that public order should not fall below some rather vague level which was generally regarded as tolerable and given a perennial tendency to see a golden age somewhere in the past, people were still quite capable of distinguishing between periods of bad order and good, or at least of picking out the less bad.[46] Despite a good deal of notorious open crime during his reign,[47] Henry V bore a high reputation for maintaining justice. In the 1440s and 1450s public order certainly declined as Henry VI and his council failed to

---

[43] e.g. The laws of Alfred, in *The Laws of the Earliest English Kings* ed. and transl. F. L. Atten-borough (1922) especially cl. 42. 'Also we enjoin, that a man who knows his adversary to be residing at home, shall not have recourse to violence before demanding justice of him. If he has power enough to surround his adversary and beseige him in his house, he shall keep him therein seven days, but he shall not fight against him if he [his adversary] will consent to remain inside [his residence]. And if, after seven days, he will submit and hand over his weapons, he shall keep him unscathed for thirty days, and send formal notice of his position to his kinsmen and his friends. . . . If, however, he has not power enough to beseige him in his house, he shall ride to the ealdorman and ask him for help. If he will not help him, he shall ride to the king before having recourse to violence.'

[44] F. M. Stenton, *Anglo-Saxon England* (3rd edn. 1971) 562–3.

[45] A. L. Poole, *From Domesday Book to Magna Carta, 1087–1216* (1955) 392. *Some Sessions of the Peace in Lincolnshire, 1381–1396* ed. E. G. Kimball, Lincoln Record Society (49) (1955).

[46] Bellamy, *Crime and Public Order, op. cit.* ch. 1.

[47] E. F. Jacob, *The Fifteenth Century, 1399–1485* (1961) 127–8.

arbitrate upon the quarrels of the nobility.[48] Decline was particularly notable in Wales and the Marches due to the absenteeism of the great landlords, who allowed the cancellation of the sessions of many of the marcher courts in return for collective fines and left their duties to be performed by corrupt Welsh deputies.[49] Under Edward IV the parliament roll of 1472-5 records bitter complaints of disorder,[50] and in a propaganda speech delivered in 1473 one of the king's officials (most probably the chancellor) pressed the argument that war abroad would reduce violence at home by removing disorderly elements. This, he claimed, could not be accomplished by the normal processes of justice, for repression would produce a remedy worse than the disease—'within few yeres such distruction of people necessarie to the defence of the lande' that enemies would be tempted to invade it.[51] The thug was unfortunately too essential for defence to be put down. Violence was such an institutional necessity that it could be restrained only within certain limits.

On the other hand, a propaganda speech of this kind should not be taken too seriously, and there is some evidence on the other side. Ralph of Diceto had claimed that Henry II tried by turns all classes of men in his efforts to find honest justices but all failed him,[52] and a century and more later Edward I's judges were notoriously corrupt.[53] By the fifteenth century, however, the bench may well have raised its standards. After the reign of Henry IV, there are no known complaints against the justices.[54] In spite of criticism in parliament in 1472 and the remarks of the chancellor, Edward IV made considerable personal efforts in the administration of justice. He issued an exceptional number of commissions of oyer and terminer for the same purpose,[55] and making the most of his position as a

---

[48] Storey *End of the House of Lancaster, op cit.* chs. 5–7.

[49] R. A. Griffiths, 'Gruffyd ap Nicholas and the Rise of the House of Dinefwr', *The National Library of Wales Journal* XIII (1964) 256–68; 'Gruffyd ap Nicholas and the Fall of the House of Lancaster', *Welsh History Review* I (1964–5) 213–31; *The Principality of Wales in the Later Middle Ages: The Structure and Personnel of Government* I; *South Wales, 1277–1536*, Board of Celtic Studies History and Law Series (26) (1972) 27 ff.; 'Patronage, Politics and the Principality of Wales, 1413–1461,' in *British Government and Administration: Studies Presented to S. B. Chrimes* ed. H. Hearder and H. R. Loyn (1974) 67–86.

[50] *Rot. Parl.* VI 8–9, 35–9, 51–4, 103–4, 132–43, 159–60. A somewhat similar argument, that the Yorkist lords and their followers should not be suppressed because this would weaken the realm's defences, had been put forward in the 'Somnium Vigilantis', an anonymous pamphlet of *c.* 1460. See below ch. 11. p. 268.

[51] See below ch. 8. pp 229–30. Also ch. 5. p. 128 n. 9.

[52] *The Historical Works of Master Ralph de Diceto, Dean of London* ed. W. Stubbs, Rolls Series (2 vols 1876) I, 434–5.

[53] A. Beardwood, 'The Trial of Walter Langton, Bishop of Litchfield, 1307–1312', *Transactions of the American Philosophical Society* new series (54) pt. 3 (1964) 3–45.

[54] Bellamy *op. cit.* 14–16.

[55] Lander, *Conflict and Stability, op. cit.* 102–3.

great landowner in Wales and the marches, in the 1470s launched a determined attack upon disorders there,[56] through the establishment of the prince of Wales's council. Although evidence and opinion about crime are always highly debatable, by the later years of his reign he may well have achieved a degree of success that was commendable to his subjects if not to modern opinion. The Bohemian nobleman Leo of Rozmital, on a grand tour of Europe, made no comment upon disorder in England during his visit in 1478, which was quite unlike his experiences in Spain shortly afterwards. Arriving at Compostella his party were at first unable to visit the famous shrine of St James. The bishop's mother, obviously a virago of parts, was defending the cathedral against a siege organized by a local baron. Only after three days' negotiation did the besiegers allow Rozmital to cross their lines, enter the church and make his devotions.[57] Nor is Sir Thomas More's statement that Edward left his realm in quiet and prosperous estates to be despised.[58] It is always unwise to reject the verdicts of observant contemporaries or near contemporaries unless there are very strong reasons for doing so. But whatever Edward IV achieved it can only be said that he reduced violence and injustice to what contemporaries regarded as acceptable levels. Apparently Henry VII was not able to go much further, for Tudor historians have now abandoned the traditional opinion that he suppressed disorder through the court of Star Chamber.[59] The decline of violence was much more gradual and probably no really major, permanent, improvement occurred until the last decades of the reign of Queen Elizabeth I.[60] Even then at the end of the sixteenth century, the council in the marches of Wales levied 270 fines for riot alone in one single year.[61] The violence of the fifteenth century was in no way an unusual phenomenon, for medieval and early modern life was perennially violent.

2   The problem of power: crown and nobility

In most spheres recent investigations have therefore led to a modest rehabilitation of the quality of fifteenth-century life. Nowhere, however, have they led to a more fundamental revision of opinion than on the nature and functions of the aristocracy in politics and in government, and the

[56] See below p. 37.

[57] *The Travels of Leo of Rozmital through Germany, Flanders, England, France, Spain, Portugal and Italy, 1465–1467* transl. and ed. M. Letts, Hackluyt Society 2nd series CVIII (1957) especially 43–65, 114–18.

[58] See below ch. 6 p. 159.

[59] *Select Cases in the Council of Henry VII* ed C. G. Bayne and W. H. Dunham Jr, Selden Society (1958) pp. cxi–cxxvi.

[60] I owe this suggestion to G. R. Elton. See also L. Stone, *The Crisis of the Aristocracy, 1558–1641* (1963) 234 ff.

[61] P. Williams, *The Council in the Marches of Wales Under Elizabeth I* (1958) appendix II.

relationships of the aristocracy with the crown. Nineteenth-century prejudice (a reflection of bourgeois complacency which instinctively ignored contemporary facts) maintained that an ancient, factious nobility to a great extent destroyed itself during the Wars of the Roses, and that the early Tudors completed the repression of its remnants and governed through bureaucrats of middle class origin. Such flights of imagination have forever vanished[62] and with them the supposition that the year 1485, with its change of dynasty, was in any way a fundamental dividing line in English history.

In the early seventeenth century James Harrington wrote in *Oceana* that government could be based either upon a nobility or upon an army.[63] English kings of the fifteenth and sixteenth centuries had no standing army for they simply could not afford one. Neither could they afford a police force, nor anything but the most exiguous bureaucracy.[64] They therefore, as Harrington wrote, had no alternative under heaven except to depend upon their nobility. Statements upon the nature of government from writers in the late fifteenth and early sixteenth centuries are well nigh unanimous in stressing this dependence, so much so that one can say that no thought of any alternative system ever occurred to them. Sir John Fortescue trenchantly stated that 'the might of the land after the might of the great lords thereof standeth most in the king's officers.' Although himself a royal judge he obviously cherished no illusions about the inferiority of bureaucratic power to that of the nobility and their affinities. His opinions are supported by those of William Worcester, the arch-conservative spokesman of the vanishing group of veterans of the Hundred Years' War. Worcester deplored the declining martial spirit of the nobility and gentry, and their civilian preoccupation with estate management and legal affairs. Yet even he somewhat grudgingly conceded that the nobility should concern themselves with civil affairs to the extent of 'maintaining' the justices and other royal officials in carrying out their mainly repressive duties. In 1483 Bishop John Russell, the chancellor, described 'noblesse' as 'vertu and auncienne richesse', compared the aristocracy with firm rocks in an unstable sea, and averred that 'the polityk rule of every region wele ordeigned stondithe in the nobles.' Fourteen years later, Raymundo de Raymundis, the Milanese envoy, reported that 'the state of the realm is in

---

[62] J. H. Hexter, *Reappraisals in History* (1961) chs 4 and 5. See below chs 4 and 5.

[63] J. Harrington, 'Oceana', in *Ideal Commonwealths* ed. H. Morley (1901) 203–23.

[64] D. A. L. Morgan has estimated that in the late fifteenth century '. . . the staffs of those stationary metropolitan offices of the crown—common pleas, king's bench, exchequer, chancery, privy seal—cannot have numbered much more than 200,' plus probably between 200 and 250 members of the royal household 'above stairs' who were important in the country's administration. D. A. L. Morgan, 'The King's Affinity in the Polity of Yorkist England', *Transactions of the Royal Historical Society* 5th series XXIII (1973) 2–3. For provincial offices at the crown's disposal and their importance, see below p. 44.

the hands of the nobles, not of the people.'[65]

The English peerage upon whom so much of the well-being of the country thus obviously depended were not a caste of ancient blood, though some of them may have liked to think so.[66] They were an agrarian plutocracy of comparatively recent origin. K. B. McFarlane demonstrated beyond all doubt that the parliamentary peerage (generally considered to form the English aristocracy) were a new creation of the later middle ages.[67] Until about the third decade of the fourteenth century a small group of powerful earls, declining in numbers owing to the conscious policy of King Edward I, had stood above three thousand or so landowners, all of whom were considered noble. From among them, together with the surviving earls, a varying number at the king's will received a personal summons to attend parliament. In Edward I's later parliaments the number of barons varied from 46 to 100, and the 53 summoned, for example, to the August parliament of 1295 were far from representative of the greater English landowners. Although the chief business to be discussed was war with France, over two thirds of them held estates near the Welsh and Scottish borders, the scenes of recent warfare, and it is quite possible that the basis of the roll of those summoned lay in an earlier list of prominent landowners called upon for military service.[68]

Within three decades the sessions of the upper house of parliament had become much more stabilized in their numbers. A small group, which thereafter became an hereditary parliamentary aristocracy, began to rise above the general ruck of landowners during the reign of Edward II,[69] and by the 1340s a new peerage (including the earls),[70] had settled down in numbers to between 50 and 60, a figure which remained remarkably constant until the end of the reign of Queen Elizabeth I. The bulk of the land-

---

[65] See below ch. 11 pp. 269–70 and n. 12.

[66] e.g. The incident at Calais in January 1460 after the Yorkists had captured the Lancastrian fleet at Sandwich '. . . As for tydyings, my Lord Ryvers was brougth to Caleys, and by for the Lords with viij^{xx} torches, and there my Lord of Salesbury reheted hym, callyng hym knaves son, that he shuld be so rude to calle hym and these other Lords traytors, for they schall be found the Kyngs treue liege men, whan he schuld be found a traytour etc. And my Lord of Warrewyk rehetyd hym, and seyd that his fader was but a squyer, and broute up with Kyng Herry the Vte, and sethen hymself made by maryage and also made Lord, and that it was not his parte to have swyche langage of Lords, beyng of the Kyngs blood.' *Paston Letters* I 506.

The scene was unconsciously ironic for, after all, the younger branch of the Neville family had been notoriously 'made by maryage.' See below ch. 4 pp. 95–7.

[67] K. B. McFarlane, *The Nobility of Later Medieval England* (1973) chs. 1, 2 and 8.

[68] J. E. Powell and K. Wallis, *The House of Lords in the Middle Ages* (1968) 227–9.

[69] *ibid.* 309–15.

[70] At this time earl and baron were the only titles known. Other and more varied titles were introduced later, some in imitation of foreign usage: duke, 1337; marquis, 1386; viscount, 1437.

owners therefore began to lose their claim to nobility, though even in the later sixteenth century some writers still described them as the minor aristocracy.[71] The term is in many ways less misleading than the more common, traditional designation 'gentry' with all its middle-class implications. The minor landowners (the top two per cent of the population or thereabouts, being less numerous in the fifteenth century than they afterwards became) were in their source of income and their way of life much closer to the peerage than to the small urban bourgeoisie. They were entitled to bear coats of arms and therefore regarded themselves as a class apart, while together with the peerage, whose clients in varying degrees many of them tended to be, they made up the ruling class and to all intents and purposes really governed the countryside.[72]

If the numbers of the parliamentary peerage remained remarkably constant, the families within the group did not. Their normal attrition rate in the male line seems to have been as high as about twenty-five per cent every quarter of a century. Neither death in battle nor execution in the Wars of the Roses made any significant difference to this decline,[73] nor even the notorious attainders of the years 1453 to 1509, most of which were ultimately reversed.[74] Such a high rate of extinction meant that the ranks of the peerage had to be maintained by constant new recruitment, from families already rich in their own right who differed but little in their way of life from the existing lords. Such families could generally expect that their wealth plus service to the crown would be rewarded with a title.[75]

Moreover, historians have traditionally and consistently underestimated the capabilities of this aristocracy and have misunderstood their attitudes to life. Like the so-called 'new aristocracy' of the Tudor period, they were a nobility of service, and rose less through military prowess (which was more often rewarded with the Order of the Garter)[76] than by civilian, governmental service. This class of course, like every other, contained within its ranks men of highly divergent intelligence and outlook, but as a group they were far from being the stupid, turbulent, military stereotypes of tradition. Some of them were the best educated laymen of their day, the patrons of literature,[77] and the builders of great houses, which set new standards of elegance and comfort, designed without much thought for the

[71] e.g. Thomas Wilson, 'The State of England, Anno Dom. 1600' ed. F. J. Fisher, *Camden Miscellany* XVI (1936) 23.

[72] See below ch. 4 p. 148 ff.

[73] McFarlane *The Nobility of Later Medieval England, op. cit.* 15, 146–9, 172–6. See also T. L. Kingston Oliphant, 'Was the Old English Aristocracy Destroyed by the Wars of the Roses', *Transactions of the Royal Historical Society* I (1875) 437–43.

[74] See below ch. 5. pp. 129–30.

[75] See below ch. 4. pp. 123.

[76] McFarlane, *The Nobility, op. cit.* 276.

[77] McFarlane, 'William Worcester', *op. cit.* 196–221. *The Nobility, op cit.* ch. 6.

needs of war.[78]

The nobility exercised two different but subtly interrelated roles, in politics and in local government, which historians have seldom if ever sufficiently distinguished. Nor until recently has a real contrast been drawn between the notorious overmighty and the essential mighty subject.

Medieval politics, until the Reformation introduced a strong ideological element,[79] was the sum of the personal relationships of crown and aristocracy (the aristocracy in the wider sense, including the greater gentry). This relationship was contained in the contemporary phrase 'good lordship', whose meaning everybody then understood but which is now so painfully elusive.

Politically, in spite of the dramatic confrontations between the king and the nobility which burst out from time to time, their normal attitude towards each other was that of cooperation. In the fifteenth century after the early conspiracies of Henry V's reign, it took a great deal to provoke the nobility into taking up arms against the king. Their long continued loyalty to Henry VI was remarkable,[80] as was their apparently growing indifference at the highest level of politics during the rest of the century.

The popularity of Sir John Fortescue's works has created something of a myth of the overmighty subject. After all there was no subject 'equipollent' to the king himself,[81] to use Fortescue's own misleading phrase. When the Lancastrians had brought their enormous accumulation of inheritances to the crown, not even the greatest subject possessed an income much more than one twelfth of that of the king, if the king exploited his potential revenues efficiently. Strong as the nobility were, the structure of English landholding made them far less powerful and independent than their continental counterparts. In England noble estates had always been scattered over many counties. Moreover, as the intelligent Venetian envoy remarked in 1497, the English nobility possessed no fortresses and only very limited judicial powers. In his eyes they were hardly noble at all, merely rich gentlemen in possession of large quantities of land.[82]

Except for the northern magnates on the Scottish marches,[83] noble

---

[78] See below ch. 2. p. 63 and Lander, op. cit. 152–3.

[79] W. T. MacCaffrey, 'England: The Crown and the New Aristocracy', Past and Present (30) (1965) 52–64.

[80] K. B. McFarlane, 'The Wars of the Roses', Proceedings of the British Academy I (1965) 94, 96, 117–19, and The Nobility, op. cit. 120–1.

[81] Fortescue, The Governance of England, op cit. 130.

[82] Relation of the Island of England, op. cit. 37.

[83] It is doubtful if a complete exception can be made even for the Percies, powerful as they undoubtedly were in the north. After all, some of their northern estates lay cheek by jowl with those of the Nevilles, the Dacres and the Cliffords and they derived a fair proportion of their income from estates in Lincolnshire, Sussex, Somerset, Dorset, Devon and Wales.

families with dispersed lands and feeble judicial control could never exercise exclusive sway over a single great block of territory, exercising all the coercive powers of landlord, military governor and judge as nobles did in other parts of Europe. No single family could defy the king from a base of strong provincial separatism. Civil war therefore, could never have been welcome as it would always constitute a threat to some part of the scattered aristocratic estate and its vital income.

These nobles, again with a few exceptions in the far north, were not the patriarchal lords of tradition, more interested in a devoted tenantry prepared to support their ambitions by force of arms than in a swelling rent roll. Some indeed were tough businessmen paying such close attention to the exploitation of their estates that their tenants very much resented their harsh efficiency.[84] By 1520 Duke Edward of Buckingham had made himself so unpopular by screwing up traditional rents, that he needed an escort of three or four hundred armed men to make a tour of his Welsh and marcher estates, and a licence from the crown[85] to recruit such an escort. His father, whom Richard III had executed, seems to have been equally unpopular.[86] Avaricious estate owners of this kind obviously attracted too little local devotion to enable them to rush headlong into wanton conflict with the monarchy.

The earl of Warwick's notorious title of 'Kingmaker' has cast a misleading spell over fifteenth-century politics. It was not a contemporary soubriquet[87] and the details of his career hardly justify it. From 1454 onwards he and his father, the earl of Salisbury, supported Richard of York entirely for their own purposes—to maintain their power against the Percies in the north of England and to advance their claim (and more) against the duke of Somerset about the division of the Despenser inheritance in south Wales.[88] In 1460 they refused to support York's claim to the throne. In fact if the Burgundian chronicler Waurin can be believed, Warwick himself was much disturbed at York's deception when the latter made his lone bid for the throne without consulting his very few allies.[89] In 1461

---

[84] K. B. McFarlane, *The Nobility, op. cit.* 41–60, 213–27.

[85] T. B. Pugh, *The Marcher Lordships of South Wales, 1415–1536,* Board of Celtic Studies History and Law Series (20) (1963) 239–61.

[86] Polydore Vergil states that Duke Henry's army against Richard III in 1483 consisted of Welshmen 'whom he, as a sore and hard dealing man, had brought to the feild agaynst ther wills, and without any lust to fight for him . . .' *Three Books of Polydore Vergil's English History, comprising the Reigns of Henry VI, Edward IV and Richard III* ed. Sir H. Ellis, Camden Series (1844) 199.

[87] The title (regum creator) is traceable no further back than the Latin history of Scotland (1521) of John Major. It was not used by any of the sixteenth century English historians. *DNB* XIV 295.

[88] T. B. Pugh, 'The Marcher Lordships of Glamorgan and Morgannig, 1317–1485', in *Glamorgan County History* II ed. T. B. Pugh (1971) 195–6.

[89] See below ch. 4. pp. 102–3.

Warwick and a very rump of supporters made Edward IV king only to escape from a desperate situation. There is no sound evidence that Warwick had any genuine enthusiasm whatever for the venture. If he hoped to make his son-in-law Clarence king early in 1470 his venture failed as a result of his political isolation. Henry VI was the only king that Warwick ever deliberately made—or restored in 1470—and even that episode was a last desperate venture to save himself.

Two explanations once favoured for the outbreak of civil war now seem unconvincing—the failure of Lancastrian foreign policy and an alleged economic decline of the nobility. There is no connection, other than a near coincidence in time, with the expulsion of the English from Normandy and Gascony and the beginning of the Wars of the Roses. From at least as early as 1431 if not before, the increasingly unprofitable nature of the Hundred Years' War had ceased to attract to its campaigns all but a section of the nobility attached to the court.[90] The Yorkist supporters of the 1450s, in spite of the prominence of York's chamberlain, Sir William Oldhall, were hardly a disgruntled war party. Those few of York's friends who were veterans of the war were by this time elderly[91] and somewhat passé in their outlook. The more prominent among them had in any case got out of France with considerable fortunes[92] and other ex-veterans are known to have fought on the Lancastrian side.[93] Most of the refugees who fled from Normandy in 1450 were a pitiful rabble, the objects of charity rather than powerful, determined men bent on revenging themselves upon an incompetent government.[94]

Nor did the nobility as a class turn to arms at home to recoup declining fortunes, for according to K. B. McFarlane most of the main figures, owing to the accumulation of inheritances by marriage, were richer than their grandfathers had been.[95] On the other hand, influence at court for finan-

[90] M. R. Powicke, 'Lancastrian Captains' in *Essays in Medieval History Presented to Bertie Wilkinson* ed. T. A. Sandquist and M. R. Powicke (1969) 371–82.

[91] e.g. Sir John Fastolf died in 1459 at the age of about 72. Sir William Oldhall in 1460 aged over 65. Sir Andrew Ogard in 1454, age unknown. Five other prominent members of York's affinity also died between 1458 and 1460, which seriously weakened his position. T. B. Pugh, 'The Magnates, Knights and Gentry' in *Fifteenth Century England, 1399–1509: Studies in Politics and Society* (1969) 108.

[92] For Fastolf's very large war profits see K. B. McFarlane, 'The Investment of Sir John Fastolf's Profits of War', *Transactions of the Royal Historical Society* 5th series VII (1957) 91–116. For Oldhall and Ogard, see William Worcestre, *Itineraries, op. cit.,* 48, 49 and n. 2, 51. J. S. Roskell, 'Sir William Oldhall, Speaker in the Parliament of 1450–1', *Nottingham Medieval Studies* V (1961) 87–112.

[93] C. A. J. Armstrong, 'Politics and the Battle of St Albans, 1455', *Bulletin of the Institute of Historical Research* XXXIII (1960) 31.

[94] On 25 August 1450 the council ordered £50 to be given to Lord Scales to relieve destitute soldiers who were embarrassing the royal household by their demands for charity. PRO, E. 28/80.

[95] McFarlane, *The Nobility, op. cit.* ch. 3.

cial reasons was extremely important if not vital, for two, and possibly three, major aristocratic politicians. It is true that the dukes of York and Buckingham were both richer than their ancestors had been, but by the 1450s Buckingham's income from his Welsh and marcher lordships had seriously declined and he may have been finding it difficult to maintain the enormous ducal household and retinue.[96] It is possible, though not proven that York, was in a similar position.[97] Moreover, the crown owed both of them very large sums of money.[98] York, in addition to the money due to him for services in France and elsewhere, was entitled to hereditary annuities at the exchequer worth £1,000, which was a vital proportion of his income.[99] His detested rival Edmund Beaufort, duke of Somerset, was much more heavily dependent upon the king. The Beaufort family had been mainly endowed with royal annuities. Partly owing to this, partly to an earlier division of family property,[100] the duke of Somerset's estates produced little more than £300 a year as against nearly £2,000 from crown annuities, pensions and offices.[101] As a result of Henry VI's reckless extravagance in rewarding his courtiers, funds at the exchequer were always inadequate to meet the demands upon them and those whose influence at court was strongest always received priority.[102] It was therefore imperative for these impecunious magnates to be in a position to influence the king. They were vitally concerned with the control of the royal funds and patronage, but under the control of a stronger personality than Henry VI such a situation need not have led to fighting, let alone to fighting which drifted into a dynastic conflict. As it was, in the early 1450s Somerset alone possessed the essential influence at court to ensure that the exchequer met his financial needs, and York's exclusion from the court, apart from his dynastic pretentions and his acute fears that he might be excluded from the succession, probably meant financial hardship. Buckingham's case is less

[96] Pugh, 'Magnates, Knights and Gentry', *op. cit.* 106.

[97] C. D. Ross, 'The Estates and Finances of Richard, Duke of York', in *Welsh Historical Review* III (1966–7) 229–302.

[98] £19,395 to Buckingham as arrears of wages for the captaincy of Calais. In 1446 York had accepted (or been obliged to accept) £26,000 as a composition for £38,066 13s. 4d., owing to him as lieutenant of France, but at least he had been treated better than Buckingham and no worse than other lesser men. Unfortunately, however, he was paid in tallies of assignment at the exchequer and many of these remained unpaid for years. In 1450 the crown also owed him £10,000 for his wages as lieutenant of Ireland and was in arrears with his hereditary pension.

[99] York's net income from land, as far as can be made out from fragmentary accounts, was about £3,800 or rather less. J. T. Rosenthal, 'The Estates and Finances of Richard, Duke of York (1411–1460)', in *Studies in Medieval and Renaissance History* II (1965) ch. 1.

[100] Upon his elder brother's death in 1444 the bulk of the estates had passed to the heir-general, his niece, Lady Margaret Beaufort.

[101] Storey, *op. cit.* 135.

[102] G. L. Harriss, 'Fictitious Loans', *Economic History Review* 2nd series VIII (1955) 187–99.

clear cut. Down to 1458 the duke always tried to keep on good terms with both sides. He was loyal to the king and, at the same time, friendly towards York who was his wife's brother-in-law. By the autumn of 1459 he was firmly on Henry's side against York. Personal loyalty to the king may well have been the decisive factor, but financial difficulties and the possibility of gain might also have influenced his decision. He certainly profited from the spoils taken from those attainted after the battles of Blore Heath and Ludford (1459).[103]

All in all, however, directly financial reasons cannot be said to have affected the actions of other peers. In view of Henry VI's character with its, to say the least, inconvenient effects upon their own lives, the loyalty of the aristocracy was remarkable. Henry and his faction-ridden council during the 1440s and the 1450s had been conspicuously unsuccessful in the most important task of contemporary politics, the exercise of 'good lordship', and they had failed to arbitrate reasonably, fairly, impartially in the disputes of the nobility, a function which the nobility traditionally had every right to expect. The result had been an escalation of private feuds into organized riots and armed clashes in the countryside.[104] These disturbances reached such horrific proportions that between 1448 and 1455 at least one sixth of the peerage were at some time or another imprisoned for disreputable conduct.[105] In spite of the development of conditions so mortifying and humiliating, the peerage remained remarkably loyal to their excessively feeble king and very few so far were prepared to take up arms against him. During the crises of 1452–6 they were distinctly cool towards York's claims to power.[106] Apart from the two Nevilles father and son, Salisbury, and Warwick, only four other peers (and two of them of somewhat dubious status) are definitely known to have fought for York before 1459, though three or four others may have been sympathetic towards him.[107] Many peers seem to have stayed away from the parliament of 1455–6 to avoid the need for taking sides when York was in the ascendant.[108] In the Parliament of Devils of 1459, which attainted the Yorkists after the battles of Blore Heath and Ludford, 32 secular peers including York's uncle Lord Abergavenny, his wife's brother-in-law the duke of

[103] Pugh, op. cit. 106–7.

[104] Storey op. cit. chs. 5–7.

[105] Between 1448 and 1455, the dukes of Exeter and Norfolk, the earls of Devon and Wiltshire, Lords Bonvile, Cobham, Cromwell, Egremont, Grey, Moleyns and Say—a sixth or so of the lay peerage—had all found themselves at some time behind bars for disreputable conduct. Storey, op. cit. 79 and appendix IV. 'John Benet's Chronicle for the Years 1400–1462', ed. G. L. Harriss in Camden Miscellany IX (1972) 199–217. In 1450 York had also imprisoned Somerset in the Tower of London, ostensibly for his own protection.

[106] See below, ch. 3.

[107] See below, ch. 4.

[108] J. S. Roskell, 'The Problem of the Attendance of the Lords in Medieval Parliaments', Bulletin of the Institute of Historical Research XXIX (1956) 189–95.

Buckingham, and his wife's nephew the duke of Norfolk, took an oath of loyalty to Henry VI and the prince of Wales.[109] Even more remarkably in the parliament of 1460, where York so suddenly and unexpectedly asserted his claim to the throne, the peers resisted his claim even though the strongest supporters of the court were far away in the north with Margaret of Anjou.[110] It was only between 1459 and 1461 that a significant section of the nobility progressively swung over to York, and even then to put him into power rather than to make him king. By March 1461 about 20 out of a total lay peerage of around 60 had fought on the Yorkist side, though owing to deaths their fighting strength at that time had been reduced to 17. Even then this new Yorkist section was particularly thin as far as the higher grades of the peerage were concerned, and in the end in March only a mere panic-stricken rump of the faction put Edward IV on the throne.[111]

Why this change then took place can be a matter only of conjecture. It may be that after a bad start, by its mere tenure of the throne over half a century the house of Lancaster had won the loyalty of the peerage. K. B. McFarlane suggested that being the greatest property holders in the country the peers may well have been among the most cautious because they had the most to lose as a result of political miscalculation, and that the past experience of their families had made them exceedingly wary of the consequences of treason. They carried in their minds the most disturbing hereditary memories of the rebellions and confiscations of the reigns of Richard II and Henry IV.[112] Some may have faltered at last in the face of York's pertinacious obstinacy. For a whole decade he had shown that he was not prepared to let his rivals govern. To give in may have seemed the only feasible exit from a now paralysing political chaos.[113] Some younger sons were certainly prepared to fight for York while their more cautious fathers and older brothers still supported the king.[114] It is of course possible that this was a deliberate policy of trimming, a kind of insurance policy to keep a foot in both camps come what may. Again, the opinions of people of lower status from yeomen to gentlemen may have begun to influence them. For many years past, in some parts of the country men had been murmuring that the king was despicable, that he had no more wits than a child.[115] The growing failure to stem the deterioration of public order may have made more and more people sympathetic towards York and thus have enfeebled the powers of the court to resist him.[116] Other nobles, in a society

---

[109] *Rot. Parl.* V 351–2.
[110] See below ch. 4 p. 103 n. 59.
[111] See below ch. 4 pp. 100, 103–4.
[112] 'Wars of the Roses', *op. cit.* 117–19.
[113] See below ch. 4 pp. 100–01.
[114] See below ch. 4 p. 99 n. 38.
[115] Storey, *op. cit.* 34–5.
[116] I owe this suggestion to G. L. Harriss.

where the sanctity of the inheritance was almost a religious conviction, may have feared a general threat to property in the confiscations resulting from the attainders of 1459.[117] Yet in the end the sources fail us. They are too impersonal to reveal the combination of emotions which in many men's minds finally destroyed their remarkably long forbearance and made possible the revolution of 1461.

In spite of Henry VI's feebleness and its malign consequences for so many of the aristocracy,[118] the king nevertheless managed to retain the loyalty of greater numbers. Between the first battle of St Albans in May 1455 and the battle of Towton in March 1461, 37 peers (and possibly 5 more), who were the heads successively of 32 noble families, fought for him, and in the end only 3 of these deserted him for the Yorkist side; 15 died for him, 12 on the battlefield and 3 were afterwards executed by their victorious foes.[119]

It is now sufficiently obvious that the greater part of the peerage—at least 49 out of about 60 families—chose to fight for Henry VI or for Richard of York, though it should be said that until October 1460, when York suddenly and unexpectedly put his claim to the throne before an astonished parliament, the nobles (including York's own closest supporters) had not yet come to regard these quarrels as a dynastic issue.

This high involvement of the peerage during the reign of the last Lancastrian forms a marked contrast to their political indifference to Henry VI's successors and dynastic rivals. The nobility showed a definite reluctance to risk their lives and fortunes for Edward, Richard III and Henry VII.

In 1461 (although he had won a decisive battle, Mortimer's Cross) Edward IV was an untried young man of 19, put on the throne by a fragment of a faction, and much too dependent on the support of one mighty family, the younger branch of the Nevilles, who moreover had been far from enthusiastic for the change of dynasty. It was not a situation to inspire widespread political confidence.

One way to buy support in times of tension and crisis—it had been tried before and it would be used again later[120] was to strengthen the peerage with loyal supporters. Edward created seven new barons in 1461, another six between that date and 1470, and during the same period also created a

---

[117] See below ch. 4 pp. 100–01.

[118] See above p. 20.

[119] See appendix A pp. 301–2.

[120] e.g. Edward III had deliberately built up the nobility. A. Tuck, *Richard II and the English Nobility* (1974) 2 ff. In the troubled years 1447–50 there were no less than fifteen new creations. Powell and Wallis, *House of Lords, op. cit.* chs. 25–9. Later, in the period of strain due to the break with Rome, there were eighteen new creations between 1529 and 1547. H. Miller, 'The Early Tudor Peerage, 1485–1547', *Bulletin of the Institute of Historical Research* XXIV(1951)88–91.

dukedom, a marquisate and eight new earldoms.[121] The recipients of these honours were already rich men in their own right. Nevertheless Edward, as for example with Lord Hastings, Lord Herbert and Lord Stafford, deliberately built up the powers of at least some of them in their own localities[122] in order to enhance their influence. The king soon tried to turn to account in a similar way his marriage to Elizabeth Wydeville, hasty and injudicious though it was. He aimed to bind existing members of the peerage to the royal family, possibly as a counterweight to the Nevilles. As I earlier demonstrated, though some of these marriages were acutely distasteful to the earl of Warwick they by no means offended the susceptibilities of the peerage as a whole, and the families particularly concerned were far from despising the advantages of so close a connection with the royal family.[123] At that time, however, I seriously underestimated the damage to Warwick's interests and the wounds to his injured pride involved in some of these arrangements. In the first place Sir William Herbert (Lord Herbert from 1461) had been a client of both Richard duke of York, and Warwick in south Wales, and Warwick and Herbert had begun to quarrel over their spheres of influence there as early as 1461.[124] The king so built up William Herbert's powers in Wales that one Welsh poet described him as 'King Edward's master lock.'[125] Warwick certainly resented the extension of Herbert's powers in the area at his expense, and therefore the marriage of Herbert's heir to Mary Wydeville. He objected even more (if a hint in the pseudo-William Worcester can be believed) to the marriage of Catherine Wydeville to Humphrey Stafford duke of Buckingham, then a minor, as he may well have intended the duke for one of his own daughters. Warwick had no son, only two daughters, the co-heiresses of enormous estates, and the provision of suitable husbands was a serious matter for any father of such rank and possessions. The matrimonial triumphs of the queen's family by 1466 had swept the board clean of possible mates among the higher nobility. Edward's subsequent

[121] Barons, 1461—Ferrers of Chartley, Hastings, Herbert, Lumley, Ogle, Stafford, Wenlock. Barons, 1462–70—Maltravers, Dunster, Dinham, Mountjoy, Morley, Howard (the first two were the sons of existing peers the earl of Arundel and Lord Herbert). Higher ranks—Henry, Viscount Bourchier, created earl of Essex (1461); William Neville, Lord Fauconberg, created earl of Kent, 1461 (died 1643); John Neville, given the Percy earldom of Northumberland, 1464, but on the restoration of the Percies in 1470, made in lieu Marquis Montagu; Edmund, Lord Grey of Ruthyn, created earl of Kent 1465; Richard Wydeville, created Earl Rivers, 1466; John de le Pole, created earl of Lincoln, 1467; William Herbert (Lord Herbert, 1461) created earl of Pembroke 1468; Humphrey Stafford (Lord Stafford 1461) created earl of Devon 1469; John Stafford, created earl of Wiltshire, 1470; George Neville, created duke of Bedford, 1470.

[122] See below ch. 8 pp. 207–8, and C. D. Ross, 'The Reign of Edward IV', in *Fifteenth Century England, op. cit.* 56. Edward also did the same for existing peers, e.g. Lord Stanley.

[123] See below ch. 4. pp. 133 ff.

[124] T. B. Pugh in *Glamorgan County History, op. cit.* II, 198.

[125] R. A. Griffiths, 'Wales and the Marches', in *Fifteenth Century England, op. cit.* 159.

refusal to allow a Warwick marriage with his brother, the duke of Clarence, left the earl with no hope of finding husbands of appropriate rank for Isobel and Anne Neville.

A great magnate was entitled to expect the benefit of royal favour in arranging marriages for his children. Although the Nevilles as a group certainly received their share of rewards in the 1460s,[126] to Warwick the combination of his defeat over foreign policy, together with such a domestic rebuff at the hands of a young king who originally he probably had no particular desire to see upon the throne, must have been exceptionally galling.[127] Edward was to some extent in a cleft stick. To have given the Nevilles even greater rewards might well have offended other members of the nobility, and to deny Warwick what he regarded as 'good lordship' was certainly unwise if not provocative.

Yet subsequent struggles show the indifference of the peerage, even of some of the newly created Yorkists, to both sides. It is true that the chronicles after 1461 are still thinner and less informative than they are for the 1450s, but even making the most generous allowance for incomplete information, the difference in the numbers known to have been actively involved is immediately striking. Only about seven great families remained irreconcilably anti-Yorkist.[128] The spread of indifference to others was remarkable.

Only four peers were prepared to fight for Warwick in the rebellions of 1469–70.[129] On the other hand only six are definitely known to have supported the king.[130] Once more, on Edward's return from his brief exile at the court of Burgundy in 1471, the majority of the peerage remained aloof from the struggle. Only eighteen took part, ten on the Lancastrian side, eight on the Yorkist.[131] They were equally indifferent in 1483. During his 'second reign' Edward alienated five major families by his manipulation of the common law rules of inheritance and property rights in favour of his own family and that of the queen.[132] T. B. Pugh has most plausibly argued that whereas in 1422 the loyalty which Henry V had inspired in the baronage had secured the peaceful succession of the infant, Henry VI, in 1483 it was the divisions and resentments of the nobility, deriving largely

[126] See below ch. 4 pp. 118–19, 121 and n. 157.

[127] Pugh, 'Magnates, Knights and Gentry', op. cit. 86–8. See also Ross, 'Edward IV', op. cit. 50.

[128] Exeter, Oxford, Beaumont, Hungerford, Roos and Jasper Tudor, earl of Pembroke. Although Lord Clifford's attainder was not reversed until 1485, he received a pardon in 1472. Somerset and Devon died without direct heirs, but the earldom of Devon was recreated for the earl's nephew in 1485.

[129] See appendix A.

[130] ibid.

[131] ibid.

[132] Howard, Berkeley, Huntingdon (Herbert), Buckingham, Westmorland. See Pugh, op. cit. 110–12.

from Edward IV's own actions, which allowed Richard of Gloucester to usurp the throne from his nephew.[133] Richard's usurpation, however, though it may have secured a passive acquiescence in his government did not convince many peers that they should risk their lives for him. When in 1485 Henry of Richmond invaded the country, more or less because it suited the interests of the French court to allow him to do so, only nine nobles, less than a quarter of the English baronage, fought for Richard, and seven of these[134] had profited greatly from his favour. The Percy earl of Northumberland on whom he had relied, stood idly by and watched the conflict, just as he had failed to fight on Edward IV's return in 1471.[135]

Henry of Richmond attracted even less support than Richard III. At the minute but decisive battle of Bosworth, only the die-hard Lancastrian earl of Oxford and his own half-uncle, John Lord Welles are definitely known to have taken part. There is a very strong presumption that another uncle, Jasper Tudor earl of Pembroke, was also there, but no contemporary source states his presence as a fact. Although troops raised by one family, the Stanleys, won Henry's victory for him, Thomas Lord Stanley, Henry's step-father, himself remained aloof, because his son Lord Strange was a hostage in Richard's camp. Altogether, as far as the nobility were concerned, only a little family group supported Henry of Richmond in arms.[136]

Even after his victory Henry seems to have been no more successful in securing active devotion than the Yorkists had been. As Wolffe has remarked, in 1485 there was very little about Henry VII, like Edward IV a quarter of a century earlier, to inspire confidence in nervous politicians.[137] He was an exile, a stranger to the English scene, with no experience in government or in administration of any kind, and at first he was as dependent upon the Stanleys as Edward IV upon the Nevilles. Henry was well aware of the fact that he had managed to seize the country with very little force at his command,[138] no more than ten thousand men, and that if one man could so easily overthrow a government so probably could another. And being so shrewd a politician he must have been equally conscious of the withdrawn attitude of the nobility. Sir Frances Bacon may well have

[133] Pugh, *op. cit.* 111–14. See also E. W. Ives, 'Andrew Dymmock and the Papers of Anthony, Earl Ryvers', *Bulletin of the Institute of Historical Research* XLI (1968) 216–29.

[134] See appendix A.

[135] The account (written 1 March 1486) of a Spanish commentator, Mosén Diego de Valera, suggests that in the interests of his own power in the north, Northumberland would have preferred the young earl of Warwick, the son of the duke of Clarence, to be king. A. Goodman and A. MacKay, 'A Castilian Report on English Affairs, 1486', *English Historical Review* LXXXVIII (1973) 92–9.

[136] For references, see appendix A.

[137] B. P. Wolffe, 'Henry VII's Land Revenues and Chamber Finance', *English Historical Review* LXXIX (1964) 230.

[138] For the minute scale of the Bosworth campaign see Lander, *op. cit.* 98–9.

been correct when he wrote, 'for his nobles, though they were loyal and obedient, yet did not cooperate with him, but let every man go his own way'.[139] This may be the reason why in military matters he relied to such an extent upon his household.[140] It is little wonder that suspicion lay with him all his days and seems to have become more acute with the passing of the years, from the insurrection of Viscount Lovell and the Staffords in 1486 to the crazy 'maumet' of 1499, a Cambridge student who dreamed of being king.[141] In 1504 or 1505, according to a spy's report, a group of officers of the Calais garrison discussed the political situation and their own future. During this talk one of them, Sir Hugh Conway the treasurer, recalled a conversation at court 'emonges many grett personages' when the king was sick, possibly in 1499. These great personages, he said, had then talked of the duke of Buckingham and Edmund de la Pole as possible successors to the crown, but they had never even mentioned the king's sons.[142] In 1508, right at the end of his reign, Henry had imprisoned Thomas Grey marquis of Dorset, and Thomas Courtenay the son of the earl of Devon, in Calais.[143] Yet once again the higher ranks of society proved to be the most cautious and aloof. There was no more of a 'Yorkist party' than there had been in the 1450s. Although sedition eternally menaced the king very few aristocratic families took part in it. After the attainders of 1485 which condemned those who had fought for Richard III at Bosworth, only five peers were attainted for raising arms against the king.[144] Yet the terrifying system of bonds and recognizances imposed in the later years of his reign shows at least by implication (we have no direct explicit statement of his motives), that he regarded the peerage, his partners in power, with the greatest suspicion and fear. This psychological brutality hardly succeeded. Most probably it transformed an earlier indifference into a dangerous backlash of resentment.[145]

[139] Sir F. Bacon, The History of the Reign of King Henry VII ed. R. Lockyer, The Folio Society (1971) 233.

[140] J. D. Alsop, 'The Military Functions of Henry VII's Household', unpublished MA thesis of the University of Western Ontario (1974), shows that Henry VII made a substantial effort to concentrate the command of castles and garrisons and (as far as he could) the control of military activities in the members of his household.

[141] Great Chronicle of London, op. cit. 289.

[142] A. F. Pollard, The Reign of Henry VII From Contemporary Sources (3 vols 1913–14) I 242–3.

[143] The Chronicle of Calais in the Reigns of Henry VII and Henry VIII to the Year 1540 ed. J. G. Nichols, Camden Series (1846) 6. Courtenay had been in the Tower of London since 1501 for supporting Edmund de la Pole, earl of Suffolk. The Anglica Historia of Polydore Vergil, 1485–1547 ed. D. Hay, Camden Series (1950) 122–5.

[144] John de la Pole, earl of Lincoln and Viscount Lovell supported Lambert Simnel, though Lincoln, in fact, probably hoped to seize the throne himself. Lord FitzWalter was the only peer who joined forces with Perkin Warbeck. Lord Audley, who took part in the Cornish Rebellion of 1497, had no Yorkist connections at that time. Edmund de la Pole, earl of Lincoln (brother of John) was attainted for treasonable activities in 1504.

[145] See below ch. 11 p. 299.

All in all, the record of the aristocracy certainly belies the long tradition which saw in their senseless turbulence the origins of the Wars of the Roses. On the contrary, it shows before 1459 a surprising fidelity to a king whose feeble incompetence had been very much inimical to their own interests, and once he had been driven from the throne a change of mood to remarkable indifference to his successors and their dynastic struggles.

Nor were the nobility in general intensely interested in court politics. Long before they began to stand aside from the dynastic struggle after 1461, they had shown a definite apathy towards parliament. J. S. Roskell has shown that in the earlier part of the century attendance in the lords was normally thin, especially among the barons (as distinct from the higher ranks of the peerage), whose attendance sometimes fell as low as one out of three. The house of lords at times could have been no more than an ample session of the continual council, reinforced by a small number of other peers.[146] In periods of crisis the barons turned up in greater force.[147] They may well have done so more from instincts of self-preservation than from any particular desire to dominate events, but once again the verdict remains in the limbo of hypothesis.

The same may be true of their attitude to the commons. If they were reluctant to attend parliament themselves one would think that they could hardly have been enthusiastic borough-mongers. Borough-mongering was already well established in political life but the impulse for it, as later in the sixteenth century, may well have come mostly from the gentry or minor aristocracy who wanted a seat in parliament.[148] Certainly peers from time to time, particularly in the disturbed middle years of the century, tried to influence elections and they may well have thought it desirable to seat some of their supporters in the commons at periods of crisis. The younger branch of the Nevilles did so in the north between 1450 and 1480.[149] As comparative arrivistes in the northern power structure they may have done

[146] Roskell, 'Attendance of the Lords', op. cit. 178–89. After 1461 the evidence is too thin to reach any firm conclusions.

[147] Roskell, 'Attendance of the Lords', op, cit. 176–8, 195. But during the crisis of 1454 an exceptionally large number of lords were so averse from committing themselves on the question of York's protectorate that they stayed away from parliament, so that York, to force a show of approval, in February 1454, decided, for the first and only known occasion in English history to fine peers for non-attendance. The fines were stiff, but they produced only the slightest effect.

[148] For rotten boroughs under aristocratic influence see McKisack, Parliamentary Representation, op. cit. chs. 3 and 6, especially 114–18. Wedgwood, Register pp. cxx ff. N. Denholm-Young, The Country Gentry in the Fourteenth Century with Special Reference to the Heraldic Rolls of Arms (1969) 53 n. 1, 60, 64, 65, 68, has found examples of gentry sitting for boroughs as far back as the 1320s and 1330s. The charters granted to Ludlow (1462) and Much Wenlock (1468) for the first time specifically permitted representation by non-residents.

[149] P. Jalland, 'The Influence of the Aristocracy on Shire Elections in the North of England, 1450–1470', Speculum XLVII (1972) 483–507.

so as a means of asserting their influence against the more firmly established Percies. The duke of York, through his wife's nephew the duke of Norfolk, tried to influence the Norfolk election in 1450. He attempted the same thing in the counties of Northampton and Oxford. His efforts were only partially successful,[150] for there was a strong tradition of independence in many counties. Magnates could hardly dominate shire elections. They could attempt only to manipulate them. There are a few other examples of peers interfering in elections but the evidence is too thin to decide whether they wanted to seat their followers in the commons or whether they acted to oblige members of their affinities.[151] Although John Paston in 1472 wrote that Lord Hastings could put a man in parliament if he wished, an investigation into the parliamentary service of his 90 retainers hardly shows a strong urge to push them into seats. Only seven (possibly ten) of them sat in the commons, at the most only three per cent of the known members of any parliament, far too few to form anything like a voting 'bloc'.[152] Even if other peers acted in a similarly modest way, the proportion of the total membership of the house which they influenced could hardly have destroyed the chamber's independence.

The explanation for this attitude to parliament may well lie in the non-ideological nature of politics. At this time men were not divided in their ideas of the state or of policy. If the great desired power at the centre they were more likely to use their influence and their powers of persuasion personally upon the king and council rather than to sway the increasingly infrequent meetings of parliament.

More important was the 'Westminster element', members of the royal household and the central government departments, the royal affinity in its widest sense, who sought seats in parliament, and may possibly even have been pressed by the king to do so. In the 1420s they were few, but towards

---

[150] McFarlane, 'Parliament and Bastard Feudalism', op. cit. 56–8; 'Wars of the Roses', op. cit. 89 and n. 2, 90 and ns1 and 2.

[151] The dukes of Norfolk and Suffolk and the earl of Oxford tried to manipulate the Norfolk elections of 1455 and 1472. Roskell, Commons in the Parliament of 1422, op. cit. 22–4. In 1459, Viscount Beaumont wrote to Grimsby asking for the election of his servant Ralph Chandler, and c. 1470 Ralph Neville, earl of Westmorland, also wrote to Grimsby asking the mayor to turn over the election writ to him so that he could appoint two members of his council to be burgesses, whose parliamentary expenses he would pay. McKisack, op. cit. 62–3. W. H. Dunham Jr. 'Lord Hastings' Indentured Retainers, 1461–83', Transactions of the Connecticut Academy of Arts and Sciences XXXIX (1955) 33 n. 9.

Various contemporary complaints about interference in elections are somewhat vague and do not mention particular lords, e.g. Huntingdon (1450) and Kent (1455), and a general complaint in the parliament of 1453. Complaints that the 1459 parliament was packed are somewhat suspect as these complaints were made by the victorious Yorkists in 1460. Proceedings and Ordinances VI 246–7. Wedgwood, Register, pp. cii–civ. R. Flenley, Six Town Chronicles (1911) 140–1. Rot. Parl. V 374.

[152] Dunham 'Lord Hastings', op. cit. 29 ff.

the middle of the century they were already numerous. In the parliament of 1478, the main business of which was the attainder of the duke of Clarence, this 'Westminster element' rose to as much as 17 per cent of the whole house, as high a proportion as in the middle years of the reign of Queen Elizabeth I.[153]

The extent of this procedure and the methods by which it was partially attained certainly suggest packing. Although the greater members of the household generally sat for the more prestigious counties,[154] minor officials grabbed borough seats. From 1439 onwards at least eight per cent of the borough returns were tampered with, either locally or by the chancery. Six distinctly over-represented counties with an exceptionally large number of small boroughs account for this activity—Dorset, Somerset, Wiltshire, Surrey, Sussex and Cornwall. Sometimes erasures and alterations in returns were no more than genuine corrections and there is nothing sinister about them, but most cases are those of complete 'carpet-baggers'. J. S. Roskell considers that in these counties in particular the sheriff conducted negotiations with the boroughs for the election of minor household retainers, and that quite possibly he received a list of recommended candidates with the writ of summons sent down from Westminster.[155] On occasion interference was even more blatant than this. In 1467 the election indentures for Bodmin and Liskeard were written in advance in what appears to be a chancery hand, including the name of one of the burgesses, and the other was added, presumably later, in a much cruder local handwriting.[156]

MPs selected in this way (and their electors) knew very well what the government expected of them. A petition to the king after a disorderly election in Huntingdonshire in 1450 states that the electors: 'discretely consideryng the grete conseil and ayde that is behovefull for your most royal estat, and conserwyng the save gard of your most gracious person entendyng the Judisiall pease of youre our erthely sourereygne lord and of your noble realm, sygnifying [?] these premysses that gentilmen of this your honorable Houshold namyed in youre checkir rolle shuld be most like the expedience and [illegible] to execute and assent to the saide aydes for yowe our sourereygne lord, youre realme and us youre trew sugetts and ligemen, for which said causes we have named and chosen for knyghtes for the said

---

[153] Roskell, *The Commons, op. cit.* 135–8. The proportion fluctuated from parliament to parliament.

[154] The election of Sir John Fogge, councillor and treasurer of the household, for Canterbury in 1467 was then unusual. Up to that time the only knights of any rank elected for a city or borough had been London merchants, and even they had been few. *ibid.* 135.

[155] *ibid.* 137–8.

[156] *ibid.* 138–9. For interference in elections in the duchies of Lancaster and Cornwall see K. N. Houghton, 'Theory and Practice in Borough Elections to Parliament during the late Fifteenth Century', *Bulletin of the Institute of Historical Research* XXXIX (1966) 136–8.

shire Robert Stonham and John Styvacle esquyers of your sayde honorable Household . . . .'[157]

The majority of the nobility, however, were far more concerned with their local powers than with the royal court and parliament. Although their estates were scattered, they were exceedingly jealous of their spheres of influence and suspicious of possible intruders. In 1451 in a 'proclamation' the duke of Norfolk stated, 'we lete yow wete that nexst the Kynge our soveragn Lord, be his good grace and lycence, we woll have the princypall rewle and governace throwgh all this schir, of whishe we ber our name, whyls that we be lyvynge, as ferre as reson and lawe requyrith, hoso ever will grutche or sey the [contrary].'[158] As previously mentioned, in the early 1460s Warwick resented exceedingly the increase in William Herbert's power in south Wales. In 1474, Henry Percy earl of Northumberland became Richard Duke of Gloucester's retainer but the wording of the indenture between them makes it amply clear that this was a method of defining their areas of power.[159] There was also long-standing rivalry between the Percies and the archbishops of York.[160]

The role of the nobility in maintaining the peace of the countryside was fundamental to their society. One of the basic problems of government was to ensure that public order did not fall below a certain acceptable minimum level. This the royal courts, in spite of their superficially brilliant development, had never been able to do because they had far too little coercive power at their command.[161] The authority necessary to ensure social peace lay largely in private hands. From the Anglo-Saxon period with its increasing emphasis on the powers of lordship, to the development of police forces in the early nineteenth century, government in England (as elsewhere in Europe) was a function of property. Through various mutations of form and style it was always government by the rich, from Anglo-Saxon lordship to classical feudalism after the Norman Conquest, from classical feudalism to bastard feudalism in the later middle ages, moving from there to a looser form of clientage in the later sixteenth century.

Until comparatively recently historians flayed bastard feudalism as a malign social development, a pathological deterioration of classical feudalism peculiar to the fifteenth century. As remarked earlier, however, the contrasts between the faith, loyalty, justice and good order of former

[157] Wedgwood, *Register* p. ciii.

[158] *Paston Letters* I 230. Undated, but probably from 1451 when Norfolk was acting as a commissioner of oyer and terminer. He, himself, was a violent man and his affinity had a particularly bad reputation. Storey *op. cit.* 79.

[159] Gloucester undertook not to accept into or retain in his service any servant retained with the earl. Dunham, *op. cit.* 77.

[160] *Select Cases in the Council of Henry VII, op. cit.* 41–2.

[161] See above pp. 8–11.

centuries and their supposed deterioration in the fifteenth have been terribly overdrawn.[162] G. A. Holmes and W. H. Dunham Jr have shown that the development of bastard feudalism long preceded the fifteenth century and long survived its close, and that it was equally associated with periods of weak or strong government, and of peace or disorder.[163] The system progressed in the later thirteenth century, and seems to have provided retinues for civil war under Edward II, and certainly did so under Richard II when the abnormally large Lancastrian retinue formed the power base for the usurpation of Henry IV.

The term 'private army' has been very loosely handled in connection with bastard feudalism. The overtones of this phrase are completely misleading as a description of the retinues of the English nobility, in that they imply a permanent force more or less constantly under arms at the disposal of a magnate. Reality was more humdrum. Magnates could of course raise considerable numbers of men in an emergency, but they could never keep them in arms for long. Too many generalizations have been based upon the quite abnormal retinue of John of Gaunt, who was far richer than any other subject in medieval England and his retinue very much greater. In the mid 1390s the duke was paying out over £3,000 a year in fees.[164] No fifteenth-century retinue so far investigated cost its patron anything like this enormous sum. The greatest, that of Humphrey duke of Buckingham in the 1450s, cost him just over £900,[165] though at one point York was paying officers and annuitants about £960 in spite of the fact that his following was considerably smaller.[166] The returns for the income tax of 1436 list the annuitants of 14 nobles (about one third of the peerage of that time). Only two had granted annuities which amounted to more than twenty per cent of their taxable income,[167] though if estate and household officials were included the proportion would rise significantly. By the 1450s however, the Percies were paying about thirty-five per cent of their income, or about £514 to officers and annuitants.[168] However, as K. B. McFarlane has pointed out, the habit of granting offices and annuities had become so indiscriminate, and so many men had become the annuitants of more than one or even several patrons, that the system must have become almost self-defeating as a method of securing the undivided loyalty of political adherents.[169]

[162] See above pp. 8–11.
[163] G. A. Holmes, *The Estates of the Higher Nobility in Fourteenth Century England* (1957) ch. 3. Dunham, *op. cit.* 7–11, 90–116.
[164] Pugh, 'Magnates, Knights and Gentry', *op. cit.* 107–8.
[165] *ibid.* 105–6.
[166] *ibid.* 108–9. But see also Ross, 'Estates and Finances of Richard, Duke of York', *op. cit.* 299–302.
[167] Pugh, *op. cit.* 101.
[168] Bean, *Estates of the Percy Family, op. cit.* 85–98.
[169] McFarlane, 'Wars of the Roses', *op. cit.* 109.

In 1471 Lord Hastings and his affinity brought 3,000 men to Edward IV's banners.[170] In 1454 it had been rumoured that the duke of Buckingham could command the services of 2,000 followers and he rewarded 90 men from Kent and Sussex alone for their services at the first battle of St Albans.[171]

Buckingham's following at St Albans may have been larger than that of other peers for the court was taken by surprise and the royalist lords, in general being therefore unprepared, could muster between them no more than 2,000 men at the most.[172] Except at the battle of Towton (1461) fighting strength in the Wars of the Roses was always small.[173] Our conventional vocabulary applied to these encounters has been intensely misleading. Contemporary specialists in the art of war knew better. In the sophisticated technical vocabulary of continental chivalry many of the so-called battles would have been designated by less grandiose terms—'besognes', 'rencounters', or 'melées'.[174] Even then there is a good deal of evidence that many men were intimidated into joining the armies rather than fighting willingly[175] and that the officials and annuitants of magnates sometimes refused to support them in times of crisis.[176]

The fifteenth-century retinue served as protection in a land otherwise ineffectively policed and added to a magnate's influence and prestige. But while it undoubtedly possessed military functions, it was less a private army than a combination of an estate bureaucracy and a series of quasi-business alliances with the gentry, for mutual profit and for the control and dis-

---

[170] *Historie of the Arrivall of Edward IV in England* ed. J. Bruce, Camden Series (1838) 8–9.

[171] Or, at least, it was rumoured that he had had 2,000 badges (bendes with knottes) made, presumably for distribution to followers. *Paston Letters* I 265.

For numbers (incomplete) of men with him at various times see McFarlane, 'Wars of the Roses', *op. cit.* 91 and ns 2 and 3, 92 and n. 1.

[172] Armstrong, 'Battle of St Albans', *op. cit.* 28.

[173] Lander, *op. cit.* 162–3.

[174] C. A. J. Armstrong, 'La Toison d'or et la loi des armes', *Publications du centre européan d'études burgondo-médianes*, Basle V (1963) 1–7.

[175] e.g. A threatened French attack on Yarmouth in 1457 roused Norwich to muster a force of 600 men, but a summons by Henry VI in 1461 to the mayor to come 'cum omne posse civitatis' produced only 120 men whom William Rokewood was persuaded 'by great labour and supplication' to command. J. J. Bagley, *Margaret of Anjou* (1948) 18 n. 1. In the same year Margaret of Anjou threatened death to all who did not come to her aid. C. L. Scofield, *The Life and Reign of Edward IV* (2 vols 1923) I 117. In 1471 Warwick threatened penalties of death when other methods of recruitment failed. *Arrivall of Edward IV, op. cit.* 8.

Polydore Vergil remarked in 1483 'whan the duke [Buckingham] with great force of Walse soldiers, whom he, as a sore and hard dealing man, had brought to the feild agaynst ther wills, and without any lust to fight for him, rather by rigorous commandment than for money, ...' *Polydore Vergil, op. cit.* 199.

[176] e.g. In 1459 Sir William Skipwith accused three of York's councillors, Sir John Neville, Sir James Pickering and Thomas Colt of putting him out of the stewardship of the duke's manor of Hatfield (Yorks) and the constableship of the castle of Conisbrough for refusing to follow York to the first battle of St Albans (1455). Armstrong, 'Battle of St Albans', *op. cit.* 27.

cipline of the countryside. W. H. Dunham Jr, for example, has strongly stressed the mainly civilian nature of the services which Edward IV's chamberlain, Lord Hastings, demanded from his numerous retainers.[177] Inevitably the system allowed undue scope for the machinations of un-scrupulous men, and demanded a king of strong character for its successful control, who would keep the peace among the nobility, and as far as he could restrain their behaviour towards others within decent bounds. As Edmund Dudley wrote, the king must not suffer the nobles of his realm 'to rune at riot as to ponisshe or reuenge there owne quarrelles.'[178] If they controlled their own affinities in the same way good order would prevail throughout the land.

Magnates frequently abused the system in their own interests. Under Richard II the question of control caused considerable contention between the lords and the commons, which led to definition and restriction in a statute of 1390.[179] The statute was realistic. It recognized retaining and at the same time placed orderly limitations upon it. In future only peers might give liveries, except to household servants, and even then only to knights and esquires who had to be retained by indenture for life. The statute was thoroughly in tune with the hierarchial opinions of the day, which held that the richer a man was the less his instincts were likely to run to oppression and corruption. In effect, its purpose was to restrict affinities, and therefore to a certain extent prime responsibility for social order, to the peerage.

Various successive acts made minor alterations, but no radical change in the law took place until 1468. A new statute then ostensibly forbade retaining completely, except for menial (household) servants, officers and men learned in the law, 'or for lawfull service doon or to be doon,' while it authorized prosecution by common informers who were to receive as their reward half the fines inflicted.[180] Mystery surrounds the operation of this statute. Edward IV certainly condoned retaining by peers after the passing of the act. Lord Hastings after 1468 issued 64 indentures of retainer, and only one of the retainers is therein described as 'counsel learned', and none as officers or resident household servants. Although lesser men were prosecuted for retaining, no single case of the prosecution of a peer is known before that of Lord Burgavenny in 1506, whose 471 retainers were described as gentlemen, clerks, yeomen and a cobbler and a tinker. As they

---

[177] Dunham, *op. cit.* 65–6. On the other hand somewhat earlier indentures, e.g. of the earls of Salisbury and Warwick and Lord Greystock, still strongly stress military service. *ibid.* 63–5. These life indentures should, of course be firmly distinguished from those completely military indentures drawn up between the king and leaders of war contingents and such leaders and their own men for foreign campaigns.

[178] E. Dudley, *The Tree of Commonwealth* ed. D. M. Brodie (1948) 103. See also 41, 44–5.

[179] Statute Roll 13 Richard II stat. 3 c. 1. *Rot. Parl.* III 265.

[180] Statute Roll 8 Edward IV c. 2. *Rot. Parl.* V 633–4.

were not knights and esquires Burgavenny had thus violated the act of 1390 which was still on the statute book.[181]

Perhaps the 'lawful service' clause provided a loophole, for certainly the phrases of Lord Hastings's indentures are carefully drafted to take account of it. An alternative explanation may be that, as the act did not mention peers who had traditionally and lawfully enjoyed the right of retaining, contemporaries assumed from the beginning that it was never intended to include them. Only later in the reign of Queen Mary did the lawyers single out the act of 1468 and interpret it as applying to the aristocracy as well as to other men. There is no evidence that under Edward IV it was ever understood to make the retaining of non-residents by peers illegal.[182]

Henry VII in 1504 again prohibited retaining. Once again peers were never specifically mentioned, though in this act there was no 'lawful service' clause. The omission therefore closed a loophole. The act, however, allowed the king to issue licences or placards under his sign manual, signet or privy seal, for the keeping of retainers.[183] During the sixteenth century the privilege of retaining was gradually restricted to peers holding office under the crown and to other royal officials, until it withered away by the early seventeenth century. Nevertheless all the early Tudors achieved was some slight control over the practice.[184]

Social and governmental conditions were such that the king was forced to rely on local control by the nobility as well as on that of his own officials, and such control could be exercised only through their affinities. Even Henry VII, who held about three quarters of the nobility under the terror of attainders, bonds and recognizances,[185] and according to Polydore Vergil intended to cow the rich and the men of substance,[186] made no frontal attack upon their local powers except in two or three cases.[187] He allowed them retainers under licence, and never attempted to deprive them as a class of either their influence or their traditional functions. They were prominent enough in his council[188] and in times of crisis like the Cornish rebellion.[189] In the north he at first pinned his faith on the Percy earl of Northumberland, in spite of that magnate's dubious record at the battle of

---

[181] Dunham, op. cit. 103–5.

[182] For a very full discussion see ibid. ch. 4. It is just possible, though incapable of proof, that the act was intended to prevent retaining by the king's enemies during the political troubles which began in 1467 and was then later ignored as far as the peers were concerned.

[183] Statute Roll 19 Henry VII c. 14.

[184] Dunham, op. cit. ch. 5.

[185] See below ch. 11.

[186] Anglica Historia, op. cit. 127–31.

[187] e.g. The earl of Kent, the marquis of Dorset and Lord Burgavenny. See below ch. 11. pp. 286–91.

[188] Select Cases in the Council of Henry VIII op. cit. p. xxix.

[189] e.g. Lord Daubeney led the royal forces against the rebels at Blackheath and the earl of Devon organized the defence of Exeter.

Bosworth. Even after the duke's murder, which had left the head of the family a minor and made reliance upon the Percies for the time impossible, the king did not turn to a council of bureaucrats for the government of the north and the defence of the realm against Scotland. Once again he committed these tasks to a nobleman, Thomas Howard earl of Surrey, who had fought against him at Bosworth, had been released from imprisonment in the Tower of London only a few weeks before he took office, and was still under attainder.[190]

Distasteful though the system may be to modern minds, it is surely pointless to condemn it on *a priori* moral grounds. Until the taxpayers were prepared to meet the cost of a much greater royal bureaucracy, bastard feudalism was local government and there was nothing to put in its place. A controlled cooperation between the king and the nobility was the desirable norm of this type of society. If the existing nobility proved insufficient to fulfil the role, kings from time to time created new peers. As Henry VI (or his council) wrote to the atrociously turbulent Lord Poynings, 'Howe it be that not long agoo we putte you to the worship and astate of baron, not for any greet service that ye hadde do to us before that tyme but for the trust and trowing that we hadde of the good service that ye sholde do us in tyme comying, *in especiall in the keping of the rest and pees of our lande*, and in letting of all that sholde mowe to the contrarye.'[191]

Indeed it seems that disorder was all the greater if aristocratic power was weak, as happened in Wales and the marches in the middle of the fifteenth century when mainly absentee great landlords, unable to give sufficient of their personal attention to the area, more or less abdicated their power to a corrupt Welsh squirearchy.[192] In fact the Venetian envoy of 1497 saw the weakness not the strength of the English nobility as a primal cause of disorder. He strongly implied in his report to the doge and senate that crime in England was so prevalent because the English nobility possessed such very limited judicial powers, and that the royal judicial system was insufficient to fill the resulting void.[193]

Even so, the execution of the law fell upon the nobility and their affinities. Noblemen were always included in the commissions of the peace and generally in the commissions of oyer and terminer, of which Edward IV made such extensive use.[194] Again, the sheriffs and the justices of the

[190] See below ch. 5 pp. 145–7. R. L. Storey, 'The Wardens of the Marches of England towards Scotland, 1377–1489', *English Historical Review* LXXII (1957) 593–615, exaggerates the switch to officials, and the decline of magnate influence in the north at this time. cf. M. R. James, *Change and Continuity in the Tudor North: The Rise of Thomas First Lord Wharton*, Borthwick Papers (27) (1963).

[191] 8 October 1453. *Proceedings and Ordinances* VI 161–2. He had been created a baron in 1449. My italics.

[192] See above p. 11 and n. 49.

[193] *Relation of the Island of England, op. cit.* 36–7.

[194] Lander, *op. cit.* 102–3.

peace may have been officials in the sense that the king formally appointed them in the chancery, but to regard them for that reason as in any sense a modern bureaucracy is to mistake the shadow for the substance. Officially appointed they may have been, but the crown's choice was automatically limited to men of standing and adequate fortune in their own districts. These men possessed sufficient powers of enforcement almost entirely derived from their own personal prestige and wealth, and moreover were rich enough to resist the grosser temptations of corruption. Widespread opinion firmly held that men of insufficient wealth were more likely than others to abuse power in their own interests,[195] and the house of commons itself insisted that the justices of the peace should be men of some substance.[196] And these lesser but essential rulers of the countryside were very closely connected with the peerage. Thirty-three of Lord Hastings's retainers for example were justices of the peace,[197] as were Sir John Howard and John Paston. Howard was a blood relation of the duke of Norfolk. John Paston, the younger brother with the same name, was in the duke's service. An uneasy relationship it was, for the duke disputed their ownership of one of their most valuable possessions and treated the family with anything but the 'good lordship' which they had a right to expect in such circumstances. Yet throughout the Pastons behaved with extreme punctiliousness and deference towards him.[198]

When Edward IV came to the throne in 1461 he naturally had no alternative but to work in this ambience. At the time when chapter 6 of this book (on Edward's personal efforts and activities) was first published in 1956, the researches on the nobility which have since so changed our views of the power structure and therefore of the politics and government of the fifteenth century, still lay in the future. It therefore suffers from omission and by today's standards from something of a false slant, in that it overemphasizes the king's personal efforts in the suppression of disorder and gives too little significance to the role of the nobility and their affinities.

Nevertheless, at the time of its publication the article broke new ground, for it at least destroyed the extreme legend, based upon the *Mémoires* of Philippe de Commynes, of Edward as a somewhat bloodthirsty, avaricious

---

[195] Lander, *op. cit.* 172–3.

[196] e.g. In 1439–40. *Rot. Parl.* V 28. Also in 1484 an act of parliament stated that jurors should be men of good substance. Statute Roll 1 Richard III c. 4. See also the act of 1478 which deprived George Neville of the dukedom of Bedford because of poverty. It emphatically states '. . . when eny Lord is called to high estate, and have not liffelode conveniently to support the same dignite, it induces gret poverte, indigens, and causes oftymes gret extortion, embracere, and mayntenaunce to be had, to the grete trouble of all such Contres wher such estate shall hape to be inhabitet.' *Rot. Parl.* VI 173. For corruption and oppression arising from an official's poverty, see case of John Newport, below ch. 2 p. 66.

[197] Including the two peers among his retainers, Lords Grey of Codnor and Mountjoy. Dunham, *op. cit.* 39.

[198] See below p. 38.

incompetent, an opinion at that time almost universally accepted. It contains nothing untrue about Edward's activities for, as an article by J. G. Bellamy a few years later showed, the king's personal efforts in conducting judicial tours round the country were very great. Bellamy indeed felt justified in speaking of an almost atavistic return to an earlier form of peripatetic monarchy.[199]

In some parts of the country royal lordship, itself after all a form of bastard feudalism, may be a clue to the restoration of order. As chapter 6 shows, Edward quite apart from his judicial tours interfered directly in various parts of the kingdom, but such action may have been most prominent in areas where he had strong interests as a landowner. Coventry, where his intervention was frequent, was one of the centres of the duchy of Lancaster, now a crown property though kept under separate administration. He was fully aware politically of the importance of the numerous officials on the crown lands,[200] and the officers of the royal household divided their time regularly between the court and their own counties[201] forming a most important link between central and local government.

In the later years of his reign Edward chose as far as he could to extend such methods. Although in the 1460s he built up the powers of the Herberts in south Wales and the Marches, even creating for William Herbert the last of the great franchises in that area,[202] after 1471 he reversed his policy. The king himself by this time was the greatest landlord in the Marches of Wales and he increased his estates by forcing an exchange of lands on William Herbert's heir. Though even then the king did not interfere directly with the jurisdictions of the existing marcher lords, the foundation of the prince of Wales's council provided a supervisory body to ensure that they performed their functions more adequately. The extension of the council's governmental and supervisory authority, especially from 1476 onwards, was based as much upon the ownership of land and the patronage connected with it as upon the inherent powers of kingship, and brought a new vigour into the administration of justice and the maintenance of public order in the west.[203] Elsewhere Edward still relied upon the nobility and their local influence.

At the same time the extent of the king's power and success should not be

---

[199] J. G. Bellamy, 'Justice Under the Yorkist Kings', *American Journal of Legal History* XI (1965) 135–55.

[200] 'Distributis namque in omnes partes Regni, ad castrorum, maneriorum, forestarium, et parcorum custodias, fiducialioribus servitioribus suis, nihil ab ullo homine quantumcunque excellenti tam subdole in aliqua parte Regni poterat attemptari in faciem restitum non fuisset.' Fulman 562. See also below pp. 44–5.

[201] Morgan, 'The King's Affinity', *op. cit.* 4.

[202] J. Otway-Ruthven, 'The Constitutional Position of the Great Lordships of South Wales', *Transactions of the Royal Historical Society* 5th series VIII (1958) 7.

[203] Griffiths, 'Wales and the Marches', *op. cit.* especially 160–62.

exaggerated. He was forced to allow his noble supporters something of a free hand in local affairs and to turn a blind eye to some distinctly questionable and oppressive activities. After the duke of Norfolk besieged Caister castle and forcibly took it from the Pastons, Edward, in spite of the family's pleas to him for justice, never effectively intervened against the duke. The Pastons recovered Caister only after Norfolk's death,[204] though in this case Edward like many other people, may have felt deeply suspicious about the validity of their claims. Caister castle was part of the Fastolf inheritance and the Pastons were widely suspected of forging Sir John Fastolf's will to obtain it. But to do him justice, Edward was neither the first nor the last English monarch to temporize in the face of a powerful nobleman or to favour him in this way. The notorious series of lawsuits about the Berkeley estates lasted for 192 years. Elizabeth I's favourite, the earl of Leicester, at one point was trying to get possession of some of the lands himself, by rather underhand methods involving pressure from the queen. He remarked that 'these titles had ever suceeded between theire houses, according to the kings favour in their times.'[205]   Not only was Elizabeth I prepared to use dubious influence of this kind on behalf of favoured courtiers, but like Edward IV she too was prepared to turn a blind eye to local feuds. She took no steps to suppress the violent conduct of the earl of Shrewsbury towards the Stanhope family in Nottinghamshire. Only when the earl fell under suspicion of recusancy did she at last clap him into prison.[206]

Sir Thomas More's verdict that Edward IV left his realm 'in quiet and prosperous astate' remains worthy of credence. But less credit than formerly must be attributed to the personal efforts of the king at local level, great though these were, and more to his cooperation with and control through the nobility and their affinities, using the lines of command of bastard feudalism.

Twenty-five years ago, taking their cue from the researches of F. C. Dietz and A. P. Newton,[207] most writers maintained that Henry VII restored the financial prosperity of the monarchy and based its organization upon the chamber. At the same time Yorkist finance (except for the proceeds of the customs) remained a dark mystery. A. Steel, after many years' work on the exchequer records, concluded that from the 1450s their nature began to change, and that from 1461 onwards omissions were so glaring that they had become quite useless as a guide to the true state of the revenues.[208]

[204] *Paston Letters* II 282, 348–9, 354–5, 371–3, 374–6, 392, 397–8, III 14, 16, n. 2, 56, 64–6, 74, 87, 127–9, 137, 139, 140, 142, 144–7, 149, 150, 151–4. Dunham, *op. cit.* 42–4.

[205] Smyth *Lives of the Berkeleys, op. cit.* II 294.

[206] W. T. MacCaffery, 'Talbot and Stanhope: An Episode in Elisabethan Politics', *Bulletin of the Institute of Historical Research* XXXIII (1960).

[207] Dietz, *English Government Finance, op. cit.* Newton, 'The King's Chamber,' *op. cit.* 348–72.

[208] A. Steel, *The Receipt of the Exchequer, 1377–1485* (1954) 322 ff.

However, while I was tentatively suggesting the Yorkist revival of the chamber as a spending department and an audit office,[209] B. P. Wolffe was publishing the first of those studies on the crown lands which have so fundamentally changed our opinions on Yorkist and early Tudor government finance.[210]

In brief, the years between 1461 and 1509 saw the rise, maturity and, in the opinion of many contemporaries, the definite abuse of a new system of royal financial exploitation, in the establishment of endowed monarchy with the great bulk of the royal income coming from the customs revenues and the crown lands.

According to Wolffe's thesis, from the Norman Conquest to the late fourteenth century English kings derived the bulk of their income from taxation, the royal estates being exploited mainly for the purposes of political patronage. In the 1380s and after, the slogan, 'the king should live of his own', became so popular[211] as to be almost a political dogma, with the house of commons and the taxpaying classes attempting to force the principle upon the king, unsuccessfully under Henry IV, successfully under Henry VI between 1450 and 1456.[212] By the middle of the fifteenth century the English landowning classes had become adamantly resistant to any reformed, realistic assessment for direct taxation.[213] Henry VI's reputation had risen immensely when he agreed to conserve his own resources by acts of resumption and therefore, to lighten taxation. Both Edward IV and Henry VII grasped the significance of these dual demands. Well aware of their insecure basis of power and wishing to avoid any excuse for discontent, they were exceedingly circumspect in their demand for direction taxation and raised in fact very little from it, Edward IV no more than an average of £10,700 a year, Henry VII doing rather better with

---

[209] See below ch. 6 pp. 166–7, 170, n. 71.

[210] For the following paragraphs see B. P. Wolffe, *The Crown Lands, 1461–1536* (1970) 1–28 and *The Royal Demesne in English History: The Crown Estate in the Governance of the Realm From the Conquest to 1509* (1971) chs. 1–3, 6–7. Chapters 6 and 7 of this latter book are revised versions of articles published in the *English Historical Review* LXXI (1956) 1–27. LXXIX (1964) 225–54. Both versions need to be used, however, as the earlier versions contain materials not included in the revisions and vice versa.

[211] *ibid.* J. J. N. Palmer. 'The Parliament of 1385 and the Constitutional Crisis of 1386', *Speculum* XLVI (1971) 477–90. But see G. L. Harriss, *History* LVIII (1973) 78 who, in a review of Wolffe's latest work, expresses doubts about this interpretation and points out that as early as 1298 Edward I declared 'que vous ne entendez a ceste fois nule aide de nous demaunder ne autre foiz si graunt besoign ne le face, mes del votre demeyne chevir vous en ceste guerre taunt come vous purrez . . .'. *Registrum Roberti Winchelsey* ed R. Graham (2 vols 1952–4) I 260. I owe this reference to G. L. Harriss.

[212] B. P. Wolffe, 'Acts of Resumption in the Lancastrian Parliaments', *English Historical Review* LXXXIII (1958) 583–613.

[213] *English Historical Documents* IV, 1327–1485 ed. A. R. Myers (1969) 379–81.

£12–13,000.[214] Although both experimented with new forms of direct taxation, their experiments turned out to be humiliatingly unsuccessful.[215] Political exigencies therefore forced both kings back on the proceeds of indirect taxation (the customs system), the royal estates and fiscal feudalism.

Edward IV in the 1470s imposed a new class of highly paid customs supervisors in all the major ports, 'men of remarkable shrewdness, but too hard upon the merchants according to the general report'[216] and Henry VII was constantly preoccupied with the system. The customs revenues amounted to £34,300 in 1478–9 and rose to an average of £40,000 during the last ten years of Henry VII's reign.[217] Unfortunately, owing to the nature of the evidence it is impossible to say what proportion of this increase was due to improved trade and what proportion was due to improved administration.

A major, even greater, thrust came with the royal lands. Edward IV and his advisers, wise in their generation, immediately in 1461 adopted as their official policy the clamours of the disgruntled house of commons of a decade earlier. An act of resumption was introduced to increase the value of the royal lands and thus avoid the need for heavy taxation. Other such acts followed in 1465, 1467 and 1473 and under Henry VII in 1485–6, 1487 and 1495.[218] Confiscations under acts of attainder further enlarged the pool, though only in a temporary way,[219] and escheats also are generally held to have increased it still more.

Equally important was a vital change in administrative methods. Traditionally the exchequer had run the royal estates. Although this government department was a ponderously persistent debt-collecting office, it worked only feebly in the sphere of estate management for it was overcentralized. Its officials rarely moved from Westminster and therefore could never adequately supervise the detailed administration of lands

[214] Edward IV also obtained an average of about £2,000 year from his two benevolences (1475, 1482–3) and he raised special local taxation from the communities of Flint and Cheshire averaging about 1,100 marks a year. Under Henry VII, the proceeds of the benevolence of 1491 would also average out at about £2,000 a year. In addition Edward IV exacted above £7,000 a year from the clergy and Henry VII about £9,000.

[215] See below ch. 9 pp. 230–34. S. B. Chrimes, *Henry VII* (1972) 198–201.

[216] See below ch. 6 pp. 168–9.

[217] Dietz, *op. cit.* 25.

[218] The act of 1461 was based on a commons' petition, but this by no means rules out the possibility that it was already official policy. Commons' petitions were often government inspired. Wolffe sees the principal act of the 1485–6 parliament as policy forced by the commons upon a king whom they had no reason to trust and one insufficiently experienced to have initiated the policy himself. The act of 1487 was more concerned with financial and administrative reorganization than with the increase of assets as such, and the acts of 1495 clarified Henry's title to the lands which Richard III had held as duke of Gloucester and lands held by the house of York under grants made by Edward III and Richard II to Edmund of Langley. Wolffe, *The Royal Demesne, op. cit.* 196–9. Chrimes, *op. cit.* 206.

[219] See below ch. 5 pp. 153, 157.

scattered throughout the country. As long as the royal estates had been used mainly for purposes of patronage this inefficiency had probably been of no great moment, but its continuation would have been disastrous once the decision had been taken to exploit the crown lands for a cash income.

Therefore, as early as 1461 the Yorkists adopted a new system based on the most up-to-date methods of private estate management such as those of the duchy of Lancaster and their own duchy of York, and common with individual variations to all the great estates of the country. To describe the new system in the simplest terms, blocks of estates (some regrouped for convenience in a way which cut across traditional boundaries) were placed under the jurisdiction of special receivers, whose accounts were checked locally by itinerant auditors instead of centrally at the Westminster exchequer.[220] These receivers were bureaucrats who spent a great part of their lives in the saddle, riding continually from estate to estate, and exercising a far stricter and tighter control than hitherto over the local officials. They were drawn from a highly trained class of professional land managers, some of whom had wide experience upon other estates as well. Their importance in the eyes of the crown (like that of the new supervisors of the customs) is firmly attested by their high pay, for their incomes exceeded all but those of the greatest of the gentry[221] and numerous landowners must have envied their professional incomes.

Henry VII, brought up abroad in complete ignorance of both governmental and private administration, for the first two years of his reign let the system lapse. Then, under the influence of ex-Yorkist administrators, he gradually revived it though in a wary and suspicious way, until by the middle of the 1490s Yorkist methods were more or less in full operation once more.

By Richard III's time cash income from the royal estates had reached between £22,000 and £25,000 a year, plus (possibly) another £4,643 from sheriffs' farms, payments by bailiffs of liberties, vacant temporalities of bishoprics, wards, marriages and various feudal incidents.[222] By 1500 the

---

[220] Wolffe, 'The Management of English Royal Estates under the Yorkist Kings', *English Historical Review* LXXI (1956) 1–16, and *The Royal Demesne, op. cit.* 159 ff.

[221] e.g. John Luthington received five shillings a day as auditor of north Wales and Chester, John Milewater as receiver-general of a group of estates in ten counties, Wales and the Marches, fees and expenses totalling £60 a year. Wolffe, *The Royal Demesne, op. cit.* 163. Such pay in many cases probably exceeded the profits of their own modest estates and their professional incomes alone were enough to place them among the two or three thousand most prosperous men in the realm. For general levels of income see H. L. Gray, 'Income from Land in England in 1436', *English Historical Review* XLIV (1934) 607–39. Lander, *op. cit.* 173.

[222] See *Rot. Parl.* VI 403. The land revenues declined from £22–25,000 p.a. under Richard III to about £11,700 in Henry's first year, most probably due to the exchequer revival of the practice of assignment. Wolffe, 'Henry VII's Land Revenues and Chamber Finance', *English Historical Review* LXXI (1956) 19–20, and *The Royal Demesne, op. cit.* 190, 199 ff.

estate revenues were about two fifths greater, but the increase was due to further accretions of land rather than to any further improvements upon the methods which the Yorkists had introduced.[223]

Edward IV's total income possibly reached between £90,000 and £93,000 in his last year, that of Henry VII between £104,000 and £113,000 towards the end of his reign.[224] Edward IV was the first English king since Henry II to die solvent. He is known to have left a 'treasure', but its extent is unknown as it quickly disappeared in the troubles after his death. Henry VII, so far from leaving the fabulous treasure erroneously attributed to him by a Milanese ambassador[225] and afterwards exaggerated by Sir Francis Bacon,[226] left on the most reliable modern estimate no more than a hoard of plate and jewels worth about £300,000, and certainly no more than £10,000 in hard cash,[227] or at the most no more than three years' income.

In chapter 2 (first published in 1965) I expressed the view that by continental standards the kings of England were so poor that financially England was 'one of the shallow, little backwaters of monarchy', and that English kings were 'compelled to shift more after the ways of a college bursar than a modern minister of finance.'[228] Although in some quarters this opinion was shortly afterwards condemned as exaggerated, a considerable body of evidence (which there had been no space to quote in so short an article) then existed to confirm it and a good deal more has since accumulated.

It has been denied that smuggling existed on any considerable scale at this period, on the ground that except for wool, the customs duties were far too low to make it worth while.[229] But all fifteenth-century kings, including

[223] Wolffe, *English Historical Review* LXXIX, *op. cit.* 251–2.

[224] Between 1502 and 1505 (the years for which the most reliable figures survive) Henry's revenue averaged £104,863 a year. If certain *ad hoc* payments such as Catherine of Aragon's dowry and arrears of the benevolence of 1491 are also included, the average for the last nine years of the reign comes to rather more than £113,000. These figures do not include normal direct taxation for none was levied during these years, but the figures do apparently include £30,000 taken in lieu of feudal aids for the knighting of Prince Arthur and the marriage of Princess Margaret. Wolffe, *The Royal Demense, op. cit.* 214–17. *Rot. Parl.* VI 532–42.

[225] 'Six millions of gold'. *Calendar of State Papers Milanese* ed. A. B. Hinds I (1912) 324. R. L. Storey, *The Reign of Henry VII* (1968) 114, apparently translates this as £135,000.

[226] Bacon estimated £1,800,000. Bacon, *Henry VII, op. cit.* 266.

[227] Wolffe, *The Royal Demesne, op. cit.* 223–5. Many historians have included Henry VII's loans to the Emperor and others as part of these assets, but if Henry ever hoped to see anything back from the impecunious Maximilian he must have been considerably more optimistic than most of his contemporaries. In any case the oldest meaning of the word 'loan' is a gift or grant from a superior and in royal accounts of this period the word was often used in the sense of 'imprests'.

[228] See below ch. 2. p. 72.

[229] For the detailed arguments see P. Ramsey, 'Overseas Trade in the Reign of Henry VII: The Evidence of Customs Accounts', *Economic History Review* 2nd series VI (1953–4) 173–82,

Edward IV and Henry VII, were undoubtedly convinced that they were being bilked of their customs duties and cheated by their officials on a very considerable scale. The sub-ports and outlying creeks were so ineffectively supervised that smuggling must have been comparatively easy,[230] and ample circumstantial evidence from the beginning to the end of the fifteenth century confirms contemporary convictions of extensive malpractice.[231]

In 1475 the barons of the exchequer sent a writ of privy seal to Roger Keyes, the chancellor of Exeter cathedral, accompanied by a 'roll of paper', signed by no less a person than the king's own secretary William Hatteclyff, giving details of the 'great deceits' perpetrated in Topsham and Dartmouth during the previous year and more, and ordering him to conduct an investigation on the basis of the information thus sent to him. This inquiry resulted in a detailed report of 69 sailings during the time in question, showing that abuses in Topsham and Dartmouth had indeed been widespread.[232] Even in the highly supervised port of London evasion was far from unknown. Some of the richest and most prominent merchants of the day were not immune from temptation. In 1478 Edward IV badly alarmed the Mercers and Merchant Adventurers by accusations of wholesale smuggling and scared them into paying a collective fine of 1,500 marks rather than face the results of numerous individual prosecutions already started in the exchequer.[233]

Henry VII between 1486 and 1488 dismissed no less than 20 officials for absence from their posts, illegally engaging in trade on their own account, or embezzlement.[234] In 1509 John Myllys, the London surveyor, was dis-

---

especially 178. E. M. Carus-Wilson and O. Coleman, *England's Export Trade, 1275–1547* (1963) 21–7.

[230] R. C. Jarvis, 'The Appointment of Ports', *Economic History Review* 2nd series XI (1958–9) 461. The difficulties presented by the creeks are apparent from a statute of 1432 which, for three years made it a felony to carry staple merchandise into any creek rather than into an assigned or appointed port. *Rot. Parl.* IV 454.

[231] *Cal. Close Rolls, 1385–1389*, 302. *Rot. Parl.* III 576–7. A. Steel, 'The Collectors of Customs of Newcastle upon Tyne in the Reign of Richard II' in *Studies Presented to Sir Hilary Jenkinson, op. cit.* 390–413, and 'The Collectors of Customs in the Reign of Richard II' in *British Government and Society, op. cit.* 27–39. J. H. Wylie, *History of England Under Henry IV* (4 vols 1884–98) I 58. R. E. Latham and I. B. Abbott, 'Caterpillars of the Commonwealth' *Speculum* XXX (1955) 229–32. F. A. Mace, 'Devonshire Ports in the Fourteenth and Fifteenth Centuries', *Transactions of the Royal Historical Society* 4th Series VIII (1925) 114–15. C. L. Kingsford, *Prejudice and Promise in Fifteenth Century England* (1925) ch. 4. J. W. Sherbourne, *The Port of Bristol in the Middle Ages* (1965). W. I. Haward, 'The Wars of the Roses in East Anglia', *English Historical Review* XLI (1926) 171–4. 'Gilbert Debenham: A Medieval Rascal in Real Life', *History* XIII (1928–9) 305–6.

[232] KR Mem. Roll. PRO E. 159/253 Trinity Term Comm. m. xxxr. and d.

[233] *Acts of Court of the Mercers' Company, 1453 to 1547* ed. L. Lyell and F. D. Watney (1936) 116–140. KR Mem. Roll PRO E. 159/255 Trinity Term Comm. ms ixd, xd, xjd, xixd, xxjd, xxijd, xxiijd, xxvd. It is true that most of the cases involved only comparatively small sums.

[234] Ramsay, 'Overseas Trade', *op. cit.* 175.

missed after only three years in office for 'manifold misdemeanours'[235] and an entry in John Heron's payments book as treasurer of the chamber reveals that 'Robert Fitzherbert, late customer of London, hath deceived the king in his customs for which he is indebted to the sum of £4,000'.[236] Even the highly trusted Sir Reynold Bray, the under-treasurer of England, one of whose jobs was to check the customs accounts, cheated and smuggled wool.[237]

Moreover neither king, except in the case of wool which was in any case a rapidly declining export, was able to impose realistic valuations. Even the famous book of rates of 1507 probably did little more than tidy-up and standardize the existing rates, merely achieving greater uniformity in the collection of the London dues. It increased the valuations of only a few staple commodities[238] and the conventional valuation of merchandise remained woefully low, in some cases as little as one seventh of its true commercial value.[239]

Similar reservations must also be expressed about the system of crown estates, and about the effect of fiscal feudalism on the value of escheats. Desirable though their cash revenue might be, the crown lands could never be run exclusively from the point of view of profit. Patronage above all kept the body politic in harmony. Even now it probably still remained the most important function of the crown lands. The Yorkists kept lists of offices available for disposal. Probably no earlier kings had ever had such a mass of detailed information at their command. They controlled the patronage of at least 800 offices worth £13,000 a year in wages (not to mention the fees which their holders collected from the public), and 700 of these derived their income from the crown lands, fee-farms and sheriffs' farms to a total of £7,000 a year. Together with annuities and pensions derived from the same sources they absorbed at least two sevenths of the value of these estates.[240] Politics and finance were in fierce competition, and the Second Anonymous Croyland Continuator thought it of supreme importance that

---

[235] *Letters and Papers Foreign and Domestic of the Reign of Henry VIII, preserved in the Public Record Office, the British Museum, and elsewhere,* catalogued by J. S. Brewer, 2nd edn. R. H. Brodie, (1920) no. 158, 45.

[236] PRO E. 36/214, 615. It is unclear whether the £4,000 was for duties evaded, or a fine—but most probably the latter.

[237] PRO E. 36/214, 474–5. After Bray's death the king forced his executors to pay 800 marks (another 400 being pardoned), 'for a forteiture of wools . . . being at Calais'.

[238] Notably, salt from 10s. to 13s. per wey, pewter vessels from 26s. 8d. to 33s. 4d. per cwt and woad from 13s. 4d. to £1 per bale. Even here, when Breton merchants the same year challenged the increase of woad, the council replied that each bale of Toulouse woad was now much heavier and of greater value than it had formerly been. H. S. Cobb, 'Books of Rates and the London Customs', *The Guildhall Miscellany* VI iv (1971) 1–12.

[239] N. S. B. Gras, *The Early English Customs System* (1918) 128 n. 6.

[240] Wolffe, *The Crown Lands, op. cit.* 63 and *English Historical Review* LXXI (1956) 20.

Edward IV had planted reliable officers in all parts of his kingdom.[241]

Owing to the amount of land which Edward IV alienated to prominent supporters during the first part of his reign, one historian has expressed doubts that he had a conscious estates policy at all.[242] This, however, appears to be pressing scepticism too far by assuming the existence of ideal conditions. Edward IV was by no means a completely free agent. As we have seen he seized the throne with comparatively little positive support. The adherents of the revolution of 1461 expected to be rewarded and they had to be rewarded.

Criticisms of the administration of the royal estates undoubtedly carry more weight. In a period of almost universal dishonesty and chicanery, the larger an organization was, the more difficult it became to supervise effectively. The royal lands were gigantic as compared with any aristocratic complex of estates in the country and a good deal of evidence survives to show that, in spite of the appointment of the new receivers and auditors, some of them were not nearly as effectively run as they might have been. On the manor of Bisley in the duchy of York for example, from 1448 onwards the manorial accounts became completely fossilized. The names and payments in the entries remained the same throughout a whole century. They were still the same at the death of Henry VIII. Through such unbelievably feeble supervision the ducal and royal owners of Bisley missed a significant opportunity for profit-taking, for during the fifteenth century the manor was going through a process of industrial expansion, the development of the manufacture of woollen cloth. Only a few miles away at Castle Combe, an area experiencing a similar process, a private landlord Sir John Fastolf, had been alert enough to cream off some of the increasing profits of his tenants. Although it is now impossible to calculate them exactly, Fastolf's increased revenues from Castle Combe must have been considerable for some of the entry fines for tenements doubled and one nearly quadrupled.[243]

Success and failure on other royal estates seem to have been very mixed. After an official progress by the duchy of Lancaster council through Lancashire and Cheshire in 1476, receipts rose from £347 in 1476–7 to £800 in 1477–8 and £885 in 1481–2. On the other hand the receipts of the duchy honour of Pontefract remained more or less stable throughout the reign. Documentary deficiencies and various alienations of land make it impossible to provide comparative figures for the entire duchy at the beginning and at the end of Edward's reign, but between 1463–4 and 1478 the gross

---

[241] Fulman 562.

[242] Ross, 'Edward IV', op. cit. 54–8.

[243] E. M. Carus-Wilson, 'Evidences of Industrial Growth on Some Fifteenth Century Manors', Economic History Review 2nd series XII (1959–60) 190–205, reprinted in Essays in Economic History II (1962) 151–67.

yield of the northern parts fell by some £700, from £7,391 to £6,696.[244] The neglect and inefficiency of Richard duke of Gloucester, as chief steward north of the Trent, may have been partly responsible for this decline in revenue, for in 1482 the duchy council told him in a remarkably outspoken letter that, through sales of timber and other things, he and his deputies had brought the lordship into great decay.[245] Evidence of static revenue also comes from other estates. The gap between the aims and the practice of estate management was often wide.

The system of fiscal feudalism also hardly lived up to the ideal form so often assumed. Although frequently stated it has yet to be proved, that the royal lands were greatly augmented by the process of escheat. Very, very few families were without common law heirs of some kind however distant, and 'natural' escheats would therefore be few. So-called escheats would in most cases be somewhat dubious seizures, rather than escheats in the exact technical sense of the term. If the families thus deprived considered such inheritances as their right, and were sufficiently powerful, royal seizures of this kind could generate dangerous political tensions, as indeed happened in the later years of Edward IV—which alienated support from his sons.[246]

Since the middle of the fourteenth century the development of trusts and uses had badly eroded the king's rights in the property of his tenants-in-chief—livery, wardship and marriage, and especially the valuable custody of estates during minorities. Edward III (who had been most successful in developing indirect taxation) tacitly allowed such evasion in the interests of political peace.[247] Henry IV had tried but failed to reassert these royal rights[248] and by the middle of the fifteenth century avoidance had become so firmly entrenched in customary thought and habit that the royal justices were refusing to take advantage in the king's interest even when there were technical flaws in the trusts and uses which would have enabled them to do so.[249] In spite of the resentment caused by the agents of both Edward IV and Henry VII[250] in searching out evasions of feudal rights, it is doubtful how successful they were. Examples are known where Edward IV failed to use his powers to enforce his rights of wardship. At the end of his reign he

[244] Ross, op. cit. 59–60.

[245] R. Somerville, History of the Duchy of Lancester I (1953) 254, PRO DL. 42–19 f. 103 v. February, 1482. Or had Gloucester been lax in the north in order to win popularity?

[246] See above pp. 24–5 and 25, n. 132.

[247] Tuck, Richard II, op. cit. 3.

[248] In the parliament of 1404. J. L. Barton, 'The Medieval Use', Law Quarterly Review 81 (1965), 562–77.

[249] In 1468 Justice Markham said that if a king's tenant had died seised to the use of x, x might have an ousterlemain cum exitibus, which was the process normally granted where land not properly seisable had been taken into the king's hand in error. According to the reporter of the case no one denied Markham's observation. ibid.

[250] See below ch. 6 pp. 167–8.

made a somewhat timid attempt to legislate against trusts and uses, but his bill covered only the duchy of Lancaster. The problem of uses was difficult and politically explosive. Henry VII had little more success in dealing with it than Edward IV.[251]

Unequal application of the law by both Edward and Henry may, at least in part, have aroused bitter resentment on these questions of trusts and uses. Those caught in the meshes of the law knew very well that others were evading them. Quite probably a kind of jungle law existed, especially under Henry VII, the king taking excessive advantage of those caught within the trap to compensate himself in some degree for the losses due to those who concealed their activities. From the king's point of view the problem was never successfully solved. After all, it should not be forgotten that in 1540, after a long struggle both in parliament and in the law courts, Henry VIII finally compromised with the landowning classes in an agreement which secured his feudal rights over one third of the lands of his tenants-in-chief, giving them the free disposition exempt from feudal exactions over all the rest.[252] 'The mighty lord who broke the bonds of Rome' could defy a distant spiritual power, but he could not exact his admitted traditional feudal rights from his own subjects.

The wheel had come full circle. A future generation is rarely satisfied with the solutions of its grandparents. The generation of the late 1440s and 1450s (and its predecessors for that matter) had become adamantly resistant to all but a minimum of direct taxation and just as strongly opposed to any kind of realistic assessment. They insisted that the king should live of his own. The government adopted their views in 1461 and in 1467 Edward IV personally announced that the system was succeeding: 'John Say, and ye Sirs, comyn to this my Court of Parlement for the comon of this my Lond. The cause why Y have called and sommoned this my present Parlement is, that Y purpose to lyve upon my nowne, and not to charge my Subgettes but in grete and urgent causes, concernyng more the wele of theym self, and also the defence of theym and of this my Reame, rather than my nowne pleasir . . .'.[253]

But his subjects, and even more those of Henry VII, wished to have their cake and eat it. They not only grudged the king taxation, they grudged him his 'own'. With one voice they clamoured that the king should live of his own, then changed the tune when patronage to some (unknown) extent was cut down and when their own pickings from the royal resources were reduced. Comparatively inefficient in all likelihood as the royal revenue

[251] J. M. W. Bean, *The Decline and Fall of English Feudalism, 1215–1540* (1968Z 215–16, 235–6, 238–42. Ross, *op. cit.* 60–61. Chrimes. *op. cit.* 180–83.

[252] E. W. Ives, 'The Genesis of the Statute of Uses', *English Historical Review* LXXXII (1967) 673–97.

[253] *Rot. Parl.* V 572.

system was, it very quickly became all too efficient for their liking. Edward IV died with an unenviable reputation for greed, which was enshrined in more than one chronicle[254] and in a vigorous anonymous poem which made him repent his financial misdeeds.[255] On Henry VII's death Lord Mountjoy wrote to Erasmus that avarice was now dead, and that a new era of liberality was dawning in the skies.[256] Sir Thomas More felt it safe enough to greet the new king with Latin poems denouncing his father's greed and the maleficent actions of his agents.[257] And even one of the most notorious of all those agents, Edmund Dudley, now a prisoner in the Tower of London, and a man who had made a very considerable personal fortune from his activities[258] in the royal service, drew up for the benefit of Henry VII's soul (or so he said) a list of 84 cases in which he thought that the late king had gone far beyond the bounds of financial decency.[259] As with the nobility and their fearsome recognizances, the young, inexperienced heir Henry VIII, immediately eased the financial pressures, relaxed the administration of the crown lands and became more generous with grants from the estates, with most deleterious results for his revenues. By 1515, his landed income had fallen from £40,000 to £25,000 a year.[260] Good lordship and efficient royal finance would seem to have been incompatible.

The attitude of the political nation, the landowning classes, is understandable if hardly justified. After all, as compared with those of the present day the functions of government were decidedly negative, confined internally to 'justice', that is the maintenance of a somewhat crude stan-

---

[254] Fulman 559. *The Usurpation of Richard III* ed. C. A. J. Armstrong (2nd edn. 1969) 66–7. Polydore Vergil, *op. cit.* 172. For the disappearance of Edward's 'treasure', see *Usurpation of Richard III, op. cit.* 80–81.

[255] 'I stored hucches, cofers and chyst
    With tresore takying off my commynalte—
    ffore there tresore that I toke
    there prayers I myst.'

Anonymous contemporary poem 'The Lament for the Soul of Edward IV' BM MS. Additional 29729 f. 8r, quoted in V. J. Scattergood, *Politics and Poetry in the Fifteenth Century* (1971) 209.

[256] *Opus Epistolarum Des. Erasmi Rotterdami* ed. P. S. Allen (12 vols 1906–58) I (215). The letter may have been written by Ammonius, whom Mountjoy was then employing.

[257] In the 'Carmen Congratulatorium', one long and four short Latin poems celebrating the coronation of Henry VIII and Catherine of Aragon.

'Now no one hesitates to show the possessions he has hitherto hidden from sight. Now it is possible to enjoy any profit which escaped the sly, grasping hands of many thieves . . .' and added that the new king 'now gives to good men the honours that used to be sold to evil men'. E. E. Reynolds, *Thomas More and Erasmus* (1965) 65, 145.

[258] Brodie, *Tree of Commonwealth, op. cit.* 10.

[259] C. J. Harrison, 'The Petition of Edmund Dudley', *English Historical Review* LXXXVII (1972) 82–99.

[260] Wolffe, *The Crown Lands, op. cit.* 76 ff.

dard of public order, and externally to warfare either defensive or offensive. As we have seen earlier, in spite of the superficially impressive development of the royal courts, 'justice' remained very largely a function of property. Therefore, once the king was adequately enough endowed to execute his own limited responsibilities the royal case in favour of taxation was exceedingly weak. In fact the reverse was quite plausible—that those who did the work locally should receive the benefits and rewards of local patronage, a cut out of the royal resources.

Nor did the political nation find demands for war taxation at all convincing during this period. The significance of the Hundred Years' War has been seriously misunderstood for the fifteenth century, largely because the enthusiasms of a small but vociferous 'war party' have been mistaken for popular, national feeling. I hesitate to use the words 'public opinion' as these convey misleadingly modern overtones.

Successful warfare in the high and later middle ages required a combination of three things: a king who was a born military leader; an aristocracy interested in fighting for his cause, and conscious at the same time of the reasonable certainty of profits for itself; and a people who were at least for a limited period prepared to pay, for after the initial campaigns during which the pump was primed, so to speak, war was generally expected to finance itself. As a means of prosecuting dynastic, hereditary claims to territory, war had always a much stronger appeal for the king than for anybody else. English historians have probably always exaggerated the popularity of war against France in the later middle ages. After indignation following the loss of Normandy under King John had died down, support both aristocratic and otherwise seems to have been far from enthusiastic until the beginning of the Hundred Years' War in 1337.[261] From then until the peace treaty of 1361 enthusiasm was high, but apparently declined after the renewal of the war in 1369 when the successive campaigns went far from well.[262]

Henry V's claim to the French throne was legal and dynastic—'the desire of justice and of his right, which every man is bounden to his power to demand and seek, only moved him to the war'—as his official biographer stated. Claiming to rule France as its rightful king he, and after his death his brother the duke of Bedford, put out considerable propaganda to convince the French that his cause was just. Therefore, as heir to the French royal family asserting his French rights, he could hardly appeal to English

---

[261] F. M. Powicke, *King Henry III and the Lord Edward* (2 vols, 1947) I chs. 5 and 6; *The Thirteenth Century, 1215–1307* (1953) ch. 14.

[262] Tuck, *op. cit.* 10 ff. See also J. Barnie, *War in Medieval English Society: Social Values and the Hundred Years War, 1337–1399* (1974) for fluctuating opinions towards the war and growing disillusionment among almost all classes by the 1380s. Unfortunately in the 1380s opinions from the greater nobility are too few for generalization about them as a class.

nationalism to support a war of conquest, for that would then have destroyed the effect of the propaganda directed at his French 'subjects'.[263] Even in the famous St Crispin's Day speech before Agincourt, as reported or invented by Edward Hall, no hint of nationalism in fact appears.[264] As Tito Livio da Forlì stated: '. . . if he shoulde pursue his conquests and subdue the lande by armes without appeasinge the minds of the gentlemen and commons, at the last he shoulde bringe all the lande in desolacion, which he intended not; insomuch as he first enterprised the warr for to conquer his inheritance, which he minded to lose with all his right in Fraunce, than to be lord of a voyde and desolate countrie'.[265]

For a time the theory seemed to work. Knowing that they could expect little or no help from the enfeebled French monarchy, the apathetic population of Normandy either fled or took the oath of allegiance to their new king. About three quarters of the landowners of western Normandy, though admittedly none of the greatest, at least quietly accepted Henry's government. Had they behaved completely in accordance with Henry's legal theories there would have been nothing of the 'Norman Conquest in reverse' as his occupation is so often, though very dubiously called, and one more reason for the cooperation of the aristocracy would have been lost.

As it was, English enthusiasm was neither complete nor long sustained. Some of the knights in a great council summoned to Westminster in September 1414 expressed their misgivings, though in a moderate way. M. R. Powicke has convincingly shown that below the ranks of the great dukes and earls warlike ardour was very much dying down even before Henry V's death, to the point where it was difficult to maintain a sizable corps of experienced commanders. After the treaty of Troyes in 1420 which recognised Henry as heir to the French throne, the English commons in effect considered that Henry was 'defending' his French territories in Normandy and that the people of those territories should therefore pay the cost of their own 'defence'.[266] This was a conveniently economical if totally unrealistic theory which enabled them to refuse taxation for the next few years. They were no more inclined to grant taxation for the expenses of the French war than they were to pay for the expenses of domestic government.[267] After 1431 the role of the nobility declined even further and moreover the recruitment of men-at-arms seriously decreased. As Powicke has remarked, the involvement of the prominent men of the countryside weakened to such a degree that the persistent interest of a small court

---

[263] Lander, op. cit. 64–5. J. W. McKenna, 'Henry VI of England and the Dual Monarchy', Journal of the Warburg and Courtauld Institutes XXVIII (1965) 145–62.

[264] Hall's Chronicle (1809) 67–8.

[265] The First English Life of King Henry V, ed. C. L. Kingsford (1911) 96.

[266] I owe this point to G. L. Harriss.

[267] Steel, Receipt of the Exchequer, op. cit. 149–202.

aristocracy was all that kept the English war effort alive.[268] Neither reluctant grants of taxation nor the very slight interest which contemporary English chroniclers showed in the later stages of the war reveal any wide support for the king's claim to his French inheritance,[269] though the question of compensation for their losses kept fiercely alive the interests of that small minority who had been granted estates in France. This is not to say that people did not regard the disasters of 1450 and 1453 in Normandy and Gascony as other than shameful and disgraceful, but the indignation of those years was to a great extent the illogical reaction of those too much inclined to blame others for the consequences of their own long continued indifference.

Edward IV's foreign policy is a hotly debated subject, often discussed with more emotional fervour than realistic grasp of the very complicated diplomacy of those times or of the restrictions which conditions at home imposed upon him. His attitudes in the end were remarkably similar to those of Henry VII. Yet Edward IV's caution in his later years has been condemned as cowardice while Henry VII's restraint has been praised for avoiding expensive foreign entanglements which would have brought little gain to English interests. One has been abused, the other praised for retiring from an overseas campaign the richer by a French pension.

Edward's policy of war with France in 1475 is said to have been popular. He has been censured for returning with money after a mere military parade, criticized for failing to interfere in the Netherlands to protect English commercial interests after the death of Charles the Bold, and accused in his last days of having been completely outwitted by Louis XI of France.[270]

These matters will probably never be other than controversial. Diplomatic history requires intimate documentation and here unfortunately our sources are desperately limited. While we can still read some of the propaganda which Edward and his advisers put out for public consumption,[271] we have no knowledge of their private discussions and debates. We are forced to deduce their motives from their actions.

It may well be that Edward IV, like Henry VIII two generations later, nourished dreams of reviving the glories of Henry V. If so, from the beginning his dreams must have been quickly transformed into the nightmares of reality. The Wars of the Roses were far from being merely an insular phenomenon.[272] From the mid 1450s England was threatened by a revived and newly confident France. Nevertheless France was still terrified of a

[268] M. R. Powicke, 'Lancastrian Captains', op. cit. 381.
[269] B. J. H. Rowe, 'A Contemporary Account of the Hundred Years War from 1415–1429', *English Historical Review* XLI (1926) 504–13.
[270] Ross, op. cit. 52–3.
[271] See below ch. 9 pp. 228–30.
[272] See below ch. 2 pp. 64–6.

resurgence of English continental ambitions, and from the mid 1460s fearful of the aggressive designs of Charles the Bold of Burgundy. From 1462 onwards Louis XI was always prepared to intrigue in English politics even to the extent of supporting an invasion, as a form of self-protection. On balance it seems that in view of Edward IV's precarious situation at home, his reactions towards France in the 1460s were defensive. At the same time, in opposition to Warwick's desire for a French alliance, he paid due regard to English commercial interests in the Netherlands by his own preference for closer ties with Charles the Bold. From 1471 onwards the tone of his propaganda still remained defensive and, assuming the lack of any ardent war spirit among the political classes, was designed for home consumption. If any illusions of conquering aggression still remained with him the events leading to the French campaign of 1475 must have shattered them beyond repair. The lack of enthusiasm outside the court and his family circle, resulting in the recruitment of an inferior army over-weighted with archers and lacking in men-at-arms, as well as the squalid story of the collection of war taxation,[273] could only have left him bitterly disillusioned, like Henry VII after a similar experience of attempts to levy war taxes in 1489.[274]

After all this it is scarcely surprising if for domestic reasons alone Edward did not later interfere in the Netherlands. In 1477 his sister, Margaret of York conceived the unrealistic plan of arranging the marriage of their dangerously unstable brother, the duke of Clarence to her stepdaughter Mary, the heiress of the rich Burgundian territories. This idea was more the product of unreasoning sisterly affection than a valid assessment of political realities for any such scheme was bound to arouse the intense hostility of both the Archduke Maximilian of Hapsburg to whom Mary was betrothed, and of Louis XI of France, scared as always that the English would regain a foothold on the continent. C. A. J. Armstrong has drawn attention to the very complicated legal and political situation existing in the Netherlands in 1477, and has pointed out that Louis XI and his successors, who did interfere, experienced immense difficulties for many years in trying to establish control there.[275] Any intervention would have involved Edward IV in a ruinously long and costly war for the occupation and defence of the Burgundian territories, and after the humiliating experiences of 1475 he knew better than to try to raise the money.

Edward has been condemned for 'deserting' Mary of Burgundy, for failing to defend her against French aggression so that he could make certain of his pension from Louis XI under the treat of Péquigny, and for imperilling English commercial interests in the Netherlands through neglect. In fact England had commercial treaties only, not an offensive or defensive

---

[273] See below ch. 9.
[274] See above, p. 40.
[275] See below ch. 10 pp. 246 n. 24.

alliance with Burgundy at this time.[276] As to neglect of English commercial interests, this contention seems to be both anachronistic and unreal. No contemporary English writer makes any such accusation and there is no convincing evidence that English trade did suffer. The French had quite enough opposition to face in the Netherlands without wantonly alienating the mercantile groups. Even the shrewd Philippe de Commynes was somewhat illogical at this point. As so often happens adverse criticism of Edward IV can be traced back to his prejudiced reflections. He reported the king as saying that the towns of Flanders and Brabant were large and strong, neither easily taken nor easily kept, and that the English had no inclination to war on account of the commerce between themselves and the Netherlands. Yet these reflections did not prevent him from censuring Edward for failing to go to war, nor from condemning Louis XI for trying to gain his ends in that area by military means.[277] A more active diplomacy, let alone war, might well have done more to hamper commerce than a passive watchfulness.

Harsh criticism has alleged that Edward's last years saw 'the ruin of his foreign policy.' The argument runs that a needless and expensive war with Scotland, which merely recovered the town of Berwick, so exhausted the king's meagre financial resources that he ceased to be either an effective support for Burgundy or a threat to France, and that the reconciliation of Maximilian and Louis XI in the treaty of Arras in December 1482 left England isolated and Edward more or less an object of contempt to both.[278]

So extreme a verdict seems to lack perspective, for pinpointing the situation at the moment of Edward's death is surely to mistake a vicissitude for permanent collapse. For three decades the diplomacy of northwestern Europe had been in a state of constant flux and change, and as succeeding events were to show it remained in a similar state for a long time to come. After all, in 1485 the French court was so acutely disturbed by the possibility of English support for Brittany that its riposte was to support Henry of Richmond's bid for the throne. It hardly appears that England had sunk so low after all. To look forward a little, the interrelated diplomatic and domestic history of Henry VII's reign demonstrates, as clearly as the Yorkist period, that England was in no condition or mood to exercise for any length of time a major influence on European affairs, let alone to consider occupying any European territory. Sir Francis Bacon remarked of Henry, 'if this king did no great matters it was long of himself; for what he minded he

---

[276] See below ch. 10 p. 246, n. 24.

[277] P. de Commynes, *Mémoires* ed. J. Calmette and G. Durville (3 vols, Paris 1924–5) II 167–9, 245–9. For a strongly unfavourable contemporary opinion, however, see Dominic Mancini in *Usurpation of Richard III, op. cit.* 58–9.

[278] Ross, *op. cit.* 52–3. See also Fulman 562–3.

compassed.'[279] Even so modest a claim is an exaggeration. Henry VII felt obliged from time to time to interfere in European affairs for dynastic reasons, in order to prevent complete isolation and, as he thought, to protect himself from the threat of pretenders—Lambert Simnel, Perkin Warbeck, the de la Poles—whom the Hapsburg and Valois courts patronized at their own convenience.

He quickly and painfully learned that domestic calamity followed hard upon the heels of even limited foreign adventure. His attempts in 1489 to raise money for war were even more humiliatingly unsuccessful than those of Edward IV had been from 1472–75.[280] Even worse, the earl of Northumberland was murdered by an angry mob at Topcliffe in Yorkshire when trying to explain the government's need for war taxation. Light as Henry's taxes were by continental standards, they were dangerous to levy even for defence let alone aggression. In 1497 the men of the southwest rose in revolt rather than pay taxes for the protection of their own fellow countrymen in the north against the Scots. The defence of the north they strongly felt to be no concern of theirs.

Harsh criticisms of timidity in English foreign policy at this time seem to be vitiated by an imperfect understanding of domestic difficulties. The tax-paying classes had tied the king's hands behind his back. The domestic situation left little room even for manoeuvre abroad, let alone a free hand.

In conclusion, the researches of the last three decades have profoundly changed the traditional view of fifteenth-century English history, particularly in their reassessment of the strength of the monarchy and of the balance of achievement between the Yorkists and Henry VII. Yet at the same time it is necessary to introduce a note of caution into these continuing debates. New conclusions were originally pushed too far and too optimistically. More recently the flaws in the system have received somewhat belated attention, tarnishing the quite considerable achievements of the revived monarchy, and in particular highlighting the weakness of its new financial system.

The adamant resistance of the commons to direct taxation and to its realistic assessment, and their successful demand after 1450 that the king should 'live of his own' had gone even further by 1509. It had turned into resentment of the king's efforts to exploit 'his own' to his full advantage, in spite of the inefficiencies of the system which allowed a good deal of evasion in the exploitation both of the royal estates and of the customs revenues, the twin pillars of the royal endowment. It may be that Henry VII had pushed the system beyond the limits of decency, but certainly by the

[279] Bacon, *Henry VII, op. cit.* 235. See also R. B. Wernham, *Before the Armada* (1966) 12–13, 27–76.
[280] The estimated yield of the tax was £100,000 but at the very most it brought in £27,000. As in 1472 very stringent, special conditions were imposed for its collection and storage. Chrimes, *op. cit.* 198–9.

end of his reign resentment had grown to a point where his son thought it politically expedient to relax the father's fiscal severity, an action very much to the disadvantage of his coffers. Such restriction left the English monarchy in a financial straitjacket for almost two centuries, denied the possibility of a sustained, aggressive foreign policy, and at home left the king as dependent as he had even been upon the cooperation of the rich and powerful. This last was in fact the fundamental trait of late medieval monarchy in England. Yet at the same time it seems more necessary than hitherto to make some distinction between the political and the governmental roles of the nobility, interrelated though of course they were.

Until the Reformation introduced an ideological, religious opposition, politics was almost entirely personal, composed of the relationships between the king and the peerage and the richer untitled landowners. In view of Henry VI's peculiar combination of weakness and wilfulness, which very adversely affected their own interests, and of his disastrous financial record during the period of his personal government, it is surprising how many of the aristocracy remained loyal to him for so long. Even at the very end of the 1450s when Richard of York at last attracted an effective following, it does not seem that the peers who swung over to his side had a great deal of sympathy for his dynastic claims. Most probably they were much more interested in bringing to an end growing political chaos and deteriorating public order. Neither Edward IV nor Henry VII at the time of their accession had much to offer to nervous and cautious politicians, and though they were prepared to acquiesce in Richard III's usurpation, few peers (except those whom he had lavishly rewarded or bribed) were prepared to risk their necks and their property to maintain him on the throne.

All in all between 1461 and 1509, unless sources are so uninformative as to be positively misleading, the nobility exhibited a caution so striking as to amount almost to indifference when it came to a question of supporting their successive kings under arms. Only a minority supported either Edward IV or his opponents. Henry VII's tardy reversal of attainders, his use of them as a kind of probationary system, and his terrorization of a large section of the peerage through bonds and recognizances, whatever the obscure causes of such a policy may have been, shows that he had very little faith in the nobility politically, in spite of the very small number who ever took to arms against him.

Even allowing, owing to the paucity of the sources, that the lists compiled above may well be incomplete, it was certainly no warlike, factious spirit in a turbulent nobility which produced the Wars of the Roses. Peers, particularly those of merely baronial rank, were not even sufficiently interested in central politics to attend the not very frequent meetings of parliament assiduously, let alone to take to arms except in the final resort.

The political interests of the nobility appear to have been pitched in a low key. Yet it may be remarked that small numbers of men, given the advantages of surprise, could overthrow a government. As we know from many contemporary examples, defence was always more difficult to organize than attack. The Wars of the Roses were very limited in scale and effect as compared with fifteenth-century wars in other parts of Europe, particularly in France. There was little devastation, little looting, few sieges. The wars had only the most temporary effects on trade, little at all on agriculture. The floods of November 1460 probably caused as much if not more, interruption to most people's lives as the five battles fought between July 1460 and March 1461. The wars left the English social structure unchanged. They may have increased to a point almost approaching indifference the political caution of an already wary nobility. They did not decrease its powers. A monarchy with no standing army, no police force, only the most exiguous of bureaucracies and with only limited, rigid financial resources, the exploitation of which its subjects did a good deal to frustrate, could not govern without the local influence and authority of the aristocracy. Though the estates of most peers were too scattered and intermingled to give them anything like a provincial hegemony, and though their judicial powers were weak in comparison with those of their continental equals, they and their gentry affinities controlled the countryside. As Sir John Fortescue said 'the might of the great lords' was greater than the might of the king's officers. Government was a function of property. Bastard feudalism was essential to the government of the country and good order depended upon a nice balance of power between crown and nobility. The nobility, jealous of each other's powers and spheres of influence, could not function without the ultimate control of a strong king, but the king was forced to exercise that control with some restraint, even to the point of turning a blind eye upon provincial iniquity. 'Good lordship' still remained the basis of government and the conventions and politics of lordship were far from being those of the modern state, for, as Harrington long ago asserted, the power of a king without an army rested upon his relationships with his nobility.

2

The Wars of the Roses

That great historical romancer, Sir Walter Scott, invented 'the Wars of the Roses'[1] to embellish a moral, almost tragical pattern of fifteenth-century English history, first set out by an Italian cleric, Polydore Vergil of Urbino. By the beginning of the sixteenth century the diplomatic and propaganda value of humanistic Latin had risen so high that the monarchs of northern Europe found it wise to justify their ancestry and their ways to the world in the fashionable prose of Italian historians. Paolo Aemiliani was already writing such a history at the French court when Polydore arrived in England in 1502 as the deputy of Adriano Castelli, diplomat and collector of the obsolete papal tax, Peter's Pence. Encouraged by Henry VII, Polydore soon began to collect the materials for a history of England and by 1513 he had completed the first draft of his *Anglica Historia*. The theme of this soon notorious work became the exemplar for all the more accomplished historians writing in Tudor England. The Henrician chronicler, Edward Hall, extended, coloured, almost hallowed, the conceptions of his Italian predecessor and passed them on to Shakespeare who, ignoring the historian's pedantic regard for 'old mouse-eaten records', as Sir Philip Sydney called them, with a poet's licence omitted or changed inconvenient facts to dramatize the moral theme.[2] Polydore Vergil drew the design of a world where institutions were more or less stable across the ages and where, within this stable framework, the personalities of individual kings determined the fate of their realms. Three powerful sentiments swayed the minds of the generations about whom he wrote—God's watchful presence over the affairs of princes, the inviolate nature of a family's inheritance and the sanctity of an anointed king.

Authors of the fifteenth and sixteenth centuries were lavish with evidence of God's intervention in the affairs of princes. Philippe de Commynes set

[1] In *Anne of Gerstein* ch. 7. I owe the phrase and information to S. B. Chrimes. Pointing out that the red and white roses were only two among many badges used by the houses of Lancaster and York, Chrimes condemns the term as misleading and would like historians to abandon it. See *History* XLVII (1963) 24, and *Lancastrians, Yorkists and Henry VII* (1964) pp. xi–xiv.

[2] E. M. W. Tillyard, *Shakespeare's History Plays* (1944). D. Hay, *Polydore Vergil, Renaissance Historian and Man of Letters* (1952).

57

down his conviction that the rulers of this world, too powerful to be controlled by other men, were subject in their doings to the peculiar interventions of the Almighty. Although the judicial duel was no longer respectable for the settlement of ordinary legal cases, it survived in the affairs of princes through the idea of the judgment of God in battle. Edward IV, according to the hints of some contemporary writers, put off his coronation until God had blessed him with victory at the battle of Towton. There was hierarchy even in wickedness. As the Lord watched more closely over princes, so he visited their transgressions with a heavier rod even in this world, and they bought their soul's peace in the next with masses on a scale which their subjects could only envy.

'Only God can make an heir.' The landed classes of the time regarded the exclusion of an heir from his lawful rights—though it was a frequent enough occurrence—as one of the worst of all crimes. As Shakespeare, following Polydore Vergil and Hall, tells the tale, Richard II first banished Henry Bolingbroke, then on the death of his father John of Gaunt, unlawfully deprived him of his patrimony, the duchy of Lancaster. Henry returned from exile to recover it with the help of part of the nobility. Henry Hotspur claimed that he had seen Bolingbroke

> A poor unminded outlaw sneaking home,
> My father gave him welcome to the shore;
> And, when he heard him swear, and vow to God,
> He came but to be Duke of Lancaster,
> To sue his livery, and beg his peace
> With tears of innocency and terms of zeal,
> My father, in kind heart and pity mov'd,
> Swore him assistance, and perform'd it too.[3]

Bolingbroke himself implied that he had returned to England with no intention of usurping the crown. Events had dragged him to his high estate—and had punished him with everlasting calamities.

> Heaven knows, my son,
> By what by-paths and indirect crook'd ways
> I met this crown; and I myself know well,
> How troublesome it sat upon my head.[4]

To deprive a man of his inheritance was one great sin to provoke God's anger. To slay a king was sin mortal and incomparable—'heinous, black, obscene'—words could scarce express the horror such sin evoked. The Lord's Anointed partook of the Lord's mystery. He shared in God's sanctity and could not be slain without divine retribution. Even at the thought of his subjects daring to condemn Richard II, the bishop of Carlisle warned of

[3] 1 Henry IV, Pt. I, IV iii.
[4] 2 Henry IV, Pt. II, IV iv.

the wrath to come:

> And shall the figure of God's Majesty,
> His captain, steward, deputy-elect,
> Anointed, crowned, planted many years,
> Be judged by subject and inferior breath,
> And be himself not present?

If such things happen

> The blood of English shall manure the ground,
> And future ages groan for this foul act;
> Peace shall go sleep with Turks and infidels,
> And, in this seat of Peace, tumultuous wars
> Shall kin with kin, and kind with kind confound;
> Disorder, Horror, Fear and Mutiny
> Shall here inhabit, and this land be call'd
> The field of Golgotha and dead men's sculls.[5]

The dread theme of guilt unfolds itself time and time again. Even on the night before Agincourt Henry V brooded on sin and expiation:

> Oh, not today!—Think not upon the fault
> My father made in compassing the crown!
> I Richard's body have interred new;
> And on it have bestow'd more contrite tears,
> Than from it issued forced drops of blood.
> Five hundred poor I have in yearly pay,
> Who twice a day their wither'd hands hold up
> Toward heaven, to pardon blood.—[6]

Henry V escaped the curse. It descended to his son, Henry VI, whose weakness and whose inability to control a quarrelsome aristocracy gave Richard of York the opportunity to revive his own stronger, legitimist claim to the throne. Tragedy developed within tragedy. Each new crime brought on its fitting retribution. The murder of Edward IV's two sons, the Princes in the Tower, punished the perjury which Richard had committed on his return from exile in 1471, for to gain support he claimed at first that he had returned to recover only the duchy of York, his family lands, not the crown. Bosworth Field finally wiped out in blood a monstrous consummation of crime in Richard III and united the houses of Lancaster and York in Henry VII and Elizabeth Plantagenet: 'Now civil wounds are stopp'd, peace lives again.' All was set for the peace and prosperity of Tudor England.

The needs of the stage forced Shakespeare to transmute all action into personal terms. He compressed the dreary annals of politics and war into

[5] Richard II, IV i.
[6] Henry V, IV i.

an unhistorical but tragic unity so intense that it overwhelms us with horror, and like Margaret of Anjou we know 'the realm a slaughter house'. From the duchess of Gloucester's demand for revenge in *Richard II*, through Prince Henry's horrifying boast that he would extinguish his frivolity in 'a garment all of blood', through the scene at Towton where father slays son and son father, the reek of death and horror rises to Queen Margaret's last envenomed taunt to the duchess of York:

> Forth from the kennel of thy womb hath crept
> A hell hound, that doth hunt us all to death.
> That dog, that had his teeth before his eyes,
> To worry lambs, and lap their gentle blood;
> That foul defacer of God's handy work;
> That excellent grand tyrant of the earth,
> That reigns in galled eyes of weeping souls,
> Thy womb let loose, to chase to us to our graves.[4]

This bloodthirsty moral theme cannot, however, be entirely laid to the door of Polydore Vergil and the Tudor writers. Its genesis may be found in Yorkist propaganda. The claim of the house of York was not as clear as this symmetrically designed history mesmerizes us into believing. In fifteenth-century England there was no definite public law governing the descent of the crown. The Lancastrians claimed as heirs male of Edward III, and by refuting the right of Richard of York, the heir general descending through a female,[8] thus assumed in England a kind of Salic law which they themselves denied in France. When Richard of York forced the issue in 1460, his claim was argued through prolonged discussions by analogy with the law of real property. By this analogy the nobility, assembled in parliament, finally and grudgingly conceded the claim to be valid. The compromise then arranged, which recognized York as Henry VI's heir to the exclusion of Henry's son, Prince Edward, soon broke down. After Richard of York was killed a few weeks later at the battle of Wakefield and Margaret of Anjou had defeated another Yorkist army under the earl of Warwick at the second battle of St Albans, to save a desperate situation a mere fragment of a fiction made York's son the earl of March, King Edward IV. The new king's supporters were by no means numerous. Necessity drove him to use every possible means to support his weak position. During his enthronement at Westminster on 4 March 1461 a speech was made setting forth his title, a statement repeated almost verbatim when his first parliament met the following November. The king and his advisers took their stand upon a declaration which his father had made a few months before—'though right for a time rest and be put to silence yet it rotteth not nor shall not perish'. They assumed that no one could possibly question

---

[7] Richard III, IV iv.

[8] Richard of York was also descended in the male line from Edward III's fifth son, Edmund of Langley, but he never put forward his claims on this ground.

the validity of Edward's title and in scathing words attributed the recent
disorders of the kingdom to God's judgment upon it for tolerating so long
the cancer of Lancastrian usurpation and the unjust denial of their rightful
inheritance to the house of York. According to this interpretation Henry
IV had taken

> upon him usurpously the crown and name of king and lord of the same realm
> and lordship; and not therewith satisfied or content, but more grievous thing'
> attempting, wickedly of unnatural, unmanly and cruel tyranny, the same King
> Richard, king anointed, crowned and consecrate, and his liege and most high
> lord in the earth, against God's law, man's liegance, and oath of fidelity, with
> uttermost punicion, a-tormenting, murdered and destroyed, with most vile,
> heinous and lamentable death; whereof the heavy exclamation in the doom of
> every Christian man soundeth into God's hearing in heaven, not forgotten in
> the earth, specially in this realm of England, which therefore hath suffered the
> charge of intolerable persecution, punicion and tribulation, whereof the like
> hath not been seen or heard in any other Christian realm. . . . unrest, inward
> war and trouble, unrightwiseness, shedding and effusion of innocent blood,
> abusion of the laws, partiality, riot, extortion, murder, rape and vicious living
> have been the guiders and leaders of the noble realm of England.[9]

The government saw to it that such propaganda had the widest possible
circulation, and the reading of this particular statement in parliament
would alone ensure that it was well known. Polydore could not have escaped from the background of such vehement opinions. For Edward IV's
reign he relied on both a popular oral tradition and the reminiscences of
men in high places who had lived through the events of those days, or who
had at least heard of them from their fathers. He therefore reflected the
judgment of Englishmen of his own day, which was strongly influenced by
Yorkist propaganda, on the end of the house of Lancaster. The 'Yorkist
myth' so strongly propagated in 1461 must surely have grown into the stem
on which he grafted the more complete 'Tudor myth'.

Since this myth prevailed, generations of authors have obviously
enjoyed writing about the fifteenth century as a degraded, blood-drenched
anticlimax to the great constructive period of the middle ages. Turbulent
and disorderly the century was by modern standards. Whether it was so
much worse than the fourteenth century or the sixteenth and whether its
disorders were due to the civil wars are other, and contentious, questions.
The highly theatrical, twopence-coloured conflation of picturesque fables,
bloody battles, proscriptions and attainders, quick reversals of fortune,
desperate flights and sudden victories, is a deceptive guide to the state of
the country. Most probably England was no more war-ridden in the
fifteenth than in earlier centuries. Between 1066 and 1377 there were only
two periods of more than thirty consecutive years when general peace

[9] *Rot. Parl.* v 464.

prevailed in the land.[10] During the Wars of the Roses the total period of active campaigning between the first battle of St Albans (1455) and the battle of Stoke (1487) amounted to little more than 12 or 13 weeks in 32 years.[11] Henry VII's progress from his landing in Milford Haven to his victory at Bosworth Field lasted only 14 days.

These almost miniature campaigns bear no comparison with the scale of warfare in the rest of Europe. The first battle of St Albans has been described, with little exaggeration, as 'a short scuffle in a street'.[12] Only at Towton (1461), the greatest battle of the period, did the numbers engaged possibly approach 50,000. Training and tactics alike were elementary. The law required every free-born Englishman between the ages of 16 and 60 to bear arms, but such a regulation did not make an army. With the exception of the Calais garrison (not in any case a field force), and from 1468 the king's personal bodyguard of two hundred archers, there was no standing military force in the country receiving constant training. The troops which fought the battles of the Wars of the Roses were hastily—and many of them unwillingly—collected as each particular climax mounted to its crisis and were as quickly disbanded once it was over. Neither side could afford the cost of anything better.[13] Strategy was equally elementary. At the second battle of St Albans Warwick was unaware of Queen Margaret's approach. Towton was fought in a snowstorm, Barnet in an April fog and even Edward's famous pursuit of the Lancastrian army to Tewkesbury in 1471 was marked more by dogged tenacity than by strategic ability.

Though several English towns were sacked from 1459–61, none suffered a prolonged siege, nor burned their suburbs to make easier their defence from besieging forces, as several French towns had been forced to do in the course of the Hundred Years' War. This urban immunity is the more significant if we call to mind that English towns were more open to attack than any in Europe. Owing to the early unification of England and the power of the central government defences had become less necessary than they were elsewhere. Little fortified market towns, so common in France, were almost unknown in England. Even major towns like Reading and Salisbury lacked fortifications.[14] The dilapidated condition of the walls of London may well, in part, account for the readiness of the city fathers to negotiate with both Yorkists and Lancastrians in the 1450s and 1460s. If so,

[10] F. M. Stenton, 'The Changing Feudalism of the Middle Ages', *History* XIX (1935) 289–301.

[11] W. H. Dunham Jr, 'Lord Hastings' Indentured Retainers, 1461–1483', *Transactions of the Connecticut Academy of Arts and Sciences* XXXIX (1955) 24–5.

[12] C. Oman, *The Political History of England, 1377–1485* (1920) 367.

[13] For the sheer financial and administrative difficulties of keeping an army together see J. R. Hooker, 'Notes on the Organisation and Supply of the Tudor Military under Henry VII', *Huntingdon Library Quarterly* XXIII (1959) 19–31.

[14] *Medieval England* ed. A. L. Poole (1958) i 65–7.

they continued to feel secure enough to take risks. A few years later they remained almost contemptuously negligent of a vigorous mayor's efforts to rebuild the fortifications.

The architecture of the day shows few concessions to warfare. After the end of Richard II's reign the science of military fortification was almost unknown in England until Henry VIII, between 1538 and 1540, built a chain of coastal artillery forts in a revolutionary foreign style. The Wars of the Roses produced nothing comparable to the fortifications and earthworks thrown up during the great civil war in the seventeenth century.[15] 'Castles' like Tattershall, Caister, Ashby-de-la-Zouch and Hurstmonceux (the first two built in the height of the latest French or Rhenish fashions) were, despite their delusive military air, magnificent dwellings rather than fortresses.

The private castles erected during the fifteenth century might never have existed as far as their significance in the Wars of the Roses counted. Lesser houses were very unmartial indeed. When John Norreys built Ockwells during one of the most acute phases of the civil war (it was not quite finished when he died in 1465), he saw fit to build a house notable for the number and size of its windows, to a design based on simple but harmonious mathematical ratios worked out for their aesthetic effect, quite unrelated to thoughts of defence.[16] Of the older royal castles only Harlech, for reasons now obscure, withstood a long blockade. The rest of the Welsh castles and the famous strongholds of northern England which figure so prominently in the struggles of the early 1460s never held out against a besieging force for more than a few weeks and often only a matter of days.

Looting was not unknown—it never can be in any war. Yet complaints of it were singularly rare. The war was highly localized. Any damage inflicted was small in comparison with the destruction wrought by the devastating raids of the Scots and the English 'scavengers' leagued with them in the early fourteenth century when, in the years between the battle of Bannockburn and the death of King Robert I of Scotland, the tithes of the churches appropriated to the monastery of Durham fell in value from £412 to £10 a year.[17] In the fifteenth century, disorders were certainly less in England than in its poorer neighbour Scotland. Seen against events in the northern kingdom—two kings assassinated within twenty years and the interminable bloody feuds of the Black and the Red Douglases, the Crichtons and the Livingstones—the Wars of the Roses seem less ferocious. Again, England seems a haven of quiet if compared with the faction fights of contemporary Bohemia.

[15] B. H. St. J. O'Neil, *Castles and Cannon* (1960) 1–64.

[16] J. Evans, *English Art, 1307–1461* (1949) 134.

[17] J. Scammell, 'Robert I and the North of England', *English Historical Review* LXXIII (1958) 385–403.

Louis XI's councillor, Philippe de Commynes, once remarked: 'England enjoyed this pecular mercy above all other kingdoms, that neither the country nor the people, nor the houses were wasted, destroyed or demolished; but the calamities and misfortunes of the war fell only upon the soldiers, and especially on the nobility.'[18] Although Commynes himself admitted that he was somewhat hazy on the details of English politics, his comparisons of conditions in different countries are exceedingly shrewd.

The English suffered hardly at all compared with the damage which they had inflicted on many of the provinces of France during the Hundred Years' War. The fortified church, almost unknown in England, once again as in earlier times became a familiar landmark in France. The chronicler, Molinet, devoted a long poem entirely to the destruction of the French abbeys. They fell into poverty of a kind they had never known since the Dark Ages and monasticism in France never recovered from the effects of this English destruction.[19] When the English were finally driven out of Gascony in 1453 they left thirty per cent of the villages ravaged or seriously damaged.[20] Nothing in English experience could compare with Limoges where it was said that in 1435 only five people were left living in the town. Recovery took twenty years and more. As late as the 1480s some districts still suffered from the wartime destruction of draught animals and men, women and children were still being harnessed to the ploughs.[21] Around Amiens damage had been so great that all the city's parish churches and most of the religious houses in the district had to be rebuilt—and they were rebuilt between about 1470 and 1490.[22] It took about the same time to clear up another of the war's more serious legacies, a tangle of conflicting property rights, for both sides during the fighting had made grants of the same estates often several times over, causing legal confusion and social conflict far more extreme than anything resulting in England from the confiscations and acts of attainder inflicted on the various combatants during the civil wars.[23]

England escaped the horrors of invasion by a foreign power, an immunity which has led historians to treat the Wars of the Roses too exclusively as an incident of English history. Although the civil conflicts

---

[18] P. de Commines, *Memoirs,* ed. A. R. Scoble (2 vols, Bohn's translation, 1855–6) i 394.

[19] J. Evans, *Art in Medieval France, 987–1498* (1948) 264–7.

[20] R. S. Lopez, 'Hard Times and Investment in Culture', in *The Renaissance: A Symposium* (1953) 19–32.

[21] *Journal des Etats Généraux de France Tenus à Tours en 1484,* ed. J. Masselin et A. Bernier, Collections de Documents Inédits sur l'Histoire de France (Paris 1835) 672–5.

[22] J. Evans, *op. cit.* 282.

[23] A. Bossaut, 'Le Rétablissement de la paix sociale sous le règne de Charles VII', *Le Moyen Age* 4th series IX (1954) 137–62.

began in a domestic crisis they were by no means an insular affair. Neither Lancastrians nor Yorkists scrupled to call in foreign help when they could get it and the rapid changes of English politics upset the calculations of statesmen in courts as far distant as Milan, Naples and Aragon. John of Calabria, Margaret of Anjou's brother, still pressed his family's claim to the throne of Naples and his Italian ambitions reacted upon his sister's fortunes in England. In the early 1450s the French still feared a renewed English invasion: in the second half of the decade they were obsessed by dread of Burgundy. From about 1456 to the death of Charles the Bold in 1477 the politics of northwestern Europe turned upon the mutual suspicions of these two powers. In this bitter conflict no holds were barred. The insincerity, chicanery and ruthlessness of its diplomacy could have taught Machiavelli as much as he ever learned from the quarrels of Italian states. As diplomacy failed war took its place. Both sides competed for an English alliance and for many years their ambitions made worse the squalid confusions of English politics.

From 1459 onwards Francesco Sforza, duke of Milan, wished to unite England and Burgundy in an invasion of France in order to frustrate French support for John of Calabria's ambitions in Genoa and Naples. He employed as his agent the papal legate, Francesco Coppini, who unscrupulously used his position to support Warwick and his friends when they mounted their invasion from Calais in 1460. In 1462 Louis XI of France, dreading once more an Anglo-Burgundian alliance, countered by supporting Margaret of Anjou, only to leave her in the lurch at the end of the year when the danger to his kingdom had passed away. France and Burgundy continued to compete for the English alliance. Charles the Bold unsuccessfully tried to persuade Edward to join with the League of the Public Weal against Louis. Later a temporary success on the part of France drove Charles to marry Margaret of York, bitterly remarking according to one chronicler, that to avenge himself of the king of France he had been constrained to marry a whore. Reacting strongly, Louis (probably as early as 1468) toyed with the idea of bringing together Queen Margaret and Warwick in the almost fantastic plan which led to their successful invasion of England in 1470, and ultimately failed because Louis, going too far, pushed his puppet Lancastrian government into an invasion of Burgundy. Duke Charles, who until that point had shown scant sympathy for the woes of his exiled brother-in-law, then quickly supported Edward's plans for a counter-invasion. Margaret and Warwick on the one side, Edward on the other, owed their triumphs in part at least to foreign interests which supported them for their own purposes. Even following Edward's restoration in 1471 his invasion of France, delayed until 1475, took place only after a bewildering progression of truces, counter-truces and contradictory negotiations between the three rivals. Henry VII invaded the country with French help and for many years nearly every court in northern Europe found it expedient, at some time or another, to support the claims of the Yorkist pretender Perkin Warbeck.

Though by continental standards England escaped the horrors of war, it was a turbulent enough land. Long before and long after the the civil wars its inhabitants complained bitterly and endlessly of 'lack of governance' and the prevalence of violent crime. In the minds of medieval men a period of good order had always existed in some erstwhile golden age and the conditions of their own day were found wanting by this legendary standard.[24] As evidence accumulates of the extensive crime of earlier centuries, it stretches credulity to think of any massive deterioration of public order in the mid fifteenth century. The execution of criminal law had always been weak[25] and the criminal records of any period in medieval or sixteenth-century England present a grim and lurid picture.[25] The respectable classes of society were as much given to violent crime as the rabble. Fifteenth-century letters often show in their writers a disturbing irascibility of temperament. Respectable members of the Mercers' company drew their knives on each other at the company's meetings. Landed families who accused each other of whole catalogues of crime from forcible entry to arson and mayhem were soon on good terms again and arranging marriages between their members. Even under Henry V outrageous assaults and the like were frequent. In 1415 servants of the members of parliament for Shropshire waylaid and attacked the tax collectors for the county.[27] A fine example of the gentleman thug was John Newport, a veteran of the French wars, whom the duke of York had appointed as his steward of the Isle of Wight. In 1450 the inhabitants of the island complained that '. . . the said John Newport, hath at this day no livelode to maintain his great countenance, but by the oppressing of the people in the country that he sit in, through the which he hath greatly enpovred and hurt the poor island ready; for what time he was Steward of the isle, he had but ten marks of fee, and kept an household and a countenance like a lord, with as rich wines as couthe be imagined, naming himself Newport the Galant, otherwise called Newport the rich, whom the country cursen daily that ever he come there.'[28]

One of the widest streams of violence flowed unceasingly from a combination of land hunger and the fantastic involutions of the law of real property. Underdeveloped agrarian societies are always fiercely litigious.

---

[24] See E. G. L. Stones, *English Historical Review* LXXII (1957) 111–12.

[25] T. F. T. Plucknett, *Edward I and Criminal Law* (1968) chs. 3 and 4.

[26] In the early thirteenth century over three hundred crimes of violence were committed in one year in the single county of Lincoln and as late as 1600–1 the council in the marches of Wales during the same short period of time levied two hundred and seventy fines for riot alone.

[27] E. F. Jacob, *The Fifteenth Century, 1399–1485* (1961) 134.

[28] *Rot. Parl.* V 204–5.

During the later middle ages and the sixteenth century men seized every chance of adding acre to acre. Few landed families went for more than a few years unentangled in a lawsuit of some kind. The law of real property was in no state to meet the demands of so acquisitive a society. Quite apart from the appalling protractions and delays of common law procedure, no statutes of limitation had been passed since Edward I's day. In real actions the term of legal memory still went back to 1189. It was not until 1540 and again in 1623 that legislation applied some limited remedies for these evils.[29] Bad titles everywhere had become one of the curses of social and economic life, and men, in angry frustration at the delays and inadequacies of the common law, took to violence to impose their 'rights'. Many of the notorious attacks on the Paston properties were supported by at least the pretext of a suddenly discovered, antiquated legal claim. It is hardly straining the evidence to suggest that the obsolete deformities of the law caused more disorder than the sporadic incidents of the civil wars.

The dramatic crises of history distort our vision of the past. Despite the periodic, spectacular clashes between them, cooperation in the government of the realm was the normal relationship between the king and the nobility. While writers from the fifteenth century to the present day have rightly condemned the intransigent ambitions of the overmighty subject and the menace to the king of the nobleman 'equipollent to himself' as Sir John Fortescue (1394?–1476) put it, they have too often passed over the less interesting, because merely mighty, subject. Edward IV and Henry VII would have regarded as little more than simple-minded the interpretation of history which saw them putting down the nobility and basing their rule on the middle classes. Politics are not played out *in vacuo*, for those who rule must work in the conditions they find. Even if the monarchs of the day had been capable of thinking in terms of ignoring the nobility, harsh realities would never have permitted them such anachronistic illusions. In the countryside royal servants of less than noble rank were unreliable. The sheriffs' offices had long been notorious centres of corruption. From their very inception experienced judges like Geoffrey Scrope had looked upon the justices of the peace with grave and justified doubts about their probable efficiency.[30] The society of the day was incapable of organizing an effective bureaucracy and in its absence no government could possibly ignore the nobility. Bishop Russell described them in a draft sermon in 1483 as the firm islands and rocks in an unstable sea and added that it was obvious 'the politic rule of every region well ordained standeth in the nobles'.

[29] W. Holdsworth, *The History of English Law* IV (3rd edn 1945) 415–61, 484 ff. C. Ogilvie, *The King's Government and the Common Law, 1470–1641* (1958) 1–33. K. B. McFarlane, 'The Investment of Sir John Fastolf's Profits of War', in *Transactions of the Royal Historical Society* 5th series VII (1957) 111–14.

[30] M. McKisack, *The Fourteenth Century, 1307–1399* (1959) 202–3.

At the same time the English nobility were hardly typical of their generation in Europe. Provincial feeling in England was weak for it was a small country early united under strong kings. It had nothing to compare with what Shakespeare aptly called France's 'almost kingly dukedoms', with their separatist tendencies and at times near-independence of the central power. As the intelligent Venetian envoy pointed out in 1497, by continental standards the English nobility, lacking compact territories and extensive judicial powers, were nothing more than rich landlords. They expected to be, and were, treated with greater consideration than other men, from such small matters as having bread baked for them on Sundays (otherwise forbidden by law) when they arrived unexpectedly in strange towns, to declaring their income on oath instead of being assessed for taxation, and having the king and council settle their major quarrels instead of suing in the law courts like other men.

Yet limited as their powers were compared with those of their peers in France, Italy and Germany, they were far too powerful for the insecure houses of York and Tudor to ignore them. Their ultimate success makes us forget that both Edward IV and Henry VII were so precariously seated on their thrones that they were compelled to make use of whatever support they could command, enforce or bribe. Their shifts and turns and essential opportunism may lend their actions a somewhat haphazard and contradictory air, but far from suppressing the nobility they welcomed the adherence of old opponents. Eight-four per cent of the attainders passed against nobles in the Wars of the Roses were reversed. The wars had no significant effect on the numbers or wealth of the English landed classes. Edward IV and the early Tudors were prepared, as and when particular circumstances made it necessary, to increase the wealth and influence of those who were loyal, and to discipline, by whatever means they could, those who were as politically unreliable as they were highly placed, or whose low intelligence, positive eccentricities or erratic conduct were likely to make them a danger to the state. The influence of the Percies, if not indispensable, was at least highly desirable in governing the north. Just as Edward IV restored Henry Percy IV to his earldom of Northumberland in 1469–70 to offset the power of the Nevilles so Henry VII soon released him from imprisonment after the battle of Bosworth to make him warden of the east and Middle Marches.

There is little to commend the traditional idea that kings at this time created a new and more subservient nobility as a counterpoise to the older aristocracy. The idea of 'old nobility' has been very much overworked. Baronial families in general seem to have died out in the male line about every third generation or so and the Wars of the Roses made little difference to this aristocratic mortality. The honours of a large section of the lay peerage did not go very far back. Between 1439 and 1504 68 new peerages were created (excluding promotions from one rank to another).

Of those 21 went to the husbands or sons of heiresses to old titles and 47 creations were completely new. The ranks of the nobility were constantly recruited from below, by promotion from a group of rich, untitled families whose way of life and political instincts differed little if at all from those of the lesser nobility. Some such peers were created and splendidly endowed by the king with a consciously political purpose in mind. In 1461 Edward ennobled William Hastings and by granting him the forfeited Leicestershire estates of the earl of Wiltshire, Viscount Beaumont and Lord Roos, transformed him from a middling landowner into a magnate capable of keeping loyal what before 1461 had been a strongly Lancastrian district in the central Midlands.[31]

Such men through their connections with the local gentry, a mixture of patronage and dominance summed up by the contemporary term 'good lordship', in no small measure kept the countryside in peace and quiet. The new Lord Hastings in the course of 22 years sealed legal indentures with 88 retainers, ranging from two other noblemen to knights and squires spread over at least five counties. The noble retinue, the affinity, in other words the 'bastard feudalism' which has been so often condemned as an unmitigated evil, was an essential part of Yorkist and Tudor government. The lack of a police force and a standing army left the personal bond between lord and man, exercised as Lord Hastings' indentures state 'as far as law and conscience requireth', essential for the peace of the countryside.[32] Law and conscience, it is true were often conspicuously absent from these relationships. The magnate had to be given a fairly free hand in his own district, and in return for his loyalty the government did not probe over-carefully into his activities.

The potential success or failure of the system lay in the personality of the king and on whether he could hold the balance between turbulent men too powerful to be ignored, prevent them from gaining undue control of his resources in land, men and money, and see that by and large they used their own in his and the general interest.

This Henry VI conspicuously failed to do. All through the middle ages and well into the reign of Elizabeth I the monarch and the royal council spent an inordinate amount of their time on settling the personal and territorial problems of the great.[33] Bastard feudalism, by putting coercive power into the magnates' hands, undoubtedly gave them the means to take advantage of Henry's irresolute character and to fight out their quarrels *vi et armis* free from the normal restraints of royal discipline. Consequently in

[31] For the nobility see T. L. Kingston Oliphant, 'Was the old English Aristocracy destroyed by the Wars of the Roses?' in *Transactions of the Royal Historical Society* I (1875) 437–43. See also below pp. 123–5, 127–58, 204–6.

[32] Dunham, *op. cit.* appendices A and B.

[33] W. T. MacCaffery, 'Talbot and Stanhope: An Episode in Elizabethan Politics', *Bulletin of the Institute of Historical Research* XXXIII (1960).

the 1440s and the 1450s more and more families took to violence to settle their disputes. This progressive deterioration of public life and the discredit which its final, swift defeat in the Hundred Years' War had brought upon the government gave Richard of York the opportunity to pit his legitimist claim to the throne against the prescriptive right of the house of Lancaster. Even so, whenever York tried to impose his will by force upon the king during the 1450s it is remarkable how little support he commanded amongst the nobles. Though turbulent and excessively prone to take to arms to settle their own quarrels, they were not prepared to cross the line which separated violence from treason. York's great rival, Somerset, may have been unpopular, but there is no evidence that York was greatly loved. York's programme, if such it can be called, was the programme of an ambitious magnate, not a party. In the 1450s the nobility was certainly not divided into Yorkist and Lancastrian. More men than we know may well have sympathized with York's complaints, and their sympathy may well have increased as support for the Lancastrian dynasty waned in the later 1450s before the court's increasing weakness. In spite of this, only after York's attainder at the Parliament of Devils in 1459 did any significant part of the nobility begin to support him. Even then at first they—and even his closest friends among them—were unaware that he planned to revive his dormant claim to the throne. The parliamentary discussions of 1460 show above all reluctance to accept and the impossibility of peacefully rejecting the duke's challenge. York himself was never able to topple Henry VI from his throne, and was forced to accept a compromise—recognition as Henry's heir. A few months later a mere fragment of the Yorkist faction which had grown up since 1459 made his son king Edward IV, but they were impelled by the desperate circumstances which had developed from York's lone policies rather than by conviction and wide support.[34]

Treason once committed tends to breed treason—and so it was at this time. The battles, attainders and proscriptions of the next twenty-five years were far from cowing the nobility and gentry into discreet behaviour. Four political revolutions in a quarter of a century tarnished ideals of loyalty and the vision of kingship and bred an atmosphere tainted with sedition which contrasts vividly with the stricter conscience of the 1450s. The 'union of the two noble and illustre famelies' of York and Lancaster in the marriage of Elizabeth of York and Henry of Richmond failed to stifle treason. There were more and wider conspiracies against Henry VII than there had ever been against Henry VI (though not on the part of the nobility) and, if a spy's report can be believed, even after 1500 some of the highest in the land could discuss the question of the succession without even mentioning the king's son.

[34] See below pp. 101–4.

Finally, in recent years historians have debated the economic condition of fifteenth-century England. Such debates still vigorously resound. After some years in which it was generally regarded as a stagnant, if not a declining economy, a recent writer has substituted the idea of an advancing economic community.[35] It is impossible to discuss this highly technical problem here except to note that the civil wars had little or no effect on agrarian and commercial life and to note a certain connection between financial power and the revival of monarchy.

The period of the 'New Monarchy', as J. R. Green in his *History of the English People* called the decades after 1461, or the 'Tudor Despotism' as others until recently described its later phases, has been analysed in a way which gives it a deceptive appearance of strength: a kind of incipient autocracy based on strong royal finances, the decline of parliament and an aristocracy weakened and demoralized by the Wars of the Roses—or alternatively as the medieval monarchy restored to new heights of secure power. In reality it was neither. Its stability must be sought in other causes.

There was no greater fundamental opposition between the king and parliament in the later middle ages than between the king and the aristocracy. Parliament occupied no static place in the constitution, it varied with circumstances. Normally its role was to cooperate with the king in the government of the realm. The great periods of parliamentary drama, apart from the peaks of revolution, were periods of financial mismanagement and financial strain, when the commons, suspicious and resentful of heavy royal expenditure which the king expected them to defray by taxation, demanded financial reforms and concessions. The so-called 'New Monarchy' coincided with one of the longest periods in English history free of prolonged and expensive foreign warfare. Between 1453 and 1544 campaigns abroad were short and took place at long intervals. The end of the Hundred Years' War of itself was enough to end the principal drain on the royal coffers.[36] Edward IV, more by luck than judgment, avoided prolonged war with France and his single expedition abroad ended in his return home the richer by a valuable pension from Louis XI. Henry VII enjoyed the like good fortune. With no wars to fight, men expected the king to 'live of his own' and thus remove the most nagging dissonance between the king and his subjects in parliament. With the great shift in English trade from the export of wool to the export of cloth, revenue from the customs duties had become much smaller than it had been in the fourteenth century. Rather than risk political discontent by radically reforming the customs dues and, even more, by reforming the antiquated and unproductive system of taxation on personal property to take account of changes in

[35] A. R. Bridbury, *Economic Growth: England in the Later Middle Ages* (1962).
[36] G. Holmes, *The Later Middle Ages, 1272–1485* (1962) ch. 12.

the distribution of wealth, Edward IV quickly adopted as his official policy demands which the commons had forced on Henry VI between 1449 and 1453—demands for less taxation and for the conservation and more businesslike management of the crown lands. By cancelling grants from these estates, adding to them by a rigid enforcement of feudal rights, placing them under a strict administration copied from the most up-to-date methods of seigneurial estate management, and with the whole removed from the control of the antiquated exchequer and entrusted to the more flexible and adaptable chamber (a department of the royal household), he greatly increased his normal revenue. When to this new system he added a more meticulous control of the customs service to avoid evasions of payment, as well as his French pension and the considerable profits of his private trading ventures, he redeemed the monarchy from chronic debt and died rich—the only English king to do so since the time of Henry I. Parliament sank into the background, content enough to accept an administration which made no demands on its purses. Henry VII continued these practices, profiting from Edward's experiments which time and his own attentive care made even more profitable.[37]

Edward IV and Henry VII, in spite of the dramatic incidents of their careers, were by no means adventurous men. Conventionally minded to the last degree, they worked within the social and political facts of the world in which they lived, not against them. Cunning to the extent of perjury if it served their turn, their moral outlook was no worse, and no better, than that of the men through whom they had to work. Though both could be hard and cruel, they were on the whole merciful towards their opponents, partly because the political conventions of the day demanded it, partly because they could not afford to be anything else. Financially, by modern standards or even by the standards of some of the more magnificent and warlike medieval kings their ancestors, their state was hardly a state at all. With inflexible incomes derived from contracted sources, capable of only limited expansion, they were compelled to shift more after the ways of a college bursar than of a modern minister of finance. To call such a monarchy strong is to mistake shadow for substance. The English monarchy emerged from the Wars of the Roses under firm, strong guidance, but inherently it was a ramshackle structure and its survival depended on the protection of the sea, serving 'as a moat defensive to a house, against envy of less happy lands' as John of Gaunt, 'time-honoured Lancaster', proclaimed. A generation later even the reforming schemes of

---

[37] B. P. Wolffe, 'The Management of English Royal Estates under the Yorkist Kings', 'Acts of Resumption in the Lancastrian Parliaments, 1399–1456', and 'Henry VII's Land Revenues and Chamber Finance', *English Historical Review* LXXI (1956), LXXIII (1958), and LXXIX (1964).

Henry VIII's minister, Thomas Cromwell, failed to obliterate its inherited weaknesses.[38] By continental standards it was one of the shallow little backwaters of monarchy.

---

[38] G. L. Harriss, 'Medieval Government and Statecraft', *Past and Present* (25) (1963).

3

Henry VI and the duke of York's second protectorate, 1455–6[1]

Most modern writers state that Henry VI twice became insane during the 1450s and that the duke of York twice became protector and defender of the realm as a result of the king's incapacity to attend to affairs of state. A close examination of the events leading up to the two protectorates, however, reveals a very different state of affairs on each occasion and provides material for some inferences about York's intentions and ambitions.

The parliament of 1453, which attainted the duke of York's chamberlain, Sir William Oldhall, for his part in York's armed demonstration in 1452 and for alleged complicity in Cade's rebellion, was prorogued on 2 July. By 10 August at the latest Henry VI was seriously ill.[2] His illness is vouched for by at least ten contemporary or near contemporary writers.[3] Abbot Whethamstede of St Albans described his symptoms in some detail[4] and the exchequer issue rolls show that attendants were specially paid for sitting with him day and night.[5] Early in January 1454 (possibly on new year's day) the queen and the duke of Buckingham presented the infant prince of Wales to the king at Windsor and asked for his blessing on the

[1] I wish to thank R. Virgoe and K. Wallis for help and criticism in writing this paper.

[2] *Paston Letters* introduction p. cxlix n. 2. Giles's Chronicle, see below, says about the feast of the translation of St Thomas the Martyr (3 July).

[3] Rawlinson B. 355, Bale, Gough London 10 (Rawlinson and Gough mention Henry's recovery only) in R. Flenley, *Six Town Chronicles of England* (1911) 108, 140, 158. 'Vitellius A XVI' in *Chronicles of London* ed. C. L. Kingsford (1905) 163. Giles's Chronicle in *Incerti Scriptoris Chronicon Anglie de Regnis Trium Regum Lancastrensium* ed. J. A. Giles (1848) 44. R. Fabyan, *The New Chronicles of England and France* ed. H. Ellis (1811) 627. *The Great Chronicle of London* ed. A. H. Thomas and I. D. Thornley (1938) 186. William Worcester (Annales formerly attributed to) in Stevenson II pt ii 771. See also below. In addition Gregory's and Davies's Chronicles mention Henry's sickness without giving specific dates though Gregory makes it clear that it was before the first battle of St Albans. *The Historical Collections of a Citizen of London* ed. J. Gairdner, Camden Society (1876) 198–9. *An English Chronicle of the Reigns of Richard II, Henry IV, Henry V and Henry VI* ed. J. S. Davies, Camden Society (1856) 78.

[4] *Registrum Abbatiae Johannis Whethamstede* ed H. T. Riley, Rolls Series (1872–3) I 163.

[5] Issue Roll E. 403/800 m. 7; E.403/801 m. 2. These payments were made on 5 February and 9 May 1455 and the entries show that they were an addition to the usual sums paid 'garconibus et pagettis Camere Regis'.

child. Henry gave no sign of recognition; he only once looked upon the prince and then cast down his eyes again.[6]

Even in these tragic circumstances there was a delay of eight months before York was made protector. The court refused to admit that the king was ill. After parliament reassembled at Reading on 12 November the chancellor had explained the king's absence by the plague then prevailing in the town and other unnamed causes. The session had been immediately prorogued to February.[7] According to a letter written at the time, the queen by mid January had already drawn up plans for exercising the regency herself.[8] By the middle of February the question could be evaded no longer. York, with the assent of the council, obtained a limited commission authorizing him to open parliament as the king's lieutenant.[9] When parliament met most people were anxious to avoid committing themselves on the major question.[10] The attendance in the upper house was very poor and for the first and only known occasion in English medieval history, fines were imposed on peers for non-attendance.[11] In spite of this only 45 peers out of a total of 105 summoned appear to have been present during the session and only 14 out of 37 lay peers below the rank of viscount.[12] It seems, in fact, that the section of the peerage whose support it was most desirable to obtain wanted to avoid committing themselves by staying away, and that York (or those who advised him) tried to compel their support or at least their approval. On 15 March Prince Edward was created prince of Wales and earl of Chester.[13] On 22 March Cardinal Kemp, archbishop of Canterbury and chancellor, died and the problem of filling two such important posts seems to have precipitated the question of the regency. The lords then commissioned 12 of their number to ride down to Windsor and put this and other matters before the king if he were well enough to discuss them.[14] When on 25 March the lords' deputation waited on the king they found his condition far worse than they had expected. They saw him three times in the course of the day. Henry was in a state of utter prostration, both

---

[6] *Paston Letters* I 263–4.

[7] *Rot. Parl.* V 238. On 24 October a great council had been held at Westminster to which York was not summoned, but then at the insistence of his friends a writ was sent to him. *Proceedings and Ordinances* VI 163–4. Sir J. H. Ramsay, *Lancaster and York* (1892) II 167.

[8] *Paston Letters* I 265. Described by the editor as a 'News Letter of John Stodeley'.

[9] *Cal. Pat. Rolls, 1452–1461*, 153.

[10] 'Many of the lords, it seems, had showed their reluctance to commit themselves personally by staying away from parliament altogether in this difficult time'. J. S. Roskell, 'The Problem of the Attendance of the Lords in Medieval Parliaments', *Bulletin of the Institute of Historical Research* XXIX (1956) 189.

[11] Roskell, 'Attendance of the lords', *op. cit.* 189–90.

[12] *ibid.* 190–1.

[13] *Rot. Parl.* V 249.

[14] *ibid.* V 240–1.

physical and mental. He had to be supported by two men as he moved from one room to another and he gave the lords no word nor sign of recognition.[15] Consequently, being unable to avoid an embarrassing decision any longer, on 27 March the lords appointed Richard of York as protector. At the same time they tried to hedge in his authority with drastic restrictions. The lords made their opinions very plain when they laid it down that 'the seid Duke shall be chief of the Kynges Counsaill, and devysed therfor to the seid Duke a name different from other Counsaillours, nought the name of Tutour, Lieutenaunt, Governour, nor of Regent, nor noo name that shall emporte auctorite of governaunce of the lande; but the seid name of Protectour and Defensour, the whiche emporteth a personell duete of entendaunce to the actuell defence of this land, aswell ayenst th'enemyes outward, if case require, as ayenst Rebelles inward, if eny happe to be, that God forbede, duryng the Kynges pleaser, and so that it be not prejudice to my Lord Prince.'[16] The arrangement was to continue only during the king's pleasure or until the Prince of Wales should become of age.[17] The poor attendance of lords at the parliament, the care taken to safeguard the interests of the prince, the restricted powers which were all that York was allowed,[18] and the definition of a narrow executive authority seem to indicate that few people were entirely happy about the arrangement.

York controlled the government for the rest of the year. Although his great rival, Somerset, was imprisoned in the Tower of London,[19] the protector behaved with moderation. By the end of December the king had recovered his sanity.[20] On 7 February Somerset was released from the Tower under recognizances which the council discharged a month later. Henry declared Somerset his faithful liegeman and both he and York entered into recognizances to abide by the arbitration of Thomas Bourchier, the new archbishop of Canterbury, and seven others on any outstanding disputes between them, the decision to be given by 20 June.[21] York's first protectorate had ended.[22] There now began the drift to

---

[15] *Rot. Parl.* V 241–2.

[16] *ibid.* V 242.

[17] *ibid.* V 243–4. *Cal. Pat. Rolls, 1452–1461,* 159. A prospective appointment for the prince on reaching years of discretion was sealed at the same time. *Rot. Parl.* V 243.

[18] York's control of patronage was also defined and limited. *Rot. Parl.* V 243–4.

[19] Somerset himself admitted that his confinement was more in the nature of protective custody than rigorous imprisonment. Ramsay, *Lancaster and York, op. cit.* II 168 n. 3.

[20] *Paston Letters* I 315. It is possible that he was on the mend by early September when people already had access to him, though William Paston's words leave the matter doubtful. *ibid.* 303.

[21] Council and PSE 28/86. *Foedera* XI 361–3. *Cal. Close Rolls, 1454–1461,* 49.

[22] The precise date cannot be determined. See C. A. J. Armstrong, 'Politics and the Battle of St Albans, 1455', *Bulletin of the Institute of Historical Research* XXXIII (1960) 8–9.

hostilities which resulted in the first battle of St Albans (22 May 1455). St Albans was not a large-scale battle; one authority has described it as 'a short scuffle in a street'.[23] The numbers engaged were small and the casualties probably numbered no more than 60. York found very little support among the peerage at the time of the battle. Apart from his brother-in-law and his nephew, the earls of Salisbury and Warwick, the only peer present in the field with him was Lord Clinton, though another of his nephews, the duke of Norfolk, came up the following day.[24]

In spite of his victory in the field there was once more considerable delay before York was appointed protector and his patent was not issued until five months later. Ever since Stubbs wrote in 1878 that before 12 November 'the king was again insane',[25] most authors have been content to follow him in giving Henry's breakdown in health as the reason for the duke's appointment,[26] though not all have gone so far as to say that the king actually lost his reason.[27] Now this assumption that Henry's health broke down completely (or nearly completely) a second time seems to be very dubious. As far as I know no definite statement of this kind was ever made until the nineteenth century.[28] None of the chroniclers who briefly refer to Henry's lapse into insanity in 1453 mention illness in 1455–6. No writer of the sixteenth, seventeenth or eighteenth centuries describes it. In fact, no statement about Henry's second illness is to be found in any chronicle or general history[29] until in 1823 Sharon Turner wrote 'in June the King again

---

[23] C. Oman, *The Political History of England 1377 to 1485* (1910) 367.

[24] *Paston Letters* I 333. Armstrong, 'Battle of St Albans', *op. cit.* 18, 19, 38, 51. It is possible that Viscount Bourchier and Lord Cobham were also with the Yorkists but this must be regarded as doubtful. *Ibid.* 21 and n. 5, 27.

[25] W. Stubbs, *The Constitutional History of England* (1878) III 173.

[26] e.g. J. R. Green *History of the English People* (1877–80) I 572. Oman, *Political History, op. cit.* 370. K. H. Vickers, *England in the Later Middle Ages* (1913) 446. M. E. Christie, *Henry VI* (1922) 261–2. K. B. McFarlane, 'The Lancastrian Kings' in *Cambridge Medieval History* VIII (1936) 413. J. J. Bagley, *Margaret of Anjou* (1949) 81.

[27] Ramsay, *op. cit.* II 185, 187, goes no further than saying that the king 'was again found to be ill'. T. F. Tout in his article 'Henry VI' in *DNB* (1908) stated, 'Henry's illness was of a different character from the absolute prostration of his first attack. He was able to transact a little business. He personally committed the government to his council, requesting that they should inform him of matters concerning his person.'

[28] The single dubious exception is Rapin de Thoyras, *The History of England* transl. N. Tindal (2nd edn 1732–3) I 580, which incorrectly speaks of York opening the session of parliament in July 'the King being then relapsed' and then refers to the king's state as an 'Indisposition, which hindered him from attending to the Affairs of the Publick'. Rapin's chronology is very inaccurate at this point and his references are to Hall, Stowe, and Cotton's abridgement, none of which mentions illness.

[29] The authors examined on this point are Polydore Vergil, Hall, Grafton, Holinshed, Stow. White Kennet, *A Complete History of England* (edn 1706). T. Carte, *A General History of England* (1747–55). D. Hume, *The History of England From the Invasion of Julius Caesar to the Accession of Henry VII* (1762). H. Hallam, *View of the State of Europe During the Middle Ages* (1818).

became diseased', though he never used the term 'insanity'.[30] Lingard, the next writer of a general history, committed himself only to the very cautious statement that about the end of October 'it was rumoured that Henry had relapsed into his former disorder'.[31] The story of Henry's illness was again asserted by James Gairdner in the introduction to his edition of the *Paston Letters* published in 1874[32] and, as we have seen, four years later it was taken over by Stubbs whose immense authority has probably been responsible for others accepting it as an undisputed fact.

It is easy to see how this legend arose. Sharon Turner juxtaposed statements made in two letters which had appeared in print for the first time during the eighteenth century in Thomas Rymer's *Foedera* and Sir James Fenn's edition of the *Paston Letters*. The first of these letters is a privy seal dated at Westminster on 5 June 1455 in which Gilbert Kemer, the dean of Salisbury, one of the most famous physicians of his day, was instructed to go to Windsor on the 12th 'for as moche as we be occupied and laboured, as ye knowe wel, with Sicknesse and Infirmitees'.[33] There is nothing in this letter which indicates an immediate or sudden deterioration in health. Even allowing for the fact that Henry had been wounded in the neck by an arrow at St Albans only a fortnight before it is probably forcing the evidence to see in it more than a letter written on behalf of a man in a chronically poor state of health.[34] Whatever interpretation is put on this letter to Kemer the king was at all events well enough to be present in person at the opening of parliament on 9 July and ten days later Henry Windsor wrote to his friends in East Anglia, 'the Kyng our souverain Lord, and all his trwe Lordes stand in hele of there bodies'.[35] On the first day of the session the chancellor, by the king's command, read out certain articles on the cause of summoning parliament, which included matters as various as

---

[30] Sharon Turner, *The History of England During the Middle Ages* III (1823) 265.

[31] J. Lingard, *The History of England from the First Invasion by the Romans to the Accession of William and Mary in 1688* IV (1849) 116.

[32] In November 'it was reported that he had fallen sick of his old infirmity—which proved to be too true'. *Paston Letters* introduction p. cxxiii (quoted from the reprint of 1896). It is fair to say that later (p. cxxiv) Gairdner stated that the infirmity 'on this occasion could scarcely have amounted to absolute loss of his faculties' though later writers seem to have lost sight of this.

[33] *Foedera* XI 366.

[34] It is unlikely that Kemer (who was a physician not a surgeon) was called in to deal with Henry's wound as on 15 July three surgeons were paid £10 (in part payment of £20 promised) 'pro diversis magnis laboribus et diligenciis suis per ipsos factis crica personam domini Regis'. Issue Roll E. 403/801 m 7. It may well be that Henry was in a weak state after St Albans though John Crane writing to John Paston three days after the battle stated that 'he hathe no grete harme'. *Paston Letters* I 334. I have not succeeded in tracing any payments made to Gilbert Kemer. William Hatteclyffe, the king's physician, received no special payments over and above his ordinary annuity at this time.

[35] *Paston Letters* I 345.

the organization of the royal household, financial provision for Calais, the defence of the realm, the settlement of differences amongst the nobility, the export of precious metals and the condition of Wales.[36] It may or may not be significant that no announcement about the king's health was included among them. No other statement on this subject is to be found before 28 October—between the two sessions of parliament. John Gresham then wrote to John Paston the second letter referred to above. This letter describes in some detail the murder of Nicholas Radford, the recorder of Exeter, by a band of men led by Sir Thomas Courtenay, the earl of Devonshire's eldest son. The letter ends with a section which is badly mutilated but as it is vital to the argument it is best to quote it in full. The text reads: 'This (i.e. the news of Radford's murder) was told to my Lord Chaunceler this fornoon . . . messengers as come of purpos owt of the same cuntre. This matier is take gretly . . . passed at ij. after mydnyght rod owt of London, as it is seid, more thanne . . . the best wyse. Summe seyne it was to ride toward my Lord of York, and summe . . . k, so mech rumor is here; what it menyth I wot not, God turne it . . . at Hertford, and summe men ar a ferd that he is seek agyen. I pray God . . . my Lords of York, Warwyk, Salesbury and other arn in purpos to conveye hym . . . &c. The seid N. Crome, berer her of, shall telle you suche tydynggs . . . in hast, at London, on Seint Simon day and Jude.'[37]

Thus, Henry has been convicted of a second attack of madness on two very flimsy pieces of evidence—that he 'sent for the doctor' on 5 June and that, nearly 21 weeks later, a London attorney hastily finishing a letter which, as he himself admitted, brought together a number of wild rumours which were floating about the capital at the time, mentioned that some men 'ar a ferd' that the king is sick again. Likewise there is no definite evidence of Henry's recovery from his alleged illness. A rumour current by 9 February 1456 that York was about to be 'discharged'[38] and the fact that on the 25th the king came in person to parliament and relieved York of his protectorate,[39] have been taken as evidence of his recovery from a bout of insanity which no contemporary source yet discovered states as a definite fact. The most that it is safe to say on the available evidence is that Henry may have been ill but he was certainly neither insane nor completely incapable of transacting business.

There are two possible ways of testing the reliability of these statements. Firstly, to reconstruct if possible Henry's personal actions during this

[36] Rot. Parl. V 279.

[37] Paston Letters I 350–2.

[38] ibid. 377. The wording of the letter implies that the king was of sound mind and refers neither to illness nor recovery; thus, 'the Kyng, as it was tolde me by a grete man, wolde have hym [York] chief and princepall counceller, and soo to be called hise chef counceller and lieutenant as long as hit shuld lyke the kyng . . .'.

[39] Rot. Parl. V 321–2.

period and secondly, to scrutinize very closely the story given on the parliament roll. Unfortunately the classes of records which would enable us to trace Henry's personal actions at this time are scrappy and incomplete. An examination of those which have survived gives only a negative result. It shows that during the time of Henry's supposed illness the longest period for which there is no document bearing the royal sign manual was 81 days. (12 December 1455 to 2 March 1456) as compared with a period of 77 days earlier in 1455 (3 February to 21 April) at a time when no illness has ever been suspected.[40] Sign manuals, in fact, continued to appear after the beginning of York's second protectorate. Such evidence must therefore be considered useless either way.

An examination of what happened in parliament is more revealing. It is doubtful if there was any enthusiasm among the peers for York's recent action. There is more likely to have been consternation and dismay. Although the prospect of renewed fines for non-attendance brought more ecclesiastical lords to parliament than had been the case recently, attendance among the lay baronage once again appears to have been poor.[41] No one wished to accept responsibility for, or even to appear to condone, what was after all the treasonable action of rearing war against the king. The duke of Norfolk most probably stayed away from parliament.[42] Even the Neville family were not completely united, for Warwick's brother, Lord Fauconberg, though he no doubt sympathized with his father and his brother, had been in the Lancastrian camp at St Albans.[43] When the inner

[40] The classes of records examined for this purpose are signet warrants, warrants under the sign manual, council warrants, council and privy seal warrants, patent and treaty rolls. There are no signet warrants at all between 18 July 1454 and 26 July 1456, yet the survival of a signet letter of 27 September 1455, copied into *London Letter Book K*, 370–1, shows that missives were being sent out under the signet at this time, as do entries on the issues rolls for payment for messengers taking out signet letters. The files of council warrants and council and privy seal warrants already show the incomplete condition which was to become so marked under the Yorkists. See below ch. 7 pp. 175 ff. For convenience the term 'sign manual' has here been somewhat loosely interpreted to include documents which bear the king's initials and enrolments which bear the note of warranty *Per Regem*. Where both the original warrant and the enrolment survive they have been counted as one. The note of warranty *Per Regem et Consilium* has been excluded as its use during Henry's first illness shows that it was employed without the king's participation.

In the period 3 February to 16 May, that is roughly the eleven weeks before the battle of St Albans (in which period no suggestion of madness has ever been made), there are only six extant sign manuals. They begin again on 6 July (the day after the privy seal to Gilbert Kemer) and the number fluctuates month by month as follows: July 4; August 14; September 1; October 1; November 1; December 1; January 0; February 0; March 6; April 2; May 6; June 5; July 10. It is interesting that they disappear entirely at the point of Henry's supposed recovery and not during his supposed illness.

[41] Roskell, *op. cit* 193–4. Only 17 out of 36 temporal lords below the rank of viscount appeared.

[42] *ibid.* 193–4. Armstrong, *op. cit.* 38, 51–2.

[43] *ibid.* 27, 65.

circle of Yorkists were thus divided among themselves, it is unlikely that they would command wide support among other lords. It has also been plausibly suggested that York's relations, the Bourchiers (the archbishop, Viscount Bourchier, their brother John, Lord Berners, and their half-brother Humphrey, duke of Buckingham) held a kind of middle place between the two main factions.[44] It would seem, therefore, that there was no large party even in the comparatively thin house of lords which assembled at the end of June likely to endorse any extreme demands which York might feel disposed to make.

Nor can the commons be regarded as exclusively partisan. Although the Yorkists used all the influence they could in the elections, and in one county at least, Norfolk, their activities went beyond the limits which local opinion considered to be decent,[45] some who were elected were definitely uneasy at finding themselves in such a parliament.[46] Even the speaker, Sir John Wenlock, was probably more affected to the Bourchiers than to York himself.[47]

During the first session of parliament the only important business transacted was the passing of an act absolving York, Warwick and Salisbury and their friends from all responsibility for 'any thyng that happened' at St Albans. The blame was thrown entirely on Somerset, Thomas Thorpe and William Joseph.[48] It was reported of this bill that 'mony a man groged full sore nowe it is passed'.[49] York rehabilitated the name of his old friend Humphrey of Gloucester by getting parliament to declare that he had died the king's true liegeman.[50] All the lords present swore a new oath of allegiance.[51] On 31 July the session came to an end. It was prorogued so that the commons might attend to the harvest and on account of an outbreak of plague in London and the suburbs. The chancellor stated that the business of the next session would be concerned 'pro bono pacis'.[52]

[44] J. S. Roskell, 'John Lord Wenlock of Someries', *Publications of the Bedfordshire Historical Record Society* XXXVIII (1958) 31. John, Lord Berners was summoned to the Lords for the first time in this parliament. Of Buckingham, *Paston Letters* I 335–6, report (how accurately is, of course, another matter) that after the battle of St Albans he had agreed to work with the Yorkists 'and ther to he and his brethern ben bounde by reconysaunce in notable summes to abyde the same'. Also in January 1456 Buckingham and Berners both entered into recognizances for the duke of Exeter which seems to indicate a somewhat anti-Yorkist bias. *Cal. Close Rolls, 1454–1461*, 109.

[45] See the letter to the sheriff of Kent in *Proceedings and Ordinances* VI 246–7. For Norfolk, K. B. McFarlane, 'Parliament and Bastard Feudalism' in *Transactions of the Royal Historical Society* 4th series XXVI (1944) 58–9, 64. Roskell, 'Lord Wenlock', *op. cit.* 30–31.

[46] 'Sume men holde it right straunge to be in this Parlement, and me thenketh they be wyse men that soo doo.' *Paston Letters* I 340–41.

[47] Roskell, 'Lord Wenlock', *op. cit.* 31–2.

[48] *Rot. Parl.* V 280–2.

[49] *Paston Letters* I 346.

[50] *Rot. Parl.* V 335.

[51] *ibid.* V 282–3.

[52] *ibid.* V 283.

A great council met on 6 November, six days before parliament was due to reassemble.[53] On 10 November the council decided that York should be commissioned to open parliament as king's lieutenant, the king being unable for certain causes to do so himself.[54] It may well be that the king was indisposed or it is possible that York's friends (he himself was not present at the meeting when the decision was taken)[55] put forward the argument later used in parliament that vigorous action was needed to deal with the disturbed state of the country. Whatever the reason, York's appointment proved to be the thin end of the wedge. When parliament assembled on 12 November the theme 'pro bono pacis' was taken up at once. On Thursday 13 November, William Burley led a deputation from the commons to the lords (where attendance was still thin)[56] asking 'that if for suche causes the Kyng *heraftre* myght not entende to the protection and defence of this lande, that it shuld like the kyng by th'advis of his said Lieutenaunt [York] and the Lordes, to ordeigne and purvey suche an hable persone, as shuld mowe entende to the defence and protection of the saide lande, and this to be doon as sone as it myght be, . . . to that entent that they myght sende to theym for whom they were commen to this present Parlement knoweledge, who shuld be Protectour and Defensour of this lande, and to whom they shuld mowe have recours to sue for remedie of injuries and wronges done to theym.'[57] To support this demand they stressed the need for vigorous action to suppress disorder, especially riots caused by the quarrels between the earl of Devonshire and Lord Bonvile in the west country.[58]

Two days later, on Saturday 15 November, the deputation, again led by Burley, came before the lords a second time and for a second time stressed the disorders in the west. This time they also suggested that if people brought their grievances to Henry himself for remedy, 'it shuld be overe grevous and tedious to his Highnesse, and that there must be a persone to whom the people of this lande may have recours to sue to for remedy of their injuries . . .'.[59] Moreover, the deputation said, or at least implied, that the commons would discuss no other business until the question of the

[53] Roskell, 'Attendance of the lords', *op. cit.* 194.

[54] *Proceedings and Ordinances* VI 261–2. *Rot. Parl.* V 453–4. The rather vague phrasing reads 'ob certas justas et racionabiles causas in persona nostra interesse non possimus'.

[55] Out of 38 people present at the meeting 24 were bishops or abbots and apart from the Neville (Salisbury, Warwick, Fauconberg) and Bourchier (Buckingham, Viscount Bourchier) groups the only others present were the earls of Arundel, Oxford and Worcester, Lords Richmond, Scrope, Fitzwarren, Grey and Stourton and the Prior of St John's.

[56] On the evidence available Roskell, 'Attendance of the lords', *op. cit.* 193–4, states that it was lower than in the previous session, particularly among the lesser lay lords.

[57] *Rot. Parl.* V 284–5.

[58] *ibid.* V 285.

[59] *ibid.*

protectorate had been settled.[60] After the commons' deputation had departed the lords discussed the matter among themselves, then gave their voices for York. The duke, after a formal denial of his fitness for the post, accepted with 'certayn protestations' which, detailed as they were, must have been prepared in advance as they were apparently debated immediately.[61] Two days later, on Monday 17 November, the commons' deputation came to the lords yet a third time to complain that they had not received an answer to their demands.[62] The same day the chancellor announced the king's assent to York's appointment as protector[63] and his patent was issued on 19 November[64]—exactly a week after parliament had reassembled.

Several points in the narrative on the parliament roll call for comment. In the first place the commons never claimed that Henry was actually incapable. The most they could say (or insinuate) was that he might become incapable, and for this reason and to relieve him from the strain and tedium of personal action at a difficult time the lords should persuade him to appoint a protector. It may be of course that we are dealing with a story like that of the emperor's new clothes, and that no one wished to mention the dreadful truth openly. This however seems unlikely in view of the fact that Henry's illness had been so openly discussed the previous year. In any case considerations of the kind put forward for relieving the king from unnecessary strain could have been suggested with equal plausibility at almost any time during his adult life. At this point also, expressions of anxiety for the king's health were joined with complaints of riots and disorders of unusual extent and violence in the west country, of which more will be said later. Secondly, someone was in a tremendous hurry to get things done. The decision that York should open the session as king's lieutenant had been taken at a great council as late as 10 November,[65] two days before parliament was due to reassemble after its recess, and as we have seen the commons had already formulated their demands, appointed a delegation and had expressed their very definite views to the lords on the second day of the session. The speed with which the commons acted must surely indicate some kind of previous discussion and planning, for the first day of any session was normally taken up to a very considerable extent with formal business. It is unlikely that so important a matter could have been decided upon in twenty-four hours unless there had been some consultation beforehand. Moreover, on the fourth day, after making the conven-

---

[60] *Rot. Parl.* V 285.

[61] *ibid.* V 286–7.

[62] *ibid.* V 285–6.

[63] *ibid.* V 286.

[64] *Cal. Pat. Rolls, 1452–1461,* 273.

[65] *Proceedings and Ordinances* VI 261–2. *Rot. Parl.* V 453–4. The patent was issued on 11 November. *Cal. Pat. Rolls, 1452–1461,* 273.

tional protest about his unfitness for the job, York was at once able to produce a list of articles setting out the conditions under which he was prepared to act.[66] Again, the commons' deputation pressed the lords outrageously in demanding three meetings with them in five days. The cumulative effect of these proceedings arouses at least suspicions of a well organized plan of campaign. These suspicions are in no way decreased by the fact that the deputation to the lords was led not by the speaker, Sir John Wenlock, but by William Burley. William Burley was no political innocent; he was one of the most experienced shire knights in this assembly. He had been one of the members for Shropshire in 19 out of the 25 parliaments which had sat between 1417 and 1455 and had been speaker in two of them.[67] He had been one of the duke of York's feofees since 1449–50[68] and was by this time a member of his council.[69]

Even when subjected to pressure of this kind the lords hesitated. Although York's 'protestations' about the conditions under which he was prepared to take on the protectorate were fairly moderate in tone they were not agreed without considerable discussion and only after a committee had been appointed to clarify certain matters of detail with York.[70] The duke in the end was appointed protector on the same limited terms as in 1454, except that he could now be dismissed only by the king in parliament instead of at the king's pleasure and his salary was increased. Once again he did not gain the powers of a regent. The rights of the prince of Wales were safeguarded and he was to take over the protectorate when he became of age.[71] Meanwhile all questions touching 'the good and politique rule and governaunce' of the land were to be decided by the council, with the proviso that the king was to be informed of all matters concerning his person.[72]

At this point it is necessary to give in some detail an account of events in Devonshire which seem to have influenced to a greater extent than is usually realized the action taken in parliament. The principal reason for which the commons had so insistently demanded the appointment of a protector was the prevalence of disorder, especially in the west country. For well over a year the earl of Devonshire and his sons had disturbed the peace in Exeter and the surrounding districts and in the last quarter of 1455 their disorderly conduct came to a violent and sanguinary climax.[73] The course of events

---

[66] *Rot. Parl.* V 286–7. On Saturday, 15 November.

[67] J. S. Roskell, *The Commons in the Parliament of 1422* (1954) 159–60.

[68] *ibid.* 160.

[69] Roskell, 'Lord Wenlock', *op. cit.* 32.

[70] *Rot. Parl.* V 287.

[71] *ibid.* V 287–9.

[72] *ibid.* V 289–90.

[73] It is said to have arisen out of conflicting claims to the office of steward of the duchy of Cornwall. Roskell, *The Commons, op. cit.* 154.

can be pieced together from a petition put to parliament asking for justice on the Courtenays, from indictments later taken before justices of oyer and terminer, and from the unpublished records of the city of Exeter.[74] It should be borne in mind, however, that accusations made in petitions and indictments must be used with caution. Stories never lost anything in the telling in such sources and the numbers of men alleged to be involved in riots and violent gatherings were often very much exaggerated. The three protagonists, the earl of Devonshire, Sir Phillip Courtenay of Powderham and Lord Bonvile were all related.[75] Taking our account of their quarrels no further back than 1450, the earl had then besieged Lord Bonvile in Taunton castle and there was 'maxima perturbatio' in the west country which had been pacified by the intervention of the duke of York, Lord Moleyns, William Herbert and others.[76] The earl took part in York's armed demonstration at Dartford in 1452 and had been accused and acquitted of treason in the lords in 1454.[77] In spite of this, Devonshire ever afterwards seems to have been opposed to York. Now in April 1454 royal commissioners (of whom Lord Bonvile was one) had arranged a meeting in Exeter with various merchants and others to negotiate contributions to a loan for the keeping of the sea and the defence of Calais. While the discussions were still in progress the earl's two elder sons, Sir Thomas and Henry, came into the city by night with, according to the indictment later laid against them, 400 men and more. The merchants were so alarmed that they went away and no loan could be collected. The Courtenays threatened to murder Bonvile and the justices of the peace were so dismayed that they dared not hold the usual Easter sessions.[78]

The earl of Devonshire had apparently been absent while all this had occurred and it may have been done without his knowledge. He returned to the west after the battle of St Albans where he had been wounded fighting on the king's side,[79] and he was certainly responsible for the outbreak of

---

[74] This was done in great part by G. H. Radford, 'Nicholas Radford, 1385 (?)–1455' and 'The Fight at Clyst in 1455', in *Transactions of the Devonshire Association* XXXV (1903) 251–78, and XLIV (1912) 252–65, hereafter referred to as *Radford I* and *Radford II*. Apart from dealing with the fight at Clyst more fully, *Radford II* also corrects mistakes in chronology in *Radford I*. As Mrs. Radford used only certain sections (without giving exact references) of Ancient Petitions, SC. 8/138/6864 and of Ancient Indictments KB. 9/16, references are here given to the originals.

[75] Bonvile had married *c.* 1426–7 as his second wife Elizabeth, widow of John, Lord Harrington and daughter of Edward Courtenay, third earl of Devonshire. He was therefore uncle by marriage of Thomas, the fifth earl. One of Bonvile's daughters was married to William, the son of Sir Phillip Courtenay of Powderham, who was the grandson of Hugh, second earl of Devonshire (d. 1377).

[76] Stevenson II pt ii 770.

[77] Ramsay, *op. cit.* II 148, 171. *Rot. Parl.* V 249.

[78] *Radford II*, 255–6. KB. 9/16/76.

[79] *Paston Letters* I 333.

violence which occurred late in 1455. The first move came when his sons again invaded Exeter. This time they bore down on the town with 600 men 'and more' and prevented the holding of the autumn sessions of the peace as they had prevented those of Easter the previous year.[80] Then, on the night of 23 October, the earl's eldest son, Sir Thomas, rode with a large number of men to Uppcotes, the house of Nicholas Radford, the aged recorder of Exeter and the godfather of his own brother Henry. He obtained entry by a stratagem and after the place had been thoroughly ransacked (the intruders even toppled Radford's ailing wife out of bed and took the sheets from it for trussing up some of the loot), Sir Thomas told Radford that he must go with him to talk with his father the earl. The party was only a stone's throw from the house when Sir Thomas, after exchanging privy words with some of his followers, spurred his horse and rode away; whereupon several of his men turned on Radford and stabbed him to death.[81] A few days later they again appeared at Uppcotes, at Radford's funeral, desecrated the corpse and performed a farce of a coroner's inquest which absolved them of all blame for the crime.[82] A week after the murder, the earl, his two sons and Thomas Carrewe assembled a gang of more than a thousand men at Tiverton. On 3 November they marched to Exeter, seized the keys of the gates from the guards and set their own watch. They held the city gates in this way until the Monday before Christmas.[83] From Exeter they immediately went on to Powderham castle and there menaced its owner, Sir Phillip Courtenay.[84]

Something of these outrages was known in London at the time the session of parliament opened on 12 November[85] and, as we have seen, the commons' delegation made good use of their knowledge during their first two interviews with the lords. They had not, as yet, heard of further violent actions committed in the west. On 11 November John Brymmore and others of the earl's men laid hold of Master Henry Weller, clerk, and so menaced and ill-treated him that for fear of his life he gave up a gold cipher and a gold chain which the earl had pledged with Edmund Lacy the former bishop for £100, and took from him 100 marks and a horse worth 10 marks.[86] On the following day, by the earl's orders, *fourteen*[87] of his men entered the cathedral and dragged Master John Morton, clerk, out of the choir where he was celebrating divine service, imprisoned and ill-treated him until he paid a 'fine' of 10 marks, handed over a horse called a 'hoby'

[80] *Radford II*, 257. KB. 9/16/76.
[81] *Radford I*, 264–7. SC. 8/138/6864. KB. 9/16/50.
[82] *Radford I*, 267–8. SC. 8/138/6864. KB. 9/16/50.
[83] *Radford I*, 269; II, 257. KB. 9/16/66.
[84] *Radford II*, 257. KB. 9/16/68.
[85] *Paston Letters* V 350–1. *Rot. Parl.* V 284 ff.
[86] KB. 9/16/66.
[87] They are actually named in the indictment.

and gave the earl an obligation in £40.[88] Heinous as these events were they were as nothing compared with the rumours which reached London just in time for the commons' delegation to make use of them in their third inter- view with the lords (17 November).[89] When the stories of the earl's entry into Exeter with 1,000 men at his back and of attacks on two clergymen by a handful of his followers appeared on the parliament roll they appeared as 'Th'erle of Devonshire, accompanied with mony riotouse persones, as it is seide with viiiC horsmen, and iiiiM. fotemen, and there have robbed the Churche of Excestre, and take the Chanons of the same Churche and put them theym to fynaunce. . .' [i.e. to ransom].[90]

The Devonshire family continued on their violent and outrageous course in Exeter and the surrounding district. In addition to various minor robberies,[91] on 15 November 500 men plundered Lord Bonvile's house at Clyft Sacheville, bore off goods to the value of 2,000 marks and £150 in money[92] and on the same day 1,000 men attacked Powderham castle. The assault is said to have lasted from eight in the morning until four in the afternoon. It failed but the earl's men continued to blockade the castle for nearly a month.[93] Meanwhile, in Exeter the Courtenays were making vigorous attempts to gain possession of Nicholas Radford's movable property. On 22 November the earl told the dean and Roger Keys, the cathedral treasurer, that unless they handed over the property which Rad- ford had deposited with the cathedral clergy for safe keeping during his lifetime he would break down the doors and carry it off. The clergy to avoid a worse evil ('in evitando magis malum') as they afterwards said, handed over plate and goods worth £600 and £700 in cash.[94] Two days later the earl's men carried off plate, jewels and other goods worth £700 from John Kelly's house, formerly Radford's own.[95]

Sir Phillip Courtenay had sent a message to Lord Bonvile for help but on 19 November the Courtenays beat off a reconnoitring party.[96] After this discomforture Lord Bonvile prepared for another attempt. The earl was also trying to strengthen his position. On the same day that he terrified the

[88] *Radford II*, 270. KB. 9/16/66.
[89] Less it should be thought that five days was too short a time for information to have reached London, the news of Radford's murder, committed on the night of 23 October, was known there at the latest by 28 October. *Paston Letters* I 350–1.
[90] *Rot. Parl.* V 285.
[91] They robbed Exeter tradesmen, Thomas Hoyle, John Hayne and John King, looted the house of Sir William Bourchier and attacked one of his servants, at Bainton. KB. 9/16/66/88, 89.
[92] KB. 9/16/67.
[93] *Radford II*, 258. KB. 9/16/65.
[94] *Radford I*, 269–70. KB. 9/16/66.
[95] *Radford I*, 270. KB. 9/16/66.
[96] *Radford II*, 258. KB. 9/16/68.

dean and treasurer of the cathedral into handing over Radford's goods he tried to browbeat the mayor and common council of Exeter into holding the city against Bonvile. The city fathers were made of sterner stuff than the cathedral clergy and steadfastly refused to have anything to do with the quarrel. Later in the day, after their failure to terrify the mayor into collaborating with them, the earl and the greater part of his men moved off to Powderham.[97] The mayor and common council then made what arrangements they could for keeping the peace within the city.[98] Shortly afterwards the earl and his forces returned and for good measure sacked Lord Bonvile's town house, looting his muniments and carrying off wine and household goods worth £20.[99] On 13 December news reached the city that Bonvile was on his way to relieve Powderham and as the mayor still refused to cooperate in resisting him the earl led his forces 'into ƿe feld by Clist and there bykered and faughte with ƿe Lord Bonevyle and his people and put them to flight and so returned again that night into the City again with his people.'[100] Two days later they sacked Bonvile's house at Shute (his third residence to suffer from their depredations) and took away goods valued at £2,000.[101] The earl then remained in the city until 21 December when he led his men away to Tiverton.[102]

Meanwhile in London York made his preparations to deal with the Devonshire family. On 5 December, after discussion in the council, privy seals were sent out to the earl of Arundel, nine other lords (including Lord Bonvile),[103] fourteen knights and three esquires ordering them to make ready to assist the protector in the west as soon as he should send them word.[104] Some days later eight sheriffs were ordered to be 'intendant' on him and among the council and privy seal documents there is the draft of a letter to the city authorities in Exeter telling them what was being done and urging them on no account to show favour to Devonshire and his men.[105] On 13 December parliament was prorogued owing to the approach of Christmas and to allow the protector to go to the west to restore order.[106] It

[97] *Radford II*, 259–60, giving verbatim the entry on the mayor's court roll, 34 Henry VI.

[98] *Radford II*, 260.

[99] KB. 9/16/66.

[100] *Radford II*, 261, quoting the mayor's court roll.

[101] KB. 9/16/69.

[102] *Radford II*, 262.

[103] This is not so fantastic as it sounds. Bonvile seems to have been drawn into the quarrels on this occasion because Sir Phillip Courtenay of Powderham had appealed to him as a justice of the peace. KB. 9/16/68.

[104] Council and PS. E. 28/87. *Proceedings and Ordinances* VI 267–70.

[105] *Cal. Pat. Rolls, 1452–1461*, 301. Council and PS. E. 28/87, 16 December. Privy seals had been sent to Devonshire, Bonvile and others as early as 19 November. Issue Roll E. 403/806 m. 4.

[106] *Rot. Parl.* V 321.

is interesting that York prorogued parliament not as protector but under a special commission approved by the council.[107] He sent Sir Robert Vere to Exeter with instructions and Vere seems to have made several journeys between Exeter and London at various times from mid December to some time after Easter.[108] York himself, as things turned out, never went to Devonshire. One chronicler reports that after the fight at Clyst Lord Bonvile 'fled, and came to Grenewiche to the kyng, and the kyng sent him agayne to the lord protectour,'[109] and another that York went as far west as Shaftesbury from where he sent for the earl of Devonshire, who submitted and after Christmas was imprisoned for a time in the Tower of London.[110] The crimes of the Courtenays were then dealt with by other means, before a commission of oyer and terminer[111] and in the king's bench.[112] In the end they received a royal pardon for every offence which they had committed, even for the murder of Nicholas Radford,[113] and even though they had tried to disperse the sessions of the peace at Easter 1456.[114]

The third session of the parliament of 1455–6 opened on 14 January. In a last effort to obtain a full attendance, privy seals had been sent a few days after the end of the second session in December to 65 lords ordering them to attend under threat of renewed fines.[115] Unfortunately there is no evidence of the actual attendance[116] but it seems most unlikely that it was larger than it had been during the second session. On 9 February John Bocking wrote to Sir John Fastolf that the duke of York and the earl of Warwick had come to parliament with a retinue of 300 armed men and 'noo lord elles' had appeared.[117] His statement, even if exaggerated, indicates that the Yorkists felt their position to be insecure and that they had misjudged the situation to the extent of making it even weaker by a tactless demonstration of armed force which gave other peers a pretext for staying

---

[107] *Proceedings and Ordinances* VI 274. *Rot. Parl.* V 321.

[108] *Radford II*, 262. Vere was in Exeter by York's orders on 19 December. After Easter the mayor and 'his fellows' made him a present of 40s.

[109] 'Vitellius A XVI' in *Chronicles of London, op. cit.* 166.

[110] Rawlinson B 355 in *Six Town Chronicles, op. cit.* 109–10. 'Vitellius A XVI', in *Chronicles of London, op. cit.* 64 n. 9, also states that York 'sent for' the earl of Devonshire and brought him to parliament in the Hilary Term but does not mention imprisonment.

[111] The indictments used above were made before justices of oyer and terminer appointed 16 March 1456. *Cal. Pat. Rolls, 1452–1461*, 304. The justices were paid the large sum of £213 6s. 8d. for their work. Issue Roll E. 403/807 m. 7.

[112] They defaulted in the king's bench and were pardoned this too. *Cal. Pat. Rolls, 1452–1461*, 358.

[113] *Cal. Pat. Rolls, 1452–1461*, 358. 10 April 1457. See also the pardon to John Brymmore and others. *ibid.* 364.

[114] KB. 9/16/64.

[115] *Proceedings and Ordinances* VI 279–82.

[116] Roskell 'Attendance of the lords', *op. cit.* 195.

[117] *Paston Letters* I 377.

away. Bocking added that he had heard that the king was disposed to keep York as his 'chief and princepall counceller' though with diminished powers, but that the queen was against it.[118] Just over a fortnight later (25 February) the king came in person to parliament and relieved York of his protectorate.[119] Although deprived of his position he was not vindictively treated, for about a fortnight later he was granted assignments on the customs of Boston and Ipswich for £1,806 2s. 4d. owing to him, partly arrears of salary from his first protectorate and partly sums promised him for expenses in the present parliament, and in May he received a valuable grant of all the gold- and silver-bearing mines in Devon and Cornwall.[120]

From this evidence some tentative conclusions may be drawn. It is clear enough that although Henry's health was poor (it was after all never anything put poor during the whole of his adult life), he suffered no second breakdown during the later part of 1455 comparable to his complete mental and physical collapse of 1453–5. He may certainly have been indisposed in the early part of November, unwell enough for a time to give York the opportunity for his first step to power in the commission to open parliament, but there is no conclusive evidence that he was incapable of transacting business even for a short period. No chronicler mentions sickness at this time and if Henry was incapable his generally well-informed friend, Abbot Whethamstede, was unaware of it. Even the deputation from the commons, anxious as they were for York to be appointed protector, were never able to allege that Henry was incapable. At the most they implied that he might become so. They had to fall back on a demand to the lords to advise the king to appoint a protector because special measures were needed for the suppression of disorder, especially in the west country. As we have seen, York's protectorate was rushed through with almost unseemly haste at the very beginning of a session of parliament by a section of the commons led by one of York's close associates. In order to get what they wanted, the delegation which Burley led gave the lords (whether deliberately or not)[121] a very much exaggerated account of recent events in Exeter, which they had seized upon the moment rumour reached Westminster. By the time parliament reassembled in January these events were seen in a truer perspective. Lord Bonvile had come to Greenwich and the earl of Devonshire was a prisoner—and all this without York having to set foot in Exeter. Many men, probably never well disposed to York's demands in the first place, may have felt (though this can only be conjec-

---

[118] *Paston Letters* I 377–8.

[119] *Rot. Parl.* V 321–2.

[120] *Cal. Pat. Rolls, 1452–1461,* 278, 291.

[121] It may not have been deliberate. For the spread of news and the prevalence of wild rumours in the fifteenth century see C. A. J. Armstrong, 'Some Examples of the Distribution and Speed of News in England At The Time of the Wars of the Roses' in *Studies in Medieval History Presented to F. M. Powicke* ed. R. W. Hunt and others (1948) 429–54.

tural) that York two months before had most unscrupulously forced the issue. At all events Henry and his advisers correctly judged that parliament would now agree to revoke York's patent and would accept that justice should be done on the malefactors of the west by the more normal method of proceedings before justices of oyer and terminer and in the king's bench.[122]

If this interpretation of events is correct, what could have been York's motives in thus attempting to force the issue of the protectorate? We possess a good deal of comparatively insignificant detail about his life and about the lives of his friends but nothing which gives us any certain insight into their motives during the successive political crises of the 1450s. So once again any attribution of motive can only be conjectural. Although he was immensely rich, York may well have been in debt[123] and wishing to profit from royal grants which he might obtain if he could influence the king. He may even (he seems to have been a very suspicious man) have regarded the protectorate as essential to self-preservation.[124] Knowing the good-natured weakness which always made Henry VI prone to trust those in power about him at the moment, he possibly thought that he could only be secure from attack if he gained complete control over the king. It may be that even after the birth of a Lancastrian heir, Prince Edward, he still thought of himself as a man with a mission—to preserve his inheritance to the throne. After all, a generation later his son, Richard, converted a protectorate into a royal title.[125] In February 1453 an Ipswich jury had in-

[122] At some time during the parliament the commons petitioned that both the earl of Devonshire and Lord Bonvile should be imprisoned without bail or mainprise until a commission of oyer and terminer had been appointed and had completed its work. The petition was refused. *Rot. Parl.* V 332. Another petition presented by John Radford, Nicholas Radford's cousin and executor, assented to by the commons and granted by the king, asked for the appointment of commissioners of oyer and terminer. The petition was not enrolled on the parliament roll. The original in the PRO, SC. 8/138/6864, is undated. Mrs. Radford, however, discovered a copy among the duke of Northumberland's MSS, together with a mandate to the justices issued as a result of it, dated 23 January 1456. *Radford I,* 264–8, 278, where part of the petition and the instructions are printed.

[123] York had stated in parliament in 1454 that non-payment of wages and expenses for his work in Ireland 'drowe and compelled me . . . to celle a grete substance of my lyvelood, to leye in plege all my grete Jowellys, and the most partie of my Plate not yit raquited, and thefor like to be loost and forfaited; and overe that, to endaungre me to all my Frendes, by chevisance of good of thaire love . . .'. *Rot. Parl.* V 255. Although this statement is certainly exaggerated, York did sell some land in the 1450s. At some time he sold the manors of Cressage and Areley to William Burley. *Cal. Close Rolls, 1468–1476,* 165. In December 1452 he had sold jewels to Sir John Fastolf, Fastolf undertaking to allow him to redeem them for £437 before June 1453. *Paston Letters,* V 249. They were still unredeemed when York was killed in 1460. *Paston Letters* II 33–5. *Cal. Pat. Rolls, 1461–1467,* 96.

[124] There is some evidence, though it is far from conclusive, that York's rivals had unduly interfered with his tenants and associates. See *Cal. Pat. Rolls, 1452–1461,* 143–4. *Six Town Chronicles, op. cit.* 107.

[125] The suggestion is by Roskell 'Attendance of the lords', *op. cit.* 192.

dicted Sir William Oldhall, who had been York's chamberlain since 1440,[126] William Assheton, Charles and Otwell Nowell[127] and others of conspiring as early as 1450 to depose the king and put the duke of York on the throne.[128] If these accusations were true (the possibility cannot be ruled out that they were part of an unscrupulous political attack by the duke of Somerset and his allies)[129] the idea of deposing the king had been in the minds of York's friends, if not of York himself, for several years. By the autumn of 1455, however, events had shown that there would be little support for any such plan in other quarters.

Polydore Vergil was the first writer to attempt an analysis of York's motives. Polydore alleged that after consultation with the Nevilles and others, 'he [York] procured himselfe to be made protector of the realme; Richard Nevill, the father, lord chauncellor of Englande; and Richard Nevell, the sonne, captaine of Calis;[130] whereby the government of the realme might rest in him, and Richard lord chancellor: thother Richard might have charge of the warres; and so Henry might be king in name and not in deede, whom they thought best to forebeare at that time, least otherwise they might stirre up the commonaltie against them, who loved, honoured and obeyed him wonderfully for the holynes of his life.'[131]

In this accusation that Richard of York intended to be king in deed, relegating Henry to the position of *roi fainéant*, all the Tudor chroniclers and some seventeenth-century writers followed Polydore Vergil.[132] In

[126] C. E. Johnston, 'Sir William Oldhall', *English Historical Review* XXV (1910), 716.

[127] The Nowells were servants of the duke of Norfolk. J. C. Wedgwood, *History of Parliament, 1439 to 1509, Biographies* (1936) 634.

[128] KB. 9/118/30. I am indebted to R. Virgoe for this reference. The indictment alleges that they realized that they could not depose the king while he remained powerful with his lords about him, that on 6 March 1450 at Bury St Edmunds they plotted the death and destruction of the king and the laws and put certain writings and ballads on mens' doors and windows attacking the duke of Suffolk and his associates, that they sent letters to divers counties, especially Kent and Sussex, urging a rising against the king, on account of which Suffolk was murdered. On 12 April, again at Bury, they incited men to levy war against the king, and on 26 May they sent letters to the men of Kent to aid the duke of York, then in Ireland, and openly counselled the duke to depose the king, and on 10 June they assembled men at Bergolt and elsewhere to levy war on the king.

[129] This was the view taken by C. E. Johnston who describes the various actions taken against York. Johnston, 'Sir William Oldhall', *op. cit.* 716–19 and the references there given. On the other hand the details in the indictment (which Johnston did not use) are too circumstantial to be lightly dismissed. The indictment gives fuller details of the alleged treasons than any other source.

[130] G. L. Harriss has shown the importance which both York and his opponents attached to the control of Calais and that its possession was the one clear gain which he obtained from his second protectorate. G. L. Harriss, 'The Struggle for Calais: An Aspect of the Rivalry Between Lancaster and York', *English Historical Review* LXXV (1960) 30–5.

[131] *Three Books of Polydore Vergil's English History* ed. Sir H. Ellis, Camden Society (1844) 97.

[132] e.g. Hall's *Chronicles* (1809) 233. Grafton's *Chronicle* (1809) I 654. Holinshed's *Chronicles* (1807–8) III 242. Stow, *Annales* (1631) 400. Kennett, *Complete History, op. cit.* 413. A somewhat modified version appears as late as Lingard, *History of England, op. cit.* 116.

Hall's words they regarded the protectorate as a 'deuise . . . polletiquely inuented'.[133] Our understanding of the fifteenth century has suffered much in the past from an uncritical use of narratives written in the sixteenth. In this case, however, the opinions of Polydore Vergil and those who followed him may not after all have been wide of the mark, although we may say that it was more probably fear of the nobility than fear of the common people that deterred York. Accusations of treason were in the air, three demonstrations of armed force had failed to secure York a position of power, and it is not beyond the bounds of possibility that the second protectorate was yet another attempt to secure permanent control and perhaps even future possession of the crown.

---

[133] Hall *Chronicle, op. cit.* n. 2.

4

Marriage and politics in the fifteenth century: the Nevilles and the Wydevilles

In spite of the notoriously fragmented nature of our sources for the mid and late fifteenth century, most general histories give a deceptively firm outline of its political events. In reality the political history of the period is a web of shreds and tatters, patched up from meagre chronicles and from a few collections of letters in which exaggerated gossip and wild rumours have been, all too often, confused with facts.[1] These defects, great enough to leave considerable lacunae in the political narrative, appear even greater when any attempt is made to elucidate the motives of statesmen and politicians. Though voluminous governmental records yield a great array of information about contemporaries, most of it is insignificant and quite useless for probing their characters and motives. Observations on character and motive are so few that some writers have set them down with an undiscriminating greed for information which seems to have atrophied any genuine critical process. Irritable words spoken in a moment of exasperation have been accepted as considered reflections upon a man's character, a unique reference in a dubious chronicle made the basis of a political agreement, or the propaganda of political rivals accepted at its face value.

Deceptively clear ideas therefore abound on the 'Yorkist party', the significance of Warwick the Kingmaker, and the scandalous greed of the Wydevilles. The Wydevilles have come down to posterity with an evil reputation. Rising to sudden eminence, they thwarted Warwick's plans 'by the art of a woman or the infatuation of a boy',[2] as Stubbs disobligingly and untruthfully remarked (Edward IV was 22 when he married Elizabeth Wydeville: his father had been appointed lieutenant-general and governor of France at twenty-five). They were, so runs the tale, one and all grasping and dishonourable from the arrogant, avaricious queen herself to her younger brother who, for money married a dowager old enough to be his grandmother. At best the family are said to have been the unworthy in-struments of Edward IV's supposed attempts to build up a new nobility to counterbalance the old, in particular to counterbalance the overwhelming

[1] e.g. see above ch. 3 pp. 77–8.
[2] W. Stubbs, *The Constitutional History of England* (1878) III 200.

might of his cousins the Nevilles.[3]

The aspirations, successes and failures of the Nevilles and the Wydevilles, if examined together, illuminate many dark places in the social and political history of the decades between 1450 and 1470, expose the weakness of that hoary myth, the 'Yorkist party', and show that the dramatic circumstances of Richard of York's claim to the throne in 1460 and Edward IV's accession a few months later make Warwick the Kingmaker's bitterness—and political isolation—in the later 1460s easier to understand.

In rather less than two centuries the Nevilles had risen from simple barons to comital rank, helped on their way by useful, though by no means unusual, marriages to heiresses. In the reign of King John, Robert FitzMaldred, lord of Raby and Brancepeth,[4] had married Isabella de Neville, the heiress of modest estates in Lincolnshire, Yorkshire and Durham.[5] From then onward the name FitzMaldred was never heard of again. Fortunate marriages and settlements brought in the baronies of Middleham and Clavering and various other estates.[6] By 1397 Ralph Neville was so rich and influential that Richard II tried to win his support by granting him the earldom of Westmorland.[7] Two years later Earl Ralph deserted the king for his wife's half-brother, Henry of Lancaster, who richly rewarded him for his services at so critical a time.[8]

In the first decade of the fifteenth century, exploiting the family connexion with the crown, the Nevilles began the great expansion which made them one of the key factors of national politics in the 1450s. Earl Ralph I (died 1425) begat on his two wives, Margaret, daughter of Hugh, second earl of Stafford, and Joan Beaufort, John of Gaunt's daughter by Catherine Swynford, no less than 22 children whose careers made up an almost interminable series of matrimonial triumphs. Three of Margaret of Stafford's daughters married north country barons[9] and the second of her two sons married Mary, the granddaughter and one of the co-heiresses of Elizabeth Ferrers of Wemme.[10]

---

[3] e.g. 'The king, unwilling to sink into the position of a pupil or a tool, had perhaps conceived the notion, common to Edward II and Richard II, of raising up a counterpoise to the Nevilles . . . .' Stubbs, *Constitutional History, op. cit.* 201. See also Sir J. H. Ramsay, *Lancaster and York* (1892) II 320. For less guarded expressions of the same theory, C. W. Oman, *Warwick the King-Maker* (1891) 164–5, and *The Political History of England, 1377 to 1485* (1906) 424. K. H. Vickers, *England in the Later Middles Ages* (1913) 465.

[4] *CP* IX 493–4.

[5] *ibid.*

[6] *ibid.* IX 496, 498 and n. (a).

[7] *ibid.* XII pt. ii 544–5.

[8] E. F. Jacob, *The Fifteenth Century* (1961) 319–21.

[9] Lords de Mauley, Dacre of Gillesland and Scrope of Bolton.

[10] *CP* II 232–3, V table between 320 and 321. *DNB* XIV 277.

This modest if substantial success fades before the triumph of Earl Ralph's plans for the children of his second wife and their descendants. Between 1412 and 1436 there occurred what must certainly be the most amazing series of child marriages in English history—eleven marriages involving 13 children under 16 years of age, a young man at the most 17, two girls of 18 or less and five men between 20 and 23.[11] One daughter Eleanor, married when she was probably no more than 9 Richard Despenser, *de jure* Lord Burghersh then aged 12.[12] Within two years she was a widow and remarried to the 21 year old earl of Northumberland.[13] Her sister Catherine at 13 married the 20 year old earl, later duke, of Norfolk.[14] Cecily aged 9 was united to the duke of York, then 13.[15] A fourth sister Anne, at the most 18 and probably younger, married the duke of Buckingham, by the standards of her family a comparatively mature male of 22.[16] Of the sons of Earl Ralph I and Joan Beaufort, the eldest Richard, at 22 or 23 married Alice Montacute, the 15 year old heiress of the earldom of Salisbury.[17] His brothers William and Edward could have been at most 17 and 14 when they married respectively Joan Fauconberg and Elizabeth Beauchamp. Elizabeth Beauchamp, the heiress of the barony of Abergavenny, was no more than 9.[18] Joan Fauconberg was about 15. She had been an idiot from birth but she was after all the heiress of the barony of Fauconberg and its broad estates.[19] By 1434 the children of Richard

[11] A list of Earl Ralph I's children is given by R. H. C. FitzHerbert, 'Original Pedigree of Tailboys and Neville', *The Genealogist* new series III (1886) 31–5, 107–11. The Neville list is taken from a manuscript then owned by Major William Martin. Its earlier history is unknown. It is said to be in a fifteenth-century hand and the portion with the Kingmaker's name ends 'cuius vite laudes etas futura post sua fata demonstrabit' which seems to date the manuscript before 1471. In any case the second earl of Westmorland (d. 1484) is described as 'qui nunc est'. The manuscript lists the children of Earl Ralph I in order of birth. To calculate their ages I have assumed that a child was born each year. This is, of course, too frequent but it has the advantage of giving each child the highest possible age (see below, n. 15), and thus strengthening the argument. For other ages and for dates of marriage see the following references to *The Complete Peerage*.

[12] *CP* II 427. It is stated, however, that he was nearly 18 at the time of his death which would make him 16 at the time of his marriage. *ibid* IV 282.

[13] *ibid*. IX 716.

[14] *ibid*. 605–7 and 606 n. (f). Earl Ralph had paid 3,000 marks for Norfolk's wardship and marriage. Jacob, *Fifteenth Century, op. cit.* 321.

[15] *ibid*. XII ii 905–9. According to my calculation (see above n. 11) she was 15 at the time of her marriage. According to the *Annales* formerly attributed to William Worcester, Stevenson, II ii 759, she was born on 3 May 1415, which would make her nine. Earl Ralph had again paid 3,000 marks for the wardship and marriage. Jacob, *op. cit.* 321.

[16] *CP* II 388–9.

[17] *ibid*. XI 395.

[18] *ibid*. I 27.

[19] *ibid*. V 281–2, 285 and n. (b). Her father had been subject to attacks of insanity. *ibid*. 276–80.

Neville and Alice Montacute were being put on the market. Young Richard Neville aged 6, and his sister Cecily, who could have been at the most 13, were married to the children of Richard earl of Warwick, Henry and Anne de Beauchamp aged 8 and 9, as a result of which 15 years later, the younger Richard became earl of Warwick.[20] In 1436 his sister Joan, aged 18, married the 21 year old earl of Arundel.[21]

For two other sons of his second marriage Earl Ralph I provided in other ways. For George he acquired by means of a very dubious conveyance which excluded the rightful heirs, the estates of the Latimer family and from 1432 George was summoned to parliament as Lord Latimer.[22] Robert made his career in the church. At 23, seven years below the canonical age, he was provided to the bishopric of Salisbury and was later translated to Durham, the richest see in northern England.[23] Between 1450 and 1455, no less than five Neville brothers and their nephew Warwick were sitting in the house of lords, as well as their nephew of the half-blood, Earl Ralph II of Westmorland, five sons-in-law and several other grandsons of Earl Ralph I.[24]

Fortunately for the English monarchy this great family connection did not work together in matters political. Inheritance, jointure and other settlement disputes were at this time the most fertile source of long and em-bittered quarrels. Property interests were just as likely to divide families as to unite them. Earl Ralph I's heir, the eldest son of his first marriage, had died during his father's lifetime. His grandson Ralph II, to whom the title passed, lived to a ripe old age, and even survived his much younger cousin, Edward IV. He played little or no part in politics, probably owing to personal grudges against the protagonists on both sides of the Wars of the Roses.[25] A deep and bitter grievance divided Earl Ralph II from the children of his grandfather's second marriage, for Joan Beaufort had obtained from her husband an excessively large jointure and settlements

---

[20] *CP* XII pt ii 383–93. Henry and Cecily became duke and duchess of Warwick and on the death of their daughter, Anne, Richard Neville's wife inherited and he was granted the earldom.

[21] *ibid.* I 248–9.

[22] *ibid.* VII 479–80. *DNB* XIV 265, 277. Jacob, *op. cit.* 321, 325–6. George Neville also married an heiress, Elizabeth Beauchamp. He had become insane before 1451.

[23] *DNB* XIV 300–1. He had received his first benefice, the prebend of Elton in the collegiate church of St Andrew, Auckland, at the age of 9 and at 17 or 18 he was provost of Beverley.

[24] *CP* XII pt ii 547 n. (h).

[25] There seems to be no ground for Oman's statement (*Political History, op. cit.* 357) that Earl Ralph II was an invalid. Nor did poverty prevent his taking part in politics for although he had been deprived of the greater part of the Neville lands (see below, pp. 111–12) he inherited, in 1436, through his mother, Elizabeth Holland, one of the co-heiresses, considerable estates from the extinct Holland earldom of Kent. T. B. Pugh and C. D. Ross, 'The English Baronage and the income tax of 1436', *Bulletin of the Institute of Historical Research* XXVI (1953) 17.

which ensured that most of the family property would pass to her own children to the detriment of the heir, their step-brother's son.[26] Ralph II was thus left poorer in land as an earl than his grandfather had been in his early life as a simple baron.[27] By the late 1430s the quarrel had reached the point of private warfare and the royal council found it necessary to intervene.[28] In these circumstances the second earl of Westmorland was hardly likely to give his support to Henry VI, some of whose chief supporters were to be found amongst the Beauforts. Nor was he likely to favour Richard of York whom the earls of Salisbury and Warwick from about 1454 strongly supported for their own purposes.

It was not until the mid 1450s that the affairs of the younger branch of the Neville family began to affect politics at the highest level. The two Richards, the earls of Salisbury and Warwick, gave no support whatever to Richard of York when he returned from Ireland in 1450 and they were both found in the king's camp during his armed demonstration at Dartford in 1452.[29] The following year, however, Salisbury's younger sons began to quarrel with their cousins, the younger sons of Henry Percy II and with their aunt, Eleanor Neville. From now on this family quarrel broke out at intervals and seriously disturbed the politics of the rest of the decade.[30] The most recent writer on these events is disposed to follow William Worcester (or, more accurately, the *Annales* which until recently he was thought to have written) in taking the quarrel between the Percies and Salisbury's younger sons as one of the main causes of the outbreak of the Wars of the Roses and in seeing the first battle of St Albans (1455) as in part at least a double faction fight, York versus Somerset and the Percies versus the Nevilles.[31]

Without the support of Salisbury and Warwick the duke of York would have been even less successful than he was in his opposition to the court during the 1450s. Until 1460 the peerage as a whole stood aloof—and in the last resort they were the people who mattered for they, and no others, commanded the most considerable military resources. At Dartford in 1452 only the earl of Devonshire and Lord Cobham took the field with the duke,[32] though Lord Cromwell may have been obscurely plotting for

[26] See below p. 112.

[27] *CP* XII pt ii 547 n. (h).

[28] See below p. 112 n. 97 and the references there given.

[29] Scofield *The Life and Reign of Edward the Fourth* (1923) I 14–17.

[30] The most comprehensive accounts (which, however, vary in detail) are given in *DNB* XIV 280–1 and CP V 33–4.

[31] Stevenson II pt ii 770. C. A. J. Armstrong, 'Politics and the Battle of St Albans, 1455', *Bulletin of the Institute of Historical Research* XXXIII (1960) 11, points out that York, Salisbury and Warwick had reached an understanding by April 1454 at the latest and plausibly surmises that the initiative came from the Nevilles. Armstrong also surmises that the decision to take up arms against the king may have come from them—in order to deal with the Percies.

[32] Scofield, *Edward the Fourth, op. cit.* I 16.

him.[33] Devonshire and Cromwell were never to support York again. At the first battle of St Albans the only peer, apart from Salisbury and Warwick, known to have fought with York was Lord Clinton, though possibly Viscount Bourchier[34] and Lord Cobham[35] might be included. Even Salisbury's brother, Lord Fauconberg, though he may have been sympathetic, was in the king's camp.[36] After the battle no large group of people could be found to approve York's plans and if the present writer's interpretation of York's second protectorate (October 1455 to February 1456) is correct, it was an attempted palace revolution which failed miserably for lack of support.[37]

Just over three years later York made his next attempt to impose his will upon the king by armed force—at Blore Heath and Ludford. The nobility gave him as little support as ever. Salisbury and Warwick apart, there were only two peers with the Yorkist forces, Lord Clinton and Lord Grey of Powys. So until October 1459, though others may have sympathized with him, only one earl and three barons (excluding the two Nevilles and possibly Viscount Bourchier) had been prepared to fight for him.[38] Even the other members and connections of the Neville family stood aloof. Of the rest not all were found in his camp on any single occasion and none of the three barons counted among the prominent of their class, or even as typical members of it. Clinton and Cobham were impoverished and even

---

[33] A priest, who claimed to have heard the last confession of one of the men executed for his part at Dartford, later accused him of treasonable activities and Cromwell found it wise to deny the accusation before the king's council. *Cal. Pat. Rolls 1452–61*, 93–102.

[34] Armstrong, 'Battle of St Albans', *op. cit.* 21 n. 5, 27 thinks it probable that Viscount Bourchier was there but points out that the evidence is not quite conclusive. Although Bourchier was made treasurer after the battle his support for York during the rest of the year was not enthusiastic. He, his brothers and their half-brother, Humphrey, duke of Buckingham, seem to have held a kind of middle place between the two main factions. See above ch. 3 pp. 81 and references there given.

[35] Cobham is said to have been present only in a late form of a document called by Armstrong the 'Stow Relation', printed by John Stow in 1580 and 1592, which includes material not found in the contemporary manuscript among the Stonor Papers. Armstrong, *op. cit.* 1 27 n. 4. Armstrong, *ibid.* 18–19, also points out that Salisbury's nephew, the duke of Norfolk, who arrived late, may have abstained deliberately from fighting and that Sir Thomas Stanley's (Lord Stanley from January 1456) loyalty to Henry VI may have been uncertain. In 1457 Norfolk obtained a licence to go abroad on a pilgrimage (perhaps an attempt to avoid faction). He committed himself unreservedly to the Yorkist cause only in 1461.

[36] One late authority states that Lord Fauconberg was present on the Yorkist side. Armstrong, *ibid.* 27 n. 7 rejects this.

[37] See above ch. 3 pp. 74–93.

[38] It is fair to add that the sons of other peers fought for York e.g. Sir William Stanley, Humphrey Bourchier (afterwards Lord Cromwell), John and Edward Bourchier. *Rot. Parl.* V 349–51. *Registrum Thome Bourgchier* ed. F. R. H. Du Boulay, Canterbury and York Society LIV (1957) p. xix.

the status of Clinton and Grey of Powys was somewhat ambiguous.[39] As far as the nobility was concerned the 'Yorkist party', which is such a feature of the general histories of the period, is a myth.

The 'Yorkist party', if we may continue to use so misleading a term, came into being over the next 15 months. Between York's flight from Ludford (12 October 1459) and Edward IV's accession (4 March 1461), three other Neville peers, two from the Bourchier family[40] (who, although Viscount Bourchier was married to York's sister, had up to this time tried to conduct a mediating policy between the two extreme groups) and ten others came over. If this list is complete, and considering the meagre quality of the sources it may well not be, the Yorkist fighting strength in peers during the early months of 1461 was 17,[41] a substantial proportion of a total lay peerage of about 60. The figure appears rather less impressive, however, if the shortage of the higher ranks is taken into account. It includes only two dukes, one earl and one viscount apart from Warwick.

The reason why so many peers went over to York at this time must remain in the limbo of insoluble problems. Some may have done so for personal reasons.[42] On the other hand, constant dripping may have worn away the political stone. For a whole decade York had shown that he was not prepared to give anyone else the chance to govern. By 1460 some may have felt that, indiscreet and violent as his conduct had been, the results of admitting him to power were at least likely to be an improvement on the growing disorders and political chaos which had resulted from his exclusion. It may be that the attainders of the Parliament of Devils (November–December 1459) had swung opinion in his favour. The sanctity of the inheritance was one of the strongest of contemporary sentiments[43] and rumours were spreading, encouraged by if not originating with York's

[39] If the figures given in the income tax of 1436 can be trusted, the Clintons were then the poorest of the English baronial families. H. L. Gray, 'Incomes from Land in England in 1436', *English Historical Review* XLIX (1934) 518. No writs of summons were issued to Clinton's father between 1432 and 1450. Clinton himself was summoned in 1450–1, 1453, 1455, 1460, 1461 and 1463 but after his death his descendants were not summoned again until 1514. It is possible that Clinton went over to York c. 1455 because of a quarrel with James Fiennes, Lord Say and Sele with whom he disputed the title of Lord Say.

Armstrong, *op. cit.* 27 also describes Lord Cobham as impoverished.

Lord Grey of Powys was 22 at this time. Neither he nor his father was ever summoned to parliament (or at least no writs survive). The son is held to have become a peer by taking the special personal oath of fidelity to Henry VI on 24 July 1455. *Rot. Parl.* V 282–3. His son John was regularly summoned from 1483 onwards. He seems to have been one of the poorer members of the baronage. Pugh and Ross, 'English baronage', *op. cit.* 19 n. 1.

[40] Viscount Bourchier has been included. See above p. 99 n. 34.

[41] See appendix B p. 306.

[42] e.g. the story told by Leland that Lord Grey of Ruthyn deserted Henry VI because the king had given Lord Fanhope's lands, which he claimed, to the duke of Exeter. *CP* VII 164 n. (j). Also n. 39 above.

[43] See below ch. 5 pp. 155–6.

friends, that the king's ministers, having alienated the king's inheritance to themselves, were now turning their covetous eyes towards other men's estates,[44] and intended the utter destruction of their opponents.[45] Whatever conjecture we adopt, the fact remains that not until 1460, the year of his death, did Richard of York attract any appreciable support from the peerage.

Even in 1460 those who rallied to him may well have done so ignorant of his real intentions. After the disaster at Ludford, York and Lord Clinton fled to Ireland, while Salisbury, Warwick and York's son the earl of March went to Calais. In March 1460 Warwick sailed for Ireland to discuss future plans with York. After he returned to Calais the earls there did their part by invading Sandwich on 26 June and marching on London.[46] It is noteworthy that the earls now, as they had always done before, protested their personal loyalty to Henry VI, claiming only that they wished for reform.[47] Early in July Warwick stated publicly in London that they had 'euer bore trew feythe and lygeaunce to the kynges persone'.[48] The events which followed give no reason to doubt their sincerity.[49] They give every reason to question York's. It is strange to say the least that York, in spite of the discussions held in Ireland, made no attempt to co-ordinate his own landing in England with that of the earls in Kent, which would surely have been the sensible proceeding in so precarious a venture. So far as we know the duke did not even begin to make his own preparations until his friends had already won the fight for him at the battle of Northampton (10 July).[50] Unless there were reasons for his conduct now unknown to us, such delay was either foolishly dangerous or it was a premeditated gamble. Even after he landed at Chester on about 8 September York's progress to London was

---

[44] An English Chronicle of the Reigns of Richard II, Henry IV, Henry V, and Henry VI ed. J. S. Davies, Camden Society (1856) 79, 82, 89. Paston Letters I 522, 535.

[45] See the pamphlet 'Somnium Vigilantis', c. 1459–60 (sometimes attributed, rather dubiously, to Sir John Fortescue), printed by J. P. Gilson, 'A Defence of the Proscription of the Yorkists in 1459', English Historical Review XXVI (1911) 512–25, especially 515–18. The plea that, if the Yorkist lords were utterly destroyed, the realm would suffer more than it had already suffered from their offences, is countered with the argument that they had now offended three times, mercy had been lost on them and they must now be plucked out like a rotten tooth. 'In conclusioun that [sic] of this poynt I say that it is more nedefull to the reyaume that thay be eternally depulsed and utterly distroyed thann to reconsile hem in eny wyse.'

[46] Scofield, op. cit. I 41–2, 59, 61, 64–6.

[47] An English Chronicle, op. cit. 89–90.

[48] ibid. 95.

[49] After the battle of Northampton, Henry had been treated with every mark of respect, installed in the bishop of London's palace (a recognized royal residence) and had taken part in thanksgiving ceremonies in Canterbury cathedral which lasted for several days. Scofield, op. cit. I 91, 95.

[50] ibid. 101.

slow, and the suspicion arises that he dallied deliberately in order to avoid meeting any of his friends before confronting parliament[51] which had been summoned for early October. Various signs on the road to London showed that, although the Nevilles had won his victory for him, York intended to use it in a manner of which he knew they could not approve and which would involve them in perjury. When he reached Abingdon the duke sent for trumpeters and clarioners, gave them banners with the royal arms of England, ordered his sword to be borne upright before him—the style appropriate only for a king—and rode on towards London.[52]

Parliament had assembled on 7 October. On the 10th York reached London. He stayed there just long enough for a formal reception by the mayor and aldermen, then at once rode on to Westminster with five hundred armed men behind him, with trumpets and clarions sounding, the sword still borne upright before him.[53] With this show of force and majesty he came to Westminster. Passing through Westminster hall he strode into the parliament chamber where the lords were in session, and laid his hand on the cushion of the empty throne as if to claim it as his by right. The expected acclamation never came. York had miscalculated badly. The lords received his demonstration in stony silence.[54] Even the pro-Yorkist Abbot Whethamstede admitted that all sorts and conditions of people began to murmur against York at this time.[55] The Burgundian chronicler, Waurin, relates that angry words ('grosses parolles') passed between Warwick and the duke when he heard of York's intentions and that even the earl of March tried to persuade his father to abandon his outrageous plans.[56] If we could accept this story, York's duplicity would be proved beyond doubt. As it is, Waurin's narrative of the events after the battle of Northampton contains so many impossible statements[57] that we can say only that circumstantial evidence from English sources makes this last story at least probable. Until his return from Ireland York had never openly[58]

[51] Waurin states that Warwick met him at Shrewsbury but no other source mentions this. Although Waurin's narrative at this point is somewhat ambiguous, his text seems to mean that Warwick heard of York's plans only later, in London. See below, notes 56 and 57.

[52] 'Gregory's Chronicle', in *The Historical Collections of a Citizen of London* ed. J. Gairdner, Camden Society (new series 1876) 208.

[53] Scofield, *op. cit.* I 103.

[54] *ibid.* 104.

[55] *Registrum Abbatiae Johannis Whethamstede,* in *Registra ... monasterii S. Albani* ed. H. T. Riley, Rolls Series (1872–3) I 377–8.

[56] J. de Waurin, *Recueil des Croniques et Anchiennes Istories de la Grant Bretaigne* ed. W. Hardy and E. L. C. P. Hardy, Rolls Series (1864–91) V 314–15.

[57] *ibid.* 299–318, in particular York's fantastic itinerary after his return from Ireland.

[58] For possible plots among some of York's friends ten years earlier see above ch. 3 pp. 91–2 and 92, n. 128. J. S. Roskell, 'Sir William Oldhall, Speaker in the Parliament of 1450–1', *Nottingham Medieval Studies* V (1961) 100–08.

suggested that Henry VI should be deprived of the crown. On balance it seems that he quite deliberately laid his plans alone, plans which he concealed from even his closest supporters because he knew that they were unlikely to cooperate in them.

It seems fair to ask the question 'How many of York's adherents among the peers would have supported him had they known of his intention to claim the crown?' If the attitude of the lords in parliament is any guide we can hardly be in doubt about the answer.[59]

The next key point to consider is the meeting at Baynard's Castle on 3 March 1461 when a 'council' chose York's son, the earl of March, as king. At the end of October 1460, parliament had reluctantly approved the act of accord which recognized York as protector of the realm for the third time and as heir to the throne on Henry VI's death.[60] Margaret of Anjou had refused to accept this arrangement which ignored completely the rights of her son Edward, prince of Wales, and she had raised an army. York had been slain at the battle of Wakefield through his own impetuous folly in refusing to wait for his scattered troops to reassemble before beginning to fight. Salisbury had been executed after the battle and Warwick had been defeated at the second battle of St Albans. Although the earl of March had won a victory in the west at Mortimer's Cross, there was still a formidable Lancastrian army in the field which was defeated only several weeks later in the desperately fought battle of Towton. It was of these ominous circumstances that the pseudo-William Worcester wrote: 'Tertio die Martii archiepiscopus Cantauariae, episcopi Sarum (Bechaump), et Exoniae (scilicet, ille reverendus Georgius Nevyll), ac Johannes dux Norfolchiae, Ricardus comes Warwici, dominus Fethwater, Willelmus Herbert, dominus de Freers de Charteley, et *multi allii*,[61] tenuerunt concilium apud Baynarde Castylle, ubi concordarunt et concluserunt, Edwardum ipsum, ducem Eboraci, fore tunc regem Anglie.'[62]

[59] The reluctance of the lords to support York is remarkable as many of Henry VI's staunchest supporters were absent. Two Lancastrian lords, the earl of Wiltshire and Lord Ryvers, did not receive writs of summons. The duke of Buckingham, the earl of Shrewsbury and Lord Egremont had been killed at Northampton and Lord Scales in London, the first two leaving minor heirs, the last two no male heirs. Viscount Beaumont was also killed at Northampton. His heir may not have been sent a writ as he did not prove his age until Sept. 1460. According to the pseudo-William Worcester, Stevenson II pt ii 774, the dukes of Exeter and Somerset, the earls of Northumberland and Devonshire and many of the northern lords did not attend.

[60] *Rot. Parl.* V 378–80.

[61] My italics.

[62] Stevenson II pt ii 777. For the dating of the events of 26 February to 4 March see C. A. J. Armstrong, 'The Inauguration Ceremonies of the Yorkist Kings and their title to the throne', *Transactions of the Royal Historical Society* XXX (1948) 55–6. Edward had been acclaimed as king by an assembly in St John's Fields on 1 March but Armstrong considers that 'in so far as Edward was elected king the substantive election took place in the council chamber and not in St John's Fields'.

A meagre list to make a king. An archbishop who was the brother of the new king's uncle by marriage, two bishops one of whom was Warwick's brother, Warwick himself, one duke cousin to both the king and Warwick, and two 'barons' of dubious status both holding such titles as they had as the husbands of old peerage heiresses. John Radclyffe, generally known as Lord FitzWater, had never been summoned to parliament and shortly before this he had been referred to in the *Paston Letters* as 'Lord FitzWater alias Master Radclyff'.[63] Walter Devereux, Lord Ferrers of Chartley, received a writ of summons for the first time later in the year.[64] So did William Herbert whose name (without the title 'dominus') appears somewhat suspiciously between the names of two dubious lords. Moreover, who were the 'multi alii'? The attempted deception is utterly naïve. It is incredible that the writer who, on the following page gives the names down to those of petty squires, of 108 men who were attainted later in the year,[65] would not have known the names of other lords had any been present at so vital a meeting.

Edward IV was made king by a faction. Though it would be unwise to stress the point unduly, the actual decision was taken by a fragment of a faction. As Francesco Coppini remarked six weeks later, when he wrote to Francesco Sforza 'in the end my lord of Warwick has come off the best and has made a new king of the son of the duke of York.'[66] Most of the peers who supported Edward (whether they had been present at Baynard's Castle or not) had resisted his father's ambitions for the crown. They had become active supporters of the house of York very late in the day, and those few of them who were in London at the beginning of March 1461 made Edward king because there seemed to be no other way out of a desperate political situation; no other way of cutting free from the disasters into which his father's ambitions had led them. Edward had become king by naked force. Warwick had made him king—probably unwillingly as a result of the chain of circumstances which had led from the duke of York's deceptions—and as an experienced man of 33 he would expect to dominate his 19 year old cousin.

We must now turn from the Nevilles to the Wydevilles. In 1464 at the time of his marriage with Elizabeth Wydeville, Edward IV was 22—a man so vigorous and handsome that he seemed to have been made for the pleasures of the flesh.[67] He may have already achieved (though the matter is

---

[63] *Paston Letters* I 512. *CP* v 485–5. The barony does not seem to have been a rich one and most of the estates were in the hands of the dowager until 1464. Pugh and Ross, *op. cit.* 19. Radclyffe's son John was summoned from 1485 onwards.

[64] *CP* v 322–3. He did not receive his writ until 26 July, more than two months after the parliament was first summoned. Wedgwood, *Register* 300 and n. 3. Wedgwood (193) states that he was present at the last session of the parliament of 1453–4, but the document which he quotes in support of this (*Proceedings and Ordinances* VI 175–7) proves the opposite. See below p. 133, n. 28.

[65] Including some who were not, in fact, attainted. Stevenson II pt ii 778–9.

[66] *Calendar of State Papers Milanese*. ed. A. B. Hinds I (1912) 69.

[67] P. de Commynes, *Mémoires* ed. J. Calmette et G. Durville (Paris 1924–5) I 203.

doubtful) that reputation for lechery[68] which has, more than anything else in modern times, diverted attention from his political successes. He married into a family which twice in as many generations profited more through marriage than they had any right to expect. Elizabeth's mother, Jacquetta of Luxembourg, was the daughter of Pierre, count of St Pol, one of the most powerful magnates in France not of the blood royal,[69] and whose eldest brother John had been among the most important of Henry V's allies in France. Her uncle the bishop of Thérouanne had in 1433 arranged her first marriage with Henry's brother, John duke of Bedford, in a futile attempt to bolster up the failing Anglo-Burgundian alliance. Jacquetta was then 17 years old. Her brief married life was probably far from satisfying to a young woman of her apparently ardent and vigorous blood. Bedford, though only 46, died just over two years later prematurely worn out by the sisyphean labours of defending the English conquests in France and holding in check the warring factions at home. Within 18 months of her husband's death, the impetuous young widow secretly married a mere knight, one of the handsomest men in England, her chamberlain's son, Sir Richard Wydeville, despite the fact that she had been given possession of her dower only on condition that she did not remarry without the king's consent. Their temerity cost the infatuated young couple the enormous fine of £1,000 which Cardinal Beaufort characteristically raised for them in return for the duchess's life interest in various manors in Somerset, Dorset and Wiltshire.

Sir Richard Wydeville was one of the most successful of the young men who had prospered at the Lancastrian court. His father, so far as we can see, had been in no way superior to the usual run of 'gentlemen bureaucrats' who entered the service of the nobility. The son possessed something of that compelling physical charm which so often accompanies great personal beauty and athletic prowess. Early introduced to the court circle, he had been one of the group of distinguished young men, headed by Richard of York, whom the child king Henry VI had knighted at Leicester on Whit Sunday, 1426. He had taken his part in the French campaigns. He and his duchess had been among the brilliant party which had escorted Margaret of Anjou to England for her marriage. Created Lord Ryvers in 1449, he and his son Anthony loyally stood by Henry VI until 1461. They were with Queen Margaret in the north at the battle of Towton. Only after her defeat there, thinking her cause then hopeless, did they go over to the Yorkists.[70] Edward treated them generously, and whatever regret for the past they may have had, they remained consistently loyal—unlike

---

[68] 'Gregory's Chronicle', *op. cit.* 226. 'Fragment of an old English Chronicle of the affairs of King Edward IV,' in T. Sprott, *Chronica* ed. T. Hearne (1719) 292–3 (hereafter referred to as 'Hearne's Fragment').

[69] For what follows see *The Coronation of Elizabeth Wydeville* ed G. Smith (1935) 41–5.

[70] *ibid.* 45–50.

some other ex-Lancastrians whom the king took into his confidence. Their loyalty paid. Lord Ryvers was already a royal councillor well over a year before his daughter became queen.[71] Though at this time Elizabeth's family was considerably less influential than many others, her marriage did not begin its advancement at the Yorkist court. It had already begun without her help.

Elizabeth Wydeville's story soon became notorious abroad: notorious enough for it to be included within four years of her marriage: in an Italian poem *De Mulieribus Admirandis* by Antonio Cornazzano, dedicated to Bianca Maria Visconti the wife of Francesco Sforza.[72] It was said, then and later, that thinking herself too base to be the king's wife but too good to be his harlot,[73] she was one of the few women who ever denied Edward Plantagenet her bed. Cornazzano made her defend herself with a dagger.[74] Dominic Mancini, writing nearly 20 years later, gave another version—she still refused him even when he 'placed a dagger at her throat'.[75] These stories may give a melodramatic colouring to rather sordid facts, which typically enough for the times, were concerned with a family squabble over property. When in 1461 Elizabeth was left a widow with two small sons, Thomas and Richard, she found her interests threatened not by the king, as might have been expected but by her former husband's relations. Although her husband Sir John Grey had been mortally wounded fighting for Henry VI at the second battle of St Albans, he had not been attainted, nor so far as we know had his lands been forfeited. His widow found it necessary to protect her jointure and what she considered to be the legitimate interests of her two sons, against the rapacity of her mother-in-law, Elizabeth Lady Ferrers.[76]

Some time between 1458 and May 1462,[77] Lady Ferrers took as her second husband Sir John Bourchier. He was one of the younger sons of Edward's aunt, Isabella Plantagenet, and of Henry, formerly Viscount Bourchier, but since 1461 earl of Essex, and among the king's most prominent councillors. Even-handed justice being unlikely in such cir-

[71] See below ch. 8. p. 210, n. 97. There is no evidence to support the conjecture, Scofield, *op. cit.* I 177-8, that Elizabeth may have been partly responsible for obtaining their pardons in 1461.

[72] C. Fahy, 'The Marriage of Edward IV and Elizabeth Woodville: a new Italian Source', *English Historical Review* LXXVI (1960) 660-63. It is significant, perhaps, of the stir the marriage caused that Elizabeth's story was one of the only two chapters devoted to contemporary women out of a total of twenty-eight. The poem cannot be taken as reliable evidence, however, for it contains numerous inaccuracies. As Fahy points out (663), 'It is essentially a pleasant tale, not an historian's or chronicler's version'.

[73] *ibid.* 665, 671-2. Sir Thomas More, 'The History of King Richard the Third' in *The English Works of Sir Thomas More* ed. W. E. Campbell I (1931) 435.

[74] Fahy, 'Marriage of Edward IV', *op. cit.* 671.

[75] *The Usurpation of King Richard III* ed. C. A. J. Armstrong (1936) 74-5.

[76] For the dispute with Lady Ferrers see *Coronation of Elizabeth Wydeville, op. cit.* 28-32.

[77] *CP* V 359-60.

cumstances, Lady Grey found it essential to 'get lordship', as the contemporary phrase went, if she were to combat with any hope of success the powerful influences which her mother-in-law could marshal against her at court. The matter of her jointure seems to have been satisfactorily settled by petitions to the chancellor, possibly with the help of her powerful Leicestershire neighbour, Lord Hastings. At all events she turned to Hastings in the second stage of her struggle for property rights. Less than three weeks before her secret marriage with the king on 1 May 1464, Lady Grey and Lord Hastings signed a very interesting indenture.[78] The agreement provided for the marriage of her son Thomas (or, in the event of his death, that of his younger brother Richard) to the eldest daughter of Lord Hastings to be born within the next five or six years, with provision for a marriage to a daughter of his brother Ralph, or of his sister Anne, if no daughter were born to him. If any manors or possessions which had once belonged to Sir William Astley[79] or any of the inheritance of Lady Ferrers could be recovered for the two boys, the rents and profits were to be divided equally between Hastings and Lady Grey until Thomas was twelve years old or until Richard reached the same age if Thomas should die. Hastings agreed to pay 500 marks for the marriage. If Thomas and Richard died before it took place or if there were no female issue in his own family, Hastings himself was to receive 500 marks.

Lord Ryvers and Lord Scales, Elizabeth's father and brother, were doing well at court themselves. Yet at the time of Elizabeth's greatest need, her father and brother may well have felt that they were not yet influential enough to intervene effectively for her against a determined group of the king's nearest relations. There was no advocate more obviously suitable than Hastings. He was the king's chamberlain, his most intimate friend, and he had quite recently married the earl of Warwick's sister, Catherine.[80] Hastings's price was high and the hard bargain which he drove with Lady Grey at this time may well have been the origin of the dislike she felt for him in later years, though her dislike never prevented her from engaging in business relations with him when she found it profitable. Knowing the way in which, in and out of season, men importuned the king on affairs of this kind, it is inconceivable that neither the Wydevilles nor the Bourchiers had 'laboured' Edward on these particular matters. That he allowed Hastings to complete the bargain just before his marriage shows how anxious the king must have been to keep his intentions secret.[81]

When the marriage was announced in the great council at Reading in

[78] Hist. MSS Comm. *Rawdon Hastings MSS* (1928–47) I 301–2.
[79] Sir William Astley of Astley, Warwickshire, was the great-grandfather of Elizabeth's husband, Sir John Grey. *CP* V 358–9.
[80] The marriage took place some time before 6 February 1462. *ibid.* VI 373.
[81] His anxiety was due at least as much to diplomatic as to domestic reasons. Scofield, *op. cit.* I 344–56.

September 1464, foreign observers reported astonishment and hostility as the immediate reactions to Edward's eccentric union.[32] Unfortunately no immediate English comment which has survived is above suspicion. With one or possibly two exceptions,[83] English comments on the marriage were all, so far as we can see, written down, at the very earliest several years later, when their writers sought an explanation for subsequent events. We are therefore quite unable to gauge the extent of the hostility expressed in 1464. That the nobility's initial disapproval of the king's marriage was great enough to alienate permanently any of their number, or even Warwick himself, may be doubted.[84]

The new queen's family could hardly avoid attracting comment. As George Eliot once remarked, 'that objectionable species, wife's kin' are generally regarded with resentful and suspicious eyes. In a court so much the centre of patronage and profit that it can be regarded almost as the stock exchange of the day, any advantages which the Wydeville family reaped from their new connection would to an unusual degree attract resentful and jealous comment, particularly among those accustomed to

[82] Foreign opinions written down immediately (in letters of varying degrees of inaccuracy) all stress the unpopularity of the marriage. *Calendar of State Papers Milanese, op. cit.* I 113, 114. *Dépêches des ambassadeurs milanais en France sous Louis XI et François Sforza,* ed. B. de Mandrot (Paris 1916–23) II 276, 292.

[83] (a) Lord Wenlock wrote to Lannoy from Reading on 3 October stating that it had caused 'great displeasure to many great lords, and especially to the larger part of all his council'. See Scofield, *op. cit.* I 354 and n. 3. It should not be forgotten, however, that this letter was written for diplomatic consumption by one of Warwick's protégés.

(b) In the Howard household books there is a draft of a letter as follows—' . . . also my lord I have bene in dyverse plasese wethein Norfolke Soffolke and Hesex, [hand] and have ad komenykasyon of thes marygge, to fel howe the pepel of the konteryes wer desposed, and in good feythe they ar despossed in the beste wysse and glade ther of; also I have ben wethe many dyverse astates to fel theyer hertes, and [in good feythe] *I fowende theme all ryte wele despossed, safe on,* the wesche I schal henforme ʒower good lordesche at my nexte komhenge to ʒowe . . .'. *Manners and Household Expenses of England in the Thirteenth and Fifteenth Centuries* ed. T. H. Turner, Roxburghe Club (1941) 196–7, (my italics). Unfortunately the draft is un-addressed and undated. The editor conjectures that it refers to the royal marriage and less happily perhaps that it was written to Lord Ryvers. The phrasing of the letter makes it at least plausible that the reference is to the king's marriage, otherwise why the phrase about 'many dyverse astates'? If it could be accepted it would give a very different view of contem-porary public opinion from that normally held.

[84] The English chroniclers who write nearest to these events and deal with them at all fully differ in their interpretations. The First Anonymous Croyland Continuator (*c.* 1470–85), a very pro-Neville author, states that the marriage was unpopular with the nobility and the chief men of the kingdom and alleges that Warwick broke with the king *c.* 1469 because he admitted all the queen's relations to his favour, promoted them to all the most dignified offices and 'fratres quoque suos et cognatos Regio de sanguine progenitos, et ipsum Comitem Warwici Richardum, cum ceteris sibi fidelibus Regni Proceribus, a sua presentia profligavit'. 'Historiae Croylandensis Continuatio' in Fulman 542. These remarks about the nobility are wildly exaggerated and record sources show that the Wydevilles were less enriched than is usually supposed. See below, pp. 112–17.

competing successfully in the speculative market of royal patronage. The customary tale of upstarts speedily enriching themselves, however, needs to be modified. Quite apart from the high birth of Jacquetta of Luxembourg, the social status of the Wydevilles and the Greys was not as lowly as many historians have assumed. The Wydevilles were a decent county family with estates in Northamptonshire, Bedfordshire, Buckinghamshire, Rutland and Kent. They had filled local offices and had occasionally provided knights of the shire since the mid fourteenth century.[85] Lord Ryvers's father had been seneschal of Normandy under Henry V.[86] Since 1450 the family had begun to marry into the peerage.[87] The Greys of Groby were related to the Greys of Ruthyn and by marriage to the Bourchiers, the Mowbrays and the Berkeleys.[88] By 1461 they might well be accounted at least the equals of some of the lordlings who made Edward IV king, or compared to William Hastings who was made a baron the same year, cashed in on the Yorkist revolution on a grand scale and less than a year later married one of Warwick's sisters.[89] From 1464 onwards the Wydevilles profited in two ways—by advantageous marriages and, to a much smaller extent, from royal grants. By the middle of 1467 they had

---

The Second Anonymous Croyland Continuator (reputedly one of Edward's councillors), writing in April 1486, claiming to correct the errors of his ill-informed predecessor, Fulman 549, denies that the marriage was responsible for any break. He claims that although there had been some murmurings on Warwick's part, the marriage was solemnly sanctioned and approved of at Reading by Warwick himself and all the great lords and prelates of the kingdom. He adds that Warwick 'Perduravitque favor Comitis in omnem ipsius Reginae parentelam, quoadusque ipsius Reginae cognati et affines istud aliud matrimonium, quod inter Carolum et Margaretam actum est pro voto Regis, amico Comite, sicut et multa alia consilia fieri procurabat' [sic]. ibid. p. 551. So the king's pro-Burgundian policy was the real cause of the break according to this writer. Although the Second Anonymous Continuator takes an obviously defensive line, his account is, in general, so superior that his testimony is more acceptable than that of the First Continuator.

Warkworth (c. 1473–98), whose narrative is compressed to the point of confusion and inaccuracy, states (J. Warkworth, A Chronicle of the First Thirteen Years of the Reign of King Edward the Fourth ed. J. O. Haliwell, Camden Society (1839) 3) 'after that [i.e. the king's marriage] rose grete discencyone evere more and more betwene the Kyng and hym, for that, and other, etc.' He adds (4) that they 'were acorded diverse tymes: but thei nevere loffyd togedere aftere'. R. Fabyan (c. 1490–1512), The New Chronicles of England and France ed. H. Ellis (1811), 654, merely mentions the marriage and rumours of sorcery. The Great Chronicle of London ed. A. H. Thomas and I. D. Thornley (1938) 202–3, states that the marriage caused 'mwch unkeyndnes' between the king and Warwick and the advancement of the Wydevilles 'kyndelid the sparkyll of envy, whych by contynuance grewe to soo grete a blase . . .'. Polydore Vergil is very uncertain as to the causes of the break between Edward and Warwick. Three Books of Polydore Vergil's English History ed. Sir H. Ellis, Camden Society, (1844) 117–18.

[85] CP XI 15–19.
[86] Jacob, op. cit. 190.
[87] See below p. 110, n. 90.
[88] J. Smyth, The Lives of the Berkeleys ed. Sir J. Maclean (1883–5) II 80. CP V 357–8.
[89] For Hastings see below ch. 8, p. 208.

arranged and completed a series of seven marriages all with members of noble families, those of Buckingham, Exeter, Norfolk, Arundel, Essex, Grey of Ruthyn and Herbert.[90] Some of these marriages deeply offended particular people, yet once again it seems doubtful whether the general advancement of the queen's family, too rapid and too great for discretion though it was, raised any opposition widespread and bitter enough to create a tense political situation.

Modern opinion on these marriages seems to be based almost entirely on a rather careless interpretation of the pseudo-William Worcester's *Annales*. Even on his evidence the marriages may be divided into two groups. Three of the seven the author merely notes without comment; four he notes with varying shades of disapproval.[91]

The earliest of the marriages in the latter group affected the interests of Warwick's second cousin, the young duke of Norfolk. In January 1465 Sir John Wydeville married Catherine Neville, aunt to both Warwick and the

[90] For a list of the marriages see D. MacGibbon, *Elizabeth Wydeville* (1938) 223–5. There are generally said to be eight marriages but the queen's sister, Jacquetta, had been married to Lord Strange of Knockyn *c.* 1450. *CP* XII pt i 356. It is fair to point out that at least three of these marriages, possibly more, were child marriages. Buckingham, William Herbert and Thomas Grey were children, so possibly were Catherine, Joan and Mary Wydeville.

[91] K. B. McFarlane has shown that William Worcester was not the author of the 'various scraps of chronicles' which Thomas Hearne fabricated into the *Annales* from a number of separate items in a miscellaneous collection entered into Arundel MS. 48 in the College of Arms after it had left Worcester's possession. See 'William Worcester: A Preliminary Survey', in *Studies Presented to Sir Hilary Jenkinson* ed. J. Conway Davies (1957) 206–7. Whoever he may have been, the author of this section of the manuscript was a very pro-Neville writer. It has been overlooked that he does not condemn all the marriages. They fall into two distinct groups. a. (1) Margaret Wydeville to Lord Maltravers, Warwick's nephew (see note p. 97, n. 21), (2) Anne Wydeville to William Bourchier, son of the earl of Essex and (3) Eleanor Wydeville to Anthony Grey of Ruthyn (son of the earl of Kent). Worcester merely notes these without comment. b. A group which Worcester condemns: (1) Sir John Wydeville to Catherine, dowager duchess of Norfolk—'maritagium diabolicum', (2) Catherine Wydeville and the duke of Buckingham—'ad secretam displicentiam comitis Warrwici', (3) Sir Thomas Grey and Anne, daughter of the duke of Exeter,—'ad magnam secretam displicentiam comitis Warrwici' and (4) Mary Wydeville to William Herbert. Here there is no comment on the marriage itself but then 'Fecitque dominus rex dictum haeredem Herberd militem, ac creavit eum dominum de Dunstarre, ad secretam displicentiam comitis Warrwici ac magnatum terrae'. Stevenson II pt ii 783, 785, 786.

It is worth noting that group A, on which no comment was made, affected Warwick's own nephew and two other families whose heads were prominent and politically active at the Yorkist court. Worcester's indignation is reserved for group b in which three out of four marriages adversely affected Warwick and his relations. Even here Warwick's displeasure is said to be shared by other magnates only in the matter of William Herbert's assumption of the title of Lord Dunster. I have found no particular reason why Warwick should have been offended at Buckingham's marriage. But see above ch. 1 pp. 23–4.

Neither Gregory, Warkworth, Fabyan nor Polydore Vergil refers to the Wydeville marriages. See also above p. 108 n. 84.

king, and the senior of the two dowager duchesses of Norfolk. Worcester called it a 'maritagium diabolicum' for the bridegroom was a young man of 20 and the bride, so Worcester alleged, was a slip of a girl ('juvencula') of about 80.[92] He libelled the lady, who could not in fact have been more than 65 or 66. Worcester's indignation was perhaps excessive, for marriages of youth and age were by no means uncommon at the time. Sixty years later a statesman as busy and as worldly as Thomas Cromwell thought of introducing legislation to prevent young men marrying aged widows.[93] The Duchess Catherine's marriage was unusual only for what the Norfolk family must have regarded as its nightmarish quality. The wretched old woman was a true daughter of Joan Beaufort. Married to the duke of Norfolk in 1412 at the age of 15 or less, she was left a widow in 1432. For 30 long years she had held in jointure a very considerable proportion of the family estates—probably far more than her grandson was holding in 1465.[94] With these expensive feathers plucked from the Mowbray wings she had flown to the joys of a second nuptial bed, then a third,[95] and now in her old age proposed to enrich a fourth. This fourth marriage seems to have implied some danger to the family property. It was not always an easy matter for a family to regain possession of jointure lands. With such powerful connections it might well prove difficult to induce Sir John Wydeville to disgorge his wife's estates after her death.[96] None knew such economic facts of life

[92] See above p. 110 n. 91.

[93] J. Hurstfield, *The Queen's Wards* (1958) 331.

[94] Excessive jointures seem to have been common enough for the Lords to wish for some kind of safeguard against them. See *The Fane Fragment of the 1461 Lords' Journal* ed. W. H. Dunham Jr (1935) 9. The Norfolk case was exceptionally blatant. It has been estimated that the greater part of the family estates were in the hands of the dowager and so never descended to her son John Mowbray, third duke of Norfolk, who predeceased her in 1461. Pugh and Ross, *op. cit.* 9. Nor did they descend to her grandson, the fourth duke, who was also burdened with a second dowager, his own mother. It was only in 1478 when the king arranged to marry the child heiress, Anne, to his son, Richard, that these outrageous settlements were, under royal pressure, broken. *Rot. Parl.* VI 169–70.

[95] She married a squire, Thomas Strangeways, and then Viscount Beaumont.

[96] The dowager duchess married Sir John in January 1465. On 25 March her grandson received livery of his lands. *Cal. Pat. Rolls 1461–7, 477.* It may or may not be significant that the patent covered not only the estates which came to him direct from his father, but also permission to enter on the deaths of the dowagers, Catherine and Eleanor, into any possessions which they held in dower or for life; an apparently unusual proviso. cf. The patent to William Herbert II in 1471 when a dowager was still alive. *Cal. Pat. Rolls. 1467–77,* 275.

Catherine seems to have been as capable as other Nevilles of conveyancing property away from common law heirs. She secured the reversion of some of the lands of her third husband, Viscount Beaumont, to her daughter, Joan, and on Joan's second marriage to Lord Berkeley in 1468 dowered her with some of the Mowbray lands of her own jointure. Although described in *Cal. Pat. Rolls 1461–7,* 179, *Cal. Pat. Rolls 1467–77,* 107, as 'sister' of John, Duke of Norfolk, Smyth, *Lives of the Berkeleys, op. cit.* II 143–6 and *CP* II 134, make her the daughter of Catherine's second husband, Thomas Strangeways.

better than Warwick, for the elder branch of the Neville family regarded the castles of Middleham and Sheriff Hutton and the estates surrounding them, some of his most cherished possessions, as illegally conveyed to his father and to him through the influence of his grandmother, Joan Beaufort.[97] Although positive proof is lacking, it may well have seemed advisable to Warwick, if he wished for the future support of a powerful nobleman and relation, to uphold either openly or secretly his young relation's grievances in such a matter.

The following year, Warwick had reason on his own account to resent two other marriage arrangements. Edward IV in 1461 had given the Herberts the lordship of Dunster which the earl claimed for himself, and in September 1466, when William Herbert the younger was betrothed to Mary Wydeville, he was permitted to assume the title of Lord Dunster.[98] The next month Warwick took another blow. The queen's eldest son, Thomas Grey, married Anne Holland, the heiress of the duchy of Exeter. The queen paid her sister-in-law, the duchess (Edward's sister, Anne), 4,000 marks for the marriage. This bargain between the king's wife and the king's sister, made presumably with the king's approval, was insulting in the extreme, for Anne Holland was already betrothed to Warwick's nephew George, Lord Montagu's son.[99]

It has been alleged somewhat inconsistently that the blindly enamoured king allowed the Wydevilles unbridled licence to indulge their ambitions in this way, and that on the other hand he married them off as part of a considered policy of building up a new nobility as a counterpoise to the old.[100] Two such different states of mind may have been compatible but it seems unlikely. The truth was probably much less dramatic. Edward at this time was ready to rely on almost anyone who was prepared to serve him. His position was far too precarious to allow him to think in terms of putting down any of the nobility,[101] new or old. It would have been difficult if not impossible for the king, unsupported as he was by a considerable section of

---

[97] Pugh and Ross, op. cit. 7–8. J. S. Roskell, 'Sir James Strangeways of West Harsley and Whorlton', Yorkshire Archeological Journal XXXIX (1956–8) 461. R. L. Storey, Thomas Langley and the Bishopric of Durham, 1406–37 (1961) 107–8. Jacob, op. cit. 320–3. The cases are not exactly parallel as these alienations were made with Earl Ralph I's connivance. However, wrongful seizure and retention of estates by powerful people under cover of legal chicanery and often backed by court influence were very common. e.g. See J. M. W. Bean, The Estates of the Percy Family, 1416–1537 (1958) 112–25.

[98] See above p. 110 n. 91. CP VI 444–5, points out, however, that there is no record of any creation of this barony.

[99] Stevenson II pt ii 786. Anne of Exeter's betrothal to Montagu's son is, itself, a good example of the business morals of the Nevilles. Her father had been bitterly opposed to them all through the 1450s but after 1461, when he was in exile, they thus arranged for his inheritance to pass to them.

[100] See above p. 95 n. 3.

[101] See below ch. 6 pp. 133 ff. Also above ch. 2 pp. 67 ff.

the higher aristocracy,[102] to work without the cooperation of the nobility in general. In fact it is unnecessarily crude to reconstruct Yorkist politics in such exclusive terms. After all, at the same time as the Wydeville marriages were being arranged Edward continued to build up the power and properties of the Nevilles.[103] Wishing to avoid excessive dependence on any one group, he may well have encouraged the development of diverse factions, but this was a very different thing from building up a new royal party.[104]

At most Edward may have hoped to strengthen his ties with men already ennobled—some for a long time, some since his own accession. Lord Herbert and Lord Grey of Ruthyn already counted among the king's supporters, Lord Herbert being one of the staunchest, while Lord Grey of Ruthyn was cousin german to the queen's first husband. The king had made Herbert a baron and relied upon him greatly in the government of Wales. Herbert's influence certainly increased after his son's marriage to the queen's sister, though his power was due more probably to his ability and his services than to the new relationship. After the father's death the king seems never to have trusted the son.[105] Lord Grey of Ruthyn had deserted Henry VI for York at the battle of Northampton (1460) and he had been made earl of Kent before his son's marriage with Joan Wydeville.[106] There was nothing either more or less scandalous in the creation or the marriage than there had been in the elevation of Warwick's uncle, Lord Fauconberg, to the same title in 1461.[107] The earl of Essex's family, the Bourchiers, were already connected with both the king and the

---

[102] There were only 8 dukes and earls in the parliament of 1461–2 and 7 in 1463–5 as compared with 15 in 1455–6 and 13 and 1460–1. Wedgwood, *Register* p. lxiv.

[103] See below, pp. 118–19.

[104] The manifesto (see notes to Warkworth, *Chronicle, op. cit.* 46–51) issued by Clarence, Warwick and the archbishop of York in 1469, though sometimes quoted for the purpose, can hardly be made to support this theory. It refers to 'the disceyvabille covetous rule and gydynge' of Lord Ryvers and his wife, William Herbert, Humphrey Stafford of Southwick, Lord Scales, Lord Audley, Sir John Wydeville and his brothers and Sir John Fogge. Although they drew attention to the fate of Edward II and Richard II, the accusations are mostly concerned with administrative corruption etc. reminiscent of those thrown out by York and his friends against the Lancastrian court a decade before. Neither Warkworth, Dominic Mancini, Fabyan, the Great Chronicle of London nor Sir Thomas More refers to any attempt to exclude Warwick or anybody else or to build up a counterpoise. Apart from the reference in the First Anonymous Croyland Continuator the story is found for the first time in Polydore Vergil who in an imaginary speech makes Warwick say *c.* 1467, 'who [i.e. Edward] resolutely maketh more honorable accownt of new upstart gentlemen than of the ancyent howses of nobylytie; wherfor ether must the nobylytie destroy him, or els he wyll destroy them.' A speech which also, significantly enough, refers to the probability of greater gains from Henry VI and his son. *Polydore Vergil, op. cit.* 119. Polydore himself, however, never attributed to Edward the intention of deliberately destroying the older nobility or of setting up others as a counterpoise to them.

[105] See below ch. 8 p. 208 and n. 86, p. 214 and n. 122.

[106] On 30 May 1465. *CP* VII 164–5.

[107] *ibid.* 163. Faconberg died 9 January 1463.

Greys of Groby.[108] So much for the active politicians. Three other marriages, that of Margaret Wydeville to Warwick's nephew Lord Maltravers, the eldest son of the earl of Arundel,[109] that of Thomas Grey to Anne Holland,[110] and that of Catherine Wydeville to the duke of Buckingham had no political effect during Edward's reign.[111] The results as well as the intent of these marriages seem to have been grossly exaggerated. The Second Anonymous Croyland Continuator states that after Edward's own marriage Warwick continued to show favour to the queen's kindred until they quarrelled on matters of foreign policy.[112] Moreover William Worcester implies that the earl dissembled his resentment of the Wydeville marriages. Only in one case, that of William Herbert, does he say that other nobles shared Warwick's displeasure, and even here it was because they objected to William Herbert's assumption of the title Lord Dunster, rather than to the marriage itself.[113] Although other nobles were undoubtedly jealous of the Wydevilles' success, there is no evidence to show how far the circle of resentment extended and, as we shall see, very few nobles were prepared to support Warwick when he took arms against the king a few years later.[114]

Nor were the Wydevilles lavishly endowed with royal grants. Their political influence, though naturally great, seems to have been neither excessive nor sinister.[115] The queen's father, Lord Ryvers, was no less

---

[108] See above pp. 106–7.

[109] William, earl of Arundel (married to Warwick's sister, Joan, who died in 1462). He had gone over to the Yorkists just before St Albans II (1461). He seems to have played little or no part in the politics of the 1460s. He was a councillor in 1472. There is no evidence that the family connection with the Nevilles in the 1450s or the Wydevilles in the 1460s had any appreciable effect on his political actions.

[110] Anne Holland died childless before 1474 and other arrangements were then made for Thomas Grey, CP V 215, n. (b), though he was given a life interest in some of the Holland lands. Cal. Pat. Rolls 1467–77, 582.

[111] Buckingham is said by Dominic Mancini, Usurpation of Richard III, op. cit. 90–91, to have detested the Wydevilles because, when young, he had been forced to marry the queen's sister 'whom he scorned to wed on account of her humble origin'. It should be noted that this statement dates from Richard III's reign when every attempt was being made to blacken the Wydevilles. The word 'forced' is in any case, misleading. Buckingham had been a child of eleven at the time. His marriage had been disposed of like that of any other child of the feudal classes whether in wardship or not. He had been no more and no less 'forced' than any of the numerous Neville children.

[112] See above p. 108 n. 84.

[113] See above p. 110 n. 91.

[114] See below p. 122 n. 163.

[115] Mancini writing under Richard III states that in Edward's later years the queen 'attracted to her party many strangers and introduced them to court, so that they alone should manage the public and private business of the crown . . . to give or sell offices, and finally rule the very king himself.' Usurpation of Richard III, op. cit. 78–9. Even of this later period the statement seems exaggerated. In 1483 the queen was unable to get a grant of lands for her second son, Lord Richard Grey, without payment. See below p. 117 n. 130.

qualified than many other men for the office of treasurer[116] in which he succeeded Warwick's protégé, Sir Walter Blount.[117] It was after all Edward himself who raised Blount to the peerage as Lord Mountjoy in 1465. Although Ryvers was made an earl, he received very little apart from the treasurership and the constableship in the way of royal grants.[118] Ryvers and his wife may have been grasping and vindictive, and if Fabyan's accusation is true that the pair of them from sheer spite brought about the ruin of Sir Thomas Cook, the story certainly shows an evil streak.[119] No one ever brought such accusations against their eldest son. By modern standards Anthony Wydeville was by no means scrupulous.[120] Yet in spite of malicious attacks and slanders which he suffered from time to time,[121] his reputation remained high. Both Dominic Mancini and Sir Thomas More, writing after the gossip of years had been directed against the family, found more good than evil to say of him. Mancini, who picked up the court gossip of the last few months of Edward's life, wrote that Anthony Wydeville 'was always considered a kind, serious, and just man, and one tested by every vicissitude of life. Whatever his prosperity he had injured nobody, though benefiting many'.[122] The king himself did not always find Lord Scales congenial. In spite of his gaiety and his skill in the tiltyard, his highly cultivated mind revealed from time to time a streak of melancholy which repelled a sybarite like Edward. The hair shirt which he wore beneath his gay courtier's clothes was afterwards venerated as a relic by the Carmelite friars of Doncaster.[123] Yet in spite of outbursts of irritation against him,[124] Edward

---

[116] W. Dugdale, *The Baronage of England* (1675–6) II 230, was of the opinion 'in respect of his valour in Arms, great integrity, and acceptable services, [Ryvers] was advanced to the degree of a Baron' (1449). If Steel's conjecture is correct, that in the 1450s and 1460s rich men were appointed as treasurers 'so that they could tide the exchequer over any pressing emergency out of their own resources', Ryvers must already have been rich. A. Steel, *The Receipt of the Exchequer, 1377–1485* (1954) 330–1. He lent £12,259 between 1466 and 1469.

[117] *CP* IX 335. The pseudo-William Worcester (Stevenson II pt ii 785) says that the change was made 'ad secretam displicentiam comitis Warrwici et magnatum Angliae'. One wonders what Lord Grey of Ruthyn's feelings had been when, in November 1464, he had been replaced as treasurer (after sixteen months in office) by Warwick's upstart friend Blount who was not even a baron at the time.

[118] *Cal. Pat. Rolls 1461–7*, 81, 83, 470. *Cal. Pat. Rolls 1467–77*, 97. His other grants consisted of two minor offices, one grant of land (jointly with others) and one valuable wardship. Others, *ibid.* 33–4, 59, only repaid debts due to him. Edward may have thought that Ryvers was already sufficiently well provided for with the duchess of Bedford's dower. She was probably one of the richest women in England. Pugh and Ross, *op. cit.* 21.

[119] Fabyan, *New Chronicles, op. cit.* 656. *Great Chronicle, op. cit.* 204–8.

[120] He was not above attempting to bring Lord Hastings into disfavour with the king and for a time succeeded. More, *English Works*, ed. W. E. Campbell (1931), 55, 428. *Usurpation of Richard III, op. cit.* 138 n. 31.

[121] See J. Gairdner, *Richard III* (new edn 1898) 338–9.

[123] J. Rous, *Historia Regum Anglie* ed. T. Hearne (1716) 212.

[124] '. . . in so myche that the Kyng hathe seyd of hym, that wen evyr he hathe most to do, then the Lord Scalys wyll sonest axe leve to depert, and weenyth that it is most be cause of

respected him enough to put him in charge of the education of the prince of Wales.[125] He had already married an heiress, the widowed Lady Scales,[126] before his sister married the king. His later gains and those of other members of the family were comparatively modest. Warwick could have found very little to attack in that quarter. Before the earl broke with Edward, Anthony Wydeville had obtained only four grants from the king, one the reversion of a grant already made to his father, one a minor office, one a minor wardship. The fourth and only immediately valuable one was the Isle of Wight with the castle and lordship of Carisbroke.[127] The younger members of the family got nothing until after 1470, after Warwick's death. Anthony's brother Lionel, though given the bishopric of Salisbury,[128] was never so far as we know a member of the royal council. As for the rest—the queen's brothers Sir Edward and Sir Richard,[129] and the queen's two sons by her first marriage, the marquis of Dorset and Lord Richard

kowardyese'. Letter of John Paston the youngest to Margaret Paston, 5 July 1471. *Paston Letters* III 10–11. Anthony Wydeville, it is said, had expressed a wish to go to Portugal at this time. Scofield, *op. cit* II 3–4. In view of Wydeville's work in London since March and the fact that he wished to go to Portugal to fight against the Saracens the accusation of cowardice was quite unjustified. The king's words spoken at an extremely busy time after months of strain are best regarded as a momentary outburst of irritation rather than a considered judgment. But see also *Calendar of State Papers Milanese, op. cit.* 1227–8.

[125] *Cal. Pat. Rolls 1467–77*, 417. *Usurpation of Richard III*, 82–3.

[126] *CP* XI 507.

[127] His principal gains came only after 1469. a. Offices and Custodies: Apart from the offices of Chief Butler (1473), constable (1467, reversion of his father's grant) and governor and lieutenant of Calais (16 June 1470 to May 1471 only) there were only five, all minor. *Cal. Pat. Rolls 1461–7*, 188. *Cal. Pat. Rolls 1467–77*, 19, 41, 415, 422, 450. *Cal. Pat. Rolls 1476–85*, 261, 315, 332. b. Annuities: £200 from the Customs (1470) and £20 reversion on the death of Philippa Wyngefeld. *Cal. Pat. Rolls 1467–77*, 206, 375, 423. c. Lands: The overlordship of the Isle of Wight, the castle and lordship of Carisbroke and all other manors and lordships etc. within the island, three other manors, the reversion of seven more and a good deal of the property of William Vaux, who was attainted. *Cal. Pat. Rolls 1461–7*, 535. *Cal. Pat. Rolls 1467–77*, 421–2, 422, 423, 424. d. Wardships: Two, both minor, *ibid.* 152, 475.

In addition in 1478 and 1479 he was granted certain lands until he should have received 1,000 marks in compensation for injuries perpetrated on him and his parents by the duke of Clarence. *Cal. Pat. Rolls 1476–85*, 115, 132, 135.

[128] He became archdeacon of Oxford at 19 and dean of Exeter at 25. Unlike Robert Neville he did not obtain the bishopric of Salisbury until he was twenty-nine. *Calendar of Papal Registers* XIII (1955) 248, 744, 806. His other preferment was by no means excessive. *Cal. Pat. Rolls 1467–77*, 541. *Cal. Pat. Rolls 1476–85*, 17, 296, 569. The promotion intended for him seems modest compared with that apparently planned for Edward's sister's son, Edward de la Pole. *Papal Registers, op. cit.* XIII 714, 274–5. See also K. B. McFarlane, *English Historical Review* LXXIII 677.

[129] Sir Edward died unmarried. He was very little employed by the king and received only two known grants, both small. Scofield, *op. cit.* II 31, 251, 284. *Cal. Pat. Rolls 1476–85*, 180, 199, 224. Sir Richard (who ultimately became the third and last Earl Ryvers) was employed on various embassies and commissions. In 1468 Edward wished him to be prior of St John's but Warwick's supporter, John Langstrother, obtained the post. Scofield, *op. cit.* 1499, n. 2. I have found no evidence of any grants to him.

Grey—Edward in his later years found them amusing enough to relax with but he seems to have allowed them little power or influence.[130]

The queen herself may have felt her 'petite extraction' (as a foreign writer called it) keenly enough to insist on the greatest personal deference being shown her.[131] One incident is usually quoted to show her haughty temperament, an episode described in the *Travels of Leo of Rozmital*: on the evening following her churching in 1465 she sat alone at table on a costly golden chair and, after a dinner lasting three hours, when not a word was spoken, dancing began; during the dance the queen's mother knelt before her all the time, except at intervals when bidden to rise.[132] The incident is, however, capable of another interpretation. The long silence was not the result of pride. It was common form. The silence which the English maintained at banquets was notorious amongst foreign visitors.[133] Protocol at the English court during the fifteenth and sixteenth centuries was strict and magnificent.[134] A similar deference had been paid to Margaret of Anjou.[135] The Yorkists, like the Tudors, seem to have used splendid ceremonial as a conscious vehicle of policy,[136] possibly imitating the court of Burgundy.[137]

[130] See below ch. 8 p. 215 n. 130. Thomas was created earl of Huntingdon in 1471 and marquis of Dorset in 1475. He was provided for by two marriages to (1) Anne Holland and (2) Cecily, daughter and heiress of Lord Harrington and Warwick's sister, Catherine. In the event of his death before the marriage was consummated Cecily was to marry his brother Lord Richard Grey, of whom very little seems to be known during Edward's reign. Although he was appointed to serve on various commissions no grants to him are recorded on the Patent Rolls. In 1483 arrangements were made to marry Dorset's infant son, Thomas, to Anne, the daughter and heiress of Anne of Exeter and Thomas St Ledger. The girl had been made Anne of Exeter's heir. As part of the arrangements Lord Richard Grey was to obtain eleven manors from the Exeter estates. The arrangement cost the queen and Dorset 5,000 marks paid to the king, probably about one-fifth of the value of the Exeter estates at current prices. Even so the price was high compared with the prices Ralph of Raby had paid for his various acquisitions earlier in the century. *Cal. Pat. Rolls 1476–77*, 32–3, 137–8, 360, 373–4, 456–7. *Cal. Pat. Rolls 1476–85*, 174, 212, 283–4. *Rot. Parl.* VI 215–18.

[131] Before she visited Norwich in 1469 the sheriff told the mayor that the queen 'woll desire to ben resseyved and attendid as wurshepfully as ever was Quene a forn hir'. *Paston Letters* II 360.

[132] *The Travels of Leo of Rozmital* ed. M. Letts, Hakluyt Society, 2nd series CVIII(1957) 5, 47.

[133] *A Relation . . . of the Island of England* transl. and ed. C. A. Sneyd, Camden Society (1847) 44 and 113 n. 75.

[134] See *Leo of Rozmital, op cit.* 45. For the Tudors see A. L. Rowse, *The England of Elizabeth* (1951) 265.

[135] 'When the wife of the Duke of Petro a Baylito, the king's son and all the duchesses speak to the queen, they always go on their knees before her.' *Calendar of State Papers Milanese, op. cit.* 119.

[136] Armstrong, 'Inauguration Ceremonies', *op. cit.* 70–72.

[137] In 1475 Edward asked Olivier de la Marche for a written description of the estate kept by Charles the Bold in his household and on the battlefield. *Mémoires d'Olivier de la Marche* ed. H. Beaune et J. d'Arbaumont (Paris 1883–8) IV 1 ff, 153–7. The influence of Burgundy on the Yorkist court needs fuller investigation.

Elizabeth Wydeville may well have been acting under orders.[138]

Avaricious Elizabeth may have been. Again convincing proof is lacking. If she loved money unduly her husband attempted to keep such passion within decent bounds. As careful of public opinion in this as in other financial matters, he saw to it that her dower was allotted with the advice of the great council of peers,[139] and it was considerably smaller than the dower which Margaret of Anjou had enjoyed. Elizabeth's household was always much more economically run than the Lancastrian queen's, her expenditure smaller, her demands in some ways less.[140] Hard-headed in her business relations she may have been, but there were few people in the fifteenth century who were not.

Contemporaries would naturally have expected the queen's family to enrich themselves as far as they could. By fifteenth-century standards they would have been quite abnormal had they not done so. Their success was great enough for open satire. Edward's court fool joked that in some counties the Ryvers were so high that it was impossible to get through them.[141] Jealousy was to be expected but the fact that this gibe was made in the king's presence might warn us against taking it too seriously. The seven great marriages apart, record sources do not support accusations that a never-ending shower of riches rained down upon the Wydevilles. Edward may have been enamoured but not so blindly that he was lavish in grants from the crown lands and royal revenues. As we have seen, the queen's dower was modest and the grants of lands and offices made to her relations, with the exception of the posts of treasurer and constable, were relatively small, especially when compared with those made to supporters like Lord Hastings and Lord Herbert.[142]

Nor were the Nevilles doing at all badly out of the Yorkist revolution. Far from it. In 1461 Edward created William Neville, Lord Fauconberg, earl of Kent and endowed him with more than 56 manors and lordships and 2 boroughs.[143] This endowment compares very favourably with the four grants which were all that Anthony Wydeville received before 1470. In 1464 Warwick's brother John Neville, whom Edward had created Lord Montagu in 1461, was made earl of Northumberland with a large part of

[138] The incident should be compared with the very different description of Louis de Gruthuyse's visit to Windsor in 1472. See *Archaeologia* XXVI (1836) 275–80. C. L. Kingsford, *English Historical Literature in the Fifteenth Century* (1913), 382–8.

[139] Stevenson II ii 783.

[140] See A. R. Myers, 'The Household of Queen Margaret of Anjou, 1452–3,' *Bulletin of the John Rylands Library*, XL (1957–8) 1–21, for a comparison of the revenues, expenses etc. of the two queens.

[141] *Great Chronicle, op. cit.* 208, under 1469.

[142] See below ch. 8 p. 208 and ns. 85 and 86.

[143] *CP* VII 163. *Cal. Pat. Rolls 1461–7*, 73, 225. He was also admiral for a time.

the Percy estates to maintain his new dignity.[144] Warwick himself had already made enormous gains under Henry VI,[145] which he now presumably kept, and in May 1461 Edward granted him all the offices, farms and custodies which his father had held or which he had held conjointly with his father or with his brothers, Thomas and John.[146] Even after 1464 the golden fountain did not run dry. Within a few days of the king's revelation of his marriage, George Neville became archbishop of York.[147] Warwick himself continued to receive valuable grants.[148] His gains from office and from the royal service were notorious at home and abroad, but as the author of 'Hearne's Fragment' put it, admittedly a writer prejudiced against the earl, Warwick's 'insaciable mynde cowde noȝt be content'.[149] Although an exact comparison of values is impossible, apart from the marriages of the mid 1460s, the Nevilles took more from the royal bounty in titles, lands, offices and money grants than the Wydevilles.

The reputation of the Wydevilles has almost certainly been distorted in the sources which have survived. Generally speaking, descriptions of the family have come down to us from authors who wrote some years later, whose information on definite political matters was often inaccurate, and who in this as in other matters collected and often distilled jealous gossip of one or more decades which may well have been inspired by Warwick's own resentment. An impression has thus been created that Warwick and the Wydevilles were irrevocably hostile from the moment that Edward revealed the fact of his marriage. In spite of the humiliation which the

[144] *CP* IX 89–91, 717. Bean, *Estates of the Percy Family, op. cit.* 109–10. Before he was created earl of Northumberland he had received the wardenship of the east marches, a grant of the Cornish tin mines, the ulnage from Yorkshire and Hull and nine manors. *Cal. Pat. Rolls 1461–7*, 19, 130, 195.

[145] The indictment of 1459 alleges that Henry VI had showed his 'grace and bounteous grauntes, in right ample wise' to both Salisbury and Warwick and among other things that 'he [Salisbury] and his had in rule, all youre Castelles and honourable Offices, fro Trent northward' except Knaresborough castle and Salisbury had the reversion even of that. *Rot. Parl.* V 347.

[146] The offices were granted for life and the farms and custodies for a term of twenty years. *Cal. Pat. Rolls 1461–7*, 95. He was, among other things, captain of Calais, admiral of England, great chamberlain and steward of England, chief justice and chamberlain of south Wales, warden of the west march, constable of Dover, warden of the Cinque ports. R. L. Storey, 'The Wardens of the Marches of England towards Scotland,' *English Historical Review*, LXXII (1957) 607, 614. He obtained various minor grants between 1461 and 1464, *Cal. Pat. Rolls 1461–7*, 45, 71, 186, 189, 215, 265, 292.

[147] Neville was given custody of the temporalities *sede vacante* on 16 September and the licence to the dean and chapter to elect was issued on the 27th. The papal bull did not reach England until the following summer. *Cal. Pat. Rolls 1461–7*, 327, 329. Scofield, *op. cit.* I 354 n. 5.

[148] See below p. 121 n. 157.

[149] 'Hearne's Fragment', *op. cit.* 299. Commynes wrote that Warwick enjoyed an income of 80,000 crowns a year from grants and pensions alone. *Mémoires, op. cit.* I 192–3. Like the rumours of the Wydevilles' gains this is obviously exaggerated but it shows what some people at least thought of Warwick.

marriage brought on Warwick in France, this extreme interpretation may well be doubted.

It remains still to assess how far such family alliances and competition for court patronage influenced mid fifteenth-century politics at the highest level. These sordid tangles of matrimonial competition and rivalry for property and influence were the absorbing interest of landed families. Rival families competed bitterly both in the country and at court. In the twenty years between 1450 and 1470 the ambitions of one overmighty family and of part of another came to dominate national politics. Lust for power, possibly intensified by heavy debts or even fears, however ill-founded, for his own personal safety, drove the duke of York to treason and ruin in the 1450s. Salisbury and Warwick joined him, probably less out of family solidarity, or to force upon the Lancastrian court recognition of what York regarded as his just claims, than to strengthen their hands in a recent feud with their other close relations, the younger members of the Percy family. Without this far from disinterested support from the two Neville earls, Richard of York would have found it difficult to maintain his factious opposition to Henry VI. No influential sector of English society gave him its support. Until 1460 the nobility as a whole watched his various attempts to seize power with aloof disapproval. Throughout the 1450s there was no such thing as a 'Yorkist party'. Only after the Parliament of devils did a substantial minority of the nobility (including at last other members of the Neville family) give him active support. Then in a desperate situation, a small and dubious group of peers on 3 March 1461 did for Edward what the nobility as a whole had consistently refused to do for his father—they made him king. Edward began his reign as the king of the Nevilles. In fifteenth-century conditions it was impossible for him to rule through the narrow clique which had given him the crown. From early days his court was open to ex-opponents, Wydevilles included, who were prepared to give him loyal service.[150] Whatever Edward's relations with his cousin Warwick had been during his father's lifetime, there were some who even before his coronation thought that recriminations might before long break out between them.[151] In the 1460s Warwick's jealousy of the Wydevilles was only one stage, and most probably not the most significant, in a career which resentment progressively and finally completely dominated. In September 1464 Warwick was justly incensed at the way in which the king had concealed his marriage while allowing him to press on with negotiations for a French matrimonial allowance. His immediate indignation, either overcome or dissembled,[152] was in the first place

---

[150] See below ch. 5 pp. 133 ff.

[151] *Calendar of State Papers Milanese, op. cit.* I 76.

[152] In spite of the fact that Louis XI drew conclusions from a letter (now lost) from Warwick that the earl was so angry he desired to make himself king of England, by Michaelmas day 1464 he had swallowed his wrath sufficiently to assist Clarence in escorting

sustained by the Wydeville success in the marriage market, and their gaining some of the prizes which he had thought to dispose of elsewhere. Again he seems to have kept his displeasure secret, or at least within decent bounds, while various members of his own family obtained other and ample rewards. It was most probably the political crisis of 1467 with the complete repudiation of Warwick's pro-French policy,[153] exacerbated by his personal hatred for Charles the Bold of Burgundy,[154] together with his failure to persuade Edward to allow the duke of Clarence to marry his daughter Isabella, which caused the final break with Edward two years later. By the middle of 1467 the king had lost patience with the Nevilles and their intrigues.[155] In June he deprived Archbishop Neville of the chancellorship[156] and for the first time Warwick himself was stripped of some of his gains including the farms and custodies though not the offices in which he had been confirmed in May 1461.[157] At the same time Edward carried on his own pro-Burgundian foreign policy, concluding a treaty of amity with Charles the Bold, and he continued negotiations for a marriage alliance.[158] The lesson 'was lost on Warwick. He nursed his grievance probably through months of intrigue. Even now Edward was not vindictive. Before the end of the year he had given the earl the valuable wardship of Francis Lord Lovell,[159] and with notable forbearance gave him chance after chance of cooperating with others in the royal council.[160] When the break finally came after a period of apparent reconciliation, it was very

Elizabeth into the chapel of Reading abbey where she was honoured as queen. Scofield, *op. cit.* I 354. Various attempts have been made to deduce the relationships between the king and Warwick over the next few years from the various social occasions at which they were or were not present. These attempts are more ingenious than convincing.

[153] It may be argued that Edward, in allowing Warwick to continue negotiations with France, was guilty of gross deception. On the other hand (a) Warwick was well aware of Edward's pro-Burgundian leanings, and (b) it was by no means unusual in current diplomacy to pursue simultaneously with different states negotiations with mutually exclusive aims.

[154] Fulman, 551.

[155] In May 1467 it was said that Louis XI had invited Margaret of Anjou to his court and there was talk in France of trying to bring her and Warwick together. George Neville had tried to put petty obstructions in the way of the Bastard of Burgundy's visit to London and he was intriguing in Rome for a cardinal's hat. Warwick was also trying to get a dispensation for his daughter's marriage with Clarence. Just how much of all this was known to Edward it is impossible to say. Scofield, *op. cit.* I 407, 410–16, 433–4.

[156] *ibid.* 416.

[157] He had been completely exempted from the resumption act of 1465 and had then received further grants. In 1467 he had to surrender all 'Graunts and dymyses for terme of yeres, to the same Erle by us made'. The offices were exempt as they were life grants. *Cal. Pat. Rolls 1461–7*, 434–5, 540. *Rot. Parl.* V 524, 579.

[158] Scofield, *op. cit.* I 429–31.

[159] *Cat. Pat. Rolls 1467–77*, 51. For others up to February 1469 see *ibid.* 132, 137.

[160] I hope to deal elsewhere with Warwick's actions during the treason scares of 1468 and with this particular point.

much of Warwick's own choosing, being the result of his temperamental incapacity (possibly influenced by his uncle the duke of York's disastrous example in the 1450s) to accept anything less than domination over a king whom he and the younger branch of the Nevilles had made. The probability that their kingmaking had been against their better judgment would (if this hypothesis be true) have sharpened the edge of his resentment.

By 1469 Warwick was ready to lay about him with any weapons that came to hand. The real reason for his discontent—failure to impose his own will upon the king and council especially in foreign policy—would hardly make a convincing platform on which to appeal for support. The queen's family and other so-called upstarts were prominent and successful enough to provide an object for attack. The hoary cliché of the discontented, by this time almost a political convention, that the king was surrounded by corrupt and grasping councillors who robbed him of his substance, was too convenient to be neglected. It was an accusation suspiciously similar to those levied against Henry VI's advisers in 1459–60[161] and part of the vocabulary of those who were out of power. If as Polydore Vergil recounts Warwick did accuse the king of making 'more honorable accownt of new upstart gentlemen than of the ancyent howses of nobylytie; wherfor ether must the nobylytie destroy him, or els he wyll destroy them',[162] he disastrously miscalculated the effects of his appeal on the nobility. Even at the end of the 1460s there was no sign that any 'ancyent howses of nobylytie' appreciated his concern for their interests against an upstart generation.[163] Even his brother the earl of Northumberland supported him tardily and reluctantly.[164] When finally he took the king prisoner at the end of July 1469, within ten weeks he was forced to release him, having found it impossible 'to cope with the situation he had created'.[165] The nobility may not have cherished very cordial feelings for the Wydevilles but by this time they knew their Nevilles. Nor were the Nevilles as a whole particularly enthusiastic for Warwick's plans.

[161] e.g. See *An English Chronicle, op. cit.* 79.

[162] *Polydore Vergil, op. cit.* 119.

[163] Only four peers had been prepared to fight for Warwick up to the time of his flight after the Lincolnshire rebellion and two of these, Lord Fitzhugh and the earl of Oxford, were married to his sisters, Alice and Margaret. In 1469 only Oxford was with him before the battle of Edgecote. Scofield I 495–6. Oxford had a special grudge as Edward had executed his father and elder brother in 1462. When Fitzhugh raised a force in the north at the end of July, Northumberland, Warwick's brother, attempted to repress him. *ibid.* 534 and n. 3. During the Lincolnshire rebellion, apart from Lord Willoughby and Welles, only Lord Scrope of Bolton rose in his favour. *Chronicle of the Rebellion in Lincolnshire, 1470* ed. J. G. Nichols, Camden Miscellany I (1847) 12. Warwick had hoped for the support of his brother-in-law, Lord Stanley, but Stanley stood aloof. *Paston Letters* II 395–6.

[164] See above n. 163.

[165] Scofield, *op. cit.* I 502. Lords Mountjoy, Dynham, Dacre of the South and Ferrers of Chartley were members of the council in London during this period (PRO Council Warrants C.81/1547/7,8) but they never fought for Warwick.

The customary assertions that the marriages arranged for the Wydevilles and the Greys were socially disparaging to the families thus united with them, and that the nobility as a whole regarded them with great hostility, are not entirely convincing. The nobility may well have viewed with some disfavour tinged with jealousy newly created peers who added to their riches by means of their close connection with the court. Some may have looked down upon Earl Ryvers because his main source of income was the duchess of Bedford's dower.[166] Nevertheless, we cannot be sure that this kind of snobbery was not in part a cover for resentment of the fact that a wider circle would be chasing a limited stock of offices, annuities and court pickings generally. The idea of 'old nobility' has been very much overworked. Baronial families in general seem to have died out in the male line about every third generation. Of the noble families in existence in 1485 half had been extinguished in the male line by 1547 and there is no reason to believe that the proportion was less in the mid fifteenth century.[167] This high mortality meant that the honours of a large section of the nobility did not go very far back. Between 1439 and 1504 there were 68 new creations of peers. Of these only 21 were for the husbands or sons of old peerage heiresses, leaving 47 completely new creations.[168] The nobility had constantly to be recruited from below and its basis was plutocratic rather than aristocratic.[169] Its numbers were maintained by promotion from a group of rich untitled families whose way of life differed little if at all from that of the lesser nobility, a pool in fact, from which the numbers of the parliamentary peerage were constantly restocked.[170]

There were extensive family connections between the peerage and other prosperous landowners and there seems to have been no objection in the fifteenth century to marriages between noble and gentry families.[171]

---

[166] I owe this suggestion to K. Wallis.

[167] H. Miller, 'The early Tudor Peerage, 1485 to 1547', *Bulletin of the Institute of Historical Research* XXIV (1951) 88. S. L. Thrupp, 'The Problem of Conservatism in fifteenth-century England', *Speculum* XVIII (1943) 367.

[168] Adapted from *Wedgwood Register* pp. lxxii–lxxiv. These figures may need some revision but they are accurate enough for this purpose. Promotions from one degree to another are excluded.

[169] Noblemen were deprived of their rank if they became too poor to maintain it: e.g. see the case of George Neville, duke of Bedford, 1478. *Rot. Parl.* VI 173. Sir Anthony Wagner points out that *c.* 1530 'as earlier' gentility and nobility were interchangeable terms and that grants of arms, their outward sign, could be made to any person 'havynge landes and possessyons of free tenure to the yerlye value of x pounds or in movable goods iiic. li. sterlynge'. A. R. Wagner, *Heralds and Heraldry in the Middle Ages* (2nd edn 1956) 9, 11, 77–9. Some contemporaries held more snobbish views however. See S. L. Thrupp, *The Merchant Class of Medieval London* (1948) ch. 7 and below p. 124 n. 172.

[170] J. S. Roskell, 'The Social Composition of the Commons in a fifteenth-century Parliament' *Bulletin of the Institute of Historical Research* XXIV (1951) 169–70.

[171] *ibid.* 167–8 for examples.

Edward's relations and supporters like the Bourchiers and the Greys of Ruthyn (both already connected with the Greys of Groby) and the Herberts were unlikely to have disdained their new and closer relationship with the court. If Warwick objected on principle, and not merely from opportunist motives, to the union of men and women of noble houses and those of lesser rank and to the employment of new men in high places,[172] it is somewhat disconcerting to find that within eleven years two of his sisters and one of his aunts married men of this kind, all of them more recently ennobled than Earl Ryvers. If Warwick's resentment was caused by principle he should have objected most strongly to his sister Eleanor's marriage to Lord Stanley,[173] his sister Catherine's to Lord Hastings,[174] and that of his aunt, the widowed duchess of Buckingham, to Lord Mountjoy.[175] The Stanleys had reached the peerage only in 1456, Hastings in 1461, Mountjoy in 1465 and Hastings had been most lavishly endowed by the king. Logically Warwick should have included Hastings and Mountjoy at least in his denunciations of the Wydevilles, Lord Herbert, and Humphrey Stafford of Southwick in 1469. They were not included because politically he could not afford to include them. Accusations of greed and corruption often fall most bitterly from the lips of those deprived of the opportunity to commit such vices. Thwarted in his own plans, he exhibited violent hypocrisy in his condemnation of the Wydevilles. In two generations the various male descendants of Ralph of Raby and Joan Beaufort had collected four baronies and four earldoms and the women between them had married six barons, one viscount, six earls and three dukes.[176] This compares very well with the Wydevilles and the Greys, who by 1469 had acquired only two baronies, one earldom, one dukedom and two rich dowager duchesses (one royal) for their males, and two barons, three earls and one duke for their females.[177] The matter may be considered in other ways. The impoverished earl of Westmorland would hardly have joined Warwick in

---

[172] In 1459 at Calais, Warwick, his father and the king (then earl of March) had all 'reheted' their newly captured prisoners, Lord Ryvers and Anthony Wydeville, as being 'made' men aspiring to political influence above their station in life. Such sentiments may have been expressed more frequently than they were acted upon. After all Edward was very soon employing the Wydevilles after he became king.

[173] *CP* IV 207. After 10 May 1457.

[174] *ibid.* VI 373. Before 6 February 1462.

[175] *ibid.* IX 336. Before 25 November 1467.

[176] Since writing this article I have discovered two other noble marriages (1) Salisbury's daughter, Cecily, after the death of her first husband, Henry de Beauchamp, to John Tiptoft, earl of Worcester and (2) his daughter Catherine, to Lord Harington. *CP* XII 845; II 219 VI 320.

[177] Marriages to heirs have been counted as equivalent to marriages to actual holders of titles. If the same man held a barony and later obtained a higher dignity both have been counted. John Neville's title of Marquis Montagu (1470) and titles which came to the Wydevilles and the Greys after 1470 have been omitted.

denouncing the covetousness of other people. Was the marriage of Sir John Wydeville more nauseating or 'diabolical' than that of Warwick's uncle, William Neville, to an idiot child of fifteen? Lionel Wydeville was at least within a few months of the canonical age when he was provided to the bishopric of Salisbury,[178] which is more than we can say of Robert Neville, or of George Neville who was seven years under age when he was hastily intruded into Exeter in 1456. Perhaps most outrageous of all to contemporaries was the creation of John Neville as earl of Northumberland in 1464 when the Percy heir, though attainted, was still alive. This was the kind of greed for which the Yorkists had condemned their opponents in 1459.[179] The sanctity of a man's inheritance was the most deeply felt of contemporary sentiments and attainders among the nobility were rarely permanent.[180] Grossly flouting contemporary sentiment in some of their gains, the Nevilles exploited the royal bounty to a degree which may well have become a source of political discontent in others.

Although marriage and politics were certainly connected in the mid-fifteenth century, the connection was far less clear and simple at the higher levels of politics than some earlier writers have alleged.[181] The extensive network of marriage alliances brought off by two generations of the Neville family engendered no corresponding group which acted consistently together in national politics. From 1454—although other members of the family may have been sympathetic, Salisbury and Warwick alone of the Nevilles supported the duke of York. They did so most probably to maintain their own quarrel with the Percies. Here the family connection had no effect for both the duchess of York and the countess of Northumberland were Salisbury's sisters. In the 1460s Warwick's failure to dominate the king's policies, rather than to obtain the marriages he wished for, was most probably the main cause of his furious resentment. His attack on the Wydevilles' success was in great part a cover for other less respectable, even inadmissible, motives. His rash and seditious plans failed to secure the mass support of his relations who had profited from the Yorkist revolution at least as much as, and probably more than, the queen's family. In both the duke of York and the earl of Warwick, personal resentment was a major cause of their violent opposition to the government of the day. Nevertheless personal resentment, inflamed in the minds of both by

---

[178] This, of course, took place long after Warwick's death.

[179] An English Chronicle, op. cit. 89.

[180] See below ch. 5 pp. 155–6. There is only one other strictly contemporary example of a man taking the title as well as taking over part of the estates of an attainted family, i.e. Humphrey Stafford of Southwick and the earldom of Devonshire in 1468 and he was accused of deliberately bringing about Henry Courtenay's death in order to get it. Scofield, op. cit. I 482.

[181] e.g. '. . . the Neville connection formed the heart of the Yorkist party'. Oman, Political History, op. cit. p. 357.

excessive ambition and greed, was too narrow an emotion to unite even their own widespread family circle behind them in a career of active treason. Still less could it unite the mass of the nobility, who, apt as they were to take to violence to settle their own quarrels, were not easily persuaded to take to violence against the king. Contrary to their wishes and their judgment, force of circumstances had led them to acquiesce in Henry VI's deposition in 1461. A few years later they were too wary to follow Warwick on the dangerous path of treason once again. By 1470 Warwick was politically isolated in Yorkist England, forced to destroy his own life's work and a cast his lot with the Lancastrian exiles for whose misfortunes he had been so largely responsible.

5

Attainder and forfeiture, 1453 to 1509[1]

Attainder was the most solemn penalty known to the common law. Attainder for treason was followed not only by the most savage and brutal corporal penalties and the forfeiture of all possessions but in addition by the corruption of blood passing to all direct descendants, in other words by the legal death of the family.[2] Before proceeding to an examination of the effects of parliamentary acts of attainder[3] in the late fifteenth and early sixteenth centuries it is necessary first of all to define the scope of forfeiture for treason as it affected landed property. Bracton's classic definition of forfeiture had involved for the traitor 'the loss of all his goods and the perpetual disinheritance of his heirs, so that they may be admitted neither to the paternal nor to the maternal inheritance'. Feudal opinion had always been very much opposed to the stringency of this conception and the Edwardian statute *De Donis Conditionalibus*, confirmed implicitly by the treason statute of 1352, had protected entailed estates from the scope of forfeiture, thus leaving only the fee simple and the widow's dower within the scope of the law. The wife's own inheritance or any jointure which had been made for her, because they antedated her husband's treason, as distinct from her right to dower which did not, were not liable to ultimate forfeiture—though a married woman could claim them only when 'her time came according to the common law', that is after the death of her husband when she ceased to be 'femme couvert'. This equitable principle was confirmed by a statute of the Merciless Parliament of 1388 which, however, included for the first time the rule that lands held to the use of a traitor were also included in the scope of forfeiture. Thus, by 1388, of the lands held by a traitor (as distinct from the wife's inheritance and jointure), only those held in fee tail fell outside the scope of the treason laws. This loophole was closed by Richard II in 1398 when parliament declared forfeit entailed es-

---

[1] I wish to thank E. B. Fryde for criticism and advice on this paper.
[2] Bracton, *De Legibus et Consuetudinibus Anglie* ed. G. E. Woodbine (4 vols 1915–42) II 335, on the heinousness of treason.
[3] This article is limited to a study of attainders for treason passed by the English parliament. Attainders for felony and attainders for treason passed by the Irish parliament, the common law courts and special commissions are not dealt with.

tates as well as lands held in fee simple and to the use of a traitor, thus reverting with one exception to Bracton's view of forfeiture.[4] This comprehensive and implacable definition was taken over completely in fifteenth-century acts of attainder,[5] although, as we shall see, public feeling against so extreme a position probably affected quite considerably the actual execution of penalties.

During the fifteenth century the penalty of attainder was for the first time imposed by act of parliament.[6] It was a procedure that had the virtues of speed and simplicity. All that was necessary to condemn opponents was the reading of a bill in the parliament chamber, the mere acquiescence of the commons and its acceptance by the king.[7] Such action became common during the Wars of the Roses when the alternations of conflict placed in power one government after another which, it has been said, from motives of both security and revenge wished to destroy its opponents 'as speedily, as utterly, and with as much appearance of legality as possible'.[8] These motives were undoubtedly the immediate objective of the acts[9] and the fullest statement by a contemporary on the point is Friar Brackley's remark that the attainder of the Yorkists in the Coventry parliament of 1459 had been contrived by the 'most vengeable labour' of Dr Aleyn, Chief Justice Fortescue, Dr Moreton, John Heydon and Thomas Thorpe.[10] Successive

[4] i.e. the wife's inheritance and estates settled on her jointly with her husband or otherwise. In the late fifteenth century the wife was entitled to them after the death of her husband and such estates could descend to her heirs not attainted, e.g. *Rot. Parl.* V 481–2.

[5] For the general contents of this paragraph see C. D. Ross, 'Forfeiture for Treason in the Reign of Richard II', *English Historical Review*, LXXI (1956) 560–75.

[6] Procedure in the treason cases of 1388 and 1397–8 had taken a different form. Acts of attainder in the fifteenth century sometimes followed judgments in the common law courts or by special commissions (increasingly so under Henry VII).

[7] Henry VII at first did not even consult the Commons but the judges held that their consent was necessary. K. Pickthorn, *Early Tudor Government: Henry VII* (1934) 119. A. F. Pollard, *The Reign of Henry VII From Contemporary Sources* (3 vols 1913–14) II 19.

[8] Pickthorn, *Early Tudor Government, op. cit.*

[9] Contemporary writers, where they mention the acts, usually state merely that revenge was taken on opponents and that they greatly enriched the exchequer. e.g. *The Great Chronicle of London* ed. A. H. Thomas and I. D. Thornley (1938) 191, 198, under 1459 merely mentions the attainders and under 1461 states that many lords and barons were convicted and their possessions escheated. It mentions no other acts under Edward IV or Richard III. Polydore Vergil, however, implies (an implication which Bacon made explicit) that avarice was one of Henry VII's motives in pressing through the attainders of his reign. *The Anglica Historia of Polydore Vergil*, ed. D. Hay, Camden Society (1950) 126–9. The Somnium Vigilantis, dated *c.* 1459–60 and sometimes attributed, rather dubiously, to Fortescue, printed by J. Gilson, *English Historical Review*, XXVI (1911) 512–25, stresses the intransigence of the Yorkists and the need for repression if orderly government were to be achieved.

[10] *Paston Letters* I 535 (see also 522). Thomas Thorpe was a baron of the exchequer and had been speaker in 1453–4. For his notorious quarrel with the duke of York at that time, see Wedgwood *Biographies* 850. The group expected that they 'schuld be made for evir' if their plans succeeded but 'yf if turnyd to contrary wyse, it schuld growe to her fynal confusyon and uttyr destruccyon'.

generations of historians have since put forward various conjectures concerning the results of attainders, which have been strongly influenced by such meagre contemporary statements about their aims—issues, in fact, which it is wiser to keep distinct. These conjectural results may briefly be described as financial and political. C. H. Plummer in the notes to his edition of *The Governance of England* states that forfeitures must greatly have increased the landed possessions of the crown under Edward IV, especially after the battle of Tewkesbury, and that the increase became even greater under Henry VII.[11] On the political side an extreme theory, dying but not yet completely dead, has been advanced that the battles, executions and attainders of the Wars of the Roses resulted in the destruction of a great part of the nobility, a destruction alleged on very flimsy evidence to have been definite government policy under both Edward IV and Henry VII. While admitting that some of the greatest names (York, Beaufort, de la Pole, Holland) disappeared, recent scholarship has spoken more cautiously of the extent of the decline of the nobility under Henry VII and of its corollary, his reliance on middle-class support, and tends to emphasize the greater tractability of the aristocracy rather than its decline.[12] It is one of the aims of this paper to attempt, if possible, to assess the effect of acts of attainder in bringing about this change.

In view of the extent of the evidence which has been in print for a long time,[14] and of the fairly general realization that the full penalties of the law were not always exacted, it is somewhat surprising that the number of people who have from time to time found it necessary to comment on the financial and political consequences of attainder have not attempted to work out the effects of the acts with any degree of precision. A glance at the figures provided in the tables (in appendix C) should be enough to show that caution is necessary in discussing the problem. Between 1453 and 1504, 397 people (excluding members of the houses of Lancaster and York) were condemned by process in parliament, and of these no less than 256 (possibly 265),[14] or about 64 per cent ultimately had their attainders reversed. It tells

[11] Sir John Fortescue, *The Governance of England* ed. C. H. Plummer (1885) 277. In fact during the 1470s attainders were notably fewer than during the 1460s and the sessions of the parliament of 1472–5 are more conspicuous for the reversal of old than for the passing of new attainders. See below pp. 136–9.

[12] For these opinions expressed with varying degrees of emphasis, e.g. H. Hallam, *The Constitutional History of England, Henry VII to George III* (3rd edn 1832, reprinted Everyman), 15. A. D. Innes, *England Under the Tudors* (1905) 7. C. Oman, *The Political History of England, 1377–1485* (1910) 450, 472. K. Vickers, *England in the Later Middle Ages* (1913), 495. W. P. M. Kennedy, *Studies in Tudor History* (1916) 4. Pickthorn, *op. cit.* 93–6. S. T. Bindoff, *Tudor England* (1950) 29–30. A. R. Myers, *England in the Late Middle Ages* (1952) 115, 118, 193, 197–8, 209. J. D. Mackie, *The Early Tudors, 1485–1558* (1952) 13, 15, 18. For a change of emphasis compare G. R. Elton, *The Tudor Revolution in Government* (1953) 33–34, and *England Under the Tudors* (1944) 7–8, 43–6.

[13] Mainly in the *Rotuli Parliamentorum* and the *Calendars of Patent Rolls, 1452–85*.

[14] See appendix C table 1, ns 5 and 6. Figures quoted in various notes to this chapter do not

very much against any theory of a calculated destruction of the nobility that the highest percentage of reversals was among the peerage as a whole (just over 84 per cent) followed by the next highest ranks the knights and squires (79 and 76 per cent, respectively) followed at a considerable distance by other ranks. Obscurity it thus appears, contrary to received opinion, was no protection and the lower a man's rank the more difficult it was to obtain restoration in blood and lands; or at any rate restoration for some reason was less usual.

It is now proposed to examine attainders and restorations in some detail to see if differences of policy can be detected at different times. No record of the attainders passed in the Re-adeption parliament of 1470 has survived.[15] The Lancastrian attainders of 1459 and those of Richard III can be quickly disposed of as they were reversed after the political revolutions which almost immediately followed. In spite of Friar Brackley's gossip about the 'vengeable labour' of the Lancastrians in the Parliament of devils, there are signs that Henry VI did not altogether approve of the proceedings of his friends and was personally inclined to a more merciful attitude.[16] Richard III's record is more debatable. After Buckingham's rebellion he attainted a hundred people. His actions seem to show that he was in the grip of something like panic. A wholesale proscription of known opponents was accompanied by bribery of possibly wavering supporters on a very considerable scale.[17] Once again, however, the quick turn of political fortune undid the effects of his own proscriptions and his ultimate intentions are doubtful.

It remains, therefore, to consider the actions of Edward IV and Henry

always tally exactly owing to the fact that a number of people were attainted twice and therefore figures vary slightly at different times.

[15] It is probable that the parliament roll was destroyed by the victorious Yorkists and any acts which it may have passed were treated as null and void.

[16] Henry gave his consent only on condition that he should be free to show mercy to any person he might wish to pardon. Three men had their lands confiscated, five were fined, but were spared the full consequence of attainder. Henry also rejected a bill for the attainder of Lord Stanley whose conduct during the Blore Heath campaign had been most suspicious. Abbot Whethamstede also testifies to the king's personal intention of showing mercy. *Rot. Parl.* V 346–50, 368–70. J. Whethamstede, *Registrum Abbatiae Johannis Whethamstede* Rolls Series (1872–3) I 355–6.

[17] e.g. See his generous treatment of Sir John Fogge, ex-treasurer of the household to Edward IV, of Lord Hastings's widow, and his brother, Sir Ralph. The Second Anonymous Croyland Continuator lays great stress on the large number of attainders under Richard though this may be due to prejudice, and Gairdner states that the king's bench controlment rolls show that there were numerous prosecutions for treason in that court. J. Gairdner, *Richard III* (new ed. 1898) 98, 111, 199. *Cal. Pat. Rolls, 1476–85,* 460, 462, 496. BM MS. Harleian 433 fos 108d–109, 159–160. J. Gairdner, *Letters and Papers Illustrative of the Reigns of Richard III and Henry VII*, Rolls Series (1861–3) I 15, 46–8. Sir Thomas More stated that Richard with great gifts won for himself unsteadfast friendships. *The English Works of Sir Thomas More* ed W. E. Campbell and others (1931) I 37. BM MS Harleian 433 fos 282 ff. show the exceptionally lavish way in which Richard rewarded his adherents.

VII whose comparatively long reigns gave them time, had they been so inclined, to work out a consistent policy. It is first of all necessary to say something about the process of reversal. An attainder could be reversed either by letters patent under the great seal or by act of parliament. With one proviso reversals by act of parliament present no difficulty—the proviso being that under Edward IV they do not always indicate the real date of restitution. There were long intervals between the meetings of parliament, and some acts of parliament, although they do not always state the fact, were in effect confirmation of pardons issued under the great seal or they completed what may be described as partial restorations[18] made by force of letters patent. As to pardons granted by letters patent under the great seal it is necessary to distinguish between various types.

Those described in the calendars of chancery rolls as 'general pardons' need to be used with caution. What is usually described as a 'general pardon' normally had no particular political significance at this period[19] (except at certain times when a general pardon was proclaimed covering a particular series of events). The stock phrasing of the pardons enrolled on the pardon rolls (nowadays called supplementary patent rolls) was changed from time to time to meet new circumstances and in 1461 the form was changed so as to exclude the pardon of attainders.[20] The pardons enrolled on the patent rolls themselves between 1461 and 1485 present greater difficulties. Unfortunately the printed calendars leave much to be desired, for although the formulae of these pardons are most divergent the summaries seem to have been made without taking this sufficiently into account (the same terms in the summaries covering a variety of offences), and it is unsafe to use them for this purpose without comparing them with the original rolls.[21] In the examples which follow, therefore, no general pardon has been accepted as evidence of the reversal of an attainder unless the full entry on the roll itself specifically states that it covers an attainder passed in some previous parliament. Nor, even more unfortunately, is this

[18] For pardons by letters patent in the 1460s see below p. 132. Those granted in 1471–2, e.g. Dr John Morton, Sir John Fortescue, may have been complete in effect as they were reversed in the next parliament and none of their lands were granted away after pardons under the great seal had been issued.

[19] The state of the law, both civil and criminal, at this time was so complicated that it was almost impossible to avoid technical offences. The supplementary patent rolls contain many pardons, e.g. to executors and accountants, with no variations of phrasing, which can only have this significance. Like the privilege of freedom from arrest for knights of the shire and parliamentary burgesses the issue of general pardons was usually intended as a protection from the vexatious processes of the common law.

[20] Supplementary Patent Roll C. 67/45 ms 47, 49. Similar clauses are found on the entries of all rolls up to 11 Edward IV C. 67/46, 47 and 48. No formula is given on the roll of 12–17 Edward IV which is merely a list of names, C. 67/49. There are no rolls extant for 18–21 Edward IV. The formula appears again for 22–23 Edward IV C. 67/50.

[21] Some entries in the calendars, like the full text on the roll, mention attainder by parliament, others do not.

the only difficulty. Pardons like people are not always what they seem. Even in this category of pardons, the formulae vary and promises given in them were not always kept to the letter. Some state that the man concerned was pardoned his offences only, others that the penalties and forfeitures involved were remitted. In fact, as far as landed property was concerned most of them irrespective of the wording seem to have been subsequently interpreted in one way only. To use the contemporary phrase the men concerned were 'enabled to the laws',[22] that is to say they were resurrected from the legal death which was the penalty of attainder and became capable in law of making contracts including the purchase of land, but the restoration of their estates (even in some cases in which the forfeitures are declared by the pardon to have been remitted) required a separate grant. Only the subsequent reversal of the attainder by act of parliament made the restoration complete.[23] It is probable that in some cases where a pardon remitted forfeitures, Edward soon found inexpedient the revocation of grants made to supporters from the forfeited estates which it involved.[24] It is also probable that he used this piecemeal process of restoration as a form of political control; ex-Lancastrians had to 'work their way back' into favour and prove their loyalty before they were allowed complete restitution. Nor can the possibility be ruled out that the process conceals bargains between Edward and the attainted under which they were made to surrender part of their estates to obtain the restoration of the remainder, though there is no proof of this.[25] Probably it was because experience had made plain ambiguities of this kind in the operation of extraparliamentary pardons that Henry VII and Henry VIII both consented to acts of parliament authorizing them to reverse attainders by patent.[26] After 1485 therefore, reversals by patent had full legal effect and no such difficulties in their interpretation arise.[27]

[22] This phrase is used in the final parliamentary reversals of Sir Nicholas Latymer, Sir Thomas Tresham and Robert Bollyng. See below p. 149.

[23] See the cases of Sir Nicholas Latymer, Sir Thomas Tresham and Sir Thomas Fulford. See below pp. 135–6, 148–50. Robert Bollyng received a pardon in 1463 but some of his estates were granted out between 1465 and 1468. Although no grant in his favour is enrolled his petition for reversal in 1472 states that although his pardon did not restore his livelihood 'by the King's grace he enjoys the same to the great relief of himself and his wife and their ten children'. *Rot. Parl.* VI 20. *Cal. Pat. Rolls, 1461–7*, 271, 476; *1467–77*, 31, 46, 50, 479. Also Thomas Cornwaille, *Rot. Parl.* VI 21–2. *Cal. Pat. Rolls, 1467–77*, 18, 45. Even in the case of Henry Percy IV whose restoration was so politically expedient, 1469–70, his estates were restored by a separate grant not by his pardon. J. M. W. Bean, *The Estates of the Percy Family, 1416–1537* (1958) 109–10.

[24] See below pp. 148–9.

[25] See below, p. 143 ff.

[26] *Rot. Parl.* VI 526; VII pp. cxxi–cxxxi.

[27] Still allowing, however, for the possibility of concealed bargains. Henry VII's act was not passed until 1504 but there were only two cases of complete reversal by patent before this date. The other pardons all contain specific limitations or other definite special features.

In the first session of the parliament of 1461–3 no less than 113 people were attainted.[28] At first sight this would indicate as vindictive and vengeful a spirit as that which Friar Brackley had attributed to the victorious Lancastrians two years earlier. So it was interpreted by J. R. Green who wrote of all these families as reduced to 'beggary and exile'.[29] Such an impression of the wholesale elimination of opponents is, however, quite incorrect. Far from being in a strong enough position to maintain its security by destroying the leaders of the vanquished, the Yorkist government was so insecure that it could not neglect any opportunity of winning over opponents especially prominent opponents. Ample opportunities were allowed to such men to make their peace, a process which was all the easier when contemporary opinion saw such changes of allegiance as a normal and far from reprehensible matter, once God had shown a cause to be righteous through victory on the battlefield.[30] Even if in the first flush of success prominent Yorkists (some of whom had every reason for harbouring bitter feelings) were set on revenge, a milder attitude prevailed at court from the beginning, even provoking resentment among some of the government's own supporters.[31] The Yorkists did not look back beyond the immediate events of 1460–61, and adherents of the house of Lancaster, such as the earl of Oxford who had not been personally involved in the recent conflicts, were not attainted, and even some who had taken part, like Lord Ryvers and Lord Scales, were allowed to take their seats in parliament.[32] Consideration of the cases of some of those who were attainted is likewise revealing. Sir Henry Bellingham, for example, had fought on the Lancastrian side at Towton, had fled after the battle, and had taken part in the Lancastrian raid on Carlisle in June 1461. For all this he was attainted later in the year. Then, captured at the siege of Naworth, after a period of imprisonment in the Tower of London he was pardoned his attainder under letters patent (though his property was not restored) and released to take part in the earl of Worcester's naval expedition along the

---

[28] The figure usually given is about 133. See below, J. R. Green n. 29. Sir J. H. Ramsay, *Lancaster and York* (2 vols 1892) II 282–3. This is arrived at by adding the defenders of Harlech and a number of people 'provisionally' attainted whom I have excluded. For reasons see appendix C notes to table 1. The Annales until recently attributed to William Worcester (see K. B. McFarlane, 'William Worcester, A Preliminary Survey', in *Studies Presented to Sir Hilary Jenkinson* (1957) 206–7), give 108 names 'et xlij plures' making a total of 150 (the author incorrectly gives a total of 154). Stevenson II pt ii 770–1. Names found in these Annals but not in the *Rotuli Parliamentorum* have been ignored.

[29] J. R. Green, *History of the English People* (4 vols 1877–80) II 27.

[30] See below ch. 8 pp. 208–10.

[31] '. . . for they grudge and sey, how that the Kyng resayvith sych of this cuntre, &c as haff be his gret eanemyes, and opresseors of the Comynes; and sych as haff assystyd his Hynes, be not rewardyt; and it is to be considered, or ellys it wyll hurt'. *Paston Letters* II 30, 16 July 1461.

[32] *The Fane Fragment of the 1461 Lords' Journal* ed. W. H. Dunham Jr (1935) 5–24.

east coast in 1463. His adherence to the house of York turned out to be shortlived and he fled to the Lancastrians at Bamborough. For this he was again attainted in 1465. Captured at the surrender of Harlech in 1468, he was again imprisoned for a short time in the Tower. In spite of all he received a pardon the following October. He apparently joined the Lancastrians under the Re-adeption and on Edward's return in 1471 a commission was issued for his arrest. There was to be no forgiveness after this and the second attainder was not reversed until after the Tudor victory in 1485.[33]

This is by no means an isolated case. The histories of Sir Ralph Percy,[34] Sir Humphrey Neville of Brancepeth[35] and Henry Beaufort, duke of Somerset, are equally outstanding in modern eyes as examples of political amnesty and political treachery. Somerset's case is the most significant of all. The enmity of the families of York and Somerset had been deep and bitter since the mid 1440s and when Somerset was captured on the surrender of Bamborough castle in December 1462, he had been Margaret of Anjou's most prominent and active supporter since 1458. Sent to Edward at Durham he swore allegiance. Edward never neglected the art of propaganda. He exulted in this very prominent conversion and flaunted it

---

[33] Rot. Parl. V 476–83, 511–12; VI 320–1. Cal. Pat. Rolls, 1467–77, 98, 288. Cal. Close Rolls, 1461–8, 167. Paston Letters II 111. William Worcester, op. cit. 791; Scofield, The Life and Reign of King Edward IV (2 vols 1923) I 180, 292, 313 n. 3. There is no means of determining the exact date of Bellingham's flight but he was with the Lancastrians in the Spring of 1464. The Paston Letters wrongly report that he was beheaded after the capture of Naworth. The attainder of 1461 had never been formally reversed but the act of 1465 states that he had received a pardon under the great seal. I have been unable to trace this pardon. He was dead by 1485 and the reversal was for his son, Roger.

[34] Sir Ralph Percy submitted by Michaelmas 1461, early enough to avoid attainder in the parliament of November. He was put in charge of the key fortress of Dunstanborough for Edward. By the end of October 1462 he had gone over to Margaret of Anjou but in December Bamborough and Dunstanborough surrendered on condition that he was given the command of both fortresses. By mid-March he had the government's confidence to the extent that he was given authority to receive repentant rebels but at about the same time he went over to the Lancastrians again. He was killed at Hedgley Moor and attainted in 1465. Scofield Edward IV, op. cit. I 204, 261, 264–5, 274, 287, 329–30, 365. Rot. Parl. V 511–12.

[35] Neville, with the Lancastrians in the north in 1461, was captured and imprisoned during the summer and attainted in November. In February 1462 he was pardoned all executions against him on account of his attainder and granted his life on condition that he would remain in prison during the king's pleasure. Escaping from the Tower he stirred up insurrection in the north in 1463 and in April a commission for his arrest was issued. In June he was received into the king's grace and pardoned all offences and most of his lands were restored. At the end of the year he fled again and joined Henry at Bamborough. In 1464 he surrendered Bamborough to Lord Montagu on condition that the garrison should be received into the king's grace. His life was spared but in 1465 he was again attainted. In 1468 he was stirring up rebellion in Northumberland and again in the north in 1469. He was then (1469) executed by Warwick and his second attainder was never reversed. Rot. Parl. V 478–83, 511–12. Cal. Pat. Rolls, 1461–7, 122, 267, 269, Scofield, op. cit. I 186, 220, 313–14, 329–30, 337, 365, 423, 501, 503.

to such an unwise degree as to produce an angry reaction. Somerset's attainder was reversed, first under letters patent and afterwards by parliament. His property was restored. The king made him gifts of money and bestowed annuities on him and on his mother.[36] The duke was sent to take part in the siege of Alnwick, jousts were specially arranged for him, he shared the king's bed and they went hunting together with no more than six horsemen of whom three were the duke's followers. Moving north in the summer of 1463 Edward even made Somerset captain of his guard and rode to Northampton surrounded by 200 of the duke's men. 'The garde of hym was as men shulde put a lombe a monge wolvysse of malyscyus bestys,' wrote the outraged chronicler and the men of Northampton, remembering the sack of the town in 1461, stormed the royal lodgings and would have torn the duke limb from limb. Edward got him safely away to north Wales, where he turned traitor again, fled to Henry in December and was executed after the skirmish at Hexham the following May and again attainted after death (1465).[37]

The story of Sir Thomas Fulford shows that ex-Lancastrians felt secure enough at times to take violent action against Yorkist supporters. In the autumn of 1461 the prominent Lancastrian captain, Sir Baldwin Fulford, had been captured by one, John Staplehill, and executed at Bristol. He was attainted in the parliament of November following, and between November 1461 and August 1464 Staplehill was granted the greater part of the Fulford estates. Baldwin's son, Sir Thomas, in spite of the attainder was evidently living unmolested in the countryside for in March 1463 he petitioned the king for permission to take down his father's head from Exeter market place and bury it. In November 1464 he was granted most of the family estates, although his attainder was not reversed and there is no record of a pardon on the patent rolls.[38] This grant to Fulford covered the estates which had been granted to Staplehill only three months before in August. Staplehill apparently refused to give up his gains and in April 1465 Fulford, according to an *ex parte* complaint made by his opponent, went to Fulford with 2000 people, broke into the house, carried off goods to the value of £300, bound and beat his servants and so menaced and disturbed his wife that her life was still in danger. Staplehill, the following month, brought a case against Sir Thomas in chancery alleging that he had been

[36] But prudently kept his brother Edmund as a hostage in the Tower.

[37] *Rot. Parl.* V 476–8, 511, 512; VI 288. *Cal. Pat. Rolls, 1461–7*, 261. C. 66/505 m. 18 (the calendar does not refer to the attainder, the roll does). Gregory's Chronicle in *Collections of a London Citizen* ed. J. Gairdner, Camden Society (1876) 219, 221, 223–5. Scofield, *op. cit.* I 117, 120–1, 129, 132, 134–5, 145, 154, 165, 169, 188–90, 208, 209–10, 220, 231–2, 241, 253 n. 2, 261–5, 273–4, 292, 312–13, 315, 320, 329–34.

[38] The only pardon I have been able to trace is one dated 28 January 1465, Supplementary Patent Roll C. 67/45 m. 7, which has no political significance as it specifically excludes the reversal of attainder and therefore merely shows that Fulford, in spite of it, was living unmolested.

wrongfully dispossessed 'by colour of' the letters patent granted to Fulford in November. Although a commission was issued for Fulford's arrest Staplehill was apparently unsuccessful.[39] The attainder was reversed in 1467. Sir Thomas was on the Lancastrian side during the Re-adeption, fled to the Westminster sanctuary on Edward's return but escaped and, making his way into Devonshire, began to stir up insurrection and was condemned by name in a proclamation. Nevertheless, he had obtained a general pardon by December.[40] Even after this, far from living quietly which one assumes it would have been wise to do, his aggressive instincts asserted themselves. He continued to harass the unlucky Staplehill and in 1477 his servants even dared to attack those of Sir Thomas St Ledger, the king's brother-in-law.[41]

Edward's first decade was the period during which nine tenths of the attainders of his reign were passed, but during the same period, as an urgent necessity of policy, he gave his opponents every opportunity to make their peace, though it is true that in some cases attainders were not reversed immediately and the terms on which individuals were taken back varied according to the king's whims or his need for their services.[42] In the 1460s when both the Lancastrians and the Nevilles had been finally defeated and the need to win over opponents was no longer so urgent as it had previously been, Edward might well have indulged an urge for revenge. New attainders however were few and reversals for those old opponents who had been condemned to forfeiture in the earlier part of his reign are far more conspicuous. No less than 30 attainders were reversed (or in some cases reversals under letters patent completed) in the parliament of 1473–5, followed by 6 more in the last two parliaments of the reign as against only 13 new attainders during the same period. Prominent ex-Lancastrians who had previously been pardoned under letters patent finally secured reversal by act of parliament,[43] and others put forward excuses plausible enough

[39] Rot. Parl. V 476–82. Cal. Pat. Rolls, 1461–7, 54, 227, 359, 372, 490–1. Cal. Close Rolls, 1461–8, 314–15. For details of Sir Thomas's exploits and the reasons for the successive grants made to Staplehill see Scofield, op. cit. I 53–4, 55–7, 61, 64, 145–6, 179, 200–01. Scofield, op. cit I 201, and C. L. Kingsford, Prejudice and Promise in the Fifteenth Century (1925) 60, seem to have overlooked the grant of November 1464 to Fulford and therefore assumed that the attack on the house at Fulford was simply a case of violent dispossession.

[40] Rot. Parl. VI 231. Scofield, op. cit. II 20. Cal. Close Rolls, 1468–76, 188–9. Cal. Pat. Rolls, 1467–77, 303.

[41] In 1475 he had to enter into a bond of £500 not to enter Devon nor maintain rioters nor prevent their arrest, in 1476 a bond of £200 to keep the peace and protect Staplehill from attacks by his servants and in 1477 a bond of 100 marks to pay Stephan Spycotte, St Ledger's servant, £20 in recompense for wounding and beating. Cal. Close Rolls, 1468–76, 428, 440; 1476–85, 68–9.

[42] Twenty people had their attainders reversed or were pardoned under letters patent by 1470, although in some cases they were subsequently condemned again.

[43] e.g. Richard Tunstall and Henry Percy, earl of Northumberland. Tunstall had been attainted in 1461 and had carried on the defence of Harlech castle until 1468. On the sur-

for the government to accept.[44] Chief Justice Fortescue returned and made his peace at the price of refuting his defence of the Lancastrian title and soon became a councillor.[45] Another prominent exile, John Morton, was soon appointed master of the rolls and during the king's later years was one of his most trusted councillors.[46] It was Edward's policy towards the offenders of his earlier years to temper justice with mercy and his attitude was vouched for later by Sir Thomas More and Polydore Vergil, who were in a position to know as they had first hand information from survivors and had no reason for giving Edward more than his due.[47]

Only 13 attainders followed the political upheavals of 1469–71. So strikingly small a figure calls for explanation. It is possible, even probable, that in 1471 Edward had in mind another mass series of attainders, but was diverted partly by the fact that when his first parliament of the 1470s met (nearly 18 months after his return to England) severe punishment in the way of heavy, even crushing, fines had already been meted out to those who had survived the hazards of the battlefield. He may also have been influenced by the persuasions of his brothers, the dukes of Clarence and Gloucester, who had very cogent reasons of their own against attainders at this time. There is a tradition, supported by fragments of record evidence, of heavy fines imposed in the period following the battle of Tewkesbury. Fines amounting in total to over £2000 were imposed by special commissioners on numerous men of Kent, the Cinque ports, Surrey, Sussex and Essex. It may well be that such punitive measures extended elsewhere for it is only from his son's inquisition post mortem taken 15 years later that we learn that Sir John Arundel of Uton, Devonshire, was fined 6000 marks for being with the Lancastrians at Tewkesbury.[48]

render of the castle he was pardoned his attainder under letters patent and a few months later served on an embassy. The attainder was reversed in parliament in 1473. *Cat. Pat. Rolls, 1467–77*, 97. C. 66/521 m. 6. The calendar does not mention the attainder but the roll does. *Foedera* XI 591. *Rot. Parl.* VI 47–8. For Northumberland, see below pp. 141, 153.

[44] e.g. Sir John Scudamore, the defender of Pembroke castle in 1461, Edward Ellesmere, Margaret of Anjou's treasurer of the chamber. *Rot. Parl.* V 483; VI 29–30, 130–1, 327. Chancery Diplomatic Documents (Domestic) no. 945. Scofield, *op. cit.* I 197. Ellesmere came under suspicion again later and because of this failed to get all his lands back; a situation which he later attributed to the malice and false accusations of the king's physician, Jacques Frus.

[45] *Cal. Pat. Rolls, 1467–77*, 296. *Rot. Parl.* VI 69. Fortescue, *Governance of England, op. cit.* 72, 78–9. S. B. Chrimes, *Sir John Fortescue* (1942) p. lxvii.

[46] *Cal. Pat. Rolls, 1467–77*, 261, 334. *Rot. Parl.* VI 26–7. For his later influence see below ch. 8 pp. 210, 214–15.

[47] For More and Vergil, see below ch. 6 pp. 159–60 and the references there given.

[48] The tradition starts with Warkworth who wrote *c.* 1478–98 and is therefore a reliable witness. J. Warkworth, *A Chronicle of the First Thirteen Years of King Edward the Fourth* ed. J. O. Halliwell, Camden Society (1839) 21–2. R. Fabyan, *The New Chronicles of England and France* ed. H. Ellis (1811) 662. *Great Chronicle of London, op. cit.* 220–1, 'Such as were Rych were hangid by the purs, and the othir that were nedy were hangid by the nekkis'. *Three Books of Polydore Vergil's English History* ed. Sir H. Ellis, Camden Society (1844) 155. *Three Fifteenth Cen-*

Even allowing that such heavy fines had been imposed on numbers of men greater than we now know, it seems suspicious that the list of those attainted was so small and even more suspicious that none of these attainders was passed until the seventh and final session of the parliament of 1473–5.[49] Apart from the earl of Oxford and his two brothers who had continued in armed rebellion until 1474 and were therefore probably attainted as a warning to others (and even so it must be remembered that Edward spared their lives), the list consists only of the three leaders of the Lincolnshire rebellion of 1470, three esquires and a yeoman who had fought at Barnet, and two knights and an esquire who had fought at Tewkesbury; ten men of whom certainly six and possibly nine were already dead by the time the act was passed in 1475.[50] The bigger fish escaped the net completely. The list is so plainly vestigial that some explanation must be sought for it, and my own conjecture is that this lies in a prolonged dispute about the Neville inheritance within the royal family itself. Edward's brothers, the dukes of Clarence and Gloucester, had married the earl of Warwick's two daughters and co-heiresses. Although the two royal dukes quarrelled bitterly about the division of the Neville estates they had at least one common aim—to gain possession of them and continue in possession, as far as possible, by inheritance at common law in right of their wives rather than by royal grant. The quarrel began in 1471. In May 1474 Edward consented to an act which treated the widowed countess of Warwick as if she were legally dead, and thus before its due time transferred their maternal inheritance to her two daughters and co-heiresses, the duchesses of Clarence and Gloucester. There still remained the question of their paternal inheritance. Now two others acts passed in 1475 debarred the heirs male of Marquis Montagu from the Warwick inheritance—a significant proceeding for Montagu's

tury Chronicles ed. J. Gairdner, Camden Society (1880) 185. Commissions for Essex and the Cinque ports. *Cat. Pat. Rolls, 1467–77,* 287–8. No commission has been found for Kent, Sussex and Surrey, but commissions certainly acted there. See the original reports sent into chancery. Ancient Correspondence LXVII nos 107–10 and 112. For the fines, see Ramsay, *Lancaster and York, op. cit.* II 387–8 and 388 n. 1. The list of names of those who received pardons after making fine and ransom covers three and a half pages in *Cal. Pat. Rolls, 1467–77,* 299–303. For Arundel, *Inquisitions Post Mortem Henry VII* no. 30. Sums totalling £12,904) appear in the Tellers' Roll E. 403/844, as gifts during the autumn of 1471. These 'dona' include £3333 in money or securities from Arundel and the sums from Kent. It may be that more of the total really consisted of fines. Ramsay, *op. cit.* II 390–1. A. Steel, *The Receipt of the Exchequer 1377–1485* (1954) 289–9, suspected that not all these sums were paid at the time. This suspicion is confirmed by the Arundel Inquisition Post Mortem referred to above.

[49] *Rot. Parl.* VI 144–9.

[50] Richard Welles was executed in 1470, Robert Welles and probably Sir Thomas de la Launde were killed at 'Lose-cote' Field, Robert Harlyston and William Godmanston were slain at Barnet, John Delves at Tewkesbury and Sir Thomas Tresham executed after the battle. Robert Baynton's attainder was reversed for his son. John Durraunt was still alive when his attainder was reversed. Robert Gybbon's case is doubtful. *Rot. Parl.* VI 218–19, 259–60, 281–3, 286–7, 307–8, 317–18, 526–7.

son was (after Warwick's daughters) the heir at law to Warwick's own estates, the paternal inheritance of the two duchesses. If the two ladies died without leaving heirs of their bodies, which seemed very like at the time, their husbands would lose these immensely valuable estates to Montagu's son. The two acts which were meant to prevent this possible loss reveal in passing that Edward had originally intended to attaint Marquis Montagu but had desisted at the request of Clarence, Gloucester and other lords. Now if Montagu had been attainted the same result would have been achieved and his son could not have inherited the Warwick estates. However, it would not have been consistent with justice to have attainted Montagu and other offenders without at the same time attainting Warwick, the greatest offender of all. If Warwick had been attainted his daughters and their husbands could have obtained possession of the estates only by royal grant and such possession (particularly in view of the recent and numerous acts of resumption) would have been much less secure than if the estates had been obtained by direct inheritance. The clauses referring to the intended attainder in these acts, together with the fact that an act of attainder, so peculiar in its contents and so long postponed, was in the end passed only in the same session of parliament as that in which the question of the Neville inheritance was finally settled, makes it reasonably plausible to suggest that the immunity of the Nevilles provided an umbrella for others. It was probably the resistance of Clarence and Gloucester which prevented the introduction of another wholesale act of attainder.[51]

[51] *Rot. Parl.* VI 101, 124–7. *Cal. Pat. Rolls, 1467–77,* 455–6, 486–7, 487–8. The marriages of Clarence and Gloucester had taken place in 1469 and 1472 respectively; Clarence, wishing to obtain all the lands himself, was vehement in opposition to his brother's marriage. Gloucester's only legitimate child, Edward, was born in 1473, and Clarence's son Edward, earl of Warwick, *c.* 21/25 February 1475 at the same time as the acts against Montagu's heir were passed. Any children which had been born previously no longer survived. In the conditions of the day the danger of the two duchesses dying without children surviving them was a real one. The oblique statement about attainder is for our purpose as important as the act itself, for it shows that the king's plans had changed under pressure. A statement of 18 March 1472 on the patent roll shows that Edward had at some previous time granted both the paternal and the maternal lands to Clarence (I have not been able to trace the grant itself) who had then been forced to disgorge a 'parcel' of them for Gloucester but had received the promise that he should not be deprived of the remainder by act of parliament or otherwise. *Cal. Pat. Rolls, 1467–77,* 330. Clarence was created earl of Salisbury and earl of Warwick on 25 March 1472. *Cal. Charter Rolls, 1427–1516,* 239–40. Clarence was clearly feeling insecure and all parties were well aware that any property settlements or grants made under any of the royal seals were automatically invalidated by an act of resumption unless exemption was obtained. The resumption acts of 1467 and 1473 expressly covered lands granted from the estates of the attainted. Clarence had obtained exemption from the act of 1467 but seems to have lost heavily in 1473. The Croyland Continuator comments on his resentment under the act of 1473 of the loss of the honour of Tutbury 'ac alias terras quam plurimas, quas ex Regia concessione prius obtinuerat'. Fulman I 561. Gloucester was exempted from the 1473 act. *Rot. Parl.* V 572, 578–9; VI 71, 75. Possession of the Warwick lands by royal grant, following attainder, would therefore have spelt insecurity. Warwick

In view of the often repeated asseverations of his cruelty and vindictiveness towards them, Edward's attitude towards the nobility deserves special consideration. These accusations are based mainly on Commynes's *Mémoires*[52] and are picturesquely but dubiously illustrated by stories of the duke of Exeter, barefoot and ragged in the Low Countries begging his bread from door to door, of the disconsolate countess of Oxford deprived of her jointure and forced to live on the charity of her friends 'or what she myght get with her nedyll or other suche conynge as she excercysed', and of Henry Clifford concealed by his mother for a quarter of a century and brought up as a shepherd for fear of Edward's vengeance. These accusations and anecdotes seem at first sight to be supported by the fact that 12 out of 16 attainders against noble families were still unreversed in 1483. The matter is, however, too complicated to be dealt with merely by reference to a few figures and a few colourful stories. Investigations of particular circumstances are called for.

Each of these cases has its special features. The Oxford family had shown very clearly that it would not cooperate with the Yorkists. Even after the twelfth earl and his eldest son had been executed for treason in 1462 his second son John, in accordance with Edward's policy of reconciliation, was soon restored to his inheritance, was made a knight of the Bath and acted as great chamberlain at the queen's coronation in 1465. Edward was so anxious to secure the friendship of the Oxfords that he even reversed Robert de Vere's attainder of 1399 and thus restored the original earldom of Oxford. In spite of all this Earl John was suspected of treason in the obscure plots of 1468, supported Warwick, fled to France and returned to fight with him at the battle of Barnet and later seized and held St Michael's Mount. Although after his capture when the Mount was taken he was imprisoned at Hammes, even then the act of attainder passed against him expressly spared his life.[53] His countess may have been living in poverty immediately after his attainder as during her husband's lifetime she was not legally entitled to either her own estates or her jointure, but in 1481 the king granted her an annuity of £100 during the life of her husband.[54] The

was, however, found guilty of treason after his death by a commission of oyer and terminer in Middlesex and Hertfordshire in 1472. *Fifteenth Century England: 1399–1509: Studies in Politics and Society* ed. S. B. Chrimes, C. D. Ross and R. A. Griffiths (1972) 165 n. 36.

[52] P. de Commynes, *Mémoires* ed. J. Calmette and G. Durville (3 vols 1924–5) I 202; II 333. Statements about the deaths of nearly all the nobles in the realm in *Calendar of State Papers Milanese*, ed. A. B. Hinds (1912) I 77, the 'First Anonymous Croyland Continuator', Fulman, 529–30, and the *Italian Relation of the Island of England* ed. C. A. Sneyd, Camden Society (1847) 69, are clearly absurd.

[53] Scofield, *op. cit.* I 231–3, 366, 376, 480–1, 494–6, 521, 529–30, 536–7, 542, 544, 547, 560, 568, 571, 573–4, 579–80; II 29, 58–60, 85–9, 190–1, 213–14. G. Smith, *The Coronation of Elizabeth Wydeville* (1935), 18, 22, 23, 51, 56. *Rot. Parl.* V 549–950; VI 144–9. He, his two brothers and others of the garrison were promised their lives when the Mount surrendered.

[54] This was confirmed by Richard III. There seems to have been no intention of depriving her permanently of her property; it would only be hers in law after her husband's death. She

story of the shepherd lord is very dubious indeed. It makes its appearance for the first time only 80 or 90 years later and in fact Henry Clifford was living unmolested in England as early as 1472,[55] though Edward never reversed his father's attainder nor restored his estates. Just as the countess of Warwick suffered from the cupidity of Clarence and Gloucester, it is probable that their sister Anne opposed the restoration of her husband, the duke of Exeter. In 1471 Anne of Exeter was already contemplating divorce in order to marry her paramour, Thomas St Ledger (one of Edward's squires of the body), and she was equally determined to keep possession of the portions of the Exeter estates which had been granted to her in addition to her jointure.[56]

If we turn to others who were not so closely connected with the royal family a different story emerges. Somerset (whose case has already been described), the only other duke attainted under Edward, had after all been ostentatiously pardoned and in the end the family died out in the male line with the death of his brothers at Tewkesbury. Of the five earls and viscounts, one, Northumberland, was restored in 1469–70. Although the earl of Devon was executed in April 1461 his brother and heir, Henry Courtenay, was given part of the family estates in Devon as early as June 1461 and but for subsequent treasons[57] might well have been allowed 'to work his way back' as others were. The earl of Wiltshire's brother, John, was recognized in 1474 as earl of Ormond and allowed the family's Irish lands.[58] Possibly the influence of Lord Hastings stood in the way of complete restoration as it also probably stood in the way of the restoration of Viscount Beaumont, for Hastings had been granted a great part of the midland estates of both these nobles. For political reasons it was essential

received general pardons in 1475 and 1479. *Cal. Pat. Rolls, 1467–77*, 507; *1467–85*, 157, 254, 450. The needlework story is found in Fabyan, *New Chronicles, op. cit.* 663. It is not mentioned in either the Paston Letters or the Howard Memoranda, the sources most closely connected with the Oxford family.

[55] W. Dugdale, *The Baronage of England* (1675) I 343. *Cal. Pat. Rolls, 1467–77*, 327. C. 66/529 m. 22. Hall tells the story that his father John, Lord Clifford slew the young earl of Rutland in cold blood after the battle of Wakefield. According to Holinshed the same Lord Clifford cut off the duke of York's head (he was killed in the battle) and sent it crowned with paper to Margaret of Anjou. The stories appear too late to be worthy of much credence. *CP.*

[56] She married St Ledger in 1472. For estates see *Rot. Parl.* V 548–9; VI 215–17. *Cal. Pat. Rolls, 1461–7*, 9–10, 486; *1467–77*, 32–3, 137–8.

[57] He was implicated in the treasons of 1468 and executed in 1469. John, the youngest and only surviving brother, was slain at Tewkesbury, 1471. The title was re-created for the heir male, Edward Courtenay of Boconnock, Cornwall, a descendant of Edward, earl of Devon (1377–1419), in 1485. *CP.*

[58] James, earl of Ormond, created earl of Wiltshire in tail male, 1449, was beheaded at Newcastle after the battle of Towton. He and his two brothers, John and Thomas, were attainted by the English parliament in 1461 and in Ireland in 1462. The attainders were reversed in Ireland in 1475, but not in England until 1485. The earldom of Wiltshire lapsed as it had been granted to John in tail male and he died without direct descendants. *CP.*

to maintain Hastings's influence in an area as predominantly Lancastrian as Leicestershire had been before 1461.[59] Jasper Tudor, earl of Bedford, was far too closely connected with the house of Lancaster and with Richmond to be trusted. Of the barons, one had been executed in 1461 leaving no heirs.[60] Apart from this only two were shown no mercy before 1483 and they both continued in rebellion, one until his capture and execution in 1469,[61] while the other, like Oxford, was imprisoned after he was taken with the earl in St Michael's Mount in 1474.[62] A fourth, after receiving very generous treatment, again became implicated in seditious activities.[63] In two other cases attainders were reversed for heirs in 1472–3.[64] When the particular circumstances of each case are examined the impression emerges that it was not difficult before 1470 for attainted nobles to make their peace if they so wished. The same seems true of the 1470s, except where powerful interests (particularly the king's siblings) intervened, greedy for property or Edward felt unable maybe unwilling in one or two instances to take a risk.

Henry VII is generally credited by modern writers with pursuing a policy of mercy and comprehension—a 'mercy of the head not heart'—which has been compared very favourably with Edward's alleged cruelty. This is certainly true with reservations[65] of his attitude towards those Yorkists who were attainted in 1485. Twenty attainders out of 28 were reversed by 1495 and 2 more by the end of his reign. Although Henry encouraged Yorkists to make their peace, he kept his head in a crisis, and consistently refused to take panic measures, early writers were much harsher in their judgments of

[59] For Edward's attitude towards Lord Hastings and the central midlands see below ch. 8 p. 208.

[60] Lord Rougemont-Gray. Nor was this attainder reversed under the Tudors.

[61] Lord Hungerford. Robert, Lord Hungerford and Moleyns, (attainted 1461), was taken prisoner at Hexham and beheaded in 1464. His son, Sir Thomas, was convicted of treason in 1469 and beheaded. For the ultimate reversal of the attainder and the division of property between the heir general and the heir male see CP.

[62] Edmund, Lord Roos. Thomas, Lord Roos was executed after his capture at Hedgley Moor, 1464. His son, Edmund, was a child and therefore could not be considered in any way a political asset. He escaped overseas sometime before 1485 for his father's attainder of 1461 was reversed before he returned to England, but even then the lands were reserved during the king's pleasure. In 1492 he was found to be weak-witted and this may already have been suspected earlier.

[63] Richard, Lord Welles and Willoughby. Leo, Lord Welles was attainted in 1461. His son Richard, in spite of the attainder, sat in parliament in his wife's right as Lord Willoughby in 1461, 1463–5, and 1468. This is all the more significant as she was dead by 1460. In 1464 he was given his father's chattels, in 1465 some of his father's lands were restored to him and the attainder was reversed in 1467. In the course of the Lincolnshire rebellion he was beheaded in 1470 and a formal act of attainder passed against him in 1475. Cal. Pat. Rolls, 1461–7, 357, 468. Rot. Parl. V 617–18; VI 144–9.

[64] John, Lord Neville and Randolph, Lord Dacre. Rot. Parl. VI 24–5, 43–5.

[65] With regard to his attitude to their property, see below p. 143 ff.

the king's attitude towards those who took part in the various plots and risings of his reign. A careful reading of the Great Chronicle of London and of Polydore Vergil shows that he could be quite ruthless in dealing with the aftermath of conspiracy.[66] Polydore Virgil indeed emphasized his notable severity and Bacon quite failed in his attempts to explain away his fluctuating attitude, now merciful now harsh, remarking 'it was a strange thing to observe the variety and inequality of the king's executions and pardons, and a man would think it at the first a kind of lottery or chance.'[67] Although at the beginning of his reign opposition to wholesale attainders made itself heard so far as we know for the first time in parliament,[68] Henry's subsequent record does not compare favourably with Edward's. Henry attainted 138 people in the course of his reign as against Edward's 140 and each king reversed 46 and 42 attainders respectively which had passed at their own instigation. But, whereas under Edward after the mass attainders of 1461–3 only 27 new names were added to the list, each crisis of Henry's reign was followed by new attainders right up to 1504 when more were passed than in any other parliament of his day.[69] Once again, however, it is unfair to pass judgment on numbers alone as Edward never had to face a major conspiracy after 1471.[70] Yet even allowing that political circumstances justified the upward curve of Henry's attainders as compared with the downward curve of Edward's, an examination of the terms on which the proscribed obtained their reversals throws an unfavourable light on Henry's attitude, and to some extent perhaps upholds the traditional but now challenged view of his avarice.

Petitions for the reversal of attainders presented under the early Tudors show that some of those suing for reversal had to compound with the king

---

[66] 'The king wished (as he said) to keep all Englishmen obedient through fear . . .'. He emphasizes Henry's fear of riches in his greater subjects and Henry's own rapacity. *Anglica Historia, op. cit.* 126–9.

[67] *The Works of Francis Bacon* ed. J. Spedding and others (6 vols 1858) VI 183. Bacon speculates on the reason for this saying that Henry must have had cause for such variation and states that he probably distinguished between 'people that did rebel on wantonness, and them that did rebel upon want' but admitted that this was mere supposition.

[68] In 1485 'Howbeit, ther was many gentlemen agaynst it, but it wold not be, for yt was the Kings pleasure'. *The Plumpton Correspondence* ed. T. Stapleton, Camden Society (1839) 49. The Third Anonymous Croyland Continuator, Fulman 581, states that although the attainders were much more moderate than under Edward IV they aroused considerable censure in parliament. This seems to have been a spontaneous protest whereas that of 1473 had been inspired by Clarence and Gloucester. See also *The Red Paper Book of Colchester* ed. W. G. Benham (1902) 64.

[69] The figures are 1485–6, 28; 1487, 28; 1489–90, 8; 1481–2, 1; 1495, 24; 1504, 51. Viscount Lovell was attainted twice—in 1485–6 and 1495. The only parliament without attainders was that of 1497.

[70] There was, however, a fair amount of disturbance and disorder in various parts of the country judging from commissions issued to various people to admit to grace those who had stirred up insurrections, e.g. *Cal. Pat. Rolls, 1467–77*, 515.

beforehand—a practice which, if it existed under Edward IV, has left no traces on the parliament rolls of his reign or elsewhere. Such petitions also seem to show that Henry VII and Henry VIII were much readier to allow courtiers and officials to hang on to their gains at the expense of those pardoned. Some of the attainted under Edward IV bought back their lands from grantees, but there are only two cases (and those quite minor) where the actual enrolled petition specifies a reservation for a particular person. Although after 1485 the legal formulae of reversals were much more carefully and precisely drafted it is hard to believe that the far richer detail given about particular reservations is entirely due to such a change of practice.[71] As far as the nobility are concerned there were only nine attainders during Henry's reign and of these he himself reversed five and Henry VIII one more. This appears to be not ungenerous, but particulars of individual transactions show a rigid aspect quite unlike Edward's ostentatious mercy in the 1460s. There is only one reversal of a nobleman's attainder under Henry VII which shows no special features.[72] All the rest exhibit reservations in some degree or other. With John, Lord Zouche, for example, Henry's attitude fluctuated at first, then hardened into meanness. In July 1486 Zouche had to produce sureties in 2000 marks to be of good behaviour and a few days later was granted a pardon under the great seal for his offences. Ostensibly the pardon also restored his lands but unless Henry changed his mind after the pardon had been issued this must be interpreted as permission merely to acquire his lands again, for when the at-

[71] The greater number of reservations in petitions for reversal may possibly be due to petitioners including clauses safeguarding the interests of grantees with whom they had previously reached some agreement. On the other hand evidence from sources other than the Rolls of Parliament is also much less for the period before 1485. Under Edward IV I have found only three cases of reservation or bargaining (apart from the sales referred to in the reversals of Sir Nicholas Latymer and Sir Thomas Tresham, see below pp. 148–50, two on the rolls of parliament (Thomas Danyell and John Delves) and one (Sir Robert Whittingham) elsewhere. *Rot. Parl.* VI 104–5, 218–19. *Cal. Pat. Rolls, 1467–77*, 329. J. S. Roskell, 'William Allington of Bottisham', *Proceedings of the Cambridge Antiquarian Society* III (1959) 51–2. In none of these cases did the king himself benefit. It should also be added that we have no evidence from before 1485 in any way comparable to the act of authority of 1523. *Rot. Parl.* VII pp. cxxi–cxxxi), which gave Henry VIII power to reverse by letters patent attainders passed under Richard III and Henry VII. Henry appears to have made very little use of the act (only one attainder was reversed under its powers) but appended to it are thirty-nine clauses exempting grantees from the consequences of reversal. Many of these clauses refer to attainders which had already been reversed and also reveal that several persons whose petitions for reversal contain no reservations had not succeeded in recovering all their property. The question could only be decided one way or the other by evidence of negotiations between parties carried on before the reversal of attainders but on balance greater difficulties after 1485 seem to be indicated.

Although there were a few royal sales of land in both periods these seem to have been exceptional.

[72] Walter Devereux, Lord Ferrers, reversed for his son John. *Cal. Pat. Rolls, 1485–94*, 61. *Rot. Parl.* VI 414–15. *CP*.

tainder was reversed in parliament in 1489, the reversal was not to extend to the estates forfeited under the act of 1485. Zouche was permitted to inherit only the lands of his grandmother Elizabeth, the wife of Lord Scrope of Bolton. The attainder was completely reversed in 1495 by another act—at a price. In November, Zouche sold five manors to Sir Reynold Bray for £1000 'since Sir Reynold helped to obtain grace for Sir John from his liege lord to repeal the attainder and recover his lande'. These five manors had previously been granted to Bray by the king. The act also protected the interests of Giles, Lord Daubeney and his heirs in certain properties which had been granted to them. The act stated that Zouche might take over any of these reserved properties only if he could persuade the grantees to sell them. Nor is this the end of the tale of losses. Other Zouche estates which had been granted to three prominent courtiers, Sir John Savage, Sir Richard Edgecombe and Robert Willoughby, were still in the hands of their descendants in 1523.[73] Lord Zouche had to pay a high price to obtain the reversal of his attainder.

The story of the Howards shows rather different features, the way in which an attainder was used as a form of control over a potentially dangerous, but also potentially useful man. Even a much less avaricious and grasping character than John, Lord Howard would have had reason to feel aggrieved against Edward IV, for the king had denied him the moiety of the lands of the Mowbray dukes of Norfolk to which he was the heir at law.[74] Richard III, who resorted to political bribery on a large scale, not only allowed him the inheritance[75] but also gave him additional rewards on a very considerable scale. By the time of his death at Bosworth Field, Howard was duke of Norfolk and a great magnate with estates extending into nearly a dozen counties. After the disasters of 1485 rumour went round that Henry intended to execute Norfolk's heir, Thomas, earl of Surrey. Although both father and son were attainted and all the Howard properties seized, Surrey escaped execution; he was imprisoned in the Tower of London under the terms of a pardon which left him completely at the king's mercy.[76] A curious incident then followed. During the earl of Lincoln's invasion of England in 1487 the lieutenant of the Tower is said to

[73] *Cal. Close Rolls, 1485–1500*, 34–5, 270. *Cal. Pat. Rolls, 1485–94*, 93, 96, 101–2, 129, 231, 315, 380. *Rot. Parl.* VI 424, 484–5; VII pp. cxxiv–cxxv, cxxviii, cxxx. The five manors sold to Bray had been granted to him successively for life, in fee tail and in fee simple. Grants of Zouche's lands were made after the act of 1489, e.g. *Cal. Pat. Rolls, 1485–94*, 315, 340–1.

[74] The king married Anne, the Mowbray heiress, to his son, Richard, then aged six, and although she died almost immediately arranged for his son to keep the lands. *Rot. Parl.* VI 168–71. *CP*.

[75] That John Howard actually received possession of the lands is shown by the statement in *Rot. Parl.* VI 478–9.

[76] '. . . provided that he stand his trial if anyone implead him of the premises, and that it shall be lawful for the King to imprison him during pleasure . . .' *Cal. Pat. Rolls, 1485–94*, 86, 27 March 1486.

have offered him the opportunity to escape. This attempt to lure Surrey to final ruin (as the episode is usually interpreted) failed, for he refused the offer saying 'he wolde not departe thens unto suche tyme as he that commaunded hym thether shuld commaunde hym out ageyn'.[77] He remained in the Tower until January 1489 when he was released after taking an oath of allegiance. Release did not mean return to the eminence and riches to which the Howards had so quickly risen under Richard III. During the session of parliament which began in the same month as his release from the Tower the act of attainder was reversed but with wide reservations. He was restored to the title of earl of Surrey only and the restoration of property was limited to the lands of his wife's inheritance, any lands which he might inherit from ancestors other than his father, and lands which the king had granted to the earl of Oxford and Lord Daubeney. Within three months of his release,[78] after the assassination of the earl of Northumberland at Topcliffe Park, he was sent north with a force to quell the insurgents. In the second session of the same parliament later in the year Surrey was rewarded with an extension of the terms of his reversal. He was now given back the lands of the Howards except those which the king had already granted away, but with the agreement of the king he might buy back such lands. This second act did not restore to him his moiety of the lands of the Mowbray dukes of Norfolk nor the grants which he had received under Richard III.[79] Further service followed when Surrey became under-warden to the young Prince Arthur in the wardenships of the eastern and western marches. In the spring of 1491 he put down a second rising at Ackworth near Pontefract and by his merciful attitude won considerable popularity in the north.[80] He received his reward the following year when another act of parliament was passed in his favour. At last Surrey was allowed to inherit all his property except for the reservation that all grants previously made by the king were to stand, though any reserved rents paid to the king were in future to go to Howard. This means that Surrey had now recovered those estates of the Howards and of that part of the Mowbray inheritance to which he was entitled which the king had not already granted away. The king, however, by certain legal concessions in the act made it easier for him to negotiate with grantees to buy them back.[81] Henry recognized loyal service and according to his own cautious lights he rewarded it. Surrey had shown both loyalty and efficiency. He had been tested and he was restored

---

[77] See the epitaph in J. Weever, *Ancient Funerall Monuments* (1631) 834–40.

[78] Weever, *op. cit.* says ten weeks, but he was not apparently sent north until after Percy's death which took place on 28 April.

[79] It also provides for exemptions of particular persons.

[80] *Cal. Pat. Rolls, 1485–94*, 314. Weever, *Ancient Funerall Monuments, op. cit. Plumpton Correspondence, op. cit.* 95–7. He severely punished the ringleaders but sued to the king for pardon for the rest.

[81] For the restoration of title and lands, see *Rot. Parl.* VI 410–11, 426–8, 448–50.

by stages. He never recovered the immense grants from the crown lands which had enriched his family under Richard III; that was not to be expected for grants which had been gained and lost under such circumstances were generally lost for ever. He received his lawful inheritance—the Howards' hereditary lands and the moiety of the Mowbray estates to which he was entitled as one of the heirs of the Mowbray family.[82] But Henry was not prepared to alienate supporters by revoking grants which he had made from these estates. Surrey apparently had to rely on negotiations with the individual grantees.[83] Nor did Henry ever restore the title of duke of Norfolk which only came after 19 more long years of service as soldier, ambassador, councillor and administrator and after his victory over the Scots at Flodden Field.[84]

The treatment of all other nobles whose attainders were reversed shows similarities to the treatment meted out to Zouche or Howard.[85] The reversals of men of less than noble rank tell the same tale. The way in which the system of control operated can be seen from the career of a 'gentleman' of London, Thomas Kyllyngworth. He was attainted in 1504 for his support of Perkin Warbeck and granted a pardon in 1506 which contained the

---

[82] In 1507 Surrey was granted licence to enter 'on lands of the inheritance of the said John (duke of Norfolk) or the said earl which Elizabeth late duchess of Norfolk held for life with remainder to the said earl'. *Cal. Pat. Rolls, 1494–1509*, 543. Elizabeth Talbot was the widow of the last Mowbray duke.

[83] For cases of Surrey buying back estates or rents see *Cal. Close Rolls, 1485–1500*, 227, 276, 362–3. In March 1490 the earl of Derby, to whom considerable estates had been granted, was sufficiently concerned at what was happening to take out an exemplification of the second act of 1489 in Surrey's favour. *Cal. Pat. Rolls, 1485–94*, 318.

[84] Together with very considerable additional grants of land. *Rot. Parl.* VII pp. xlv–xlvi, xlvii–xlix.

[85] (1) Lord FitzWalter, attainted 1495, and later executed after attempted escape from imprisonment in Calais. Under indentures dated 24 July 20 Henry VII, his son Robert bound himself to pay the king £5000. It seems reasonable to connect this payment with the reversal of his attainder under letters patent the following November. He was allowed to pay in instalments of £1000 p.a. This did not mean complete restitution, for grants were made from his property in 1506, and 1509 he was granted the lease at a rent of £100 p.a. of the manors of Hampnell and Disse, Norfolk, which had been forfeited under the act of attainder. He took the precaution of getting the attainder repealed in Henry VIII's first parliament. At least two payments of £100 each were made under the indentures. *Cal. Pat. Rolls, 1494–1509*, 444–5, 454, 467, 483, 522. *Letters and Papers Foreign and Domestic of the Reign of Henry VIII*, I nos. 341, 811, 4347. PRO E. 36/214, 511. BM Lansdowne MS. 127. f 18*d*.

(2) Lord Audley, attainted 1497. The act of reversal of 1514 for his son John exempts grants made to Lord Dudley and others. In 1523 John had still not recovered an advowson granted away in 1508. Parliament Roll C. 65/132 m. 4. *Rot. Parl.* VII pp. liii–lv, cxxvi–cxxvii. *Cal. Pat. Rolls, 1494–1505*, 592.

(3) The de la Poles were, because of their royal blood and extreme unreliability, atypical. Nevertheless their treatment shows similarities to that of other families, e.g. the allotment in 1493 for £500 to Edmund de la Pole of certain lands and manors as though his brother had never been attainted and his reduction from duke to earl. See *Rot. Parl.* VI 397–400, 474–8; VII cxxii. *Cal. Pat. Rolls, 1494–1509*, 259–61.

proviso that whenever the king wished to examine him alone or cause him to be examined by someone of the royal council upon any matter touching the king's majesty or the security of the realm on any treasons and misprisions done with his knowledge and consent, he should clearly declare them and the circumstances surrounding them.[86] Other cases show Henry imposing much harsher conditions on those who sought the reversal of their attainders[87] and even obscure yeomen were made to pay.[88]

Under both the Yorkists and the early Tudors the way to reversal for men of less than noble rank was not always the simple process of petitioning the king in parliament for a pardon under the great seal. It was often a case of 'working one's way back' to the king's satisfaction from legal oblivion to full legal rights. Some achieved their restoration step by step, either being pardoned their offences but having their lands restored to them only some time later, or, conversely, receiving a grant of a fraction of their forfeited estates followed some time later by the reversal of the attainder and fuller restitution. Others were less fortunate in that they found it necessary to buy back their lands between the date of their pardon under the great seal and the formal reversal of their attainder in parliament. Edward IV, though he does not seem to have made offenders compound to his own advantage, was not always prepared to risk alienating useful friends by depriving them of their gains when exercising his prerogative of mercy. One of the most interesting cases is that of Sir Nicholas Latymer. After fighting on the Lancastrian side at the battles of Wakefield and Towton, Latymer was attainted in 1461 and some of his lands were granted to Sir John Howard and to Edmund Grey. Latymer was still with Queen Margaret in the north and was at Dunstanborough when the garrison surrendered in December 1462. He swore allegiance to Edward at the same time as Somerset and received his pardon at the end of June 1463, the period in which Edward, for urgent political reasons, was trying to win over all the ex-Lancastrians he could. In his final petition for reversal Latymer stated that the earls of Warwick and Worcester had promised him all his former possessions and this is allowed

---

[86] *Rot. Parl.* VI 544-8. *Cal. Pat. Rolls, 1494-1509,* 468. The pardon of 1506 was limited in its application. It only 'abled to the laws'. The attainder in this case was never apparently reversed.

[87] Thomas Tyrell had to pay £1738 for the reversal of his own and his father's attainders. E. 36/214, 519. BM Lansdowne MS. 127 f. 41*d*. Roger Wake, attainted 1485, in order to obtain reversal in 1487, agreed to leave the king free to grant away certain of his lands and grants already made to Viscount Welles, Sir Humphrey Stanley, and others were reserved. *Rot. Parl.* VI 275-8, 393-4. Elizabeth Brews paid the king £500 for the lands of Sir Gilbert Debenham and a promise to get his attainder reversed at the next parliament. *Cal. Pat. Rolls 1494-1509,* 238-9. For the hard conditions imposed on George, son of William Catesby (attainted 1485), see *Rot. Parl.* VI 275-8, 490-2. A priest, James Harrington, had to pay 80 marks. E. 36/214, 445.

[88] e.g. the Cornish yeoman Thomas Polgreven paid £40 and six others paid £30 between them. See BM Lansdowne MS. 127 f. 34*d* (entry on Thomas Gosworthdogga).

in the full text of his pardon, but in fact it was interpreted only as 'habled unto youre Lawes, but not restored unto his lyflode'. Frustrated though he must have been by this interpretation Latymer lost no time in setting about the recovery of his property. During the next few months some of his actions can be traced in the financial memoranda kept by Sir John Howard and his household officials. At the end of October Howard paid William Farnevelle for riding to Sir Nicholas, a matter which Howard must have regarded as of some importance, for the payment was made in the middle of his journey to take part in the northern campaigns. This is the first of a number of entries scattered among the Howard Memoranda recording negotiations between Howard and Latymer for Sir Nicholas to buy back the manors of 'Develeche' and 'Donteche', properties which the king had granted to Howard. On 26 March Howard and Latymer discussed certain matters at the Mermaid inn in Bread street following which an indenture was drawn up. Under this indenture various payments were made to Howard. Some time still early in 1464 they met again at Sonning where various payments were made and others agreed upon. Then on 12 March 1465 a new agreement was made (possibly as a result of difficulties which Latymer was experiencing in raising money punctually) stating that Howard should receive 1000 marks of which £40 were to be paid cash down the same day and arrangements were made to pay the balance in instalments. Judging from the terms of his reversal Latymer had also been buying back land from other people besides Howard. This case raises the problem of how a man like Latymer, who was supposed to have forfeited every acre and every penny in 1461, contrived to raise very considerable sums of money both in cash and loans until at least the middle of 1466, when the king made him a special grant of some of his former estates—a period of rather over two years from the time he received his pardon. The Howard jottings, though tantalizingly obscure, make it clear that the sale of the two manors was not the only financial transaction between Howard and Latymer. Howard was powerful at court. Latymer needed help in high places.[89] Howard presumably knew the terms of Latymer's pardon and, fully aware of Edward's very conciliatory attitude towards ex-Lancastrians at this time, was shrewd enough to realize that it might become more difficult for him to retain the two manors if Latymer petitioned for reversal at the next parliament and therefore drove a hard bargain while he could.[90]

[89] Latymer had manors of Howard's at farm, though they were not his own former manors. It is tempting to think (although there is no proof) that Howard, having obtained his pound of flesh, used his influence in the grant of 1466 and the reversal of 1468.

[90] Wedgwood, *Biographies* 526. Scofield, *op. cit.* 1 265. *Cal. Pat. Rolls, 1461–7*, 269, 525. *Manners and Household Expenses of England in the Thirteenth and Fifteenth Centuries* ed. T. H. Turner, Roxburghe Club (1841) 176, 177, 231, 251–2, 466, 468–9. It has to be remembered that these notebooks consist of jottings only and are by no means a complete record of Howard's final transactions. William Worcester, *op. cit.* 780, incorrectly states that his lands were restored in 1462. The full text of his pardon shows that it was originally intended to

At least one man recovered all his property by purchase. This was Sir Thomas Tresham, one of the most notorious of all Lancastrians, who had been speaker of the parliament of 1459 which had proscribed the Yorkists.[91] His petition for reversal is of great interest for it shows the insecurity in which a man under attaint was forced to live even though he had received a pardon and had recovered his lands: 'the seid Sir Thomas, by the Licence of your Highnes, hath bargayned and agreed with all suche persones as it hath liked your Highnes to graunte his Lyvelode unto, and the same Lyvelode he hath aswell by your Graunte to hym and to his heires, as by the releases, astates and confirmations of the seid persones, the whiche sommes by hym content for the same, amounte to the somme of MM Marc and more, for which of grete parte he resteth yette endetted to dyvers of his frendes, for the contentment whereof he can make noo chevysaunce of his Lyvelode, in asmuche as noo persone wolle take it for any suerte of their payment, nor bargeyn, nor marye with his sonne and heire, because of the seid Acte, withoute that he, by the merciable favour and socour of your good grace, may be restored by auctorite of youre Parlement.'

The effects of attainders on different families varied enormously. We have just discussed the cases of two men who were pardoned their treasons within three years of their proscription and had been restored in blood and lands within seven, but were presumably left saddled with a heavy load of debt because powerful interests ranged against them had seen to it that they paid heavily for their restoration. Others like the squire Robert Bollyng and his wife and children were reduced to 'povert and miserye',[92] and Sir James Harrington who was attainted in 1485 and admitted to allegiance in 1486 died in 1488 too poor, it is said, even to pay the chancery clerks for his pardon.[93] Yet by no means all families were reduced to debt or destitution. Some had settlements outside the scope of the acts which left various of their members with considerable incomes. Dowagers, whose length of days could be such a curse to their heirs under normal conditions, became a blessing when the head of the family was attainted, for their jointures rescued a considerable proportion of the family income from forfeiture. In the 1460s for example, during the attainder of Henry Percy IV, the two

restore his lands '. . . relaxavimus eidem Nicholo universa et singula forisfacta . . .' Patent Roll, C. 66/505, m. 10. His petition for reversal in 1468, *Rot. Parl.* VI 230–1, states, 'he hath bargayned and agreed *with dyvers such persones* as it hath lyked your seid Highnes to graunte his said lyvelode unto . . .; the which somes he hath content unto the seid persones by payment and suerte, to his importable charge.'

[91] *Rot. Parl.* V 616–17. By his pardon he had merely been 'abled unto youre Lawes'.

[92] There is less reason to doubt this statement than some of a similar kind for it was made after some of his property had been restored. Although his attainder was not reversed in Parliament until 1473 he had received a pardon which covered the attainder and the king had separately granted him some of his lands. *Cal. Pat. Rolls, 1461–7* 271. C. 66/505 m. 7.

[93] *Rot. Parl.* VI 275–8. *Inquisitions Post Mortem Henry VII* II no. 44. W. Campbell, *Materials for a History of the Reign of Henry VII etc.*, Rolls Series (1873–7) I 542.

dowager countesses of Northumberland may have enjoyed between them as much as £1850–£1900 a year gross from their own estates and join-tures.[94] The private estates and jointures of Margaret, Lady Hungerford, Katherine, Viscountess Beaumont, and Eleanor, duchess of Somerset, were by no means insignificant. Other types of settlements were also useful in such circumstances. Even where there were no settlements outside the scope of the law of forfeiture, wives and families were not always left destitute. Small allowances were made sufficient for their support but in-sufficient to allow their diversion to treasonable political activities.[95]

Although attainder did not necessarily mean beggary, on the other hand reversal did not necessarily imply complete restitution. Even if all his es-tates were ultimately returned to their owner they may have been much im-poverished. It was generally realized that the tenure of forfeited estates was insecure[96] and some of the new owners undoubtedly took the opportunity to squeeze as much as possible out of such estates while the going was good.[97] Worse still, the reversal of an attainder was one thing; persuading the grantees to whom the estates concerned had passed to give them up was another, and often much more difficult. It was easiest to recover possession if, in the meantime, the grantee had died without heirs or had turned against the government.[98] Others, particularly under the early Tudors, found it impossible to compel restitution from powerful grantees who were determined to hang on to their gains. Some people, as has been said,

[94] The widow of the second earl had a dower interest of £500 p.a. from her first husband Richard, Lord Despenser and settled estates worth £650–700 p.a. She also had a annuity of £200 on the Yorkshire estates. The widow of the third earl held the Ponyings' inheritance worth £500 p.a. in her own right. J. M. W. Bean, *Estates of the Percy Family, op. cit.* 83, 85, 91. For proof that the second earl's widow was still living in 1465 see *Cal. Pat. Rolls, 1461–7*, 455. For a general account of the incomes enjoyed by dowagers in the fifteenth century see T. B. Pugh and C. D. Ross, 'The English Baronage and the Income Tax of 1436', *Bulletin of the Institute of Historical Research* XXVI (1953) 4–13, 26–8.

[95] Isabel Horne, 40 marks p.a., Catherine Arundel £100 p.a. *Cal. Pat. Rolls, 1461–7, 7; 1476–85*, 417. It was more usual, however, to place a small income or lands in the hands of reliable officers to be administred for their use, e.g. Elizabeth Fulford, Philippa, Lady Roos, Elizabeth Tailboys, Eleanor, Lady Hungerford, Anne Hampden, Joan, Lady Zouche. *Cal. Pat. Rolls, 1461–7*, 64, 87, 89, 181; *1485–94*, 222, 223.

[96] See remarks on public opinion and forfeiture below, pp. 155–6 and nn. 104 and 105).

[97] When Thomas, Lord Roos's estates were restored to him in 1485 after a quarter of a century in other hands he alleged that they had suffered great waste and destruction—a plausible enough complaint, for it is known that Lord Hastings (to whom most of his midland properties had been granted) had stripped the lead from the roofs of Belvoir castle c. 1475 and had left the building to tumble into ruin. Stoke Albany, another Roos property, is said to have suffered the same treatment. *Rot. Parl.* VI 310–11. N. H. Bell, *The Huntingdon Peerage* (1820) 20.

[98] e.g. The greater part of Sir John Fortescue's lands had been granted to Lord Wenlock who was killed in the battle of Tewkesbury in 1471, leaving no heirs, and they were therefore in the king's hands again when his attainder was reversed in 1473.

recognized such harsh facts when they petitioned for reversal and the wording of their petitions, which include exemption clauses in favour of particular people, shows that they had previously come to an agreement with some of the grantees. Sir Humphrey Stafford of Grafton, whose father had been attainted in 1485, never managed to recover his paternal lands. They had been granted to far too powerful a man, Sir Gilbert Talbot. He managed to recover only his maternal inheritance and even that was denied him until 1514, ten years after the reversal of his father's attainder (an interval of time which probably shows the difficulty encountered), and henceforward the Staffords of Grafton became the Staffords of Blatherwick.[99] The Berkeleys of Welley never managed to recover the manor of Northfield and Welley which Lord Dudley had bought from the king in 1486 for 1000 marks after the attainder of Sir William Berkeley, even though they were prepared to buy it back and Sir Richard Berkeley even obtained parliamentary authority to bargain with the Dudleys for the purchase of his family's former property. The struggle went on for years but in vain.[100]

Nor did the acts affect only those specifically condemned. The prospect of forfeiture could adversely affect the prosperity of near relations and excessive zeal or mistakes in administration could cause inconvenience and loss of property to quite innocent parties from the dowager duchess of Somerset to a simple squire, thus adding to the already very considerable risks and troubles of fifteenth- and early sixteenth-century landowners.[101]

---

[99] Wedgwood, *Biographies* 792–3. *Rot. Parl.* VI 275–8. *Victoria County History, Worcestershire* III 125–6. Stafford's name is included in the act of 1504. (*Rot. Parl.* VI 526) giving the king power to reverse attainders by letters patent but no reversal is enrolled on the patent roll.

[100] The story, though very interesting, is too long and complicated to give in detail here. It was also somewhat confused by grants made to Jasper Tudor. The matter came before parliament in 1495, 1504 and 1523 as well as being the subject of numerous discussions elsewhere. In 1531 Lord Dudley sold the manor to Richard Jervaise, a London Mercer. *Rot. Parl.* VI 483–5, 487–8, 552–4; VII p. cxxix. *Cal. Pat. Rolls, 1485–94*, 64, 83–4, 260, 266; *1494–1509*, 59, 224. *Cal. Close Rolls, 1485–1500*, 115–16. *Victoria County History, Worcestershire* III 194–5. Northfield and Welley were one manor though records often refer to 'manors'.

For other cases of reservation see Edward, duke of Buckingham and John, Lord Audley. *Rot. Parl.* VI 43–4, 213, 285–6; VII pp. liv–lv.

[101] In 1464 when the dowager duchess of Somerset was imprisoned for a time after her son's flight she complained that certain of her tenants were refusing to pay their rents. Scofield, *op. cit.* I 313; C. L. Scofield, 'Henry, Duke of Somerset, and Edward IV', *English Historical Review* XXI (1906) 300–02. In February 1461 Sir John Fortescue attempted to settle his wife's jointure. Because he was then 'in trouble and jeopardy' the conveyances were hastily and carelessly drafted and there was trouble and uncertainty about the settlement as late as 1480. *Cal. Close Rolls, 1476–85* 199. See also the cases of Hugh Moyne and John Fauntleroy. *Rot. Parl.* VI 495–6. *Cal. Pat. Rolls, 1494–1509*, 88–9. For other allegations of wrongful seizure, *Cal. Pat. Rolls, 1461–7*, 231, 549–50; *1467–77*, 127–8, 193–4, 200, 445–6, 453–4, 522–3, 584–5; *1476–85*, 364–5, 508, 523, 523–4, 530, 539–40; *1485–94*, 208, 307–8, 397–8, 399–400, 439–41, 473–4; *1494–1509*, 208. In some cases those who had been attainted are alleged to have wrongfully occupied the lands. For the normal hazards of the

On the other hand, one exceptionally fortunate family emerged from the confusion of an attainder with its estates increased. When the third earl of Northumberland was attainted in 1461 his family had not completely recovered the lands which they had lost as a result of their rebellion under Henry IV. Under the terms of their restoration of 1414, confirmed in 1439, the family had recovered only the lands which they had held in fee tail; those held in fee simple were excluded. When, however, in 1469–70 Edward restored the fourth earl because at that moment he so badly needed his influence to counteract that of the Nevilles in the north, some of the manors held in fee simple were also restored.[102]

It is now possible to draw at least some tentative conclusion from these investigations. It seems, in the light of the evidence available, that a reappraisal of the actual effects, as distinct from the consequences possible if the law of attainder had been fully enforced, is appropriate. If Friar Brackley's statement is correct the first comprehensive act passed in the Parliament of Devils was intended by its authors to compass the utter ruin of their political opponents and we may well believe that in 1461 the triumphant Yorkists were no less revengeful in their attitude towards those who had proscribed them. If the letter of the law had been carried out and the proscriptions had remained permanently enforced, a number of noble (and other) families would have disappeared from English life, vast estates would have escheated permanently to the crown, and attainders would have been one of the major factors in renewing the landed endowment of the crown—the system which in its most advanced form has come to be known as 'Tudor feudalism'. For various reasons, however, attainders in the majority of cases were not permanent. The acts of attainder passed under Henry VI and Richard III were quickly and completely reversed. Of the attainders of Edward's reign which were never reversed, only 9 affected men above the rank of esquire, while the corresponding figure for Henry VII is 13. Within this total of 22, 5 attainders (affecting 4 families) were those against nobles and in five of these cases there were no

---

fifteenth-century landowner see K. B. McFarlane, 'The Investment of Sir John Fastolf's Profits of War', *Transactions of the Royal Historical Society*, 5th series VII (1957) 111–14. P. S. Lewis, 'Sir John Fastolf's Lawsuit over Tichwell 1448–1455', *The Historical Journal* I (1958) 1–20.

[102] For the very complicated history of the Percy estates in the fourteenth century, see Bean, *op. cit.* 69–111. The manors formerly held in fee simple which were restored in 1470 were Shilbotle, Pennington, Guyzance and Beauley. Bean suggests that the crown then lost sight of the distinction between the entailed estates and those held in fee simple. This confusion was partly due to the fact that in 1461 the third earl had been holding them on lease from the crown. Moreover, Henry Percy IV seems to have been able to bilk some of his father's creditors as the attainder of 1461 had extinguished certain of the financial dispositions made by the third earl. *ibid.* 134 n. 4. Henry Percy IV made very considerable acquisitions under Richard III. *ibid.* 112.

direct male heirs to carry on the line.[103] Acts of attainder as such can therefore hardly be said to have produced any significant diminution in the numbers of the greater English families.

Though Edward IV and his advisers may for a short time have intended that attainders should stand for ever, there is no evidence that they ever intended to exact the extreme penalty. In 1461 itself the process of attainder seems to have been somewhat haphazard. A considerable number of quite obscure men were condemned while prominent Lancastrians were allowed (possibly intentionally) to escape. During the 1460s the desperate need for support from almost any quarter led the king to pardon and make use of prominent Lancastrians like Sir Henry Bellingham, Sir Humphrey Neville of Brancepeth, the duke of Somerset, and rather later Sir Richard Tunstall and the earl of Northumberland. The 1470s saw few attainders, possibly due almost accidentally to disputes within the royal family, but perhaps we should offset against this a policy of severe fines and heavy financial penalties. At the same time Edward adopted a policy of comprehension and mercy towards those who had suffered attainder in his earlier years and even the notorious exiles of St Mighiel-sur-Bar made their peace and recovered most of their property, while some like Morton became trusted councillors at the court of the monarch whom they had so long opposed.

Henry VII's reign, if the evidence is strictly comparable, shows a marked contrast to Edward's. Although Henry was merciful to the Yorkists who were attainted in 1485, his reign as a whole much more than Edward IV's shows a continued resort to the process of attainder. Each new conspiracy against the king was followed by punitive action in parliament. Only one parliament of Henry's reign—that of 1497—was without its act of attainder. Moreover, towards the attainted noble especially, but also towards others (unless again the evidence is uneven), Henry's attitude seems to have been more severe than Edward's had been, and his attitude towards the bargains which he allowed his courtiers and servants to make with the attainted was distinctly cynical. When attainders against nobles were reversed he rarely allowed complete restitution of their property. Men like Lord Zouche and Thomas, earl of Surrey were pardoned their lives but their estates were in a greater or lesser degree withheld from them and the hope of recovery was held out often over long years as an incentive to loyalty and good service. With lesser men, when the attainted sued for pardon, Henry in some cases unlike Edward reserved to himself a proportion of their property, and he was much more inclined to countenance and even to assist his courtiers and officials in their determination to retain grants of forfeited land when their former owners were in law restored to their rights. This is not to say that Henry on the whole showed less inclination

[103] Henry, duke of Exeter, Francis, Viscount Lovell (left only daughters), Thomas, Lord Rougemont-Grey. The other two were John de la Pole, earl of Lincoln, and Edmund de la Pole, earl of Suffolk. The last male representative of the family died *c.* 1539 or later.

than Edward to allow his opponents to make their peace, but they certainly had to submit to stiffer conditions. The contrast traditionally drawn between Edward IV's cruelty and Henry VII's inclination to mercy can hardly be sustained. Though this particular contrast must not be pushed too far, in Edward's later years proscriptions died away; under Henry they reached a ferocious climax in his last parliament. Although under both kings men had to 'work their way back' to restitution, Henry imposed by far the harder conditions.

Apart from the very sensible desire of these insecure régimes to encourage support from whomever was prepared to give it, contemporary opinion among the landed classes had a strong effect on the attitude of rulers. Stubbs summed up this point in his usual concise, clear way: 'The landowner had a stake in the country, a material security for his good behaviour; if he offended against the law or the government, he might forfeit his land; but the land was not lost sight of, and the moral and social claims of the family which had possessed it were not barred by forfeiture. The restoration of the heirs of the dispossessed was an invariable result or condition of every political pacification; and very few estates were alienated from the direct line of inheritance by one forfeiture only'.[104]

Throughout the fifteenth century opinions of this kind were forcibly expressed, in action as well as in theory. The tenant in fee simple had the sole interest in his estate. It could therefore be confiscated without necessarily injuring others. By contrast the tenant in fee tail had only a life interest. Consequently, in spite of the confiscatory legislation of the 1390s and later, men felt very strongly that lands held in fee tail should go to the heir, sentence of forfeiture notwithstanding, when his time came at common law after the death of the convicted traitor.[105] To fly in the face of this

[104] W. Stubbs, *The Constitutional History of England* (1878) III 610. It may also be added that Stubbs's opinion is given added force by the fact that the number of reversals passed in favour of collaterals is by no means insignificant. e.g. The following attainders were reversed for other than sons—Sir Robert Whittingham, John Floryl, Sir Anthony Notehill, Sir Walter Notehill, Sir Alexander Hody. The act of 1489 for the reversal of Sir Robert Brakenbury's attainder in favour of his sisters and co-heiresses even contained a proviso that if the co-heiresses died without leaving direct descendants his bastard son should inherit. *Rot. Parl.* VI 27–8, 108–9, 175–6, 219, 433–4.

[105] In 1423 it was declared in parliament that Henry V on his deathbed had been greatly troubled in conscience because he had granted away certain forfeited lands of Henry, Lord le Scrope of Masham which were asserted to be entailed. It was stated that the grantees were willing to surrender the lands if this were so. It was therefore decided that the question of fact should be tried at common law. In 1425 the case was settled in favour of John le Scrope, brother and heir of Henry. *Rot. Parl.* IV 212–13, 287–8. There had been some vacillation as to what type of lands attainder covered. In the de Vere case, 1392–3, entailed lands were not to be forefeited by attainder. *Rot. Parl.* III 302–3. The rebels of 1 Henry IV, the earls of Kent, Huntingdon and Salisbury, Thomas, Lord Despenser and Sir Ralph Lumley, were to forfeit all lands and tenements which they held in fee simple. *Rot. Parl.* IV 18. On the other hand the forfeitures of those condemned in 1406 extended to entailed lands. *Rot. Parl.* IV 604–7, but a declaration in parliament in 1439 confirmed restorations of lands held in fee tail but not in

opinion would have been to outrage one of the strongest of contemporary sentiments.

It may be that this insistent public opinion so strongly in favour of ultimate restoration, contributed to one aspect of attainders which a close examination of the acts quite clearly brings out. As time went on, however unpremeditated such a thing may have been in 1459 and 1461, attainders came to work at least in part as a kind of probation system.[106] They became a method of political control, the extreme form of the current system of recognizances for good behaviour (the close rolls both under the Yorkists and under Henry VII are crowded with recognizances exacted from men as highly placed as they were unreliable) and of the heavy suspended fines imposed on prominent men and others by Henry VII. The workings of the system must certainly have appeared thus to men who were first pardoned and then allowed to recover their lands by purchase or partial grant before the final act of oblivion and mercy.

It remains to assess the effect of attainders on the holding of property. In the present state of research on the subject it is impossible to assess accurately either the extent or the value of the property which passed into the royal hands at one period or another of the civil strife. Nevertheless, it is clear enough that vast estates and goods and chattels of enormous value passed to the crown as a result of the acts. After the attainder of Sir William Stanley, Henry VII netted the prodigious sum of £9062 in cash and

---

fee simple. *Rot. Parl.* V 12. For the Percies see above, p. 153 and n. 102. There was a similar proviso in St. 9 Henry VI cl 3, which confirmed the proceedings against Owen Glendower. Fortescue, *op. cit.* 278. The petition against William de la Pole in 1451 seems to represent the opinion of the landowner. It asks that his heirs should be corrupt of blood and unable to inherit any lands, tenements, rents, services or any other manner inheritance or possessions of fee simple as heirs to him. His goods and chattels were also to be seized. *Rot. Parl.* V 226. The petition does not mention entailed estates or estates held to his use. As late as 1453 a proviso exempting entailed estates was expressly introduced into the act of attainder against Sir William Oldhall. *Rot. Parl.* V 265–6. The provisions of the acts of attainder from 1459 onwards for the confiscation of estates in fee tail were therefore flying strongly in the face of public opinion. According to Polydore Vergil, when Edward IV returned in 1471 none dared for fear of Warwick join him in his attempt to recover the crown. He therefore gave out that he sought only for his dukedom of York 'to thintent that by this reasonable and rightewouse request he might get more favor at all handes. And yt ys incredible to be spoken how great effect that feygnyd matter was of, suche ys the force of righteuousnes generally among all men; for whan they herd that King Edward mynded nothing lesse than to require the Kingdom, and sowght simply for his inhertyance, they began to be movyd ether for pyty to favor him, or at the leest not to hinder him at all from thattayning of that dukedome.' Polydore Vergil, *op. cit.* 137.

[106] The method was not new. Very similar measures had been taken under Edward II. See the case of Bogo de Knovill in 1326. *Cal. Pat. Rolls, 1324–7*, 333. I owe this reference to E. B. Fryde. It may also be compared as a method of governmental discipline with the taking of hostages from feudal tenants under the Angevins and the enormous fines imposed (but generally uncollected) under King John.

jewels,[107] and similar though smaller windfalls must have been very useful to Edward IV in the 1460s when he so desperately needed money.[108] As to estates, sums obtained from the sale of custodies, a few outright sales of estates, and sums taken from the attainted before the restoration of their lands were by no means negligible.[109] The income received from the estates themselves in comparison with the crown's annual budget must at certain times have been very considerable.[110] The permanent effect on the landed endowment of the crown is, however, a different matter. It is true that after each successive revolution and conspiracy the lands of the dispossessed were available for distribution to the victors, thus reducing the insistent pressure for grants of crown lands. The relief of pressure is, however, a very different thing from the permanent building up of the landed endowment of the monarchy. After all only 5 or at the most 7 noble estates were never returned,[111] either in whole or in part, to their original owners,[112] and only 17 estates of men of knightly rank. The remaining 119 estates which were permanently forfeited were those of squires, yeomen, merchants and minor ecclesiastics, the greater number of them most probably of small value.

Perhaps more important was the effect of attainders on the fortunes of individual landowners. The probability that the possession of forfeited

[107] W. C. Richardson, *Tudor Chamber Administration 1485–1547* (1952) 12.

[108] e.g. From Edward Ellesmere £2000. See above p. 137 n. 44. Henry, duke of Exeter, £1100 (jewels and silver plate), Henry, duke of Somerset, £1000 (jewels and plate). *Cal. Pat. Rolls, 1467–77*, 121. William Tailboys (cash and debts), £108. *Cal. Pat. Rolls, 1461–7*, 295.

[109] e.g. For part of the estates of the following—Henry, duke of Exeter, £4666. 13s. 4d. Ramsay, *op. cit.* II 459. Clarence, £2000. *Cal. Pat. Rolls, 1476–85*, 212. Berkeley of Welley, £666. 13s. 4d. *Cal. Pat. Rolls, 1485–94*, 83–4. Sir Henry Bodrugan, £320. *Cal. Pat. Rolls, 1494–1509*, 503. Including 600 marks which Lord Audley paid to Edward IV to save his brother Humphrey's lands from forfeiture (*Rot. Parl.* VI 127–8), £5000 paid by Edmund, earl of Suffolk, £5,000 by Lord FitzWalter, £1728 by Thomas Tyrell and other smaller sums the total amounts to over £20,000 and it is by no means complete.

[110] A list of 16 estates (and the values of some of these are far from complete) gives a total value of nearly £18,000 p.a. Not all these estates, however, were in the crown's hands simultaneously. The figure includes the estates of Clarence and Gloucester, £3500 and *c.* £3666 net respectively. It seems legitimate to include these as the figures include the old Salisbury, Spenser and Warwick lands as well as royal grants. As the figures are only an approximation detailed references have been omitted to save space.

[111] Those of the dukes of Exeter, Somerset, and Suffolk, Viscount Lovell and Lord Rougemont-Grey. The figure is brought up to six if the Salisbury and Warwick estates are counted. These fell to the crown after the attainders of Clarence (1478) and Richard III (1485).

[112] It is also improbable that attainders to any great extent permanently reduced the acreage of land in the hands of the aristocracy, though the distribution of lands between its various members may have been altered or diverted. e.g. The Howards, although they had to wait for many years, finally emerged with their lands greatly increased, including their moiety of the Mowbray estates and the grants made to Surrey from the crown lands after Flodden.

estates was likely to be temporary may well have led to excessive exploitation by those to whom they had been granted and to their return wasted and impoverished to their original owners. Others of the proscribed ran deeply into debt to get back their estates and may have done so in order to live. The process may also have increased the considerable hazards of the fifteenth-century land market by adding further complications to titles already insecure and uncertain. It must have embittered some to the extent of making them the more ready to plot treason again. Even so, the system as it actually operated, as distinct from the way it could have operated (and has so often been assumed to have operated) if the full penalties allowed by the law had been exacted, cannot have brought about any significant numerical reduction of the aristocracy nor even the decimation of an unruly element in English society. The cooperation of the nobility was essential to firm government as the history of both Edward IV and Henry VII shows.[113] What the attainder system ultimately achieved in combination with other things like fines, bonds and recognizances, was to hold the sharpest of legal swords over recalcitrant heads and to help to bring about that greater tractability which some historians have noted as one of the more prominent characteristics of the upper ranks of English society in the early sixteenth century.

[113] See below ch. 8 pp. 206–11.

6

Edward IV:
the modern legend and a revision[1]

1 The growth of the modern legend

In *Little Arthur's History of England*, Maria, Lady Calcott quickly disposed of Edward IV; she was able to say very little good of him, except that he was brave and handsome and good humoured in company. Alas, these valuable social qualities were offset by more sinister trains for he loved his own pleasure too much to do anything for the good of his people 'and he did them much wrong'. This is but the crudest copy of the conventional portrait of Edward IV which historians have drawn for the last two hundred years—a portrait of a handsome, powerful but politically immature prince, given over in his later years to lust and luxury, neglecting affairs of state except when roused to momentary bursts of energy and cruelty by a crisis or a fit of avarice. It is enlightening to trace the growth of this legend, for it is not to be found in any contemporary or near contemporary English writer. Fifteenth-century English writers, with the exception of the Second Anonymous Croyland Continuator, give only superficial details of Edward's work and character.[2]

The Croyland Continuator apart, the first real characterizations of Edward come from Sir Thomas More and Polydore Vergil. Both based their descriptions on the reminiscences of a wide circle of men, some of whom had been active in Yorkist administration and others partisans in exile of Henry of Richmond;[3] both give balanced, sensible portraits, compiled from many men's information, quite unlike the sharp black and white judgments of later historians. Both state that Edward was diligent, that he restored his kingdom to prosperity, that his rule was judicious and

---

[1] I would like to thank E. F. Jacob for suggestions and criticism.

[2] Fabyan, *The New Chronicles of England and France* (1811) 667. *The Great Chronicle of London* ed. A. H. Thomas and I. D. Thornley (1938) 228–9.

[3] A. F. Pollard, 'The Making of Sir Thomas More's *Richard III*', in *Historical Essays in Honour of James Tait* (1933) 223–38. D. Hay, *Polydore Vergil, Renaissance Historian and Man of Letters* (1952) 93–5. See also C. L. Kingsford, *English Historical Literature in the Fifteenth Century* (1913) chs 6, 7 and 10.

popular.[4] This tradition, early established on the oral evidence of contemporaries, maintained itself for a century and more among reputable historians. Hall held the same views and Grafton, Holinshed and Stow copied More's description almost verbatim.[5]

Meanwhile, an important though unconscious step towards creating the modern legend was taken in William Habington's *Edward IV*. This life of Edward, though written much earlier, was not published until 1640.[6] The high-water mark of seventeenth-century publications on the Yorkists, it is in many ways a surprise after the Tudor chroniclers. Habington retained all their abhorrence of rebellion against the powers that be, whether de facto or the Lord's legitimately anointed. Yet the horror of the social disorders of the fifteenth century had vanished and he assumed the calmer social background of the late sixteenth-century. For Habington the main preoccupation of fifteenth-century England was political faction and succession disputes. To see the situation in terms like these was to invite misconception, and there is an uncertain, ambivalent attitude throughout his work. For example, he condemned the king's apparent negligence in face of the danger from Warwick and Clarence in 1469 in terms in which the later legend is almost completely formulated. But after this his conclusion is astounding—nothing less than a complete endorsement of the best sixteenth-century tradition. His eulogy of Edward's strong government even surpasses that of the Tudor historians: '. . . this king was, if we compare him with the lives of princes in general, *worthy to be numbered among the best*.' Any severities which seem to blemish his later years were 'but short tempests or rather small overcastings during the glorious calm of his government.'[7] We are still a long way from the bloody tyrant of later authors.

This attitude was maintained by all the more discriminating writers throughout the seventeenth century. Neither the volume nor the quality of seventeenth-century writing on the Yorkists is at all impressive. Nothing appeared in any way comparable to the erudition of Dr Brady on the Norman Conquest or Fabian Philipps on feudalism. The Yorkist period had little attraction for contemporary controversialists, for its incidents had little to add to their store of arguments and they were bewildered by the source materials. At the end of the century William Nicolson, a judicious critic, summed up the position admirably when he stated that historians were too perplexed 'to form a regular History out of such a vast Heap of

[4] *The English Works of Sir Thomas More* ed. W. E. Campbell (1931) I 35–6. *Three Books of Polydore Vergil's English History* ed. Sir Henry Ellis, Camden Society (1844) 172.

[5] Hall, *Chronicle* (1809) 341. Grafton, *Chronicle* (1809) II 79–80. Holinshed, *Chronicles* (1807–8) III 360–1. Stow, *Annales of England* (1631) 434–5.

[6] *DNB*.

[7] W. Habington, from White Kennett's edition of *The Complete History of England* (1706) 444, 469, 478–9.

Rubbish and Confusion' and took the safe, if unenterprising, course of recommending Habington's book.[8] Yet it is important to note that both Habington and these seventeenth-century authors[9] had one common characteristic. This was reliance on the *Mémoires* of Philippe de Commynes for details of their narrative at certain points, coupled with a marked reluctance to accept his conclusions on the character of late fifteenth-century England in general, and of Edward IV in particular.

With the eighteenth century there came a new turn both in the historians' knowledge of the late fifteenth century and in their attitude towards it. Unfortunately for strict historical truth, the new attitude was not based on the new knowledge. The points at issue are best illustrated from two eighteenth-century 'best sellers', Rapin and Hume.

Rapin's *History of England* was first published, in French, in 1723 and translated in 1725. It went through seven editions before it was superseded in popular esteem by the shorter *History* published by David Hume in 1761.[10] Rapin's narrative of the late fifteenth century was a great advance on anything which had so far appeared. During the years when Rapin was planning his work Rymer was publishing his selections from the public records.[11] Working from the *Foedera*, Rapin was able to establish for the first time an accurate chronological basis for the events of the late fifteenth century. Yet most of the corrections which he made were after all minor corrections of detail. In his attitude to those sources of information which were likely to influence his final estimates of character, Rapin's methods showed no advance over those of his predecessors. In fact he was much less cautious than they had been and he accepted Commynes's verdict completely. Following Commynes he asserted that Edward's life was one long continued scene of lust, stained by avarice due to the heavy cost of his pleasures and by the wanton cruelty of a large number of needless political executions.[12] Rapin's book was a turning point. Under the disguise of a more detailed and accurate scholarship it placed greater reliance than ever before on an untrustworthy authority. Rapin was measured in his language. Hume dropped all qualifications and 'improved' on him at every point.[13]

Commynes's *Mémoires*, which are incomparably more vivid and richer in detail than any other contemporary narrative, have always strongly attracted historians of the late fifteenth century. Yet until the last few years

---

[8] W. Nicolson, *The English Historical Library* (1696–9) 83.

[9] Lack of space makes it impossible to give references to the numerous seventeenth-century authors whose works have been consulted for this section.

[10] *DNB*.

[11] *DNB*.

[12] Rapin de Thoyras, *The History of England* (2nd edn 1732) 1607, 624, 627–8.

[13] D. Hume, *The History of England from the Invasion of Julius Caesar to the Accession of Henry VII* (1761) II 418.

discussion of Commynes, as an authority for English history at least, has been appreciative rather than critical. C. A. J. Armstrong has convincingly shown how unreliable Commynes is when he discusses English internal affairs. He points out that Commynes himself stressed his ignorance of English affairs, and his work is in fact full of inaccuracies.[14] To his mistakes of fact he added a gift for distortion which has done even more than his ignorance to create the modern legend of Edward IV. His desire to show that Louis XI stood far above any other prince of his time in shrewdness and statecraft led him consistently to write down the abilities of contemporaries until they become of stature small enough to serve as foils for the king of France. Edward, like Charles the bold and the emperor, also fellow sufferers, came badly out of this process of denigration. He became a king who indulged himself so continually in debaucheries that he thoroughly merited the political disasters which came upon him towards the end of the 1460s. All the rest of the legend is there too—cruelty, avarice, neglect of busines in times of security, and lack of energy and decision in times of danger.[15]

Thus, Commynes's slanders, sceptically treated by seventeenth-century writers, had become well established by the middle of the eighteenth century. Nineteenth-century historians accepted them almost without reserve, Stubbs, in addition allowed his ideas of a Lancastrian constitutional experiment to lead him into an equally untenable theory of tyranny and constitutional backsliding on the part of the Yorkists.[16] Others were content to follow and exaggerate where he had led.[17] It would be mistaken to condemn their attitude. Commynes's statements could only be tested against detailed research into contemporary institutions based on the public records and such studies of fifteenth-century institutions had hardly begun when their works were written.[18] Even so, this atmosphere of condemnation did not pass without challenge. As long ago as the 1870s, when J. R. Green formulated his famous theory of the 'New Monarchy', he surmised that Edward was a king of iron will and great fixity of purpose.[19] Others have since taken up the idea though with little more than suggestions as to the way in which the verdict should be modified.[20]

[14] The Usurpation of Richard III ed. C. A. J. Armstrong (1936) 53. See also P. de Commynes, Mémoires ed. J. Calmette and G. Durville (1924–5) I 203, 206, 214–17; II 334.

[15] Commynes, op. cit. I 203; II 5, 153–8, 239–40, 334.

[16] W. Stubbs, The Constitutional History of England (1878) III 194, 275–6. S. B. Chrimes, English Constitutional Ideas in the Fifteenth Century (1936) pp. xvi–xvii.

[17] Sir J. H. Ramsay, Lancaster and York (1892) II 269 and n. 2. C. Oman, The Political History of England IV (1910) 450–2.

[18] C. L. Scofield's Life and Reign of Edward IV (2 vols 1923), an exhaustive narrative history based largely on records, treats the development of institutions only very superficially.

[19] J. R. Green, History of the English People II (1878) bk v, and especially 27–8. See also J. D. Mackie, The Earlier Tudors, 1485–1558 (1952) 6.

[20] L. B. Stratford, Edward IV (1910). K. H. Vickers, England in the Later Middle Ages (1913) 460–3, 481–2, 486. A. R. Myers, England in the Late Middle Ages (1952) 181 ff.

2 The character of Edward IV: a revision

Let us now deal with some of Edward's activities as recorded in contemporary sources. Only a very small selection of the evidence for dealing with Edward's work and character can be reviewed here, for it would be quite possible to pile up page after page of detail in cumulative demonstration of the points baldly set out in the following account.

John Warkworth, the contemporary master of Peterhouse, in the *Chronicle* attributed to him and written some time after 1478, makes it quite clear that by 1469 Yorkist government was so unsuccessful that it was as discredited as Lancastrian government had been ten years before.[21] Yet during the next decade opinion completely changed. Two historians who wrote shortly after Edward's death, Dominic Mancini and the Second Anonymous Croyland Continuator, held very different opinions about later developments. Both give the impression that, in spite of his debaucheries, Edward applied himself closely to government business and that he was well advised by experienced councillors. The Croyland Continuator more particularly stresses his wealth, his attention to financial detail and the secure position which he achieved towards the end of his reign when, he says, the king was held in dread by all his subjects and 'by glory and tranquility' had 'made himself illustrious'.[22]

Public order was one of the main problems facing the Yorkists and soon after his accession Edward had to take vigorous measures to put down disorder in Norfolk. The Tuddenham-Heydon gang, which had grown up under the protection of Henry VI's minister, the duke of Suffolk, and afterwards of Lord Moleyns, rioted unchecked. Tuddenham had been treasurer of Henry's household and Daniel, another prominent member of the affinity, a squire of the body,[23] and consequently there had been little hope of redress from the central government. After the political crisis of 1460–61 had brought the chronic disorder to a head,[24] the more peaceful elements in East Anglia could think of no other remedy than an appeal to the king.[25] Whether a petition was actually sent or not Edward was well-informed of the state of affairs there. His solution was to appoint as sheriff one of his most trusted household officers. The new sheriff, Sir Thomas Montgomery, accompanied by William Yelverton, went down to the country after Montgomery's appointment. Yelverton, Margaret Paston wrote

[21] J. Warkworth, *A Chronicle of the First Thirteen Years of the Reign of King Edward the Fourth* ed. J. O. Halliwell, Camden Society (1839) 12.
[22] *Usurpation of Richard III, op. cit.* 75–85. 'Historiae Croylandensis Continuatio', in Fulman 559–60, 564.
[23] Wedgwood, *Biographies* 880–1, 253–5.
[24] See *Paston Letters* II 3–4, 11–12, 20–7, 32, 35–6, 47–8, 57, 60. C. H. Williams, 'A Norfolk Parliamentary Election, 1461' *English Historical Review* XL (1925) 79–86.
[25] *Paston Letters* II 22.

'seyd opynly in the Seschyons they to come downe for the same cause to set a rewyll in the contre. And yet he seyd he woste well that the Kynge myth full evyll have for bor ony of hem bothe; for as for a knyth ther was none in the Kyngys howse that myth werse a be for bore than the Scheryfe myth at that tyme.'[26] Not only had Edward sent a servant whom he could ill spare from the pressing problems of the central government, but he had had a long discussion on East Anglian affairs with Yelverton and Montgomery before they left and discussed with them the best means of restoring order.[27]

High Lancastrian officials had also been involved in piracy in the south-west. Once again Edward took action where his predecessor's administration had been corrupt. In this case, however, success was delayed and it was not until 1474 that the piracy of the western ports was successfully put down.[28] It is possible by the collection of scattered evidence to show that this kind of activity was not confined to the two areas of East Anglia and the south-west. It was exerted as and where it was necessary. In 1464, Edward seems to have gone on an extended judicial progress which took him to such widely separated districts as Gloucestershire, Cambridgeshire, Kent and Yorkshire.[29] In later years the same kind of thing continued. The demobilization after the French campaign of 1475 produced such a crop of unrest and disorder, particularly in Hampshire, Wiltshire, Wales, the Marches and Yorkshire, that Edward personally took his justices to some of the disturbed districts, sent Gloucester to others, and spared no one, not even his own servants, if they were guilty of theft or homicide.[30]

References in town records tell the same story. Nowhere on the evidence available does the royal supervision of a town's activities seem to have been so pronounced as at Coventry. From 5 March 1461, the day after his accession, when the city authorities received their first letter under Edward's signet, to the end of the reign, they received a stream of signs manual, signet letters and privy seals inquiring into and directing their affairs.[31] The city authorities were trained to order by a series of admonitions over 20 years. An incident of 1480 shows how well they had learned their lesson. When Sir Thomas Everyngham sent one of his servants to Coventry to retain men to go with him to Burgundy to fight for the emperor Maximilian,

[26] *Paston Letters* I 179.

[27] *Paston Letters* I 179; II 75–7.

[28] C. L. Kingsford, *Prejudice and Promise in Fifteenth Century England* (1925) 78–106. E. Power and M. M. Postan, *Studies in English Trade in the Fifteenth Century* (1933) 122–9.

[29] Scofield, *Edward IV* I 318–19. Issue Roll E. 403/836, 17 June. Warrants for Issues E. 404/74/2/28. *Paston Letters* II 150–1; Supplement to introduction, 84.

[30] Fulman 559. BM Cottonian MS. Vespasian CXIV f 572. *Cal. Pat. Rolls 1467–77*, 574. R. Davies, *York Records* (1843) 50–52.

[31] *The Coventry Leet Book* ed. M. D. Harris, EETS (1907–13) 314, 315, 319–20, 322–8, 340–3, 345–6, 353–4, 373–5, 381 n. 1, 402–5, 408–13, 420–5, 475–7.

the city authorities dared not assist him because he had no written authority from the king. The mayor therefore wrote to Earl Ryvers and other members of the royal council for instructions. The king himself replied by a signet letter within three days saying that the scheme had his full approval.[32]

The history of the provincial councils, the prince of Wales's council in the marches and the council in the north under Richard of Gloucester, and their revival by the Tudors, is too well known to need much comment here.[33] The prince of Wales's council, however, seems to have exercised jurisdiction over a much wider area than is generally realized. On more than one occasion we even find it intervening in the affairs of a city as far east as Coventry,[34] (Coventry always seemed to attract attention).

Nor is evidence of financial activity lacking although it is incomplete and extremely difficult to interpret. It is generally stated that by private trading and economical administration, assisted after 1475 by his French pension and the revival of trade which swelled the customs receipts, Edward died a rich man.[35]

Steel's analysis of the exchequer receipt rolls has shown that it is improbable that a definitive verdict on Yorkist finance can ever be given.[36] During the first half of the fifteenth century the rolls give a fairly reliable general picture of the trends of government finance. In the 1450s their character rapidly changed. From this time onwards important sources of revenue came, in whole or in part, to be habitually omitted from them. Under Edward IV most of the benevolences were left out, so was a large proportion of the French pension after 1475, a good deal of the profit of Edward's trading ventures, the Calais customs from 1466, certain parliamentary grants and the revenues from some estates.[37]

If the evidence of these receipt rolls were to be accepted at face value we should have to agree with Steel that 'the Yorkist kings were always even worse off than Henry VI had ever been . . . and yet we know that this conclusion is absolutely untrue.'[38] The receipt rolls in fact by this time have ceased to be a useful index to the state of the crown finances and as, Steel says, for many terms and even years it is difficult to say what if anything they really do mean.[39]

[32] *Coventry Leet Book, op. cit.* 426–8.

[33] C. A. J. Skeel, *The Council in the Marches of Wales* (1904) 1–30. R. R. Reid, *The King's Council in the North* (1921) 41–7.

[34] *Coventry Leet Book, op. cit.* 430–43, 484–501, 504–11.

[35] See Ramsay, *Lancaster and York, op. cit.* II 457–68. For trading ventures, Scofield, *op. cit.* II 404–16. E. Power, *Cambridge Historical Journal* II 21–2.

[36] A. Steel, *The Receipt of the Exchequer, 1377–1485* (1954) chs 8, 9 and conclusion.

[37] Steel, *op. cit.* 300 ff., 326 n. 1, 354 and n. 1. See also below p. 166 and n. 46.

[38] Steel, *op. cit.* 324, 355.

[39] Steel, *op. cit.* 322–3.

As the receipt rolls are proved to be misleading we must turn to other evidence for indications of the trend of crown finance. This can be done fairly safely by examining Edward's relationships with some of his main creditors—the Florentine Caniziani, the city of London, and above all the merchants of the Staple. In each case, if our evidence reveals the full story, the decline of the royal debt in Edward's later years is very striking.

In 1471 the King owed Caniziani £14,391 7s. 8d; in 1476 Caniziani agreed that £3,000 would be enough to pay off all outstanding items and payment was made in three instalments.[40] In 1478 Edward took steps to liquidate his debt to London, which then stood at £12,923 9s. 8d. It was arranged that the revenue of various offices should be assigned until the whole sum was repaid.[41] The king's most important creditor was undoubtedly the Staple, and the Staple loans were mainly though by no means exclusively connected with the administration of Calais. Only these Calais loans will be dealt with here. In the 1450s the garrison at Calais was unpaid and mutinous,[42] which in view of the arrears of wages due is hardly a matter for surprise. Henry VI's government had owed over £37,000 in Calais.[43] The arrangement made under the first act of retainer in 1466, under which a debt of £32,861 was to be paid off and the Staple was to take over financial responsibility for Calais, very soon broke down owing to the outbreak of war in the Netherlands, with its consequent interruption to trade and loss of customs revenue. When the act was redrafted in its final form in 1473, arrangements for repayment at last worked smoothly. The royal debt was steadily reduced according to plan, until at the time of Edward's death it stood at only £2,616 0s. 10d.[44]

What the exchequer lost it is possible that the chamber in part gained. During the period of Henry VI's personal rule the chamber had been insignificant in national finance. In some years its known receipts were less than £800. Apart from the year 1444–5, when it received over £6,000 to meet the expenses of the king's marriage, its highest receipts were in 1455–6, totalling £1,957 16s. 8d.[45] By contrast the Yorkist chamber became very prominent. Although its income fluctuated violently, it is known to have received from the exchequer over £21,000 in one half year of very heavy expenditure and the figures are probably incomplete.[46] As no chamber records have survived we have no means of calculating its income

[40] Scofield, op. cit. II 215 and n. 5, 421–5. Warrants for Issues E. 404/75/3/64.
[41] Scofield, op. cit. I 89–91, 118, II 215 and n. 6.
[42] W. I. Haward, in Power and Postan, Studies in English Trade, op. cit. 301–7.
[43] Scofield, op. cit. I 298 and n. 3.
[44] Rot. Parl. v 613–16; VI 55–61. Warrants for Issues E. 404/74/1/9, E. 404/77/3/79, E. 404/78/2/65.
[45] I am indebted to G. L. Harriss for this information about Henry VI's chamber.
[46] Calculated from Issue Roll E. 403/844, Easter Term 2 Edward IV.

from non-exchequer sources, though it must have been far from inconsiderable. From 1461, the revenues of some, probably all, of the hereditary Yorkist lands and possibly those of certain other estates were paid into the chamber and their receivers-general accounted to the treasurer of the chamber.[47] Even without allowing for its income from non-exchequer sources, it is obvious that the chamber was one of the chief spending departments and it had once again become an auditing department. In his use of the chamber Henry VII was certainly drawing on Yorkist experience.

It has been surmised that Henry VII based other financial reforms on a memorandum, never put into effect, drawn up for Richard III in 1484.[48] In fact some practices common to both can be detected earlier. For example, under Edward IV the treasurer and barons of the exchequer were already merely custodians of some accounts audited elsewhere,[49] and this part was allotted to them for certain accounts in both Richard's memorandum and under Henry VII. Too little is yet known, however, of the details of Edward's financial administration or Henry's exchequer reforms for us to be certain of the extent to which one was indebted to the other.[50]

Contemporaries and sixteenth-century writers believed that Edward IV was a careful administrator, and careful, even harsh, in enforcing his rights.[51] They also believed that in his later years he was rich. His household and the household finances covered by the wardrobe organization were drastically reformed in 1478.[52] The king applied a much stricter supervision over the distribution of local offices. In 1475 Godfrey Greene was constrained to assure a hard-headed businessman like Sir William Plumpton that requests for local offices were being much more closely scrutinized than ever before.[53]

In view of the importance of revenue from lands and customs in the early Tudor budget,[54] Yorkist action in such matters may well have considerable significance. Although general inquiries into feudal tenures had been

---

[47] e.g. KR Mem. Roll E. 159/259 Brevia Directa Hilary Term m. iijd.

[48] *Letters and Papers Illustrative of the Reigns of Richard III and Henry VII* ed. J. Gairdner, Rolls Series (1861–3) I 81–5. A. P. Newton, 'The King's Chamber under the Early Tudors', *English Historical Review*, XXXII 350–3.

[49] e.g. KR Mem. Roll E. 159/254 Brevia Directa Easter Term m. iir. *Cal. Pat. Rolls, 1476–85*, 14, 213. KR Mem. Roll E. 159/259, Brevia Directa Michaelmas Term m. vjr. See also F. C. Dietz, *English Government Finance, 1485–1558* (1920) 66 n. 14.

[50] Steel, *op. cit.* 355 and n. 1. See also *Ministers' Accounts of the Warwickshire Estates of the Duke of Clarence, 1479–80* ed. R. H. Hilton, Dugdale Society (1952) pp. xxiii–xxiv.

[51] See below p. 168. n. 58.

[52] The Queen's College MS. 134. Scofield, *op. cit.* II 217, incorrectly states that this document has disappeared.

[53] *The Plumpton Correspondence* ed. T. Stapleton, Camden Society (1839) 33.

[54] Dietz, *English Government Finance, op. cit.* 21, 25.

going on more or less continuously under Henry VI,[55] they were probably ineffective as they are not known to have aroused any protest. Under Edward IV similar action was successful enough to be resented. The tentative beginnings at least of that strict inquiry into feudal tenures generally associated with the names of Empson and Dudley were made, not under Richard III, as Dr Brodie has claimed,[56] but under Edward IV. By 1474 commissions had already been issued covering ten counties and three cities, and others followed.[57] The Croyland Continuator referred to their effects and the Tudor chroniclers preserved a tradition of the heavy fines exacted in Edward's later years.[58] Though it is not possible to check these statements for the whole country, corroboratory evidence is to be found in a recent study of the duchy of Lancaster. R. Somerville has found evidence of 'an active and competent administration, and of an enterprising and reforming spirit' at work in the duchy. He has claimed that 'it is no disrespect to Henry VII's great qualities as a shrewd and careful administrator to say that he carried on and extended the work that had been developed under Edward IV.'[59] In particular in the last four or five years of Edward's reign 'there was intense activity over these feudal dues.'[60] Nor should it be forgotten that Empson during this period was gaining experience as attorney general of the duchy.[61]

Stricter methods of supervision and control were simultaneously being imposed on the customs system. By the beginning of 1481 an official called the surveyor had been reintroduced into 11 of the principal ports.[62] Such surveyors (who should not be confused with a minor official called the surveyor of the search) had only been sporadically appointed under Henry VI, and none seem to have been appointed after 1447.[63] The new surveyors were given almost absolute authority over existing officials and their importance is attested by their high pay. William Weston, who held office in the port of London, had the large salary of 100 marks a year and £10 for his clerk.[64] It does not seem rash to identify these new highly paid surveyors with those inspectors of customs whose appointment the Croyland Continuator made so much of, 'men of remarkable shrewdness but too hard

[55] Cal. Pat. Rolls, 1429–36, 275, 276, 425–6, 526; 1436–41, 269, 314–16, 368–9, 371, 413, 535, 574; 1441–6, 198, 203, 370; 1446–52, 138–40; 1452–61, 169, 225, 255–6, 305–6.

[56] D. M. Brodie, The Tree of Commonwealth (1948) 7.

[57] Cal. Pat. Rolls, 1461–7, 276, 553; 1476–77, 408–9, 427, 464; 1476–85, 543, 546.

[58] Fulman, op. cit. 559. Hall, Chronicle, op. cit. 329. Stow, Annales, op. cit. 431.

[59] R. Somerville, History of the Duchy of Lancaster I (1953) 255.

[60] Somerville, op. cit. 242–6.

[61] Somerville, op. cit. 392. See also 243 and 252 for his work.

[62] Cal. Pat. Rolls, 1467–77, 391–2; 1476–85, 101, 225, 231, 236.

[63] Cal. Pat. Rolls, 1436–41, 519–20, 545; 1446–52, 60, 81–2.

[64] Cal. Pat. Rolls, 1476–85, 225.

upon the merchants according to the general report.'[65]

The Croyland Continuator and the sixteenth-century writers were without doubt correct in believing that Edward was rich in his later years. As they were, however, unacquainted with the details of his finances, their views cannot unfortunately be taken as evidence of financial stability as well, which is after all a more important consideration than mere riches. On the evidence of the receipt rolls Steel believes that Edward's financial success was nothing more than a personal *tour de force* of a somewhat shady and shaky nature, and that at the time of his death it was already cracking. It is fair to remember, however, that Edward was in a good enough financial position to do without any parliamentary grant between 1475 and 1483. It was not until war with Scotland had already been going on for two years and the treaty of Arras between Louis XI and Maximilian made additional war preparations necessary that he called upon parliament for money in 1483.[66] In view of the admittedly inadequate and puzzling character of the receipt rolls and the loss of the vital chamber records we have no means of formulating an exact judgment, and it perhaps seems fair to leave the question open, while admitting that, although Edward could now get along well enough in time of peace, a war on two fronts would have caused serious financial difficulties.

What therefore is it safe to say about Edward IV's character and administration? Even to the more discerning of his contemporaries he was a somewhat enigmatic figure; a compound, perhaps less unusual than is often admitted, of dissipation and ability. His was an ability normal enough, using nothing but conventional medieval methods, and taking the form of a natural capacity for detail and a care in financial matters which his subjects termed avarice. It was this combination which so surprised and impressed the Croyland Continuator. He was astounded that a man given to fits of debauchery like Edward's 'should have had a memory so retentive in all respects that the names and estates used to recur to him just as though he had been in the habit of seeing them daily of all the persons, dispersed throughout the counties of his kingdom and this, even, if in the districts in which they lived they held the rank only of mere gentlemen.'[67]

His love of pleasure did not prevent a close application to work. The great increase in the amount of public business dealt with at this time under the signet and the sign manual is especially noteworthy.[68] Although he could be ruthless, as in the case of Clarence's execution, Edward was, as early writers claimed, generally merciful towards his enemies. Even so prominent a Lancastrian as Edward Ellesmere, who had been treasurer of

---

[65] Fulman 559.
[66] Steel, *op. cit.* 356–8. Scofield, *op. cit.* II 384.
[67] Fulman 564.
[68] J. Otway-Ruthven, *The King's Secretary and the Signet Office in the Fifteenth Century* (1939) 41.

the chamber and keeper of the jewels to Margaret of Anjou, was able to obtain a pardon and the restoration of some of his lands.[69]

Any attempt to estimate the degree to which Edward's methods were successful brings us on to more debatable ground, especially in matters of public order and financial stability. Official records of their very nature cannot be used either to confirm or deny the testimony of early writers that the state of public order greatly improved during Edward's later years. However, the contrast between the late fifteenth and the sixteenth century here, probably as elsewhere, has been far too strongly drawn. Until recently it has too often been assumed that bastard feudalism vanished under the Tudors. Henry VII did not suddenly suppress maintenance. Government pressure, among other things, gradually transformed it into the sixteenth-century clientage system, which at times bore such a strong resemblance to earlier conditions that one writer has alleged 'the survival of bastard feudalism far into the sixteenth century'.[70] We must reduce the contrast to its true proportions.

That Edward's work suffered during the troubled period which immediately followed his death was only to be expected. His time had been short for dealing with the manifold problems which faced him on his return to England in 1471. The margin between order and disorder was still small, as it remained for a long time to come, and it depended on the action of a strong king. Yet the opinions of contemporaries on this point and on his wealth, the evidence of his interest in the disturbed parts of his kingdom, the extensive use of the signet and sign manual, of the regional councils and the chamber, go far to confirm J. R. Green's guess that Edward was a king of iron will and great fixity of purpose. These factors are enough to warrant at least a challenge to the conventional view of his reign and to suggest that we may plausibly substitute for it the picture of a strong man who began to 'break the teeth of the sinners', to restore order and even possibly financial stability, and who made easier the work of Henry VII.[71]

[69] Wardrobe Books E. 101/410/11. *Rot. Parl.* V 477; VI 130–1. *Cal. Pat. Rolls, 1461–7*, 8, 270; *1467–77*, 344, 533.

[70] K. B. McFarlane, 'Bastard Feudalism', *Bulletin of the Institute of Historical Research* XX 178–80. See also C. H. Williams, *The Making of the Tudor Despotism* (1926) 177.

[71] Since this article was written, B. P. Wolffe has published the results of his investigations into Yorkist estate management. 'The Management of English Royal Estates under the Yorkist Kings', *English Historical Review* LXXI 1–27. This article shows that Edward IV was responsible for the policy of building up the royal estates and for the creation of the chamber system as the centre of estate administration, payment and audit for which Henry VII has generally been given credit. The system was extended under Richard III, who was receiving from it an income of £35,000 and an actual cash income of £25,000 per annum after the deduction of running costs and the payment of various pensions and annuities with which the estates were charged. The system actually began to disintegrate in Henry VII's early years, and it was reconstructed, on the advice of former Yorkist administrators, only after Henry had come to realize its value.

7

The Yorkist council
and administration, 1461–85[1]

The administrative history of the fifteenth century has received little attention until recent years and most of our notions about it must still be
regarded as provisional. Within the century itself no part of it has been so
much neglected as the period of the Yorkist kings.[2]

This is particularly true of the council. Although much research must
still be carried out on the history of the Lancastrian council before its position in government at various times can be accurately defined, it seems to
be accepted, broadly speaking, that it was an abnormal development due
to certain constitutional defects of which the greatest was the prolonged
weakness of the monarchy.[3] The theory of the Lancastrian council as the
balancing force between king and parliament[4] must follow the rest of the
Lancastrian constitutional experiment into oblivion. As a corollary we
must abandon as equally untenable any theory of tyranny or constitutional
backsliding on the part of the Yorkists, or of the Yorkist and early Tudor
council as a somewhat perverse deviation from established usage and from
the good example of the past.[5] The state of politics, not constitutional
theories and aspirations, is the real key to changes in the council in the
fifteenth century. Such changes had more political than immediate constitutional significance. If after 1461 the turn of politics brought to the

---

[1] I wish to thank A. L. Brown and R. L. Storey for criticism and advice on this paper.
[2] For a general survey see S. B. Chrimes, *An Introduction to the Administrative History of
Mediaeval England* (1952) 241–2. For Yorkist administration, J. Otway-Ruthven, *The King's
Secretary and The Signet Office in the Fifteenth Century* (1939), and B. P. Wolffe, 'The Manage-
ment of English Royal Estates Under the Yorkist Kings', *English Historical Review*, XXI 1–27.
[3] J. E. A. Joliffe, *The Constitutional History of Mediaeval England* (3rd edn. 1954), 472–3. For
Joliffe's account of the late fourteenth and fifteenth century council, *ibid.* 468–85, 490–1. In
his discussion of the Yorkist period Joliffe follows J. F. Baldwin, *The King's Council in England
During the Middle Ages* (1913). For the most detailed account of the Lancastrian council see
Baldwin, *op. cit.* 147–207.
[4] W. Stubbs, *The Constitutional History of England* (1878) III 252.
[5] S. B. Chrimes, *English Constitutional Ideas in the Fifteenth Century* (1936) pp. xvi–xvii.
Stubbs, *op. cit.* III 250, describes the council at this period as 'an irresponsible committee of
government, through the agency of which the constitutional changes of that period were
forced on the nation, were retarded or accelerated'.

throne a king of sufficient strength of mind and application to rule as well as reign, we should logically expect a change in the form and powers of the council[6]

The following pages will be mainly concerned with an analysis of the sources available for the study of the Yorkist council and with the problems involved in their use, though incidentally the council's part in administration will also appear.[7]

The greater part of the material extant[8] for the history of the council during the years 1461–85 is indirect and casual in nature. Nothing comparable to John Prophet's *Journal*, or to the collection of conciliar records such as we have for parts of the Lancastrian period in Nicolas's *Proceedings and Ordinances of the Privy Council* is available to show the discussions of the Yorkist council. There are a few references in chronicles and collections of correspondence both English and foreign. Evidence from such sources, however, is small in volume though not perhaps in significance, when compared with the details which a search of the records of the central administration yields.[9]

It must be admitted that the number of references in any particular class of records is limited. Yet collected they reveal more about the position of the council in government than we should expect at first sight. As Scofield long ago pointed out, though her words have generally been ignored, 'in spite of the almost complete lack of council records of Edward's reign, there is plenty of evidence that the council met frequently while he was king.'[10]

This evidence has somewhat narrow limitations. It may indicate that at some particular time some particular decision was taken by the king and

[6] See above ch. 6. Both Edward IV and Richard III were vigorous personalities who applied themselves assiduously to government.

[7] See also below ch. 8.

[8] In addition to the documents in the files of Chancery Warrants and the Council and Privy Seal files references have been found in the following: Patent, Close, Treaty and Fine Rolls, Warrants to the Privy Seal, Signet Warrants, Signed Bills, Issue, Tellers' and Memoranda Rolls (KR and LTR), Warrants for Issues. There are also references in various less important classes in the Public Record Office. There is also scattered material amongst the Cottonian, Harleian and Landsdowne MSS. In particular Harleian MS. 433 gives valuable information for the reigns of Edward V and Richard III. The entries relating to Edward V's reign were printed by J. G. Nichols, as *Grants of King Edward V*, Camden Society (1854). J. Gairdner published a few documents from Richard III's time in *Letters and Papers Illustrative of the Reigns of Richard III and Henry VII*, Rolls Series (1861–3). For discussions on the nature of Harleian MS. 433, see Sir H. Maxwell-Lyte, *Historical Notes on the Use of the Great Seal of England* (1926) 27–8 and J. Otway-Ruthven, *The King's Secretary, op. cit.* 117 n. 3, 118 n. 1.

[9] See note 8 above.

[10] Scofield, *The Life and Reign of Edward IV* (1923) II 374. This book is, in fact, a mine of evidence on the council. Unfortunately, this is concealed as it is most inadequately indexed for institutions. A careful reading of the book reveals example upon example of conciliar activity.

council or by the council alone. It can even reveal periods of intense conciliar activity. Yet, although we are informed of numerous decisions which
the council took or assisted in taking, in most cases we are ignorant of the
deliberations which preceded these decisions. It gives only very uncertain
indications of the size of the council at any particular time, of divisions of
opinion at its meeting, and of the relative influence of different councillors.

A much more fundamental difficulty is to decide from the surviving
evidence on the nature of conciliar activity. It has already been noted that,
for the Yorkist period, there is no collection of conciliar records comparable to the *Proceedings and Ordinances*. Nicolas thought that records
similar to those which he published had once existed but had been lost.[11]
Baldwin took the opposite view. While admitting the possibility of accidental loss, and further admitting that Tudor writers, such as Sir Julius Caesar,
were familiar with documents now unknown, on balance he attributed the
diminution in the volume of records to 'a failure in the operations of the
council itself' especially in the years immediately following the revolution
of 1460–61. He pointed out that the number of documents in the single file
of council warrants and in the council and privy seal files (the classes of
documents issued directly by the council) is much smaller after 1461 than
during the preceding years. Using a limited selection of collateral sources
he found that references to the council in these are also much fewer.[12] From
this and from the fact that no new statutes were framed by the council or
entrusted to it for execution,[13] and that grants of the crown were generally
made on the king's authority[14] he deduced a great recession of conciliar activity in administrative matters.

Baldwin held that it was Edward's intention, departing both from certain Lancastrian precedents and from the policy pursued by his father
between 1453 and 1455, to maintain a council composed mainly of
officials. He thought that Edward was successful in so far as the composition
of his council was concerned, but that this very change left its activities

[11] *Proceedings and Ordinances* VII p. iii.

[12] Baldwin, *op. cit.* 420–6. The collateral sources which Baldwin used were the Parliament
and Statute Rolls, the *Calendars of Patent Rolls*, the Issue Rolls, Warrants for Issues and Early
Chancery Proceedings. It is true that he had closely examined these classes of documents
over a long period and that such comparative evidence should not be lightly disregarded.
On the other hand, as will be seen below, pp. 181 ff, this selection is far too limited par-
ticularly in view of the increased importance of the sign manual and the signet at this time.
Plucknett also thought that its administrative activities were curtailed but in view of the
slender evidence in the Council and Privy Seal files expressed himself more cautiously. T. F.
T. Plucknett, 'The Place of the Council in the Fifteenth Century', *Transactions of the Royal
Historical Society* 4th Series I (1918) 185–6.

[13] Baldwin, *op. cit.* 426. This is not true. The council was certainly concerned with the
preparation of acts of parliament and although new statutes did not specifically give the
council executive powers it certainly exercised them. e.g. *Cal. Close Rolls, 1468–1476*, 238–9.

[14] Baldwin, *op. cit.* 426.

much reduced in face of a more vigorous, personal exercise of authority.[15] Although Baldwin was careful to admit that the deliberative functions of the council may have been of more weight than was revealed by the bare statements of the selection of documents which he examined.[16] The impression given by his account remains that the Yorkist period was dominated administratively by the personal action of the king—the implication being at the expense of the council.

Objections to these opinions were registered as soon as Baldwin's book appeared, but have never been followed up with detailed evidence. Tout, when reviewing the book, pertinently asked whether it was safe to argue the reduced activity of the Yorkist council from such entirely negative evidence as Baldwin relied upon. Baldwin himself had pointed out that the council was under no obligation to record its actions. It did so from time to time only when a record was found useful.[17] Any notes that were made were generally brief, and little care was taken to preserve them once their period of immediate utility was past. Tout asserted that we have no real documents of the council preserved until the reign of Henry VIII, and that there no longer survives any special *fonds* of council records for 'such acts as have survived owe their existence to the fact that they were preserved in the archives of the two great record-preserving departments, the chancery and the exchequer'.[18] In other words, there has survived among the records of the central government only those documents which initiated action in other departments,[19] and as we shall see later even this selection is probably incomplete.

Tout also pointed out in the same review that the essential function of the council was not to act but to give advice. The council might give any advice and the king might or might not take it, but before Tudor times at least the executive measures necessary to carry it out generally involved a mandate from one of the secretarial offices (the signet office, the privy seal office and the chancery) or from the exchequer.[20]

This view of the position is certainly exaggerated. Without going into the matter in detail it seems reasonable to assert that although the council could act in an executive capacity its executive activities fluctuated while its

---

[15] Baldwin, *op. cit.* 421–5.

[16] *ibid.* 428.

[17] *ibid.* 374, 392–4.

[18] *English Historical Review*, XXX 117–23; reprinted in *Collected Papers of Thomas Frederick Tout* (1932) I 190–98. Baldwin himself admitted this. He stated that the council recorded its actions 'only so far as the utility of the moment required.' Baldwin, *op. cit.* 374. If I read Tout rightly, however, he thought that Baldwin did not always keep this sufficiently in mind.

[19] Tout, *Collected Papers, op. cit.* I 195.

[20] *ibid.* 192.

advisory activities remained more constant.[21] As medieval government was personal government the forms and functions of the council were highly mutable and ultimately depended on the part the king allotted to it or at least on his acquiescence. It is a likely assumption that the form of executive action taken, after business had been discussed at a council meeting, would vary with a number of factors. These would include the interests and business capacities of the king, his presence in or absence from the realm and the strength of organized opposition to his policies.

Under Edward IV conditions were hardly such as to favour independent action on the part of his council. Before 1467 (the turning point in their careers) the influence of Warwick and the Nevilles though exceedingly strong was from time to time successfully resisted by other groups. With their disappearance in 1471 the field was left clear for the king. Edward, except in 1470–71 and a few weeks in 1475, was continuously present in the realm and, in spite of his debaucheries, he showed a marked application to the business of government.[22] We might therefore expect the king to be responsible for action which some years earlier the council might have initiated.

We have now to examine the record material for the Yorkist council with this background in mind. The following questions then arise. Is it possible to show (1) that there have been losses from the council warrants and council and privy seal files; (2) that collateral sources, such as enrolments, do not show the full extent of the council's participation in the decisions recorded there, owing partly to the practice not uncommon in the secretarial offices of failing to note the entire contents of their warrants; and (3) that parallel to the changed position of the monarchy there was a change in the form of executive action by which, after important matters had been discussed in the council, directions were more frequently issued under the sign manual and signet, instead of under direct warrants from the council to the chancellor or to the keeper of the privy seal, authorizing them to use the deals under their control?

(1) For the whole of the Yorkist period there is only one file of direct warrants from the council to the chancellor for the issue of letters patent

[21] Chrimes, *Administrative History, op. cit.* 163, thinks that Tout's arguments are based too much on 'the subsidiary question of whether the council could use a seal'. Tout himself later adopted the view that the council was at times an executive body. See his discussion of the council under Richard II's personal rule, *Chapters in the Administrative History of Mediaeval England* III (1928) 465–75. Nevertheless in his latest expression of opinion he once more stressed that the essential nature of the council was consultative and advisory not executive. *ibid.* V (1930) 61. For the fourteenth century see B. Wilkinson, *Studies in the Constitutional History of the Fourteenth and Fifteenth Centuries* (2nd edn 1952) especially 129–33. W. A. Morris in Willard and Morris, *The English Government at Work, 1327 to 1336* I (1940). For Baldwin's views, which at this point seem not to be explicit but only implied, see Baldwin, *op. cit.* 129–61.

[22] See above ch. 6 pp. 163–70.

under the great seal.[23] It should be mentioned here that the chancery seems to have found great difficulty in noting warrants exactly and its practice was always somewhat inconsistent.[24] These notes of warranty are never therefore completely reliable for determining the exact nature of the part played by the king and the council respectively. We can with few exceptions, however, say that the council played a prominent part in making the decision recorded in any enrolment warranted *Per Consilium* or *Per Regem et Consilium*. Although only a proportion of such enrolments (varying at different periods) originated in written warrants,[25] these written warrants if they exist should normally be found in the files of council warrants. Documents warranted *Per Regem*, however, as we shall see, require a much more cautious approach for such a note of warranty by no means eliminates the possibility of conciliar action.

With these reservations in mind we can now proceed to an examination of such enrolments for the Yorkist period and a comparison of the enrolments with the surviving file of council warrants. This file[26] contains only 14 documents. It has been possible to trace 11 resulting enrolments. The appended notes of warranty vary considerably.[27]

Of immediate interest here, however, are enrolments warranted *Per ipsum Regem et Consilium* and *Per Consilium*. Of 61 which have been found on the *Calendars of Patent* and *Close Rolls*, the treaty rolls and the Scottish rolls, only 6 are backed by warrants in the file.[28] Seven other warrants have, however, been found in other classes of records of which 5 may possibly,

---

[23] C. 81/1547.

[24] Maxwell-Lyte, *Use of the Great Seal, op. cit.* 181-4. H. Maxwell-Lyte has pointed out how the chancery clerks sometimes in the note of warranty to an enrolment, credited the king with a share in warranting instruments which had really been passed by the council only, or, alternatively they sometimes added the note of warranty *Per Consilium* to an instrument of the king to which the council had merely made some alteration. Moreover, different documents covering the same case issued after the same meeting of the council, and enrolled on different rolls could bear different notes of warranty. *ibid.* and the example cited on 182.

[25] *ibid.* 182.

[26] C.81/1457.

[27] See note 28 below.

[28] *Cal. Pat. Rolls*, 4 warranted *By K. and C., 35 By C. 1461-1467*, 34 (2), 65, 98, 201 (2), 201-2, 203, 204, 205, 229, 231; *By K. and C. 1467-1477*, 259, 285, 366; *By K. and C.* 474, 493 (2); *1476-1485*, 60, 145, 264, 313, 320, 321, 321-2; *By K. and C.* 355, 356, 446, 447, 453 (2), 457 (2), 493 (2), 494. Three based on warrants in the file are: *Cal. Pat. Rolls, 1461-1467*, 262; *By K. and C. 1467-1477*, 259; *By K. and C.* 544; *By K. and C.* The warrants in the file are unnumbered. Date references are, 26 March, 3 Ed. IV, 27 April, 11 Ed. IV, 7 September, 15 Ed. IV. On *Cal. Pat. Rolls, 1461-1467*, 204, 7 other documents were to be issued on the same lines and on *Cal. Pat. Rolls, 1476-1485*, 320, another 20 which would if counted separately bring up the total *By C.* to 31 and the total of both to 65. *Cal. Close Rolls*, two *By K. and C.*, one

though not certainly, be described as misplaced.[29] Three of these resulted in enrolments *By K. and C.* and three *By K.* Thus we have a grand total of 61[30] enrolments only 12 of which are backed by surviving warrants. Such a ratio (5 to 1) would indicate either very considerable verbal communication between council and chancery or losses from the file of warrants or both. The state of the file suggests that losses are not improbable.

Conciliar memoranda as distinct from warrants to secretarial offices are very rare indeed at this time. There are only three such memoranda on the file. One of these dealing with parliament is discussed below.[31] Another dating from September 1469, shows that the council in London decided to send Lord Ferrers to south Wales 'for the sueretie and defence thereof and resistence and repressing of the Kinges enemyes and rebelles in cas they wolde presume or take upon thaim to arrive there'. The council decided that the chancellor should make out a commission for Lord Ferrers authorizing him to call on the sheriffs of Gloucester, Worcester and Hereford for help.[32] The result was a commission of array enrolled on the

---

By C. 1461–1468, 424, *By K. and C.* with one more of the same type; *1468–1475*, 299. The only one based on a warrant in the file is *Cal. Close Rolls, 1461–1468*, 424, File reference, 17 November, 7 Ed. IV. Treaty Rolls C. 76/146 m. 2, C. 76/147 m. 3 and 9, C. 76/149, m. 18 (*Foedera* XI 543–5) c. 76/151 m. 5, C. 76/152 m. 23 (*Foedera* XI 618–24) C. 76/159 m. 6 (all *Per ipsum Regem et Consilium*); C. 76/160 m. 10 (*Foedera* XII 29–30) C. 76/164 m. 5, C. 76/168 m. 12, C. 76/169 m. 2 (all *Per Consilium*). There are no surviving warrants. C. 76/147 m. 9, is followed by another document on the same lines and C. 76/149 m. 18, by two more, thus bringing the total up to 10. *Rot. Scot.*, 6 warranted *Per Regem et Consilium* and two *Per Consilium*, II 415 (2), 417, 418, 423, 442 (all *Per Regem et Consilium*), 451 and 452 (both *Per Consilium*). Those based on warrants, 423, 442. File references, 18 July, 10 Ed. IV and 14 July, 15 Ed. IV. (The latter wrongly dated in *Rot. Scot.* II 442.)

[29] I am aware that it is not possible in every case to contend that a document is misplaced because it is not in the series of files where an investigator expects to find it. But in five cases here misplacement seems undoubted. The three warrants resulting in enrolments *By K. and C.* are among the Signed Bills, although none of them bears the sign manual and they all have endorsements similar to the documents in the Council Warrants file. Signed Bills C. 81/1493/21 and 22; C. 81/1502/22. Treaty Roll C. 76/155 ms. 7 and 9. *Cal. Pat. Rolls, 1467–1477*, 259. The other three enrolments are warranted by *K.* C. 81/1502/50 is a warrant confirming the act of retainer, enrolled *Cal. Pat. Rolls, 1467–1477*, 270, does not bear the sign manual but bears the statement that it was passed by the king on the council's advice and gives a list of councillors present. The king himself was present at this meeting and this may be the reason why the enrolment is *By K.* C. 81/1508/21 and C. 81/1530/49 (enrolments printed *Foedera* XI 814; XII 231) are commissions for embassies. Both bear the familiar conciliar endorsement and the sign manual. Diplomatically they might be put quite legitimately in either the Council Warrants file or the Signed Bills file. They are noteworthy as showing that matters agreed before the council went to the king. The fifth warrant is described on a paper slip between the sixth and seventh document in the Council Warrants file. It is dated 18 March 1468, ordering an exemplification of letters patent to Louis XI. It is now in Chancery Misc. Box 30/10/23. No enrolment has been traced.

[30] 91 if various examples of stock forms are included.

[31] Below p. 185 n. 63.

[32] Council Warrants C. 81/1547, 12 September, 9 Ed. IV.

patent roll under the date of the following day. The text of the commission does not mention the council nor is a note of warranty appended.[33] Possibly no formal warrant was required in this case because the chancellor had been present at the meeting at which the decision was taken and the memorandum made.

Whether such practice was normal or abnormal it is impossible to say,[34] but the council certainly authorized the chancellor on its own authority to use the great seal on occasions for which no warrants have survived and no mention of the fact is found on enrolments. It is equally difficult to determine the extent to which it directly authorized the use of the privy seal. The history of the privy seal records has been calamitous. They have suffered losses by theft and fire among other things and 'rearrangement' at the hands of eighteenth-century 'methodisers'.[35] The gaps in the series of signs manual and signet bills sent to the privy seal office known as the warrants to the privy seal (PSO 1) are very great.[36] The council and privy seal files (E. 28) present more complicated problems. This title, accurate enough for earlier years, is misleading for the four files for Edward IV's reign. (There are none for Edward V and Richard III.) As the files stand at present they seem to be the miscellaneous rag-bag of the privy seal office containing a variety of documents, of which 70 per cent bear the sign manual, mostly petitions with a few drafts of indentures. These two classes of documents together with the warrants for issues (E. 404) were in fact amalgamated during the eighteenth century,[37] and it may be suspected that the signs manual in the council and privy seal files (E. 28) would be more appropriately placed in the files of warrants to the privy seal (PSO 1). Only 24 documents in these files (E. 28) are, diplomatically speaking, genuine council warrants bearing the superscription *De mandato Regis per avisamentum sui consilii* or similar

---

[33] *Cal. Pat. Rolls, 1467–1477*, 172. No additional information is to be found on the Roll itself.

[34] Both these memoranda were made after meetings of the council in London during September 1469, when Edward was imprisoned by the Nevilles at Middleham. The circumstances were, therefore, somewhat exceptional, but I do not think that it affects the general validity of my argument on the relationship of conciliar activity and enrolments.

[35] Maxwell-Lyte, *op. cit.* 29–31. The records for Richard II's reign and for the fifteenth century were, as is well known, subjected to the depredations of Sir Robert Cotton and some of his acquisitions perished in the fire of 1731. Moreover, during the Whitehall fire of 1619 other records were only saved by being thrown out of windows in blankets. At the end of the eighteenth century a 'methodiser' arranged the classes of Warrants for Issues (E. 404), Council and Privy Seal Warrants (E. 28) and Warrants to the Privy Seal (PSO 1) in bundles together per Exchequer terms. They remained in this condition until they were transferred to the Public Record Office where they were separated into their natural classes. R. L. Storey of the Public Record Office has allowed me to use the results of his unpublished researches and I am indebted to him for this information.

[36] M. S. Giueseppi, *A Guide to the Manuscripts Preserved in the Public Record Office* (1924) II 132.

[37] Above n. 35.

words at the foot or on the dorse. Four similar warrants have been found in other files—almost certainly misplaced during various rearrangements[38]—bringing the total up to 28. Once again the state of the files suggests that losses of council warrants are highly probable.

(2) We now come to our second question—whether collateral sources such as enrolments are a fair test of conciliar activity? To answer this it will be necessary to carry out an investigation of the archives of the various secretarial offices and the passage of documents through them to the final stages of enrolment.

Firstly, it may be noted that for this period the entries in the *Calendars of Patent Rolls* are not to be relied on; they are sometimes overcondensed and omit important information. Even a comparison with the *Calendar* of the limited selection of documents from the patent rolls printed in Rymer's *Foedera* reveals four instances where the *Calendar* omits to record that a decision was taken on the advice of the council, and other cases omits various details about the council.[39] Instances can be multiplied by comparing the *Calendars* with the patent rolls themselves. For example, the *Calendar* for 11 Edward IV when subjected to this process reveals no less than 22 such omissions.[40] For nearly every year there are some omissions though no other provides so many examples.

This, however, is merely a marginal phenomenon. Of much greater importance is the fact that documents originating in the council often lost all trace of that origin in their passage through one or more of the secretarial offices. Notes of warranty, especially those giving the authority of the king or the privy seal on the various chancery enrolments, must at this period be treated with the utmost caution. It has long been known that in the fifteenth century the note of warranty *per breve de privato sigillo* in many cases

[38] (1) A writ authorizing a commission to treat with the Scots (misplaced among the files for Henry VI), Council and PS. E. 28/54/13, 5 February (11 Ed. IV).

(2) A warrant for the payment of ambassadors to the duke of Burgundy, Warrants for Issues E.404/72/3/84 reproduced in full in *Foedera*, XI 504.

(3) A writ addressed to Warwick as Warden of the Cinque Ports ordering him to arrest Thomas Howard of Faversham and others and bring them before the king and council. Warrants for Issues E. 404/72/3/83.

(4) A writ to Lord Dynham, Lieutenant of Calais, giving a decision in a case concerning three Breton ships. Warrants to the PS. PSO 1/57/2917. All are subscribed with the words *Rex de avisamento sui consilii mandavit custodi sui privati sigilli* or similar—the usual formula appended to documents of this kind. The fact of misplacement in these last three cases is undoubted as all are found amongst the previously amalgamated classes.

[39] *Foedera* XI 478–9, 488–9, 639–40; XII 117–18. *Cal. Pat. Rolls, 1461–1467*, 102, 176; *1467–1477*, 130; *1476–1485*, 213–14. On other occasions the entry in *Foedera* XI 478, describes Robert Botyll as a councillor and the *Calendar, 1461–1467*, 52, does not. Another entry in the *Calendar* correctly gives the note of warranty *By K. and C.*, but omits any note of the council's advice in the text when Rymer reads *de avisamento concilii nostri*. *Foedera* XI 506. *Cal. Pat. Rolls, 1461–1467*, 282.

[40] If various stock entries are treated as separate cases the total is brought up to 60. Detailed references have been omitted owing to lack of space.

conceals the ultimate origin of the matter with which the document deals. It may have been the king who set the privy seal in motion or the council may have authorized the use of that seal on its own authority. The privy seal office often has the effect of a screen which conceals the preceding processes of administration. Thus we are forced back from the privy seal to the warrants which authorized its use if we wish to find the real source of authority.[41]

If at this stage we turn to those documents in the council and privy seal files which bear an endorsement that they come from the council, and compare the resulting enrolments, we find that in every case where the enrolment can be traced it gives no indication whatever that the council had dealt with the matter.

For example, when in February 1472 the merchants of Cologne were regranted their ancient privileges, the entry on the patent roll has the note of warranty *By p.s.* The council is not mentioned. The grant had, however, originated in a petition addressed to the king. This petition is to be found on the council and privy seal files. The council is not mentioned in the text of the petition but on the dorse is the statement: 'The xiiij daye of ffebruary the xj yere . . .'[42] in the Stere Chamber the King or Souueraigne lorde by thavis of his counsail wold and commaunded the Keper of his priue seel to be addressed unto the Chaunceller of England commaundeying him to do make letters patentes under the great seel after the tenour and fourme within writen.' Thus, a petition presented to the king was granted by him on the advice of the council and, so endorsed, was passed to the privy seal office. The details of the endorsement were omitted as unnecessary from the privy seal addressed by that office to the chancellor, and so left out of the final enrolment. As the council was not mentioned in the text of the petition the final enrolment gives no indication of its origin.[43]

We can trace the same kind of progress from the council chamber via the privy seal office not only to the chancery but also to the exchequer. Thomas Gale and Thomas Grayson, the customs officers in the ports of Exeter and Dartmouth, were authorized to rent buildings there for use as customs houses. There is a privy seal writ on the KR memoranda roll for 18 Edward IV authorizing the treasurer and barons of the exchequer to allow them 40s. a year in their accounts for the rent of the houses and £13 11s. 7d. for moving-in expenses. There is no indication whatever on the memoranda roll of the authority which moved the privy seal. The council and privy seal files, however, contain a petition on the subject from Gale and Grayson

---

[41] Plucknett, 'Place of the Council', *op. cit.* 162–5. See also V. H. Galbraith, *An Introduction to the Use of the Public Records* (1934) 24 ff.

[42] Several words are illegible at this point.

[43] Council and PS. E. 28/90/40. Chancery Warrants C. 81/832/3137. *Cal. Pat. Rolls, 1467–1477*, 307.

which bears on the dorse the formula *de mandato Regis per avisamentum sui consilii.*[44]

Altogether there are 25 council and privy seal documents of this kind of which 22 could have resulted in further writs or in enrolments. Eighteen in fact did result in privy seals or in enrolments with notes of warranty *Per breve de privato sigillo.* None of these privy seals or enrolments gives any indication of the council's hand in the matter.[45] If we can show this from the few documents which have survived on the council and privy seal files (files almost certainly incomplete), allowance must obviously be made for the distinct possibility that a good many patents under the great seal and many writs authorizing allowances in accounts and issues of money or assignments, which ostensibly bear no other sign of their passage through the administrative machine than issue from the privy seal office, ultimately came from the council.

(3) We must now leave this examination of the privy seal documents and turn to the signed bills and signet warrants addressed directly to the chancellor authorizing him to use the great seal and to the keeper of the privy seal.

One of the most striking features of the Yorkist period was the vast increase in the amount of public business which passed under the sign manual and the signet.[46] It was long ago suggested, though with considerable reservations, that a good deal of the business which came before the council was passing under these instruments.[47]

An examination of the files of signed bills and signet bills (which unfortunately Baldwin did not use) certainly shows that only a small proportion contain specific statements that the matters dealt with in them had been before the council. The number fluctuates violently from year to year but for the whole period there are 161 such signed bills and signet bills which

---

[44] Council and PS. E. 28/91, 13 April, 18 Ed. IV. KR Mem. Roll E. 159/255 Easter Term Brevia Directa m. iij.

[45] e.g. The following examples will illustrate the point: (1) Treaty with the Scots. E. 28/54/13. *Rot. Scot.* II 430–1, *Foedera*, XI 733–4. (2) Inspeximus and confirmation of letters patent for the deputy lieutenant of Ireland. E. 28/89, 3 March, 3 Ed. IV. *Cal. Pat. Rolls, 1461–1467,* 275–6. Though the roll itself mentions the council for the original grant it does not do so for the inspeximus. (3) Order to the lower exchequer for payments to Sir John Scotte. E. 28/90/21. Warrants for Issues E. 404/74/3/21.

[46] Otway-Ruthven, *op. cit.* 41.

[47] Plucknett, *op. cit.* 186. The use of the sign manual and signet does not, of course, *ipso facto* means that the king was aware of everything that passed. It would be begging the question to assume that the use of these instruments during the personal rule of Henry VI or during the reign of Edward V meant the active personal supervision of the ruler but even estimating this system of attestation at its lowest there seems no valid reason for doubting it for Edward IV and Richard III. For the development of immediate warrants in the fifteenth century, the technicalities of drafting, sealing, etc. see Maxwell-Lyte, *op. cit.* 147–57. For warrants to the privy seal, *ibid.* 75–91—though it is doubtful whether the procedure was ever as complete in practice as there outlined.

specifically refer to the council as against only 48 direct council warrants to the chancellor and the keeper of the privy seal.[48] These figures become significant once it is realized that there was no necessity for the clerks who wrote them to state that their contents had been discussed in council. Their authentication with the signet or sign manual was the only authorization which the chancellor and the keeper of the privy seal needed in order to use the seals under their control. It is probable therefore that conciliar discussion lies behind many more of the numerous documents in the series.

There is, however, more direct indication that reference to the council's part in decisions was sometimes omitted from such documents, and moreover that the chancery officers did not trouble to repeat, in their enrolments, any information which they may have had about circumstances in which decisions were taken.[49] A revealing example of the process is to be found in the issue in 1466 of a safe-conduct for the Bastard of Burgundy and his retinue to come to England for his famous tourney with Lord Scales. On 6 June, a warrant under the signet (with no mention of the council) was sent to the chancellor commanding the issue of a safe conduct. George Neville, the chancellor, queried the warrant ostensibly because it laid down no maximum number of men for the Bastard's retinue and because it did not forbid him to bring any of the 'king's rebels' with him.[50]

The matter was cleared up by another signet warrant issued the following day. In this the king agreed that, although in a discussion with the Bastard's herald the question of numbers had been left open, an upper limit of 1,000 should be fixed. As to rebels, the chamberlain had obtained a verbal assurance that no rebels should be included in the retinue; nevertheless rebels were to be forbidden in the safe conduct.

The interesting point about the second signet warrant is the light which it throws upon the omissions of the first. The second warrant states that the terms of the first had been approved by 'meny Lordes of oure Counsell then beeing present'. This was now evidently mentioned in order to meet,

<hr/>

[48] The figure 161 is arrived at from the documents among the Signet Warrants and Signed Bills. C. 81/1377–1392, 1486–1528, and Warrants to the Privy Seal PSO 1/22–60, which mention the council in their text but omitting eight documents bearing superscriptions which seem to show that they may be misplaced council warrants, but plus thirteen documents in the Council and Privy Seal files (E. 28/89–92) which mention the council in their text and bear the Sign Manual. The figure 48 is arrived at from Council Warrants C. 81/1547, and Council and Privy Seal files plus twelve similar and possibly misplaced warrants found in other series. For the fluctuations, e.g. 1 Ed. IV (10), 2 Ed. IV (10), 6 Ed. IV (2), 11 Ed. IV (13). The signet clerks were on occasion given additional pay for dealing with conciliar business. Issue Roll E. 403/825 m. 8, 14 July.

[49] For this general point see Maxwell-Lyte, *op. cit.* 149.

[50] Scofield, *Edward IV, op. cit.* 1 407, considers that the real motive was that Neville did not relish the visit as it might forward Edward's pro-Burgundian leanings. The Nevilles were, at this time, trying against the king's inclinations to bring about an alliance with France.

or perhaps stifle, the chancellor's objections.[51]

Another example shows that a course of action recommended by the council in London might have to be approved by the king even if he was away in a different part of the country. In 1464 the government was faced with the urgent problem of raising money to meet a new Lancastrian threat. Towards the end of 1463 the Lancastrian exiles, their position at the Scottish court growing more and more insecure, resolved on another effort to overthrow the Yorkists. The duke of Somerset left north Wales to join his old friends. There were risings in Wales, Cheshire and Lancashire. Troubles thickened. About the beginning of March 1464, the Lancastrians moved Henry from St Andrews to Bamborough. Norham and Skipton-in-Craven (the centre of the Clifford influence) declared for him.[52] This was the beginning of the movement which led to the battles of Hedgeley Moor and Hexham. The government resorted to various expedients to raise money immediately[53] and finally tried to provide for the future by trading in cloth. On 21 May the king, then at Doncaster, sent a signet letter to the chancellor enclosing a patent which had been sent to him by the council. The signet letter states that the king was forwarding to the chancellor 'the copie of a patent unto us sent by the lordes and other of oure Counsail from our Citie of London', and which he himself had signed for shipping 8,000 woollen cloths to raise money 'for chevisance of good towardes oure grete charges borne and to be borne at this tyme'.[54] Two days later James de Sanderico was commissioned to ship the 8,000 cloths and the commission was enrolled on the treaty roll with note of warranty *Per ipsum regem*. Nowhere on the roll is the council mentioned.[55]

Again in November 1478, William Herbert and three other people were pardoned at the request of the queen. The pardon enrolled merely states that they had failed to appear before the king and council when summoned.[56] No details of the reason for the summons are given, and for these we have to turn to the signet warrants. A warrant under the signet had been

---

[51] Signet files C. 81/1379/14 and 15. The form *counsell* is often found when the council is quite clearly meant. Different spellings were, of course, used indiscriminately until much later. See A. F. Pollard, 'Council Star Chamber and Privy Council under the Tudors', *English Historical Review* 5 XXXVII 338–9. In the following pages if there is any possible doubt of the meaning of a particular entry I have given the form of the word.

[52] Sir J. H. Ramsay, *Lancaster and York* II (1892) 301–2. Scofield, *op. cit.* I 312 ff.

[53] Including loans from London and others and a special levy from their own supporters. See Scofield, *op. cit.* I 331.

[54] Signet Files C. 81/1377/25.

[55] Scofield, *op. cit.* II 331. Treaty Roll C. 76/148 m. 14. The patent which the king signed does not appear to have survived, but if it had mentioned the council in its text the reference would have been reproduced in the text on the roll.

[56] *Cal. Pat. Rolls, 1476–1485*, 128. The original warrant ordered patents to be issued covering the other accomplices but only three appear to have been enrolled. Warrants to the PS. PSO 1/46/2386.

sent to the keeper of the privy seal on 8 September informing him that letters missive had gone out to Arnold Botelar and others who had been fortifying and victualling Pembroke castle against the king's peace, commanding them to quit the place and ordering that writs of privy seal to the same effect should be sent to them. This warrant does not mention the council but another signet letter sent the same day to the keeper of the privy seal shows that the council had already discussed the affair. The second letter also shows that William Herbert was behind the whole business and that writs of privy seal had already been sent, on the advice of the council, to Herbert himself ordering him to get his gang out of the castle.[57] Herbert and his accomplices were summoned to appear before the council to answer for their actions. They failed to obey and apparently sued to the queen for a pardon.

So in three cases discussion by the council was followed by action under the sign manual and the signet. We know of the council's part only by accident—from the fact that in the first case the chancellor, for reasons of his own, challenged the warrant, and that in the other two cases covering letters (which mentioned the part played by the council) were dispatched to the chancellor and the keeper of the privy seal respectively which was as far as we know a comparatively unusual proceeding. In the first two cases the resulting enrolments do not mention the council at all, and in the third case only in another connection.[58]

Business in which the council was involved, dealt with under the signet and sign manual, often covered matters very similar to those dealt with by conciliar warrant to the privy seal office and the chancery. But business of an altogether different and more important class such as the summoning of parliament was dealt with under these instruments.

All the extant writs of summons to parliament for the period contain the phrase *de avisamento et assensu consilii nostri*.[59] This is unfortunately a stock form which, although it cannot be taken into account in any accurate

[57] Warrants to the PS. PSO 1/46/2395 B. and C. Both are signs manual. The whole matter may be connected with Herbert's surrender of the earldom of Pembroke for that of Huntingdon the following July. Scofield, *op. cit.* II 250. Edward was anxious to extend the jurisdiction of the prince of Wales's council and keep a firmer hand on Wales and the marches.

[58] For the Bastard's safe-conduct see Treaty Roll C. 76/154 ms. 8 and 15. It was enrolled twice—dated 6 June and 30 October. The two entries are exactly similar. The safe-conduct for 30 October is printed in *Foedera* XI 573–5. For Sanderico's patent, Treaty Roll C.76/150 m. 14. All three cases are warranted *per ipsum Regem* and the formula in the text is *de gratia nostra speciali*.

[59] The phrase *de avisamento consilii nostri* is first found in the writs of 12 Ed. III. It becomes the usual form from *c.* 47 Ed. III and with only five exceptions (2 Henry IV, 3, 7, 20 and 23 Henry VI) is the usual form under the Lancastrians. The formula changes to *de avisamento et assensu . . .* with the Yorkists but there is no significance in this. *Report on the Dignity of a Peer* IV 497 ff., 695 ff., 773 ff., 869 ff., 902 ff., 907 ff., for the Yorkists, 950–998. The notes of warranty are varied.

assessment of the council's part in the matter, nevertheless fairly certainly expresses the facts. It is very unlikely that the king would take so important a step as summoning parliament without some kind of preliminary discussion with his advisers. An examination of the documents preliminary to the writs of summons, however, definitely shows the action taken. Parliament was summoned eleven times during the Yorkist period though only seven parliaments actually sat.[60] The preliminary documents tell us that the council was concerned in the decisions to summon, postpone or cancel six of these parliaments. For four parliaments the mandate to the chancellor to issue the writs of summons was a signed bill each of which mentions the council[61] and the evidence for a fifth also comes from a signed bill.[62] A sixth parliament was summoned by the chancellor on the authority of a privy seal writ which mentioned the council, and it was postponed on the authority of a signet warrant also authenticated by the sign manual. This signet warrant also mentions discussion in council.[63]

Thus it was a conventional practice established long before Yorkist days to state in the writs of summons that parliament was to meet on the council's advice. Though most likely to be true, the phrasing of these writs is therefore worthless as evidence for our particular purpose. There is no particular reason, however, why any preliminary warrants sent to the

[60] The parliament of 2 Ed. IV was never held owing to irregularities in the elections; that of 9 Ed. IV was postponed ostensibly on the ground of the danger of a Scottish invasion and in the end never met; Edward V's only parliament assembled but no business was done and no speaker elected; the first parliament summoned in 1 Richard III was cancelled owing to Buckingham's rebellion. Wedgwood, *Register* 331, 363, 465, 473.

[61] The parliaments of 22 Ed. IV, 1 Ed. V, and the two parliaments of 1 Richard III. Signed Bills C. 81/1522/28, C. 81/1529/3, C. 81/1531/61, C. 81/1530/6. C. 81/1531/61 bears no regnal year but internal evidence makes the date quite certain.

[62] The parliament of 2 Ed. IV. Signed Bills, C. 81/1492/15. This is a writ ordering the cancellation of the parliament of 2 Ed. IV. It reveals that the original decision to summon parliament had been taken on the council's advice. The warrant ordering the issue of writs for the parliament immediately following, that of 3 Ed. IV, does not mention the council. Signed Bills C. 81/1492/17. See also *Cal. Close Rolls, 1461–1468*, 159–60.

[63] For the circumstances see Scofield, *op. cit.* I 499–502 and Baldwin, *op. cit.* 427. The chancellor issued the writs of summons on the authority of a privy seal which mentions the advice of the council. Chancery Warrants C. 81/827/2875. (I have been unable to trace any warrant to the privy seal. It is possible that it may have been moved by word of mouth.) It was then decided to cancel the meeting. The process is described in the council memorandum in Council Warrants C. 81/1547, 7 September, 9 Ed. IV. The section of the council with the king and Warwick at Middleham decided on the cancellation and sent a signet warrant authenticated with the sign manual dated 30 August from Middleham to the chancellor and others informing them of the decision. It was then discussed by the section of the council in London. Signet Warrants C. 81/1381/31. The memorandum mentions a second letter written by Warwick to the chancellor from Sheriffhoton on the 2 September confirming the credence given to Richard Scrope the bearer of the letters in the first. Warwick's letter does not appear to have survived. *Cal. Close Rolls, 1468–1476*, 115 ff., does not mention the council's advice on postponing the parliament though the writ itself does. Close Roll C. 54/321 m. 3d, printed in *Dignity of a Peer, op. cit.* IV 972 ff.

chancellor should mention the council unless that body had actually discussed the matter. So although the wording of the actual writs is not to be trusted that of the preliminary documents can be accepted. This contention is strengthened by the fact that in some cases the preliminary documents do not mention the council at all. So it seems that as often as not the council discussed the summoning of parliament and that it was also fairly normal practice to authorize the summons under the sign manual or signet—both in cases where the council is known to have been concerned and in others. It is worth noting too that on several occasions the decision to summon convocations was taken on the advice of the council and the necessary writs were issued on the authority of a signed bill.[64] Thus the council discussed matters of the most important kind and action followed under the sign manual and signet.

There is a good deal more evidence covering these points. It can best be used by examining the various sources together at three different periods. Whenever the council's activities are examined over a selected period no particular class of documents covers or nearly covers its work. There are no documents in the files of council warrants or council and privy seal files for the first year of Edward's reign[65] and none for Edward V and Richard III. A search of other records, however, has given 54 specific references to conciliar action for 1 Edward IV[66] and 79 for Edward V and Richard III.[67] Many others mentioned particular councillors. It is thus evident that the council was sitting and advising on a wide variety of matters at times when the two series of records, generally considered to be most particularly its own, fail completely.

In case these examples from the beginning and the end of the period are suspected to be abnormal, let us examine a more normal period in some detail, the year 18 Edward IV. This year is marked by two outstanding matters—an attempt to put certain administrative matters in order and the condemnation of the duke of Clarence. Council warrants are completely absent and there are only five council and privy seal warrants. One deals with the payments of the king's debts outstanding since before 1470 and mentions the advice of the council in its text.[68] Another is the writ to the

---

[64] Signed Bills, C. 81/1502/9, C. 81/1503/34, C. 81/1508/54, convocation of both Canterbury and York 10 and 12 Ed. IV, and York alone 14 Ed. IV. Another signed bill for summoning the convocation of Canterbury 18 Ed. IV does not mention the council. C. 81/1513/45. For the writs see *Dignity of a Peer, op. cit.* IV 979–80, 984, 988.

[65] The first council warrant is dated 8 March, 2 Ed. IV, C. 81/1547. The first warrant to the privy seal office which mentions the council is dated 5 March, 3 Ed. IV, E. 28/89.

[66] Distributed as follows: Patent Rolls 19, Close Rolls 1, Fine Rolls 3, Scots Rolls 5, Treaty Rolls 3, Signed Bills 10, Issue Rolls 2, KR Mem. Rolls 9, Warrants for Issues 2.

[67] Distributed as follows: Patent Rolls 25, Close Rolls 13, Scots Rolls 3, Treaty Rolls 7, Signed Bills 6, Warrants to the Privy Seal 8, KR Mem. Rolls 10, Warrants for Issues 7.

[68] Council and PS. E. 28/91, 20 July, 18 Ed. IV.

treasurer and barons ordering them to allow Thomas Gale and Thomas Grayson expenses for the customs houses at Exeter and Dartmouth.[69] A third deals with an alleged case of smuggling,[70] a fourth with an instruction to pay Clarenceux, king-at-arms, sent on an embassy to the king of Denmark,[71] and a fifth with directions to the upper exchequer about the accounts of Austin and John Russe, customs officials in Great Yarmouth.[72] There are two other documents which if they were in a better state might be added to the list.[73]

The KR memoranda roll adds to the tale—in opposite but equally significant ways, both in what it omits and in what it adds. Neither of the writs about the Exeter and Dartmouth customs houses nor the accounts of Austin and John Russe as enrolled mention the council.[74] On the other hand, a search of the brevia directa section of the roll alone reveals another five writs which state that they had been issued after discussion in council.[75]

Proceeding with the exchequer records, both the warrants for issues and the issue roll for the Easter term partly duplicate information about wages for the Calais garrison found on another section of the memoranda roll.[76] The warrants for issues give additional information about tasks performed by individual councillors and the remuneration given them.[77] In another case a warrant tells us that it was on the council's advice that John Fitzherbert and John Sorrell had been appointed tellers of the exchequer and it was also decided on the council's advice that they should each be paid 40 marks a year which was higher than the pay normally given.[78]

There are another 18 entries on the issue rolls showing various payments made on the orders of the council. These brief entries are tantalizing in

---

[69] Council and PS. E. 28/91, 13 April, 18 Ed. IV.

[70] Council and PS. E. 28/91, 14 April, 18 Ed. IV.

[71] Council and PS. E. 28/91, 28 April, 18 Ed. IV.

[72] Council and PS. E. 28/91, 23 November, 18 Ed. IV.

[73] A petition from a Duchy of Lancaster tenant which bears no regnal year. Council and PS. E. 28/91, 30 November (18 Ed. IV?) and the draft of an indenture between the king and Lord Hastings setting out his terms of service as Lieutenant of Calais. E. 28/91, 11 February 18 Ed. IV. This is too badly mutilated to be certain whether it was issued on the council's advice.

[74] In each case the instruction to the privy seal office contained the council's authority in an endorsement. It was therefore omitted from the enrolment. KR Mem. Roll Brevia Directa Easter Term m. iij, Michelmas Term m. vij.

[75] KR Mem. Roll E. 159/225. Brevia Directa Easter Term Ms, ii, v, vj, Trinity Term M. ij, Mich. Term m. iijd. The last orders the treasurer and barons to take the account of John Elryngton, treasurer for war, for the French campaign of 1475. It gives very detailed instructions. No warrants to the privy seal have been found in these cases.

[76] KR Mem. Roll E. 159/255 Hilary Term Communia m. xx, gives details of Lord Hastings's retinue in Calais.

[77] Warrants for Issues E. 404/76/4/12.

[78] Warrant for Issues E. 404/76/4/24. In this case executive action was taken in the Signet Office. Warrants to the PS. PSO 1/45/2343.

their lack of detail but they at least tell us that there was a council in London at times sending letters to the king and his council in the provinces[79] and that the council had dealings with at least five receivers of landed revenue[80] and with five customs officers.[81] Altogether these sources give 49 entries not counting duplicates.[82]

The year 1478 was to some extent a year of financial clearance and reform.[83] We have already seen how the council was concerned in the decisions to pay the king's long-standing debts.[84] It also instructed the exchequer to deal with the accounts of the 1475 campaign.[85] The king put his household in order and a signet warrant to the chancery tells us that the reform was undertaken after consideration by the council.[86] Judging from the details given in the *Orders and Regulations* drawn up as a result of the work the household was very much in need of it.[87]

A most important piece of political information is supplied by the Croyland Continuator. He tells us that in the period of strained relations before the duke of Clarence's final quarrel with the king, Clarence absented himself more and more from the king's presence, would not willingly eat or drink in the king's house and spoke scarcely a word in

[79] Issue Roll E. 403/845 m. 10, 26 August.

[80] Entries on Piers Beaupie, Nicholas Leventhorpe, Richard Welby, John Agard and Richard Spert. Issue Roll E. 403/845 m. 2, 23rd October (4), m. 3, 11 November.

[81] Issue Roll E. 403/848 m. 8, 17 February. Those in Exeter and Dartmouth, Bridgewater, Plymouth and Fowey. Poole, Chichester, Southampton. Other entries are Issue Roll E. 403/845 m. 1, 29 April (2), m. 4, 22 May, m. 8, 26 August; E. 403/848 m. 5, m. 1, 12 October, m. 3, 28 October, m. 5, 18 November, m. 9, 27 February, m. 11, 1 April, m. 12, 1 April.

[82] Distributed as follows: Patent Rolls 5, Scots Roll 1, Signed Bills 2, Signet Warrants 1, Warrants to the PS 3, Issue Rolls, 25, KR Mem. Rolls 7, Warrants for Issues 5. About an additional 20 per cent duplicate or partly duplicate information.

[83] Scofield, *op. cit.* 216–17 and 216 n. 3.

[84] Above p. 186 and n. 68. Scofield, *op. cit.* II 216.

[85] Above p. 187 n. 75.

[86] 'Right reverend fader . . . wheras we by thadvis of oure Counsell have made certain ordinennces for the stablysshing of oure howshold comprised in a booke which by oure commaundement shalbe deliuered unto you by oure trusty and right welbeloued clerc and counsellor Thomas Langton . . .'. Signet Warrants C. 81/1386/8.

[87] The Queen's College MS. 134. This manuscript is beautifully preserved. Its early provenance is unknown but it was given by Thomas Barlow, the Provost of the Queen's to Sir Joseph Williamson. Williamson left in 1701 with other manuscripts and books to the College. Myers informs me that on-paleographical evidence he considers the document to be a copy of a lost original made probably not later than the 1490s. It should not be confused with the better known Liber Niger Domus Regis Edwardii iiij published by the Society of Antiquaries in the *Collection of Ordinances for the Government of the Royal Household* (1790). The manuscript has now (1975) been edited by Myers. A. R. Myers, *The Household of Edward IV: The Black Book and the Ordinance of 1478* (1959).

council.[88] He goes on to show that the events leading up to Clarence's condemnation were to some extent played out in the council. Stacey and Burdet (who was a member of Clarence's household) after being found guilty of several crimes, were sentenced to death in the king's bench and executed at Tyburn—both declaring their innocence, Burdet most emphatically. On the following day Clarence with Dr. William Goddard went to the council chamber at Westminster and read the declaration of innocence to the council there assembled. The king who was then at Windsor, seems to have regarded this as the last straw. Immediately he heard of it he summoned the duke to appear before him on a certain day at the palace of Westminster.[89] The rest of the story and Clarence's execution are too well known to need repeating here.

Thus for the year 18 Edward IV at least, only a small proportion of the information still available about the council comes from documents which it issued itself. Nor are the matters dealt with in these documents among the most significant. The important question of the reform of the household was dealt with under the signet. All the references to the council in the official records examined, apart from petitions for justice, deal only with administrative matters, and even here the picture is incomplete. Although the official documents give information about payment for additional troops for Calais, we learn only from the accidental survival of a private letter about discussions between the council and the merchants of the Staple on the currency in which the normal Calais establishment was to be paid, and that finally they were paid in sterling.[90] The official records examined do not mention politics in the wider sense at all, and for information about one of the most dramatic events of Edward's reign we are forced back on a chronicler who, though better informed and more detailed than any other contemporary writer is really only the best of a bad lot. It is hardly surprising therefore, that we hear so little of conciliar activity at the highest level of politics.

So during the Yorkist period there were several channels through which decisions taken in the council could be implemented. The privy seal, for the time, had lost the position of 'the direct and authoritative organ of the

---

[88] Historiae Croylandensis Continuatio in Fulman 561. It is worth noting that Polydore Vergil, when describing the Clarence affair says that he sought information from 'many who at the time had been of importance among the royal counsellors'. D. Hay *Polydore Vergil, Renaissance Historian and Man of Letters* (1952) 93. It is perhaps significant that the Croyland writer's phrasing implies that Clarence had attended the council frequently but only two official documents have been found which mention his presence. Signed Bills C. 81/1502/50 and Council and PS. E. 28/54/13.

[89] Fulman 561.

[90] *The Cely Papers* ed. H. E. Malden, Camden Society (1900) 6.

king's council' which it had occupied earlier and was later to assume again.[91]

Documents which went direct from the council to the privy seal office, chancery and exchequer did not necessarily contain any statement of their origin in their text. The same is certainly true of the signs manual and signet warrants, by means of which a good deal of the more important administrative business was now being initiated. This was naturally reflected in the succeeding enrolments. From 1461, if not before, it may be argued that the nature of the executive action changed and with it the position of the council. The council, although it could, and from time to time did, take independent executive action, became in the main an advisory body. This change in position and method led (from our point of view) to the concealment of a good deal of its activity.

'Personal government' is a highly misleading phrase as applied to the middle ages. The tasks of government were always so multifarious that, both in theory and practice, the king had of necessity to act with counsel. The Yorkist kings certainly did so. It seems reasonable to suggest that two things in this period obscure the action of the council from the historian—the loss of some unknown proportion of its records, and the changes suggested in the methods by which decisions were implemented after conciliar discussion. It would be rash at this point to attempt to say to which of these factors the obscurity is mostly due. Yet taking into account the demonstrable omissions of the sources, the fact that nearly 1,500 references to the council have been found between 1461 and 1485 (an average of about 60 a year), besides numerous references to individual councillors and their work, seems significant enough to cast grave doubts on any theory of 'a failure in the operations of the council'. All the evidence points the other way—that the council was a most important factor in the 'personal government' of the Yorkists.

[91] Baldwin, op. cit. 257. For previous and later history, L. W. Labaree and R. E. Moody, 'The Seal of the Privy Council', English Historical Review XLIII especially 192. Willard and Morris, English Government, op. cit. 75–6, 178–82 and the references there given. Plucknett, op. cit. 185–6. The relations between the council and the privy seal of course remained close. Thomas Kent was secondary in the privy seal office as well as clerk of the council.

8

Council, administration and councillors, 1461–85

In the previous chapter I have shown, from a study of the sources, that the importance of the Yorkist council has been unduly underestimated.[1] Owing to the lack of detailed chronicles for the period there is very little information about its activities at the highest level of politics and, generally speaking, there remain only its decisions on the details of administration. Even here information is regrettably patchy, owing partly to the loss of some unknown, though probably quite considerable proportion of the council's records, partly to the fact that the participation of the council in decisions was only haphazardly recorded in the documents issued from the various secretarial offices ordering the execution of those decisions, and partly to a shift in govermental methods which resulted in action under the signet and sign manual instead of under direct conciliar and privy seal warrants. It remains to show something of the extent of the council's activities and of its composition. The references to the council which still remain, widely scattered as they are through many classes of documents, show that its activities covered almost every subject with which the government had to deal. The fragmentary nature of the evidence, however, permits the demonstration of a continuous oversight of affairs in only a limited number of matters. Two subjects, military and financial affairs, with particular reference to the defence of Calais, will serve as examples to show the continuity of the council's work throughout the years.

Military affairs took up a good deal of the government's energies during most of Edward IV's reign, particularly during the earlier years when rebels at home and in Ireland and danger from enemies abroad were all serious threats. We can trace the council's hand almost continuously in military and naval affairs from preparations against an expected French invasion in 1461, through measures for resistance to the Lancastrian rising of 1463–4, and abortive preparations for an invasion of France in 1468, to the

[1] As the printed calendars of Patent, Close and Fine Rolls often omit references to the council and even the original rolls sometimes omit information contained in privy seal warrants, signet warrants and signs manual (see above pp. 179 ff.), I have given references in the following pages to both the original rolls and warrants where it seems desirable to show the whole administrative process involved.

actual campaign in France in 1475 and the expeditions against Scotland from 1480 onward.[2] The extent of the attention which the council gave to military matters appears most clearly in its dealings with Calais. As the defence of the town was so closely bound up with financial questions the two will be dealt with together in order to show the frequency with which the council discussed its affairs. The protection of Calais was always one of the major preoccupations of fifteenth-century governments, and equally of the Yorkist council, for references to the council are nowhere more numerous than they are in connection with the town's affairs. Constant vigilance was required in its defence, and its safety was threatened by every adverse turn of diplomatic relations with France.[3] From the beginning the situation was full of danger. In the 1450s the garrison had been unpaid and mutinous,[4] which in view of the arrears of wages due to them is hardly a matter for surprise. A commission appointed by the king and council which reported in 1464 revealed that Henry VI's government had owed over £37,000 in the town.[5] Unless the Yorkists contrived to meet their obligations more promptly the garrison's loyalty would be uncertain and the safety of the town in jeopardy. Sometime before mid August 1461, the king on the council's advice ordered Sir Walter Blount, the treasurer of Calais, to pay £7,000 and more to the garrison in part payment of their wages.[6] Sometime before the beginning of October, £1,900 was borrowed for current wages and the council discussed arrangements for repayment.[7] In November the council advised on the payment of arrears of wages for the garrison of Hammes.[8] During the next three months Blount came over to England several times and he himself, his deputy and the Calais council sent messages to impress upon the king and the royal council the 'excessive indigence and importable poverty' of the garrison, and to plead for more money for wages and for repairs to the fortifications. It was not until 17

[2] Detailed references have been omitted owing to lack of space.

[3] Scofield, *The Life and Reign of Edward IV* (2 vols 1923) I 249–57, 295–8, 323–4; II 175–6, 197, 314, 318–19, 358. J. Calmette and G. Périnelle, *Louis XI et l'Angleterre* (1930) 2, n. 5, 23 and n. 7, 33 and n. 3, 47 n. 4, 155, 218–21, 249–54, and Pièces Justificatives nos 11 and 12.

[4] W. I. Haward, 'The Financial Transactions between the Lancastrian Government and the Merchants of the Staple from 1449 to 1461', in E. Power and M. M. Postan, *Studies in English Trade in the Fifteenth Century* (1933) 301–7.

[5] The exact sum was £37,160 4s. 10½d. The reckoning was taken to the last day of Henry's reign except in the case of Hammes where it was extended to 25 October 1461, the day the fortress surrendered. Scofield, *Edward IV, op. cit.* I 298 and n. 3.

[6] KR Mem. Roll E. 159/238 Brevia Directa Michaelmas Term m. xxxviijd.

[7] *ibid.* Michaelmas Term m. xlj.

[8] Signed Bills C. 81/1488/3. They had been part of the duke of Somerset's retinue and this was probably an attempt to make sure of their allegiance to the Yorkists. Their arrears to the day of surrender were to be paid. At the same time they received a general pardon.

March 1462, however, that Blount obtained another £2,000.[9]

From this time onwards we can trace a succession of hand-to-mouth arrangements, in most of which the council was involved, showing the government's reliance on the merchants of the Staple for the maintenance of Calais. These arrangements ultimately led to the famous act of retainer.[10] In August 1462 the situation in Calais was so alarming it was thought the king himself would have to go to the rescue. The rumour was going round that two hundred of the disgruntled garrison were prepared to go over the Lancastrians. Margaret of Anjou had moved from Rouen to Boulogne with, it was said, money to pay their wages.[11] The earl of Worcester, the prior of St John's and other members of the council went to plead with the common council of London for a loan. This appeal, together with an earlier one which had been made to the city, brought in something over £2,000,[12] mere chicken feed in comparison with the government's need. The accumulated claims of the Staple for the defence of Calais acknowledged by the government at this time amounted to £40,917 19s. 2¼d.[13] In spite of this they were prevailed upon in September to advance half a year's wages (£6,872 7s. 4d.) and to write off 3,000 marks of the debt. At the same time it was agreed, on the council's advice, that until the balance of the debt was paid off, all customs and subsidy on wool and wool fells which members of the society shipped through any port of the kingdom should be remitted, and that the society should take half the customs and subsidy on the same commodities shipped by non-members through Boston and Sandwich.[14] A few weeks later the other half of these dues was allotted to the Calais garrison towards their arrears.[15]

[9] Scofield, *op. cit.* I 205–6 and 205 m. 6, 206 n. 1. Issue Roll E. 403/824 m. 10, 17 March 1462. Foreign Accounts E. 364/97 m. E. The visits and messages took place between 6 November 1461 and 10 October 1462. The Foreign Account refers to details given in the account book of Richard Whetehill, the comptroller of Calais. E. 101/196/2. The £2,000 had to be borrowed from Angelo Tany and Simon Nory.

[10] In the following pages only Staple loans for the defence of Calais are discussed. There were, of course, others. No attempt is made to give a complete and detailed history of Calais finance. The council is always mentioned in the original documents referred to unless the contrary is stated.

[11] Scofield, *op. cit.* I 256 and n. 2.

[12] *ibid.* 255–6 and 256. n. 1.

[13] *Cal. Pat. Rolls, 1461–1467,* 222.

[14] Treaty Roll C. 76/146 m. 12, *Per ipsum Regem.* Signed Bills C. 81/1492/4. *Cal. Pat. Rolls, 1461–1467,* 222, *By K,* does not mention the council but the roll itself and the Signed Bill read *de avisamento et assensu concilii nostri.* C. 66/500 m. 11, C. 81/1491/28. Scofield, *op cit.* I 256–7 puts the arrangements for the settlement of the debt before the new loan, but the Treaty Roll makes it clear that the new loan was agreed on 2 September. The patent for the repayment of the debt (Patent Roll) is dated 16 September. Probably both were agreed at the same time, but the details of the debt settlement being more complicated, drafting and execution took longer.

[15] Signed Bills C. 81/1491/76. Treaty Roll c. 76/146 m. 2, *Per ipsum Regem et consilium.*

What happened is revealed in considerable detail in a memorandum preserved among the signed bills.[16] This indicates that the discussions with the Staple had been carried on by the archbishop of Canterbury, the treasurer and others of the council. It goes on to show that although the 3,000 marks released to the king were part of Henry VI's debt, Edward intended to repay the balance of the sums which his predecessor had owed to the Staple as well as the new debts which he had incurred himself. The memorandum gives the dates for paying the half year's wages in two instalments and the arrangements made for their repayment to the Staple. It also reveals that between Christmas 1461 and the agreement made in September 1462, the Staple had lent an additional £4,322 7s. and arrangements were also made for this to be repaid.[17] Various other details being noted, a section occurs which although cancelled is significant for future developments. It runs: 'And ouer that to graunte that thees said articles may be made in due forme and enacted in the Kings Counsaill And thereupon to be exemplyfied under his greet seal wt a promisse of him and his said Counsaill to doo their part that the said articles may be enacte in the next parlement.'

Acts of parliament in favour of the Staple were not of course new. There was nothing, therefore, very important in this part of the proposal in the cancelled clause. What was significant was the procedure there outlined—discussion and agreement in the council followed by the issue of letters patent under the great seal to be more solemnly recorded in an act of parliament. Action of this kind, as we shall see later, was the genesis of the act of retainer. By 1 July 1463, the Staple had advanced yet another quarter's wages which the council advised should be repaid from the second half of the aid recently granted by parliament,[18] and the treasurer and victualler were given assignments on the same aid for payment of a further quarter's wages.[19] This, however, was only a stopgap, for the means of

---

[16] Signed Bills C. 81/1492/4, dated 18 Nov. Scofield, *op. cit.* I 257 ns. 2 and 3 (who uses the old numbering of these documents), wrongly describes this as an indenture whereas in fact the last clause states that the chancellor and the keeper of the privy seal were to make and deliver to the Staplers any letters and privy seals necessary to put the agreed arrangements into effect without any further warrants from the king and to give it effect the king signed it. In fact, it covers patents already issued as well as some to be issued. It is a rough memorandum in which points agreed were written down. Its many alterations and erasures indicate that it was mostly likely the result of prolonged and tough negotiations between the parties.

[17] The patent for repayment was not issued until 29 January, 1463. *Cal. Pat. Rolls, 1461–1467*, 220, *By K.*, does not mention the council, but the roll, C. 66/500 m. 13, reads *de gratia nostra speciali ac de avisamento et assensu consilii nostri concessimus.*

[18] The aid granted in the first session of the parliament of 1463–5. *Rot. Parl.* V 497–8. *Cal. Pat. Rolls, 1461–1467*, 271, *By K.*, omits mention of the council but the roll and the signed bill read *de avisamento et assensu concilii nostri.* C. 66/505 m. 8. C. 81/1493/8.

[19] Scofield, *op. cit.* I 297–8. Warrants for Issues E. 404/72/3/85. This does not mention the council.

repaying the debt was hardly yet in sight. The government simultaneously tried another tack—another desperate stop-gap. It attempted to raise money by trade.[20] On 1 July a decision was taken to hand over to Sir Walter Blount, the treasurer of Calais, £20,000 with which to trade in wool and wool fells, and to use the profits towards paying off the arrears due at the end of Henry VI's reign.[21] Seven days later the council appointed the commission already mentioned to investigate the extent of the Lancastrian debt.[22] When the commission finally reported in December 1464, besides giving detailed figures, it recommended extensive repairs at all three fortresses (Calais, Hammes and Guisnes) and an increase in their artillery and war stores.[23]

We can now trace the series of events which led to the act of retainer. Royal cutting-in on the wool trade was naturally distasteful to the Staplers and as soon as they could they took steps to protect their interests. In the parliamentary session of January to March 1465, they obtained a statute against the issue of licences and exemptions for trading to non-Staplers,[24] and in spite of the cancelled clause of the memorandum of November 1462, they gained an act securing them payment of £32,861, the detailed arrangements for repayment being the same as those outlined in the memorandum.[25] In January 1466 letters patent were issued *de gratia nostra speciali ac de avisamento et assensu consilii nostri* confirming the statute against licences and exemptions,[26] and furthermore granting an eight year extension to a statute of 1463 that no wool (that of the four northern counties only exempted) should be shipped except to Calais.[27] The way being thus prepared, further letters patent intended to make a definitive agreement

---

[20] This was not, of course, the only occasion on which Edward's government resorted to trade to raise money. See *English Historical Review* LXXIII (1958) 39.

[21] Scofield, *op. cit.* I 298. Council and PS. E. 28/89, 1 July 3 Ed. IV. Warrants for Issues E. 404/72/44. Treaty Roll C. 76/147 ms 11 and 14. None of these documents mention the council or show that they were involved in the decision to allot £20,000 to Blount, but in view of the fact that they discussed Calais wages and a loan on the same day and only a week later appointed the commission to investigate the king's debts to the Staple it is hardly likely that they had no hand in the matter.

[22] Council Warrants C. 81/1547, 8 July. Treaty Roll C. 76/147 m. 3, *Per ipsum Regem et consilium.*

[23] Chancery Miscellanea C. 47 bundle 2 no. 50. The report begins by reproducing the text of the original commission in full but omitting the note of warranty, *Per consilium.* There is nothing in this document therefore to show that the original decision to appoint the commission was taken in council. So easily could reference to the council be lost.

[24] Ed. IV c. 2. *Rot. Parl.* V 563–4. *Statutes of the Realm* II 407–9. No council evidence.

[25] *Rot. Parl.* V 550–1. It seems doubtful whether the act became operative as the debt stood at the same figure in July 1466. The act differs from the act of retainer in that it is only concerned with the outstanding debts and not with administrative arrangements etc. for Calais generally.

[26] Treaty Roll C. 76/150 m. 24, *Per ipsum Regem.*

[27] Ed. IV c. 1. *Rot. Parl.* V 503–4. *Per ipsum Regem.*

with the Staplers, were issued on 13 July after discussion in the council. These letters patent show that the debt to the staplers stood at £32,861. The provisions for the defence of Calais and for the repayment of the debt, known as the act of retainer, follow.[28] It was soon found however that the revenues assigned to the Staple were insufficient to cover their outgoings, and the arrangement was revised by the issue on 15 December of further letters patent,[29] which were confirmed later in the first session of the parliament of 1467–8.[30] The details are too well known to need repeating here.[31] The important thing from our point of view is that the procedure contemplated but abandoned in the meetings of 1463 was now adopted. There was to be discussion between the council and the Staple followed by the issue of letters patent on the council's advice and the confirmation of these letters patent in the parliament next following. If all had gone according to plan the debt would have been paid off by 1474 and the arrangement ended. It was upset however by external factors as early as 1468,[32] and of course broke down as a result of the troubles of 1470–71.

In July 1471, very soon after Edward's return another temporary agreement was reached. To settle various debts amounting to £20,276 8s. the act of retainer, after discussion in council, was confirmed by letters patent[33] before being redrafted in a new and final form in February 1473. There is no evidence of the council's hand on this last occasion, though in view of its previous and subsequent activities it is unlikely that it took no part.[34] Even when the act was passed there were still temporary difficulties. Richard Whetehill, the lieutenant of Guisnes, was unable to pay the garrison there and a supplementary arrangement was made in April under which the Staple lent £3,734 to meet his needs. In return the king handed over certain lands and tenements for a period of seven years, part of the revenues to be

---

[28] Treaty Roll C. 76/150 m. 22, *Per ipsum Regem.*

[29] *ibid.* m. 29, *Per ipsum Regem.*

[30] *Rot. Parl.* V 613–16.

[31] For a summary see Power and Postan, *Studies in English Trade, op. cit.* 74–5.

[32] In 1468, owing to the interruption of trade with the Netherlands caused by war, it was alleged that the revenues assigned brought in less than £10,000 instead of £15,000 as estimated. Warrants for Issues E. 404/74/1/9. The figures given by Carus-Wilson show a fall of about 22 per cent in the year 1467–8. E. Carus-Wilson, *Mediaeval Merchant Venturers* (1954) table facing p. xviii. The Staplers' claim, therefore, though somewhat exaggerated, was certainly valid.

[33] Neither the *Cal. Pat. Rolls, 1467–1477,* 270 *By K.,* nor the roll itself, C. 66/527 m. 15, mentions the council, but the warrant among the Signed Bills C. 81/1502/50, is endorsed with the statement that it was passed by the king on the council's advice, the king himself being present at the meeting. A list of members present follows. No mention of the council appears in the enrolment because the information is in the endorsement and not the text of the warrant.

[34] *Rot. Parl.* VI 55–61.

paid to him, part retained to pay off the debt.[35] The final provisions under the act of retainer were temporarily upset by the interruption of trade brought about by the French campaign of 1475. Complaint was made that 'thutterance of wolles and felles have of longe tyme be gretely stopped and letted' to the detriment of the Staplers. The matter was discussed both in council and with the society and a scheme produced for their relief, which was accepted on the advice of the great council which met at Westminster on 9 February 1476, and issued as an ordinance.[36] Plans for repayment from this time at last worked smoothly. The Staplers received sufficient revenue from the sources earmarked for them to cover the upkeep of the defences and the garrison, the various other payments which they had undertaken to make, the annual payments against the debt and to leave an annual 'surplusage' for payment into the exchequer. This particular problem was now solved, no doubt much to the council's relief.[37] From the late 1470s arguments in which the council was involved were still going on, but they were arguments with a difference. Whereas formerly disputes had been concerned with the fundamental question whether the money for wages and defence could be raised at all, they now turned on the comparatively minor question of exchange rates—whether payment should be made in sterling or in Flemish groats.[38] Discussions about the garrison not immediately connected with financial ways and means were also frequent. The indentures between the king and the lieutenant generally contained a provision that any danger which threatened the town should be reported immediately to the king and council so that reinforcements could be sent.[39] Between 1461 and 1485 in fact the council added to or reduced the garrison

[35] Warrants for Issues E. 404/77/2/58. This document, which finally clears up the somewhat complicated arrangements involved, describes the issue of the original patent, which itself does not mention the council. Treaty Roll C. 76/157 ms 20–23.

[36] Signed Bills C. 81/1511/26. Treaty C. 76/160 ms 1 and 2, *Per ipsum Regem*. The phrasing of these documents makes the distinction between the council (*dominis et aliis de consilio nostro*) and the great council (*dominorum spiritualium et temporalium de consilio nostro*) clear. The latter phrase was generally the formula for the great council at this period. The patent contains a mass of detailed and complicated regulations which must have been drafted beforehand for the consideration of the great council if they were informed of the details and not merely the general outlines of the scheme. Various relaxations were to be allowed till June 1478.

[37] By June 1481 the debt due under the act of retainer had been reduced to £2,616 0s. 10d. By the end of the reign, and probably a good deal earlier, the garrison were paid monthly. Warrants for Issues E. 404/78/2/65. J. Gairdner, *Letters and Papers Illustrative of the Reigns of Richard III and Henry VII*, Rolls (1861–3) 113.

[38] *The Cely Papers* ed. H. E. Malden, Camden Society (1900) 6, 98–100, 111–12, (this reference is to the council at Calais). Warrants to the PS. PSO 1/50/2564–5. A good deal of inferior money was current on the marts and the king insisted on specifying the currency and sometimes apparently fixed a rate of exchange in his own favour. Power and Postan, *op. cit.* 78.

[39] e.g. Lord Hastings's indenture of 1471. Treaty Roll C. 76/162 m. 3, *Per ipsum Regem*. The draft of an indenture drawn up in 1479 specifies the number of men to be sent in such circumstances. Council and PS. E. 28/91, 11 Feb. 18 Ed. IV.

on several occasions and supervised security arrangements in other ways.[40]

In comparison with the Calais evidence, the material available for a discussion of financial matters generally and of the part, if any, which the council played in improving the financial position of the monarchy is comparatively meagre.[41] The two main sources of revenue at this time were the customs and the crown lands. The administration of both can only be reconstructed from piecemeal evidence. No general declarations of policy have survived.[42] In his later years Edward's newly appointed customs surveyors had the reputation of being over-severe towards merchants[43] and the customs revenues were increasing.[44] There are a number of com-

[40] Issue Roll E. 403/827, m. 1, 6 Oct. 1462. In 1466, Treaty Roll C. 76/150 m. 6, *Per Ipsum Regem*. In 1471, Signed Bills C. 81/1502/49. The international situation after the death of Charles the Bold in 1477 was particularly dangerous. In Feb. 1477 a great council was held in London to discuss the situation. Scofield, *op. cit.* II 176. Lord Hastings went to Calais in March and stayed there until June. He took with him large reinforcements for the garrison. Shortly afterwards the council authorized him to pull down any buildings which might impede the town's defences. Treaty Roll C. 76/161 m. 6, *Per Consilium*. It seems from a writ later issued in Hastings's favour authorizing payment for the addition to the garrison, that the council put forward details of the scheme for increasing it, the great council approved the scheme and it was left to the ordinary council to vary the number of troops from time to time at their discretion. They did so twice within eighteen months, in September and the following April. The writ was issued in 1479 when a financial settlement was made with Hastings. Warrants for Issues E. 404/76/4/113, 115 (duplicates). KR Mem. Roll E. 159/255, Communia, Hilary Term, m. xx, gives full details of Hastings's retinue. In May 1482, Calais was again in danger as a result of Edward's new alliance with Brittany and in July one thousand archers were ordered to be retained in Kent and sent to Calais. They were to be mustered before embarkation and the results of the muster reported to the king and council. *Cal. Pat. Rolls, 1476–1485*, 322, *By K.* Two days after Richard III's accession a commission was issued on the advice of the council for taking possession of Calais, followed six weeks later by a similar commission for Guisnes. Treaty Roll C. 76/168 m. 29, *Per breve de privato sigillo*, m. 27, *Per ipsum Regem*. In June 1484 a series of ordinances for the conduct of the Calais garrison, originally drawn up by Warwick when he was lieutenant of the town and issued under his own seal in 1465, were reissued. Treaty Roll C. 76/168 m. 4, *Per ipsum Regem.* The original is enrolled C. 76/149 m. 14. In the same month a proclamation was ordered in the Cinque ports that the men of the ports should hold themselves ready with ships, guns and supplies to assist in the defence of Calais when called upon by the king or council. Signed Bills C. 81/1531/3.

It is worth commenting at this point on the means by which these decisions were put into effect. Instructions under the sign manual and the signet were the predominant method even for such important business as the arrangements made with the Staple in 1466.

[41] A financial revival under the Yorkists seems now to be definitely established. See A. Steel, *The Receipt of the Exchequer 1377–1485* (1954) chs 8, 9 and conclusion and especially 322–4, 354–5, 357–8, as qualified by B. P. Wolffe, 'The Management of English Royal Estates under the Yorkist Kings', *English Historical Review* LXXI (1956) 1–27.

[42] The only exception is the statement *c.* 1484 published by Gairdner, *Letters and Papers, op. cit.* 81–5. Wolffe, *op. cit.* 20–22.

[43] 'Historiae Croylandensis Continuatio', in Fulman 559.

[44] The increase is generally attributed to a revival of trade but part of it may be due to a tightening up of the customs administration. See above chs 1 and 2.

missions and reports of investigations into smuggling in which the council was concerned and numerous individual cases in which it authorized exemptions from customs, the issue of sums of money (generally from the customs revenues), or safe conducts for trade in restitution for piracy.[45] On 24 February 1484, for example, a writ of privy seal addressed to the upper exchequer ordered the remission of £2,353 10s. 4d. of customs and subsidy due from the merchants of the Staple. In March the previous year the wool fleet on its way to Calais had sighted pirates and put back to London. A good deal of wool was ruined through lying too long in the ships. Besides taking the decision to remit the customs and subsidy on this ruined wool, the council itself went so far into details as to decide from the evidence of the port books which merchants were to be reimbursed, and to send in a list of their names and the amounts due to the exchequer.[46]

B. P. Wolffe has shown that the revival of the chamber as both a treasury and audit office was a Yorkist achievement. The proceeds of confiscated and resumed estates, together with the more efficient practices of private estate management on the royal lands and careful administration from the chamber raised the known income from land to at least £35,000 gross by Richard III's day.[47] For our purposes these lands can be divided into two groups—those permanently in the king's hands, and lands which fell in during the reign for various reasons. In the first group, a connection can be shown between the council and the administration of several estates including the duchy of Lancaster. Richard Fowler and Thomas Thwaytes, both prominent councillors, were successively chancellors of the duchy of Lancaster. Other councillors were included in commissions to tour the duchy estates.[48] In 1478 a letter was sent to Nicholas Leventhrope, the

---

[45] e.g. In June 1472, a proclamation was issued on the council's advice ordering that the statute of 1463 forbidding certain malpractices in the sale of wool should be observed and that the names of offenders should be certified to the king and council. *Cal. Close Rolls, 1468–1476*, 238–9. *Rot. Parl.* v 503–4. In December 1475, commissions were issued for enquiries into the smuggling of Staple merchandise from Kent and Sussex. The results were to be reported to the king and council. They were followed two months later by a similar commission for the Cinque ports. *Cal. Pat. Rolls, 1467–1477*, 571, 573. In 1478 alone they dealt with a number of cases, and sent letters to various customs officers in five ports. See above Ch. 7, p. 188 and n. 81. In May 1482, they discussed the evasion of duty on cloth exported from London and sent instructions both to the customs officers and to the mayor (who controlled the office of packer) ordering the packing of cloths to be more rigidly supervised. Warrants to the PS. PSO 1/59/3039, 3046 both under the signet. They authorized payment for keeping guards in the port of London. Tellers' Roll E. 405/66 m. 4r, entry on William Martyn and John Draper, and for the cost of the wool convoys to Calais. Warrants to the PS. PSO 1/59/3033 (Signet). Warrants for Issues E. 404/78/2/61. KR Mem. Rolls E. 159/258, Communia, Hilary Term, m. iijr, E. 159/259 Communia, Michaelmas Term, m. xlvr.

[46] KR Mem. Roll E. 159/260, Brevia Directa, Hiliary Term, ms xlr and d, and xlir.

[47] Wolffe, *op. cit.* 20. But see also ch. 1 above p. 41.

[48] Below p. 215 n. 135.

receiver-general, for certain special causes and matters moving the king and his council[49] and on at least one occasion the duchy accounts were cleared after discussion in council.[50] When in 1472 new appointments of surveyors were made for various crown lands administered in seven regional groups, the appointments were made 'pro diversis causis et consideracionibus nobis et consilio nostro moventibus'.[51] Their commissions also instructed the new surveyors to ascertain the value of the lands and rights and report back to the king and council. In 1461 and 1473 the council was concerned in the appointment of commissions to administer the Marches of Wales.[52] In the second group, the forfeited Beaufort, Percy, Roos, Richmond, Wiltshire and Clarence estates fell within this new system and also those of the Talbot earls of Shrewsbury, which were in Edward's hands for most of his reign owing to two long minorities.[53] It can be shown that at some time or other the council was concerned with all these estates except the first two[54] and, moreover, dealt with other confiscated estates

---

[49] Issue Roll E. 403/848 m. 2, 23 Oct.

[50] Warrants for Issues E. 404/77/2/31.

[51] For the general significance of these arrangements see Wolffe, *op. cit.* 2 and ns 1–3, who states that there were no precedents for such action between the thirteenth century and 1462. Two sets of patents for these appointments exist. Both instruct the surveyors to report back to the king and council. Only the earlier set issued in March and April mentions the council's part in the appointments. The entries on *Cal. Pat. Rolls, 1467–1477*, 329, 332, *By K.*, omit this information but it is given on the roll and in the Signed Bills. C. 66/529 ms 17 and 20. C. 81/1504/8, 15, 18. The patents were reissued in August when more detailed information about their charge was given to the surveyors. On this occasion no mention of the council's advice was made though the surveyors still had to report as before. *Cal. Pat. Rolls, 1467–1477*, 347–8. C. 66/529 m. 1. C. 81/1504/39. Earlier commissions of the same type issued in 1462 do not mention the council at all and were warranted by the treasurer, *Cal. Pat. Rolls, 1461–1467*, 110–11.

[52] *Cal. Pat. Rolls, 1467–1477*, 283, *By K.* Patent Roll C. 66/527 m. 1. Signed Bills C. 81/1502/38. Information about the council is omitted from the Calendar. *Cal. Pat. Rolls, 1467–1477*, 366. *By K. and C.* At this early date the prince of Wales's council was concerned in the main with administration only. It only acquired military and judicial powers piecemeal during the next few years. C. A. J. Skeel, *The Council in the Marches of Wales* (1904) 19–29.

[53] Wolffe, *op. cit.* 6, 7–9.

[54] In July 1461, the king on the council's advice allotted 100 marks to Philippa, Lord Roos's wife, to be taken from the income of the forfeited estates. Warrants for Issues E. 404/72/1/21. In 1478, Richard Welby, the receiver of the Richmond lands in Lancashire, Peter Beaupie, the receiver of Clarence's forfeited lands at Warwick, and John Agard, receiver of the honour of Tutbury, all received letters after discussion in council. Issue Roll E. 403/848 m. 2, 23 Oct. Beaupie, in 1478, had to furnish relevant accounts of Clarence's lands to a commission consisting of five councillors, four of them very prominent—Sir Thomas Vaughan (treasurer of the chamber), Sir John Say, Sir John Elryngton, Sir Robert Wingfield and Henry Butteler. Wolffe, *op. cit.* 8 ns 1 and 2. In 1478–9 the constable of Warwick castle sent the Warwick bailiff to discuss repairs to the castle walls *cum domino Rege et aliis de consilio suo. Ministers' Accounts of the Warwickshire Estates of the Duke of Clarence 1479–80* ed. R. H. Hilton, Dugdale Society (1952) p. xxv n. 1, and 24. In 1470 and 1478 the council discussed the position and maintenance of Eleanor, countess of Wiltshire. Council and PS.

and estates in hand.[55] A letter in the *Plumpton Correspondence* written about 1475 by Godfrey Greene to Sir William Plumpton throws more light on the system. Greene stated: 'And as for the labour for the bailiships and farmes, Sir, your worship understands what labour is to sue therefore; first, to have a bill enclosed of the King, then to certein lords of the Counsell, (for there is an act made that nothing shall passe fro the King unto time they have sene it,) and so to the privie sealee and Chauncellor: so the labour is so importune, that I cannot attend it without I shold do nothing ells, and scarcely in a month speed one matter.[56] The terms of this letter are so definite that it seems to allow of no doubt that offices and farms on the crown lands were much more difficult to come by than they had been and that the council held a key position in this stricter administration. The letter after all only summarizes what contemporaries had long regarded as sound administrative practice.[57] The statement lacks definitive proof for England, but evidence from Ireland indicates the development of this practice there

E. 28/90/23. (A petition to the king, the resulting enrolment, *Cal. Pat. Rolls, 1467–1477*, 211, *By p.s.*, does not mention the council) *Cal. Pat. Rolls, 1476–1485*, 106, *By K.* Signed Bills C. 81/1514/45. A writ to the privy seal about the Shrewsbury estates runs 'We considering that thissues and profuytes of the said lyvelode by thaduise of or Counseill have been assigned for the contentacion of the charges and expenses of or household. . . .' Warrants to the PS. PSO 1/55/2833K. The date unfortunately is mutilated.

[55] e.g. The council appointed a commission, which consisted of four prominent councillors, Sir John Wenlok, Sir John Fogge, Sir John Scotte and John Say, to deal with the earl of Oxford's forfeited estates. *Cal. Pat. Rolls 1461–1467*, 229, *By C.* Sir John Wenlok was also appointed governor of John, duke of Norfolk, with control of his estates during minority. *Cal. Pat. Rolls, 1461–1467*, 105, *By K.*, 112. In March following, the council confirmed this. Council Warrants C. 81/1547, 18 March 2 Ed. IV, but no enrolment. The council was still dealing with questions about the Norfolk estates in 1472. Council and PS E. 28/90/36. *Cal. Pat. Rolls, 1467–1477*, 293, *By p.s.* does not mention the council. Wenlok was also placed in charge of the wives or widows of three attainted Lancastrians, Lady Hungerford, Anne Hampden and the countess of Wiltshire. *Cal. Pat. Rolls, 1461–1467*, 178, 181. The council is not mentioned in the writs covering Lady Hungerford and Anne Hampden and only in a later document for the countess of Wiltshire. See above n. 54. In 1471 the council dealt with the temporalities of Llandaff. *Cal. Pat. Rolls, 1467–1477*, *By K.*, 287. Patent Roll C. 66/527 m. 19. Signed Bills C. 81/1502/51. The *Calendar* omits the reference to the council.

[56] *Plumpton Correspondence* ed. T. Stapleton, Camden Series (1839) 33. The editor dates this letter *c.* 1475.

[57] *The Governance of England* ed. C. Plummer (1885) 142–4, 150–53, 349–53. *Proceedings and Ordinances* I 9–10, 85–6. J. F. Baldwin, *The King's Council in England during the Middle Ages* (1913), 148, 157, 163, 172, 198, 201. Greene regarded the 'act' as new, but it may have been a recent revival of an old practice. For this possibility see the regulations of 1443. For opinions on these regulations see Baldwin, *op. cit.* 188–9. T. F. T. Plucknett, 'The Place of the Council in the Fifteenth Century', *Transactions of the Royal Historical Society* 4th series I (1918) 180–83. Sir H. Maxwell-Lyte, *Historical Notes on the Use of the Great Seal of England* (1926) 83. J. Otway-Ruthven, *The King's Secretary and the Signet Office in the Fifteenth Century* (1939) 34–7. I have followed Maxwell-Lyte and Otway-Ruthven in regarding them as an attempt to secure administrative efficiency rather than as political moves. The possibility cannot be ruled out that Greene was making excuses for his own negligence, though this is unlikely.

from the late 1470s.[58]

The council discussed the spending as well as the raising of money. In June 1461 standing orders were sent to the treasurer and chamberlains of the exchequer authorizing payments 'by thavise of or counsaill' for a variety of offices including the household, the chamber, the great wardrobe, 'or werkes', the exchequer officials, the judges of all the courts, the customs officials, and officials of 'livelodes'. The lieutenant of Ireland, the wardens of the marches and the captain of Berwick were also to be paid their 'wages assigned by us and or counsaill after thendentures of thayr witholdying'. Such orders were renewed on seven occasions between 1462 and 1471 and once under Richard III. A draft for similar orders also exists for Edward V.[59] These documents probably indicate a formal more or less routine approval of expenses, but they do at least show that a whole range of payments periodically came before the council for authorization and that important officials had their pay decided by the council on other occasions.[60] A good deal of miscellaneous financial business (much though by no means all of it of a minor character) came before the council.[61] From

[58] For England only seven petitions granted on the advice of the council have been found, i.e. those concerning the Roos, Wiltshire (2), Norfolk and Llandaff estates and the mines (see above p. 200, n. 54 and p. 201, n. 55), and one from Sir Thomas and Sir George Lumley for the office of constable of Scarborough castle. *Cal. Pat. Rolls, 1461–1467*, 427, *By K.* Patent Roll C. 66/512 m. 21. Signed Bills C. 81/1487/2. The *Calendar* omits mention of the council. Baldwin points out that grants were generally made in the king's name and seldom mention the council. The changed character of executive action would account for this. See above ch. 7 pp. 181–90.

The disposal of offices and confiscated and deserted lands in Ireland had generally been left to the lieutenant who had power to grant such lands to suitable persons though the government had frequently interfered. *Cal. Pat. Rolls, 1461–1467* 142, 437; *1467–1477*, 205, 335–6; *1476–1485*, 90. When after Clarence's fall the lieutenants were the king's young children, the patents of appointment stipulated that ecclesiastical patronage and lands acquired should be disposed of on the advice of the king and council ('nec terras aut tenementa illius terre adquisica seu adquirenda aliis applicetur usibus quam in defensionem eiusdem terre et hoc iuxta discrecionem et avisamentum nostrum et consilii nostri'). *Cal. Pat. Rolls, 1476–1485*, 118, 153, 210, 403. Patent Rolls C. 66/543 m. 28; C. 66/544 m. 28; C. 66/545 m. 2; C. 66/554 m. 26.

[59] Warrants for Issues E. 404/72/1/7; E. 404/72/2/20; E. 404/72/3/78; E. 404/73/1/32; E. 404/73/3/55; E. 404/74/2/37, 78 and 79 (duplicates); E. 404/75/1/5; E. 404/78/2/54. *Grants of King Edward V* ed. J. G. Nichols, Camden Series (1854) 68–9. All covering more or less the same range of subjects but they contain some interesting variations which show that their issue was not completely routine.

[60] This is confirmed from other sources. Council and PS. E. 28/90/24; E. 28/92, 7 and 8 May 19 Ed. IV. Signed Bills C. 81/1512/30.

[61] See, for example, the long list of expenses authorized in January 1467, including among other things payments for the expenses of Henry Beaufort in the Tower of London, the expenses of various heralds and messengers, payment for new seals for the customs and aulnage officials, and sums to Lord Herbert for military operations and bringing rebels from the Isle of Wight before the council and the expenses of the earl of Worcester for a journey to Wales. Warrants for Issues E. 404/73/2/53.

time to time it supervised the expenditure and accounts of the household, and this was obviously intended to be a normal arrangement.[62] On at least three occasions exchequer officials were paid quite large sums for compiling financial statements for the king and council or for the council alone.[63] The council also kept an eye on the general course of business in the upper exchequer. Once in 1482 the king, being informed by the council of delays which officials coming to present their accounts had to put up with, ordered the treasurer and barons to arrange for additional sittings every Wednesday and Friday and 'othir tymes behouefull' in the council chamber next the exchequer to relieve the congestion.[64]

In addition to its oversight of normal revenue matters the council was active in times of crisis. Sometimes Edward found it expedient to ignore the exchequer and the established, but exceedingly slow, official methods of raising money. Two such occasions will be dealt with here—on both of which the king needed money for war. The first was to meet a crisis brought about early in 1464 by renewed civil war.[65] On the council's advice, the king imposed a special levy on his own supporters. All who had received grants and pensions of the value of ten marks a year or more since his accession were to contribute a quarter of their annual value.[66] The second occasion

[62] I have already discussed elsewhere the reform of the household carried out on the council's advice in 1478. See above ch. 7 p. 188 and ns. 86, 87. For expenditure and the payment of creditors see the grants for expenses to Sir John Fogge and Sir John Howard. *Cal. Pat. Rolls, 1461–1467*, 442, By K.; *1467–1477*, 98, By p.s. Patent Rolls C. 66/512 m. 7; and C. 66/521 m. 5. Signed Bills C. 81/1497/9. Warrants to the PS. PSO 1/32/1664. In both cases reference to the council is omitted from the *Calendar*. Also for Thomas Markham, the purveyor of sea fish (1467), the chaplains and clerks of the royal chapel (1469). Warrants for Issues E. 404/73/2/63; E. 404/74/2/51. In 1472 the treasurer and barons were instructed to look into the question of certain sums of money paid by Sir John Fogge, when he was treasurer of the household, to Sir John Scotte, the former controller, and his subordinates. Warrants to the PS. PSO 1/35/1850. For payment of other debts see Warrants to the PS. PSO 1/55/2833 K & N; PSO 1/58/2984. Warrants for Issues E. 404/75/2/60. In 1475 the exchequer auditors, Hugh Fenne and Nicholas Lathell, declared before the king and the lords of the council that John Elryngton, the treasurer of the household, had rendered account for the period May 1471 to September 1474. As £3,729 1s. 4d. was still owing to creditors on 31 March 1475 the king, on the council's advice, granted Elryngton £600 a year until the sum should be paid off. *Cal. Pat. Rolls, 1467–1477*, 537, By p.s. Patent Roll C. 66/536 m. 15. The entry on the *Calendar* is over-condensed, omitting the information that action taken was on the council's advice and stating only that the auditors reported to the council. The Orders and Regulations of 1478 state that each year the steward, treasurer and controller must inform the king of his creditors so that he could arrange to settle with them on the council's advice. Oxford, The Queen's College MS. 134 f. 15d.

[63] Issue Rolls E. 403/827 m. 11, 11 Feb., E. 403/831 m. 5, 22 June, m. 6, 23 June. Entries on Hugh Fenne, Nicholas Lathell and William Essex and Richard Forde.

[64] Warrants to the PS. PSO 1/51/2605A. KR Mem. Roll, Communia, Easter Term, m. ijr.

[65] See above ch. 7 p. 183 and ns. 53 and 54.

[66] *Cal. Close Rolls, 1461–1468*, 230. A proclamation was issued at the end of March and a household officer, Stephen Preston, placed in charge of the collection. He was to receive the

occurred in 1475 with the problem of raising money for the French campaign. More normal methods having failed to produce enough money, Edward with enormous personal trouble resorted to a benevolence assessed under his own eye and collected under the supervision of his household officers.[67] There is no evidence that the council discussed the original decision to levy the benevolence. On the other hand, the council was concerned with its collection in 14 counties and in the Cinque ports and with overcoming the resistance of certain persons to it and to other war taxation in Coventry and London.[68] The council was also concerned in the disbursement of funds for the campaign[69] and the final audit of accounts.[70]

There are in fact, in spite of the defects of the sources, a large number of scattered references which show the council to have been frequently occupied with military and financial affairs. Although these documents with only a few exceptions are concerned merely with details, their number, together with the fact that in the 1470s it was the treasurer who most often presided over the council when the king was not present,[71] makes it highly probable that the council played a major part in shaping financial policy and in bringing about the revival of the royal finances.

II

The names of 124 people to whom the title *councillor* was given at different times between 1461 and 1483 have been collected.[72] Although so

money at York and draw up indentures with those who paid. *ibid.* 259–60. The second document (addressed to Preston) does not mention the council.

[67] Edward's difficulties in raising money have been vividly described by H. L. Gray and A. Steel. H. L. Gray, 'The First Benevolence', in *Facts and Factors in Economic History* ed. A. E. Cole, A. L. Dunham and N. S. B. Gras (1932) 90–113. Steel, *Receipt of the Exchequer, op. cit.* 300–07.

[69] Kent, Southampton, Somerset, Dorset, Devon, Cornwall, Gloucestershire, Rutland, Surrey, Sussex, Essex, Bedfordshire, Buckinghamshire and Leicestershire. Tellers' Roll E. 405/60 m. 8. A councillor, Robert Martyn, was paid the large sum of 20 marks for attending to the business of the benevolence in the Cinque ports. Warrants for Issues E. 404/76/1/6. In December 1472, a signet letter had been sent to Coventry ordering that all persons who refused to pay taxes should be imprisoned and, if need be, the stiff-necked sent before the king and council for punishment. *The Coventry Leet Book* ed. M. D. Harris, EETS (1907–13) 383–4. For London see J. O. Halliwell, *Letters of the Kings of England* (1846) I 144–7, quoting from BM Harleian MS. 543 fos 148–9. As Scofield, *op. cit.* II 127 n. 5, 128, has pointed out, the correct date of this letter is 17, not 22 June, as Halliwell gives it.

[69] Warrants for Issues E. 404/76/4/112. On the council's advice Thomas Bulkeley was sent to Canterbury to pay the army wages and remained there for three weeks.

[70] KR Mem. Roll I. 159/255, Brevia Directa, Michaelmas Term, m. iijd.

[71] This is shown by numerous entries on the Issue Rolls between 11 and 18 Ed. IV.

[72] In addition there were two clerks until 1465 and one thereafter. James Goldwell is also once mentioned as acting as clerk in 1472 and William Lacy once in 1478. The influence of the clerks was such that they should be classed as councillors themselves and not as mere agents of the council.

large a number might at first sight seem to imply a loose use of the title it was in fact used with discrimination.[73] Nineteen of these men are mentioned only in connection with diplomatic missions or negotiations. It is possible that in some cases they were given this title to add to their dignity as the king's representatives but more likely because councillors were required to take an oath of secrecy. Thus 105 people are left who had more than this casual importance. This large figure is meaningless without subdivision and analysis.[74] The period has therefore been divided between the troubled years before 1470 and the more peaceful years after Edward's return in 1471 when he personally was in much firmer control. For the first period 60 names have been collected, of whom 20 were nobles, 25 ecclesiastics (16 bishops, 1 abbot and 8 others), 11 officials and 4 others. For the second period there are 88 names, of whom 21 were nobles, 35 ecclesiastics (22 bishops, 2 abbots and 11 others), 23 officials and 9 others.[75] The most striking point about these figures is the comparatively large number of nobles[76] and the increase in the number of lay officials during the second period. Although officials always had been and always must be an important element among the king's councillors, the view has sometimes been put forward, expressly and by implication, that Edward made a deliberate attempt to exclude the nobility from his council in their favour and that this led to protests from the lords, who were accustomed to regard themselves as the king's natural councillors.[77] In spite of the increase in the number of lay officials in the second period it may be doubted whether there was any deliberate policy of this nature. The figures hardly support the view that nobles were deliberately excluded. The nobles

[73] Baldwin, *op. cit.* 426. A perusal of Rymer's *Foedera* quickly shows that in the lists of names given in commissions care was taken to distinguish those who were councillors from those who were not.

[74] The method of classification and the somewhat arbitrary way in which the period of service of councillors has been determined is explained in appendix D p. 309.

[75] Three of the ecclesiastics died shortly after the re-adeption and it is possible that they were not councillors in the second period. In the first period I have classed as bishops one abbot (Milling) and four ecclesiastics (Alcok, Goldwell, Martyn and Russell) who became bishops only between 1471 and 1483. Ecclesiastics who became bishops only after 1485 I have classed as 'Ecclesiastics: Others'. Of other classes Sir Guy Fairfax and garter king-at-arms are only mentioned in documents of foreign origin and should possibly be discounted.

[76] Out of a total of 34 nobles (which figure excludes four on diplomatic commissions only) 15 were either relations of the king or created during the period. In attitude (in spite of the notoriety of the Wydevilles) there seems to be very little to distinguish them from others and I have not therefore made them a separate class.

[77] Baldwin, *op. cit.* 421–5. The manifesto of the rebels in 1469 (incidentally before the great increase in the second period) quoted in support of this view is merely conventional propaganda. Polydore Vergil, however, took the opposite view—that Edward did not try to exclude the nobility. *Three Books of Polydore Vergil's English History* ed. Sir H. Ellis, Camden Series (1844) 172.

provided 20 members in the first period and 21 in the second. The average number of lay peers summoned to parliament during the same periods works out at 45 and 39 and the number who actually attended was probably considerably less. The fact that so considerable a section of the lords summoned (44 per cent at the lowest computation) at some time bore the title of councillor makes a policy of deliberate exclusion unlikely.[78] The regularity with which they attended, and consequently the extent of their influence, poses however another question which the sources hardly permit us to answer.

Edward's own experiences no doubt reinforced in his mind the traditional distrust of medieval kings for the overmighty subject, but like his predecessors it is *a priori* unlikely that he could do without the support of the mighty who were prepared to give him loyal service. Especially in the early part of his reign he needed all the support he could get and the local

[78] The average number of lay peers summoned to Edward's parliaments was 43 with a range of 36 (1478) to 49 (1461). Divided into periods again the average for the first period is 45 with a range of 42 (1469) to 49 (1461) and for the second an average of 39 with a range of 36 (1478) to 45 (January 1483). Compiled from Wedgwood, *Register*. If the position is examined at any one point there seems to be good reason for the omission of a number of great names from the list of councillors, e.g. in the parliament of 1472-5, 38 peers were summoned of whom 25 (including one diplomatic only) were already councillors or became councillors in the course of the parliament. Of the remainder, the dukes of Norfolk and Suffolk were probably regarded as unsuitable, in spite of the fact that Suffolk was Edward's brother-in-law. Their territorial rivalries in East Anglia were notorious and they were a hindrance rather than a help to good government there. Moreover, Edward evidently had a very poor opinion of Norfolk's abilities. *Paston Letters* II 356. The earl of Westmorland was the only earl summoned but not a member of the council and he was 68 in 1472. (Another, Shrewsbury, it is true, was on a diplomatic commission only). Ralph, Lord Sudeley, died in 1473, aged 77, leaving no heir. As early as 1461 he had received letters patent excusing him from attendance at parliaments and councils on account of age and debility. W. Dugdale, *The Baronage of England* (1675-6) I 596-7, quotes a rumour, following Leland, that Edward distrusted him on account of his Lancastrian connections. Lord FitzWarin was also granted exemption in 1474 (*CP*). Apart from minors and those attainted, only 14 were not councillors at some time. It is interesting that one non-councillor was Thomas, Lord Lumley, whom Edward himself had raised to the peerage (*CP*). The others were Lords Abergavenny, Berners, Cobham, Grey of Wilton, Scrope of Masham, Strange, De la Warr. Apart from active disloyalty, political factors do not seem, on the whole to have entered into the matter.

My argument seems to be strengthened in the context of Roskell's discoveries on the poor and haphazard attendance of the lay peers (especially those below the rank of viscount) at fifteenth-century parliaments. Although the evidence for Yorkist parliaments is thin, a comparatively poor attendance at most seems to be indicated. The large attendance in 1461 shown by the *Fane Fragment* was most probably abnormal. J. S. Roskell, 'The Problem of the Attendance of the Lords in Medieval Parliaments', *Bulletin of the Institute of Historical Research* XXIX (1956) 153-204 and especially 196-7. If lords were reluctant to attend the infrequent sessions of parliament, many may well have been even more reluctant to become councillors.

influence of the magnates was indispensable.[79] The system of maintenance was inherent in Yorkist and early Tudor government and Edward seems quite deliberately to have built up the power of some of his followers in certain districts.[80] The extent of the Neville territorial influence is well known.[81] Among others, Edward released Henry Percy from his imprisonment in the Tower in October 1469, restored him to his earldom, and made him warden of the east march in 1470 as a counterpoise to the influence of the Nevilles in the north. It was Percy's forces which prevented decisive action by Marquis Montagu in 1471.[82] The Bourchier influence countered that of the de Veres in Essex.[83] Lord Stanley is said to have raised 2000 men to the civil wars in 1459 and 3000 for Scotland in 1481.[84] His influence in a strongly Lancastrian district like south Lancashire and

---

[79] This was probably the reason for his treatment of Laurence Booth, bishop of Durham. Booth had been Henry VI's keeper of the privy seal and Margaret of Anjou's chancellor and had obtained Durham as a result of her support. Up to 1460 he was a decided Lancastrian partisan. Edward probably realized how desirable it was to win over the man who controlled the great palatine bishopric of the north and made him his confessor in April 1461. He helped to resist the Lancastrians in the north, but, suspected of disloyalty, his temporalities were seized in December 1462 and only returned in April 1464. He was almost certainly a councillor during his period as king's confessor, though I have found no record of it. He does not appear as a councillor again until 1470 and was probably not completely trusted again until after Henry VI's death. *DNB* Scofield, *op. cit.* I 174, 186, 243–4 and 244 n. 3, and 248.

[80] W. H. Dunham Jr has recently convincingly argued that retaining was a politically stabilizing force under Edward IV. See below p. 208 n. 85. These methods were certainly being employed as late as the 1503s. Henry VIII deliberately built up the territorial properties of the Russells to give them sufficient power and prestige to control the southwest. H. P. R. Finberg, *Tavistock Abbey* (1951) 268–9. J. A. Youings, 'The Terms of the Disposal of the Devon Monastic Lands, 1536–58', *English Historical Review* LXIX (1954) 23. Peers regarded their spheres of influence with a jealous eye. See *Plumpton Correspondence, op. cit.* 33. The indenture made between Gloucester and Northumberland at Nottingham in May 1474 was probably due to this. W. H. Dunham Jr, 'Lord Hastings' Indentured Retainers 1461–1483', *Transactions of the Connecticut Academy of Arts and Sciences* XXXIX (1905) 77–8 and n. 21. For the way in which various peers had the 'rule' in various shires under Edward VI, see Hist. MSS Comm., *12th Report*, App. pt 4, 32.

[81] C. W. Oman, *Warwick the Kingmaker* (1891) 25–34, gives a rough account of the Neville estates.

[82] *Historie of the Arrivall of Edward IV in England* ed. J. Bruce, Camden Series (1838) 6–7. J. Warkworth, *A Chronicle of the First Thirteen Years of the Reign of King Edward the Fourth* ed. J. O. Halliwell, Camden Series (1839) 13–14. *DNB*. Scofield, *op. cit.* I 505. R. L. Storey, 'The Wardens of the Marches of England towards Scotland, 1377–1489', *English Historical Review* LXXII (1957) 607, 615. For Northumberland's feedmen in 1485, see *Plumpton Correspondence, op. cit.* pp. xcvi-xcvii.

[83] *Victoria County History, Essex* II 217.

[84] *Victoria County History, Lancashire* II 213–15. Scofield, *op. cit.* II 316. Edward did not try to diminish his power, he rather added to it by making Lord Stanley chief justice of Chester (1461). In March 1470 Stanley refused to give any assistance to Warwick and Clarence but joined Henry VI under the Re-adeption.

Cheshire must have been extremely useful. Among those whom Edward more particularly favoured and enriched, Lord Hastings's influence in the central Midlands[85] and William Herbert's in south Wales[86] was probably deliberately built up. Nor was the influence of Lord Dynham in Devon,[87] Lord Howard and Earl Ryvers in East Anglia to be despised.[88] Others exercised similar influence in other districts.[89]

By present-day standards no political tests (if so consciously modern a

[85] Before 1460, Leicestershire, which included estates of James Butler, earl of Wiltshire, John, Viscount Beaumont, Thomas, Lord Roos and John, Lord Lovell as well as the Greys, was predominantly Lancastrian. In 1462 Hastings was given large grants of forfeited lands including the Leicestershire estates of the earl of Wiltshire, Viscount Beaumont and Lord Roos. It is significant that the county played no part in the Lincolnshire rebellion of 1470 although Leicester was the place at which Clarence and Warwick had arranged to meet the Lincolnshire insurgents. By the 1470s Hastings was the most prominent magnate in the county. *Victoria County History, Leicestershire* II 98–100. By 1483 Hastings's known retainers numbered 90 and they must certainly have extended his influence into Staffordshire, Nottinghamshire and Derby and to a lesser degree perhaps into Rutland, Lincolnshire and Yorkshire. Dunham, 'Lord Hastings', *op. cit.* 15–26. Although only six of these retainers are definitely known to have been in Hastings's employ by 1471, the statement in the *Historie of the Arrivall*, *op. cit.* 8–9, that the majority of the three thousand men who came in to Edward at Leicester for his march on London were raised by Hastings, does not seem impossible.

[86] Herbert possessed considerable estates in north and south Wales. Edward increased his local influence by making him chief justice and chamberlain of south Wales (1461), justice of Merioneth (1463), chief justice of north Wales (1467), besides other offices, the stewardship of Buckingham's lands and castles in Wales and extensive grants of lands. *DNB* Dugdale, *Baronage*, *op. cit.* II 266–7. His influence in Wales may be compared with that given to Buckingham by Richard III. In the 1460s the Herbert influence was probably also looked upon as a useful counterpoise to the Neville influence in south Wales. After 1471 it was less favourably regarded, possibly at first owing to the youth of William Herbert II (born *c.* 1455), and in this area at least where the Yorkists themselves were very considerable landowners, Edward seems to have intended the special arrangement of the prince of Wales's council in the marches to replace the method of trusting to the loyalty of local magnates. William Herbert II was made in 1479 to exchange his title of earl of Pembroke for that of earl of Huntingdon. See Ramsey's remarks on Edward's policy in Wales at this time. Sir J. H. Ramsey, *Lancaster and York* (1892) II 430–1. Ramsay wrongly dates the exchange in 1478.

[87] Lord Dynham's career and local influence are admirably described in R. P. Chope, 'The Last of the Dynhams', *Transactions of the Devonshire Association* I (1918) 431–92.

[88] W. I. Haward, 'Economic Aspects of the Wars of the Roses in East Anglia', *English Historical Review* XLI (1926) and especially 178–89.

[89] e.g. The influence of Lords Audley, Stanley, Mountjoy and Dudley (Sutton) in Staffordshire. *Victoria County History, Staffordshire* I 242–3. Of Lord Grey of Ruthyn and Lord Wenlok in Bedfordshire, which had been a particularly disturbed county in the 1450s. *Victoria County History, Bedfordshire* II 35–7. Also the Arundel interest in Surrey. *Victoria County History, Surrey* I 364. To a lesser degree, perhaps, the influence of such men as Sir John Fogge and Sir John Scotte in Kent. Fogge was one of the most active members of the commission which sat from October to December 1471 to investigate the Bastard of Fauconberg's rebellion. Ancient Correspondence LVII nos 107–10 and 112. He and Scotte were both concerned locally with every conceivable subject from commissions of array to the care of deer parks and the morals of the clergy. e.g. *Christ Church Letters* ed. J. B. Sheppard, Camden Series (1877) 26–7. *Literae Cantuarienses* ed. J. B. Sheppard, Rolls Series (1887–1889) III 274.

term may be used) were applied to such people. Conventions of behaviour and public morality were so alien from our own that it is difficult always to bear in mind the very different relationships of the fifteenth century while discussing them in the vocabulary which we ourselves are accustomed to use. A superficial violence of life and conduct often went hand in hand with a tolerance of situations which would be quite inconceivable today[90] and with a mingling of personal and public affairs which from our point of view seems immoral, not to say sinister. Personal and family interests then and for long afterwards affected political affiliations in a most dangerous way. These interests were most profitably served at court, and it was therefore wise to transfer allegiance to the winning side. No loss of honour was involved in such shifts of loyalty. Certain ingrained mental attitudes—political thought would be too dignified a term—gave a moral justification, if any were needed, to these practical considerations. Although the judicial duel was no longer a respectable method of settling legal cases, the idea that God still disposed of kingdoms in battle was widely held. The ultimate decisions in high affairs lay not with men but with God. The *Mémoires* of Philippe de Commynes teem with references to the intervention of the deity in the affairs of kings.[91] The contemporary attitude is well expressed in the speech which Sir Thomas More put into the mouth of Bishop Morton in conversation with the duke of Buckingham which, though not authentic, is certainly a truthful enough comment on Morton's own attitude and career: 'Surely my lord [the bishop said] foly wer it for me to lye, for yf I wold swere the contrary, your lordship would not I weene beleue, but that if the worlde woold haue gone as I would haue wished, king Henryes sone had had the crown & not kinge Edward. But after that god had ordered hym to lese it, and kinge Edwarde to reigne, I was neuer soo mad, that I would with a dead man striue against the quicke. So was I to king Edward faithfull chapelyn, & glad wold haue bene yf his childe had succeded him. Howbeit if the secret iudgement of god haue otherwyse prouided: *I purpose not to spurne against a prick, nor labor to set up that god pulleth down.*'[92] It is completely misleading, therefore, to see in the

---

[90] The Pastons remained on surprisingly close terms with the duke of Norfolk's family all through the famous quarrel about Caister. Although he considered going to Calais with Lord Hastings in November 1472, John Paston the Youngest seems to have continued in Norfolk's service and in the same year one of the duchess's servants wrote to the bailiff of Malden asking that Sir John Paston should be elected to parliament, a letter in which Sir John is described as 'one of my Ladys consayll'. *Paston Letters* III 51–2, 52–6, 58–60, 60–61, 63–6, 143–4.

[91] P. de Commynes, *Mémoires* ed. J. Calmette and G. Durville (Paris 1924–5) e.g. II 227–30, 306, 332 and many others. For English evidence see Edward's proclamation of 1471. *Foedera op. cit.* XI 709–10. *Cal. Close Rolls, 1468–1476*, 188–9. *Historie of the Arrivall*, 13–14. *The Boke of Noblesse* ed. J. G. Nichols, Roxburghe Club (1860) 41–2, 74, 74–6, 82. C. H. Williams, 'England: the Yorkist Kings, 1461–1485', in *Cambridge Medieval History* VIII 420–21.

[92] Sir Thomas More, *English Works* ed. W. E. Campbell (1931) I 70.

terms 'Lancastrian' and 'Yorkist' implications of anything resembling a modern party affiliation. A man might be Lancastrian or Yorkist at any particular time, that is all we can safely say. Competence and willingness to give loyal service were the main claims to advancement. It should come as no surprise therefore that from the beginning of his reign Edward was sensible enough to take service from whoever would offer it.[93] Although at least 11 of his councillors had been on the duke of York's council after the first battle of St Albans,[94] others like Sir John Wenlok[95] and Walter le Hert[96] the bishop of Norwich, who had formerly been prominent members of Margaret of Anjou's household, were also found there. None could have been more Lancastrian than the Wydevilles before 1461, but Lord Ryvers was a councillor by March 1463, long before the king married his daughter.[97] The process of absorption continued. Sir John Fortescue, the chief justice, was in exile with Queen Margaret all through the 1460s but he was a member of Edward's council by November 1474, a few months after the reversal of his attainder.[98] John Morton, later bishop of Ely and archbishop of Canterbury, was also with the exiles at St Mighiel-sur-Bar was attainted but made his peace, became keeper of the rolls in 1472 seven months before the reversal of his attainder, and was a councillor by December 1473 at the latest.[99] Even some who had been Yorkist in the 1460s but had gone over to Henry VI during the Re-adeption were later found on the council.[100] On the other hand, prominent Yorkists were not

[93] Thorold Rogers long ago correctly claimed that Edward was merciful towards old opponents. J. E. Thorold Rogers, *Six Centuries of Work and Wages* (1884), II 316. See also above pp. 169–70. The list of pardons of attainders and restorations of estates on the parliament roll of 1472–5 is impressive. *Rot. Parl.* VI 16–23, 24–33, 45–6, 46–8, 69–70, 104–5, 108–9, 130–31. Commynes several times laments the folly of Louis XI in dismissing his father's servants (whom Louis regarded as enemies) on his succession and praises him for taking some of them back later. Commynes, *Mémoires, op. cit.* 19–20, 39–40, 85, 91; II 311. Commynes was himself, of course, a fine example of change of political allegiance.

[94] Archbishop Bourchier, the bishops of London and Winchester, the earls of Warwick and Worcester, Viscount Bourchier, Lords Fauconberg and Stanley, the prior of St John's, Sir John Say and Peter Taster. *Proceedings and Ordinances* VI 257–8. Baldwin, *op. cit.* 202 n. 1.

[95] J. J. Bagley, *Margaret of Anjou* (1948) 57. Wenlok was on the Yorkist side by 1455. See Appendix D for all dates of service.

[96] Bagley, *op. cit.* 68.

[97] Ryvers and Scales had both been present at Edward's first parliament (Wedgwood, *Register* p. LXVII, quoting the *Fane Fragment*), although neither, according to the Close Roll, had been summoned. It is hardly likely that they came against the express will of the king. *Calendar of State Papers Venetian* ed. R. Brown (1864) I 111, states that Ryvers had already come to tender obedience to Edward by August 1461.

[98] *Governance of England, op. cit.* 72. S. B. Chrimes, *Sir John Fortescue* (1942) p. lxvii. See also below Appendix D n. 65.

[99] *DNB* and Appendix D.

[100] e.g. Lord Stanley. In March 1471 he was besieging Hornby castle on behalf of the Lancastrians. *Victoria County History, Lancashire* II 215. Peter Courtenay served as Henry VI's secretary in 1470–71. Otway-Ruthven, *The King's Secretary, op. cit.* 155 n. 5.

included.[101] This may seem surprising to us because we are in the habit of thinking so exclusively in terms of parties which are either 'in' or 'out' of office, but it is doubtful if it was a matter of surprise to contemporaries, though it must have been the occasion of some very human resentment. Many may have grudged the rewards given to those who had formerly fought against them.[102]

Biographical information is often fuller for ecclesiastics than for laymen, but it casts little light on their influence in the council chamber. Lawyers were predominant. Well over half were canon or civil lawyers and they were prominent on judicial and diplomatic commissions.[103] Though a few bishops[104] were noted for their piety, it was naturally less pronounced in most of them than administrative ability. Their bishoprics were in most cases the reward of administrative service and the class of ecclesiastics might well be considered for the great part as a class of officials. Most of the lay officials came from the ranks of the country landowners and they seem to have begun their political life at a fairly high level round the court, as knights or squires of the body at least. The few exceptions such as Sir William Nottingham[105] and Sir John Elryngton[106] only serve to point the rule. Elryngton's family origins are obscure and he rose from the humble position of clerk of the kitchen to banneret and knight of the Garter. So successful a career from such lowly beginnings was highly exceptional and Elryngton must have been a man of outstanding abilities or backed by very powerful patronage.

Now these 124 men (105 if those on diplomatic commissions only are excluded) were called councillors at different times in the course of 22 years. The number of councillors about the king at any particular time during this period must certainly have been much smaller. After all, the total of the members of modern cabinets over a similar period would probably amount to about the same figure. Thirty-nine documents have

---

[101] e.g. The dukes of Norfolk and Suffolk and Thomas, Lord Lumley. Above p. 206 n. 78.

[102] In 1461 John Berney reported dissatisfaction in Norfolk with Edward's moderation towards opponents and alleged that some of his followers were not sufficiently rewarded. *Paston Letters* II 30–31. See also the Neville jealousy of the Wydevilles. For evidence of similar feelings during the English occupation of Normandy, see B. J. H. Rowe, 'The "grand Conseil" under the Duke of Bedford, 1422–35', in *Oxford Essays in Medieval History Presented to H. E. Salter* (1934) 207, 225.

[103] For suggestions as to the political and administrative importance of lawyer ecclesiastics at a slightly earlier period, see E. F. Jacob, *Essays in the Conciliar Epoch* (2nd edn 1953) 183–4.

[104] e.g. Alcok was the author of devotional works and, according to Bale, was admired for his sanctity. *DNB*.

[105] Nottingham came of a humble family of weavers in Cirencester. Wedgwood *Biographies* 642, n. 7.

[106] *ibid.* 297–9, subject to the following corrections. He was a servant of the household by 1463/4, not 1466 (Wardrobe Accounts E. 101/411/13 l. 37), cofferet of the household in 1471 and treasurer 1474 (E. 101/412/3. *Cal. Pat. Rolls, 1467–1477*, 395, 398, 477–8).

been found noting councillors present at meetings. The number named never exceeds 20 and the average is much lower.[107] Unfortunately these documents were mostly concerned with administrative and judicial matters and not with political policy. It would not therefore be legitimate to use such lists to draw any positive conclusions about the composition of the small inner group that was most probably the core of the council. All that we can say is that membership fluctuated violently even at meetings fairly close together, but that ecclesiastics generally formed the principal group.[108] It is, however, possible to detect attendance of a more political kind and even small groups of men prominent at particular times. The archbishop of Canterbury, George Neville, bishop of Exeter (the chancellor), Lord Fauconberg, Lord Hastings, Sir John Fogge and John Say are known to have served on the council within a day or two of Edward's accession.[108] Although there is no documentary evidence for the earl of Warwick he must certainly be added to the list.[110] The bishop of Salisbury and Lord Wenlok were there by early April, the earl of Worcester and Bishop Stillington of Bath and Wells by 1 November.[111]

Our information about the influence of individual councillors in these early days of Edward's reign is scanty. According to the bishop of Salisbury's unsupported word he was one of an inner group of three high in the king's confidence or at least he was trying to give this impression abroad.[112] One of the others was most probably Warwick and the third possibly Lord Hastings.[113] The immense influence of the Nevilles in

[107] These lists, however, frequently end with the phrase 'et cetera'. We may be certain that the names of the less important laymen are omitted on these occasions.

[108] At two meetings held in May and June 1482 dealing with the same case fourteen and ten people were present including six and seven ecclesiastics respectively. Only five members were common to both and four of these were ecclesiastics. Council and PS. E. 28/92, 26 June.

[109] Baldwin, *op. cit.* 422, states 'the formation of a council was mysteriously left in the background'. It is true that there was no formal announcement or formal appointments, but the council was there. A good many appointments of all kinds were made by word of mouth in the early weeks of the reign.

[110] The *Annales* until recently attributed to William of Worcester (see K. B. McFarlane, 'William Worcester, a Preliminary Survey', in *Studies Presented to Sir Hilary Jenkinson* (1957) 206–7) state that on 3 March the archbishop of Canterbury, the bishops of Salisbury and Exeter, the duke of Norfolk, the earl of Warwick, Lords Fethwater (FitzWalter), Herbert and Ferrers of Chartley 'et multi alii, tenuerunt concilium apud Baynarde Castylle'. Stevenson II 777. If this statement could be accepted it would add the duke of Norfolk and Lord FitzWalter to the list besides considerably antedating the presence of Warwick and Herbert, but considering the time it is safer to interpret the phrase as meaning merely a meeting of Yorkist supporters.

[111] Scofield, *op. cit.* I 217. Warrants for Issues E. 404/72/1/103.

[112] *Calendar of State Papers Milanese* ed. A. B. Hinds (1912) I 64, also 67.

[113] Five prominent people bestowed offices or annuities on him during 1461. K. B. McFarlane, 'Bastard Feudalism', *Bulletin of the Institute of Historical Research* XX (1943–45) 168. In December 1462, John Paston the Youngest reported that Lord Hastings and Lord Dacre

Edward's early years may have been exercised in the council mainly through George Neville, the chancellor.[116] Yet from a very early date various people suspected that the relationship between the king and the Nevilles was uneasy.[115] Alienated by the Wydeville marriage, further exasperated by Lord Ryvers's appointment as treasurer,[116] Warwick grew more and more disgruntled as Edward opposed the Neville pro-French policy by rapprochement with Burgundy. By the middle of 1467 his name disappears from the commissions printed in Rymer and by October the rumour was going round that Warwick was favouring Queen Margaret's party.[117] Early in 1468 William Monypenny reported to Louis XI that Warwick was striving to prevent an alliance with Burgundy and that he himself had done all he could to edge Edward's advisers in the same direction. In spite of their efforts the king's pro-Burgundian policy prevailed. During the council meetings held in January and February at Coventry and London, where the question was discussed, we can detect some group affiliations. Lord Wenlok and Thomas Kent were Warwickites.[118] William Herbert, Lord Stafford of Southwick, Lord Audley (with whom the Nevilles were temporarily reconciled),[119] the earl of Essex, Earl Ryvers, Lord Scales and Sir John Howard were on the other side.[120] Of others pre-

were then 'gretest about the kyngys person'. *Paston Letters* II 122. Lord Dacre was a councillor from June 1462 at the earliest. Also in 1462 the York city authorities paid William Eleryk for riding from York to Durham on three occasions to speak with Lord Hastings and others of the council and William Worell for going to Newcastle-on-Tyne and Alnwick on several occasions to confer with Hastings and once with the earl of Kent. R. Davies, *Extracts from the Municipal Records of the City of York* (1843) 20, 24. See also *ibid.* 6, 22, for other references to Hastings.

[114] Scofield, *op. cit.* II 374, has plausibly suggested that Warwick himself was too much away from court at this time, either in the north or in Calais, to attend council meetings very often.

[115] As early as April 1461, Prospero di Camulio, in a letter to Francesco Sforza, mentioned grievances and the possibility that recriminations might break out between them. In February 1465, the rumour was going round that they had 'come to a very great division and war together'. The source of the information is suspect. It was reported by the Milanese ambassador in France that Louis XI had been informed of it by Margaret of Anjou. *Calendar of State Papers Milanese, op. cit.* I 76, 116.

[116] Stevenson II 785.

[117] *Foedera* XI 574 ff. See also the remarks of Rapin de Thoyras, *History of England* (2nd edn 1732) I 603–4. Dunham, *op. cit.* 79 and n. 24.

[118] Scofield, *op. cit.* I 441. Monypenny had previously met these two in London and according to his own account they gave him valuable information on the state of the kingdom. Scofield, *ibid.* 443, points out, however, that Edward seems to have been unaware of Kent's attachment to the Warwick interest.

[119] *ibid.* I 444. Stevenson II 789.

[120] Ryvers and Scales, for the sake of peace, apparently did not attend, although it was Ryvers, strangely enough, who had previously arranged through George Neville for Warwick to come. Scofield, *op. cit.* I 443–4. Howard, who was unable to go to Coventry owing to an injury to his leg, wrote offering to lead a contingent at his own expense if the king should decide on war with France. *Manners and Household Expenses of England in the*

sent the prior of St John's (Robert Botiller), Sir John Say and John Grene were possibly anti-Warwick, though it is impossible to be certain.[121] With the decline of the Nevilles the name of William Herbert, earl of Pembroke, appears much more frequently. The Croyland Continuator stresses Herbert's influence in 1469,[122] and together with Sir John Fogge, Lord Audley, Humphrey, Lord Stafford, and the Wydevilles, he was one of the evil councillors (i.e. political opponents) singled out for condemnation in the manifesto issued by Clarence, Warwick and Archbishop Neville the same year.[123] So opposed to the Nevilles there was a group round Edward made up of the Herberts, the Wydevilles, Fogge, probably Sir John Scotte,[124] the earl of Essex, Edward's uncle by marriage, and his Bourchier connections, Humphrey Stafford of Southwick,[125] Lord Audley and Sir John Howard. To these must be added the chamberlain, Lord Hastings.

After Edward's return in 1471, Lord Hastings's power soon attracted attention again.[126] A more certain index of influence in these later years are the pensions which Louis XI assigned to councillors after the treaty of Péquigny in 1475. The largest pension of all—2,000 crowns a year—went to Hastings.[127] Sir John (by this time Lord) Howard, and Sir Thomas Montgomery got 1,200 crowns a year each, Bishop Rotheram the chancellor, 1,000 crowns, and Dr John Morton keeper of the rolls, 600.[128] The fact that a newly created peer (Howard) and a mere knight got more than a bishop-chancellor and the chamberlain twice as much, seems to lend credibility to these figures as an indication of their sway with the

Thirteenth and Fifteenth Centuries ed. B. Botfield, Roxburghe Club (1841) 172–3. There are drafts of two letters about the war, both undated, but early 1468 is the only possible date to which they can be referred.

[121] Say was under-treasurer and closely connected with Essex. The prior and Grene were on a commission to treat with Brittany dated 26 December 1467—an anti-French move. But so was Kent. Scofield, *op. cit.* I 443.

[122] Fulman 551—'multum enim praeeminebat ille hac tempestate in consilio Regis et Reginae'.

[123] Printed by J. O. Halliwell in his notes to Warkworth's *Chronicle, op. cit.* 46–51.

[124] Scotte had been controller of the household since 1461. Wedgwood, *Biographies* 750–52.

[125] Created earl of Devon, 1469.

[126] James Arbalaster wrote to the bailiff of Malden, 'what my seyd Lord Chamberleyn may do with the Kyng and with all the Lordys of Inglond, I trowe it be not unknowyn to you. . . .' At the same time the Pastons were trying to use Hastings's influence in elections and in the Caister affair. *Paston Letters* III 51–6, 67–9.

[127] Possibly because he was already receiving a pension of 1,000 crowns from the duke of Burgundy and Louis wished to counteract this. How long Hastings continued to receive the Burgundian pension is not known, possibly not after 1475. Scofield, *op. cit.* II 7 n. 3.

[128] According to Commynes, Howard also received as much as 24,000 crowns in money and plate and Hastings got 1,000 marks worth of plate on a single occasion alone. *ibid.* 146–7.

king.[129] Apart from the Wydevilles, Dominic Mancini writing shortly afterwards,[130] picked out Hastings, Rotheram and Morton as being most in Edward's confidence in his last years.[131] It is noteworthy that these were singled out by both Louis XI in 1475 and by Mancini towards the end of the reign as being specially prominent. There was undoubtedly continuity of influence among a small group although there was certainly strain and rivalry between the Wydevilles and the rest. Groups which had formerly been united in face of danger from the Nevilles now lived only uneasily together.

Although the councillors were sworn,[132] the working council at any given moment never had a definite, nominated membership.[133] Even the most important councillors were frequently away from the king's side for long periods. They were employed on embassies, on special work in the countryside, the royal estates and the like. Lord Hastings spent long periods in Calais after he became lieutenant of the town.[134] In 1476 Richard Fowler and John Elryngton accompanied various duchy of Lancaster officials on a three week progress round the duchy properties in Yorkshire.[135] Elryngton went with Gloucester on his Scottish campaigns from 1480 onwards to act as treasurer for war.[136] Lord Howard,[137] John Russell and Thomas Kent were extensively employed on diplomatic missions. For nearly twenty years under Henry VI and Edward IV Thomas Kent is held to have been the

---

[129] 'Les pensions ainsi offertes, à l'exemple de la pension royale, se tarifent proportionnellement à l'importance et aux exigences de chacun.' Calmete and Périnelle, *Louis XI, op. cit.* 215. There has been some dispute as to the identity of the chancellor at this time, but the receipts given to Louis XI prove that it was Rotheram who got 1,000 crowns. *ibid.* Pièces Justificatives no. 71.

[130] Towards the end of 1483. *The Usurpation of Richard III* ed. C. A. J. Armstrong (1936) 14, 128.

[131] *ibid.* 82–4. He specially noted Hastings's position. Mancini's words seem to indicate that, apart from Earl Ryvers, the Wydevilles were more prominent about the court than in the council. There is no other evidence that the marquis of Dorset, Lord Richard Grey and Sir Edward Wydeville had any great influence in the council at this time. As I have found no reference to them in official sources I have not included them in my list of councillors. It is perhaps noteworthy that Richard III thought it necessary to imprison both Morton and Rotheram as well as to execute Hastings in order to carry out his plans.

[132] This is known only from one incidental reference, an order for payment for Richard Martyn. Warrants to the PS. PSO 1/42/2199. The form of the oath was most likely that of 1424–5, omitting the section referring to the king's minority. Baldwin, *op. cit.* 353–4.

[133] Only a small minority of councillors were appointed by letters patent and even some of these served before their formal appointment.

[134] *Paston Letters* III 16, 160, 161, 173–4, 183–4, 195.

[135] R. Somerville, *History of the Duchy of Lancaster* (1953) I 250–51. Also Thomas Thwaytes's position as chancellor of the duchy meant that he was often occupied elsewhere between 1478 and 1483.

[136] Wedgwood, *Biographies* 298.

[137] For Howard, see *DNB*.

leading spirit in negotiations with the Hanse and he was often absent on such business. After Kent's death his mantle fell on Edward's secretary, William Hatteclyff, and on John Russell. Russell took charge of certain diplomatic matters at least until the treaty of Utrecht was concluded in September 1473.[138] At council meetings others would presumably listen with some respect to opinions based on such long experience and detailed knowledge. Like his predecessors, Edward was accompanied by some of his councillors when he went on his numerous progresses. The council with the king dealt with matters of the highest political importance and councillors might find themselves summoned to some provincial town for discussions. Other councillors remained at Westminster and conducted business there, after 1471 with the treasurer, the earl of Essex, as president. The councillors at Westminster kept up regular communication with the king and referred important matters to him. Thus, the council was a fluctuating group. This irregular membership and lack of formal structure would confirm the opinion expressed elsewhere that the council did not normally act as an executive body. Its members were present at the king's will, and although there were groups within the council advocating different policies and showing certain personal animosities, it was the king who had the last word, who ultimately decided important matters, and possibly even many minor matters, which were then executed under the sign manual and the signet.

Membership of the council meant hard work, and at least until 1471 often hardship and even danger.[139] The rewards, however, could be very great. Some councillors were paid,[140] although more obvious inducements lay in the special grants which it was now customary to make to councillors for their services, and in the *douceurs* which many were ready to bestow on those in influential positions. Lord Hastings's gains were enormous. By

---

[138] The question of the council's dealings with the Hanse is very involved and deserves a separate study. Kent had been concerned as early as 1449 when he headed an English delegation to a conference in Lubeck. The Hanseatics regarded him as one of the most powerful opponents of their interests and the prime mover in the seizure of their goods in England after the taking of the English fleet in the Baltic in 1467. The Nevilles (Warwick, Montague and the archbishop of York) were also supposed to be against their interests and Howard and Fogge in favour. For a general account of negotiations with the Hanse, see M. M. Postan, 'The Economic and Political Relations of England and the Hanse from 1400 to 1475', in Power and Postan, *op. cit.* 91–153, 374, 376–7 and the references there quoted. For other cases and instructions concerning the Hanse, Signet Warrants C. 81/1381/27. Signed Bills C. 81/1528/22. KR Mem. Roll E. 159/238, Brevia Directa, Michaelmas Term, m. xxij. Tellers' Roll E. 405/60 m. 7r. For various negotiations in which Hatteclyff and Russell were concerned, Scofield, *op. cit.* II 30–31, 46, 50–51, 63–4, 67–84.

[139] Richard Langport lost 20 marks and a book worth 5 marks 'in the feld at Shirbourne'. Warrants for Issues E. 404/72/1/26. For capture by pirates, see Scofield, *op. cit.* I 147, 161–2, 188, 210. Warrants to the PS. PSO 1/39/2026.

[140] At rates varying from £200 for an archbishop to £40 for a knight. Baldwin, *op. cit.* 442–3.

1482 his return from grants on the duchy of Lancaster revenues was £127,[141] while the offices and pensions bestowed on him by nobles and religious houses were worth well over £200 a year.[142] His income from grants of offices and pensions in England at the lowest and most conservative estimate must have been between £600 and £700 a year besides the unknown profits from grants of lands and wardships.[143] From 1471 he had his profits as lieutenant of Calais, his pension from Burgundy and later from France, with valuable gifts of plate from Louis XI. He was certainly the most successful of the administrator politicians of Yorkist days and it is little wonder that he could afford not only to rebuild Ashby de la Zouche magnificently and Kirby Muxloe only less so, but also to build at Slingesby and to contemplate building at Bagworth and Thornton.[144] Others attracted by no means inconsiderable rewards. Sir Thomas Montgomery began life as an almost penniless cadet who had to fend for himself. He early deserted the Lancastrian cause, fought with the Yorkists at Towton and from 1461 was numbered among Edward's most trusted supporters. Edward gave him annuities and offices worth nearly £100 a year (where the value is given), four wardships and extensive grants of land.[145] By the end of 1483 the royal service had certainly brought him wealth, for in addition to the gains which he had accumulated under Edward, Richard III bought his

<hr />

[141] BM MS. Harleian 433 fos 317–21. These grants on the duchy estates were known to Dugdale, *op. cit.* 1580–83, but he does not mention the fees attached to them.

[142] *ibid.* Other councillors held similar offices, e.g. Lord Dudley and his son, Sir Edmund, from the duke of Clarence. We know of the Dudley grant only because it was confirmed by the king after Clarence's execution. *Cal. Pat. Rolls, 1476–85*, 137. The common council of Bristol granted Oliver King 40s a year while he held the office of king's secretary. *The Great Red Book of Bristol* ed. E. W. W. Veale, Bristol Record Society (1931–53) pt ii 152–3. Under Richard III, St Albans granted to William Catesby the office of steward previously granted to Hastings and John Foster jointly. *Registrum Abbatiae Johannis Whethamstede*, Rolls Series (1872–3) II 263–7.

[143] In addition to the grants referred to above ns 141 and 142, he had £100 a year as a councillor, £41 as receiver general of the duchy of Cornwall and portage fees on its revenues bringing in perhaps another £25. Warrants for Issues E. 404/73/3/41; E. 404/74/1/111; E. 404/76/1/59; E. 404/76/2/36; E. 404/76/3/23; E. 404/77/2/40. *Cal. Pat. Rolls, 1461–1467*, 9. Foreign Accounts E. 364/96 m. 16d.

[144] Nothing remains of the house Hastings built at Slingesby; only the moat can be traced. *Victoria County History, Yorkshire North Riding* I 558. Apparently no building was actually carried out at Bagworth and Thornton but there may have been a definite strategic intention in the proposal to fortify four houses in a southeast to northwest line across part of Leicestershire. Licence to crenellate was given in April 1474 (*Cal. Charter Rolls, 1427–1516*, 242) not 1471 as stated in Dunham, *op. cit.* 23.

[145] Wedgwood (*Biographies* 605–6) considered Montgomery a young man of almost unbelievable precocity already occupying the responsible position of marshal of the Hall to Henry VI at the age of 17. Unfortunately he conflated the careers of two different men. His judgment of Montgomery is therefore most unjust. For grants under Edward, *Cal. Pat. Rolls, 1461–1467*, 18, 46, 79, 121–2, 124, 125, 126, 180, 367; *1467–1477*, 173, 528, 532, 538; *1476–1485*, 173, 206, 238.

support with a life grant of lands worth the enormous sum of £412 a year.[146] The successful politician and administrator had travelled far from the young squire who, 33 years before, had alleged that he had very little to live on apart from £23 a year from the royal gift.[147] A good deal of 'labouring' went on about the court and council. Councillors were under considerable pressure from their affinities for favours. During the 1460s and early 1470s, in addition to Lord Hastings with whom they had a very close connection, the Pastons lobbied or considered lobbying no less than eleven councillors for their favour on various matters, particularly on the question of the Fastolf inheritance and Caister.[148] Again after the death of Sir John Paston in 1479 the family found it advisable to seek the help of Lord Hastings and the bishop of Ely in settling their affairs.[149] Gifts certainly passed from supplicants to councillors. In a society where customary gifts were common form it is not always easy to distinguish between corruption and the legitimate *pourboires* taken by powerful patrons. However by modern and even contemporary standards, some Yorkist councillors were certainly corruptible.[150] Nor is evidence of violent conduct lacking.[151]

The similarity between the Yorkist council and that of Henry VII is striking. The names of 227 people who bore the title 'councillor' under Henry are known and the division among various classes of people is very similar to that of Edward IV's council.[152] Moreover, there was a con-

---

[146] BM MS. Harleian 433 f. 284. *Cal. Pat. Rolls, 1476–1485*, 430.

[147] *Rot. Parl.* V 193. This is, of course, an *ex parte* statement and should not perhaps be taken at its face value.

[148] The dukes of Clarence and Gloucester, the earls of Warwick, Essex and Pembroke, Earl Ryvers, the archbishop of York, the bishop of Ely, Lord Scales, John Morton and Sir Thomas Montgomery. *Paston Letters* II 9–10, 39–42, 324–6, 340–42, 343, 355–8, 366–7, 373–6; III 127–9, 136–7. I have excluded the bishop of Winchester (*ibid.* III 145) from the list as he was made administrator of Fastolf's estate in 1470.

[149] *ibid.* III 261–3, 263–5, 265–7.

[150] e.g. in 1461 the burgesses of Beverley gave Sir John Fogge a horse, saddle and bridle when he went there to raise soldiers. Scofield, *op. cit.* I 167. The Celys, on one occasion in trouble for alleged infringement of the game laws, gave Sir Thomas Montgomery the value of a pipe of wine and possible more for his help in suppressing the evidence against them. *Cely Papers, op. cit.* 73, 78, 80. See also *Paston Letters* II 11 for suspicions of bribery.

[151] e.g. on the part of Sir John Howard. *ibid.* II 10–11, 12, 42, 52–4, 61–4, 97–8. C. H. Williams, 'A Norfolk parliamentary election 1461', *English Historical Review* XL (1925) 81–6. *Acts of Court of the Mercers' Company 1453–1527* ed. L. Lyell and F. D. Watney (1936) 63–5. See also accusations made in parliament in 1485 and 1488 against William Herbert and the Bourchiers. *Rot. Parl.* VI 292–4, 417. It should be mentioned, however, that a good many accusations, some probably of an *ex parte* nature, were being made against Yorkist government just after Henry Tudor seized the throne.

[152] Agnes Conway compiled an index of Henry VII's councillors using (1) Patent Rolls, (2) MSS connected with the Liber Intracionum, (3) MSS connected with the Court of Requests, and (4) Polydore Vergil. This index is now in the possession of Mrs S. T. Bindoff, who has very generously allowed me to use it. See also C. G. Bayne and W. H. Dunham Jr. *Select Cases in the Council of Henry VII*, Selden Society (1958) pp. xix 77.

siderable transfer of personnel into the Tudor period, and Henry VII was able to draw on the experience of men who had been prominent in affairs under both Edward IV and Richard III.[153]

So Edward certainly destroyed any idea of a 'de facto' independent council such as that which, for example, had conducted affairs for a time after 1406, but he did not as has sometimes been supposed go to the other extreme and rely almost entirely on officials. It was his immediate example (if any example in such matters were needed) that Henry VII followed when he ignored men's past history if he thought they were prepared to give loyal service. Loyalty and ability were the only criteria of service—mighty lord, bishop, doctor of canon or civil law, or official, all were there,[154] but only at the king's will. The Yorkist council was not an independent body; no council ever could be with a strong and vigorous monarch on the throne. It was a collection of men well under the king's control as it always had been under a competent king. Its composition was fluctuating, fixed neither by ordinance nor even by recent custom. The doctrine that the magnates were the king's natural councillors was not very much in evidence. Nor was it by any means a predominantly official body. It was quite impracticable to exclude members of the nobility if they were prepared to give loyal service. It is probable that there was a small inner council, irregular and indefinite, consisting of those whom the king saw fit to consult from time to time.

In view of the scattered and casual material which has survived it would be improper to suggest that we can come to any definitive conclusions about the Yorkist council. We shall probably always see it as through a glass darkly—the dark glass of records not its own. Although it was composed of those whom the king wished to consult and its discussions covered all the many topics with which the government had to deal, the extent to which its advice was accepted on particular aspects of administration and policy is a more intricate question which it is impossible to answer from the evidence available. Yet the volume of evidence which still exists, fragmentary though it is, makes it possible at least to suggest that in the past its influence has been very much underestimated, and that it may well have been that central co-ordinating body necessary to every governmental system.

[153] Out of 40 of Edward's councillors who were still alive after 1485, 22 were councillors to Henry VII and even 20 of Richard III's councillors served in the same capacity. In addition Henry was also served as councillors by 15 people who were near relations of various Yorkist councillors including the Bourchiers and Wydevilles. Others, such as Sir Richard Croft and Richard Empson, had had prominent careers under the Yorkists.
Although the activities of Richard III's council were so similar to those of Edward IV's that examples have been taken from both to demonstrate the council's activities, it would be misleading, owing to the shortness of Richard's reign, to attempt an analysis of the personnel of his council on these lines.

[154] This was, of course, a practical application of the views which Fortescue expressed in a more doctrinaire form. *Governance of England, op. cit.* 145–9. Baldwin, *op. cit.* 206–7 very strangely sees Fortescue as advocating 'the strongly aristocratic point of view'.

9

The Hundred Years' War and Edward IV's 1475 Campaign in France

In the later middle ages success in warfare depended upon a threefold combination: a king who was an able military leader, an enthusiastic ruling class (both aristocracy and gentry) prepared to fight and command the armies, and a people willing to bear the cost through taxation. Traditionally, most historians have held that the reign of King Henry V fulfilled this recipe for success, that war against France was popular and continued so throughout the century. Consequently Edward IV was politically astute when, in 1475, he set out to revive the glories of his usurping predecessor.[1] A closer examination of events, however, hardly supports the age-old glamour of the St Crispin's day tradition and the campaigns following the battle of Agincourt.

Of Henry V's military genius there is no possible doubt, but though the campaigns and conquests of the last five years of his reign were brilliantly successful, opinion about him was already deeply divided before his death. Some warriors worshipped him as the splendid hero-king who led his lords to victory to recover his just rights as the legitimate heir to the kingdom of France. These sentiments were carefully fostered after the king's death by his devoted brother Humphrey, duke of Gloucester, who commissioned an official biography in praise of the noble dead from the Italian humanist, Tito Livio da Forlì.[2] The London chronicles also maintained this laudatory tradition,[3] and the hero's fame captivated Henry VIII when he too, young, romantic, and reckless, against all the dictates of political and financial common sense, plunged into war to recover his 'French inheritance'.[4]

---

[1] The standard biography of Edward IV states that the king's subjects showed 'their willingness, even eagerness' for war with France. Scofield, *The Life and Reign of Edward IV* I 452, II 10.

[2] Titi Livii Forojuliensis, *Vita Henrici Quinti* ed. T. Hearne (1716).

[3] R. Fabyan, *The New Chronicles of England and France* ed. H. Ellis (1811) 578–89. *The Great Chronicle of London* (also written by Fabyan) ed. A. H. Thomas and I. D. Thornley (1938) 91–123.

[4] J. J. Scarisbrick, *Henry VIII* (1968) ch. 2. A compilation, in English from Tito Livio da Forlì, and to a lesser extent from other writers, including information which the anonymous author had obtained from the earl of Ormonde was composed in 1513. Henry VIII himself commissioned the work, and the translator, in turn, calls upon him to emulate

This carefully fostered tradition, enriched, embellished, and immortalized by William Shakespeare, has tended to obscure rather more brutal and prosaic facts. An examination of some contemporary sources throws serious doubts upon Henry's wisdom in embarking on a policy of war with France to enforce what he regarded, under feudal laws of descent, as his personal claim to a foreign territorial inheritance. It throws even more doubts upon how far, even during his own lifetime, the popularity of his achievements among large sections of his subjects survived the cost of their attainment.

Richard II, realistic at least in this, knew that the Hundred Years' War had become an intolerable drain on the resources of the English monarchy, so much so (or he may have been merely indifferent to his 'French inheritance'), that he was ready to abandon it with the exception of Calais, to John of Gaunt, to hold directly as a vassal of the king of France.[5] Other people also shared his views for some of the knights in a great council held at Westminster, summoned for 30 September 1414 on the very eve of the war's renewal, though they expressed themselves in a moderate way, obviously felt that Henry's diplomatic demands were extravagant and they were certainly not enthusiastic for war.[6]

Moreover, none of the Lancastrian kings had the slightest financial sense, and Henry V badly misjudged his capacity to pay for a prolonged war. Henry's income was considerably less than that of his great-grandfather Edward III, and unfortunately he also thought in strategic terms which were much more costly.[7]

Owing to almost insatiable demands for English wool from the weavers of Flanders and Italy, Edward III had been able to pay approximately half the cost of his French campaigns out of an immensely high export levy on this article—an indirect tax borne in very great part by the foreign con-

Henry V. See, C. L. Kingsford, *The First English Life of Henry V* (1911), and *English Historical Literature in the Fifteenth Century* (1913, reprinted 1964) 64 ff. Scarisbrick, *op. cit.* 23 n. 3.

[5] J. J. N. Palmer, 'Articles for a Final Peace between England and France, 16 June 1393,' *Bulletin of the Institute of Historical Research* XXXIX (1966) 180–85, and 'The Anglo-French Peace Negotiations, 1390–96,' *Transactions of the Royal Historical Society* 5th series XVI (1966) 81–94.

[6] *Proceedings and Ordinances* II 140–42. Sir J. H. Ramsay, *Lancaster and York* (2 vols 1892) I 187.

[7] As K. B. MacFarlane noted, in the fourteenth century 'It was very far indeed from being total or continuous war. Until Henry V decided upon piecemeal conquest it was a war of raids in which the English chose the time and place of their descent upon France. If sufficient troops or transport were not available, the raid could be called off. In fact it often was.' 'England and the Hundred Years War,' *Past and Present* (22) (1962) 5. For the expensive nature of Henry V's new strategy and campaigns see the comments of the experienced veteran, Sir John Fastolf. Stevenson II pt ii 579. Fastolf's report, made in 1435, commented in particular, upon the methods of Henry's brother, John, duke of Bedford, after the king's death, but Bedford had merely continued Henry's own strategy. For the decline of Lancastrian income from that of the level of Richard II, see A. Steel, *The Receipt of the Exchequer, 1377–1485* (1954) chs 2–5.

sumer.[8] By Henry V's time the English domestic cloth industry was absorbing a high proportion of English wool,[9] and cloth exports could not be taxed at the same high rate or they would not have sold abroad.[10] The king was therefore forced back into politically much more explosive demands for direct taxation. Englishmen of the late fourteenth and fifteenth century had become adamantly resistant to realistic assessments for taxation[11] and Henry's reputation quickly fell as a result of his demands for money. Already in 1417 at the beginning of his most expensive campaigns, the king was deeply disturbed that the clergy, resenting his heavy taxation, *tepide causante*, were ceasing to pray for the success of the war.[12] The parliament of 1420 and the first parliament of 1421 made no grants of money,[13] and in this latter year Adam of Usk's chronicle broke off with the vehemently disparaging words: 'Our Lord and King, rending every man throughout the realm who had money, be he rich or poor, designs to return again into France in full strength. But, woe is me! mighty men and treasure of the realm will be most miserably foredone about this business. And in truth the grievous taxation of the people to this end being unbearable, accompanied with murmurs and with smothered curses among them from hatred of the burden, I pray that my liege lord become not in the end a partaker, together with Julius, with Asshur, with Alexander, with Hector, with Cyrus, with Darius, with Maccabeus of the sword of the wrath of the Lord!'[14]

M. R. Powicke has attempted to gauge the popularity of the war among the supposedly militarily-minded classes by an analysis of the contingents which the aristocracy and the gentry led into Normandy.[15] This is a sure

---

[8] MacFarlane, *op. cit.* 3–9.

[9] MacFarlane, *op. cit.* 3–9. He points out that 'Edward III and Richard II together received well over three million pounds from this source (i.e., export duties on raw wool, wool fells, and hides), Henry VI perhaps as little as £750,000 between 1422 and 1453, an annual average of less than half that of his fourteenth-century predecessors.' After reaching a peak in the 1350s and early 1360s these exports began to decline rapidly. See E. M. Carus-Wilson and D. Coleman, *England's Export Trade, 1275–1547* (1963) 122–23.

[10] The export tax on wool was about $33\frac{1}{3}$ per cent, that on cloth no more than 2 or 3 per cent.

[11] A. R. Myers, *English Historical Documents* IV 1327–1485 (1969) 379–81. See also Adam of Usk's remarks upon the almost blasphemous iniquity of taxation. He commented on the sinking, by a storm, of a fleet under Sir John Arundel in 1379 'causa infortunii sui pecuniis clero et populo exactis non inmerito imponebatur.' *Chronicon Adae de Usk, A.D. 1377–1421* ed. Sir E. Maunde Thompson (2nd edn 1904) 8, 149.

[12] *The Register of Henry Chichele, Archbishop of Canterbury, 1413–1443* ed. E. F. Jacob (4 vols 1943–47) IV 176. Also E. J. Jacob, *Essays in the Conciliar Epoch* (2nd edn 1952) 59 n. 2.

[13] Ramsay, *Lancaster and York, op. cit.* I 288.

[14] *Chronicon Adae de Usk, op. cit.* 133, 320. The manuscript breaks off at this point, the remainder being lost.

[15] For the contents of the next five paragraphs see M. R. Powicke, 'Lancastrian Captains,' in *Essays in Medieval History Presented to Bertie Wilkinson* ed. T. A. Sandquist and M. R. Powicke (1969) 371–82.

enough method since 'the armies of the fifteenth century were composed of companies of irregular numbers serving under captains who first recruited and then commanded them.'[16] Under this system a captain raised a number of men-at-arms and archers, a proportion of three archers to one man-at-arms generally being regarded as the most effective combination, and Powicke rightly took this as a useful standard of efficiency.

His conclusions demonstrate clearly enough that doubts about Henry's war policy grew very quickly, and the original enthusiasm for it did not long survive. In 1415 20 peers recruited and led just over one half the total forces. In the same campaign knights, who tended to be prominent men in their local communities and who served in parliament led all the larger non-noble companies. Local gentlemen of the same type also raised the smaller contingents, and a high proportion of important local men, esquires and gentlemen either served alone or with one companion or follower. This group was composed of 'the essentially non-military country squire setting off to do his duty in the wars.'

In the campaigns of 1417–21 the picture changed. The contribution of the titled aristocracy fell from one half to just over one third. There was a larger proportion of small contingents (less than 20 men) and their leaders were less likely to be knights than they had been in the days of Agincourt. Moreover the captains of Agincourt did not lead the campaigns of conquest in the years 1417–22. Although the great dukes and earls still remained prominent as contingent leaders, no single parliamentary baron now led a company to the wars. Moreover, only 31 out of 177 contingent commanders during these years were veterans of Agincourt, and even of this remnant of 31, only 25 went on to serve in the armies of Henry VI. This failure to maintain a sizeable corps of experienced captains suggests a fundamental weakness in the English forces, and as Powicke states the whole trend shows 'a decline, not cataclysmic but noteworthy in the involvement of the politically leading class after the high point of the Agincourt campaign.'

One last revival of interest occurred in the 'coronation march' of 1430–31, but at the same time the contingents were now of lesser quality, for the proportion of archers to men-at-arms had begun to increase. In the companies led by the great nobles the ratio increased only slightly, rising from three to one, to four to one. In most of the lesser companies it rose a little higher, but in some of the greater non-noble companies it rose to the very high ratio of sixteen to one, and a few companies became little more than bands of archers. As Powicke again remarks, this significant

[16] Powicke, 'Lancastrian Captains' op. cit. 371. For the change from the feudal levy to this type of army recruited under indentures between the king and captains see A. H. Burne, The Agincourt War (1956). C. Oman, A History of the Art of War in the Middle Ages (2nd edn 2 vols 1924) II F. Lot, L'Art militaire et les armées (Paris 1949). R. A. Newhall, The English Conquest of Normandy (1924), and Muster and Review (1940). M. R. Powicke, Military Obligation in England (1962).

deterioration 'probably represents a drying-up of the source of men-at-arms rather than a deliberate military policy and, as such, reflects the growing disenchantment of the English middle-class with war in France.'

After the 'coronation march' this deterioration continued, and the change in the increased ratio of archers to men-at-arms became a typical feature of Henry VI's reign. Moreover, the involvement of the prominent men of the countryside declined to such a degree that 'the persistent interest of *the court aristocracy* in the war was all that kept the English effort alive,' and even this all but disappeared in the closing campaigns of the war. Long before the final collapse in the 1450s the idea of a military career must have been distinctly passé. Contemporary English chroniclers showed so little interest in the later stages of the war that when the Tudor historian Edward Hall came to write about them he had to cull most of his information from Monstrelet, Waurin, and other Burgundian and French authors.[17]

Nor could Henry V and his successors make up for this growing lack of enthusiasm among the politically prominent by appealing to a wider national feeling. As we have already seen, some of the knights in a great council gave voice to misgivings about war in 1414, and in the parliament of December 1420 (the same parliament which refused any further grant of direct taxation), the commons' debates showed considerable constitutional fears about the future if the king carried through his plans. They demanded his early return to England and the reaffirmation of a statute of 1340 guarding against any subjection of the people of England to their king as king of France.[18] Moreover, Henry was forced to deny any intention of appointing a joint chancellor for both England and France. Also, as I have pointed out elsewhere,[19] Henry could not afford to whip up any kind of aggressive nationalistic feeling in England, for that would have boomeranged in France where he claimed his 'rights' not as a foreign conqueror but as a Frenchman, the legitimate descendant and representative of the French royal family. After the king's death, his brother John duke of Bedford, developed around this concept an intensive propaganda campaign in Normandy, emphasizing in a flood of political literature and sym-

---

[17] B. J. H. Rowe, 'A Contemporary Account of the Hundred Years War from 1415 to 1429,' *English Historical Review* XLI (1926) 504–13. Moreover, at the Winchester parliament of 1449, when the situation of the English possessions in France was desperate, we are fortunate in possessing an authentic account of a parliamentary debate, a rare document at this period. At the king's command Reginald Boulers, the abbot of St Peter's, Gloucester, appealed to both lords and commons for aid for the duke of Somerset, lieutenant of France, but all that came of the appeal was a discussion in the lords which showed very little sense of urgency and the meagre grant of a half subsidy by the commons. See A. R. Myers, 'A Parliamentary Debate of the Fifteenth Century,' *Bulletin of the John Rylands Library* XXII (1938) 388–404. Myers discusses the situation in great detail.

[18] *Rot. Parl.* VI 125, 127.

[19] J. R. Lander, *Conflict and Stability in Fifteenth Century England* (1969), 62.

bolic objects the equal status of English and French under a king descended from the blood royal of both realms. Moreover, by 1426 the government also found it necessary to issue propaganda to justify to the English public Henry's title to the throne of France.[20] Henry V's takeover of France was, both in legal theory and in practice, the warlike enforcement of a legal right which had been denied, not the conquest of one people by another. Although an unknown number of Englishmen received grants of estates in Normandy, Frenchmen who swore an oath of allegiance were left in possession of their estates,[21] and apart from small settlements at Harfleur, Honfleur, and Caen, Henry made no attempt to anglicize the population of Normandy,[22] and John, duke of Bedford, left the civilian administration as far as possible in Norman hands.[23]

Henry V therefore held only major card—his undeniable military genius. It was not enough to ensure the success of his plans. In the absence of any ardent nationalistic spirit he was forced to rely on the enthusiasm of the ruling segment of English society to fight for (and upon the populace to pay for) the warlike enforcement of his legal claims. However great their ancestors' enthusiasm for such projects had been in the fourteenth century, theirs rapidly vanished, and they quickly ceased to relish the part which the king's plans had assigned to them.

It is now time to turn to Edward IV, to try to assess his policy and actions by the same criteria. Edward has come down to posterity with the reputation of a great general. His reputation, however, seems to be based solely on the fact that he never lost a battle, a consideration that hardly decides the question one way or the other. His success may well be due to the fact that his opponents were as comparatively inexperienced as he was himself. Edward never faced a veteran continental commander and the battles of the Wars of Roses (when they were not mere skirmishes as some of them were) were hardly notable for the strategic or tactical skills of their protagonists.[24] Even Edward's famous pursuit of Queen Margaret to Tewkesbury 'was tenacious rather than able.'[25]

[20] J. W. McKenna, 'Henry VI of England and the Dual Monarchy: Aspects of Royal Political Propaganda, 1422–1432.' *Journal of the Warburg and Courtauld Institutes* XXVIII (1965) 145–62.

[21] Although most of the greatest proprietors fled, at least three quarters of the landowners stayed on their estates. Henry V's invasion of Normandy was certainly not 'the Norman Conquest in reverse' which some writers have imagined.

[22] W. T. Waugh, 'The Administration of Normandy, 1420–1422,' in *Essays in Medieval History Presented to Thomas Frederick Tout* ed. A. G. Little and F. M. Powicke (1925) 352.

[23] B. J. J. Rowe, 'The *Grand Conseil* Under the Duke of Bedford,' in *Oxford Essays in Medieval History Presented to Herbert Edward Salter* ed. F. M. Powicke (1934) 207–34.

[24] J. R. Lander, *The Wars of the Roses* (1965) 20–21.

[25] C. A. J. Armstrong, 'Politics and the Battle of St. Albans, 1455,' *Bulletin of the Institute of Historical Research* XXXIII (1960) 25.

Nor does enthusiasm in the country appear to have been at all conspicuous. William Worcester, more or less the spokesman of the remnant of the dispossessed war captains of the previous generation, had in the 1450s written his *Boke of Noblesse*[26] and had made a collection of documents about the war[27] to encourage Henry VI and his advisers to renew it. Worcester revised the *Boke* in the early 1470s, touched it up again, and presented it, together with the collection of documents, to Edward IV on the eve of the 1475 campaign.[28] His enthusiasm for war by this time, however, may well have been no more than an echo from a vanished past. By contrast, an anonymous writer of c. 1470 or slightly later, in discussing Henry V hardly mentions the French war after the triumph of Agincourt, and ends his brief account of the reign with the somewhat frigid words, '[Henry] departed this life at Bois de Vincent in Paris, after having ably reigned nine years and five months.'[29] The Second Anonymous Croyland Continuator, traditionally, though perhaps dubiously, described as one of Edward IV's councillors,[30] remarked that in the parliament of 1472–5:

The principal object of the King was to encourage the nobles and people to engage in the war against France: in the promotion of which object, many speeches of remarkable eloquence were made in Parliament, both of a public and private nature, especially on behalf of the duke of Burgundy. The result was that all applauded the King's intentions, and bestowed the highest praises on his proposed plans; and numerous tenths and fifteenths were granted, on several occasions, according to the exigencies of the case, in assemblies of the clergy and such of the laity as took any part in making grants of that nature. Besides this, all those who were possessed of realty and personal property, all of them, readily granted the tenth part of their possessions. When it now seemed that not even all the grants before-mentioned would suffice for the maintenance of such great expenses, a new and unheard of impost was introduced, everyone was to give just what he pleased, or rather just what he did not please, by way of benevolence. The money raised from grants so large and so numerous as these amounted to sums, the like of which was never seen before, nor is it probable that they will ever be seen in times to come.[31]

No other English writer of the day has left any account of contemporary opinion,[32] and although the Croyland Continuator describes accurately, if

[26] William Worcester, *The Boke of Noblesse* ed. J. G. Nichols (1860).

[27] Lambeth MS. 506, printed in Stevenson II pt ii 521–742.

[28] K. B. MacFarlane, 'William Worcester, A Preliminary Survey,' in *Studies Presented to Sir Hilary Jenkinson* ed. J. Conway Davies (1957) 210–13.

[29] 'The First Anonymous Croyland Continuator,' in Fulman 514.

[30] Sir G. Edwards, 'The Second Continuation of the Croyland Chronicle: Was It Written in Ten Days?', *Bulletin of the Institute of Historical Research* XXXIX (1966) 117–29.

[31] Fulman 557–8.

[32] Admittedly the English sources for this period are pitifully meagre. Foreign sources, however, are almost equally uninformative. e.g. *The Calender of State Papers Milanese* ed. A. B. Hinds (1912) frequently mentions English war policy but except for references to resistance to taxation and descriptions of the benevolence (177, 184, 193–4) mentions public opinion

somewhat vaguely, the course of proceedings in the commons, the rolls of parliament themselves and the transcript of a speech preserved at Christ Church, Canterbury, show that his testimony to the enthusiasm of the members gives, to say the least, somewhat wide bounds to truth. These sources show that enthusiastic, warlike feeling was hardly conspicuous. Both royal propaganda and debates seem to have been conducted in a low key, quite different from the earlier appeals of King Henry V, with an emphasis squarely and firmly placed on defence rather than on aggression.

This emphasis upon defence may be easily explained by the development of Anglo-French relations since the loss of Normandy and Guienne in the early 1450s. As the Wars of the Roses progressed they became more than a series of domestic crises. Neither Lancastrians nor Yorkists scrupled to call in foreign help when they could get it, and the rapid upheavals of English politics upset the calculations of statesmen in distant parts of Europe—and they still particularly affected France. Even after 1453 the king of France dreaded a renewed English invasion, and within a few years fear of Burgundy became an even greater obsession with him. From about 1456 to the death of Charles the Bold in 1477, the mutual suspicions of Burgundy and France developed into a bitter diplomatic contest in which no holds were barred and in which both sides alternately dreaded and wooed the English.

In 1462 Louis XI of France, alarmed once more at the prospect of an Anglo-Burgundian alliance, countered by supporting the exiled Margaret of Anjou, only to abandon her cause at the end of the year when the Burgundian threat to his kingdom had diminished. France and Burgundy then competed for an English alliance. Charles the Bold unsuccessfully tried to persuade Edward to join the League of the Public Weal against Louis XI. Later a temporary success on the part of France drove Charles to marry Margaret of York, and in 1468 Edward IV was threatening to invade France. Reacting strongly, Louis (probably as early as 1468) toyed with the idea of bringing together Queen Margaret and the earl of Warwick: the almost fantastic plan which led to their successful invasion of England in 1470, and to their ultimate failure, because Louis, going too far, pushed their puppet Lancastrian government into plans for an invasion of

only twice. In December, 1473, Christopher Bollati, the Milanese ambassador to the French court, wrote home that 'King Edward is not so eager to make war on the King of France as his subjects' (177), and in August 1474, he wrote of the duke of Burgundy stirring up 'the English people to make war on France' (183). The Milanese state papers are, however, crammed with the wildest rumours about English affairs and should be used only with the greatest caution. Scofield, *Edward IV, op. cit.* II 53–54, states that in 1473 James III of Scotland proposed to Louis XI that for the sum of 10,000 crowns he should keep Edward at home 'by attacking him if that proved to be necessary, or by promising to protect him against his subjects if they should rise in revolt when he gave up his expedition to France.' This does not, however, prove that the war policy was popular. It may merely indicate the probability of fury against what would then have appeared to be fraudulent war taxation.

Burgundy. Duke Charles, until then coldly unsympathetic to the woes of his exiled English brother-in-law Edward IV, in self-defence quickly supported plans for a counter-invasion. After his return Edward tried to come to terms with Louis XI, and his attempts at rapprochement, though unsuccesful, may well have been sincere.[33] At any rate they failed and the suspicion-laden diplomatic manoeuvrings of the 1460s began all over again. Among other things, Louis tried to egg on the Scots to invade England, and to keep up disturbances in Wales where in 1471 Jasper Tudor still held out, and he gave some help to that irreconcilable Lancastrian, the earl of Oxford, to whose treasonable activities rumour persistently linked Edward IV's brother, the duke of Clarence.[34] We should therefore see the campaign of 1475 not as a revival of the genuinely aggressive policies of Henry V, but as a reaction to this background of deep, intense suspicions and fears, and as a somewhat defensive response to the development of Anglo-Burgundian-French relationships over the past two decades.

From the beginning of the parliament of 1472–5 Edward made intensive efforts to popularize his war policy with the commons. At some point he presented them with a 'declaration in writing' on the subject and informed them of his intentions 'dyvers tymes' through speeches by the chancellors.[35] Unfortunately, the rolls of parliament at this period rarely record the full text of speeches, but the roll does very briefly summarize an oration made on 1 February 1474 by the chancellor, the bishop of Durham, on the dual themes of good and stable government at home and the recovery of France.[36]

More fortunately however, the same themes are dealt with and the connection between them made absolutely explicit in the full text of a speech in English preserved in the letter books of Christ Church, Canterbury.[37] This oration obviously one of the 'many speeches of remarkable eloquence' mentioned by the Croyland Continuator, was probably delivered in the

[33] Edward apparently thought of a French alliance as early as the middle of 1472. Scofield, *op. cit.* II 16–17.

[34] Scofield's very detailed account brings out this atmosphere of suspicion, duplicity, and Constant diplomatic flux extremely well. *ibid.* I 1–151.

[35] *Rot. Parl.* V., III. The declaration is mentioned in the subsidy bill of the sixth session of the Parliament (23 January–14 March, 1474) as having been delivered to the commons 'afore this tyme.' It is also mentioned in the seventh session, *ibid.* 150. The same bill of the sixth session also informs us of the chancellor's speeches. There were three chancellors in the course of this parliament—Robert Stillington, bishop of Bath and Wells (April 1471–July 1473), Laurence Booth, bishop of Durham (July 1473–May 1474) and Thomas Rotheram, bishop of Lincoln (May 1474–May 1483).

[36] *Rot. Parl.* VI 88–89. 'Ut idem Cancellarius recitavit, inter alia fuerunt, ad bonum regimen infra Regnum plantand', idemque Regnum per ministrationem justicie stabiliend', ac personas in ociositate nimium degentes per medium guerre exterius in labore ponend', necon jus Regium in Regno Francie recuperand'.'

[37] *Literae Cantaurienses* ed. J. B. Sheppard, Rolls Series (3 vols 1887–89) III 274–85.

first session of the parliament (6 October–30 November 1472).[38] It is indeed eloquent and very long, covering no less than eleven printed pages. The most significant, and perhaps surprising, thing which emerges from its considerable emotional rhetoric, however, is its markedly defensive tone. The king's title to the crown of France is not even mentioned until almost the end of the fifth page, and even then it is rapidly disposed of in fourteen lines as part of a long argument that attack is the best form of defence.[39]

The speech begins with a peroration that internal peace and tranquillity are the means by which a country waxes to abundance and riches. Although the king's recent 'moost victorious prowesse'[40] has extirpated the worst causes of dissension, 'extorcions, oppressions, robberies and other grete myscheves' still abound.[41] The severest justice would be insufficient to repress the perpetrators of such deeds without a remedy worse than the disease, that is, 'within fewe yeres such distruction of people necessarie to the defence of the lande' that enemies would be tempted to invade it. In other words many of the country's thugs are part of its ruling class. They cannot

[38] J. B. Sheppard, the editor of *Literae Cantuarienses*, assigned the year 1474 as the probable date of the speech, but as Scofield, *op. cit.* II 44 n. 1, has pointed out, this date is disproved by internal evidence. The speech mentions that Edward was hoping for a treaty with the Hanseatic league, and such a treaty was signed on 28 February 1474. It also refers to instructions given by the duke of Burgundy to the Lord Gruthuyse and there is a statement that 'last summer' the duke of Burgundy had been on French territory. Both these things can be dated to the summer of 1472. Moreover, the speech refers to Denmark and Scotland threatening England, but treaties were made with these countries respectively on 11 May 1473, and 30 July 1474. Scofield, *op. cit.* II 50, 102. Scofield suggested that the archbishop of Canterbury made the speech, but there seems to be no evidence for this beyond the fact that the text is preserved in the Canterbury archives. It could have been made by the chancellor, Robert Stillington, bishop of Bath and Wells.

[39] *Literae Cantuarianses, op. cit.* 279. After a long passage on the danger of foreign attack the speech goes on, 'it is thought to the Kyngs Highness most expedient, that rathe than he shuld abide the defence of the werre atte home, and leve his lande in the jeopardie that Rome stode in by the comyng of Hanyball out of Carthage, and, like as Scipio, when the Romanes were in dispair of their defence in their owne contre ageynst Hanyball, departed fro Rome and went to Cartage and victoriously behad him there, to the grettest comforte of the Romaynes that he came fro; right soo our Souverayne Lord thynketh that [he], considered his just and rightwys title whiche he hath to the corone and reame of Fraunce, whereof a grete partie was but in late daies in the possession of Englissh men, seeyng also that he hath largely doo his parte in requisicion of justice or of some resounable recompence in that partie, as is aboveseid, coude doo thynges better for the recomforte, sewertie and welthe of his subgetts, than, now havying noon other remedie, to entre and begynne in his owne querell a werre in tho parties ageinst the seid adversarie, for the recoverie not oonly of the duchies of Normandie and Guyenne, but also of the corone of Fraunce . . . .'

[40] A euphemistic reference to Edward's victories over the Lancastrians at Barnet and Tewkesbury and his restoration in 1471.

[41] This statement is made the more plausible by the fact that the commons themselves complained of such things in certain parts of the country in the session of October–November 1472. *Rot. Parl.* VI 8–9.

without peril be destroyed, but their exuberant surplus energy must be diverted into socially less abominable channels.

Moreover, the Scots and the Danes are threatening England, and the subtle and crafty enterprises of King Louis XI of France have for long been, and still are, a constant danger in spite of Edward's efforts to reach a friendly agreement with him.[42] Therefore war abroad, taking the aggressive line, is demonstrably the surest guarantee against invasion and the road to internal order and prosperity. For the first time in Edward's reign, the state of the country and the king's foreign alliances combine to make this policy feasible.

Pelion is then piled upon Ossa in the way of subsidiary, negative arguments to make this long appeal more attractive: possession of the French coast would make the English Channel safer for English shipping and reduce the intolerable financial burden of keeping the sea; many gentlemen, younger sons, and others could be rewarded with land; 'men of werre that have none other purveaunce' could be settled in garrisons and live by their wages—the type of men, who otherwise unoccupied, would cause mischief at home; then, in an appeal to history, the chancellor reminds the king's subjects that since the Norman conquest internal peace has never for long prevailed 'in any King's day but in suche as have made werre outward.'

These long, emotional, at times even eloquent appeals are in the end distinctly negative. The gist of them—fight in France to avoid more trouble at home, reduce (in the end) the king's expenses, and make something for yourself in the process—are a very far cry from Henry V's aggressive clarion calls to conquest. He after all would never have slipped in his claim to the French crown as a short aside in a long argument about defence. The claim to the throne had been the very core of his policy.[43] It looks as if Edward IV realized that he must use all the arts of propaganda at his disposal to whip up an aggressive spirit in a blasé and indifferent people.

Efforts to raise taxation for the campaign show an equally indifferent, if not a definitely hostile, spirit toward the king's plans. In November 1472, instead of the standard levy of a fifteenth and tenth on personal property granted by both houses of parliament, the lords voted a special tax of one tenth of their incomes from lands, annuities, and offices, and the commons separately granted a similar tax from non-aristocratic revenues to pay the wages of 13,000 archers for one year,[44] for which a sum of £118,625 was

[42] See above p. 228.

[43] This is not, of course, to say that Henry V never used the appeal for defence; he did, but it was never the central theme of his propaganda.

[44] Both bills state that the grants were made for the 'defence' of the realm by means of war abroad. *Rot. Parl.* VI 4–6, 6–8. There were several precedents earlier in the century for this form of taxation. See H. L. Gray, 'Incomes from Land in England in 1436.' *English Historical Review* XLIX (1934) 607–39.

needed. Both houses were obviously in a suspicious mood, for both made their grants with the grudging stipulation that the money was to be returned to the taxpayers if the army were not mustered by Michaelmas 1474, and both houses added other intensely humiliating conditions. They refused to trust the king with the money. It was not to be paid into the royal exchequer. Instead the lords instructed the collectors of their grant to pay the proceeds to the archbishop of Canterbury, the bishop of Ely, the prior of the hospital of St John of Jerusalem in England and John Sutton, Lord Dudley. They in turn were to commit the money for safe keeping to the dean and chapter of St. Paul's cathedral, to hold until such time as parliament authorized its release to the king. The commons in their bill ordered the commissioners who had been appointed to supervise the collection of their tenth to place the money in provincial repositories, local castles, towns, houses of religion, and other suitable places, again until parliament authorized its use. Either the lords and commons bitterly grudged the money or they doubted the sincerity of Edward's war policy.[45] Possibly both.

In the next session of the same parliament in April 1473, the lords confirmed their grant of the tenth and now allowed the proceeds to be paid into the exchequer. According to Sir James Ramsay, the exchequer tellers' roll for Michaelmas 1472, reveals that the lords' tenth had produced only £2,461 3s. 4d.[46] If the figure is complete they must have underassessed themselves in a big way.

The commons' tenth was to have been levied by the Feast of the Purification of Our Lady (2 February), but by April no certificates of collection had come in from the local tax commissioners appointed under the terms of the commons' grant. Because no records were available from previous taxation of this kind, it was impossible to calculate what the tenth would yield.[47] As the king's preparations called for money urgently, the commons now granted (in addition to the tenth on incomes) a standard fifteenth and tenth on the value of movable property. Yet they still restricted the new grant to the payment of the archers' wages, and in view of their own admission that the king's needs were urgent, illogically withheld it in the local repositories until the proclamation of the army musters.[48]

---

[45] Parliament had made a grant for war on France in 1468, when, owing to political complications at home, no campaign had followed. In 1472 Edward was forced to remit the still unpaid portion of this grant and any claim he had to a grant made for archers to Henry VI as far back as 1453. *Rot. Parl.* VI 6.

[46] *ibid.* 42–43. Ramsey, *op. cit.* II 393–4.

[47] Records survived from the income tax of 1436 (see above n. 44), but parliament and the government were either unaware of them or chose to ignore them.

[48] *Rot. Parl.* VI 39–41. The collectors were to certify to the chancery within twenty-two days after the Feast of St John. (Probably either the Nativity of St John, 24 June, or the Decollatio of St John the Baptist, 29 August.)

Delay followed upon delay, expedient upon expedient—and all of them unsatisfactory. In the seventh session of the parliament in July 1474, the government revealed to the commons that by the previous January the commissioners had returned most of the certificates for the original levy of the tenth on incomes, from which it appeared that their assessments amounted to £31,410 13s. 1½d.[49] To exert pressure upon recalcitrant districts, the commons then allotted specific numbers of archers (558 in all) to be supported by those areas from which the commissioners had so far returned no certificates of assessment.[50] Moreover, upon hearing that the fifteenth and tenth had not yet been collected they somewhat oddly granted another in its place[51] and extended the time limit for the sailing of the army to the Feast of St John the Baptist (29 August 1476).

The government also revealed that the combined sum for the tenth and the fifteenth and tenth from those shires where the commissioners had made assessments would not exceed £62,094 0s. 4d. The king therefore asked the commons to make up the balance of the money needed to pay the archers' wages, £5,147 3s. 7½d. This they granted, but only on condition that it should be raised from sections of the community normally untaxed—from the order of St John of Jerusalem in England (except for the prior himself) and from 'the Goodes and Catalles of such persones not havyng any or but littell Lond, or other frehold, nor to the XVe and X^e afore tyme but litell or not charged, in ease and relyef of other persones to the said Xth part and other charges afore tyme gretly charged, specially at this tyme to be chargeable and charged.' To make things firmer, definite sums were allotted for collection in each county. In other words the commons now attempted to shift part of the burden of war payments off the shoulders of the customary classes of taxpayers and on to those of an exempt religious order and those of the poor. Once again the grant was to be void if the king exceeded the time limit for the expedition.[52]

Even after this, worse was to come and worse was to be revealed. The roll of the seventh and last session of the parliament, held from 23 January to 14 March 1475, tells a horrifying story of inefficiency, resistance, and corruption:

And howe be it that grete part of the said Xth part in every Shire, Cite, Towne and Burgh, is levied by the Collectours thereof, it is so, that some of the Collectours

[49] Slightly more, in fact, than the yield of the standard fifteenth and tenth which, at this time, was about £31,000.

[50] In compensation £5,383 15s. 0d. was to be deducted from the contributions of other shires and districts. The districts were Cheshire, Northumberland, Cumberland, Westmorland, the bishopric of Durham, the town of Newcastle upon Tyne, the city of Lincoln, the wapentake of Ewcrosse in Yorkshire, and the hundred of Wormelowe in Herefordshire. In the past some of these northern areas had often been exempted from taxation for war against France owing to their obligations for the defence of the Scottish border.

[51] 'a XVe and X^e for and yn the name and place of the forsaid XVe and X^e.'

[52] *Rot. Parl.* VI 111–19.

have not delyvered the sommes by theym receyved to the place lymyted and appoynted by the said Commyssioners, but have converted it to their owne use, and some that have receyved it, and not so delivered it, bee nowe dede, and some of the said X[th] part both be delyvered by the Collectours thereof to the place lymyted by the said Commyssioners, and the Governours of the same place have converted it to their owne use, and some of the said Commissioners have receyved parcell of the said X[th] part, and will not delyvere it to the Kyng's Commissioner, ordeyned by the Kyng to be receyvour therof, and some personnes to whom parcell of the said X[th] part have be delyvered by the Collectours, therof, saufly to be kept to the Kyng's use, will not make payment therof to the receyvour of the same. and some persones that with strong hand have taken parcell of the said X[th] parte oute of the place where it was put to be kept by the said Collectours, accordyng to the said Graunte. . . .[53]

Twenty-six months after the first war grant had been made, the king still had no money in his hands except the meagre proceeds of the lords' tenth on incomes. Everything else was in a welter of confusion. The commons at last, however, released to the king what money had been collected. Admitting also that their attempt in the previous session to shift part of the burden on to the order of St John and on to the poor had been overingenious and the money (owing to difficulties in the assessment of new taxpayers) could not be collected in time for the expedition,[54] on 15 March they granted one and one third fifteenths and tenths to raise the outstanding £51,147 7s. 7½d.[55]

Edward, in the end, through parliament had raised nearly the equivalent of four normal fifteenths and tenths, almost as much as Henry V had raised in a similar period,[56] but with infinitely more trouble than Henry had ever encountered and against far greater resistance to payment. Even now after all this time, haggling, and confusion, money for the campaign was still so short that Edward, taking immense personal trouble, begged, cajoled, flattered, and bullied contributions from some of his richer subjects and sent out commissioners to do likewise with others, placing the collected funds in the hands of a trusted official of the royal household. This was the

---

[53] ibid. 121.

[54] It was to have been delivered to the exchequer on Ascension Day, but as the commons now admitted, 'The fourme of the Levie by your Commissions to be made of the said LIMcxlvii li iiijs vijd. ob.q. is so diffuse and laborious . . . cowed not by that tyme be convenyently levied.' New assessments had to be made by commissioners given powers of investigating incomes, while the standard fifteenth and tenth could be collected against longstanding, traditional assessments.

[55] Estimated to yield £53,697. The fifteenth and tenth was to be paid by the quindene of Easter, the third by the Feast of St Martin in winter (11 November). Rot. Parl. VI 149–53. Between 1473 and 1475 the clergy were also taxed, the convocation of Canterbury granting three and a half tenths, that of York Two. Ramsay, op. cit. II 401.

[56] Henry V had received six fifteenths and tenths between Martinmas 1413 and Martinmas 1417. ibid. II 401.

notorious first benevolence.[57]

We may now turn to the other preparations for the campaign and to the composition of the army. In spite of the immensely frustrating financial difficulties already noted, the government lavished great care on these preparations.[58] Military leaders also carried on their recruiting in good time. Some were already organizing their contingents in the middle of 1474. Sir Richard Tunstall for example entered into indentures in August

[57] A fair amount of scattered evidence confirms the impression, derived from the rolls of parliament, of unwillingness to pay and tardiness in paying. In March 1473, before the second parliamentary grant was formally made, John Paston the younger, writing to his brother, Sir John, who was apparently an MP said, 'God send yow . . . rather the Devyll in the Parlement House . . . we sey, then ye shold grante eny more taskys.' In May 1475, Margaret Paston alleged that heavy taxation had depressed prices and wrote, 'The Kyng goth so nere us in this cuntre, both to pooer and ryche, that I wote not how we shall lyff.' *Paston Letters* III 82, 135. See also 126. On 21 April 1475, the king sent a signet letter to the collectors of the subsidy in Nottingham urging the quicker collection of money, pointing out that payments for the second quarter's wages of troops, due at easter, were in arrears. *Records of the Borough of Nottingham* (11 vols 1882–1956) II 387–8. See also BM Harleian MS. 543 fos 148–9.

For the benevolence, see *The Great Chronicle of London, op. cit.* 223. The Second Anonymous Croyland Continuator in Fulman 558. H. L. Gray, 'The First Benevolence' in *Facts and Factors in Economic History Presented to J. F. Gay* ed. A. E. Cole, A. L. Dunham and N. S. B. Gras (1932) 90–113. In London in January, the mayor was ordered to present all persons with incomes of £10 a year, or personal property worth £100. As late as 17 June (less than three weeks before the expedition sailed) the property qualification was reduced to 100 marks and the mayor and aldermen were ordered, with the help of the two chief justices and the chief baron of the exchequer, to obtain a grant from everybody in the city who had not yet contributed. This latest levy, however, seems to have produced only £282. The mayor and aldermen passed on both orders to the livery companies, and the mercers alone presented 119 people between January and July. *Acts of Court of the Mercers' Company, 1453–1527* ed. L. Lyell and F. D. Watney (1936) 78–80, 84. Scofield, *op. cit.* II 127–8.

The Great Chronicle, op. cit. 244–5, commenting upon a later benevolence under Henry VII notes the advantages of this method of raising money: 'The kyngis grace was well contentid with the lovyng demeanure of his subgectys. And soo he hadd good cawse ffor [by] thys waye he levyed more money. Then he shuld have doon with ffowyr ffyfftenys, and also wyth less grudge of hys comons, ffor to this charge payd noon but men of good substaunce, where at every ffyfftene ar Chargid pore people, which make moor grudgyng for payying of vjd., than at this tyme many did for payyng of vj noblys.' The same reluctance to provide money for war with France was notable under Henry VII. See G. R. Elton, *England Under the Tudors* (1955) 24.

[58] Military stores were being collected and workmen impressed from the end of 1472 and such efforts were intensified from the middle of 1474 onwards. *Cal. Pat. Rolls, 1467–77,* 362, 365, 366, 372–3, 379, 395, 398, 462, 474, 479, 492, 494–6, 515, 524, 525–7. Great care was taken over the supply of ordnance, bows, bowstrings, and arrows. *ibid.* 462, 492. Over 10,000 sheaves of arrows were brought back after the campaign was over. J. Calmette and G. Périnelle, *Louis XI et l'Angleterre* (Paris 1930) Pieces Justificatives n. 63. Three London merchants who were apparently prepared to speculate in army supplies were licensed to requisition all things needful everywhere in England except on ecclesiastical lands. Scofield, *op. cit.* II 118. Large supplies of food were purchased and instructions issued for transporting it overseas. *Cal. Pat. Rolls 1467–77,* 515, 516, 527, 529, 532, 537.

to provide ten spears and one hundred archers,[59] and the majority of the contingent leaders had their indentures drawn up and sealed by the end of December.[60] They were retained for one year and they were to be paid their first quarter's wages at Westminster on 31 January 1475, the date on which they were to muster and their service formally began. Compared with Henry V's preparations, Edward IV's were made in very good time. In Henry's day, February had been the usual month for drawing up indentures for the year's campaigning. In 1415 they had been drawn up as late as the end of April, and some even later.[61]

Although the campaign was bloodless[62] and ended in a peaceful settlement, there is no reason to believe that from the first Edward intended it to be a mere military parade. Louis XI of France certainly regarded the English threat seriously. During the early months of 1475 he was most agitated and in a state of acute nervous anxiety. In his pious and yet worldly way, he did everything he could by both prayer and diplomacy to break the alliance between Edward IV and Charles the Bold, and to induce Charles to agree to a truce. The bloodless dénouement was mainly due to Charles's irrational folly in carrying on his war against the Swiss, continuing the seige of Neuss, and ignoring his treaty obligations towards Edward.[63] Edward, let down by his temperamental ally, took the wise if unheroic course of leaving France in return for a large payment and an annual pension. Yet the long preparations for the campaign, Edward's immense labours in raising money and war stores, and Louis's anxiety to break the Anglo-Burgundian alliance all point strongly to the supposition that everybody concerned expected a hard campaign. We are therefore surely justified in supposing that Edward intended to lead overseas the largest and finest army he could assemble and transport to France.

At this point government records can provide a good deal of information on both the nature of recruitment and on the quality of the troops ultimately assembled. There are three sets of easily accessible records dealing with the forces engaged: (1) a declaration of payments made at Canterbury in June 1475, by the tellers of the exchequer to leaders of troops for the second quarter of their engagement, preserved in the College of Arms and

[59] *Foedera* XI 817–18.

[60] Exchequer Various Accounts PRO E. 101/71/5/956–70; E. 101/71/6/971–988, 990–1,000; E. 101/72/1/1001–1030; E. 101/72/2/1031–1045. Only 4 out of the 94 surviving indentures for men-at-arms and archers were sealed after the end of December. PRO E. 101/72/2/1046, 1048, 1057, 1058.

[61] Newhall, *The English Conquest, op. cit.* 24 n. 109. J. H. Wylie and W. T. Waugh, *The Reign of Henry V* (3 vols 1914–29) I 455–56, 466.

[62] Except for a skirmish between an English foraging party and some Frenchmen near Noyon in which fifty Englishmen were said to have been killed. Scofield, *op. cit.* II 132.

[63] *ibid.* II 114, 122–4, 126, 129, 131–5. Scofield is, in general, hostile to Edward in discussing this campaign. Her testimony on this point is, therefore, all the more weighty.

published in facsimile by Francis Pierrepoint Barnard in 1925; (2) a number of indentures, preserved in the Public Record Office, drawn up between the king and the various contingent leaders; and (3) the exchequer tellers' rolls, also preserved in the public record office.

The indentures are incomplete. There were at least 192 contingent leaders, but only 95 of their indentures have survived.[64] Although they supply interesting details of the conditions of service, they are, therefore, useless for any discussion of the numbers engaged. Again, at first sight, the College of Arms roll seems to be a most impressive document, but a closer examination shows it to be inaccurate and incomplete.[65] We are therefore

[64] See above n. 60. There are eight indentures dealing with specialized services, transport, artillery, etc. Exchequer Various Accounts PRO E. 101/71/6/989; E. 101/72/2/1051–56. E. 101/72/2/1049 is an interesting example of a subcontract: an indenture between the duke of Clarence and James Hyde, esquire, to bring five archers to the duke's retinue and to serve himself as a man-at-arms. Clarence agreed to pay Hyde from 19 March 1475, and he was to be ready for muster by that date.

[65] F. P. Barnard, *Edward IV's French Expedition of 1475: The Leaders and their Badges, Being MS. 2. M.16 College of Arms* (1925). The roll bears the title 'A declaracion Aswell of Capitegnes theire Speires and Archers Reiteigned wyth our Sou[er]eigne lord Kyng Edward the iiij[th] in his s[er]uise of Guerre into his Duchie of Normandye and his Realme of ffraunce as of theire wages for the second q[ua]rter paid by John Sorell and John ffitzherberd Tellers of the Kynges mony in his Receyt at Canterbury the moneth of Jun the xv yere of the Reigne of our said sou[er]eigne lord Kyng Edward the iiij,' Thomas Bulkeley, an official of the Exchequer of Receipt, was sent there for the payment of the troops. He and six others stayed there for four weeks to guard the money. PRO Warrants for Issues E. 404/76/4/112. Tellers' Rolls E. 405/60 m.2d; E. 405/61 m.5d.

The roll begins with a summary of the numbers of men-at-arms and archers led by dukes, earls, barons, bannerets, knights, and others, and the numbers of artificers and tradesmen, together with the payments made under each heading. Grand totals of both numbers and money are then given. Detailed entries from which this summary was partially compiled then follow, giving the names of the individual dukes, earls, barons, bannerets, and knights with the numbers of their individual contingents. On the right side of each entry is a drawing of their coats-of-arms. But with the knights these generous details unfortunately end.

The roll is incomplete because (a) a number of contingent leaders must have been paid their wages elsewhere than at Canterbury. For example, the roll states that 173 esquires and gentlemen led contingents whereas the Tellers' Rolls supply the names of 194. Also, although the roll includes the names of the marquis of Dorset, Lord Clinton, and Sir Simon Mountford, it gives no figures for either the men-at-arms or archers in their contingents, and no figures for archers for Sir Thomas Burgh, Sir Richard Brandon, Sir Richard Corbett and Sir John Crokke—all of which figures the Tellers' Rolls supply. There are also a good many other omissions.

The arithmetic of the roll is highly inaccurate even by medieval standards. (1) The totals in the first section of the roll very often differ from the addition of the detailed figures in the second section of the roll from which they were ostensibly compiled and (2) in the first section of the roll itself the grand total of the archers gives an excess of more than 1,500 over the figures from which it is supposed to be made up.

The College of Arms Roll is, therefore, useless for my particular purpose. The relationship between the Tellers' Rolls and the College of Arms Roll remains obscure. The College Roll may have originated as an attempt to calculate the cost of the second quarter of the expedition—but if so, it can hardly be considered a very successful attempt.

forced back upon our third source, the tellers' rolls.[66] These seem to give a reasonably full record of those taking part in the campaign. Unfortunately, however, although the rolls always supply the numbers of men-at-arms and archers which each commander led, they generally give no more than the mere names of these commanders, which often makes very difficult a precise identification of some of the leaders below the knightly class.[67]

Edward's preparations did in fact produce a total of at least 11,451 combatants, the largest army which had so far crossed the English Channel during the fifteenth century.[68] An analysis akin to that made by Powicke for the contingents of the earlier part of the century, can now be used to suggest both the quarters from which Edward IV obtained support for his war policy and the comparative quality of the forces which he was able to recruit.

As appendix E shows, the army divides into two parts: firstly, contingents led by men who were part of, or had very close connections with, the royal court; and secondly, contingents led by men who had no such strong court connections, whose involvement we may regard as the response of the coun-

[66] There are three Tellers' Rolls with entries relating to the payment of troops (a) Michaelmas Term 14 Edward IV PRO E. 405/59 ms 8r and d; 9r and d. (b) Easter 15 Edward IV PRO E. 405/60 ms 1r and d; 3r and d; 4r and d; 5r and d; and E. 405/61 ms 1r and d; 2r and d; 3r and d; 4r and d. Although E. 405/61 is incomplete it contains most of the entries for the Easter Term relating to the war. To this degree it duplicates the entries on E. 405/60. Rymer printed most of the entries concerning men-at-arms and archers from E. 405/61 but he misdated it Michaelmas Term, 14 Edward IV, and stated that the payments recorded were made during the first quarter. The Roll itself has no headings and is not dated. Internal evidence, however, proves that it was compiled during the Easter Term, 15 Edward IV, as there is an entry on m.5d recording a payment to John Fitzherbert for going to Canterbury with money to pay the troops for the second quarter. Fitzherbert went to Canterbury for that purpose in June and stayed there for four weeks (see above n. 65). The payments recorded were therefore for the second quarter; the matter is put beyond doubt by the fact that the payments tally with those recorded on E. 405/60 which is dated Easter Term 15 Edward IV. Rymer's caption, *Foedera* XI 844–8, indicates that the roll is an Issue Roll, but it is in fact a Teller's Roll.

[67] Many of these, however, can be more precisely identified by comparison with the returns of the knights of the shire, lists of sheriffs, appointments of justices of the peace, and other local officers.

[68] The fighting men who went to France in the Agincourt campaign had numbered not more than 9,000. In 1417 there were something like 10,000 mobile troops, increased by reinforcements during 1418 to over 13,000. E. F. Jacob, *Henry V and the Invasion of France* (1947) 85. Newhall, *op. cit.* 192–4, 204–6. Edward, therefore, took to France a bigger army than any which Henry V had been able to muster at the beginning of a campaign. Allowing for noncombatants the whole host was probably much greater. P. de Commynes, *Mémoires* ed. J. Calmette and G. Durville (3 vols Paris 1924–25) II 10–11, states that there was a numerous body of camp servants, although there was not one page in the whole army. If the army contained the same proportion of non-combatants as Henry V's the numbers crossing to France would have to be quadrupled. There were in addition 2,000 archers sent to the duke of Brittany under the command of Lords Audley and Duras and Lord Dynham commanded a fleet with 3,000 men to protect the crossing. Scofield, *op. cit.* II 122, 124, 127.

tryside to the war effort.

The leaders of the court section of the army comprised peers who were closely related to the king and queen or held appointments in the royal household, officials of the household, and a few officials from other government departments. This group between them led approximately 63 per cent of the men-at-arms and 66 per cent of the archers. The second group, consisting of peers who had no strong connection with the court and a number of non-nobles ranging from prominent bannerets to quite obscure countrymen, produced only 37 per cent of the men-at-arms and only 34 per cent of the archers.

The most prominent among the military leaders were the 'court' peers, with 11 peers leading 516 men-at-arms and 4,080 archers.[69] The most conspicuous of all the individual contingents were on average three times larger than those of the 'country' peers in the second category with 12 'country' peers producing 231 men-at-arms and 1,619 archers.[70] Members of the court aristocracy were thus overwhelmingly important as recruiting agents for the campaign. To add to the recruiting of the court circle, the household officials produced 50 contingent leaders with a total of 270 men-at-arms and 2,587 archers, and 9 other officials,[71] 29 and 134 respectively. By contrast the whole country in general produced 108 non-noble leaders who raised only 220 men-at-arms and only 1,639 archers, forming individual contingents roughly no more than one third the size of those which the officials led.

Of these non-noble 'country' leaders 5 were bannerets and 13 were knights, that is men whose fairly prominent social position speaks for itself.

[69] The duke of Clarence (brother to the king), duke of Gloucester (brother), duke of Suffolk (brother-in-law), duke of Buckingham (married to the queen's sister), marquis of Dorset (stepson), Earl Ryvers (brother-in-law), Sir Anthony Grey of Ruthyn (married to queen's sister and heir-apparent of Edmund, earl of Kent), Lord Stanley (steward of the household), Lord Hastings (chamberlain), Lord Howard (treasurer of the household, October 1468–December 1474), Thomas Howard, his son and heir and an esquire of the body. (I have included in this category the eldest sons of two prominent peers, since they appear logically to fit here better than with any other group.)

[70] The duke of Norfolk, the earls of Northumberland, Pembroke, and Ormonde, Lords Cobham, Ferrers, Fitzwarren, Sir John Fenys (son and heir of Lord Dacre of the South), Grey of Codnor, John Grey (son and heir of Lord Grey of Wilton). Lysle, Scrope. Once again two heirs of peers have been included. Lord Clynton is named in the College of Arms Roll, but the roll gives no figures for him. He does not appear in the Tellers' Rolls and, therefore, presumably did not take part in the campaign. Two Scottish lords (the earl of Douglas and Lord Boyde), in exile at Edward's court, also took part in the campaign. These have been separately classified (see table in appendix E p. 321.)

[71] John Crabbe (servant of William Hatteclyff, the king's secretary), Peter Curteis (keeper of the great wardrobe), Thomas Downes (clerk of the ordnance), Geoffrey Gate (marshall of Calais), Robert Radclyff (master porter of Calais), John Sturgeon (master of the ordnance), Thomas Swan (clerk of the ordnance), William Tymperley (servant of John Morton, master of the rolls of chancery), Thomas Ustwayte (servant of John Gunthorpe, king's almoner, secretary to the queen and clerk of parliament).

Of the rest, the tellers' rolls designate 52 of them as esquires, 6 as 'gentlemen,' and there are 32 others to whom no description is attached—most of them (though not all) falling below even the rank of gentlemen. Of these 90 (responsible between them for only 136 men-at-arms and 972 archers), as many as 70 led only archers, and 27 of the 70 as few as 3 archers or fewer. As to their standing in their county communities, only 8 were at some time or other both members of parliament and justices of the peace, 3 certainly and possibly 6 were justices of the peace, and another may have been a member of parliament.[72]

Thus, with 18 bannerets and knights and 15 other prominent men, below the ranks of the peerage[73] the country in general produced only 33 men really notable in their own local communities, plus 75 minor figures, all but a few of which led only a handful of archers. Hardly an impressive figure for the entire country;—in fact, a miserable total which seems to indicate that most people were indifferent, if not hostile to the war policy.

Another of Powicke's criteria was the ratio of archers to men-at-arms. In 1475 this was astonishingly high. Nowhere was the highly desirable figure of three to one attained. In only two small contingents did the figure approach this standard and amongst the bannerets of the royal household it rose as high as ten to one. For the army as a whole it was over seven to one.

Therefore by means of intensive propaganda, immense efforts in raising money, and other preparations, the government, despite indifference or even hostility to the war, managed to put a large army into the field. It is, however, doubtful if in addition to size the government also managed to produce quality. Since the army was never put to the test of fighting, one should not be dogmatic about its efficiency, but the probabilities would seem to lie strongly against military distinction.

As we have seen, after 1430 the quality of the English forces in France had notably declined, and even such permanent military organization as then existed had disappeared with the loss of Normandy and Guienne. The campaign of 1475 was therefore based upon an improvised organization called into being for a particular occasion and hurriedly disbanded with its passing, mounted by a generation with little or none of the professional

---

[72] (1) MPs and JPs—James Blount, esquire, Derbyshire; Thomas Cokesay (no descr.), MP Gloucestershire, JP Warwickshire; Egidius Daubeney, esquire (created Lord Daubeney, 1486), Somerset; Thomas FitzWilliam, esquire, Lincolnshire; John Fortescue, esquire, Hertfordshire; Walter Hungerford, esquire, Wiltshire; William Meryng, esquire, Nottinghamshire; John Risley, esquire, Middlesex. JPs—John Blount, esquire, Derbyshire; Halnath Malyverer, esquire, Devon; Robert Palmer (no descr.), Devon; Possibly JPs—Thomas Fenys, esquire, Sussex; William Redmyle (no descr.), Somerset; Brian Talbot (no descr.), Lincolnshire. And Thomas Mauncell, esquire, may possibly have been MP for High Wycombe.

[73] The participation of some gentry may, however, be concealed since they raised men for peers. e.g. Sir John Paston raised a group which seems to have been absorbed into Lord Hastings' contingent. *Paston Letters* III 122. See also above n. 64.

experience and expertise which prolonged warfare brings with it. All over Europe at this time such particular mobilizations, after long periods of peace, were generally amateurish affairs. Commynes commented upon this very strongly when, in 1464–5, Charles the Bold of Burgundy embarked upon his first military expedition in the *Ligue du Bien Public:* 'car je ne croy pas que de douze cens hommes d'armes ou envyron qu'ilz estoient, qu'il en y eust cinquante qui eussent sceu coucher une lance en l'arrest. Il n'y en avoit pas quatre cens arméz de cuyrasses et sy n'avoyent pas ung seul serviteur armé, *à cause de la longue paix*, et que en ceste maison ne tenoit nulles gens de soulde pour soullager le peuple de tailles.'[74]

Commynes again, basing his statement upon observation of Englishmen serving as mercenaries in continental armies, both before and after the campaign, thought that they became excellent soldiers with experience, but that having little knowledge of foreign warfare and being unpracticed in seige methods, they were more or less useless when they first crossed the seas. He thought that Charles the Bold was most unwise to carry on the seige of Neuss, since the English army was no longer formed of the experienced soldiers who had fought in France with so much valour in earlier days, but all raw soldiers unaquainted with French affairs, whom he should have been at hand to guide during their first campaign.[75] Commynes's words seem to be true enough. It was now 22 years since the last English soldier had been thrown out of Guienne in 1453. Most of the battles of the Wars of the Roses were insignificant by continental standards, fought by non-professional soldiers, and the seiges being minor affairs.[76] Apart from the garrison of Calais, which was not after all a field army, the only standing force available was the king's bodyguard of two hundred archers formed in 1467.[77] The army of 1475, unlike Charles the Bold's army of

[74] Commynes, *Mémoires, op. cit.* I 27. See also the similar description, I 13. For similar remarks upon other occasions, I 176–8, 177–8, 188–9. In 1478 he also made similar observations upon the weakness of the Florentine forces under threat of attack from the Papal and Neapolitan armies. See II 272–3.

[75] *ibid.* II 8, 15, 120–22, 134. He seems to ignore the seiges of the northern and Welsh castles in Lancastrian hands in the 1460s, but these, except for Harlech, were very short affairs compared with continental seiges and his opinion is undoubtedly correct.

[76] See Lander, *The Wars of the Roses, op. cit.* 20 ff. See also above n. 75.

[77] The garrison of Calais was 1,120 in war, reduced to about 780 in peacetime, but none of it was available for this campaign. The only other large permanent forces at this time, those of the wardens of the Scottish marches, can be neglected for this purpose since they obviously could not be taken out of the country. According to the pseudo-William Worcester, Edward IV formed a bodyguard of 'CC Valettos probos et valentissimos sagittarios Anglie, ordinando quod quilibet eorum haberet viij.d. per diem, equitando et attendendo super personam suam propriam.' Stevenson II pt ii 788. This bodyguard, considerably expanded, was most probably represented in the campaign forces by the 'Archers of the King's Chamber' (See appendix E. p. 320). It has not, however, been possible to trace a definite connection between them, though Worcester's phraseology and that of the Tellers' Rolls makes such a connection highly probable.

1464–5, seems to have been well enough armed because preparations had been underway for a long time. Its fighting quality however was a different matter entirely, and a verdict upon it must at best be left in doubt.

As we have seen, the response from the countryside to the king's call to arms was hardly fervent, and the proportion of men-at-arms to archers in the army was woefully low. It may well be that from about 1430, certainly from 1453 onwards, the numbers of men trained for this role had declined.[78] As William Worcester bitterly lamented, the English were not the martial race they had formerly been.[79] It is perhaps no exaggeration to claim that the majority of the aristocracy and gentry were no longer enthusiastic for continental war, nor particularly fitted for it, and that Edward IV's claim to be waging defensive war was true. The old enthusiasm (such as it had been) for the king's claim to the French throne had long since departed, and the campaign of 1475 was not so much a fervid renewal of ancient glories as a defensive reaction of the government to the complications and dangers of the international situation in northwestern Europe as it had developed since 1453.

[78] It may be objected that the provision of a large ratio of men-at-arms to archers may have been deliberate policy, but this seems implausible. The fact that the parliamentary grants mention only archers proves nothing for no army could be composed of archers alone. Since war tactics in northern Europe do not seem to have changed since the earlier part of the century, the logical deduction seems to be as Powicke suggested (see above pp. 223–4), a drying up of the supply of men-at-arms.

[79] Worcester, *The Boke of Noblese, op. cit.* 77–8.

10

The treason and death of the duke of Clarence: a reinterpretation[1]

In February 1478 a few days after the execution of George, duke of Clarence, one of Edward IV's councillors, Dr Thomas Langton, laconically remarked in the middle of a letter to the prior of Christ Church, Canterbury, 'ther be assignyd certen Lords to go with the body of the Dukys of Clarence to Teuxbury, where he shall be beryid; the Kyng intendis to do right worshipfully for his sowle.'[2]

Even by the easy moral standards of the late fifteenth century Clarence's soul cried out for all the masses which his brother or anyone else saw fit to endow. A family liability and a public nuisance from the age of 18 the duke united fantastic lack of political judgment with beauty of person and dangerous eloquence,[3] a combination which made him an almost fatal menace to an insecurely established dynasty. Yet when at last the end came to his long career of folly and treason, men seem to have been as uncertain of the reasons for his condemnation as they were of the manner of his death, despite a long and detailed indictment signed by the king, his brother, which had been given the maximum publicity by its presentation to parliament. One outstanding section of this indictment, his contemporaries, one and all, ignored a statement that after Clarence's arrest there had been found among his possessions an exemplification under the great seal of Henry VI: a copy of an agreement presumably made during the re-adeption of 1470–71, for it promised him the succession to the throne failing heirs male to the house of Lancaster.

An examination of this royal indictment and the scepticism about it implied by the silence of contemporary writers after the considerable publicity which it undoubtedly received, may well lead to a reinterpretation of one

[1] I wish to thank E. B. Fryde for criticism and advice on this article.

[2] *Christ Church Letters* ed J. B. Sheppard, Camden Series (1877) 36–7.

[3] e.g. Dominic Mancini wrote 'Augebat hunc regine timorem, quod dux Clarentie elegantissime forme, ut dignus videtur imperio: preterea popularis eloquentie vero habebat tantum, ut nihil quod cuperet difficile ei factu visum esset.' Quoted in *The Usurpation of Richard III* ed. C. A. J. Armstrong (1936) 76–7. John Rous, the contemporary Warwick antiquary, described him as 'right witty and wel visagid.' BM Rows Roll no. 59. See also *Historie of the Arrivall of Edward IV in England* ed. J. Bruce, Camden Series (1838) 11, and the Second Anonymous Croyland Continuator in Fulman I 557.

of the most notorious episodes in the struggle between the houses of Lancaster and York.

Clarence had been brought up in the household of his cousin Richard Neville, earl of Warwick, a magnate of talents incomparably greater than his own, and leader of the tiny faction of nobles which had placed Edward IV on the throne in 1461 as their only way out of a desperate political impasse, in a revolution which they had consistently refused Edward's father, Richard of York.[4] Having brought about the Yorkist revolution *faute de mieux* after long opposing it, Warwick expected at least to rule the new king, his cousin, then aged 19. But Edward's marriage to Elizabeth Wydeville in 1464 provided a firm indication that he was no longer to dominate the king in matters of major importance. He became increasingly exasperated by his lack of success in disposing of court patronage, particularly the feudal marriage market, in the Neville interest, and by his failure to impose his own pro-French foreign policy in place of the king's preference for an Anglo-Burgundian alliance. Although for a time Warwick dissembled his grievances and remained outwardly at least on good terms with the king, his grudges drove him step by step into dubious intrigues and at last into open treason.[5]

By the middle of 1467, if not earlier, Richard Neville had already gained the most powerful influence over Clarence. As early as April the Milanese ambassadors at the French court sent word home that Louis XI had told them that Warwick had married Clarence to his own elder daughter, Isabella.[6] The news was premature. The same year, however, Warwick sent a certain Master Lacy[7] to Rome to obtain a dispensation for the marriage, as Clarence and Isabella Neville were within the prohibited degrees of relationship. Lacy failed to obtain it. The king was adamantly opposed.[8]

Edward IV at last reached agreement with Burgundy early in 1468.[9] Warwick, already suspected of intriguing with the exiled Lancastrians in France,[10] averted suspicion from himself by taking an active part together

---

[4] See above ch. 4 pp. 98–104.

[5] *ibid.* pp. 110–23.

[6] *Calendar of State Papers Milanese* ed. A. B. Hinds I (1912) 119.

[7] Probably William Lacy, who in 1478 was acting as clerk of the royal council, and had become a councillor by 1480. See above 8 Appendix D, pp. 313 and 316.

[8] *Annales,* formerly attributed to William Worcester, in Stevenson II pt ii 788.

[9] On 5 January 1468, Edward IV confirmed a commercial treaty with Burgundy, and on 16 February the Burgundian marriage treaty was signed at Brussels. Scofield, *The Life and Reign of Edward IV* (1923) I 442–8.

[10] Stevenson II pt ii 788. As early as May 1467, the Milanese ambassadors in France wrote that if Edward IV continued his pro-Burgundian policy the French 'talked of treating with the Earl of Warwick to restore King Henry in England.' *Calendar of State Papers Milanese, op. cit.* I 120. Polydore Vergil (for what his account is worth at this point) states that as early as 1467 Warwick planned to restore Henry VI, and that all his subsequent intrigues with Clarence were to this end. *Three Books of Polydore Vergil's English History* ed. H. Ellis, Camden Series (1844) 118 ff. J. Calmette and G. Perinelle, *Louis XI et l'Angleterre, 1461–1483* (Paris

with Clarence in the treason trials of the year.[11] Then in July 1469, during Robin of Redesdale's rebellion, they at last threw off the mask and fled to Calais, where Clarence and Isabella Neville were immediately married, a dispensation having been obtained from Rome through the duplicity of James Goldwell, Edward IV's own agent as the papal court.[12] Then, by one of the sudden reversals of fortune notable in those times when, given the advantage of surprise, a very small military force could overthrow a government, Warwick and Clarence within less than three weeks of the marriage had returned to England, taken Edward prisoner, and executed some of his principal supporters, including the queen's father, Earl Ryvers, and her brother, Sir John Wydeville.

This palace revolution, however, attracted so little support that their immediate attempt to rule the country in the name of a captive king failed on the rocks of passive resistance.[13] After six or seven weeks they were compelled to release him. Yet within five months Clarence and Warwick were deeply implicated in the Lincolnshire rebellion of 1470, fomented with the intention of putting Clarence on the throne.[14] On the swift collapse of the revolt the conspirators fled the country. They made for Calais (Warwick was its captain), the port from which the Yorkist earls had mounted their invasion of England in 1460. For reasons now obscure Lord Wenlock, Warwick's lieutenant of the town, refused to admit them.[15] Driven forth

1930) 104, and Pièce Justificatif n. 28. This document, a digest of four memoranda by Sir John Fortescue, is undated. It has generally been attributed to 1470, but the editors date it 1468. On internal evidence (which I hope to demonstrate in detail elsewhere), I have accepted their dating.

[11] *Cal. Pat. Rolls, 1467–1477*, 102, 103, 126–7, 128. *The Great Chronicle of London*, ed. A. H. Thomas and I. D. Thornley (1938) 205–6.

[12] Scofield, *Edward IV, op. cit.* I 493–5 and 495 n. 1.

[13] The rebels attracted very little support from the nobility either at this time or a few months later. See above ch. 4 p. 122 n. 163.

[14] At least according to the propaganda which Edward put out. See the statements in *The Chronicle of the Rebellion in Lincolnshire, 1470* ed. J. G. Nichols, Camden Miscellany I (1847) 11, and Sir Robert Welles's confession, *ibid.* 21–3. In *English Historical Literature in the Fifteenth Century* (1913) 173–4, C. L. Kingsford described the 'Chronicle' as 'a purely partisan document' deliberately designed to implicate Clarence and Warwick in the rebellion. Also, a proclamation issued at Nottingham on 31 March 1470, runs '. . . the said duke and earl unnaturally intending his destruction and the subversion of the realm and to make the said duke king of the realm against God's law and all reason and conscience, dissimulated with his highness and under colour thereof, provoked and stirred up by their writing Sir Robert Welles late captain of the commons of Lincolnshire . . .' *Cal. Close Rolls, 1468–1476*, 135–6. Although all these sources are very much *ex parte* statements it would be unrealistic to reject their testimony completely. The attempt to turn Edward into a *roi fainéant* a few months before having failed, the obvious course would now be his deposition. For a full account of the rebellion see Scofield, *op. cit.* I 509–18.

[15] Scofield, *op. cit.* I 519 ff. According to Philippe de Commynes, Wenlock was playing a double game, secretly remaining loyal to Warwick but convinced that, at the time, it would be too dangerous to attempt to admit him to the town. Commynes, *Mémoires* ed. J. Calmette and G. Durville (Paris 1924–5) I 193–6.

from his expected asylum in Calais, Warwick took refuge at the French court. The idea of an alliance between Margaret of Anjou and Warwick had been in the air for at least two years by this time.[16] Louis XI for his own purposes, in discussions which took place mainly at Angers, now urged such a scheme upon them both, and Warwick was finally reconciled to the queen whom he, above all men, had been responsible for driving into exile ten years before. The new allies made their plans for an invasion of England, drove Edward IV a penniless refugee to the Netherlands, released Henry VI from his imprisonment in the Tower of London, and set him on the throne again.

Success, however, was brief. Edward returned to defeat Warwick and the Lancastrians in the two hard-fought battles of Barnet and Tewkesbury: victories which owed a good deal to Clarence's continued treacheries. He deserted Warwick, and with considerable forces which he had collected for the rebels, went over to the other side.

After so black a record of double-dealing and treason, Clarence would have been well advised to walk more carefully. Yet as pugnacious as ever, he now quarrelled with the king over estates formerly granted to him and now taken back under an act of resumption.[17] He tried, possibly even to the point of kidnapping the prospective bride, to prevent his younger brother, Richard of Gloucester, marrying his sister-in-law, Anne Neville.[18] Foiled in his attempt to prevent the marriage, he split the royal family by a bitter quarrel lasting for more than three years, over the division of the Neville inheritance between the co-heiresses, the duchesses of Clarence and Gloucester. This dispute most probably thwarted the passing of an act of attainder against most of the rebels of 1469 to 1471 and thus deprived the king of immensely valuable forfeitures.[19]

All might yet have been well had Clarence stayed within the bounds of avarice and estate-building. Indiscreet as ever, he was soon dabbling in higher and more dangerous affairs. As early as November 1472 Pietro Aliprando, the malicious and rumour-mongering papal envoy, reported from Bruges (for what the statement is worth) that Edward before invading France would have to 'decide about the regents and lieutenants to govern, so that he may not be overthrown by his brother, the duke of Clarence.'[20] It

---

[16] See above pp. 2–3 and no. 10.

[17] The act of 1473. *Rot. Parl.* VI 71–98. The act was fully enforced against Clarence, and according to the Croyland Continuator (who admittedly is a little hazy about its date), the duke resented it bitterly. Fulman, 561. By the middle of 1474, many crown lands in Nottinghamshire and Derbyshire had already been recovered from Clarence. B. P. Wolffe, 'The Management of English Royal Estates under the Yorkist Kings.' *English Historical Review* LXXI (1956) 7.

[18] Fulman 557.

[19] See above ch. 5, pp. 137–9.

[20] *Calendar of State Papers Milanese, op. cit.* I 166.

is possible that Clarence was implicated in the earl of Oxford's attempted landing in Essex in May 1473.[21] On the last day of September, Oxford captured St Michael's Mount. In November rumours once again connected Clarence with treason,[22] and in September 1475 the duke of Burgundy (admittedly a disgruntled and prejudiced witness) claimed that Edward did not wish his brothers to leave France for England before him lest they, and in particular Clarence, should seize the opportunity to stir up trouble there.[23]

From 1472 rumours which murmured treason against Clarence were thus never lacking, though it is impossible to decide how reliable they were. On the other hand, the transgressions which could be proved against him, mainly defiance of his brother in matters financial and his quarrel with Gloucester, though they dangerously weakened an insecure dynasty, were hardly indictable offences. Early in 1477 the point came at which Clarence's ambitions and resentments drove him to actions perilous internationally and scandalous at home.

When Charles the Bold of Burgundy was killed at the battle of Nancy on 5 January 1477, his widow, Margaret of York, conceived the unrealistic plan of arranging the marriage of her brother Clarence, himself a widower of about a fortnight's standing, to her stepdaugher Mary of Burgundy, the heiress of one of the richest accumulations of land in Europe. Any such plan was certain to arouse the bitter hostility of the Archduke Maximilian of Habsburg to whom Mary had been betrothed, and of Louis XI of France scared as always that the English would regain a foothold on the continent. If carried out the plan would have involved Edward IV in a ruinously long and costly war for the defence of the Burgundian territories.[24] Edward made

[21] Scofield, *op. cit.* II 58–9, tentatively connects Clarence with Oxford's conspiracy. See also *Paston Letters* III 92–3.

[22] *Paston Letters* III 98.

[23] *Calendar of State Papers Milanese, op. cit.* I 217.

[24] War meant money and that, in turn, taxation. Edward IV had met almost fantastic difficulties in raising money for the French campaign of 1475—grudging, inadequate grants from parliament, paid not to the exchequer but to special local repositories, refusals to pay, thefts and losses from sums which were paid. See *Rot. Parl.* VI 4–8, 39–41, 42–3, 111–19, 120–1, 149–53. J. R. Lander, *The Wars of the Roses* (1965) 203–5, and above ch. 9 pp. 230–34. Resentment had been strong because only Edward and a few councillors and courtiers had profited through pensions from Louis XI, plus the contractors who provided supplies. Edward knew very well that he was in no position to wage prolonged war abroad at this time.

See also C. A. J. Armstrong, *The New Cambridge Modern History* I (1957) 224–58, for an account of the complicated legal and political situation in the Netherlands in 1477 and the immense difficulties which Louis XI and his successors experienced for many years in trying to establish control there. Also F. W. N. Hugenholtz, 'The 1477 Crisis in the Burgundian Duke's Dominions,' in *Britain and the Netherlands* ed. J. S. Bromley and E. H. Kossman II (Groningen 1964) 33–46. Edward has generally been condemned not only for 'deserting' Mary of Burgundy (although he had commercial treaties only, not an offensive or defensive alliance with the Burgundian state at the time) to make sure of his pension under the Treaty

it plain, possibly in a meeting of the great council on 13 February, that he would neither be drawn into so expensive a tangle nor permit his brother so great and dangerous a marriage.[25] Then, fearing that Louis XI might break the agreement made two years before at Pécquigny for the marriage of the dauphin to Princess Elizabeth of York, or that he might cease payment of his pension made under the same treaty, Edward proposed his brother-in-law, Earl Ryvers, as a husband for Mary of Burgundy. This suggestion, probably a mere move in the diplomatic duel[26] to bring pressure to bear upon the king of France, further inflamed Clarence's discontent, but otherwise produced no effect whatever, for it seems that Mary never at any time in 1477 thought of abandoning her engagement to Maximilian.

Clarence appears to have brooded in ever-growing resentment on what he thought to be his great injuries. By early April his self-control, never very strong, had given way completely. Frustrated abroad, he vented his spite at home. His wife had died on 22 December, 1476, about six weeks after giving birth to her third child. Now on 12 April two of his hirelings, backed by a gang of men fourscore strong, rode to Cayford in Somerset, kidnapped Ankarette Twynyho, one of the duchess's former attendants, from her own house, and carried her across three counties to the duke's own stronghold of Warwick. Here on 15 April she was indicted before the Warwickshire justices of the peace of poisoning her former mistress, falsely convicted by a terrorized jury, and forthwith hanged, all within the short space of three hours.[27] At the same time John Thuresby of Warwick was

of Pécquigny from Louis XI, but also for imperilling English commercial interests in the Netherlands. This contention seems both anachronistic and unreal. No contemporary English writer makes any such accusation. Nor do later events justify the criticism. English commercial interests did not suffer, and the French had quite enough opposition to face without alienating the mercantile groups. Commynes himself, while condemning Edward for not entering the Netherlands, also condemns Louis XI for rashly trying to gain his ends by military means instead of more peaceful methods, and reports Edward IV as saying that the towns of Flanders and Brabant were large and strong, neither easily taken nor easily kept, and that the English had no inclination to such a war on account of the commerce between them and the Netherlands. Commynes, *Mémoires, op. cit.* II 167–9, 245–9.

[25] This question was most probably discussed, for the great council dealt with the situation as it threatened the safety of Calais, and the garrison was strengthened as a precaution. *Paston Letters* III 173. See above ch. 8 p. 198 n. 40.

[26] No one abroad seems to have taken the suggestion seriously. See Commynes, *op. cit.* II 247–8. Olivier de la Marche mentions it without comment, *Mémoires* ed. H. Beaune and J. d'Arbaumont III (Paris 1885) 243.

[27] *Third Report of the Deputy Keeper of the Public Records* (1842) appendix II, 214. *Cal. Pat. Rolls, 1476–1485,* 72–73. See also L. W. Vernon Harcourt, 'The Baga de Secretis,' *English Historical Review* XXIII (1908) 508–29. Roger Twynyho, Ankarette's grandson and heir, even claimed that '. . . diverse of the same Jurre, after the said Judgment yoven, came to the seid Ankarette, havyng grete remorce in their consciens, knowyng they hadde yoven an untrue Verdyt in that behalf, humbly and pituously asked foryefnes thereof of the seid Ankarette. . . .' *Rot. Parl.* VI 174.

also tried and hanged for the murder of Clarence's infant son, Richard. A third victim, Roger Tocotes, who was accused of assisting at both crimes, fortunately escaped. The accusations, those against Ankarette in particular, were so fantastically implausible that only a seriously disturbed mind could have produced them.[28]

This violent perversion of justice by noblemen was not uncommon at this period or considerably later, and governments unable to exist without the support of the powerful generally turned a blind eye towards such oppressions, unless they involved active treason and the security of the king and the country. Even now Edward IV showed considerable restraint, for the crime of embracery committed by a royal duke must have had a most adverse effect on the popularity of the king himself, and he chose for the time not to attack his brother directly. He may have retaliated deliberately by means of an oblique warning, or possibly the following incidents may have begun independently, if very conveniently for the purpose.

About this time—we cannot date the event exactly[29]—an Oxford gentleman, an astronomer called John Stacy, was accused of practising sorcery and 'of having made leaden images and other things to procure thereby the death of Richard, Lord Beauchamp at the request of his adulterous wife.'[30] During a very severe examination about his practice of the black arts, he made a confession which led to the arrest of Thomas Burdett of Arrow, a member of the duke of Clarence's household, and of Thomas Blacke, an Oxford clerk. By 12 May the king had appointed a commission of oyer and terminer to deal with these offences. Again proceedings were swift, but not so indecently swift as in the Twynyho affair. A week later the commissioners convicted Stacy and Burdett of disseminating treasonable writings and of treasonably imaging and compassing the death of the king by necromancy and other means at various times from April 1474 until 5 May, only a week before the appointment of the commission.[31] On 20 May Burdett and Stacy were hanged, drawn, and quartered at Tyburn, both protesting their innocence at the foot of the gallows.[32] It may well be coincidence only, but on the same day as the

---

[28] Ankarette was accused of giving the Duchess Isabella poisoned ale on 10 October 1476, of which she died on 22 December. The child Richard died on 1 January, 1477, allegedly of poisoned ale drunk on 21 December. There was, of course, no poison then known having so delayed an effect. It is curious, and if correct, possibly indicative of perjury, that a Tewkesbury chronicle (printed W. Dugdale, *Monasticon Anglicanum* II 64) states that the duchess was at Tewkesbury until 12 November, whereas the indictment accused Ankarette of administering the poisoned drink at Warwick on 10 October.

[29] Fulman 561.

[30] *ibid.*

[31] *Third Report, op. cit.* 213–14.

[32] Fulman 561. Thomas Blake, though convicted, was pardoned at the request of the bishop of Norwich. *Third Report, op. cit.* 214.

execution a writ of *certiorari* was issued to the Warwickshire justices ordering the transfer to Westminster of the records of the proceedings in the Twynyho and Thuresby cases.[33] On the following day, or the day after, the king then being at Windsor, Clarence burst into the royal council chamber at Westminster and there made Dr. John Goddard read to the assembled councillors the declaration of innocence which Burdett and Stacy had made at the gallows' foot.[34] His choice of a spokesman was tactless to the point of folly, for Goddard was none other than the Minorite preacher who had expounded Henry VI's right to the throne at St Paul's Cross on 30 September 1470.[35]

Under this last provocation, an accusation of injustice from a brother so recently guilty of the crimes of embracery and judicial murder, and with possibly a suspicion that Clarence was connected with an impostor calling himself the earl of Oxford who was trying to raise disturbances in Cambridgeshire or Huntingdonshire,[36] Edward's long-tried patience broke. Even now, however, he acted far from precipitately, allowing himself time for reflection. He ordered Clarence to appear at Westminster Palace and there, about three weeks after the scene in the council chamber, publicly denounced his conduct in the presence of the mayor and aldermen of London 'as being derogatory to the laws of the realm, and most dangerous to judges and jurors throughout the kingdom.'[37] Either then or shortly afterwards Clarence was arrested.

For a whole decade Clarence had been a public nuisance and a menace to a family insecure in its possession of the throne. During the two months before his arrest, his conduct had mounted to a frenzy of indiscretion. He had committed judicial murder, had impugned the king's administration of justice, and possibly at this very time was fomenting rebellion (though nothing ever was or could be proved). Influenced by the dowager duchess of Burgundy, he had tried to push his brother into an expensive foreign commitment of little advantage to anybody but himself, which would certainly have ended in war, most probably with dangerously unpopular reactions in England itself.[38]

Louis XI of France now chose to exploit Clarence's fall for the advantage of his own Burgundian policy. The marriage of the Archduke Maximilian to Mary of Burgundy on 18 August 1477, made it necessary to secure at

[33] *Third Report, op. cit.* 214.
[34] Fulman 561.
[35] Scofield I 538; II 190.
[36] Scofield II 190–1; also the same author's 'The Early Life of John de Vere, Thirteenth Earl of Oxford,' *English Historical Review* XXIX (1914) 242–3. These disturbances were over by 23 June at the latest.
[37] Fulman 561–2. Edward had left London for Windsor on 21 May, the day of the scene in the council chamber, and did not return until 10 June. PRO C. 81/861/4452–4474.
[38] See above p. 246 n. 24.

least England's neutrality towards Louis's own attempt to gain control in Burgundy. Some time in late August or early September Louis sent his envoy, Olivier Le Roux, to Edward to poison the king's mind against his sister, the dowager duchess, and incidentally against Clarence. He instructed Le Roux to rouse Edward's fears with statements that a marriage between Clarence and Mary of Burgundy would have done more harm to the king of England than to the king of France. Le Roux was to report to Edward remarks commonly made about this marriage proposal overseas, and in particular things which Madame de Bourgogne had secretly told her confidents and certain great lords, but which had not been concealed from Louis XI. Although somewhat vague about the marriage and what Clarence intended to do in England once he obtained possession of the Burgundian lands,[30] these obscure hints were intended to plant the suggestion that he had planned to use Burgundian men and money to turn on his brother. A wild tale, but wild tales seemed plausible enough in an atmosphere already tense with suspicion and resentment.[40]

After an interval of four months, in mid January 1478 the king at last exhibited to parliament an indictment signed with his own hand, a catalogue of Clarence's offences drawn up in fairly precise terms, and including heinous accusations now levelled against him for the first time. These were that he had intrigued for the throne, and by implication that during Henry VI's re-adeption it had been entailed upon him failing heirs male in the house of Lancaster, in return for his support.

Although the choice of parliament as the place for Clarence's trial gave this *cause célèbre* maximum publicity, contemporaries and near-contemporaries who wrote about it chose to speculate upon the reasons for Clarence's destruction rather than to accept and reproduce the indictment. Can it be therefore that, doubting the truth of at least part of it, they preferred rumour and speculation to the details of the record statement?

Dominic Mancini, who was in England from the late summer of 1482 until some time before Richard III's coronation on 6 July 1483, had written his book *De Occupatione Regni Anglie Per Riccardum Tercium* by

---

[39] Calmette and Périnelle, *Louis XI, op. cit.* 218–26. Their dating of this episode seems more convincing than that of Scofield, *op. cit.* II 191 ff; owing to lack of space it is impossible to give full reasons for this. Le Roux's instructions are printed in Scofield II appendix XI. Calmette and Périnelle, Pièce Justificatif, *op. cit.* no. 72.

[40] Scofield, *op. cit.* II 206, connecting this by inference with the obscure rising of May or June (see above p. 249), considered it to be one of the strongest counts against Clarence. The story was the more plausible in that the house of Burgundy considered themselves to have a claim to the English throne. On 4 November 1471, Charles the Bold, as a descendant of John of Gaunt, had signed in the presence of his chancellor and two other witnesses a statement that his mother, Isabella of Portugal, had declared herself the rightful heir to all the possessions of Henry VI and had ceded her claim to him, and that he intended to make good his claim to the English crown as soon as a suitable opportunity offered. Scofield *op. cit.* II 24, 164–5, 175.

December 1483. Therein he reported accounts of these events, picked up in London and at the Yorkist court. He states that the Wydevilles, the queen's family, procured Clarence's death because he had publicly denounced them, and because the queen feared that if he remained alive he would never permit her children to succeed for he had impugned her marriage to the king on account of her widowhood.[41] This tale may be exaggerated, since Richard III's court was very hostile to the queen mother and her entire family.

The Second Anonymous Croyland Continuator, who was well-informed about events at the Yorkist court, and most probably completed his chronicle not long after Henry VII's accession, gives the fullest contemporary account which we possess.[42] The Croyland writer narrates in detail the various dissensions between the king and Clarence during the 1470s. He then describes the king as inveighing to the mayor and aldermen of London against Clarence's conduct 'as being derogatory to the laws of the realm' among other matters—an obvious reference to the Ankarette Twynyho scandal. From this point onwards, however, he seems to become almost deliberately evasive. He fails to discuss or enlarge upon these 'other matters.' He leaves studiously vague the account of events in parliament which immediately follows, though not without some tart comment upon the procedures there adopted. In the end, 'Parliament, being of the opinion that the informations which they had heard were established, passed sentence of condemnation upon him.'[43] The writer nowhere describes these informations.

A quarter of a century later, Sir Thomas More discussed Clarence's trial in his History of Richard the thirde. More's bias in this work is so obvious and so commonly assumed, that its readers are apt to ignore the care which he took to distinguish what he accepted as fact and what he regarded as rumour, in dealing with any particular event. Although he is known to have drawn his information from a wide circle of men who had been alive in Yorkist times and from their immediate descendants,[44] Sir Thomas remained bewildered and undecided between the envy of the Wydeville family against Clarence and 'a prowde appetite of the Duke himself enten-

[41] Usurpation of Richard III, op. cit. 74–7; also 82–3 and, for the feeling or prejudice against English kings marrying widows, 133 n. 13.

[42] Kingsford wrote that this author's 'accounts of events at court, and especially of the scene at the trial of Clarence, read like the work of an eye-witness.' English Historical Literature, op. cit. 182. For the most recent analysis of this chronicle see Sir Goronwy Edwards, 'The second continuation of the Croyland Chronicle: was it written in ten days?', Bulletin of the Institute of Historical Research XXXIX (1968) 117–29.

[43] Fulman 561–2.

[44] A. F. Pollard, 'The Making of Sir Thomas More's Richard III,' in Historical Essays in Honour of James Tait ed. J. G. Edwards, V. H. Galbraith, and E. F. Jacob (1933) 223–8. The Complete Works of Sir Thomas More ed. R. S. Sylvester II (1963) pp. lxv ff.

dinge to be king.'[45] Polydore Vergil writing at about the same time, certainly collecting information from among the same people as More, and just as scrupulous as Sir Thomas in attempting to sift fact from rumour,[46] was equally cautious or equally puzzled. Although, he wrote, he had enquired of many men who were not of least authority in the king's council at that time, he was quite unable to make up his mind between divers conflicting accounts—the influence of a soothsayer's prophecy on the king's mind, the Burgundian marriage affair, or sorcery practised by one of the king's servants and Clarence's defence of the sorcerer.[47] Various stories had obviously become somewhat garbled as they were handed down. Even Edward Hall, whose statements about the Yorkists are often so much more definite than those of earlier writers in a better position to gather the facts, gave up in despair at this point, confronted by what he called 'coniectures, which as often deceyve the imaginacions of fantastical folke.'[48] Foreign writers were equally vague and undecided.[49]

So, the king's brother died violently and mysteriously. He was condemned on a detailed indictment signed by the king himself, and in parliament, the highest court in the land, which as the king intended, gave the greatest possible publicity to the whole affair. Yet not one of these authors even mentions completely new accusations in what may well be the key clauses in the indictment, and in particular the claim that Clarence had 'laboured by parliament' to obtain the crown in 1470 and 1471, and that he had concealed an exemplification under the great seal of Henry VI which entailed the succession upon him failing heirs male to the house of Lancaster. No contemporary writers quite knew why Clarence died, and they seem to have been reluctant to accept official accusations at their face value. Such reluctance and suspicion obviously require investigation.

[45] *The English Works of Sir Thomas More* ed. W. E. Campbell I (1931) 37, 401.

[46] It is true that he did not always succeed; e.g., he absorbed very thoroughly Yorkist propaganda about the fifteenth-century dynastic conflict. See above pp. 59–61.

[47] Polydore Vergil, *op. cit.* 167–8.

[48] E. Hall, *Chronicle* (1548) f. ccxxxix (b) ed. H. Ellis (1809) 326.

[49] e.g. 'Le duc de Clarence querella contre sa marâtre, et fut vaincu par procès et jugé à mourir,' according to the text of Molinet's *Chroniques* ed. J. A. Buchon (Paris 1827–8) II 377. Armstrong (*Usurpation of Richard III, op. cit.* 134 n. 15) suggests that by 'marâtre' Molinet probably intended Elizabeth Wydeville but was ignorant of her actual relationship to Clarence. But the definitive edition of the *Chroniques* ed. G. Doutrepont and O. Jodogne (Brussels 1935–7), gives the reading '. . . le duc de Clarence querela contre *sa majesté* et fut vaincu parprochèz et jugiét à morir.' (I 415) Commynes, *op. cit.* I 53 merely remarks 'le roy Edouart fist mourir son frère, duc de Clarence, en une pippe de malvoisye, pour ce qui'il se voulait faire roy, comme l'on disoit.' The *Chronique Scandaluse* remarks that in 1477 Edward heard that his brother intended to go to Flanders to help his sister, so took him prisoner, detained him for a long time, then assembled his council. By their deliberation Clarence was condemned to hanging, but at the request of his mother was less publicly done to death. *Journal de Jean de Roye, connu sous le nom de Chronique Scandaleuse* ed. B. de Mandrot (Paris 1894–6) II 63–4.

Modern writers, on the other hand, have generally overlooked these contemporary doubts, and by the dual process of deducing more from the parliament roll of 1478 than the letter of its text will support and treating Warkworth's *Chronicle*[50] as an independent authority, have confidently asserted that Clarence obtained the succession to the crown by agreement with Margaret of Anjou. These modern accounts of the episode take two forms, sometimes found separately, sometimes combined. According to one version, Clarence, though by 1470 a political embarrassment to the earl of Warwick, could not be entirely overlooked in the settlement made at Angers during July and August before the Lancastrian invasion of England. As he was now disappointed in his immediate expectation of the crown, Margaret was induced to promise in addition to more immediate rewards, that if her son Edward prince of Wales died without lawful male heirs, Clarence should succeed. The alternative version runs that the re-adeption parliament of 1470–71 passed an act so entailing the crown. To render their narratives doubly convincing, some writers have conflated the two accounts so that the act of parliament confirms the compact made at Angers.

On close examination, however, the evidence for any such compact turns out to be dubious in the extreme. The story of the agreement made in France was first written down in Warkworth's *Chronicle*, as will be shown later, between 1478 and 1483. It cannot therefore be treated as an authority independent of the parliament roll, and the story did not appear in print until John Stow adopted it in 1580.[51] On the other hand, the tale of the act of parliament which is alleged to have given Clarence the right to the succession appeared for the first time only in Hall's *Chronicle* in 1548.[52] Hall knew nothing, however, of the agreement supposedly made in France.

It is odd, to say the least, that seventy years later Hall's *Chronicle* should confidently relate one episode which nobody so far had heard of, and that thirty years after Hall's book had appeared Stow should print another story buried for a full century in an obscure manuscript chronicle and only once copied, never published, in the intervening years. It was a story moreover which contemporaries and near-contemporaries either had never heard or had chosen to ignore.

This obscure exception, Warkworth's *Chronicle*, tells of an agreement made in France between Margaret of Anjou and Warwick,[53] though it never mentions Angers. John Leland, in his travels across England between 1534 and 1543, saw the unique manuscript at Peterhouse, Cambridge, whence

---

[50] See below pp. 259 ff.
[51] See below pp. 261–2.
[52] See below p. 262 and n. 97.
[53] See below pp. 259–60 and n. 83.

he copied the story into his *Collectanea*,[54] from which manuscript Stow in turn obtained it. Stow, always more the avid collector than the discriminating critic, chose to repeat the story despite the fact that he himself transcribed 'The Maner and Gwidynge of the Erle of Warwick at Aungiers,'[55] the fullest account now extant of these negotiations. Judging from internal evidence, this document was almost certainly written before Warwick and Clarence sailed from La Hogue on 9 September 1470.[56] It merely confirmed Clarence in possession of his estates and promised him the duchy of York and 'many other.'[57] The succession to the crown is never mentioned. For reasons to be given later, it seems wiser to accept the evidence of the 'Maner and Gwidynge' than to follow Warkworth's allusion to the discussions in France.

If we examine events in both France and England during 1470–71, such generosity towards Clarence appears to be improbable to say the least. By this time he was something of a political liability, and his associates treated him with almost open contempt. Possibly already on bad terms with the earl of Warwick,[58] Clarence was excluded from the negotiations at Angers in order to appease Margaret of Anjou.[59] The *Arrivall*, the official Yorkist account of Edward IV's recovery of his kingdom in 1471, claims that the die-hard Lancastrians who had suffered exile for Henry of Lancaster's sake held Clarence 'in great suspicion, despite, disdeigne and hatered', and that 'he sawe also, that they dayly laboryed amongs them, brekynge theyr ap-

---

[54] *ibid.* Although the *Collectanea* were known to a good many sixteenth- and seventeenth-century writers, they were printed for the first time, by Thomas Hearne, as late as 1716.

[55] BM MS Harleian 543 f. 168a–169b, 'The Maner and Gwidynge of the Erle of Warwick at Aungiers from the XVth day of July to the iiij of August, 1470, which day he departed from Aungiers,' printed in *Original Letters Illustrative of English History*, ed. H. Ellis 2nd Series I (1827) 132–5. Its provenance is unknown.

[56] 'Towchinge the poynt concerninge th'Erle of Warwicks passage, trewthe it is that th'Erle every day gave to understand, and yet dothe to the Kynge of Fraunce, that he hath Lettars often from Lords of England conteynyng that assone as he shalbe londed there, he shall have moe then L.M.¹. fighters at his commaundement; wherfore the seyde Earle promysed the Kynge that yf he wold helpe hym with a fewe folk, shipps, and money, he shall passe over the sea without any delay. . . .' *ibid.* 135.

[57] *ibid.* 134.

[58] A note in the Milanese archives contains information from an English knight on his way to Jerusalem that Warwick and Clarence had 'left London' on bad terms. *Calendar of State Papers Milanese, op. cit.* I 137. The Milanese state papers, however, are crammed with wild, incredible rumours during these months. Unless 'left London' may be interpreted as 'left England' the story is dubious. The Burgundian chronicler Chastellain, however, also reported differences between them: 'Mesmes le duc de Clarence . . . se porta contraire encontre son frère, pour avoir la couronne, et contre nature et contre honneur, l'aida à persécuter avecques Warwyc; mais enfin, ne demoura gaires que division ne sourdist entre Warwyc et lui, pour la préminence en autorité at par quoy le fait de Warwyc en devint moindre. . . .' *Oeuvres de Georges Chastellain* ed. M. Le Baron Kervyn de Lettenhove (Brussels 1863–6) V 494.

[59] Scofield, *op. cit.* I 533.

poyntments made with hym.'[60] Admittedly, the *Arrivall* is heavily biased. Circumstantial evidence, however, lends support to its contentions. Queen Margaret herself, though the idea of alliance with Warwick had first been mooted two years earlier,[61] hesitated when it came to the point for fear of alienating her Lancastrian supporters.[62] Back in England Warwick, as ever, took the lead.[63] There was considerable delay in restoring even the lieutenancy of Ireland to Clarence,[64] and despite the agreement at Angers guaranteeing him possession of all the lands which he already held, he was forced to disgorge to Queen Margaret and the prince of Wales certain of these estates, for which at the time he was only partially compensated.[65]

Excluded from the key negotiations at Angers, at best only scornfully tolerated by the die-hard Lancastrians, relegated to a subordinate position in England, the victim of agreements quickly broken, he was hardly likely, even if he demanded it, to be granted the succession to the crown.[66]

The second version—the story about the act of parliament of 1470–71—rests entirely upon Edward Hall's statement, shored up by implausible modern conjectures. The act itself, presuming that it was ever made, has not survived, for if the roll of the re-adeption parliament was ever made up it was afterwards destroyed by the triumphant Yorkists. We are therefore driven back upon the chroniclers for information about this parliament. These state, as one would expect, that the parliament passed acts which declared Edward IV a usurper, disinherited both Edward and

---

[60] *Arrivall of King Edward IV, op. cit.* 10.

[61] By a group of Lancastrians in exile with Queen Margaret at St Mighel-sur-Bar. Calmette and Périnelle, *op. cit.* 104, and Pièce Justificatif no. 28.

[62] 'Maner and Gwidynge,' *op. cit.* 132.

[63] Scofield, *op. cit.* I 543, following earlier writers, alleges that Warwick *took* the title 'lieutenant' and this caused hostility between him and Clarence. This is most likely true. I have nowhere found any reference to Warwick as lieutenant in record sources, where all the other titles formally granted him are used, but he is so designated in a proclamation concerning sanctuaries preserved in Stow's collections and in the *Arrivall*. BM Harleian MS. 543, f. 171b–172a. *Arrivall, op. cit.* 1, 8. Moreover, on 27 March 1471 a patent was issued making Edward, prince of Wales, lieutenant in anticipation of his landing in England. *Cal. Pat. Rolls, 1467–1477*, 252.

[64] The instruction for his appointment was drawn up on 18 December, but not delivered to the chancellor until 21 January, and the letters patent were not sealed until 18 February, Scofield, *op. cit.* I 543.

[65] *Cal. Pat. Rolls, 1467–1477*, 241–3, dated 23 March 1471. He had to surrender lands which had formerly belonged to Queen Margaret and Prince Edward and 'certain lands attainted,' or estates forfeited by Lancastrian supporters under the attainder acts passed in the 1460s. In partial recompense he received the lordship of Richmond, twelve manors, various small parcels of land plus various fee farms, annuities, etc., worth £380 p.a.

[66] It is unfortunately impossible, as the authorities are too conflicting, to decide at what point Clarence decided to go over to Edward IV again. It seems certain that secret negotiations began before Clarence left France for England, but he may have taken his decision only after he reached England.

his brother Richard of Gloucester, and restored their former possessions to the Lancastrians. No chronicler before Edward Hall in 1548 refers to any act of parliament settling the succession on the duke of Clarence. Although a strict patrol of the English Channel by the Burgundian fleet made communications with the continent difficult during the re-adeption,[67] it would be strange if tidings of such importance, just the kind of scandalous story about ruling families that was the breath of life to the French and Burgundian chroniclers, never filtered through either at the time or later. It is even more incredible that, with parliament sitting at Westminster, none of the London chroniclers knew of such an act.[68]

Various historians claim that this act is known from its rehearsal in another act repealing it in 1478[69] In fact the parliament roll of 1478 contains no repeal of any particular act dealing with the succession. The act misleadingly described in this way was a general act based on a common petition (no doubt inspired by the king), annulling *all* legislation of the re-adeption parliament, on the ground that it was 'inconvenient' to the king, the blood royal, the nobles, and all the king's subjects, as many of the acts still remained 'in writyng and some exemplified.'[70] Thus the repeal act was so phrased that it disposed of danger to the subject as much as of danger to the king.[71] That this repeal was introduced in 1478, after any apparent need for it had been ignored in the five sessions of parliament held between 1472 and 1475, rouses the suspicion of an ulterior motive. Though it was obviously intended to set the atmosphere for Clarence's trial, it nowhere referred to the duke. The king dealt with him in a second stage and in another way, by putting into parliament the bill referred to above, signed with his own hand, indicting his brother of treason.[72]

The indictment, after a preamble referring to 'manyfold grete conspiracies' which had taken place during the king's reign, proceeds with a statement that there had 'comen nowe of late' to Edward's knowledge, 'a moch higher, moch more malicious, more unnaturall and lothely Treason, than atte eny tyme heretoforn hath been compassed, purposed and conspired.' After making great play of Edward's generosity to Clarence, the document returns to the theme of treason, denouncing in a general but unmistakable way Clarence's offences between 1468 and 1469, then accusing him during the king's exile of 1470–71 of 'laboryng also by Parlement, to exclude hym and all his from the Regalie, and enabling hymself to the

---

[67] *Calendar of State Papers Milanese, op. cit.* I 155. See also 149–50 on attacks by Breton ships.

[68] See *Great Chronicle of London, op. cit.* 213–14. R. Fabyan, *The New Chronicles of England and France* ed. H. Ellis (1811) 660.

[69] e.g. W. Stubbs, *The Constitutional History of England* (1878), III 208 n. 5.

[70] *Rot. Parl.* VI 191.

[71] i.e. The legal threat to the property rights of loyal Yorkists caused by the legislation of the re-adeption Parliament.

[72] *Rot. Parl.* VI 193–5.

same, and by dyverse weyes otherwyse attemptyng.'

All this the King had forgiven him, but more recently the duke had conspired new treasons—details of which are rehearsed. Then follows what is, for our immediate purpose, a key passage:

> And overe this, the said Duke, continuyng in his false purpose, opteyned and gate an exemplification undre the Grete Seall of Herry the Sexte, late in dede and not in right Kyng of this Lande, wherin were conteyned all suche appoyntements as late was made betwene the said Duke and Margaret, callyng hereself Quene of this Lande, and other; amonges whiche it was conteyned, that if the said Herry, and Edward his first begoton Son, died without Issue Male of theire Body, that the seid Duke and his Heires, shulde be Kyng of this Lande; whiche exemplificacion the said Duke hath kepyd with hymself secrete, not doying the Kyng to have eny knowlegge therof, therby to have abused the Kynges true subgetts for the rather execucion of his said false purpose.

Thus, the story is tracked down to its source. It appeared for the first time on the parliament roll of 1478, and is entirely unsupported by any independent contemporary source. Moreover, its presentation seems to be quite as ambiguous as its revelation was convenient. The entire episode was premeditated and managed with considerable skill. Although rumours of his death were circulating as early as September 1477,[73] Clarence was not hurriedly done to death in an uncontrolled outburst of regal passion. After the king's first angry, but far from precipitate, denunciation of his brother before the mayor and aldermen of London in June 1477, seven months went by before parliament met. Then on 16 January 1478 the chancellor Thomas Rotheram, bishop of Lincoln, preached at the opening of parliament, taking as his text the first verse of the twenty-third psalm, 'Dominus regit me et nichil michi de-erit'—words more apt and pointed for the occasion in the Latin of the Vulgate than in the usual English translation, and in this context loaded with menace.

He supported his text with examples, from both the Old and New Testaments, of the retribution which followed upon broken fealty and quoted St Paul's awesome phrase 'Non sine causa Rex gladium portat.' Against this threatening overture there followed the act nulifying the proceedings of the re-adeption parliament, which, it should be recalled, contained a general reference to the survival of 'inconvenient' writings and exemplifications. Thus prepared, parliament was presumably in a receptive mood to hear the king's fierce and detailed, yet withal somewhat evasive, indictment of his brother.

It may be noted that the statement accusing Clarence of 'labouring by parliament' in 1470–71 to exclude the king and his heirs and to 'enable himself', is separated by over five hundred words of vehement denunciation and accusations (many of them already notorious) from the specific

[73] *Calendar of State Papers Milanese, op. cit.* I 230.

reference to an exemplification under the great seal of Henry VI about arrangements for the succession. Moreover, the indictment does not claim that his efforts to 'enable himself' in parliament succeeded.[74] On the other hand, Edward's description of the exemplification refers only to agreements made between Clarence, Margaret of Anjou and others. It never mentions ratification of such agreements by parliament or any parliamentary proceedings whatsoever. With its mixture of notorious actions and accusations hitherto unknown, this document has all the appearance of being drafted with a deliberately ambiguous cunning to create a false impression of events in 1470–71, without committing its writer to a completely untruthful statement about the proceedings of the re-adeption parliament.[75]

These proceedings carry an air of careful stage management. It is hardly conceivable that Edward would first have heard the story of the succession plan in 1477 had such a plan been discussed in 1470 and 1471. Even had he known of it and decided to ignore it in the interest of reconciliation with his brother, the London chroniclers, the foreign chroniclers and the Milanese ambassadors had no such reason for suppression. The exemplification, so opportunely discovered, was never shown to parliament, and there is no evidence that anybody else ever saw it. Clarence's possessions had been seized after his arrest in 1477 and it is of course quite possible that such a document was found among them. Yet the fact still remains that Edward IV, at a time when he had ample cause to wish to do away with his brother, suddenly discovered a treasonable document which no one has ever seen, which adds a completely new agreement to one of the most notorious political contracts of the day and implies parliamentary proceedings which no man at the time or for seventy years later ever mentioned.

Nor is the presence of these accusations in an official record any guarantee of their truth. Forgery was by no means unknown among the well-born or even in royal circles,[76] and in the course of the century unscrupulous politicians and triumphant factions placed a number of highly mendacious statements on the very rolls of parliament.[77] If it served his

[74] See above p. 257. Note how the accusation is tied to the truthful statement that parliament excluded Edward and his heirs. The accusation that Clarence attempted to 'enable himself' and failed may, of course, be correct. If so, Edward tacked the story of a frustrated attempt by Clarence on to the general story of the re-adeption. But, once again, the same arguments apply, that the chroniclers would surely have noted any attempt of this kind.

[75] It is possible, of course, that too much is being read into all this, but repeated readings of the indictment at long intervals seem to reveal skilled and careful drafting.

[76] e.g. Their enemies accused the Pastons of forging Sir John Fastolf's will; the papal dispensation for the marriage of Ferdinand of Aragon and Isabella of Castile in 1469 was forged.

[77] e.g. In 1398 Richard II forged the roll of the Shrewsbury parliament in order to condemn his political enemies more easily. See J. G. Edwards, 'The Parliamentary Committee of 1398,' *English Historical Review* XL (1925) 321–33. Henry IV placed a misleading account

turn, Edward himself was quite capable of unblushing perjury.[78] And as the well-informed Croyland Continuator tartly remarked of Clarence's trial 'some parties were introduced ... as to whom it was greatly doubted by many, whether they filled the office of accusers rather, or of witnesses: these two offices not being exactly suited to the same person in the same cause.'[79] Should we not be equally sceptical about the king's indictment? Was it less truth than an *ex parte* statement in a political battle?

No independent confirmation of the succession story which Edward IV made so much of has yet been found. As stated earlier, Warkworth's is the sole chronicle written during the fifteenth century to allege that any agreement made in France[80] entailed the succession upon Clarence, whence the story was copied by Leland and then by John Stow. Even this chronicle, however, nowhere states that parliament ratified the agreement.[81]

The chronicle owes its name to John Warkworth, master of Peterhouse from 1473 to 1500. He either wrote it or commissioned it as a continuation of the *Brut Chronicle*, one of the most popular books of later medieval England.[82] The first part of the unique vellum codex is strangely enough a manuscript copy of Caxton's printed text of 1480.[83] The continuation was almost certainly added to the *Brut* text before Warkworth presented the

---

of Richard II's deposition on the roll of 1399. See G. Lapsley, 'The Parliamentary Title of Henry IV,' *English Historical Review* XLIX (1934) 423–49, 577–606. In 1444 and 1450, Suffolk placed on record highly favourable statements of his own actions, and in 1455 York and his friends their own highly tendentious version of the events leading up to the first battle of St Albans. *Rot. Parl.* v 73–4, 176. C. A. J. Armstrong, 'Politics and the Battle of St Albans, 1455,' *Bulletin of the Institute of Historical Research* XXXIII (1960) 19–20, 33, 57–61. The preamble to the 1459 act of attainder was a violent indictment of York and his supporters, the act of 1461 declaring Edward IV's title to the throne extreme anti-Lancastrian propaganda, and that declaring Richard III's title a vehement denunciation of his brother's rule. *Rot. Parl.* V 346–9, 463–7, VI 240–2. S. B. Chrimes, *English Constitutional Ideas in the Fifteenth Century* (1936) 197–8. See also Richard of York's request to the earl of Salisbury in 1450 on the state of Ireland '. . . that this language maie be inacted at this present parlement for mine excuse in time to come.' R. Holinshead, *Chronicles of England, Scotland and Ireland* (1807–8) VI 268.

[78] Polydore Vergil, *op. cit.* 137. *Arrivall, op. cit.* 3–9. Above ch. 5 p. 155, n. 105.

[79] Fulman 562.

[80] Warkworth, *Chronicle* (see below n. 83) 9–10.

[81] For his account of the re-adeption Parliament, see *ibid.* 12–13.

[82] The *Brut* in its final form ends in 1461, and in this form was composed some time before 1470. A number of continuations were attempted. See F. W. D. Brie, *Geschichte und Quellen der mittelenglishcen Prosachronik, The Brute of England* (Marburg 1905), and *The Brut or the Chronicles of England*, EETS (2 vols 1906–8).

[83] Peterhouse MS. n. 190. The continuation was edited for the Camden Society in 1839 by J. O. Halliwell as *A Chronicle of the First Thirteen Years of the Reign of King Edward the Fourth*. See M. R. James, *A Descriptive Catalogue of the Manuscripts in the Library of Peterhouse* (1899) 221, and Kingsford, *English Historical Literature, op. cit.* 171–3. A comparison with the manuscript shows that apart from a few insignificant mistakes in transcription the printed text is sound.

manuscript to his college in 1483.[84] The text as it has come down to us, however, ends in 1474, thus giving the superficial impression that it was written at that time and is therefore for the events of 1470–71 an authority independent of the parliament roll of 1478. This is not the case. An examination of the manuscript shows that either it is an incomplete copy or the author (whoever he was) abandoned his narrative unfinished.[85] There is nothing whatever to show that he meant to end his work in 1474, and internal evidence puts the composition of the continuation between Clarence's death and July 1482 or shortly afterwards,[86] that is after the publicity surrounding the king's indictment of his brother in parliament.

So Warkworth's *Chronicle* is a strictly contemporary source; but the date of its composition unfortunately cannot vouch for its reliability. It is short, covering only 27 printed pages. It deals very briefly and very inaccurately with the first eight years of Edward's reign. Obviously the work of a man writing without notes, whose memory of events has become compressed and confused, the chronology of events is chaotic. The *Chronicle's* real interest (and greater accuracy) begins with Robin of Redesdale's rebellion in 1469, and it is of very considerable value for events in England in 1470 and 1471. By contrast, events in France during the same months are dismissed in one single paragraph, a significant point perhaps, as the *Chronicle* places

[84] See below n. 86.
[85] See below n. 86.
[86] An examination of the manuscript shows that the *Brut* ends on f. 214b and Warkworth continues to f. 225a. On f. 214b occurs the statement that the copy was finished on 2 July 1482. The Caxton text used was, therefore, that of 1480—not 1482, as stated by M. R. James, as the latter was not published until 8 October 1482. See *DNB* III 1296. The continuation, however, is in the same hand. Two scribes were employed, but the change from the first to the second takes place earlier, in the middle of f. 196b; so it may be presumed that the continuation was copied very shortly, if not immediately, after the second scribe completed the transcription of the Caxton text. Though copied in the second half of 1482, or shortly afterwards, the text of the continuation as it stands ends early in 1474. There is nothing to show that the author planned to end his narrative at this point and several indications that he did not. F. 225a contains five lines and twelve words followed by a series of dashes, dots, and curls, which was the usual way in which the scribes had divided sections of the book. J. O. Halliwell, the Camden Society's editor, suggests (p. xxiii) that there were two copies of the whole work—one Warkworth's own (now lost), and the other the existing codex which he presented to the college. On the evidence which he cites, the hypothesis is plausible and it may well be that the second scribe never completed the existing copy. The fact that Warkworth (25) mentions Archbishop Neville's imprisonment at Hammes but not his release and death might be taken to indicate that an original draft from which the copy was made was completed before June 1476 or even by the summer of 1475 (*DNB* XIV 256). On the other hand he had already remarked (15), commenting on Clarence's desertion of Warwick and the Lancastrians in 1471, 'so alle covandes of fydelite, made betwyx the Duke of Clarence, and the Erle of Warwyke, Quene Margarete, Prince Edwarde hir sonne, bothe in Englonde and in Fraunce, were clerly brokene and forsakene of the seide Duke of Clarence; which, in conclusione, *was distruccion bothe to hym* and them.' So emphatic a statement about Clarence himself can surely refer only to his condemnation and death. It could hardly have been written before his execution.

the agreement with Clarence in France, not in the English parliament. Moreover, the author seems to have had no special 'inside information' about the events of the 1470s.[87]

We cannot therefore accept this jejune continuation of the *Brut* as an authority independent of the parliament roll of 1478. Its statement about Clarence's claim to the throne is thus less likely to be that of an independent witness than a garbled echo of Edward's own accusation made in parliament. As we have seen, the Croyland Continuator chose to ignore that particular accusation, while Dominic Mancini, Polydore Vergil and Sir Thomas More, who all had ample opportunity at the centre of court life to glean information from survivors, also ignored it completely.

It remains to suggest how, after its seeming early rejection, the tale was promoted to the historical canon. We know that John Leland saw the Peterhouse manuscript, for he paraphrased the section of it which deals with the agreement about the succession and noted the origin of his information.[88] Before his death in 1552 the London printer Reyner Wolfe (whose earliest publications included Leland's own writings) acquired part of his collection of manuscripts. About 1548 Wolfe planned to publish a universal history and cosmography and began himself to compile the English, Scottish and Irish sections. Wolfe died in 1573, after twenty year's work on the project, with nothing completed.[89] After his death Stow bought part of his collections and used them extensively in his own works.[90] It is interesting to note how the Clarence story grew in successive editions of the works of the same Tudor writers. Stow's first historical work, *A Summarie of Englyshe Chronicles*, a brief set of annals given to the world in 1565, and the abridgements of it which he published in 1566, 1567, and 1573, contain nothing relevant under the year 1470. For 1477 (sic) he baldly relates that Clarence was drowned in the Tower in a barrel of Malmsey.[91] In the *Chronicles of England*, published in 1580, in form an

---

[87] Very little is known about Warkworth himself. He was elected a fellow of Merton College, Oxford, in 1446, was principal of Neville's Inn in 1453, and was chaplain to William Grey, bishop of Ely, who appointed him to Peterhouse in 1473. Grey was at Ely and then at Downham from February 1478 until his death on 4 August. *DNB* VIII 656. The *Chronicle* shows signs of sympathy for Henry VI, but it is critical of Edward IV rather than pro-Lancastrian, and it is hostile to Clarence and the Nevilles. See Kingsford, *English Historical Literature, op. cit.* 172.

[88] Warkworth, *Chronicle, op. cit.* 9–10. *Joannis Lelandi Antiquarii De Rebus Britannicis Collectanea* ed. T. Hearne (1770) II 471, 502.

[89] *DNB* XXI 776.

[90] But although Stow knew the *Collectanea*, it was not among the documents which he bought. It passed to Humphrey Purefoy and then to William Burton. Stow also prepared for publication a history of England which he described as 'Reyner Wolfe's Chronicle.' Archbishop Whitgift urged him to send it to the press, but he died without doing so. *DNB* XIX 3, XXI 776. J. Stow, *A Survey of London* ed. C. L. Kingsford (1908) I p. xxi.

[91] J. Stow, *A Summarie of Englyshe Chronicles* (1565) 158d.

expansion of his earlier *Summarie*, he accepts the story (found in Leland's collection) of the agreement made in France in 1470,[92] in spite of the fact that his own transcript of the 'Maner and Gwidynge,' by far the fullest account of the negotiations at Angers, says nothing about it.[93] Yet although Stow's account of the events of 1466 and 1478 is now much fuller, he does not connect them with the earlier episode of 1470. Nor does he link up Thomas Burdett's execution with Clarence's fall.[94] It is not until the publication of the *Annales* in 1592, which in spite of their title modified the annalistic form to create a smoother narrative, that Stow for the first time gives an account of the exemplification,[95] in words which are simply a rough paraphrase of about one quarter of the king's indictment on the parliament roll of 1478.[96]

We must now turn to Hall's *Chronicle*.[97] It is here, in 1548, that the story of the entail made in the parliament of 1470–71 is first found, whence it was adopted by Grafton in his later works[98] and by Holinshed[99] but never by

---

[92] J. Stow, *The Chronicles of England* (1580) 723.

[93] Nor, oddly enough, does the story appear in the second edition of Holinshed (1586), for which Stow gave some help. See Stow, *Survey, op. cit.* I xxi. Holinshead, who had worked for Reyner Wolfe, and had access to all his collections, after his death cut down the plan of the Universal History to more manageable size. The result was the famous *Chronicles*, first published in 1578.

[94] *Chronicles of England, op. cit.* 747. He merely states that Burdett was executed for treasonable words spoken in fury against Edward IV after the King, while hunting in Burdett's park at Arrow, had slain his favourite white buck.

[95] J. Stow *The Annales of England* (1592) 707–9. Here Stow also comes closer in other ways to the accepted version of events. In addition to the story of the white buck, he relates that Burdett was condemned for poisoning and sorcery and that Clarence protested.

[96] As he remarks, 'In the which attaindor (which I have read) . . .' *Annales, op. cit.* 708. The *Annales* contains a much longer list than any of his earlier works of the authorities which he had consulted, and the list for the first time includes 'Parliament Records.' 'Ingulphus' (i.e., the Croyland Chronicle) also appears in the list for the first time. However, in spite of increasing knowledge, Stow had little means of discriminating between his various authorities and seems rather to have pecked here and there. So he now takes the story of the exemplification from the parliament roll, rejects (or at least does not mention) Hall's statement about the entail of 1470–1 and the possible hint in the parliament roll of Clarence's attempt to procure it, takes the story of Burdett and the white buck from a now lost 'Register of the Grey Friars,' but ignores the Croyland Chronicler's account of John Stacey and either misreads or misinterprets his account of Burdett's trial.

[97] Hall, *Chronicle, op. cit.* 1548 f. ccx (d), edn of 1809 H. Ellis 286. The supposed edition of 1542 is a ghost. See G. Pollard, 'The Bibliographical History of Hall's Chronicle,' *Bulletin of the Institute of Historical Research* X(1932–3) 12–17.

[98] Grafton's continuation of Hardyng, published in 1543, repeats various conjectures under the year 1477 and then in a section on Edward IV copies Sir Thomas More. This was, of course, the first printing of any English version of 'The History of King Richarde the thirde.' See *More's Complete Works, op. cit.* II pp. xx ff. *The Chronicle of John Hardyng* ed. H. Ellis (1812) 465.

The various editions of Grafton's *Abridgement* published between 1562 and 1572 and the *Manuell* of 1565 say nothing either of agreement in France or parliamentary action in

Stow. Yet Hall himself never connected this incident with Clarence's death. Of the causes of the duke's death, he remarked, '. . . the certayntie thereof was hyd, and coulde not truely be disclosed, but by coniectures, which as often deceyue the imaginacions of fantastical folke . . .' These conjectures claimed that both the king and queen were disturbed by a foolish prophecy, and that the king and his brother quarrelled over the Burgundian marriage question and over Clarence's indignation at the execution of one of his servants (unnamed) for poisoning and sorcery. In the end Hall evaded a choice, merely remarking that the duke was arrested, 'cast into the Towre, where he beyng taken and adiudged for a Traytor, was priuely drouned in a But of Maluesey.'[100]

Two traditions can thus be traced: first, the story of an agreement made in France (just possibly hinted at in Edward IV's indictment) descending through Warkworth, Leland, and Stow, the last of these three authors also tacking on the tale of the exemplification which he read in the parliament roll of 1478; and second, the story of the entail made in the parliament of 1470–71, introduced as far as we can see by Edward Hall and copied by Grafton and Holinshed. The stories were first brought together in a single volume in William Habington's *Edward IV*[101] published in 1640, though part of it at least had been written many years before. The rather superficial historians of the eighteenth century more or less 'mixed according to taste'[102] and then, during the nineteenth century, the whole combination was generally accepted.[103]

After all this, why was Clarence executed? By 1478, seven years had passed since he had last made war against the king, and his treason of those days had been forgiven if not forgotten. It is true that for years he had been a dangerous focal point for disturbances, that his quarrel with Gloucester since 1472 had weakened a still somewhat insecure dynasty, that his name had been linked, if vaguely, with a number of conspiracies against the king, and that foreign observers had at various times surmised that he might

1470–71 and give no reason for Clarence's death in 1478. The *Chronicle at Large . . . of* 1568 copies Hall for both 1470 and 1477–8. *A Chronicle at Large . . .*, (1809) II 27, 68. Hall had, of course, in his will left Grafton his own chronicle in the hope that he would print it, which Grafton did. As to Grafton's own book of 1568, Stow contemptuously alleged that he had just patched it up from Fabian, Hall, and others. See *Survey, op. cit.* I pp. lii·liii.

[99] Holinshed, *Chronicles, op. cit.* III 301.

[100] Hall, *Chronicle, op. cit.* (edn 1809) 326. Then, in his section on Edward V, he reproduces (342) Sir Thomas More's remarks on Clarence.

[101] *The Historie of Edward the Fourth, King of England* (1640), 59, 70–71, 188–95.

[102] See Rapin de Thoyras, *The History of England* transl. N. Tindal (2nd edn 1732–3) I 608–9, 624. Thomas Carte, *A General History of England* (1747–50) II 782, 785, 796–8. D. Hume, *The History of England from the Invasion of Julius Caesar to the Accession of Henry VII* (1762) II 400–01, 404, 415–17.

[103] e.g. J. Lingard, *The History of England* (6th edn Dublin 1854–5) IV 87, 89, 103. Sir J. Ramsay, *Lancaster and York* (1892) II 353–4, 361–2.

attempt to seize the throne. In 1477 his conduct reached a frenzy of indiscretion in procuring a judicial murder and then in impudently denouncing the trial of Stacy and Burdett and the king's own administration of justice. The last action indeed Edward must have resented most bitterly, for he had worked almost unceasingly to uphold the royal function of giving firm justice throughout the country.[104]

Was Edward at last out of patience with the constant scandals provoked by this unmitigated family nuisance[105] or did he quite genuinely fear that his brother was once again plotting for the throne? At this point we move on to very debatable ground, for, as with many other episodes in medieval English history, we know some of the external facts, but nothing of the inner thoughts, or motives of the protagonists. Clarence had recently revived an old slander that Edward IV was illegitimate. Even if he did not impugn the validity of Edward's marriage to Elizabeth Wydeville as some historians have suspected,[106] he may have been indiscreet enough to leave a desperate fear in the queen's mind that he would never permit the succession of her children.[107] Edward may or may not have taken seriously the vague accusations thrown out by Louis XI,[108] and have linked them with the obscure rising of May or June 1477, though if we can accept certain sections of his indictment for truth, he believed that Clarence was at this time making extensive preparations for revolt.[109]

[104] J. Bellamy, 'Justice Under the Yorkist Kings,' *American Journal of Legal History* IX (1965) 135–55.

[105] A statement in the indictment runs '. . . his said Brother by his former dedes, and nowe by this conspiracye, sheweth hymself to be incorrigible, and in noo wyse reducible to that by [sic] bonde of nature, and of the grete benefices aforn reherced . . .' *Rot. Parl.* VI 194.

[106] For a full discussion see M. Levine, 'Richard III—Usurper or Lawful King?,' *Speculum* XXXIV (1959) 391–401. On balance, Levine is inclined to reject the story, together with P. M. Kendall's suggestion in *Richard III* (1955) 217–18, that Edward discovered that Clarence knew the story of his alleged pre-contract with Lady Eleanor Butler and that this signed Clarence's death warrant. There is no evidence that Clarence made use of this story. He was so impulsive that he could hardly have refrained from using it had he known it, as he had repeated the equally dangerous story of Edward's bastardy. This story seems, originally, to have been put about to assist the first of Warwick the Kingmaker's plans against Edward, in 1469. Calmette and Périnelle, *op. cit.* Pièce Justificatif n. 30. Commynes, *op. cit.* II 50. Charles the Bold knew of it in 1475. Accusations of bastardy were, however, part of the common stock of political smears in the fifteenth century and should not be taken too seriously.

[107] See above p. 251 and n. 41.

[108] 'Whether the hint thrown out by the King of France through Olivier Le Roux was based on truth or falsehood, it offered only too good an explanation of Clarence's strange actions, and it sealed his fate.' Scofield, *op. cit.* II 206.

[109] e.g. The accusation that Clarence had caused men '. . . to be sworne uppon the blessed Sacrament to be true to hym and his heires, noon exception reserved of theire liegeaunce.' *Rot. Parl.* VI 194. For comment see W. H. Dunham Jr, 'Lord Hastings' Indentured Retainers, 1461–1483,' *Transactions of the Connecticut Academy of Arts and Sciences* XXXIX (1955) 93.

The indictment also refers to Clarence's plans to subvert the realm 'by myght to be goten as well outewarde as inwarde,' which seems to hint at foreign, possibly Burgundian help,

All is vague, cloudy, indefinite. Evasions, even worse, hints of perjury, abound in the main narratives. After the Croyland Continuator's detailed descriptions of the quarrels which had taken place since 1472, it is disconcerting to find that he avoided discussing or even reproducing the final charges laid against Clarence in the king's indictment, although he must have known them very well.[110] Dominic Mancini ominously wrote, '. . . *whether the charge was fabricated*, or a real plot revealed, the duke of Clarence was accused of conspiring the king's death by means of spells and magicians.'[111] Polydore Vergil was completely bewildered as to Edward's motives, and there is more than a hint of doubt in Sir Thomas More's remark, '. . . at the last heinous treason was laid to his charge, and finallye, were he faulty or were he faultlesse, attainted was he by parliament, and iuged to death.'[112]

The story of the settlement in the parliament of 1470–71 may certainly be rejected as a fabrication. It is inconceivable that the chroniclers would ignore such a story. They enjoyed scandals in high places, and in this case there was no particular restraint which would have kept all of them silent. Leaving aside the truth or falsehood of many other details in the king's indictment, nowhere does a tale of any agreement with Margaret of Anjou about the succession whether in England or in France, or any reference to the notorious exemplification, appear before Edward IV suddenly produced it in 1478. In the complete absence of any previous knowledge of this vital document, and given the fact that no-one ever saw it, together with the lack of any circumstantial evidence of its treasonable contents, and its suspiciously opportune discovery, is it too much to suggest that either the whole story was a fabrication or that if the document did exist it was a forgery? If we adopt the suggestion that this unseen document was forged. the question of authorship still remains. It is possible that Clarence himself forged it and that the royal officers found it among his papers when, after his arrest, they seized his possessions. His whole career shows that he would stop at nothing to realize his ambitions. Alternatively, the king himself had

and includes accusations of a plot (fortunately foiled) involving the abbot of Tewkesbury and others to smuggle a strange child into Warwick castle and substitute him for Clarence's son and heir while the latter was conveyed out of the country to Ireland or Flanders, 'wherby he myght have goten hym assistaunce and favoure agaynst oure said Sovereigne Lorde . . . commaunded and caused dyverse of his Servauntes, to goo unto sundry parties of this Royaulme, to commove and stirre the Kynges naturall Subgetts, and in grete nowmbre to be redy in harneys within an Houre warnyng, to attend upon hym, and to take his parte to levy Werre agaynst the Kynges moost Royall persone . . .' *Rot. Parl.* VI 193–4. These accusations are also completely unsupported by independent evidence.

[110] It is, of course, possibly, though unlikely, that he kept silent out of respect for Elizabeth of York, Henry VII's queen and Clarence's niece, but Dominic Mancini had no such motives for silence.

[111] See above p. 251 and no. 41. Clarence, himself, was not, of course, accused of sorcery, but that does not affect my argument.

[112] See above pp. 251–2.

ample motives for such action. Outrageous as Clarence's behaviour had always been, his past treasons had been pardoned, and neither his proved offences since 1471 nor his recent dangerous ways were enough by the standards of the day to inflict the death penalty upon a prince of the blood royal. Evidence of overt treason was highly desirable, if not essential, and such evidence the concealment and opportune discovery of the mysterious exemplification provided[113]—or at least it made more plausible Edward's accusations, so far as we know unsubstantiated, about his brother's most recent plots against him.[114] Perjury was one of the commonplace vices of the times, and long before this Edward IV had shown himself quite capable of it. As we consider the silences and evasions of contemporary writers and the doubts and suspicions of the following generation, we may well begin to wonder if Edward committed this particular crime yet again in order to dispose of his intolerable brother under the semblance of a fair trial. Must we, therefore, add yet another official falsehood to the growing list which modern scrutinies of the parliament rolls have revealed, and reject completely one of the more dramatic incidents in the brief re-adeption of King Henry VI?

[113] Carte, two centuries ago, although he believed the stories, thought that the exemplification was included in the indictment to secure sufficient evidence; thus '. . . the rest of the charge being founded upon bare words, it was necessary to find some overt act to countenance his being condemned of treason . . .' A General History, op. cit. II 798. C. Oman, History of England, 1377–1485 (1910) 462, remarked of this incident 'no real proof of it was produced'.

[114] See above pp. 256–7, 264 and n. 109.

11

Bonds, coercion and fear: Henry VII and the peerage

One of the main themes of English history has been the increasing degree of control attained by government over society. Historians have all too often assumed that the monarchy achieved such increased control by frontal attacks on the power of the aristocracy. The two main points of attack, widely separated in time, are considered to have been Henry II's assault on the feudal courts of the lords through the development of royal courts staffed by a judicial bureaucracy, and Henry VII's repression of the nobility in favour of middle-class servants. Both conceptions are somewhat tarnished. It is now generally recognized that, in meeting contemporary demands for justice, Henry II had no idea of destroying the courts of his tenants-in-chief. To have done so would have been to deny great and powerful men their just rights. Moreover, in a turbulent, undisciplined society, attacks upon any institutions which helped to maintain public order would have been dangerously unrealistic. Henry II introduced new instruments which offered supplements and more efficient alternatives to the old. The royal courts of justice ultimately replaced the baronial courts because these withered away, gradually becoming incompetent to serve the needs of a society where feudal relationships and land tenures had become too tangled and complicated for baronial courts to deal with. More immediately, however, as Glanvill's great legal treatise makes amply clear, the royal court could be expected to strengthen feudal justice by advising barons on the treatment of difficult cases which sub-tenants brought to their own courts.[1] Henry VII was no more consciously revolutionary than Henry II had been. The first Tudor continued to rely on the aristocracy in government, and yet at the same time attempted to control them by methods which, although short-lived, are in themselves interesting.

All late medieval and early modern societies lived in fear that their in-

[1] 'The lord himself can place his court into the court of the lord king, so that he may have the advice and agreement of the lord king's court touching the matter in doubt. And this lord king owes his barons as a matter of right . . . But when a baron's doubts are resolved in the lord king's court he can return with his plea and determine it in his own court.' Glanvill. *De legibus et consuetudinibus regni Anglie* ed. G. E. Woodbine (1932) II 123, quoted from D. M. Stenton, *English Justice between the Norman Conquest and the Great Charter*, Memoirs of the American Philosophical Society LX (1964) 78.

adequate institutions would fail to hold the terribly thin line between order and chaos.[2] English society had proved quite incapable of producing an effective bureaucracy (even had Henry VII found the money to pay it, which he could not). In the thirteenth century one enquiry after another had revealed an almost sempiternal corruption of local government. The sheriffs' offices were notorious from at least the early part of the fourteenth century, and experienced judges like Sir Geoffrey Scrope (d. 1340) had looked upon the system of justices of the peace from its very inception with justifiable doubts about its probable efficiency.[3] Since many of the justices of the peace were corrupt and violent themselves, they had failed to improve the standard of law and order in any notable way.[4] Moreover, control of the countryside at the village level was far less adequate than it afterwards became. Even in the 1500s, if a recent investigation of Buckinghamshire and Rutland can be accepted as typical, probably only one village in five had a resident squire, whereas by 1680 more than two out of three had one.[5]

In these conditions the king could not possibly ignore, much less suppress, any class of men who could assist in maintaining public order and the defence of the realm. Indeed, statements of the time show that nobody at the time was so wildly eccentric as to harbour the slightest idea of suppressing the nobility. Contemporary writing of all kinds constantly stressed their power and with equal frequency emphasized the need for upholding it. Even violence and disloyalty could not destroy the nobleman's essential role in society. In 1459 an anonymous pamphlet, the *Somnium Vigilantis*, could even argue, though it is true that the author in the end rejected the argument, that the utter destruction of the Yorkist lords, outrageous and treasonable though their actions had been, would harm the realm far more than the injury which their earlier offences had already inflicted upon it. Considering, so the pamphlet runs, that the realm was surrounded by enemies on every side, 'it were more need for to procure to have more heads and lords for the tuition and defence of the same than for to depose and destroy any of them.'[6] In draft sermons written for delivery to parlia-

---

[2] See J. R. Lander, *Conflict and Stability in Fifteenth Century England* (1969) ch. 7.

[3] M. McKisack, *The Fourteenth Century* (1959), 201–2.

[4] For the sixteenth century, see F. W. Brooks, *The Council in the North*, Historical Association general series (25) (revised edn 1966).

[5] J. Cornwall, 'The Early Tudor Gentry,' *Economic History Review* 2 Ser., XVII (1964–5) 459–61. L. Stone, 'Social Mobility in England, 1500–1700,' *Past and Present* (33) (1966) 52.

[6] J. P. Gilson, 'A Defence of the Proscription of the Yorkists in 1459,' *English Historical Review* XXVI (1911) 515. The Yorkist lords themselves stressed the same point in a letter sent to Henry VI at Ludlow in 1459, commenting on the action of their enemies who had shown '. . . ne any tenderness to the noble blood of this land such as serve to the tuition and defence thereof, ne not weighing the loss of your true liegemen of your said realm.' *An English Chronicle of the Reigns of Richard II, Henry IV, Henry V and Henry VI.* ed. J. W. Davies, Camden Series (1856) 82. I have modernized spelling and punctuation in all quotations in this chapter.

ment in 1483, Bishop John Russell described nobility as 'virtue and ancient riches,' went on to compare the nobles themselves to firm rocks in an unstable sea, and averred 'the politic rule of every realm standeth in them[7]; they like Moses and Aaron approach the king, the commons stand afar off.' Their quarrels were to be settled by the king, other men's affairs in the ordinary courts of law. Finally, in at least two different passages William Caxton described the government of the realm as more or less a cooperative effort between the king and the nobles.[8]

Impressive as the development of English governmental and legal institutions had been during the high middle ages, in practice these institutions had always been defective. Their working to a great extent depended upon the local support of the aristocracy. In October 1453 Henry VI or his council reminded Lord Egremont that the king had made him a baron, not for any past services 'but for the trust and trowing that we had of the good service ye should do to us in time coming, in especial in keeping of the rest and peace of our land and in letting of all that should mowe be to the contrary'.[9] Sir John Fortescue thought the aristocracy the most influential group of people in the country,[10] and even William Worcester, who vehemently deplored the declining martial spirit of the nobility and gentry[11] and their preoccupation with estate management and legal matters, admitted that they should concern themselves with civil affairs to the extent of 'maintaining' the justices and other royal officers in carrying out their duties.[12]

[7] *Grants, Etc., From the Crown During the Reign of Edward the Fifth* ed. J. G. Nichols, Camden Series (1854) pp. xxxix–lxiii.

[8] 'And therefore my right redoubted lord I pray almighty god to save the king our sovereign lord, to give him grace to issue as a king, to abound in all virtues, to be assisted with all other his lords in such wise that his noble realm of England may prosper, abound in virtues, and that sin may be eschewed, justice kept, the realm defended, good men rewarded, malefactors punished, the idle people to be put to labour, *that he with the nobles of his realm may reign gloriously.' The Prologues and Epilogues of William Caxton* ed. W. J. B. Crotch, EETS (1928), 14–16, see also 81.

[9] *Proceedings and Ordinances* VI 161.

[10] '. . . the might of the land *after* the might of the great lords thereof standeth most in the king's officers.' *The Governance of England* ed. C. Plummer (1885) 150–1.

[11] So, incidentally, did Caxton.

[12] *The Boke of Noblese* ed. J. G. Nichols, Roxburghe Club (1860) 77–8. See also Edmund Dudley, *The Tree of Commonwealth* ed. D. M. Brodie (1948) 44–5, 66. For Dudley the functions of the nobility entailed the duty of 'true defence,' that is, the protection of the poor from injury and the defence of the king. Instances can be multiplied almost indefinitely, e.g., 'For so much as the great surety, defence, honour and the politic governance of this noble realm standeth and oweth to be in the noble persons, born of high blood, and exalted to high estate and power . . .' (creation of the duke of York) *Rot. Parl.* VI 168. In 1497 Raymundo de Raymundis, commenting on the Cornish rebellion, Perkin Warbeck, and the Scottish attack, wrote, 'Everything favours the king, especially an immense treasure, and because all the nobles of the realm know the royal wisdom and either fear him or bear him an extraordinary affection . . . and *the state of the realm is in the hands of the nobles not of the people.' Calendar of State Papers Milanese* ed. and trans. A. B. Hinds (1912) I 325. See also *ibid.* 316–17.

The influence of noblemen followed naturally enough from their wealth and territorial power. As G. A. Homes has pointed out, the English were highly realistic about status. In the fourteenth century no man was elevated to an earldom unless he had built up, or unless the king granted him, an inheritance sufficient to maintain the dignity.[13] A poor nobleman was almost a contradiction in terms.[14] The same held true in the fifteenth and early sixteenth centuries, though deliberate endowment by the king then became less frequent.[15] Moreover, contemporary feeling that government was naturally better in the hands of the rich who, almost from the mere fact of their wealth, were less openly corrupt and self-seeking than other people, also reinforced the position of the aristocracy.[16]

Although Tudor England showed most of the characteristics common to Renaissance states elsewhere it was with a difference, for such traits were there less extreme in degree. Its smaller area and the peculiar development of both the monarchy and feudal institutions had given England greater unity. Although dialects were so divergent still that people from different parts of the country found difficulty in understanding each other, and as late as 1497 Cornishmen rose in revolt rather than pay taxes to defend the remote inhabitants of the north against the Scots, regional feeling never combined with the discontents and ambitions of the nobility. In England noble estates had always been scattered over many counties. Moreover, as an intelligent Venetian envoy remarked in the same year as the Cornish revolt, the nobility possessed no fortresses[17] and only very limited judicial powers. He claimed indeed that by continental standards they were hardly nobles at all, merely rich gentlemen in possession of great quantities of land.[18] Such conditions meant that, even when granted royal offices in districts where their estates lay, no single great family ruled a compact block of territory combining all the coercive powers of landowner, military commander, and judge. Therefore no single family could rely for its own enhancement on attracting strong feelings of provincial separatism. There was nothing in England to compare with what Shakespeare so rightly

---

[13] G. A. Homes, *The Estates of the Higher Nobility in Fourteenth-Century England* (1957) 4–5.

[14] In 1478 George Neville was degraded from the dukedom of Bedford, ostensibly on grounds of poverty. *Rot. Parl.* VI 173. Also, see below, p. 290–91 for the case of the earl of kent.

[15] See below p. 294–5.

[16] See Lander, *Conflict and Stability, op. cit.* ch. 7.

[17] This seems to be true except for a few castles in the northern marches. Fifteenth-century 'castles' were built as comfortable residences, not fortresses, and by this time most of the older private castles, even in Wales and the Marches, were so dilapidated that they were probably indefensible. See B. H. St. J. O'Neil, *Castles and Cannon* (1960) 1–64. T. B. Pugh, *The Marcher Lordships of South Wales, 1415–1536*, Board of Celtic Studies University of Wales History and Law Series (20) (1963) 247. See also above ch. 2.

[18] *A Relation, or Rather a True Account of the Island of England* ed. and trans C. A. Sneyd, Camden Series (1847) 37.

called France's 'almost kingly dukedoms.' Even though the greater peers showed intense jealousy of any encroachment upon their local spheres of influence, they never, even during Henry VI's minority, attempted formally to parcel out the country among themselves like the Scottish nobles during the minority of James IV.[19]

Yet, in spite of their somewhat weak position as compared with other aristocratic groups, the English peers were still the natural leaders and disciplinarians of their local communities.[20] No king could govern unsupported by their wealth and prestige. Even in the late sixteenth century the local lord, knight, or even esquire, set the tone of his district and, for example, the survival of catholicism and the development of puritanism depended to a marked degree upon their influence and protection.[21] Ideally therefore a higher standard of behaviour should prevail among such people,[22] partly to set an example to lesser folk, partly because when powerful nobles quarrelled their neighbours and clients tended to be drawn into the disputes and whole districts might be disturbed by affrays and riots.[23] In practice of course, such a system was often by modern standards rank with self-seeking, oppression, and injustice. To make the system work the king had to enforce sufficient control over powerful men to keep their activities within decent bounds. In the imaginary exhortation from God to a monarch at the end of Dudley's *Tree of Commonwealth* the deity is made to say:

'Thou hast kept the temporal subjects in a loving dread, and hast not suffered them, nor the mightiest of them, to oppress the poor, nor yet woldes not suffer thine own servants to extort or wring any other of my people, thy subjects, nor hast not suffered the nobles of thy realm, nor any

---

[19] R. L. Mackie, *King James IV of Scotland* (1958) 50–51.

[20] L. Stone, *The Crisis of the Aristocracy, 1559–1641* (1965) ch. 5.

[21] J. Bossy, 'The Character of Elizabethan Catholicism,' *Past and Present*, (21) (1962) 39–59. J. Hurstfield, *The Elizabethan Nation* (1964) 30.

[22] As the household ordinances of November 1454 state, 'In so much as faith and truth and liegance compelleth every subject to do all that in him is for the honour, estate and welfare of his sovereign lord—it must natheless be thought and understand that lords and such as be called to be councillors with a prince must more tenderly take to heart those things wherein resteth his renown, honour, worship and politique rule of his land and ease of his people.' *Proceedings and Ordinances* VI 220.

[23] See the observations, made in 1504, upon a quarrel between the earl of Northumberland and the archbishop of York: '. . . considering that they both were men of great honour and authority many enormities might and were like thereupon to ensue. Wherefore the king's highness then and there commanded my Lord Chancellor to show unto them on his behalf that for as much as they both being men of honour and such persons as the King's grace had chiefly committed to governing and authority in the parts of the north his highness would not otherwise take it but as a great fault in them both and that it should rather have been to both their honours to have given good example to other men than to have been of such demeanour . . .' *Select Cases in the Council of Henry VII* ed. C. B. Bayne and W. H. Dunham Jr, Selden Society (1958) 41–2.

other of thy subjects [so] to run at a riot as to punish or revenge their own quarrels.'[24] If the king himself were spotless, setting his nobles an example which they faithfully followed, what a realm there would be![25]

Self-help had been endemic in medieval life; even the administration of the law itself had always been a violent matter although the growing sophistication of society had tended somewhat to reduce its worst excesses. Royal harryings of the countryside—which in late Anglo-Saxon days kings had from time to time deliberately commanded in the name of discipline—were past long since, and the seizure of estates by force, though by no means unknown, was far less common than it had been in Anglo-Norman days. Moreover, reform of the law of distress under Edward I had made more peaceable the relationship between landlord and tenant.[26] Nevertheless, the still deplorably weak sanctions of the criminal law and the confused obsolescence of the law of real property worked against improvement,[27] and unfortunately the nobility upon whom so much depended were probably no less violent and corrupt than any other group of people. From time to time the king or the royal council found it necessary to remind them of the need for higher standards of conduct. In 1425 and 1430 the nobility agreed not to take to violence to settle their own quarrels[28] and in 1426, 1461 and 1485 they were either forbidden to receive or maintain criminals or had sworn oaths against so doing.[29] However, self-help and the oppression of lesser men tended to go on as before.

Late medieval and early modern kings could not suppress the nobility. To govern at all they were forced to sustain it and yet, at the same time, to control it. Such a policy meant, among other things, the maintenance of aristocratic numbers. The great mortality of individual noblemen during the Wars of the Roses did not abnormally reduce the number of aristocratic houses. Aristocratic mortality had always been extremely high, so high that during the fourteenth and fifteenth centuries about one quarter of the peerage families died out in the male line about every twenty-five years.[30] Only the custom of allowing men who married the heiresses of peers to assume their titles[31] and the practice of deliberate new creations kept up their numbers. Though the earliest example dates from

---

[24] Dudley, *Tree of Commonwealth, op. cit.* 103.

[25] *ibid.* 39.

[26] T. F. T. Plucknett, *The Legislation of Edward I* (1949) ch. 3.

[27] See above ch. 2 pp. 66–7.

[28] *Proceedings and Ordinances* III 174–7; IV 36. *Rot. Parl.* V 407.

[29] *Proceedings and Ordinances* III 217–18. *Rot. Parl.* V 408, 487–8, VI 287–8.

[30] K. B. McFarlane, 'The Wars of the Roses, *Proceedings of the British Academy* L (1964) 115–16. The tendency continued. Between 1485 and 1547, 28 out of 55 families (56 peers) were extinguished in the male line, only 27 remaining. H. Miller, 'The Early Tudor Peerage, 1485–1547,' *Bulletin of the Institute of Historical Research* XXIV (1951) 88–91.

[31] Between 1439 and 1504, 21 peerages were continued in this way.

1397, the creation of parliamentary baronies by royal letters patent first became established in the mid fifteenth century when Henry VI and his advisers began, quite consciously, to create new peers to support the throne and its occupants during times of political stress.[32] The practice continued well into the sixteenth century. Just after Henry VIII's death a patent issued in favour of John, Viscount Lisle, stated quite clearly that Henry had intended to ennoble and endow certain of his councillors and servants in order to strengthen his nobility.[33]

At the same time many historians have noted that the early Tudor nobles were more cautious and more docile than their ancestors had been, though the contrast with those of the mid fifteenth century has probably been too strongly drawn. K. B. McFarlane suggested that the nobility had long memories of the consequences of violence and treason and, possibly, had become more tractable following the quarrels and disastrous confiscations of estates during the reigns of Richard II and Henry IV.[34] I have myself suggested elsewhere the possibility of a failure of nerve and a disinclination to take responsibility during both the minority and the personal rule of Henry VI.[35] Certainly the reluctance of the peers to follow Richard, duke of York into treason in the 1450s, and their even greater disinclination to support the earl of Warwick in the late 1460s, disposes of any idea that the aristocracy were unusually turbulent and treacherous during the Wars of the Roses.[36] This already existing caution was undoubtedly strengthened in

[32] Lander, *op. cit.* 174. In the difficult years between 1447 and 1450 there were no less than 15 new creations, in 1460 and 1461 9 followed by another 11 between 1464 and 1470. Henry VII added only 5; significantly enough, all but 2 during the first three years of his reign. See J. E. Powell and K. Wallis, *The House of Lords in the Middle Ages* (1968) chs 25–9. In the period of calm between 1509 and 1527 his son created only 7. In the years of strain between 1529 and 1547 the number of new creations rose to 18. This tendency was at least as important as the ferocious attainders which, temporarily in most cases, permanently in a few, deprived peerage families of their wealth and position. Excluding members of the royal families, 34 peers were attainted between 1459 and 1504. 9 were attainted and executed. All but 5 (84 per cent) were ultimately restored between 1536 and 1540. See above ch. 5 pp. 127–58 and appendix C. Miller, 'Early Tudor Peerage' *op. cit.* 89.

[34] McFarlane, 'Wars of the Roses,' *op. cit.* 119. One of the most constant themes of the later middle ages (as probably earlier too) was fear for property. After the extensive treason trials, executions, and confiscations of estates under Edward II, Edward III had restored a feeling of security to the landed classes by gradually returning forfeited property and by conceding in 1352 a statute which narrowly restricted the definition of treason. Richard II's confiscations, particularly his withholding of the great Lancastrian inheritance from Henry of Derby in 1399, had revived these terrors. For his reign in general, see C. D. Ross, 'Forfeiture for Treason in the Reign of Richard II,' *English Historical Review* LXXI (1956) 560–75. During the 1450s Richard of York constantly harped on these fears in his propaganda against the court. e.g. See his letter to the citizens of Shrewsbury in 1452. *Original Letters Illustrative of English History* ed. H. Ellis (1824) I 11–13. It may well be that the threat to property in the attainders of 1459 brought over to York a number of peers who had hitherto declined to support him. *An English Chronicle, op. cit.* 79–80.

[35] Lander *op. cit.* ch. 3.

[36] See above ch. 4 pp. 97–102, 122–3.

two ways during the second half of the fifteenth century: from 1459 onwards by parliamentary attainders for treason, and by the wide extension under Henry VII of a system of bonds and recognizances.

It is now proposed to investigate the effect of this combination of attainder and financial sanction on the attitude of the nobility, dealing first of all with the most extreme form of control, attainders. Parliamentary attainders, though originally intended as confiscatory measures against political opponents, came in the end, especially under Henry VII, to operate as a sanction for good behaviour. During Henry VII's reign, nine peers were attainted. Of these attainders three were permanent,[37] and six were ultimately reversed, five by Henry himself, one after his death.[38] Only one of these five reversals, that of Walter Devereux, Lord Ferrers, in favour of his son John in 1489, shows no special features. Pardon and restitution of property were apparently complete in their case. All other attainted families suffered from considerable reservations imposed on reversal.

In July 1486 John, Lord Zouche, produced securities in 2,000 marks to be of good behaviour and a few days later the king granted him a pardon under the great seal for his offences. Ostensibly the pardon also restored his lands but, unless Henry changed his mind after the pardon had been issued, this must be interpreted as permission merely to acquire his property again by some means or other, for when parliament formally reversed the attainder in 1489 the reversal did not extend to the estates confiscated under the original attainder act of 1485. In 1489 Zouche was permitted to inherit only the lands of his grandmother, Elizabeth, the wife of Lord Scrope of Bolton. A further act of 1495 allowed the return of his own paternal lands, at a very considerable price. In November, Zouche sold two manors to Sir Reynold Bray for £1,000 (a figure undoubtedly far below their real value), 'since Sir Reynold helped to obtain grace for Sir John from his liege lord to repeal the attainder and recover his land.' The acts also protected the interests of Giles, Lord Daubeney, and his heirs in certain properties which had been granted to them.[39] Other Zouche estates which the king had granted to three prominent courtiers, Sir John Savage, Sir Richard Edgecombe, and Sir Robert Willoughby, were still in the hands of their descendants in 1523.

John, Lord Fitzwater, was attainted in 1495 and later executed after attempting to escape from imprisonment in Calais. Restitution cost his son Robert very dear. In July 1505 he bound himself to pay the king £5,000,

---

[37] John de la Pole, earl of Lincoln, Edmund de la Pole, earl of Suffolk, and Francis, viscount Lovell.

[38] Lord Audley, attainted 1497. The reversal of 1514 in favour of his son John was, like Henry VII's reversals (see below), incomplete. It exempted grants made from the estates to Lord Dudley and others.

[39] The act states that Zouche might take over any of these reserved properties only if he could persuade the grantees to sell them.

obviously the price for the reversal of the attainder under letters patent the following November. Robert Fitzwater paid the king at least £2,000 under the agreement. These were immense sums for a family which probably ranked amongst the poorer barons.[40] Even so, he did not obtain complete restitution of his father's property, for grants were made from it in 1506, and in 1509 he took at an annual rent of £100 the manors of Hampnell and Disse in Norfolk, which had been part of the paternal estate.

John de la Pole, earl of Lincoln, slain fighting for Lambert Simnel at the battle of Stoke, was attainted during the lifetime of his father, John de la Pole, duke of Suffolk. After the father's death, the younger brother Edmund, in return for a payment of £5,000 and the surrender of the dukedom, was allotted certain lands and manors as though his brother had never been attainted and given the title of earl of Suffolk only. Edmund himself was later attainted in 1504 and this second attainder was never reversed.

The story of the Howards is perhaps the most intriguing of all. John Howard, duke of Norfolk, and his son Thomas, earl of Surrey, were both attainted for their support of Richard III at the battle of Bosworth. The father had been slain on the battlefield and rumours spread that the king intended to execute the son. Instead Surrey remained a prisoner in the Tower of London until January 1489 when he was released after taking an oath of allegiance. From then onwards he served Henry VII and his son faithfully for nineteen long years as soldier, ambassador, councillor, and administrator, gradually and only gradually, receiving back sections of his property. First in 1489 he was restored to the title of earl of Surrey, and was granted the lands of his wife's inheritance, lands which he might inherit from ancestors other than his father, and lands which the king had granted to the earl of Oxford and Lord Daubeney. From 1492 onwards more of his estates were restored and, after his victory over the Scots at Flodden Field in 1513, Henry VIII gave him back the dukedom of Norfolk. Even so, however, he never recovered all the Howard estates.[41]

So one noble family was eliminated by attainder, another after considerable reduction in property and rank was also finally eliminated in the male line. One, and only one, apparently achieved complete restitution. Three suffered more or less severe losses.[42] The example of such severity

[40] The family income is unknown but in 1433 the marriage of the Fitzwater heiress and the keeping of her lands had been sold 'for the comparatively small sum of £533.' T. B. Pugh and C. D. Ross, 'The English Baronage and the Income Tax of 1436,' *Bulletin of the Institute of Historical Research* XXVI (1953) 19.

[41] In effect Surrey recovered the hereditary estates of the Howards and that part of the Mowbray estates of the duchy of Norfolk to which his family was entitled as co-heirs, which the king had not already granted away. The king, by certain legal concessions, made it easier for him to negotiate with the grantees to buy them back. Surrey, however, never recovered the immense grants from the crown lands which had enriched his family under Richard III.

[42] As also a fourth, the Audley family, restored under Henry VIII. See above n. 38.

would certainly not be lost on the rest of the aristocracy.[43]

The second method of discipline and control (if so it may be called) lay in bonds and recognizances, a terrifying system of suspended penalties.[44] K. B. McFarlane remarked on a change which came over the nature of the entries in the close rolls of the chancery especially in Henry VII's later years. He pointed out that after 1500 over one third of the entries in the close rolls consist of recognizances in favour of the king and that over fifty of them bear the condition that those entering such recognizances should keep their allegiance to Henry VII and his heirs. Plausibly assuming that many more recognizances which merely acknowledge a debt to the king were imposed with the same intention in mind, McFarlane suggested that the king was so suspicious of those who surrounded him that 'the point had almost been reached where it could be said that Henry VII governed by recognizance.' In this he was neither 'medieval' nor 'modern' but *sui generis*. The possibility that the difference in the entries, and therefore any theory built upon it, may be due to an order of December 1499 tightening up the procedure for enrolment cannot be entirely ruled out,[45] but this is unlikely for, as far as the nobility was concerned, the number of recognizances taken did not increase until 1502.

Before discussing the application of this system it may be well to say something of its origins. Apart from somewhat similar methods used from time to time in earlier centuries but by then probably forgotten,[46] bonds and recognizances were part of normal methods of estate management during the fifteenth century. Dishonesty and corruption were endemic in all administration, both royal and private. Methods of criminal procedure against defaulting officials being inefficient in the extreme, it was standard practice on many estates to demand the production of bonds carrying a heavy financial penalty, and of mainpernors or guarantors, as a condition

---

[43] For a more detailed account and evidence for these attainders, see above ch. 4 pp. 142 ff.

[44] The legal, technical differences between obligations, bonds, recognizances and mainprises are irrelevant to this study. The crucial point is that they all involved promises or guarantees under financial penalties.

[45] *English Historical Review* LXXXI (1966) 153–5. McFarlane allowed the possibility that the difference in the entries from 1500 onwards may be somewhat misleading owing to a tightening up of procedural methods, but on the whole discounted this factor. The order of December 1499 alleged that, owing to the negligence of the royal officers, recognizances 'in cases of high treason or misprision of the king's majesty by his subjects or strangers' had failed to be enrolled and laid down heavy penalties for failure to enrol within eight days. *Cal. Pat. Rolls. 1485–1500*, no. 1199. McFarlane argued that the royal officers 'as a precaution . . . decided thereafter to enrol all recognizances to which this order might conceivably apply.' Many, in fact, seem to fall somewhat outside the regulation. McFarlane's argument is strengthened by the fact that chroniclers noted a more rigid attitude on Henry's part shortly after this time. See below pp. 292–3.

[46] See below pp. 295–6.

of appointment for officials.[47] Mainprises were also usually taken from customs officials. Similarly, bonds and recognizances were extremely common among private people in such matters as binding them to keep the peace towards each other, guaranteeing the execution of family settlements, and in commercial transactions, arbitrations over land disputes, and many other matters. Bonds and recognizances were in fact very much a part of the normal texture of the late medieval life.

At government level they were common enough all through the fifteenth century, covering most of the matters for which Henry VII exacted them and even some for which he did not.[48] In the 1470s their use in some areas may have become more systematic, particularly in the Marches of Wales. At the great sessions held at Newport in 1476 recognizances were taken from 72 people, mostly for 100 marks, but from some for up to 500 marks, although most men from whom they were exacted had not been charged with any crime. T. B. Pugh has suggested that the recognizances were taken because the crown demanded them, and that the system may well have been a quite recent development, perhaps the result of discussions between the marcher lords and the prince of Wales's council at Ludlow shortly before.[49] Whether this surmise be true or not, Henry VII early adopted this system for the Marches and it continued in force until the reforms of Thomas Cromwell in the 1530s.[50]

The nobility were accustomed to give and take bonds and recognizances on ordinary matters of business both among themselves and with lesser men. The Lancastrian kings had also demanded financial guarantees from them for various purposes. However, the first Lancastrian, Henry IV, can hardly be said to have used such methods as a form of discipline against the nobility itself. During his reign thirteen nobles (including one widow) gave mainprises in chancery. All but one were guarantees for keeping the peace

---

[47] e.g. In the marcher Lordships of the Stafford dukes of Buckingham the steward and other officers had to give recognizances as guarantees of good conduct and they were liable to forfeit large sums of money if they defaulted. When Thomas Vaughan of Hergest (d. 1469) was appointed receiver of the lordship of Brecon in 1451 he had to find at least six mainpernors with freehold estates in England, each of whom was bound in the sum of 2,000 marks, and at least six other mainpernors bound jointly and severally in a further 2,000 marks in the ducal exchequer at Brecon. Pugh, *The Marcher Lordships, op. cit.* 246 and n. 2. For the duchy of Lancaster and the Burgavenny estates see R. R. Davies, 'Baronial Accounts, Incomes and Arrears in the Later Middle Ages,' *Economic History Review* end series XXI (1968) 221 and n. 7, 227 n. 6. For examples on the crown lands see *Calendar of Fine Rolls, 1471–1485* nos 48–57, 61–71 and many others.

[48] e.g. Not to sue in foreign courts, to serve the king faithfully in the French wars. *Cal. Close Rolls, 1419–22,* 38–9, 44, 66.

[49] Pugh, *op. cit.* 29–30.

[50] See *ibid.* and T. B. Pugh, 'The Indenture for the Marches between Henry VII and Edward Stafford (1477–1521), Duke of Buckingham,' *English Historical Review* LXXI (1956) 436–41.

given on behalf of lesser men. One involved the custody of a royal ward.[51] The most important, and probably the only one of any political significance (though even this is doubtful) was a recognizance for 10,000 marks in 1409 from the earl of Arundel to keep the peace towards his uncle, the archbishop of Canterbury.[52]

At the beginning of Henry V's reign such matters took on a more political turn. In November 1413 the earl of Arundel, the earl of March, the earl marshal, Lord Roos, and Lord Morley each gave a recognizance for 10,000 marks and Lords Talbot, Willoughby, Clinton, Haryngton, and Ferrers of Chartley, each gave one of £4,000 'to be of good behaviour towards the king and people.'[53] Later in the reign Lady Burgavenny gave a mainprise of £2,000 for her appearance before the council, and another of £1,200 not to harm Nicholas Burdet or any other people, and four commoners also gave mainprises for her good behaviour in this matter.[54] Five peers gave mainprises for the good behaviour of other men, including one peer, Lord Poynings, who was already bound in 1,000 marks himself.[55] Thus under Henry V 15 peers and a peeress were under some form of financial obligation to the crown, 10 for their own actions, 5 for those of other men. During Henry VI's minority 16 peers found themselves in similar situations though no recognizance at this time seems to have borne any particular political significance.[56]

The same kind of practice continued during the period of Henry VI's personal rule. Between 1437 and the beginning of 1458, 22 peers were at

[51] *Cal. Close Rolls 1399–1402*, 93, 413; *1402–5*, 506–17; *1405–9*, 134 (2), 370, 525 (Arundel).

[52] A similar recognizance was also taken from the archbishop. Uncle and nephew had apparently been on bad terms since 1405 and the earl had become a political ally of his uncle's rivals, the Beauforts. *DNB* VII 101–2.

[53] *Cal. Close Rolls, 1413–19*, 97–99.

[54] *ibid.* 500.

[55] *ibid.* 451, 515; *1418–22*, 63. Figures given in the text do not exactly tally as one peer, Lord Clinton, was involved in two of these transactions. Non-nobles also gave mainprises for the good behaviour of Lady Lestraunge and the countess of Arundel. *1413–19*, 458, 459, and two citizens of London gave recognizances that the duke of Exeter should content the king for the value of the goods taken from a Genoese carrack wrecked off the Devonshire coast. *1419–22*, 38.

[56] The duke of Gloucester, the duchess of Clarence, the earls of Huntingdon, Northumberland, Ormond, Oxford, Salisbury, Stafford, Westmorland. Joan Beaufort, Countess of Westmorland, Lords Daker, Fauconberg, Fitzhugh, Greystoke, Grey of Ruthyn, and Talbot. *Cal. Close Rolls, 1422–9*, 53, 58–59, 66, 69, 132, 259, 277, 325, 342, 343, 448; *1429–35*, 67, 125, 190–1, 322, 346–7, 348, 351, 359; *1435–41*, 102, 157–8. The most interesting are those taken in the course of the notorious quarrel about the Westmorland inheritance which continued for well over a decade. See E. F. Jacob, *The Fifteenth Century, 1399–1485* (1961) 321–3. Several of these guarantee repayment of a loan which Humphrey of Gloucester had taken from the royal treasury and that of 1432 in which Richard of York had to find friends sufficient to put up ten recognizances of 100 marks each as security for payment by the duke, within five years, by two instalments each year of 1,000 marks demanded for livery of his lands.

various times under bonds and recognizances.[57] Particularly notable is a series of bonds and recognizances imposed upon John Mowbray, duke of Norfolk, the nephew of Richard, duke of York, and once of his political associates. Even by the standards of his own day John Mowbray was an exceptional ruffian and he was twice, in 1440 and in 1448, imprisoned for violent conduct.[58] In July 1440 Norfolk gave a recognizance for 10,000 marks that he would remain in the royal household until he found security to keep the peace towards people in general and towards John Haydon in particular. This was cancelled as Norfolk fulfilled the condition. In December the duke was in trouble again, giving another recognizance for £500 that he and certain other people would pay a fine, to be settled apparently by negotiation, for the improper disposal of certain lands without a royal licence. This too was cancelled. Then in 1443 the earl of Stafford, Lord Fauconberg, Lord Latimer, and Lord Willoughby gave a mainprise of £500 in chancery for Norfolk. Norfolk himself under 'a pain of £2,000' undertook to appear in person before the king and council in the quinzaine of Easter to answer certain charges against him, and in the meantime not to molest Sir Robert Wingfield, his household, servants, and tenants. The council put his dispute with Wingfield to arbitration. It appeared that Norfolk had attacked and ransacked Wingfield's house at Letheringham, for which the arbitrators ordered him to pay 3,500 marks compensation, and also made certain other dispositions.[59] Even this was not the end of Norfolk's violent course. In December 1453 he gave another enormous recognizance, this time for £12,000 to appear in chancery on the Monday of the first week in Lent and in the meantime to refrain from harming Alice, duchess of Suffolk.[60]

During the same period the duke of Exeter, the earl of Northumberland, and Lord Grey of Codnor were all, at some time, placed under recognizances to keep the peace.[61] So were the earl of Devon and Lord Bonvile during their notorious quarrels in the southwest.[62] It seems that the king and council were at this time using such instruments to quell the growing recalcitrance of nobles and the personal feuds between magnates, which as R. L. Storey has shown[63] preceded the Wars of the Roses.

[57] The dukes of Buckingham, Exeter, and Norfolk, the earls of Devon, Northumberland, Oxford, Salisbury, Westmorland, and Wiltshire, Lords Berners, Bonvile, Camoys, Clinton, Fauconberg, Grey of Codnor, Grey of Ruthyn, Grey of Wilton, Latimer, Roos, Rougemont, Welles, Willoughby. Cal. Close Rolls, 1435–41, 178–9, 239, 276, 279, 381, 384, 388, 446, 471; 1441–7, 144, 149, 196, 460; 1447–54, 398, 476, 512; 1454–61, 44, 109, 171, 173, 227.

[58] In the cases of John Heydon and Robert Wingfield mentioned below. R. L. Storey, The End of the House of Lancaster (1966) 79, 226–7.

[59] ibid. 226–7.

[60] See note 57 above.

[61] Storey, House of Lancaster, op. cit.

[62] ibid., and see above ch. 3 pp. 84 ff.

[63] Storey, op. cit. chs 5–9.

In 1458 and 1459 recognizances took on a more directly political note. A great council, held from 29 January to the fourth week of March 1458, tried to patch up the differences between the king and the families who supported him on the one side, and Richard, duke of York and his supporters, the Nevilles, on the other. Various arrangements were agreed to settle the personal and political feuds of all the great families concerned and after the agreements were sealed on 24 March the participants ostentatiously displayed their reconciliation in a grand procession to St Paul's.[64] More practically, the previous day the king had taken recognizances making a grand total of £68,666 13s. 4d. that they would abide by the awards from the duke of York, the earls of Salisbury and Warwick, the dowager duchess and the duke of Somerset, the earl and countess of Northumberland and Lord Clifford.[65] Six other peers also gave recognizances during these years.[66]

Under the Yorkists the use of recognizances continued as before, though for almost all purposes except routine administrative matters they were few in number. Under Edward IV only two groups, involving six peers and a peeress, were of any high political significance. In 1470, on the same day as Henry Percy earl of Northumberland, still under attainder, was released from imprisonment in the Tower of London, he guaranteed his allegiance and his appearance before the king in chancery at a certain date by a bond in £5,000, supported by a joint bond in £3,000 from the bishop of Ely, the earls of Arundel and Kent, and Lord Ferrers.[67] In March 1473 the countess of Oxford, whose husband had been, and still was, actively engaged in treason,[68] gave a bond in £3,000, supported by bonds of £2,000 each by the earl of Essex and Lord Howard, and others by commoners, that she would appear daily before the king in council at Easter next, and within three days after due warning given her, answer certain matters pending against her until she was dismissed.[69] Other bonds concerning seven noblemen dealt with legal arbitrations and the keeping of the peace and one guaranteed the sale of certain estates to the king.[70]

[64] Sir J. H. Ramsay, *Lancaster and York* (1892) II 208–9.

[65] *Cal. Close Rolls, 1454–61*, 292–3. Three more recognizances totalling £9,333 6s. 8d. were taken from minor members of the Percy family. *ibid.* 293.

[66] In May 1458, William Neville, Lord Fauconberg, and the duke of Buckingham, the earl of Warwick and Viscount Bourchier on Fauconberg's behalf. In April 1459 the duke of Exeter and Lord Roos on Exeter's behalf. *Cal. Close Rolls, 1454–61*, 287–8, 350. These do not seem to have had the same political significance.

[67] *Cal. Close Rolls, 1468–76*, nos 403, 404.

[68] *DNB* XX 240–1.

[69] *Cal. Close Rolls, 1468–76*, no. 1103.

[70] In 1468 the earl of Shrewsbury, and Lords Dudley and Mountjoy gave a joint recognizance for £1,000 binding the earl not to molest certain jurors and to keep the peace towards Henry, Lord Grey. Lord Grey, Lord Hastings, and a squire, Thomas Wyngfield, gave a similar guarantee regarding the earl. In 1472 Lord Stanley gave a bond in 3,000 marks to abide by the award of arbitrators chosen by the king in his quarrel with Sir James Harrington; in 1476 Edward, Lord Burgavenny, gave a bond in 4,000 marks to appear in

Considering the brevity of his reign, bonds and recognizances were more frequent under Richard III than under Edward. Only seven, however, affected noblemen.[71] Surprisingly enough, in view of the political tensions of Richard's reign, none of these directly dealt with the question of allegiance, although bonds for this purpose were certainly taken from commoners.[72]

So, in the course of 24 years some 20 nobles, including one woman, the countess of Oxford, were placed under bonds or recognizances of some kind, 10 for themselves, 10 on behalf of other people. In addition, Edward IV attainted 17 peers and Richard III another 4,[73] thus making a total of 30 under some form of direct discipline themselves and 10 more on behalf of others. By 1485 the nobility were thoroughly accustomed to sanctions on their behaviour which involved financial penalties and the forfeiture of estates.

From the point of view of the nobility, matters changed considerably for the worse under Henry VII. During the Yorkist period about two thirds of the titled families of England were, at some time or other, under the discipline of either attainders or recognizances. Between 1485 and 1509 the proportion rose to slightly more than four fifths. Although in comparison to the Yorkists Henry inflicted few attainders, his conditions for reversal became more severe,[74] and as we shall see his employment of bonds and recognizances became much more intensive and stringent than even the numbers so far quoted might indicate. As before, evidence of these instruments comes mainly from the close rolls of chancery, though a seventeenth-century copy of Edmund Dudley's notebook in the British

---

chancery on the morrow of All Hallows and not to molest William Culpepyr of Aylesford, and in 1478 his son, George, Lord Burgavenny, gave a bond of £4,000 guaranteeing the sale of estates to the king. *Cal. Close Rolls, 1468–76* nos 93, 94, 403, 900, 1103, *1476–85*, nos 44, 407.

[71] Three concerned land transactions. John, duke of Suffolk, together with four commoners, gave a bond in 2,000 marks, for John Wynfield, concerning the transfer to the king of some of the property of the late duke of Norfolk; John, Lord Audley, a bond for £5,000, also concerning the transfer of property to the king; William Berkeley, earl of Nottingham, a bond in £10,000 concerning the very complicated transfer to the king of the inheritance of the Mowbray dukes of Norfolk, of whom he was one of the co-heirs. Four others were imposed for good behaviour: 1,000 marks on Viscount Lisle to remain within a mile of London and generally keep the peace; a bond in £1,000 from Lord Ferrers to keep the peace towards the abbey of Waltham, and a bond given by Lord Stourton for the good behaviour of Sir William Berkeley which is known only from a reference to the payment of part of it. *Cal. Close Rolls, 1476–85*, nos 1184, 1218, 1225, 1317, 1412, 1423.

[72] *Cal. Close Rolls, 1476–85* nos. 1194, 1242, 1243, 1244, 1245, 1258, 1259, 1417, 1456.

[73] See below, appendix C, p. 307.

[74] See above, pp. 274–6. The eighteen reversals of Yorkist attainders (four under Edward IV, the rest in 1485), appear to have been unconditional, except for that of Dorset in 1485.

Museum adds to the numbers.[75] The same notebook, together with Sir John Heron's payments book as treasurer of the chamber for the years 1505–9, containing a list of the bonds and recognizances which passed through Heron's hands,[76] also provides a good deal more detail about their operation. An investigation of other sources would undoubtedly reveal more details of particular cases, but it is most likely that it would not materially alter the observations now offered.

Things did not change rapidly. Judging from the close rolls, between Henry's accession and the end of 1499 11 peers gave bonds and recognizances varying in amount from £100 to £10,000.[77] Even then, in spite of the order, earlier mentioned,[78] of December 1499 for the enrolment of bonds and recognizances, numbers did not rise immediately. There was, in fact, only one more before the beginning of 1502.[79] From then onwards, however, the close rolls show an immense increase, no less than 27 peers giving bonds and recognizances between that date and the end of the reign.[80] To these can be added another 9 for which evidence is provided from Dudley's notebook and Heron's payments book.[81]

[75] BM MS. Lansdowne 127 (hereinafter BM L 127), covering the period of 9 September 1504, to 28 May 1508. A special list of obligations taken by Dudley for 21 Henry VII is also contained in BM MS. Harleian 1877 f. 47.

[76] PRO Exchequer treasury of receipt, miscellaneous books E. 36/214. In the back part of this book Heron kept careful lists of all the obligations and recognizances in his hands from 1505 to 1509. These lists were from time to time annotated by the king. They also give a fuller description of the bonds, etc., than is to be found in the receipt books. See F. C. Dietz, *English Government Finance, 1485–1558*, University of Illinois Studies in the Social Sciences IX (1920) 33.

[77] *Cal. Close Rolls, 1485–1500*, nos 52, 82, 616, 618, 753, 894, 942, 973, 974, 1008, 1056, 1060. The earls of Westmorland and Devon, Viscount Beaumont, Lord Grey of Wilton, and Charles Somerset, Lord Herbert, each gave a recognizance on his own behalf; in a similar way Lord Burgh gave two. The marquess of Dorset, the earls of Devon and Kent, Viscount Lisle, Lords Burgh, Grey of Codnor, Grey of Wilton, and Willoughby de Broke gave them on behalf of others. They covered such varied matters as feudal custody and marriage, rents, the safekeeping of royal castles, good behaviour in office and appearance before the king at specified dates.

[78] See note 45 above.

[79] *Cal. Close Rolls, 1485–1500*, no. 1222, 20 July 1500, concerning Edward Lord Dudley. No condition was specified.

[80] *Cal. Close Rolls, 1500–9*, nos 131, 226, 228, 290, 304, 331, 332, 347, 361, 377, 408, 415, 423, 428, 459, 499, 518, 543, 549, 550, 559, 602, 605, 609, 622, 635, 658, 669, 675, 686, 705, 756, 773, 798, 814, 818, 821, 822, 825, 851, 904, 955, 963. The peers concerned (some being involved in several bonds and recognizances) were: the duke of Buckingham, the marquess of Dorset, the earls of Arundel, Derby, Essex, Kent, Shrewsbury, and Surrey, Viscount Lisle, Lords Burgavenny, Clifford, Conyers, Darcy, Dacre of Gilsland, Daubeney, Edward Sutton, Lord Dudley, Grey of Powys, Hastings, Mountjoy, Seyntmount, Stourton, Scrope of Upsall, de la Warre, Willoughby de Broke, Willoughby of Eresby, and Lady Hungerford.

[81] BM L 127, r.4, 16d, 20r, 48d. PRO E. 36/214, 256, 381, 445, 472, 491, 492, 499. Lords Berners, Dacre of the South, FitzWarren, Grey of Ruthyn, Ogle, Scrope of Bolton, Herbert (Charles Somerset), and Lady Arundel.

It would be tedious to go into the details of these bonds and recognizances in great numbers. A random selection must suffice to show their purpose and conditions. In December 1485 Viscount Beaumont gave a bond payable at Christmas for his good behaviour.[82] In the same month the earl of Westmorland gave the king the custody and marriage of Ralph, his son and heir, guaranteeing the grant with bonds totalling 1,000 marks.[83] In 1504 the earl of Northumberland and the archbishop of York each gave a bond of £2,000 to keep the peace towards each other.[84] In 1505 Lord Clifford gave a recognizance for £2,000 that he would keep the peace both for himself, his servants, tenants, and 'part-takers' towards Roger Tempest of Broughton, and that he would endeavour within forty days to bring before the king and his council 'such as were present at the late pulling down of Roger's place and house at Broughton.'[85] In August 1506 the duke of Buckingham entered into an obligation to pay the king 300 marks 'for the king's gracious favour in the recovering of the 800 marks assessed upon the tenants of Brecknock.'[86] In 1508 Lord Willoughby de Broke gave a recognizance for 1,000 marks, the condition being payment of £2,000 within two months of warning given by the king's letters missive or privy seal.[87]

These examples so far quoted are what may be called 'simple' recognizances, that is they affected nobody but the single person concerned. Other types, what one might call 'composite' recognizances, involved several or even a great many people. In such cases one man's misbehaviour or failure to fulfil specified conditions could bring other people into financial peril. In 1500 Lord Grey of Powys, Richard ap Thomas and Richard Pole gave a recognizance for £100, Master John Tolley another for 100 marks, and Sir William Sandys and Sir Hugh Vaughan jointly a third also for 100 marks, that Pole would be true in his allegiance as constable of Harlech castle. Pole would also pay any debts due to the king by prisoners permitted to escape, and various heavy fines, whose amounts are specified, for any escapes of prisoners incarcerated for murder, rape, or felony.[88] In 1504 Thomas Wyndham of Felbrigge, Norfolk, gave a recognizance for £2,000 supported by another for the same amount given jointly by the earl of Essex and the earl of Kent, guaranteeing that Wyndham would find sufficient security before Pentecost next for keeping his allegiance, appearing when required before the king and council, paying 2,000 marks

[82] *Cal. Close Rolls, 1485–1500*, no. 52.

[83] *ibid.* no. 82.

[84] Bayne and Dunham, *Select Cases, op. cit.* 41–2, 44.

[85] *Cal. Close Rolls, 1500–9*, no. 499.

[86] BM L 127 m. 29d. PRO E. 36/214, 502.

[87] *Cal. Close Rolls, 1500–9*, no. 955 (xii).

[88] *ibid.* no. 377 (xii).

by instalments, or else surrender to imprisonment in the Tower of London.[89]

One of the most complicated of all these transactions concerns William Blount, Lord Mountjoy, the student and later the patron of Erasmus, and the companion of the child Prince Henry. He had served in the army against Perkin Warbeck in 1497, and in May 1503 was appointed keeper of Hammes castle, one of the subsidiary fortresses of Calais. His indentures, besides laying down his duties and various other arrangements, stipulated that he should give a recognizance of 10,000 marks himself and find guarantors in a similar sum that he would keep the castle safely and surely to the king's use, deliver it up when required in writing under the great or privy seal, appear personally before the king and council upon reasonable warning under any of the king's seals and keep his allegiance.[90] Mountjoy duly gave his recognizance for 10,000 marks but his guarantors put up recognizances totalling only 8,180 marks. There were, however, no less than 28 men involved, including five other peers, the earl of Shrewsbury, Viscount Lisle, and Lords Burgavenny, Hastings, and Strange; Mountjoy himself had to put up yet another recognizance for £1,000 to find substitutes in the event of death and for allowing the castle treasurer £200 from the local revenues towards the cost of repairs.[91] Mountjoy did in fact later find four replacements, including the earl of Arundel, the earl of Kent, and the marquess of Dorset.[92] Nor were these the only recognizances in which Mountjoy was involved for there were at least another 21 in which he was at various times concerned.[93]

Although some of these bonds and recognizances were small and remained in force for limited periods only, others could have been ruinous, for they involved immense sums of money and even, in some

[89] ibid. no. 332. For other recognizances involving seventeen more people in Wyndham's affairs, see ibid. nos 361, 419, 579, 741.

[90] ibid. no. 226.

[91] ibid. no. 228.

[92] ibid. nos. 290, 428, 756. Henry VIII cancelled all these recognizances on 3 November 1509 but at the same time took another recognizance of £10,000 from Mountjoy whom he had re-appointed on 6 October. Letters and Papers Foreign and Domestic of the Reign of Henry VIII, preserved in the Public Record Office, the British Museum, and elsewhere I, catalogued by J. S. Brewer 2nd edn R. H. Brodie (1920); II-IV, catalogued by J. S. Brewer (1864–72), I no. 257 (5); see also no. 257 (4).

[93] Seven for £100 each jointly with Sir Thomas Griesley and Sir John Montgomery for payment of 100 marks at each of seven terms down to Pentecost, 1505. They were then cancelled when, presumably, the debts had been paid; eleven for 240 marks each together with Sir William Say, Robert Newport, and Thomas Periunt for various payments totalling 2,300 marks down to Christmas 1511, when they were then cancelled; in 1507 he gave a recognizance of £100 for Sir Richard Carew who had become keeper of Calais under terms rather similar (but considerably less onerous) to his own tenures at Hammes. Cal. Close Rolls, 1500–9, nos 228, 549, 773. PRO E. 36/214, 395. For two other smaller ones, see E. 36/214, 409, 463.

cases, put part or all of a nobleman's estates within the king's grasp. An examination of four of the greatest cases will show the nature and extent of the perils threatening the families concerned and the way in which the system operated. The cases chosen for study are those of the earl of Northumberland, the marquess of Dorset, Lord Burgavenny, and the earl of Kent.

Henry Percy V, the earl of Northumberland, first gave a recognizance for £2,000 in 1504 in the course of his quarrel with the archbishop of York.[94] Four years later in 1506, with others he gave a recognizance in £200 for the payment of a debt of £100 to the king by his probable relation, William Percy, and in 1507 another of £100 as a guarantor for the safe-keeping of Castle Cornet, Guernsey, by Richard Weston, and the same year replaced the earl of Kent in giving a bond of £200 for Sir Nicholas Vaux as keeper of Guisnes.[95] All this, however, was very small beer compared with difficulties in which the earl was already involved. In 1505 he was condemned to pay the enormous sum of £10,000 for 'ravishing' Elizabeth Hastings, a royal ward, that is interfering in some way with royal rights of wardship. The king suspended the fine 'during his pleasure,' when the earl agreed that he and four others would enter into a recognizance of 6,000 marks to pay 3,000 marks in annual instalments of 500 marks each Candlemas.[96]

In November 1507 this arrangement, which may not in fact have come into effect, was changed. On the tenth of the month the earl gave a recognizance of £5,000 payable at the king's pleasure.[97] Another recognizance made ten days later stiffened conditions by making the money payable the same day.[98] Even worse, according to an entry dated 13 November in Sir John Heron's payments book, the earl had levied a fine to put certain of his estates into the hands of feoffees to the king's use until £5,000 of his fine had been paid by half yearly instalments of 500 marks;[99] moreover, payment of the remaining £5,000 of the fine was still to hang at the king's pleasure.[100] It has not been possible to trace payments under these arrangements. Even if the feoffees paid the instalments as they became due, however, the earl could not have lost more than £1,000. In

[94] See above p. 283.
[95] *Cal. Close Rolls, 1500–9*, nos. 602, 675 (i), 767.
[96] W. C. Richardson, *Tudor Chamber Administration 1485–1547* (1952) 150. J. M. W. Bean, *The Estates of the Percy Family, 1416–1537* (1958) 143. PRO E. 36/214, 474, 1 October 1505. Another entry mentions ravishment of the king's ward 'and other retainers.' *ibid.* 479, 6 December 1505.
[97] PRO E. 36/214, 403.
[98] *Cal. Close Rolls, 1500–9*, no. 821 (i).
[99] PRO E. 36/214, 530. See also *ibid.* 403. Bean, *The Estates, op. cit.* 143.
[100] BM L 127 50d. The net value of the Percy estates *c.* 1523 was something under £3,900. Bean, *op. cit.* 140.

this he was fortunate in the king's death, for Henry VIII on his accession in 1509 cancelled all the outstanding recognizances. Thus, as Bean has remarked on these transactions, 'if the earl did suffer financially from the crown's policy, his losses in the event were much less than those threatened by the agreements he was forced to make. Nevertheless, the harshness of the terms, and the fact that some of his estates were temporarily in the crown's hands, emphasize the threatening and humiliating nature of the situation in which he was placed.'[101]

If the king's treatment of the earl of Northumberland is considered humiliating, there are hardly words left to describe his dealings with Thomas Grey, marquess of Dorset, 13 years earlier. Thomas Grey, the eldest son of Edward IV's queen, Elizabeth Wydeville by her first husband, Sir John Grey of Groby, had been created marquess of Dorset by his stepfather in 1475. Under Richard III he joined in Buckingham's rebellion, on its failure fled to Henry of Richmond in Brittany, and in his absence was attainted. In Brittany his conduct was somewhat two-faced and, apparently despairing of Richmond's success, he prepared to return to England and make his peace with Richard. Richmond, however, sent a messenger to him and persuaded him to abandon the idea. During Richmond's invasion, Dorset and John Bourchier were left behind in Paris as surety for a loan. Presumably as a result of his duplicity in Britany, to achieve the reversal of his attainder he had to renounce all grants which Edward IV had made to him other than those associated with his creation as marquess of Dorset, and in particular to repudiate any agreements concerning property which had belonged to Henry, duke of Exeter, as well as the wardship, marriage, and custody of Edward, earl of Warwick.[102] This hard bargaining may well have rankled deeply. Henry, perhaps suspecting Dorset's resentment, seems never to have trusted him again. In 1487 he fell under suspicion of complicity with Lambert Simnel, was imprisoned in the Tower of London, but was restored to favour after the battle of Stoke (16 June 1487).[103]

Dorset took part in the expedition against the French in 1492, but on 4 June, just before the fleet sailed, the king and the marquess entered into a very interesting indenture.[104] This ran that if the marquess would find sureties and demean himself loyally the king would admit him to favour and grant him letters of pardon. The cost of the royal forgiveness, whatever offence he may have committed, and the royal favour turns out to have been very high indeed. Dorset was forced to make a lawful estate in fee simple to twelve trustees named in the indenture of 'all castles, honours,

[101] ibid.

[102] Rot. Parl. VI 315–16. Dorset's first wife had been Anne Holland, daughter and heiress of the last Holland duke of Exeter. There had been complicated property settlements at the time of the marriage.

[103] DNB VIII 644–5.

[104] Cal. Close Rolls, 1485–1500, no. 612.

manors, lands, rents and services, whereof he or Cecily his wife is seised, or any other persons to his use or by recovery,' saving only two manors in Essex which were to be left in the hands of their farmers to the use of the marquess and marchioness and for the performance of the marquess's last will.[105] Then follow a number of extremely stringent conditions. If Dorset did not in future offend the king, 'nor do misprision to the king's person, but disclose such treason to his highness in writing, and the parts be proved and the plotters convicted,' the trustees should be seised to the king's use in the lands. If, however, the marquess was taken prisoner overseas, sufficient manors might be sold to pay for his ransom. The marquess was in addition to 'labour' to place all his and his wife's remaining lands in Lancashire 'or elsewhere' under the same conditions. All these arrangements were to be ratified in the next parliament and this was, in fact, done in the parliament of 1495.[106] The indenture, and the act of parliament, continue that if the marquess remained innocent of any of the specified offences during his lifetime, after his decease the arrangement should be void and his heir would be allowed to inherit according to the normal course of the law.

Even now Henry had not finished. Dorset had also to grant to the king the wardship and marriage of Thomas, his son and heir, 'to be found in the king's service at the cost of the marquess.' The marquess was also to pay the king £1,000 if the boy was redelivered to him unmarried under the age of 19. Dorset himself gave a recognizance for £1,000 for the performance of all this and also undertook to find 'sureties of divers persons bound in recognizances of £10,000,' and to be prepared if necessary to replace any of them with others at three weeks' notice.[107] Dorset had, in fact, already found 55 people, including the earl of Kent, Viscount Lisle, Lord Grey of Codnor, and Lord Grey of Wilton, to put up mainprises totalling £9,225.[108] In February 1495 another peer, Lord de la Warre, gave a bond of 500 marks for Dorset's loyalty during life.[109]

As with many other of Henry VII's arrangements, this was a disposition *in terrorem*, probably only partially carried through. Had the terms of the agreement of 1492, confirmed in 1495, been fully executed, the unfortunate marquess of Dorset would have been left without an acre to his name except for the manors of Stobbyng and Fairested in Essex. He was not however,

---

[105] The indenture details the property as two manors in Lincolnshire, two manors and a pasture in Leicestershire, and all lands in Kent, London, and Coventry.

[106] *Rot. Parl.* VI 472–3. This act makes it clear that the remaining lands had, in fact, by this time been placed in the hands of the trustees.

[107] *Cal. Close Rolls, 1485–1500*, no. 612 '. . . after due notice given by the king he will after three weeks cause other persons to be bound to the king by recognizances so that his highness or his heirs may discharge the executors.'

[108] *Cal. Close Rolls, 1485–1500*, no. 618. All these arrangements must have been under discussion for some time for the fifty-five 'mainprised for the loyalty of Dorset' on 19 and 22 May, a fortnight before the indenture was enrolled.

[109] *Cal. Close Rolls, 1485–1500*, no. 836.

completely denuded of income, and possibly not even of land. In 1495 he was still in possession of an annuity of £35 granted to him on his creation as marquess in 1475,[110] and in 1495 certain offices which he held were exempted from the act of resumption covering the principality and other estates held by the prince of Wales.[111] Moreover, in September 1492 he sold three manors in Kent to the archbishop of Canterbury for £120.[112] It is possible that he was granted an income from the estates which he made over to the trustees or that he was allowed to retain at least part of them.[113] Dorset seems in the end to have satisfied the king of his loyalty, for the arrangement was ended some time before August 1499, possibly as early as May 1496.[114]

Dorset continued loyal and took part against the Cornish rebels in 1497. He died in 1501. Yet, even after such harsh sanctions against him, his son may possibly have dabbled in treason, for under the year 1508 the *Chronicle of Calais* states, 'the Lord Marquess Dorset and the Lord William of Devonshire, which were both of kin to the late Queen Elizabeth[115] and her blood,' after being imprisoned in the Tower of London 'a great season' were brought to Calais and were there 'kept prisoners as long as King Henry VII lived and should have been put to death if he had lived longer.'[116]

---

[110] *Reports from the Lord's Committees touching the Dignity of a Peer of the Realm* (1829) V 402–3. In 1495 the act assigning revenues for the expenses of the royal household was not to be prejudicial to Dorset 'touching any annuity granted to the said marquess, in, of, or upon the creation of him into Marquess Dorset.' *Rot. Parl.* VI 502.

[111] Exempted 'for any office to him by my Lord Prince given by his Letters Patents.' *Rot. Parl.* VI 466.

[112] *Cal. Close Rolls, 1485–1500*, no. 650.

[113] It is just possible that in spite of their apparently comprehensive language the indenture and the act of parliament did not, after all, cover all Dorset's estates. The act of parliament states 'except such manors, lands and tenements, rents, reversions and services, as be excepted and forprised in the said indentures . . .' This may possibly indicate that some property was exempted in the second arrangement concerning the lands not immediately enfeoffed in 1492.

[114] In May 1496 Dorset was able to make a marriage contract for his daughter, Elizabeth, which involved the payment of 1,000 marks. *Cal. Close Rolls, 1485–1500*, no. 945. The original indenture of 1492 has a note appended in a schedule stating that it was vacated by a writ signed by John Blythe, keeper of the chancery rolls. Unfortunately the note is undated but Blythe died in August 1499. See J. Le Neve, *Fasti Ecclesiae Anglicanae 1300–1541* III Salisbury diocese, compiled by J. M. Horne (1963) 3. The arrangement may possibly have been cancelled in September 1496 when nine men, including the earl of Devon, put up mainprises for Dorset's allegiance totalling £2,766 13s. 4d. *Cal. Close Rolls, 1485–1500*, no. 972. These new arrangements do not mention the indentures of 1492 so that these men were not substitutes for earlier guarantors. So this seems to be the most likely point for the replacement of one set of arrangements by another less severe.

[115] Henry VII's wife died in 1503.

[116] *The Chronicle of Calais* ed. J. G. Nichols, Camden Series (1846) 6. In Paril 1509 Dorset had been excepted by name from the general pardon, but in July he was brought back from

As far as sums of money were involved, during the whole reign the most extreme case involving a peer was that of George Neville, Lord Burgavenny. In the Michaelmas term 1507 the court of king's bench fined Burgavenny the grand total of £70,650 for unlawfully retaining 471 men below the rank of knight or squire.[117] This was a fine which no one at the time could possibly have paid, so now bargaining began. On 5 November 26 people and institutions entered into recognizances totalling £3,233 6s. 8d. that Burgavenny would be the king's true liegeman for life.[118] On 23 December he himself gave a recognizance for £5,000 to be true to his allegiance and to find substitutes for any of his recognitors whom, before the utas of the Purification next, the king or any of his councillors should deem insufficient,[119] and the following day gave a second recognizance for 5,000 marks not to enter the shires of Kent, Surrey, Sussex, and Hampshire at any time during his life without the king's licence.[120]

The details of all Henry's dealings with Burgavenny seem to be incomplete, for in an indenture also dated 24 December Burgavenny admitted that he was indebted to the king in £100,000 'or thereabouts' for unlawful retainers. He also admitted in this indenture that the execution and levy of the debt was clearly due, both in law and conscience, and that the king might attach his body, keep him in prison and take all the issues of his lands until the whole sum was paid. The king however, was gracious enough to eschew the full severity of the law and accepted instead, as parcel of the debt, the sum of £5,000 payable in instalments over ten years at Candlemas.[121]

So in the end Lord Burgavenny got away with the prospect of losing £500 a year for ten years. The recognizances and the indenture were in this case all cancelled during the first year of Henry VIII's reign.[122] So Burgavenny probably paid no more than £1,000.[123] We do not know what Burgavenny's income was. In 1436 his grandparents were assessed for an income tax at £667, but this certainly did not represent the total income of

Calais and in August he was pardoned and granted the office of forester of Sawsey forest, Northamptonshire. *Letters and Papers, op. cit.* I nos. 11 (10), 104, 158 (49), (75). In September the lieutenant of Calais stated that he could not have made ends meet but for the money he had received for Dorset's board and lodging. *ibid.* I 170.

[117] Bayne and Dunham, *op. cit.* pp. cxxi–cxxii. W. H. Dunham, Jr, 'Lord Hastings' Indentured Retainers, 1461–1483,' *Transactions of the Connecticut Academy of Arts and Sciences* XXXIX (1955) 103–4.

[118] *Cal. Close Rolls, 1500–9,* no. 825 (i).

[119] *ibid.* no. 825 (ii).

[120] *ibid.* no. 825 (iii).

[121] *ibid.* no. 825 (iv). BM L 127, 53r notes the delivery, on Lord Burgavenny's behalf, of the various documents concerned.

[122] *ibid.*

[123] The first instalment due was paid at Candlemas 1508 in ready money. BM L 127, 55r, dated 12 February.

their estates.[124] At this time, however, the conventional figure for the income of a baron was £1,000 a year. A few had more, some had a good deal less. Whatever Burgavenny's income was, the prospect of losing a very large proportion of it for a whole decade was a sufficiently shattering blow in a society where ostentatious display was a considerable factor in maintaining a man's prestige. And moreover the shadow of absolute ruin hung over him for two years.[125]

After all this, it seems somewhat ironical that in 1510 he was granted in reversion for life the constableship of Dover castle and the wardenship of the Cinque ports. In 1512, in preparation for the king's invasion of France, Henry VIII issued Burgavenny a licence 'to retain as many men as he can get in Kent, Sussex and Surrey and elsewhere . . . and he shall give them badges, tokens or liveries as he thinks convenient.'[126]

There are numerous references in the close rolls to the exceedingly involved affairs of Richard Grey, third earl of Kent, who succeeded to the earldom in 1503, and whose father in his will had expressed the fear that 'he will not thrive but will be a waster.'[127] Traditionally he is held to have dissipated his estates by gambling and the king certainly took advantage of his difficulties. At the time he inherited, his father owed the king 'certain moneys' for the payment of which a number of manors had been specially enfeoffed.[128] In 1506 Earl Richard owed the king £1,683 6s. 8d.[129] For this, under a recognizance of 4,000 marks, he had to make 'surety of lands' worth 500 marks a year from which payments by half yearly instalments of 200 marks could be made until the debt was cleared off; moreover, he was to make an estate, described as 'freely offered', of lands worth £100 a year to the use of himself and his heirs male with remainder in default to the king and his heirs.[130] The following year he sold a manor to Sir John Huse

---

[124] H. L. Gray, 'Incomes from Land in England in 1436,' *English Historical Review* XLIX (1934) 617. This seriously understates their income. Underassessment was considerable. See Pugh and Ross, 'The English Baronage,' *op. cit.* 1–28. There was a dowager alive at the time, whose income was apparently not included, nor did this particular tax cover Welsh estates. In 1559 the gross rental of the estates was between £2,000 and £2,999 p.a. Stone, *The Crisis, op. cit.* 760. But by this time very considerable additional estates had fallen in from the Beauchamp family. *CP* I 27–34.

[125] Although this is not made explicit in the main indenture, Sir John Heron's book states that Burgavenny, over and above the £5,000 agreed upon, was still obliged to pay the residue of the acknowledged debt at the king's pleasure. PRO E. 36/214 535.

[126] *Letters and Papers, op. cit.* I 632(4), 1356(16).

[127] *CP* VII 169.

[128] *Cal. Close Rolls, 1500–9,* no. 473. By the time of the second earl's death he still owed 2,500 marks (apparently for a wardship) of which the king now pardoned £1,000. *ibid.* no. 482. See also BM L 127, 6d. PRO E. 36/214, 466.

[129] Made up of £750 for livery of his lands, 1,000 marks remaining for the wardship of Elizabeth Trussell and 400 marks for livery of his mother's lands.

[130] *Cal. Close Rolls, 1500–9,* no. 553. BM L 127, 27d.

for 300 marks in return for a life annuity of £42 which was to be used for the payments of his debts to the king.[131] Eleven weeks before this particular arrangement was made the earl had also given an indenture stating that he still owed the king £1,800 of earlier debts, namely those of his father and other sums due for livery of his lands, plus the earlier recognizance of 4,000 marks.[132] The indenture went on to state that the earl could not pay these sums 'without in manner his utter undoing.' The king therefore, 'consented' (a distinct euphemism in the circumstances) to a recovery being made against him, by Edmund Dudley and others, of 10,000 acres of land, 4,000 of meadow, 4,000 of woodland and a rent of £120 in lordships in Wales and Shropshire. The king was to take the issues and profits of these lands to the annual value of £216, together with the profits of various other manors bringing up the total to £300 a year, until £1,800 had been paid. If the earl was still alive when this debt was settled, he in turn was to receive an annual rent of £212 from the Welsh lands and the rest were to be handed back to him. His heirs, however, would suffer most under this arrangement, for all the lands named in the recovery to Dudley and the other feoffees were to revert to the king and his heirs forever after the earl's death.[133]

Then in August of the following year, 1507, the king forced a recognizance of £10,000 from the wretched peer that he would make no sale, lease, or any other grant of land, and that he would grant no office or annuity nor sell growing timber on his estates without the king's consent in writing under his sign manual or one of his seals. Under the same recognizance he suffered the humiliation of having a royal servant placed in charge of his household,[134] whose activities he was not to meddle with nor hinder in any way. The earl himself was to appear once a day in the royal household and not to depart without licence in writing, 'except for eight days in each quarter to be taken at his liberty.'[135] How much of the estate was left at the end of Henry VII's reign it is impossible to say but when the spendthrift earl died in 1523 it was so wasted that Henry Grey, his half-brother and heir, never assumed the title 'by reason of his slender estate' and his descendants were not summoned to parliament again until 1572.[136]

---

[131] *Cal. Close Rolls, 1500–9*, no. 724. This apparently replaced the slightly earlier sale of the reversion of the manor (together with other lands). *ibid.* no. 702.

[132] Here incorrectly stated as £4,000.

[133] *Cal. Close Rolls, 1500–9*, no. 765. BM L 127, 32d, 44r.

[134] Apparently Sir William Gascoigne was put in charge of the household, for an entry of 10 August 1507 in Dudley's notebook records repayment of £43 6s. 8d. which the king had advanced to Gascoigne for the charges of the earl's household. BM L 127, 47r.

[135] *Cal. Close Rolls, 1500–9*, no. 797.

[136] CP VII 169–71.

All in all, as the result of these activities, out of 62 peerage families[137] in existence between 1485 and 1509, a total of 46 or 47 were for some part of Henry's reign at the king's mercy. Seven were under attainder, 36 gave bonds and recognizances, of whom 5 were also heavily fined, another was probably also fined,[138] and 3 more were at some time under subpoenas which carried financial penalties. Only 16 (possibly 15) remained free of these financial threats.[139]

As we have seen, the system was by no means new. Attainders had been prominent enough in late Lancastrian and Yorkist times and bonds and recognizances were part of the normal discipline and the normal hazards of fifteenth-century life. Never before, however, had any monarch developed the disciplinary use of such financial instruments to so systematic and involved a degree. The mere numbers of families, great as they were, give only an inadequate idea of the complications and dangers which this intensified system brought with it. Under the Yorkists only a single peer, Lord Ferrers of Chartley, gave more than one recognizance.[140] Under Henry VII the number giving more than one rose to 23, 11 gave 5 or more, 2 (Edward Sutton, Lord Dudley, and Lord Dacre) as many as 12, and Lord Mountjoy 23. Moreover, as noted earlier, many of the peers concerned gave bonds, recognizances, and mainprises for the good behaviour and the contracts of other noblemen, and, for that matter, of a great many commoners too, as well as for their own conduct. John Talbot, fourth earl of Shrewsbury, for example, besides giving the king recognizances totalling £466 13s. 4d. on his own behalf, between 1505 and 1507 stood guarantor for Lord Mountjoy in the sum of £500 and up to the end of the reign was jointly endangered with five different groups of people in sums totalling over £5,000.[141] There thus

[137] The parliamentary peerage was, in fact, somewhat smaller than this figure suggests as not all these families were members of it at the same time. e.g. John, Lord Cheyne, was made a baron in 1487 and his peerage became extinct on his death without heirs in 1499 and the barony of Dinham, created in 1467, died out in 1501. I have excluded (a) two foreign families, that of Louis de Gruthuyse, earls of Winchester between 1472 and 1500, and Philibert de Chandée, earl of Bath from 1486, (b) members of the Plantagenet and Tudor royal families who held peerages.

[138] Lord Beauchamp of Powicke, though his indentification is somewhat doubtful.

[139] Earl Ryvers, the earls of Huntingdon, Stafford, and Westmorland, Viscount Welles, Lords Cheyne, Cobham, Dinham, Egremont, Fitzhugh, Welles and Willoughby (Richard Hastings), Latimer, Lumley, Morley, Rochford, and Roos. See also note 138 above.

[140] Two recognizances were taken from the Burgavenny family, but one each from father and son during the time each held the barony.

[141] Cal. Close Rolls, 1500–9, nos 599, 904. PRO E. 36/214, pp. 392, 402, 403, 493, 495. See also the petition which Lord Dacre presented to Henry VIII in 1509 for discharge from recognizances, alleging (1) that bonds in 2,000 marks had been wrongfully taken for the keeping of Herbottle castle from Sir George Tailboys and still retained after Dacre had been discharged from keeping that office, (2) for £500 in which he was bound for keeping the peace against Lord Greystoke and for his own and others' appearance in the Star chamber, (3) £200 of which he was bound jointly with others, allegedly wrongly forfeited, (4) a recognizance of 3,000 marks wrongly transformed by Empson and Dudley into a debt

developed in the later years of Henry VII's reign an immensely tangled, complicated series of relationships in which a majority of the peerage were legally and financially in the king's power and at his mercy, so that in effect people were set under heavy penalties to guarantee the honesty and loyalty of their fellows. The system was so extensive that it must have created an atmosphere of chronic watchfulness, suspicion, and fear.

Polydore Vergil, who was in England during the later part of Henry's reign, had a very good idea of the king's motives. In his account of the year 1502, a date which exactly coincides with the remarkable increase in the number of recognizances enrolled on the close rolls, he remarked that Henry VII 'began to treat his people with more harshness and severity than had been his custom in order (as the king himself asserted) to ensure that they remained more thoroughly and entirely in obedience to him' although people in general attribute his motives to greed. Vergil went on to allege that the king wished to keep his subjects obedient through fear, that he inflicted heavy financial penalties thinking that they derived from great wealth the courage to commit offences, and that his policy of financial terror was eminently successful.[142] Vergil's opinion, which Edward Hall exactly followed,[143] and Sir Robert Cotton and Sir Francis Bacon as usual exaggerated, deserves respect, for although the fragmentary and limited sources still available allow no calculation of the income which the king derived from these methods, it is most probable, as Dietz surmised, that except for the fines levied on the Cornish rebels of 1497, the returns from fines, recognizances, and pardons sold was not great.[144]

payable at Michaelmas and (5) of 1,000 marks (600 of which had been paid) in which he had been bound with George, Lord Fitzhugh, for his mother Dame Mabel Dacre accused of (wrongfully, it is alleged), and imprisoned for ravishing a royal ward. Another entry reveals that he had also given a recognizance for 1,000 marks jointly with Sir Edward Musgrave. *Letters and Papers, op. cit.* I nos 131, 132 (50). For the original indenture with Musgrave, see *Cal. Close Rolls, 1500–9*, no. 582; for no. (3) above, *ibid*, no. 315. See also, *ibid.* no. 818. For six more recognizances in which Dacre was bound see *ibid.* nos 543 and 601. The grand total of recognizances for Dacre from various sources reaches at least twelve.

[142] '. . . all people, in terror of losing their wealth, at once began to behave themselves and (as the saying goes) to withdraw into their shells.' In discussing the actions of Empson and Dudley, Vergil added 'they proceeded not against the poor but the wealthy churchmen, rich magnates, even the intimates of the king himself, and any and every individual of fortune' and '. . . the king claimed that he tolerated these exactions of set plan, in order thereby to maintain the population in obedience.' *The Anglica Historia of Polydore Vergil, A.D. 1485–1537* ed. and transl. D. Hay, Camden Series (1950) 126–31. It is interesting to note that in 1541 Henry VIII 'graciously remarked that he had an evil people to rule and promised that he would make them so poor that they would never be able to rebel again.' J. J. Scarisbrick, *Henry VIII* (1968) 428.

[143] Though he was slightly more inclined to give Henry the benefit of the doubt on the question of greed. E. Hall, *Chronicle* (1809) 499, 502–3.

[144] At least up to Michaelmas 1505, when Heron's receipt book ends. Dietz, *English Government Finance, op. cit.* 34. Payments 'by obligation' begin to appear in the chamber records in 1493, and towards the end of the reign, together with similar payments 'by recognizance,'

Side by side with such financial sanctions as these, Henry VII's strictness in enforcing his feudal rights is notorious and, although there is no space to discuss such matters here, the king's transactions in the land market with various noble families also reinforce the impression of harshness and deserve investigation. So does the question of the sale of justice and payments for royal favours in legal cases,[145] a question which had been difficult and contentious all through the middle ages.[146] As usual, the whole atmosphere was probably made far worse by the corruption of the royal agents.[147]

To sum up, as remarked earlier, status and wealth went hand in hand at this time. As the monarchy possessed little coercive power at its direct command, it was forced to rely on the rich, that is on the titled nobility and the greater gentry, to keep order in the countryside and to provide the bulk of the military forces both to suppress revolt at home and to wage its campaigns overseas. Far from destroying the peerage, the crown found it essential to maintain the numbers of nobility. Periods of political tension, significantly enough, saw not only attainders but the greatest number of new creations. In their own interest kings had either to endow new peers or to promote men already rich enough to sustain the dignity. Between the late fourteenth century and the Reformation they generally preferred the latter course.[148] The later part of the fifteenth century and the first three decades of the sixteenth century were a period of remarkable stability for noble property. From 1450 onwards political miscalculation was the only conspicuous cause for loss of property. Neither land nor money was granted to the peerage in any great degree. On the other hand, theories of

they became very important, though, of course, only a minority were from peers. In the year, Michaelmas 1504 to Michaelmas 1505, Dietz states that £34,999 was received in this way. Unfortunately most of the entries are brief and do not specify the cause. Elsewhere Dietz implies that it was 'bonds of various sorts' together with jewels, plate, and loans that made up the bulk of the immense fortune Henry VII is alleged to have left at his death. *ibid.* 33, 87. For serious doubts about the extent of this fortune, see B. P. Wolffe, 'Henry VII's Land Revenues and Chamber Finance,' *English Historical Review* LXXIX (1964) 253–4.

[145] e.g. See Bayne and Dunham, *op. cit.* pp. xxxix. BM L 127/34r, 37r, 55r.

[146] W. Stubbs, *The Constitutional History of England* (1873–8) II 636–7. J. C. Holt, *Magna Carta* (1965) 226.

[147] As noted earlier courtiers and officials made considerable gains at the expense of unfortunate peers suing for the reversal of their attainders. Dudley, a poor man in the mid 1490s before he entered the royal service, died possessed of lands in thirteen counties and goods worth £5,000. Many years after his death he was accused of forgery. It should be remembered, however, that few people at this time were over-scrupulous about forgery if it suited their own interests and accusations of corruption after the death of powerful men were common enough. Sir Robert Plumpton accused Empson of trying to dispossess him of his lands for the heirs general of his father, Sir William Plumpton, to one of whom Empson planned to marry his daughter. Dudley, *Tree of Commonwealth, op. cit.* 10. Dietz, *op. cit.* 46–67. *The Plumpton Correspondence* ed. T. Stapleton, Camden Series (1839) pp. cii ff.

[148] See above p. 270.

their economic decline appear to have been greatly exaggerated. As in any other age, reckless incapacity might ruin an individual, like the third Grey earl of Kent, and estates, like those of the Percies or the dukes of Buckingham, might suffer from poor administration and over-exploitation during periods of attainder or during minorities. Otherwise no peer is known to have been in more than temporary difficulties. The greater lords who fought in the Wars of the Roses were all richer than their grandfathers had been.

Though history of course never crudely repeats itself, various writers have noted a marked tendency in the Yorkists and early Tudors to bypass ancient institutions which had become formalized, cumbersome, and over-rigid, and to adopt more directly personal forms of government which bear a very close resemblance to the practices of earlier times. An increased reliance on revenue from the crown lands was one of these methods; so was financial administration through the chamber rather than the exchequer and J. G. Bellamy has described Edward IV's judicial methods as a return, at least in part, to the peripatetic tradition of Angevin kingship.[149] The arbitrary element in medieval English kingship was always strong. The king, as well as being the fount of that justice and discipline which flowed through the law courts, still exercised justice tinged with favour through his own will, especially upon his richer subjects. Great landed fortunes, and the power which they carried with them, could be profoundly affected by the royal favour or displeasure and the success of government still depended upon keeping a balance between the powerful. Indeed, the powerful expected the king to arbitrate fairly in their quarrels rather than to have to take their disputes to the law courts like ordinary men.[150]

Given this centuries-old tradition, direct interference in the affairs of the great can hardly of itself be considered new or unusual. Although many of Henry VII's actions may seem to us the very negation of justice, we should at least bear in mind that his conduct was less violent than that of many earlier kings. A good deal of the violence of the Anglo-Norman period is now attributed to the fact that William the Conqueror and his sons refused even to recognize the hereditary tenure of many estates.[151] King John had compelled men to seal deeds allowing him to seize their lands at his pleasure and he had imposed enormous fines on his tenants-in-chief, manipulating the huge resulting debts for political purposes.[152] K. B.

---

[149] J. G. Bellamy, 'Justice under the Yorkist Kings,' *American Journal of Legal History* IX (1965) 135–55.

[150] See above p. 269.

[151] R. H. C. Davis, 'What Happened in Stephen's Reign,' *History* XLIX (1968) 1–12; *King Stephen* (1967) 6, 8–10, 14, 24–5, 41, 53, 121 ff.

[152] S. Painter, *The Reign of King John* (1949) ch. 2 and 110 ff.

McFarlane excoriated Edward I's treatment of his earls, his violent 'arrangement' of escheats which, on very flimsy pretexts, deprived a number of great families of wide inheritances for the benefit of the royal house and its members.[153] It may also be stressed that the somewhat evil reputation of Henry VII which has come down to posterity owes more to contemporary and near-contemporary denunciation of his greed than to comments on the disciplinary aspects of his policy. In spite of its evil reputation the fifteenth century was no more violent than earlier times—indeed it may have been rather less so. Certainly Edward IV and Henry VII were in some ways extremely cautious in their relations with their subjects in general,[154] and Henry VII's dealings with the nobility had at least a conventional background both in political tradition and in the way in which the king and the great lords themselves dealt with their own estate officials and dependents and in the way in which government was carried on in Wales and the Marches.

As James Harrington wrote in the middle of the seventeenth century, monarchy could be of two kinds, 'the one by arms, the other by a nobility', and he added, 'a monarchy, divested of its nobility, has no refuge under heaven but an army.'[155] Henry had no army. As his taxation policy, like that of Edward IV, was principally aimed at avoiding discontent among large numbers of his subjects, he could not afford to maintain one. Foreign visitors noted with continual surprise how small the English military forces were.[156] Henry therefore could do no other than rely upon his nobility. In the north of England, the Marches against Scotland were still a frontier and, as M. E. James has pointed out, a frontier at this time was not a neat line of barbed wire fence, but a march many miles deep, given over to endemic violence.[157] Although Henry experimented with the abolition of aristocratic wardens of the marches,[158] he was soon forced to resort once again to the appointment of powerful noblemen.[159] The famous council in the north, if indeed it had anything more than a sporadic existence under Henry VII, was only a limited success. Even in the late 1530s when Henry VIII and Thomas Cromwell deprived the Percy earl of Northumberland of all his power and most of his estates, they replaced him in office by a former

---

[153] K. B. McFarlane, 'Had Edward I a "Policy" towards the Earls?' *History* L (1965) 145-9.

[154] e.g. In their demands for taxation.

[155] J. Harrington, 'Oceana,' in *Ideal Commonwealths* ed. H. Morley (1901) 203, 223.

[156] e.g. *Calendar of State Papers Milanese, op. cit.* I 324.

[157] M. E. James, *Change and Continuity in the Tudor North: the Rise of Thomas, Lord Wharton*, St Anthony's Hall Borthwick Papers (27) (1965) 3.

[158] R. L. Storey, 'The Wardens of the Marches of England towards Scotland,' *English Historical Review* LXXII (1957) 608-9, 615.

[159] *Rot. Scot.* II 470-1, 484-5. Even when lieutenants, not wardens, were appointed they were generally magnates. *ibid.* 472-3, 479, 486, 501-2, 515, 519.

Percy client, Thomas Wharton, endowed from the Percy lands and suitably ennobled for the purpose, a man in fact belonging to the same landed society as the magnates. It was only after 1570 that the power of the Percies and other great northern families finally passed to civil servants from London.[160]

Even in less abnormal areas the king exercised insufficient power through his own officials. Therefore as S. T. Bindoff once wrote, 'the keystone of the many arched temple of the Tudor peace were the noblemen and gentlemen of the kingdom . . . The problem before Henry VII was how to suppress the magnates' abuse of power while preserving the power itself. He could no more do without a ruling class than he could do with a class that refused to be ruled.'[161]

If also, as MacCafferty has remarked, for 55 years after Henry VII's accession the Tudors succeeded in keeping the greater aristocracy cowed,[162] this success was due in part to the fact that they gave the aristocracy no great cause for political and social offence. As long as the king was not actively evil or politically stupid the magnates had no particular wish to dominate the central government but cared far more for the maintenance of their inheritances and their local influence. Henry VII's oppressive disciplinary measures, which after all affected the nobles' conduct rather than their powers, exercised in varying degrees against at least three quarters of the titled families of the kingdom, were perhaps the more effective because the disturbing political experiences of a century and more had probably left the greater and more ancient families in a cautious mood.[163] Though far from being without precedent, the degree to which Henry VII took the use of bonds and recognizances was so extreme that, as McFarlane wrote, during the last few years of his reign it produced a form of government that was indeed *sui generis*.

Henry VIII at once eased the system as part of a general reaction against the harsher aspects of his father's rule. The Venetian ambassador reported the new king's liberality,[164] and Lord Mountjoy wrote to Erasmus just after the arrest of Empson and Dudley that 'all England is in ecstasies. Extortion is put down, liberality is the order of the day.'[165] However, Henry, or his advisers, mixed his popular gestures with considerable financial caution. When granting a more comprehensive general pardon than the one which his father had issued just before his death, the new king included the reser-

---

[160] James, *Change and Continuity, op. cit.* 39.

[161] S. T. Bindoff, *Tudor England* (1950) 53.

[162] W. T. MacCaffery, 'England, the Crown and the New Aristocracy,' *Past and Present* XXX (1965) 52–64.

[163] See above pp. 272–3.

[164] Dietz, *op. cit.* 49. *Calendar of State Papers, Venetian* I ed. R. Brown (1864) 942, 945.

[165] *Opus Epistolarum Des. Erasmi Roterodami* ed. P. S. Allen *et al.* (1906–58) I no. 215.

vation 'for all things except debts.'[166] With something of a flourish, to demonstrate 'how favourable and benevolent sovereign lord we have been unto divers our nobles and other our subjects' he merely respited, not pardoned, 'divers recognizances and other weighty matters drawn by our special commandment out of divers books signed with the hand of our dearest father', concerning 50 people, including 10 aristocrats, 3 of them women.[167] As late as 1512, Thomas Lucas, Sir James Hobart (Henry VII's attorney), and the late king's executors were ordered to investigate debts due to the crown upon recognizances, obligations, recoveries, and deeds of feofment, long respited by the executors.[168] Such discrimination was after all to be expected, for a majority of bonds and obligations had always been made for purposes recognized as legal and just. For a decade and more the chamber went on collecting money in settlement of recognizances made under Henry VII, and the practice of collecting the king's debts and dues in instalments by means of obligations continued, to fall into disuse during Henry VIII's later years, but even then to be revived under Mary.[169]

Nevertheless, Henry VIII cancelled at least 45 recognizances during the first year of his reign and 130 more over the next five years.[170] In 51 cases the recognizances were stated to have been unjustly extorted.[171] Henry seems to have been as careful in dealing with recognizances taken from peers as with those of lesser men. A number concerning what might be called normal debts and contracts were allowed to stand,[172] or at least no record of their cancellation appears to have been made. However, Henry reduced the use of the system *in terrorem* over peers to minute proportions, though he did not discard it completely.[173] The ruinous sanctions hanging

---

[166] *Letters and Papers, op. cit.* I no. 11(i).

[167] *ibid.* I no. 309.

[168] *ibid.* I no. 1493. They were provided with the names of 49 people under recognizances and 125 owing other kinds of debts. Their instructions also gave them scope to include other people not named.

[169] Dietz, *op. cit.* 49–50. Richardson, *Tudor Chamber Administration, op. cit.* 145.

[170] These figures are calculated from the calendar of *Letters and Papers, op. cit.* They are certainly incomplete as other cancellations, not found here, are entered after the original recognizances on the close rolls of Henry VII's reign.

[171] e.g. '. . . were made without any cause reasonable or lawful, and that the parties recognizing the same were without ground or matter of truth, by the undue means of certain of the learned council of our said late father thereunto driven, contrary to law, reason and good conscience, to the manifest charge and peril of the soul of our said late father . . .' *Letters and Papers, op. cit.* I no. 448. See also nos 651 (7), 731 (7), (20), 749 (16), 804 (9), 1123 (45), 1524 (38).

[172] From the earls of Essex, Kent, Northumberland and Westmorland, Lords Berkeley, Darcy, de la Warre, Mountjoy, Scrope of Upsall, and Willoughby.

[173] Recognizances of this kind affecting the earl of Kent and Lords Burgh, Clifford, Darcy, and Daubeney, seem to be uncancelled. Possibly also recognizances from Lords de la Warre, Grey of Powys, and Willoughby come into this class. Henry VIII obviously made

over Lord Burgavenny and their humiliating conditions of payment were cancelled.[174] So was the earl of Northumberland's fine of £10,000.[175] Henry cancelled bonds and recognizances affecting ten other peers during the first year of his reign.[176] In two cases the recognizances were stated to have been unjustly taken.[177] Even some of the land which Empson and Dudley had questionably wrung from peers for the crown was restored.[178] Henry VII himself had, of course, cancelled many other recognizances at various times, so by the middle of 1510 possibly nine peers at the most remained bound for other than normal debts or mainprises (generally small in amount) for the good conduct of themselves and other men in office.[179]

The reasons for this new policy can be a matter only of opinion. F. C. Dietz thought that 'the stern justice of Henry VII's day was no longer needed to ensure respect for the laws.'[180] Since Dietz wrote, however, others have shown that the repression of lawlessness and violence was a much less rapid phenomenon than his generation held it to be and that its occurrence was the result, not so much of action taken by Henry VII, as of a more gradual process extending over most of the sixteenth century.[181] It is far more probable that by the end of the reign Henry VII's ruthless methods were producing a dangerous backlash of resentment,[182] and that his son's immediate, though by no means precipitate or incautious, relaxation of his methods was an avowed policy of appeasement to soften the resentment

---

some distinction between recognizances for good behaviour in office and those of a more directly coercive nature. Recognizances taken from Lord Mountjoy by Henry VII were cancelled, those of Hammes castle in 1 Henry VIII. *Cal. Close Rolls, 1500–9*, nos 226, 228, 290, 428, 756. At the same time, however, he was forced to give a new recognizance for £10,000 for Hammes and another for 1,000 marks concerning victual money for Calais. *Letters and Papers, op. cit.* I no. 257 (4) (5). Other recognizances of Mountjoy's were cancelled at various times, one as late as 4 Henry VIII. *Cal. Close Rolls, 1500–9*, nos 549, 955 (xiv). Henry VIII also made Mountjoy find sureties as master of the Mint and give recognizances for various other purposes. *Letters and Papers, op. cit.* I nos 110 (2); 2578 (80).

[174] See above pp. 289–90.

[175] See above p. 286. But a recognizance given in 1506 on behalf of Richard Weston for the sake-keeping of Castle Cornet, Guernsey, stood. *Cal. Close Rolls, 1500–9*, no. 765.

[176] The earls of Arundel, Buckingham, Kent and Shrewsbury, the marquess of Dorset, Lords Dacre, de la Warre, Hasting, Mountjoy, Somerset. Not all the recognizances affecting Kent and Mountjoy (see note 174 above) were, however, cancelled.

[177] Lords Daubeney and Mountjoy. *Letters and Papers, op. cit.* I nos 749 (24), 1524 (38).

[178] e.g. To Lord Darcy and his wife. Dietz, *op. cit.* 49. *Letters and Papers, op. cit.* I nos 132 (115), 289 (5).

[179] See notes 172 and 173 above.

[180] Dietz, *op. cit.* 49.

[181] e.g. Stone, *The Crisis, op. cit.* ch. 5.

[182] This is also the opinion of B. P. Wolffe on Henry VII's financial practices generally. See 'Henry VII's Land Revenues and Chamber Finance,' *op. cit.* 252–4, and *Yorkist and Early Tudor Government*, Historical Association (1966) 18–20.

and anger of those aggrieved by the potentially ruinous fines and recognizances hanging over them—and the most important and dangerous of the aggrieved were the resentful nobility.

Appendix A   Peers known to have fought in the Wars of the Roses, 1455–85.

1   The Lancastrian peers, 1455–1461

To the time when Edward IV seized the throne in March 1461, the following peers fought in battle on the Lancastrian side:[1]

St Albans I (1455)—Humphrey Stafford, duke of Buckingham, Edmund Beaufort, duke of Somerset*, Thomas Courtenay, earl of Devon, Henry Percy II, earl of Northumberland*, Jasper Tudor, earl of Pembroke, James Butler, earl of Wiltshire, Lord Berners, Thomas, Lord Clifford*, Lords Dudley, Fauconberg (William Neville), Sudeley, Roos. John Tiptoft, earl of Worcester was also in the king's camp as at one point he was sent to York to act as a mediator. Owing to the rapidity with which events developed, a number of lords arrived only the day after the battle. Of these the following would certainly have been on the royalist side—John de Vere, earl of Oxford, John Talbot, earl of Shrewsbury, Ralph, Lord Cromwell. C. A. J. Armstrong, 'Politics and the battle of St Albans, 1455', *Bulletin of the Institute of Historical Research* XXXIII (1960) 18–24. John Mowbray, duke of Norfolk, also arrived a day late and he may, perhaps, be suspected of deliberately abstaining. He was a bitter enemy of Somerset and was sympathetic to the duke of York, and at one point before the battle the duke of Buckingham thought that he might be in the Yorkist camp. Thus the message which occurs in an account written to Sir John Fastolf by one of his servants, possibly an officer of arms, most probably written before the end of the battle, runs 'Vous me recommanderez a mes beaux freres d'York et de Salisbury a mon nepveu de Warrewyk et a mon frere de Norffolk ou cas qu'il soit en leur compagnie comme vous dites qu'il est pres'. 'Fastolf Relation,' College of Arms Arundel MS. 48 fos 341ᵣ –342ᵣ quoted *ibid.* 65–7. In spite of the fact that he was twice imprisoned by Henry VI for disreputable conduct,[2] in 1457 he obtained a licence to go on a pilgrimage to the Holy Land for the recovery of the king's health. In 1458 he and his wife were serving the queen and in December 1459 he was one of the peers who swore allegiance to Henry VI at the Coventry Parliament. Only in 1461 did he fully champion the Yorkist cause. He fought with Warwick at the second battle of St Albans (1461) but it should be remembered that Henry VI was then in Yorkist hands and it could be argued that he was fighting with King Henry against those who had broken the Act of Accord of 1460. *ibid.* 19. *CP* IX 607–8.

Blore Heath (1459)—James, Lord Audley*, Lord Dudley. *Rot. Parl.* V 348. *CP* IV 479. An *English Chronicle of the Reigns of Richard II, Henry IV, Henry V, and Henry VI* ed. J. S. Davies, Camden Society (1856) 80. Although Sir William Stanley fought for the Yorkist his brother Thomas, Lord Stanley, who had collected forces at the command of Margaret of Anjou, remained idle (probable deliberately) six miles away.[3] *Rot. Parl.* V 348, 349, 369–70.

Ludford (1459)—There was, in fact no battle at the so-called 'rout of Ludford' as the Yorkists fled before any troops engaged. Chronicle evidence fails at this point and no peers are mentioned by name on the Lancastrian side.

Northampton (1460)—Humphrey Stafford, duke of Buckingham*, John Talbot, earl of Shrewsbury*, John, Viscount Beaumont*, Lord Egremont*. An *English Chronicle, op. cit.,* 96–7.

Wakefield (1460)—Henry Beaufort, duke of Somerset (son of Duke Edmund, killed at St Albans I). Thomas Courtenay, earl of Devon, Henry Percy III, earl of Northumberland, (son of

[1] Those killed in battle are marked with an asterisk.

[2] See above p. 20 n. 105.

[3] The Burgundian Chronicler, Waurin, also notes the following as present at Blore Heath—Henry Holland, duke of Exeter, John Beaufort, duke of Somerset, James Butler, earl of Wiltshire, John Viscount Beaumont. Thomas Courtenay earl of Devon, (le comte d'Enchier') and Lord Welles. Jehan de Waurin, *Recueil des Croniques et Anchiennes Istories de la Grant Bretaigne, A Present Nomme Angleterre* ed. W. Hardy and E. L. C. P. Hardy, Rolls Series (5 vols 1864–91) V 319. Waurin's account of events at this point, however, is so confused that his testimony must be regarded as somewhat dubious.

301

Henry Percy II, killed at St Albans I), John, Lord Clifford, (son of Thomas, Lord Clifford, killed at St Albans I), Lords Harrington*, Neville (brother of the earl of Westmorland) Roos of Helmsley. *Rot. Parl.* v 477. *An English Chronicle, op. cit.* 106. *CP* III 293, v 213, VI 320, VII 480, x 778, XI 105.

Gregory's Chronicle states that Lord Greystock and Lord Latimer were with the duke of Exeter at Hull shortly before. It is, therefore, quite likely that they were also present at the battle. *The Historical Collection of a London Citizen in the Fifteenth Century* ed J. Gairdner, Camden Series (1876) 209–10.

Mortimer's Cross (1461)—Jasper Tudor, earl of Pembroke, James Butler, earl of Wiltshire. *An English Chronicle, op. cit.* 108, 110. William Worcestre, *Itineraries* ed. J. H. Harvey (1969) 203.

St Albans II (1461)—Henry Beaufort, duke of Somerset, Henry Percy III, earl of Northumberland, Thomas Courtenay, earl of Devon, John, Lord Neville, Lord Roos. *Rot. Parl.* v 476–7. The 'Annales' formerly attributed to William Worcester (Stevenson II pt ii 776) also state that the following were present in a preliminary scuffle at Dunstable the previous day—Henry Holland, duke of Exeter, John Talbot, earl of Shrewsbury, Lords Fitzhugh, Grey of Codnor, Greystock, Welles, and Willoughby. It is, therefore, most likely that they were at the battle itself, although they are not mentioned in the act of attainder of 1461 as being present, and may have made their peace with the Yorkists in the meantime.

On the other side with Warwick, were John Mowbray duke of Norfolk, John de la Pole, duke of Suffolk (who had been recently married to York's daughter, Elizabeth), and Lord Bonvile. The issue now, however, was hardly as clear-cut as in the other battles, for Henry VI was in Warwick's hands, and the Yorkists could claim to be fighting perjurors who had broken the act of accord of 1460 to which Henry VI had agreed, and which left him king during his lifetime, disinherited his son Prince Edward and made Richard of York heir to the throne.

Towton (1461)—Henry Holland, duke of Exeter, Henry Beaufort, duke of Somerset, Thomas Courtenay, earl of Devon (beheaded after the battle), Henry Percy III, earl of Northumberland*, James Butler, earl of Wiltshire (beheaded after the battle), William, Viscount Beaumont (son of John, Viscount Beaumont, killed at Northampton), John, Lord Clifford* (son of Thomas, Lord Clifford killed at St Albans I), Dacre of Gillesland, Rougemont-Grey, (executed after the battle), John, Lord Neville*, Roos, Anthony Ryvers, Lord Scales, Leo, Lord Welles*, Richard, Lord Willoughby. *Paston Letters* II 5. 'Gregory's Chronicle' in *Collections of a London Citizen, op. cit.* 216–7. *Rot. Parl.* v 477–8. *CP* IV 18, 326, XII pt ii 443–4, 445, 734.

In addition, in October 1459, Henry Beaufort, duke of Somerset, Lord Audley and Lord Roos tried to take Calais from the Yorkists. They failed. Somerset fled to Guisnes, Roos to Flanders. Audley was captured, taken to Calais and there joined forces with the Yorkists. *An English Chronicle, op. cit.* 84.

Between 1459 and 1461 three of these peers went over to the Yorkists, John, Lord Audley, Lord Berners and William Neville, Lord Fauconberg. See above appendix B.

The following are described as being in the Tower of London in the Lancastrian interest when the Yorkists arrived in the city from Calais in July 1460—Lords Delaware, Hungerford, Lovell, Thomas, Lord Scales (murdered by a London mob when trying to escape), Vesci—and a Gascon called Lord Kendal. *An English Chronicle, op. cit.* 98.

The act of attainder of 1461 accuses the following of encouraging resistance in the Lancastrian interest after Edward IV's accession on 4 March 1461—Henry Holland, duke of Exeter, Henry Beaufort, duke of Somerset, Jasper Tudor, earl of Pembroke, James Butler, earl of Wiltshire, Lord Hungerford, and accuses the dukes of Exeter and Somerset and Lords Roos and Rougemont-Grey of handing over Berwick to the Scots on 25 April 1461. *Rot. Parl.* v 478.

(The eldest sons of magnates who held courtesy titles are not included.)

2 Yorkist Peers to March 1461

See below ch, 4 p. 100, and appendix B p. 306.

3 Peers supporting Warwick 1469–70

The earl of Oxford and Lord Fitzhugh, both of whom were married to sisters of Warwick, Lord Scrope of Bolton, and Lord Willoughby and Welles. Lord Willoughby and Welles was probably much more concerned with his own quarrel with Sir Thomas Burgh than with Warwick's interests. Warwick's own brother, the earl of Northumberland (later Marquis Montagu) tried to suppress Fitzhugh, and sided with Warwick only during Henry VI's Re-adeption. See below ch. 4 p. 122 n. 163.

4 Peers supporting Edward IV 1469–70

At Edgecote (1469), Humphrey Stafford of Southwick, earl of Devon*, William Herbert, earl of Pembroke*, Richard Wydeville, Earl Ryvers*. All three were executed by Warwick after the battle. The earl of Arundel, Henry Percy, earl of Northumberland, and Lord Hastings were also with the king's forces elsewhere. *Three Books of Polydore Vergil's English History, Comprising the Reigns of Henry VI, Edward IV and Richard III*. ed. Sir H. Ellis, Camden Series (1844) 123. 'Gough London 10', in *Six Town Chronicles of England* ed. R. Flenley (1911) 164. In 1470, John Tiptoft, earl of Worcester, was executed by the Warwick-Lancaster faction. *CP* XII pt ii, 844–5.

5 Warwick-Lancaster peers 1470–71

In 1470 Lord Fitzhugh led a small insurrection in Yorkshire to divert Edward IV's attention from Warwick's invasion. 'Vitellius A XVI,' in *Chronicles of London* ed. C. L. Kingsford (1905) 181. Between Edward's landing at Ravenser (14 March 1471) and the battle of Tewkesbury (4 May), the following are known to have been in arms against him—Henry Holland, duke of Exeter, Edmund Beaufort II, titular duke of Somerset* (the attainder of 1465 was still unreversed), John Neville, Marquis Montagu* (Warwick's brother), John Courtenay, titular earl of Devon* (the attainder of 1461 of his brother, Thomas, was still unreversed), John de Vere, earl of Oxford, Lord Wenlock, Richard Neville, earl of Warwick*. Jasper Tudor, earl of Pembroke, is included as he was recruiting troops in Wales although he did not get them to Tewkesbury in time to fight. Just before Edward's landing Lord Stanley was beseiging Hornby castle on behalf of the Lancastrians and also as part of his own personal feud against the Harrington family. Lord Sudeley was in London with the Lancastrians but apparently did not fight. When Edward arrived in London he ordered him to be arrested. *Historie of the Arrivall of Edward IV in England* ed. J. Bruce, Camden Series (1838) 8, 24, 27, 29–30, 45. *Paston Letters* III 9. *A Chronicle of Tewkesbury Abbey*, in C. L. Kingsford, *English Historical Literature in the Fifteenth Century* (1913) 376–7. *Foedera*, XII 699. The *Arrivall* (*op. cit.* 8) also mentions Lord Bardolf, but *CP* does not list a Lord Bardolf living at this date. Several modern works, including the *Complete Peerage* (*CP* II 63) state that Viscount Beaumont was in arms in 1470–1, but I know of no contemporary reference to this. On the other hand he was with the earl of Oxford in St Michael's Mount in 1473. J. Warkworth, *A Chronicle of the First Thirteen Years of the Reign of King Edward the Fourth* ed. J. O. Halliwell, Camden Series (1839) 27.

6 Yorkist peers 1470–71

Anthony Wydeville, Earl Ryvers, Lords Cobham, Humphrey Bouchier, Lord Cromwell, Grey of Codnor, Hastings, Howard and Say. *Arrivall, op. cit.* 3, 9, 10, 11, 20, 37. *Paston Letters* III 9. PRO E. 404/74, writ of privy seal dated 24 May 1471. The duke of Norfolk took part in judgments in Tewkesbury two days after the battle (*Arrivall, op. cit.* 31) so it is possible he may have been there.

See also T. B. Pugh, 'The Magnates, Knights and Gentry', in *Fifteenth Century England, 1399–1509: Studies in Politics and Society* (1969) 110. Henry Percy, who Edward had recently restored to the earldom of Northumberland, provided no active support, though his presence probably prevented other northerners from attacking the king. *Arrivall, op. cit.* 1–7. Pugh, *op. cit.* 109, 126 n. 124, suggests that Northumberland could not support the king because the majority of his tenants were still Lancastrian in sympathy. The *Arrivall* (*op. cit.* 6, 31–32) which after all was the official Yorkist account of these events, states that a new Lancastrian rising in the north was probable early in May, but Edward's final victory at Tewkesbury (4 May) put an end to it.

On the other hand when Edward entered London on 21 May, in addition to Clarence and Gloucester, twenty five peers were with him, including the following who do not appear in the above list of those fighting—the dukes of Suffolk and Buckingham (aged sixteen), the earls of Northumberland, Essex, Pembroke, Shrewsbury and Wiltshire, Lords Audley, Stanley, Grey of Ruthyn (son and heir of the earl of Kent), Dacres, Maltravers (son and heir of the earl of Arundel), Dudley, Scrope and Ferrers. 'Yorkist Notes' in C. L. Kingsford, *English Historical Literature, op. cit.* 375. This list is, however, inaccurate and should be regarded with caution, as it contains the names of Lords Bourchier (son and heir of the earl of Essex) and Cromwell who were both killed at the battle of Barnet.

7 Peers supporting Richard III 1485

The duke of Norfolk and the earl of Surrey, father and son, and the earl of Nottingham (Berkeley), had received the lands of the Mowbray dukes of Norfolk (through co-heiresses) which Edward IV had denied them, as well as other valuable grants. Viscount Lovell and Lords Scrope of Bolton and Dacre of Gillesland had also profited financially from royal grants. The others were Lord Ferrers and Lord Zouch. The earl of Northumberland who had also profited from grants, came to the battlefield but did not fight. J. R. Lander, *Conflict and Stability in Fifteenth Century England*, (1969) 99 and n. 1.

8 Peers supporting Henry VII 1485

The earl of Oxford. *Fulman* 574. *Polydore Vergil, op. cit.* 223. John, Lord Welles. *Fulman* 574. Welles was the son of Margaret, widow of John Beaufort, first duke of Somerset, who died *spm*, 27 May 1444. In 1485, Welles, himself, was under attainder for his part in Buckingham's rebellion, and he had not enjoyed his title owing to the (unreversed) attainder of his elder brother, Robert, in 1475. Welles had joined Henry of Richmond in exile. *CP* XII pt ii 444, 448.

Jasper Tudor, earl of Pembroke. *Polydore Vergil, op. cit.* 216, guardedly states, 'But thinhabytants of Pembrough at the same very time comfortyd all ther dysmayed myndes, for they gave intelligence, by Arnold Butler, a valyant man, demanding forgeavenes of ther former offences, that they wer ready to serve Jaspar ther erle.' The earliest statement of Pembroke's presence seems to have been made in Hall's chronicle, published in 1548. E. Hall, *The Union of the Two Noble and Illustre Famelies of Lancastre and Yorke* ed. H. Ellis (1809) 414. Grafton, Holinshed, Stowe and the anonymous author of the seventeenth century 'Life of Sir Rhys ap Thomas' followed Hall and thus the statement has entered modern books.[4]

Thomas, Lord Stanley. Although his brother Sir William fought there is no hard evidence that Thomas himself did, though he may have done so in the final stages of the battle. Once again the chronicle of Hall, *op. cit.* 418, states that Lord Stanley fought. *Polydore Vergil, op. cit.* 226, states only that after the battle Stanley crowned Henry with Richard III's crown 'found among the spoyle in the feilde', but in a deposition concerning Henry VII's marriage with Elizabeth of York, Stanley later said that he had 'known the aforesaid king well since the 24th day of August', that is two days after the battle of Bosworth. *Calendar of Entries in the Papal Registers Relating to Great Britain and Ireland, Papal Letters, 1484–1492* XIV ed. J. A. Twemlow (1960) 17. The possibility that the date is an error cannot, however, be completely ruled out.

---

[4] I wish to thank S. B. Chrimes and R. S. Thomas for information and assistance on these points.

Thomas Grey, marquis of Dorset, having been implicated in Buckingham's rebellion in 1483 and attainted, was also in exile with Henry, but on receipt of letters from his mother, Elizabeth Wydeville, whom Richard III had won over, attempted to flee and return to England. With the help of the French king, he was intercepted at Compiègne and brought back to Paris. When Henry embarked for England he left Dorset and Sir John Bourchier with the king of France as pledges for the money which he had borrowed from him. J. Gairdner, *History of the Life and Reign of Richard III* (1898) 50, 59, 113, 141, 152, 158, 186, 187, 212. He can, therefore, scarcely be considered as being prepared to fight for Henry.

Appendix B   The Yorkist nobility, 1459–61

Anyone individually summoned or known to have attended parliament before 1461 has been classed as a peer. Though not completely accurate this is the most convenient definition for the purpose.

Between the flight from Ludford (12 October 1459) and Edward IV's accession (4 March 1461) part of the peerage swung over as follows.

A. *A Neville–Bourchier group* which, though sympathetic, had never been completely committed before this time. Lord Fauconberg held Calais for the Yorkists after Ludford and thereafter fought with them. Viscount Bourchier and Lord Abergavenny were with March and Warwick in July 1460, the duke of Norfolk, the earl of Arundel (Warwick's brother-in-law) and Lord Berners with Warwick on 12 February 1461.

B. *A non-Neville group.* Lord Audley, whose father had been killed on the Lancastrian side at Blore Heath, was taken prisoner during an attempt to relieve the duke of Somerset in Guisnes. During his subsequent imprisonment at Calais he went over to the Yorkists. Some time before October 1460, the 18 year old duke of Suffolk married Elizabeth, York's second daughter, and then supported his father-in-law. Lords Say and Sele and Scrope of Bolton had come over by July 1460. Lord Grey of Ruthyn treacherously deserted Henry VI at the battle of Northampton. Lord Bonvile was with Warwick in February 1461. Lord Grey of Wilton and Humphrey Stafford of Southwick were with Edward at Mortimer's Cross. *Johannis Whethamstede, op. cit.* I 368–75, 374. *An English Chronicle, op. cit.* 91, 95, 107. Stevenson II pt ii 773. *Three Fifteenth-Century Chronicles* ed. J. Gairdner, Camden Series (1880) 76–7. *Itineraria Symonis Simeonis et Willelmi de Worcestre* ed. J. Nasmith (1778) 327–9. *Calendar of State Papers Milanese, op. cit.* I 51. *CP* XII pt i 448–50. Scofield, *op. cit.* I 94–5.

Humphrey Stafford of Southwick is included as although this peerage is generally held to date from 1461, A. R. Myers has shown that his father (d. 1450) attended the parliament at Winchester, 1449. Humphrey was a minor at his father's death. A. R. Myers, 'A Parliamentary Debate of the Fifteenth Century', *Bulletin of the John Rylands Library* XXII (1938) 388–404. See also W. H. Dunham Jr, 'Notes from the Parliament at Winchester, 1449,' *Speculum* XVII (1942) 407–8.

The pseudo-William Worcester (Stevenson II pt ii 775–6) states that in December 1460 the Lancastrians were suspicious of Lords Fitzhugh and Greystock. Nevertheless they fought on the Lancastrian side at St Albans II. Scofield, *op. cit.* I 93, 140, also adds the earl of Kendal and Lords de la Warr and de Vesci to the Yorkist group. All three were with the Lancastrians in the Tower of London in July 1460 (*An English Chronicle, op. cit.* 95) and no evidence has been found of any Yorkist activity on their part before Edward's accession.

Of earlier adherents the earl of Devonshire had died in 1458 and his son was loyal to Henry VI, being beheaded and attainted in 1461. *CP* IV 326–7. *Rot. Parl.* V 476–83. Lords Clinton and Cobham continued their support. *An English Chronicle, op. cit.* 95. Scofield, *op. cit.* I 77.

Thus, *c.* 1459–61, 14 peers came over to the Yorkists, 4 of the Neville group, 2 Bourchiers and 8 others. Between 1452 and 1461 there were 20. So omitting Devonshire, Grey of Powys and Salisbury (executed after Wakefield) the actual fighting strength known early in 1461 was 17.

Lords Stanley, Stourton, Dudley and Fitzwarine all attended the royal council after St Albans II. Scofield, *op. cit.* I 94–5. Evidence is lacking, however, that they fought at the battle.

Appendix C   Attainders and reversals, 1453–1509

Table 1

A   Total figures of attainders and reversals (excluding royal families)

(*a*, number attainted; *b*, number reversed or ultimately reversed for heirs; *c*, number unreversed.)

attainder under	Henry VI a	b	c	Edward IV a	b	c	Richard III a	b	c	Henry VII a	b	c	total	reversals	unreversed	per cent reversed
Dukes	—	—	—	2	1	1	1	1	0	1	1	0	4	3	1	75
Marquises	—	—	—	—	—	—	1	1	0		1	1	0	100
Earls	3	3	0	5	5	0	1	1	0	3	1	2	12 } 34	10 } 29	2 } 5	83 } 84
Viscounts	—	—	—	1	1	0	—	—	—	1	0	1	2	1	1	50
Barons	2	2	0	8	7	1	1	1	0	4	4	0	15	14	1	93
Knights	7	7	0	38	31	7	17	17	0	23	13	10	(84)* 85	(67)* 68	17	79
Squires	9	9	0	55	31	24	53	53	0	53	22	31	170	115	55	76
Yeomen	—	—	—	15	5	10	20	19	1	30	8	22	65	32	33	47
Ecclesiastics	—	—	—	11	3	8	3	3	0	5	1	4	(18)* 19	(6)* 7	12	36
Merchants	—	—	—	5	2	3	2	2	0	10	1	9	17	5	12	29
Miscellaneous	—	—	—	—	—	—	1	1	0	8	1	7	9	2	7	22
Grand totals	21	21	0	140	86	54	100	99	1	138	52	86	(397)*400	(256)*258	141	64

Figures in brackets marked * give the actual number of persons involved as distinct from the number of attainders and reversals—allowing for the fact that Sir Nicholas Latymer and Dr John Morton were each attainted in two periods.

B   Member of royal families

Yorkist	attainted	Lancastrian	attainted
(1) Richard, duke of York	1459	(1) Henry, earl of Richmond (Henry VII)	1484
(2) Edward, earl of March (Edward IV)	1459	(2) Margaret, countess of Richmond	1484
(3) Edmund, earl of Rutland	1459	(3) Henry VI	1461
(4) George, duke of Clarence	1478	(4) Margaret of Anjou	1461
(5) Richard, duke of Gloucester (Richard III)	1485	(5) Prince Edward	1461
(6) Edward, earl of Warwick (Clarence's son)	1504		

Notes to Table 1

General

(a) If a man has been attainted *twice* in *one* period, e.g. Edward IV and the attainders twice reversed once 'in' and once 'out' of the period, only the reversal in the period 'out' has been counted for this table; e.g. Sir Thomas Tresham, attainted 1461, pardoned by patent 1464, reversed by parliament 1468, attainted 1475, reversed for heir 1485, therefore included in Tudor reversals only. If a man was attainted in *two* different periods he is included as attainted in *both*; e.g. John Morton, attainted 1461, reversed 1473, attainted 1484, reversed 1485.

(b) 'Provisional' attainders. In the parliaments of 1461–3 and 1463–5 a number of men were to be regarded as attainted unless they surrendered for judgement by certain dates. Where it is known that these 'provisional' attainders become effective they have been included in the figures in the table. The residue for which no further information has been found is as follows: esquires and gentlemen 12, yeomen 3. Of the three yeomen one later received a general pardon but as this is enrolled on the pardon roll (C. 67/48 m. 2) it has no political significance.

(c) *Defenders of Harlech.* In 1461 eighteen of the defenders of Harlech were declared attainted unless they surrendered by the Feast of the Purification of our Lady. I have no evidence that any of them gave themselves up to the royal officers. These have not been included in the table. One was definitely attainted and two more 'provisionally' attainted in 1463–5.

Special cases

(1) Somerset. Although the family was extinct in the male line Henry VII reversed his attainder in 1485.

(2) Wiltshire. James Butler (see above p. 141 and no. 58).

(3) Sir Robert Chamberlain's attainder (1491–2) was reversed in 1531 but no property was to be restored.

(4) Dan Miles Salley, attainted 1489–90, after the Abingdon conspiracy. A monk of Abingdon, of the same name, received a pardon in 1492 (which does not cover attainder) (*Cal. Pat. Rolls, 1485–94*, 381). The name is unusual and (in spite of that fact that there is no evidence of the reversal of attainder) he may be the man who afterwards became abbot of Eynsham and bishop of Llandaff and whose splendid tomb is in John of Gaunt's Hospital, Bristol.

(5) In addition the following seven men received general pardons (which do not, however, specifically mention reversal of attainder) and should possibly be counted as restored: esquires and gentlemen, James Dalton, Thomas Tunstall, Thomas Blandrehassett, William Antron, Richard Cockerell; ecclesiastics, John Whelpdale; yeomen, Thomas Carr.

(6) John Hooe of London was the only man attainted by Richard III who was not included in the mass reversal of 1485. This was probably merely due to inadvertence.

Table 2   *Details of attainders and reversals*

attainted under	dukes	marquises	earls	viscounts	barons	knights	squires	yeomen	ecclesiastics	merchants	miscellaneous	attainder reversed under
Henry VI	—	—	3	—	2	7	9	—	—	—	—	
	—	—	3	—	2	7	9	—	—	—	—	Henry VI*
	—	—	—	—	—	—	—	—	—	—	—	Richard III
	—	—	—	—	—	—	—	—	—	—	—	Henry VII
	—	—	—	—	—	—	—	—	—	—	—	Henry VIII
Edward IV	2	—	5	1	8	38	55	15	11	5	—	
	—	—	1	—	3	16	15	3	3	1	—	Edward IV
	—	—	—	—	—	—	—	1	—	—	—	Richard III
	1	—	4	1	4	15	16	1	—	1	—	Henry VII
	—	—	—	—	—	—	—	—	—	—	—	Henry VIII
Richard III	1	1	1	—	1	17	53	20	3	2	1	
	1	1	1	—	1	17	53	19	3	2	1	Henry VII
	—	—	—	—	—	—	—	—	—	—	—	Henry VIII
Henry VII	1	—	3	1	4	23	53	30	5	10	8	
	1	—	1	—	3	12	19	7	1	1	1	Henry VII
	—	—	—	—	1	1	3	1	—	—	—	Henry VIII

* In the parliament of 1460, which was Yorkist controlled.

Appendix D Councillors of Edward IV, Richard III and Henry VII

1 List of Edward IV's councillors

Notes are added below, pp. 316–8, indicating the principal offices held by minor ecclesiastics and laymen and sources where detailed biographical information is to be found. The notes of offices are not exhaustive. The following abbreviations are used: *F*, Foss, *Judges of England*; *O-R*, J. Otway-Ruthven, *The King's Secretary and the Signet Office in the Fifteenth Century*; *VCH*, *Victoria County Histories. The Complete Peerage* deals with all nobles, and J. C. Wedgwood, *History of Parliament, 1439 to 1509*, and the *Dictionary of National Biography* with many others. References to these are omitted. None of these sources give either detailed or accurate information about conciliar activities but they are useful for family connections and general careers.

The first date on which a man is described as a councillor is given, followed by the reference to the source in the next column. As a method of determining the date from which a man first served on the council this is, of course, inaccurate, but no other method is available. In many cases it is reasonably certain that a man served before the date noted; e.g. Warwick, Essex, Hastings, Sir Thomas Burgh, Sir John Elryngton, Sir Thomas Montgomery, Sir Thomas Vaughan. The date of death has been given where known as there is no evidence of retirement from the council. Some are described as councillors during the French campaign of 1475 before they are so described on other occasions. This information has been disregarded as the conditions were abnormal.

The various categories, are of course, very loose and other classifications could be adopted; e.g. most ecclesiastics could be considered as civil servants.

The names of those found on diplomatic commissions only are given in italics.

Name	1461	1461–70	1471–83	Date first mentioned as councillor, followed by date of death	First reference as councillor
1 NOBILITY					
George, duke of Clarence			×	20 vii 1471 18 ii 1478	C. 81/1502/50
Richard, duke of Gloucester			×	5 ii 1472	E. 28/54/13
John Neville, (Lord Montagu 1461, earl of Northumberland 1464, Marquis Montagu 1470)	(×?)	×		5 iii 1463, 14 iv 1471 (battle of Barnet)	E. 28/89
William FitzAlan, earl of Arundel			×	5 ii 1472, 15 ii 1487	E. 28/54/13
Humphrey Stafford (Lord Stafford of Southwick 1461, earl of Devon 1469)		×		i 1468, 17 viii 1469	Stevenson II 789
Henry Bourchier, earl of Essex	×	×	×	18 iii 1462, 4 iv 1483	C. 81/1547
Edmund Grey, Lord Grey of Ruthyn (earl of Kent 1465)		×	×	5 iii 1463 22 v 1490	E. 28/89
William Neville, Lord Fauconberg (earl of Kent 1461)	×	×		5 iv 1461 9 i 1463	E. 404/72/1/56

Name	1461	1461–70	1471–83	Date first mentioned as councillor, followed by date of death	First reference as councillor
Henry Percy IV, earl of Northumberland[1]		x	x	vi 1470, 25 iv 1489	*Chronicle of John Stone*, ed. W. G. Searle, Cambridge Antiquarian Society (1902) 114
William Herbert (Lord Herbert 1461, earl of Pembroke 1468)		x		i 1468, 27 vii 1469	Stevenson II 789
Richard Wydeville, Lord Ryvers, (Earl Ryvers 1465)		x		7 iii 1463, 12 i 1469	E. 28/89
Anthony Wydeville, Lord Scales, Earl Ryvers			x	29 iv 1471, 25 vi 1483	C. 81/1547
John Talbot, earl of Shrewsbury			x	26 viii 1471, 26 vi 1473	*Foedera* XI 717
Richard Neville, earl of Warwick[2]	(x?)	x		5 iii 1463, 14 iv 1471 (battle of Barnet)	E. 28/89
John Tiptoft, earl of Worcester[3]	x	x		1 xi 1461, 18 x 1470	Scofield I 217
John Stafford (Earl of Wiltshire 1470)			x	26 viii 1471, 8 v 1473	*Foedera* XI 717
Thomas Stanley, Lord Stanley (earl of Derby 1485)			x	5 ii 1472, 29 vii 1504	E. 28/54/13
William Berkeley, Lord Berkerley (Viscount Berkerley 1481, earl of Nottingham 1483)			x	20 v 1482, 14 ii 1491	E. 28/92
John Audley, Lord Audley		x	x	1 xi 1468, 26 ix 1490	Stevenson II 789
Humphrey Dacre, Lord Dacre of Gillesland			x	26 viii 1471, 30 v 1482	*Foedera* XI 717
Richard, Lord Beauchamp of Powicke			x	20 v 1482, 19 i 1503	E. 28/92
Humphrey Bourchier (Lord Cromwell 1461)		x		5 iii 1463, 14 iv 1471	E. 28/89
John Dynham (Lord Dynham 1466)[4]		x	x	iv 1462, i 1500	E. 404//72/2/25
Walter Devereux (Lord Ferrers of Chartley 1461)		x	x	7 ix 1469, 22 viii 1485 (battle of Bosworth)	C. 81/1547
Richard Fenys, Lord Dacre of the South[5]		x	x	3 vii 1462 25 xi 1483	*ibid.*
John Dudley (or Sutton), Lord Dudley		x	x	17 vii 1470, 20 ix 1487	E. 28/90/23
Henry, Lord Grey of Codnor			x	27 vii 1473, 1496	*Cal. Close Rolls, 1468–1476*, 320

Name	1461	1461–70	1471–83	Date first mentioned as councillor, followed by date of death	First reference as councillor
Ralph Greystock, Lord Greystock			x	26 viii 1471, 22 xi 1501	*Foedera* XI 717 C. 81/1503/6
William Hastings (Lord Hastings 1461)[6]	x	x	x	5 iv 1461, 13 vi 1483	E. 403/73/3/41
John Howard (Lord Howard 1470)		x	x	ii 1468, 22 viii 1485 (battle of Bosworth)	*Manners and Household Expenses* 172–3
Walter Blount (Lord Mountjoy 1465)		x	x	4 iii 1466, 1 viii 1474	E. 404/75/3/19
John le Scrope, Lord Scrope of Bolton			x	29 vii 1474, by 13 xi 1481	*Foedera* XI 815
William Stourton, Lord Stourton[7]			x	27 vii 1473, 18 ii 1478	*ibid.* 783
John Wenlok (Lord Wenlok 1461)	x	x		23 vii 1461, 4 v 1471 (battle of Tewkesbury)	E. 403/822 m. 6

2 ECCLESIASTICS

(a) *Bishops*

Name	1461	1461–70	1471–83	Date first mentioned as councillor, followed by date of death	First reference as councillor
John Alcok bishop of Rochester (1472–), Worcester (1476–), Ely (1486–1500)		x	x	7 ix 1469, 1 x 1500	C. 81/1547
Richard Beauchamp, bishop of Hereford (1449–), Salisbury (1450–81)[8]	x	x	x	7 iv 1461, 4 xi 1481	*Calendar of State Papers Milanese* 64
Richard Bell, prior of Durham (1464–), bishop of Carlisle (1478–96)[9]			x	26 viii 1471, 1496	C. 81/1503/6
Lawrence Bothe, bishop of Durham (1457–), archbishop of York (1476–80)		x	x	18 vii 1470, 1480	C. 81/1547
John Bothe, bishop of Exeter (1465–78)			x	27 vii 1473, 5 iv 1478	*Foedera* XI 783
Thomas Bourchier, archbishop of Canterbury (1454–86)	x	x	x	5 iii 1461, 30 iii 1486	E. 404/72/3/6
John Chedworth, bishop of Lincoln (1452–71)		x		5 iii 1463, 23 xi 1471	E. 28/89
Peter Courtenay, bishop of Exeter (1478–), Winchester (1487–92)[10]			x	12 iii 1477, 22 ix 1492	PSO I/44/ 2274
William Dudley, dean of the Chapel, bishop of Durham (1476–83)			x	31 iii 1472, 24 xi 1483	E. 404/75/2/7
William Grey, bishop of Ely (1454–78)		x	x	5 iii 1463, 4 viii 1478	E. 28/89
James Goldwell, bishop of Norwich (1472–99)[11]		x	x	1 i 1469, 15 ii 1499	*Calendar of Papal Registers* XII 325–7

Name	1461	1461–70	1471–83	Date first mentioned as councillor, followed by date of death	First reference as councillor
John Hals (Hales), Bishop of Coventry and Lichfield (1459–90)			x	27 vii 1473, 30 xii 1490	*Foedera* XI 783
Thomas Kempe, bishop of London (1450–89)		x	x	5 iii 1463, 28 iii 1489	E. 28/89
Walter Le Hart, bishop of Norwich (1446–72)		x	(x?)	3 vii 1462, 17 v 1472	C. 81/1547
John Marshall, bishop of Llandaff (1478–96)			x	2 v 1482, 1496	E. 28/92
Richard Martyn, bishop of Waterford and Lismore (1472–), St David's (1482–83)		x	x	17 vii 1470, by 11 v 1483	E. 28/90/23
Thomas Milling, abbot of Westminster (1469–74), bishop of Hereford (1475–92)[12]		x	x	4 vii 1470, 1492	E. 28/90/21
John Morton, bishop of Ely (1479–', archbishop of Canterbury (1486–1500)			x	7 xii 1473, 15 ix 1500	C. 81/1384/13
George Neville, bishop of Exeter (1458–64), archbishop of York (1465–76)	x	x		4 iii 1461, 8 vi 1476	E. 404/72/1/20, 99
Richard Redeman, abbot of Shap (1458–1505), bishop of St Asaph (1471–), Exeter (1495–), Ely (1501–5)[13]			x	15 viii 1474, 24 viii 1505	*Foedera* XI 815–16
Thomas Rotheram, bishop of Rochester (1468–), Lincoln (1472–), archbishop of York (1480–1500)		x	x	4 vii 1470, 29 v 1500	E. 28/90/21
John Russell, bishop of Rochester (1476–), Lincoln (1480–94)		x	x	5 i 1467, 30 xii 1494	*Foedera* XI 591
Robert Stillington bishop of Bath and Wells (1466–91)[14]	x	x	x	1 xi 1461, v 1491	E. 404/72/1/103
Edward Story, bishop of Carlisle (1468–), Chichester (1478–1503)		x	x	7 ix 1469, 29 i 1503	C. 81/1547
William Waynflete, bishop of Winchester (1447–86)[15]			x	27 vii 1473, 11 viii 1486	*Cal. Close Rolls 1468–1476*, 319–20 *Foedera* XI 782

(b) *Abbots*

Name	1461	1461–70	1471–83	Date first mentioned as councillor, followed by date of death	First reference as councillor
William Albone, abbot of St Albans (1465–76)[16]		x	(x?)	4 vii 1470, vii 1476	E. 28/90/21
John Sante, abbot of Abingdon (1468–96)[17]			x	15 viii 1474, 1496	*Foedera* XI 816–17

(c) *Heads of religious orders*

Name	1461	1461–70	1471–83	Date first mentioned as councillor, followed by date of death	First reference as councillor
Robert Botiller, prior of St John of Jerusalem in England (1439–69)		x		18 iii 1462, ix 1469	C. 81/1547
John Langstrother, prior of St John of Jerusalem in England (1469–71)[18]		x		5 iii 1463, 4 v 1471 (Executed after the battle of Tewkesbury)	E. 28/89
John Weston, prior of St John of Jerusalem in England (1477–91)			x	26 xi 1474, 1491	C. 81/1508/21

(d) *Others*

Name	1461	1461–70	1471–83	Date first mentioned as councillor, followed by date of death	First reference as councillor
Dr Henry Aynesworth[19]			x	22 ii 1482	*Foedera* XII 146–7
Dr (Thomas?) Bonyfaunt[20]		x		7 ix 1469, 1470	C. 81/1547
Dr Robert Bowthe			x	15 viii 1474	*Foedera* XI
Dr John Coke[21]			x	30 x 1475, by 1495	*Cal. Pat. Rolls, 1467–1477*, 554, 569–70
Richard Coke[22]			x	26 iv 1482	E. 404/77/3/6
Edmund Coningsburgh[23]			x	10 viii 1471	*Calendar of State Papers Venetian* 130
John Doget			x	5 vii 1480, iv 1501	*Foedera* XII 121–2
Thomas Danet[24]			x	29 vi 1481, 18 ix 1483	PSO 1/50/2572C
John Fox[25]			x	14 iv 1478, 1482	E. 28/91
Louis Galet[26]	x	x		9 viii 1461	C. 76/145 m. 25
Dr John Gunthorp[27]		x	x	13 iii 1470, 25 vi 1498	*Foedera* XI 653–4. C. 81/1501/38
Oliver King[28]			x	20 vi 1475, 29 viii 1503	*Foedera* XII 12
William Lacy[29]			x	5 vii 1480	*ibid.* 121–2
Dr Thomas Langton[30]		x	x	30 xi 1467, 22 i 1501	*ibid.* XI 591
Robert Morton[31]			x	1 viii 1480, iv (or v) 1497	C. 81/1518/21
Dr Roger Ratcliff[32]		x	(x?)	7 ix 1469, by 28 vii 1471	C. 81/1547
Dr Henry Sharp		x	x	5 i 1468	*Foedera* XI 591–9
Peter Taster[33]	x	x	x	8 viii 1461	C. 76/145 m. 24
Dr Thomas Wynterbourne[34]		x	x	7 ix 1469, 7 ix 1478	C. 81/1547

Name	1461	1461–70	1471–83	Date first mentioned as councillor, followed by date of death	First reference as councillor
3 OFFICIALS					
Sir William Alyngton[35]			×	11 viii 1478, 16 v 1479	Cal. Pat. Rolls, 1476–1485, 142
Sir Maurice Berkeley[36]			(×?)	(See notes) 27 iii 1474	ibid. 337
Sir Thomas Billing[37]			×	22 vi 1475, 5 v 1481	Halliwell, Letters of the Kings Kings of England i 144–7
Sir Thomas Bryan[38]			×	22 vi 1475, c. x 1500	ibid.
Hugh Bryce[39]			×	18 xii 1478, 1496	Foedera XII 96–7
Sir Thomas Burgh[40]			×	2 v 1482, 18 iii 1496	E. 28/92, 26 June 22 Ed. IV C. 81/1547
Thomas Colt[41]		×		18 iii 1462, viii 1467	C. 81/1547
Sir John Donne[42]			×	20 v 1477, by iv 1506	Foedera XII 42–3
Sir John Elryngton[43]			×	13 ix 1480, xii 1483	C. 81/1389/1
Hugh Fenne[44]		×	×	9 viii 1464, vi 1476	Scofield i 354 n. 1
Sir John Fogge[45]	×	×	×	4 iii 1461, vii 1490	E. 404/72/3/9
Richard Fowler[46]		×	×	4 vii 1470, 3 xi 1477	E. 28/90/21
William Hatteclyff[47]		×	×	1 v 1468, 1480	Foedera XI 591–9
Sir William Huse[48]			×	14 vii 1475, 9 x 1495	C. 81/1547
Sir John Markham[49]		×		7 viii 1464 (See notes)	E. 404/73/1/6
Sir Thomas Montgomery[50]			×	30 vi 1475, 2 i 1495	Cal. Pat. Rolls 1467–1477, 532
Sir William Nottingham[51]		×	×	28 viii 1465, 7 ix 1483	Cal. Pat. Rolls, 1461–1467, 467
Sir William Parre[52]			×	20 vii 1471, viii/xi 1483	C. 81/1502/50
Richard Quartermains[53]		×	×	17 xi 1467, 6 ix 1477	C. 81/1547
Sir John Say[54]	×	×	×	4 iii 1461, 12 v 1478	E. 404/72/3/20
Sir John Scotte[55]		×	×	7 iii 1463, 18 x 1485	E. 28/89
William Slyfeld[56]			×	13 vii 1482, 1483–5	PSO 1/53/ 2711A
Thomas Thwaytes[57]			×	22 vi 1482, c. 1495	E. 28/92
Sir Thomas Urswicke[58]			×	22 vi 1475, 19 iii 1479	Halliwell, i 144–7

Name	1461	1461–70	1471–83	Date first mentioned as councillor, followed by date of death	First reference as councillor
Sir Thomas Vaughan[59]		×	×	4 ii 1470, 23 vi 1483	*Foedera* xi 651
Richard Whetehill[60]		×	×	8 v 1465	*ibid.* 541–2
Sir Robert Wingfield[61]			×	25 iii 1474, by 13 xi 1481	C. 76/158 m. 30
John Wode			×	18 v 1482, 15 x 1484	E. 404/77/3/ 24; PSO1/ 52/2659
4 OTHERS					
Henry Butteler[62]			×	28 i 1478, 1490	C. 81/1513/37
James Douglas, earl of Douglas			×	14 iv 1478, 1491	E. 28/91
Gaillard de Dureford, Lord Duras[63]		×	×	4 ii 1470 (See notes)	*Foedera* xi 651
Sir Guy Fairfaxe[64]		×		13 ii 1470, 1495	*Calendar of Papal Registers* xii 772
Sir John Fortescue[65]			×	26 xi 1474, after 12 v 1477	C. 81/1508/21
John Grene		×	×	27 ii 1468, 1 v 1473	C. 81/1499/21
Thomas Grey(e) (of Crawdon?)			×	2 v 1481, 1495	E. 28/92, 26 June 22 Ed. IV *ibid.*
Sir Richard Harecourt			×	26 vi 1482, 1 x 1486	
Sir Robert Harecourt		×		6 v 1467, 14 xi 1470	*Foedera* xi 578
Sir Richard Tunstall[66]		×	×	30 xi 1467, iii/iv 1492	*ibid.* 591
Sir Thomas Tyrell[67]			×	26 xi 1474, 1510	C. 81/1508/21
Sir John Wingfield		×	×	vi 1470, 10 v 1481	E. 404/75/1/64
Garter King-at-Arms[68]		×		4 ii 1469	*Foedera* xi 651
5 CLERKS					
Thomas Kent[69]	×	×		4 iii 1461, 1466	E. 159/238 Brevia Directa Michaelmas Term m. vijd.
Richard Langport	×	×	×	4 iii 1461	*ibid.*

1 E. B. Fonblanque, *Annals of the House of Percy* (1887). G. Brennan, *A History of the House of Percy* (1902). J. M. W. Bean, *The Estates of the Percy Family, 1416–1537* (1958) has been published since this article was written.

2 C. W. Oman, *Warwick the Kingmaker* (1891). P. M. Kendall, *Warwick the Kingmaker* (1957).

3 R. J. Mitchell, *John Tiptoft* (1938).

4 *Transactions of the Devonshire Association,* 1. Although he was a councillor from 1462 he was 'appointed' by patent with a salary of 100 marks in 1475. *Cal. Pat. Rolls, 1467–1477,* 559.

5 Although he was a councillor from 1462 he was 'appointed' with a salary of 100 marks in 1475. *ibid.* 534, 550.

6 Writ dated 16 October 1467 orders reward as chamberlain and councillor 'for six years and more'. He was certainly chamberlain by 31 July 1461 and probably had been from March. In all probability, therefore, he was a councillor from March. Warrants for Issues E. 404/73/3/41.

7 His father, John Lord Stourton, had been treasurer of the household 1446–53.

8 This reference gives his own statement. The first reference in records is 7 March 1463. E. 28/89.

9 This is the signed bill behind the patent in *Foedera* XI 717. The prior's name is omitted from Rymer's text.

10 *O–R.* Acted as secretary to Henry VI during the re-adeption and to Edward IV, 1472–4.

11 These dates do not clash with those of Walter Le Hert as Goldwell was a councillor long before he became bishop. He was Henry VI's secretary for a short time in 1460. He was also acting as clerk of the council in 1472. Signed Bills C. 81/1504/24.

12 E. H. Pearce, *The Monks of Westminster* (1916).

13 H. M. Colvin, *The White Canons in England* (1951).

14 *The Registers of Bishops Stillington and Fox* ed. Sir H. C. Maxwell-Lyte, Somerset Record Society (1937). Writ states that he was to be paid as councillor and keeper of the privy seal.

15 S. H. Cossan, *Lives of the Bishops of Winchester* (1827).

16 *V.C.H. Hertfordshire.*

17 *V.C.H. Berkshire.*

18 He was a councillor before he became prior. Edward opposed his election in 1469 as he was a Warwickite. Scofield I 499 and n. 1.

19 Prebendary of Lincoln 1483–1516.

20 Prebendary of London 1464(?).

21 Archdeacon of Lincoln 1481–94, archdeacon of Chichester 1494, secondary in the privy seal office 1475.

22 Treasurer of Chichester 1479, chancellor of Salisbury 1485, Lichfield 1489, provost of King's College, Cambridge, 1499–1501.

23 Archbishop of Armagh 1477–9, but never gained effective possession of the see *DNB.*

24 King's almoner, prebendary of Lichfield 1473–83, Lincoln 1480–83, dean of Windsor at death (1483).

25 Archdeacon of Salop 1464, prebendary of Lichfield 1470, Lincoln 1476, chancellor of Lichfield at death (1482).

26 He may have been a member of the Calais council only.

27 R. J. Mitchell, *John Free* (1955). Queen's secretary, prebendary of Banbury 1471–98, archdeacon of Essex 1472–8, dean of Wells 1472–8, warden of King's Hall, Cambridge, 1468–77, clerk of parliament 1471–85, keeper of the privy seal 1483–5.

28 *O–R.* King's secretary 1480–83, 1487–95, French secretary 1476–80. He had also been secretary to Edward, prince of Wales (Henry VI's son). Bishop of Exeter 1492, Bath and Wells 1495–1503.

29 Once mentioned as clerk of the council in 1478. E. 404/845 m. 3.

30 Chaplain to the king 1476, treasurer of Exeter 1478, bishop of St David's May 1483, provost of the Queen's College, Oxford, 1487, bishop of Salisbury February 1485, bishop of Winchester 1493–January 1501, when elected archbishop of Canterbury, but died before consecration. There is no reference to Langton as a councillor between a diplomatic commission of 1467 and another of 31-3-1477 (*Foedera* XII 42), shortly after he became king's chaplain. He may, therefore, belong to the 'diplomatic only' class for the first period.

31 Nephew of Cardinal Morton, prebendary of Thorngate (Lincolnshire) 1471, archdeacon of Winchester 1478–86, Gloucester 1482–6, bishop of Worcester 1486–97, master of the rolls 1479–83, 1485–97.

32 Prebendary of Salop 1465, dean of St Paul's 1468, chancellor to Elizabeth Wydeville.

33 Dean of St Severin's, Bordeaux.

34 Archdeacon of Canterbury 1468(?)–71, dean of St Paul's 1471–8.

35 Tutor and councillor to the prince of Wales 1473–9, speaker 1472–5, 1478. He was most probably a councillor before the patent of appointment dated 11 August 1478.

36 Squire and knight of the body 1467–74. Only called councillor in a document issued after his death.

37 *F.* Common serjeant of London 1443–9, recorder 1450–54, judge, king's bench 1464–, chief justice king's bench 1469–81.

38 *F.* Chief justice common pleas, 1471–1500.

39 A. B. Beavan, *The Aldermen of the City of London* (1908–13). Keeper of the exchange and alderman of London. Concerned with currency affairs only.

40 Squire and knight of the body 1461–83, master of the horse 1465–83, summoned to parliament as Lord Burgh of Gainsborough 1487.

41 Chamberlain of the exchequer 1454–9, 1460–67, chancellor of the earldom of March 1463/7, councillor of the duke of York 1453–60, and in 1463 of the earl of Warwick.

42 Usher of the chamber 1461–5, squire of the body 1465–9(?), one of the Calais council 1471.

43 Clerk of the kitchen 1463/4, cofferer of the household 1471–4, treasurer of the household 1474–83, treasurer for war 1475–83, knight of the body 1483.

44 Auditor of the exchequer 1452–76, under treasurer of England 1463–7.

45 *Archaeologia Cantiana* II V, XXVIII. W. Hasted, *History of Kent* (2nd edn 1797–1800) III, VII, VIII, IX. Treasurer of the household 1461–8.

46 Somerville, *Duchy of Lancaster* 391. King's solicitor 1461–7, chancellor of the exchequer 1469–71, chancellor of the duchy and county palatine of Lancaster 1471–7, under treasurer of the exchequer 1471–7.

47 King's physician from 1454, first to Henry VI and then to Edward IV, king's secretary c. 1466–80.

48 *F.* Attorney general 1471–8, serjeant at law 1478–81, chief justice king's bench 1481–95.

49 Justice, king's bench 1444–61, chief justice, 1461–9. He was dismissed after Sir Thomas Cook's case, and though he did not die until 1479 there is no evidence that he ever attended a council after 1468.

50 Knight of the body 1461–83. Although first mentioned in the records as a councillor in 1476, in view of his general importance he was probably on the council much earlier.

51 *F.*, R. Bigland, *History of Gloucester* (1819). King's attorney 1452–83, baron of the exchequer 1461–83.

52 Controller of the household 1471–4, 1481–3.

53 Steward of Woodstock 1467–77.

54 Under-treasurer of the exchequer 1455–6, 1460–63, 1470–71, 1477–8, keeper of the great wardrobe 1476–8.

55 *Archaeologia Cantiana* V, X, XXI. Hasted, *History of Kent*. J. R. Scott, *Memorials of the Family Scott of Scot's Hall* (1879), an inaccurate monument to family piety. Controller of the

household 1461–71, lieutenant of Dover 1460–70, marshal of Calais 1471–6.

56 King's secretary 1474–80(?), treasurer of Calais 1481–3.

57 Somerville, *Duchy of Lancaster* 391. Victualler of Guisnes 1468–, chancellor of the duchy of Lancaster 1478 to *c.* 1495, chancellor of the exchequer 1471–83, treasurer of Calais 1483–90.

58 *F., Records of the Family of Urswick of Urswick* (1893). Common serjeant of London 1453–4, recorder 1454–71, chief baron of the exchequer 1471–9.

59 Master of the ordnance 1450–61, squire of the body 1450–59, 1462–75, keeper of the great wardrobe 1460–61, treasurer of the chamber 1465–82/3, chamberlain and councillor of the prince of Wales 1471–83.

60 Comptroller of Calais, lieutenant of Guisnes.

61 J. M. Wingfield, *Some Records of the Wingfield Family* (1925). Controller of the household 1474–81.

62 Recorder of Coventry 1455–90.

63 Came to England after the loss of English possessions in France in 1453, was made a knight of the Garter and lieutenant of Calais, returned to France in 1476 and was killed in the French service in Burgundy in 1487.

64 *F.* Described as a 'councillor' in a papal indult allowing him and his wife to have a portable altar. He is probably the Guy Fairfax of Walton, Yorkshire, who became serjeant at law 1468, recorder of York 1476, and a justice of the king's bench *c.* 1477.

65 C. Plummer, *The Governance of England* (1885). S. B. Chrimes, *Sir John Fortescue* (1942). His attainder was reversed in the session of October–December 1473. He himself states that he was made *one of the King's counsell* soon after he was pardoned in October 1471, *viz.* before the reversal of his attainder and the restoration of his estates. I have found no other reference to him as a councillor until 1474.

66 Squire of the body 1452–5, king's carver 1450–60.

67 Squire of the body 1478–85, master of the horse 1483–5.

68 Described as a councillor in a letter under the great seal of the duke of Burgundy.

69 E. Power and M. M. Postan, *Studies in English Trade in the Fifteenth Century* (1933), R. J. Mitchell, *John Free* (1955). Kent was not merely clerk. He was an experienced and trusted councillor and is found in lists of councillors signed by Langport, as clerk. e.g. C. 81/1499–20.

2 Richard III's councillors

Key: E—Edward IV's councillor
H—Henry VII's councillor

Thomas Bourchier, archbishop of Canterbury (E)
Thomas Rotheram, archbishop of York (EH)
John Alcok, bishop of Worcester (EH)
Thomas Langton, bishop-elect of St David's (EH)
Richard Redeman, bishop of St Asaph (EH)
John Russell, bishop of Lincoln (EH)
John Shirwode, bishop-elect of Durham
Robert Stillington, bishop of Bath and Wells (E)
John Kendall, turkopellier of Rhodes (H)

John Howard, duke of Norfolk (E)
William FitzAlan, earl of Arundel (E)
Henry Percy IV, earl of Northumberland (E)
William Berkeley, earl of Nottingham (EH)
Thomas Boteler, earl of Ormond (H)
James Douglas, earl of Douglas (E)
Francis Lovell, Viscount Lovell
John Audley, Lord Audley (EH)

John Blount, Lord Mountjoy
Humphrey Dacre, Lord Dacre of Gillesland (E)
John Dynham, Lord Dynham (EH)
John Dudley (Sutton), Lord Dudley (EH)
John Le Scrope, Lord Scrope of Bolton (son of Edward IV's councillor)
John Le Scrope, Lord Scrope of Upsall
Thomas Stanley, Lord Stanley (EH)

Thomas Barowe
John Coke (E)
John Gunthorp (EH)
Dr Thomas Hutton (H)
Alexander Lye

Sir Robert Brakenbury
Sir Thomas Bryan, Chief Justice (EH)
Sir Thomas Burgh (E)

Sir Richard Fitzhugh
Sir John Grey of Powys
Sir William Huse, chief justice (E)
Sir Thomas Montgomery (EH)
Sir Richard Ratclyff
Sir George Stanley of Straunge
Sir John Scotte (E)
Sir Humphrey Talbot
Sir Richard Tunstall (EH)
Sir James Tyrell

William Catesby

Edmund Chaderton (H)
Avery Cornburgh (H)
John ffineux
Bernard de la Forse
John Fortescue, mayor of Calais
John Kendall[1]
Morgan Kidwelly (H)
Richard Salkeld
Thomas Thwaytes (E)
Adrian Whetehill
Mayor of the Staple[2]

There were two clerks of the council, William Lacy and John Haryngton. *Cal. Pat. Rolls, 1476–1485*, 413, 461. The entry in the *Cal. Pat. Rolls* might be taken to imply that John Haryngton was clerk of 'requests' only, but Warrants for Issues E. 404/78/1/50, makes it clear that he was clerk of the council.

[1] The king's secretary—a different John Kendall from the turkopellier of Rhodes.
[2] Treaty Roll C. 76/168 m. 28. The mayor of the Staple of Calais at this time was Thomas Otley. Foreign Accounts E. 364/117 m. C.

3 (a) Overlap of councillors 1461–1509

	Served on				Served on		
	Ed. IV	R. III	H. VII		Ed. IV	R. III	H. VII
Thomas Bourchier, archbishop of Canterbury	x	x		John Kendall, turkopellier of Rhodes		x	x
John Morton, bishop of Ely, archbishop of Canterbury	x		x	John Howard, Lord Howard, duke of Norfolk	x	x	
Thomas Rotheram, bishop of Rochester, Lincoln, archbishop of York	x	x	x	William FitzAlan, earl of Arundel	x	x	
John Alcok, bishop of Rochester, Worcester, Ely	x	x	x	Edmund Grey, Lord Grey of Ruthyn, earl of Kent	x		x
James Goldwell, bishop of Norwich	x		x	Henry Percy IV, earl of Northumberland	x	x	
Thomas Langton, bishop of St David's	x	x	x	Thomas Stanley, Lord Stanley, earl of Derby	x	x	x
Robert Morton, bishop of Worcester	x		x	James Douglas, earl of Douglas	x	x	
Richard Redeman, bishop of St Asaph, Exeter, Ely	x	x	x	William Berkeley, Viscount Berkeley, earl of Nottingham	x	x	x
John Russell, bishop of Rochester, Lincoln	x	x	x	Thomas Boteler, earl of Ormond		x	x
Robert Stillington, bishop of Bath and Wells	x	x		John Audley, Lord Audley	x	x	x
Edward Story, bishop of Carlisle	x		x	Richard, Lord Beauchamp of Powicke	x		x
John Weston, prior of St John of Jerusalem in England	x		x	Humphrey Dacre, Lord of Gillesland	x	x	
				John Dudley (Sutton), Lord Dudley	x	x	x
				John Dynham, Lord Dynham	x	x	x

	Ed. IV	R. III	H. VII		Ed. IV	E. III	H. VII
Dr Henry Aynesworth	×		×	Sir Thomas Montgomery	×	×	×
John Coke	×	×		Sir John Scotte	×	×	
Dr Thomas Hutton		×	×	Thomas Thwaytes	×	×	
Oliver King	×		×	Sir Richard Tunstall	×	×	×
Dr John Gunthorp	×	×	×	Sir Thomas Tyrell	×		×
Sir Thomas Bryan, chief justice	×	×	×	Edmund Chaderton		×	×
Sir Thomas Burgh	×	×		Avery Cornburgh		×	×
Sir William Huse, chief justice	×	×		Morgan Kidwelly		×	×

(b) Henry VII's councillors who were near relations to those of Edward IV

Thomas FitzAlan, earl of Arundel
Edmund Grey, earl of Kent
Henry Percy V, earl of Northumberland
George Talbot, earl of Shrewsbury
Thomas Fenys, Lord Dacre of the South
John Scrope, Lord Scrope of Bolton
Henry Bourchier, earl of Essex
Richard Wydeville, Earl Ryvers
Edward Stafford, earl of Wiltshire
Edward Hastings, Lord Hastings
Thomas Howard, earl of Surrey
William Blount, Lord Mountjoy
Sir John Huse
Sir John Wingfield
Sir Thomas Bourchier

Appendix E Figures of combatants, 1475[1]

	Number of contingent leaders[2]	Men-at-arms	Archers	Average no. per leader Men-at-arms	Average no. per leader Archers	Ratio of archers to men-at-arms
1 Household						
Bannerets	7	69	720	10	103	10
Knights[3]	5	39	370	8	54	7
Esquires	28	107	910	4	32	8
Gentlemen	2	2	7	1	3½	3½
Others	7	10	80	1½	11½	8
Gentlemen of the house of the lord king	1	43	316	43	316	7½
Archers of the king's chambers			184			
Total of 1	50	270	2,587			
2 *Peers:* Royal relations and holding household appointments	11	516	4,080	47	371	8–
3 *Other officials*	9	29	134	3	15	5
Total of 1, 2, 3	70	815	6,801			
4 *Other peers*	12	231	1,619	16	135	9–
5 *Other: nonhousehold*						
Bannerets	5	32	272	6	54	8½
Knights	13	52	449	4	35	9
Esquires	52	91	672	2	13½	7–
Gentlemen	6	5	32	1	5	5
Others	32	40	268	1	8	8
Total of 4 and 5	120	451	2,312			
6 *Scottish lords*	2	8	60	4	30	7½
Total of 4, 5, 6	122	463	3,372			
Total of all six categories	192	1,278	10,173			
Total men-at-arms (including leaders) and archers						11,451
Add technical personnel (transport, miners, carpenters, medical, etc.)						387
Grand total						11,838
Plus secretaries, councillors, royal servants, possibly another 10 or 12 per cent						1,182
						13,020

1 Small numbers may be omitted from all these sources, e.g. the city of Salisbury sent and paid 54 men under Sir Edward Darrell. R. C. Hoare, *The History of Modern Wiltshire* (4 vols 1843) IV 195–6. It is possible that other cities may have acted in the same way.

2 These figures are also included in the column 'men-at-arms,' and therefore are not included again in the total figures.

3 Sir John Elrington, the cofferer of the household, led a contingent as a knight as well as leading the gentlemen of the household of the lord king.

Index